FEDERAL TAX RESEARCH

A PRACTITIONER'S GUIDE TO FEDERAL TAX RESEARCH AND COMMUNICATION

ANTHONY KIM

2ND EDITION

FEDERAL TAX RESEARCH

Second Edition
Anthony J. Kim, B.A, J.D., M.B.A.

ISBN-13: 978-1790716098
Amazon Kindle Direct Publishing

Dedication

To my mom, who guided me to be a lawyer. Mom always knows best. To my dad, I miss you so much and hope to make you proud every day. To my sister, who never stops looking after her little brother. To my son, Jonathan, and daughter, Chloe, who taught me that love is boundless and forgiving. And, to me dear wife Michelle, thank you for your incredible strength, humor, guidance and our wonderful life together.

With grit and grace, the hardworking civil servants of the Internal Revenue Service carry out their mission in ensuring that the United States tax law is properly interpreted and applied so that our country has the financial stability to operate and flourish. It is no secret that the men and women who make up the IRS are the most hated civil servants in the federal government. And, yet these employees continue their work without complaint and with hardly anyone to stand up for them. I have been honored to serve as counsel to IRS employees for over two decades. I dedicate this book to the civil servants who will never be appreciated by the public but whose work strengthens the country that we cherish.

Foreward

Whether you are a student, tax practitioner, government official or someone who wants to better understand the complexities of tax law, administration and research, this book provides a great foundation for that understanding. Tony Kim takes you step by step into the often daunting task of tax law research. He begins with how legislation is enacted and why uncertainty may exist. He then moves on to the forms of regulation and guidance. Next he covers how to minimize risk and uncertainty using appropriate research tools, and even includes an introduction to the administrative audit process with some "words of wisdom". His case studies and questions at the end of each chapter allow the readers to test their knowledge, each with interesting examples that capture your attention.

As a former internal revenue agent, IRS executive, partner at EY and college professor, I would have used this "nuts and bolts" guide as a reference to learn and teach. Tony's years of practical experience working with complex tax law, performing research of complex issues, serving clients and imparting that knowledge as a college professor and IRS instructor, come together as he shares all of that with the readers of this book.

Tony Kim brings his technical experience, practical insights and his wonderful ability to convey that knowledge with the reader in mind. He is a true tax professional, in search of the "right answer" and serves his client, whether it be a Fortune 500 company or an IRS audit team, with integrity and efficiency. I have had the privilege of seeing him in action on both fronts. Tony has a passion for coaching and mentoring that shines through in his approach to _Federal Tax Research: A Practitioner's Guide to Effective and Efficient Federal Tax Research and Communications_.

-Debbie Nolan
Former IRS Commissioner, Large and Mid-Size Business Division
Former Partner EY, Americas Director of Tax Controversy and Risk Management

Tax Professionals Who Recommend This Textbook

- **Maria Hwang**, retired/former Director of Servicewide Operations and Director of Field Operations, Large Business & International, Internal Revenue Service (Arlington, VA)

- **Joe Calderaro**, retired/former Internal Revenue Service Technical Coordinator for Northern California District, currently an IRS Enrolled Agent (Walnut Creek, CA)
  - "Tony's challenge to take on the ever changing Tax Code is nothing less than admirable."

- **Ray Cassabonne**, retired/former Team Manager, Large Business & International (Communications, Technology & Media), Internal Revenue Service (Concord, CA), currently site supervisor, AARP TaxAide Program, in Concord, California

- **Melvin Louie**, retired/former Senior Program Analyst, Large Business & International (Communications, Technology & Media), Internal Revenue Service (Union City, CA)
  - "This book provides honest, practical advice, which Tony provided when I worked at the IRS with him. It is a must-read for anyone who needs to perform tax research."

- **Patricia Montero**, retired/former attorney with the Office of Chief Counsel, Internal Revenue Service (San Francisco, CA)

About the Author

 Anthony Kim received his bachelor of liberal arts degree in political science from Amherst College, a masters degree in business administration from the College of William & Mary and his law degree from Brooklyn Law School. Upon graduating from law school, Tony began his tax career with the Internal Revenue Service, Office of Chief Counsel in 1995. During his government career, he worked in three field offices with IRS Chief Counsel (New York, San Francisco, Oakland), served as an Associate Area Counsel in two divisions (Small Business/Self -Employed and Large & Mid-Size Business), and as Deputy Area Counsel with the Large & Mid-Size Business Division (precursor to the new Large Business & International Division). In his role as Deputy Area Counsel, Tony supervised national industry programs covering Sports, Gaming, Telecommunications, High Technology, Research Credit and Media/Entertainment working closely with IRS Technical Advisors to propose/draft published guidance. Additionally, Tony served as the lead instructor for the Office of Chief Counsel's new manager training program, as an instructor for IRS revenue agent technical update sessions and as a member of two Tier I issue management teams.

In 2008, Tony left the Office of Chief Counsel to become an Executive Director of Tax Controversy and Risk Management Services with Ernst & Young, LLP ("E&Y"). At E&Y, he led the Pacific Northwest tax controversy practice for E&Y assisting clients address a wide range of IRS issues including compliance with IRS procedures and developing strategies to resolve proposed tax adjustments. Tony returned to IRS Office of Chief Counsel and now works in the San Francisco field office as part of the Large Business & International Division. As part of his duties, Tony serves as one of five national Counsel to the new Global High Wealth Industry and assists local teams in the Bay area. During his career with the Office of Chief Counsel, Tony has received multiple awards including the Office of Chief Counsel's National Innovation Award (2007), Legal Opinion Award (2010), Manager's Award, several Special Act awards, as well as the U.S. Department of Justice's award for special contribution in litigation (2018).

Tony is a member of the New York State bar and admitted to practice before the United States Tax Court as well as the United States Supreme Court. He has served as an adjunct professor at Golden Gate University ("GGU") located in San Francisco, CA since 2003. In 2016, Tony received the Distinguished Adjunct Faculty award from GGU. In 2014, Tony became an adjunct associate professor at St. Mary's College in Moraga, CA teaching individual Federal income tax and supervising the Volunteer Income Tax Assistance community engagement program partnering with the Unity Council, a non-profit community organization that provides services to needy families in Oakland, CA. Tony has been married to his wife, Michelle, for 25 years and they have two children, JK and Chloe.

Table of Contents

Preface

This book is written by a tax practitioner as a "nuts & bolts" introduction for individuals who desire to get up to speed as quickly as possible to the practice of federal tax. In other textbooks, publishers include hundreds of end of chapter questions that offer opportunities for students to either simply recite definitions or address numerous scenarios that are too complicated. As a practitioner who has taught tax to students for over 14 years, I have routinely assigned 5% or less of the questions provided in textbooks because students cannot reasonably take time to answer all of the questions included in these publications. And, over time, I've realized that the best approach is to provide limited, practical exercises at the end of each chapter to solidify students' grasp of the elements discussed. As such, this book includes a very limited number of questions and exercises designed to reinforce important core practice skills for students.[1]

This book is a compilation of material that I have developed over 14 years to teach my graduate tax students on how to understand federal tax as quickly as possible. I've drawn on publicly available government sources (IRS, IRS Chief Counsel, Department of Justice), examples used in my graduate tax classes and court cases that provide the best examples, in my view, to show students who are new to tax how to get up to speed in tax practice as quickly as possible.

The overall objective of this text is to provide the reader with practical examples to become proficient in tax practice. Each chapter will engage the reader with plain text explanations and examples in a deliberate attempt to avoid the abstruse technical vocabulary of tax law. Tax is difficult enough without adding confusing jargon to the journey. I hope that you enjoy the material as presented in this book.

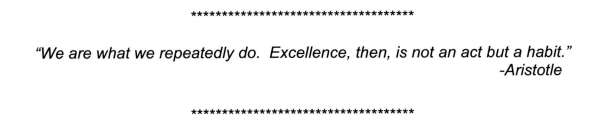

****

"We are what we repeatedly do. Excellence, then, is not an act but a habit."
-Aristotle

****

---

[1] A free supplement to this textbook which contains a recommended answer key for all end-of-chapter questions and exercises is available to instructors/professors who select this publication for their course. Please contact the author at amjck2@yahoo.com using your official school email address to request the supplemental guide and the author will respond immediately.

CHAPTER 1 - INTRODUCTION TO TAX RESEARCH & DECISION-MAKING

1. Introduction

The goal of tax research is to determine an answer to a tax question or to assess potential tax implications based on a given set of facts. As we consider this task, many

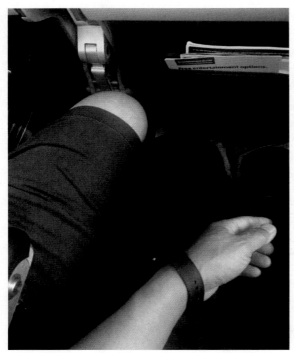

of us complain about the enormity of the tax code. But, let's be honest. We understand the need for rules and <u>we really want rules to be followed</u>. Have you ever had a car signal left only to make a right turn on the roadway? Have you ever patiently waited for your turn at a store, Department of Motor Vehicles, public transportation or some other establishment when another person decides that waiting on line is not convenient and decides to cut in front of you? How about when you board an airplane and sit next to someone who decides to take up your personal space as well. See the picture to the left. Yes, your author is sitting on the right forced to endure the steady leg invasion of a stranger seated next to me who felt entitled to his seating space and half of mine as well. There is no law that requires someone to avoid leg "creep" on to an adjoining seat. But, don't you want such a rule in place to keep order? Admit it. You want people to follow rules.

And, even when people seem to be following the rules, you know that in some instances the true intent of the rule is not being followed. Consider the picture to the right. The car owner has properly displayed his/her handicap placard in their car to use the designated parking space. But, do you feel that something is not right with this picture, as if a rule is being abused?[2] The point is that we want rules to provide order to our chaotic world and the equity that rules promote. But, why does the tax code engender such a different view in most of us? Could it be that we don't like to part with our money? Regardless of whether you like rules or not, tax professionals must tackle the labyrinth of the tax maze beginning with

---

[2] A 2017 California state audit presented a report concerning California's DMV disabled person parking placard program. See http://bsa.ca.gov/pdfs/reports/2016-121.pdf. In part, the State Auditor reported, "As of June 30, 2016, nearly 26,000 placard holders with active, permanent placards in DMV's data were age 100 or older. This number is significantly higher than the estimated 8,000 individuals that comprised California's entire centenarian population as of 2014. These results indicate that DMV's process for canceling placards of deceased individuals is inadequate, given that thousands of individuals age 100 or older who are likely deceased still have active placards."

understanding the research process. So let's begin with an introduction to the four basic steps in this process.

Four Step Tax Research Process

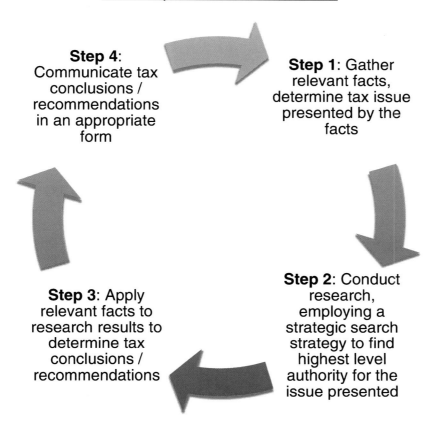

Step 4: Communicate tax conclusions / recommendations in an appropriate form

Step 1: Gather relevant facts, determine tax issue presented by the facts

Step 2: Conduct research, employing a strategic search strategy to find highest level authority for the issue presented

Step 3: Apply relevant facts to research results to determine tax conclusions / recommendations

While this four-step process appears basic, it is not. For example, Step 1 provides that the tax practitioner obtain "relevant" facts. However, determining the difference between relevant, aka, key/material facts vs. irrelevant facts will require an understanding of the facts required by applicable authorities on the issue presented, a process involved in Step 2. Thus, this process does not present a clean separation between Steps 1 thru 4 but rather a blending, reiterative engagement by the tax practitioner.

With the recognition of this continuous, evolving process, tax practitioners must always be cognizant of time and client budgets that dictate how long we can devote to each step. The complexity of facts and law may lead practitioners to spiral into a vortex of seemingly endless searches. In practice, tax professionals do not have the luxury of unlimited time to complete their work because clients have defined budgets for tax matters. And, unlike some other professions, say a mechanic who can assure the client that an automotive issue is 100% fixed, there are often-times results that leave tax practitioners with uncertainty rather than a clear-cut answer. Thus, we must understand how to use secondary sources to provide us with efficient guidance to obtain primary source authorities to support our answers and when we must decide that a good answer, rather than a perfect answer, is the best professional outcome.

To illustrate the practical problem confronting tax professionals with respect to this four-step process, let's look to Step 1 in the diagram, above, that instructs practitioners to gather relevant facts. A relevant fact is a fact that, if present or absent, alters the tax conclusion. Now, to determine whether a fact is relevant or not requires that we find applicable primary source tax authority that informs us whether a fact is material in reaching a conclusion. Reading complicated tax material and determining with some degree of certainty which facts are material to a tax conclusion presents a challenging task. And, in the process of a tax professional attempting to proceed with Step 1, there is the ever present practical pressure that the clock is ticking and a decision must be made to proceed to Step 2.

Let me provide a practice example from my experience as a private sector tax practitioner. As an Executive Director at a large accounting firm, my job was to provide expert tax advice and bring in new clients. When I did secure a client, I would assess their tax requirements and provide an engagement letter which set forth the scope of work, expected hours and rate per hour of various levels of employees: Executive Director at $800/hr; Senior Manager at $500/hr; Associate at $200/hr.[3] In addition, I had to determine an estimated fee based on the anticipated work of each level of employee making up the engagement team for the tax issue(s) impacting the client.

As an Executive Director, I would plan an engagement with the goal of leveraging lower level employees to provide a streamlined plan in order to come below budget in charging my client. Depending on the complexity of the tax assignment, I would pull in lower or higher level employees to complete each task. If I tapped an Associate level employee for a task that I deemed simple, then I'd estimate a certain number of hours, say 10 hours x $200/hr, for the Associate to complete his/her assignment. If the Associate returned with the completed assignment reporting to me that they worked 20 hours, then I had to determine whether I underestimated the complexity of the assignment or whether the Associate was inefficient. In most instances, my tendency was to determine that the Associate was inefficient. And, this assessment of the employee's competency with respect to tax research would leave me with a poor view of the employee's capabilities. Ultimately, because there are so many other employees at every level to place on my team, an inefficient employee would never be invited to become part of my team.

So, why didn't I take the time to train an inexperienced employee on how to become a more efficient researcher? Every hour that I devoted to train an employee reduced the time I had to develop new clients. And, at $800/hr of my charge out time, training an employee was an investment that did not improve the revenue that I produced on behalf of the firm. Since I was primarily measured on my revenue production, training new employees was not a priority. This is a harsh reality but a reality nonetheless in private practice. What is the lesson for new tax professionals? Get trained **now**, become exceptional at tax research **now**. When you are hired at a firm, be the employee that every partner seeks out because you are known at the firm as the most efficient tax researcher.

---

[3] See Appendix A, which provides a sample engagement letter.

In some cases, I've witnessed employees "ghosting" hours. Employees who are not efficient will work 20 hours on a project but report to their engagement partner that he/she devoted only 10 hours to charge out to the client for the task with the other 10 hours just a "ghost" of real work that disappears. In this way, the employee is meeting the expectations of the client engagement partner. This is a tactic to mask an employee's deficiency in tax research. Firms will counsel employees not to employ "ghosting" of their hours stating that it remains the partner's decision whether they will pass along the actual hours worked as part of the client bill or a reduced number of hours or at a reduced rate of the actual hours worked.

In my graduate tax class, I provided a writing assignment to five teams made up of three students. Each team was provided a tax topic along with instructions that they must break down their time spent on the project between writing and research time. In addition, each team was to provide me with the rate that they would bill the client for each hour worked. Finally, each team was told that the firm's tax partner had estimated that the project would be billed out to the client for a fixed fee of $2,500. Consider the following table summarizing the reported number of hours worked for the assignment by each team. Although the teams were made up of CPAs with various levels of practical tax experience, each and every team provided hours of work that reflected the underlying pressure of charging time below the expectations of their supervisor.

Team	Topic	Writing Time	Research Time	Rate	Bill to Client
1	How to Report Child's Summer Earnings	11	13	$100	$2,400
2	How to Report Child's Summer Earnings	7	7	$170	$2,380
3	Tax Impact from Ebay Sales	10	20	$80	$2,400
4	Tax Impact from Ebay Sales	4.25	4.25	$125	$1,063
5	Tuition for Child to Attend a Special School	10	10	$125	$2,500

In tax practice, there exists a strong undertow of pressure to complete research and writing assignments quickly. If you devote the time now to become an effective, efficient researcher, you ensure that you will always be sought after by partners for multiple engagements and never be forced to consider whether to "ghost" hours. My advice: devote the time and effort to read the material in this book NOW to become a valued employee from Day 1 with your firm.

2. Primary Source Authority vs. Secondary Source Material

Tax practitioners may only cite to certain primary source authorities to support tax conclusions. Primary source authorities are comprised of tax material issued by governmental entities - the executive, legislative or judicial branch. Secondary sources relate to material not issued from governmental sources, such as treatises published by other tax professionals, material developed by fee-based tax services or academic papers authored by law professors.[4] These secondary source materials can never be cited by a tax professional to support a tax conclusion or recommendation. So, if you can't cite to secondary sources, then what is the value of reading/using secondary source material? Secondary sources provide tax professionals with concise summaries on various topics that guide the reader to applicable primary source authorities. Thus, the value of secondary source material is that it provides tax professionals with an efficient tool to reduce time to locate primary source authorities resulting in the most efficient research process.

3. Tax Uncertainty

Before we begin our journey together to learn the basics of tax law, it is essential that we accept the unavoidable presence of tax uncertainty. Generally, uncertainty exists in every aspect of our lives. How is my retirement account performing this month? Will the value of my home increase or decrease this year? Will my child gain acceptance to the college of his/her choice? In the face of this unwelcome reality, we strive for the highest measure of predictability in our affairs. While we readily acknowledge the inevitable uncertainty in these areas of our lives the topic of tax occupies a particularly disquieting presence.

Uncertainty may not apply strictly to tax law, but uncertainty in tax result, where often the "right answer" is *within a range* where reasonable people can disagree. Valuation and transfer pricing are two areas that come to mind, where the law may allow for a methodology that can result in several different answers within a range.

The complexity of the Code may sometimes lead to unintended results. On the one hand, taxpayers who honestly seek to comply with the law often make inadvertent errors, causing them either to overpay their tax or to become subject to IRS enforcement action for mistaken underpayments of tax. On the other hand, sophisticated taxpayers search the Code for loopholes that enable them to reduce or eliminate their tax liabilities.[5] Individual taxpayers find the return preparation process so overwhelming that more than 80 percent pay transaction fees to help them file their returns. About 60 percent pay preparers to do the job, and another 22 percent purchase tax software to help them perform the calculations themselves.[6]

---

[4] Some tax research textbooks refer to secondary sources as secondary source "authorities." However, there is nothing "authoritative," e.g., of value, that a tax professional can cite to in order to support his/her tax conclusion or recommendation. As such, secondary sources should never be referenced as authorities, in this author's opinion. There are "primary source authorities" and "secondary source materials."

[5] 2008 Annual Report to Congress by the Taxpayer Advocate Service.

[6] Id.

The Code currently contains at least 11 incentives to encourage taxpayers to save for and spend on education; the eligibility requirements, definitions of common terms, income level thresholds, phase-out ranges, and inflation adjustments vary from provision to provision. The Code also contains at least 16 incentives to encourage taxpayers to save for retirement; these incentives are subject to different sets of rules governing eligibility, contribution limits, taxation of contributions and distributions, withdrawals, availability of loans, and portability. Taxpayers wishing to choose the optimal vehicle to save for college must know the difference between a Section 529 plan, a Coverdell Education Savings Account, and the Hope and Lifetime Learning Credits, among other alternatives. Taxpayers wishing to choose the optimal plan in which to save for retirement must know the difference between a traditional IRA, a Roth IRA, a Section 401(k) plan, a Section 403(b) plan, and a SARSEP[7], among others. The point of a tax incentive, almost by definition, is to encourage certain types of economic behavior. But taxpayers can only respond to incentives if they know they exist and understand them. Choice is good, but too much choice is overwhelming.[8]

The oft-repeated saying goes that "the only things certain in life are death and taxes." Anyone who has tried to tackle the Internal Revenue Code will tell you that the topic of taxes is anything but certain. So, what is "tax uncertainty?"

Long ago, U.S. Supreme Court Justice Holmes said, "Taxes are what we pay for civilized society."[9] In collecting this toll, Congress enacted the Internal Revenue Code to provide the rules for taxing and collecting this payment. But, the presence of ambiguity in these rules creates "tax uncertainty." Taxpayers who have labored through tax law to complete their forms and returns are understandably frustrated when they encounter confusing language. Likewise, the government suffers where taxpayers find it difficult to easily comprehend tax law. Such confusion in tax law is a counter-force to taxpayer compliance. And, the presence of confusion in tax compliance by the taxpayers presents a burden to the proper and efficient operation of our government.

While the difficult text of the tax code draws the most notoriety, tax law does not exist alone in presenting challenges to its readers. A Wall Street Journal entitled "Here's a Funny Idea: Medicare Laws That Are Easy to Read," on March 9, 2012, noted the cries of foul from judges who must read and decide the proper application of Medicare and Medicaid laws. Despite the difficulty of the code, whether it is tax law or Medicare/Medicaid law, we cannot escape complexity. We live in a complex world.

And, tax complexity triggers an enormous investment of time to make sense of our obligations under Title 26. How much time is devoted to tackle tax complexity?

---

[7] A SARSEP is a simplified employee pension (SEP) plan set up before 1997 that includes a salary reduction arrangement. Under a SARSEP, employees can choose to have the employer contribute part of their pay to their Individual Retirement Account or Annuity (IRA) set up under the SARSEP (a SEP-IRA). A SARSEP may not be established after 1996. However, for SARSEPs set up before 1997, eligible employees hired after 1996 must be allowed to participate.

[8] Id.

[9] Compania General De Tabacos De Filipinas v. Collector of Internal Revenue, 275 U.S. 87, 100 (1927) (Justice Holmes).

Chapter 1: Introduction to Tax Research

Consider a slice of time in 2006 and the number of hours spent preparing tax returns and information reporting documents.[10]

Type of Return	Number (in millions)	Average Total Hours/Minutes	Total Hours (in millions)
Tax Returns			
Individual Income Tax (1040)	134.6	26.40	3,553.44
Estate and Trust Income Tax (1041)	3.6	116.27	418.56
Estate and Trust Est'd Tax (1041-ES)	0.7	3.28	2.30
Partnerships (1065)	3.0	126.75	380.25
Electing Large Partnerships (1065-B)	0.0001	113.95	0.01
S Corporations (1120S)	3.9	145.97	569.27
Corporations (1120)	1.8	193.77	348.78
1066	0.03	54.25	1.63
1120-A	0.2	115.08	23.02
1120-C	0.001	107.60	0.11
1120-F	0.02	222.45	4.45
1120-FSC	0.006	152.90	0.92
1120-H	0.2	32.62	6.52
1120-L	0.001	178.20	0.18
1120-PC	0.006	212.33	1.27
1120-POL	0.005	36.62	0.18
1120-REIT	0.01	130.37	1.30
1120-RIC	0.009	118.15	1.06
Estate Tax (706)	0.5	7.75	3.88
Gift Tax (709)	0.2	5.77	1.15
Employment Tax (940 series)	6.0	37.32	223.92
Employment Tax (941 series)	24.0	15.40	369.60
Tax-Exempt Organizations (990)	0.4	152.33	60.93
Excise Tax (720) (data from 10/2008)	0.1	28.67	2.87
Form 1040X (data from 11/07/2006)	3.7	3.50	12.95
Tax Returns Subtotal			**5,988.56**

---

[10] 2008 Annual Report to Congress by the Taxpayer Advocate Service.

Information Reporting	Number (in millions)	Average Total Hours/Minutes	Total Hours (in millions)
W-2	243.3	0.50	121.65
K-1 (1041)	3.5	12.47	43.63
K-1 (1065)	17.8	45.87	816.49
K-1 (1120S)	6.7	42.03	281.62
1096	5.6	0.22	1.21
1098	105.2	0.12	12.27
1098-C	0.2	0.25	0.05
1098-E	18.2	0.12	2.12
1098-T	24.2	0.22	5.24
1099-A	0.5	0.15	0.08
1099-B	538.1	0.33	179.37
1099-C	1.7	0.17	0.28
1099-CAP	0.002	0.18	0.00
1099-DIV	103	0.30	30.90
1099-G	72.7	0.18	13.33
1099-H	0.02	0.30	0.01
1099-INT	231.7	0.22	50.20
1099-LTC	0.2	0.22	0.04
1099-MISC	83.5	0.27	22.27
1099-OID	4.1	0.20	0.82
1099-PATR	1.6	0.25	0.40
1099-Q	1.0	0.18	0.18
1099-R	76.3	0.30	22.89
1099-S	4.2	0.13	0.56
1099-SA	1.0	0.13	0.13
5498	108.5	0.20	21.70
5498-ESA	0.8	0.12	0.09
5498-SA	1.4	0.17	0.23
W2-G	9.7	0.30	2.91
Information Returns Subtotal			**1,630.69**
Grand Total			**7,619.25**

Except as noted, all data is for Tax Year 2006. Sources: IRS Form Instructions for Tax Year 2006; IRS Fiscal Year 2007 Data Book; Document 6961 (Calendar Year 2007 Projections); Document 6149 (Calendar Year 2007 Projections); and Document 6186 (Calendar Year 2007 Projections).

Chapter 1: Introduction to Tax Research

a. Why Does Tax Uncertainty Exist?

The legislative branch drafts law, including the tax code, known as the Internal Revenue Code or Title 26 of the United States Code. In writing tax law, Congress crafts language expressing the government's goals for raising revenue as well as establishing a system of incentives and penalties. But, in this process, a number of factors form uncertainty in tax law.

First, language itself presents an obvious obstacle. Words can be read in different ways. "A word is not a crystal, transparent and unchanging...it is the skin of living thought and may vary greatly in colour and content according to the circumstances and time in which it is used."[11]

Second, Congress cannot draft tax law with such precision to cover every factual variation that may potentially fit within their targeted area for a tax provision. Recognizing this limitation, Congress must provide general guideposts in many instances when drafting law. Of course, some guideposts present definitive, predictable guidance to taxpayers. However, many areas of the Code do not offer such precise direction.

Third, the unique formulation of tax law can seem to present an almost ancient Egyptian hieroglyphic structure that defies common sense. But, tax law demands careful wording to avoid unintended consequences or loopholes. And, this diligence to protect policy goals and the fisc in writing tax provisions can lead to language that tests many of us.

Finally, tax law presents a quasi-existential problem for its readers. Not questions such as "Who am I?" or "Why do I exist?" Rather, we must ask, "What version of the law governs my specific situation?" As Congress enacts new provisions or revisions of existing sections of the Code, we must understand the changes and determine the applicable effective period with respect to these changes. Wading through historical amendments to track down changes to tax law can present quite a challenge which we will address later in Chapter 5.

b. Why Do We Seek Certainty in Tax Law?

Almost everyone seeks certainty in all aspects of life. One of the primary goals of the Internal Revenue Service is to provide certainty in tax law. A high level of certainty promotes compliance in a voluntary tax system. If taxpayers understand their tax obligations as set forth in the Internal Revenue Code, then this should rightly promote compliance since there are predictable results. Supreme Court Justice Oliver Wendell Holmes, Jr. famously stated, "[C]ertainty generally is illusion, and repose is not the destiny of man."[12] Yet, we will strive for certainty in many things, including in our tax affairs.

---

[11] Towne v. Eisner, 245 U.S. 418, 425 (1918)
[12] "The Path of Man," 10 Harvard Law Review 457 (1897).

What are the consequences where uncertainty dominates tax law? First, the level of compliance drops because people are confused on how they can comply with their tax obligations. Second, time and costs burden taxpayers as well as the tax system as everyone awaits guidance or, in some instances, receives untimely guidance.[13] It is estimated that taxpayers annually spend 7.6 billion hours and over $100 billion in an effort to comply with the Internal Revenue Code.[14]

Third, opportunists will exploit gaps and loopholes in tax law leading to unintended consequences. In order to eliminate, or at least minimize uncertainty, we must take steps to understand the fundamentals of tax law.

4. Various Roles in the Tax System to Address Tax Uncertainty

   a.   The Federal Government – Executive Branch (IRS), Judicial Branch (Courts), Legislative Branch (Congress)

✓ **Executive Branch - Internal Revenue Service** - The IRS is a bureau of the Department of the Treasury and one of the world's most efficient tax administrators. In fiscal year 2015, the IRS collected almost $3.3 trillion in revenue and processed almost 240 million tax returns. Beyond the monetary results achieved by the IRS, it is important to appreciate the mission of the tax agency – "provide America's taxpayers top quality service by helping them understand and meet their tax responsibilities and enforce the law with integrity and fairness to all." This mission statement describes its role and the public's expectation about how this agency should perform that role:

- In the United States, the Congress passes tax laws and requires taxpayers to comply.
- The taxpayer's role is to understand and meet his or her tax obligations.
- The IRS role is to assist the majority of honest, hard-working taxpayers efficiently comply with their tax obligations, while ensuring that the minority who are unwilling to comply pay their fair share.

Thus, in order to achieve an efficient tax system, the IRS focuses on reducing uncertainty for taxpayers by providing guidance to promote tax compliance.

✓ **Judicial Branch - Courts** - The U.S. Courts were created under Article III of the Constitution to administer justice fairly and impartially, within the jurisdiction established by the Constitution and Congress. The federal judiciary operates separately from the executive and legislative branches, but often works with them as the Constitution requires. Federal laws are passed by Congress and signed by

---

[13] Consider an example of tax uncertainty that impacted taxpayers in 2018 who contributed to their health savings account ("HSA"). An HSA is a type of savings account that lets you set aside money on a pre-tax basis to pay for qualified medical expenses. By using untaxed dollars in a HSA to pay for deductibles, copayments, coinsurance, and some other expenses, a taxpayer can lower their overall health care costs. An HSA can be used only if a taxpaye
r has a High Deductible Health Plan ("HDHP") — generally any health plan (

the President. The judicial branch decides the constitutionality of federal laws and resolves other disputes about federal laws.[15] However, judges depend on our government's executive branch to enforce court decisions.

Courts decide what really happened and what should be done about it. They decide whether a person committed a crime and what the punishment should be. They also provide a peaceful way to decide private disputes that people can't resolve themselves. Depending on the dispute or crime, some cases end up in the federal courts and some end up in state courts.

When a tax dispute arises between the IRS and taxpayers, the courts provide a forum to resolve uncertainty.[16] Decisions reached and published by courts present guidance to the IRS and to taxpayers on the proper interpretation and application of various tax sections that are presented to courts for ultimate resolution.

✓ **Legislative Branch - Congress** - What if the legislative branch decides after a court decision that it disagrees with the judiciary's interpretation of a statutory provision? Congress always has the option to amend or repeal any statute as it deems appropriate. Until that time, the judicial branch has the final say on the proper meaning of tax code.

b. Private Tax Practitioners

Tax practitioners must comply with various rules in conducting their work. Section 6694 provides baseline levels of tax confidence that must be reached by practitioners in order to approve of their clients' tax positions. Along with statutory responsibilities regulating their conduct, practitioners are subject to follow rules set forth under Circular 230 for "practice" before the Service and various professional rules of conduct, such as the AICPA rules. Circular 230 is discussed in greater detail in Chapter 2.[17]

5. The Need for Decision-Making Given the Presence of Tax Uncertainty

Before we embark on our journey through the Internal Revenue Code, I believe that we must address two fundamental questions: (1) why do we need to pay any taxes at all; and (2) why is there so much confusion or uncertainty in tax law? Let's get a basic

---

including a Marketplace plan) with a deductible of at least $1,350 for an individual or $2,700 for a family. As of the end of 2017, a taxpayer was advised that he/she could contribute up to $3,450 for self-only HDHP coverage and up to $6,900 for family HDHP coverage in the subsequent tax year, 2018. See, e.g., www.Healthcare.gov. The observer would conclude that the purpose and effect of section 107(2) is to provide financial assistance to one group of religious employees without any consideration to the secular employees who are similarly situated to ministers." See USDC opinion at https://ffrf.org/images/DOCKET087_CORRECTEDORDERreOPINIONANDORDER.pdf. The second District Court opinion is pending before the Seventh Circuit Court of Appeals. On June 22, 2018, a group of tax professors filed an *amicus curiae* brief in support of appellees (and against the appellants – U.S) in support of their position that the lower court's decision should be affirmed as correctly decided. See the amicus curiae brief at: https://ffrf.org/images/AmicusBriefofTaxLawProfessors.pdf.

[16] In chapter 7, we will address the U.S. Tax Court, the primary judicial forum for federal tax controversy matters.

[17] See also Appendix B.

understanding of these two matters so that we can better appreciate our role and approach in this tax system.

Justice Oliver Wendell Holmes of the Supreme Court of the United States famously observed, "the greatness of our nation is in no small part due to the willingness of our citizens to honestly and fairly participate in our tax collection system which depends upon self-assessment."[18] Without a source of funds from the public, how can the government provide for our country's common defense against foreign threats, fund police for safety on our neighborhood streets, create nationwide roads or public libraries, spend resources to be prepared against pandemic viruses along with numerous other expenditures for the public good?

"By enacting and amending the Internal Revenue Code, Congress, the people's elected representatives, has accomplished the purpose of providing the primary means of financing the costs of the Federal Government. This is the system under which both individuals and corporations will be required to pay their shares of the burden, at least until such time as Congress decides to repeal the income tax and try another way to raise the necessary revenue."[19] As with many things in life, balance is the key. Judge Learned Hand famously noted the role of citizens within our tax system stating:

> "Anyone may arrange his affairs so that his taxes shall be as low as possible; he is not bound to choose that pattern which best pays the treasury. There is not even a patriotic duty to increase one's taxes. Over and over again the Courts have said that there is nothing sinister in so arranging affairs as to keep taxes as low as possible. Everyone does it, rich and poor alike and all do right, for nobody owes any public duty to pay more than the law demands: Taxes are enforced exactions, not voluntary contributions. To demand more in the name of morals is mere cant."[20]

Why does uncertainty exist in the Internal Revenue Code? First, the nature of drafting law presents unavoidable difficulties in creating precision in language that leaves areas open to interpretation. To test this statement, try writing your own short version of tax law that reflects your desire for an incentive program. For example, you wish to provide a "green" incentive for those individuals who buy and use bicycles to commute to work to receive $100 tax credit towards the purchase price of the equipment. Did you adequately define "bicycle"? If a person uses a scooter with two small wheels, does the scooter fit the definition in your draft tax law? How about a person using a tricycle? A bicycle with motor assist feature? A person using a wheel chair? So, many factual circumstances in life cannot be adequately considered in tax law as written. Given this reality, the tax law often provides the skeletal framework expressing the desire of law makers for a stated purpose. And, it remains up to governmental personnel, tax practitioners, and taxpayers to engage in the process of understanding and complying with the will of Congress.

---

[18] Compania de Tabacos v. Collector, 275 U.S. 87, 100 (1927).
[19] Liddane v. Commissioner, T.C. Memo. 1998-259.
[20] Helvering v. Gregory, 69 F.2d 809 (1934).

Second, the process of analyzing law as written is imbued with differences of approach, understanding and conclusions. The text of tax law presents inherent issues in properly determining the meaning of words. When Congress provides that taxpayers may deduct "ordinary and necessary" business expenditures under section 162 of the Internal Revenue Code, we are left to define this subjective term. Congress provides the skeletal framework of tax law given the reality that law cannot set forth with exact precision the endless permutations of facts that life will present to test the proper application of law.

Understanding that the nature of language creates uncertainty in tax law does not stop citizens from complaining about this situation. Deborah Messina petitioned the U.S. Supreme Court for review of a Fourth Circuit decision that affirmed the U.S. Tax Court's holding that she was liable for tax and penalties arguing that the complexity of the tax laws and lack of availability of legal advice deprived her of her Constitutional due process rights under the Fifth Amendment.[21] The Supreme Court denied her petition for review of her case. Scream at the moon, or in Ms. Messina's case petition to the highest court in the land, that the tax law is too complex. Ultimately, we should accept that the nature of language conspires to leave all of us in this situation together to understand and apply the tax law through proper tax research.

6. Hierarchy of Authorities That Provide Tax Guidance

Tax law begins with Title 26, the Internal Revenue Code, that is enacted by Congress. Below the code, additional guidance assists to interpret and apply tax law. Although the IRS issues thousands of publications in a variety of different forms to help taxpayers and their advisors understand the law, it has stated that only guidance published in the Internal Revenue Bulletin ("IRB") contains the IRS's authoritative interpretation of the law (see figure 1, below, sourced from GAO-16-720).

---

[21] Messina v. Commissioner, Sup. Ct. Dkt. No. 09-1463 (October 4, 2010).

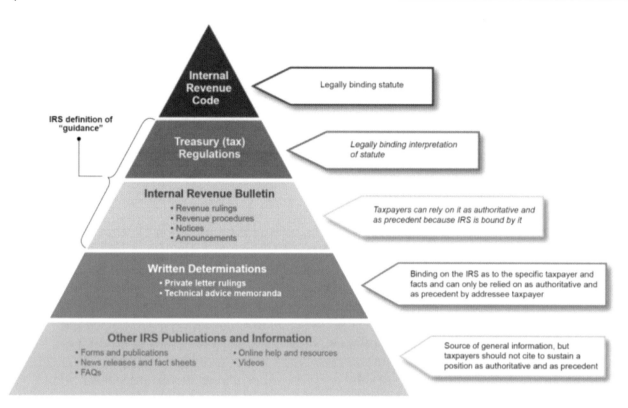

- Internal Revenue Code (IRC). Federal tax law begins with tax provisions enacted by Congress and codified in title 26 of the U.S. Code as the IRC. Consequently, the IRC is the most authoritative source of information for taxpayers. It is the codified collection of U.S. laws on income, estate and gift, employment, and excise taxes, plus administrative and procedural provisions.

- Treasury (tax) regulations provide Treasury's and IRS's official interpretation of tax laws. Regulations are the most authoritative source of published guidance, and they are binding on taxpayers and IRS since they have the force and effect of law. They are published both in the Internal Revenue Bulletin ("IRB") and the Federal Register.

- Other IRB guidance (revenue rulings, revenue procedures, notices, and announcements) do not have the same "force and effect" of Treasury regulations, but taxpayers can still rely on them as authoritative. For example, taxpayers can use IRB guidance to support a position knowing that IRS is bound by IRB guidance because IRS employees must follow it.

- Written determinations are Chief Counsel letters to, or memorandums regarding, individual taxpayers; but IRS cautions that only the taxpayer addressed by the guidance can rely on it as precedent. Every year, the Chief Counsel issues thousands of private letter rulings to taxpayers or their advisors who request (for a fee) answers to technical questions about potential tax consequences of particular transactions. The Chief Counsel also issues technical advice memorandums to IRS offices that have technical or procedural questions about an individual taxpayer case. When written determinations are later published via the IRS website, they often contain disclaimers noting any legal limitations.

Other IRS publications and information are described in the Internal Revenue Manual (IRM) as "a good source of general information." However, the IRM states that these documents cannot be relied upon by taxpayers as authoritative or as precedent for their individual facts and circumstances since they are not binding on IRS.[22] Tax practitioners and other tax law experts note that courts have ruled that taxpayers cannot rely on IRS documents published outside the IRB to support a position. The form that information in this category can take varies widely, and includes IRS videos, online tools, forms and publications, and Frequently Asked Questions (FAQs).

Guidance published in the IRB goes through a multi-step clearance process at both Treasury and IRS, involving review and approval by officials in a wide variety of Treasury and IRS offices. The weekly IRB is described as the "authoritative instrument" for publishing official IRS rulings and procedures and tax regulations. This distinction is important because, according to IRS officials, only guidance published in the IRB is binding on IRS and can be relied upon by taxpayers as authoritative. The five types of guidance published in the IRB are: regulations, revenue rulings, revenue procedures, notices, and announcements. Tax regulations are also published in the Federal Register and codified in the Code of Federal Regulations like other federal agency regulations. Table 1, below, describes the types of IRS guidance published in the IRB.

Table 1: Descriptions and Examples of IRS Guidance Types Published in the Internal Revenue Bulletin

Type	Description	Example
Regulation[a]	Treasury's and IRS's interpretation of how a particular Internal Revenue Code (IRC) section is to be applied. Final regulations carry the force and effect of the law. Proposed regulations convey the IRS's position on a topic.	T.D. 8784 (REG-122488-97) provided rules for substantiating certain business expenses.
Revenue Ruling	An official interpretation of the IRC, related statues, tax treaties or regulations as applied to a specific set of facts.	Rev. Rul. 2006-56 provided guidance on the tax treatment of reimbursements to employees for certain travel-related expenses.
Revenue Procedure	An official statement of a procedure that affects the rights or duties of taxpayers or other members of the public under the IRC, related statutes, tax treaties and regulations.	Rev. Proc. 2010-51 specified how taxpayers can compute deductible automobile expenses by applying a mileage rate.
Notice	A public pronouncement that may contain guidance that involves substantive interpretations of the IRC or other provisions of law.	Notice 2016-1 announced a change to the mileage rate used to deduct certain automobile expenses.
Announcement	A public pronouncement that has only immediate or short-term value.	Announcement 2015-31 notified taxpayers of amendments to previously issued guidance.

Source: GAO analysis of IRS documents. | GAO-16-720

---

[22] See Chapter 7, supra, for a discussion of "precedents" or "precedential authority."

Temporary or final regulations called Treasury Decisions (TDs) take effect upon a specified date after they are published in the Federal Register. Proposed regulations do not take effect upon publication; rather they only become effective when issued as final regulations after Treasury and IRS have considered public comments on the proposed regulations.

From 2013 to 2015, the IRB (52 weekly issues) contained nearly 300 guidance documents per year, as shown in figure 2, below, that total about 2,000 pages.[23] From 2002 to 2008, the number of IRB items published annually was higher (about 500 items), but starting in 2009 that number began to decline.[24] From 2002 to 2003, IRS Chief Counsel diverted resources away from litigation and toward the issuance of guidance, in particular revenue rulings, which contributed to the increasing counts of guidance documents during these years.[25] Regarding the recent decline in the number of guidance documents issued, IRS officials said that hiring freezes have reduced the total number of chief counsel attorneys by 14 percent from 2011 to 2015.[26] Issuance of complicated regulations to implement the Patient Protection and Affordable Care Act (PPACA) and the Foreign Account Tax Compliance Act (FATCA) has contributed to fewer overall guidance documents being issued in recent years.[27]

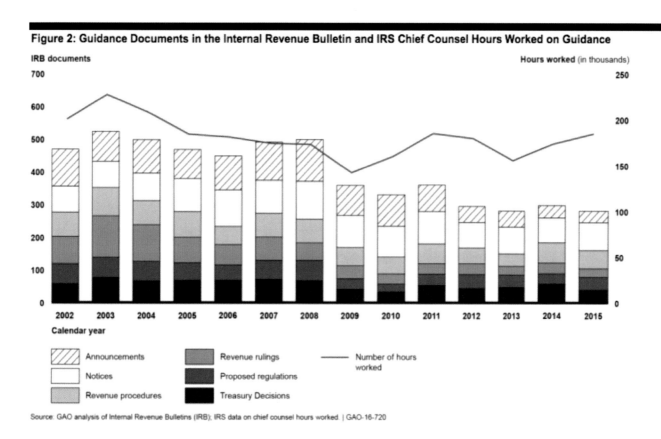

Figure 2: Guidance Documents in the Internal Revenue Bulletin and IRS Chief Counsel Hours Worked on Guidance

Source: GAO analysis of Internal Revenue Bulletins (IRB); IRS data on chief counsel hours worked. | GAO-16-720

---

[23] U.S. Government Accountability Office, Report to Congressional Requesters, September 2016.
[24] Id.
[25] Id.
[26] Id.
[27] Id.

This hierarchy of authorities provides guidance for tax practitioners to provide their professional judgment on the strength or weakness of tax positions, also referred to as "tax confidence levels."

7. Tax Confidence Levels

Tax practitioners must appreciate that effective tax law requires compliance by taxpayers. Tax compliance occurs when taxpayers understand how to follow tax law. But, language is not a simple vehicle in which to express rules. Language is difficult. Language can be beautiful and inspiring. Consider the following quote from Elbert Hubbard: "To avoid criticism, do nothing, say nothing, be nothing." What do you think these words mean? Different individuals may have slightly different perspectives on the meaning of these words. And, each person's perspective regarding the meaning of these words may offer a unique and viable view. But, in law, different perspectives on the meaning of written law presents confusion. And, confusion in law drives non-compliance – taxpayers are so confused that even with sincere intentions to follow law, individuals may not reasonably be able to do so. However, if tax law is not drafted with precision, then the law may be subject to misunderstanding or aggressive reading leading to abuse. Thus, the tax law is drafted to provide precision and just a bit of room to allow for reasonable interpretation consistent with the intent of the drafters of the law.

Understanding how the tax law is meant to apply promotes compliance. And, tax compliance is the bedrock of financing the operations of any government. Where we have uncertainty in understanding tax law given the nature of language and difficulty of navigating this language, what guides taxpayers and practitioners? The answer - tax confidence levels.[28]

---

[28] Note that these confidence levels may be different than for financial accounting purposes. For example, on July 13, 2006, the Financial Accounting Standards Board ("FASB") issued FASB Interpretation No. 48 ("FIN 48"), Accounting for Uncertainty in Income Taxes. FIN 48 is an interpretation of FASB Statement No. 109 regarding the calculation and disclosure of reserves for uncertain tax positions. FIN 48 clarifies the accounting for uncertainty in income taxes recognized in an enterprise's financial statements. FIN 48 is effective for fiscal years beginning after December 15, 2006, is applicable to all enterprises subject to US GAAP (including non-profit enterprises), and applies to all income tax positions accounted for in accordance with FASB Statement No. 109. Under FIN 48, one occasion when the remaining benefits of uncertain tax positions can be fully and finally recognized in US GAAP financial statements is when an enterprise determines that "effective settlement" of the uncertain position occurs. FIN 48 states:

> An enterprise shall evaluate all of the following conditions when determining whether effective settlement has occurred:
>> a. The taxing authority has completed its examination procedures including all appeals and administrative reviews that the taxing authority is required and expected to perform for the tax position.
>> b. The enterprise does not intend to appeal or litigate any aspect of the tax position included in the completed examination.
>> c. It is remote that the taxing authority would examine or reexamine any aspect of the tax position. In making this assessment management shall consider the taxing authority's policy on reopening closed examinations and the specific facts and circumstances of the tax position. Management shall presume the relevant taxing authority has full knowledge of all relevant information in making the assessment on whether the taxing authority would reopen a previously closed examination.

Various sections of the Internal Revenue Code provide references to "tax confidence levels" as the basis for relief or imposition of penalties. Section 6694 imposes a penalty upon tax return preparers based on the following tax confidence levels: reasonable basis, substantial authority, and more likely than not. Section 6662 imposes a penalty upon taxpayers but offers relief in certain circumstances if "reasonable basis" exists.

In addition to the Code, the applicable standards required to be followed by certified public accountants ("CPAs") refer to tax confidence levels as well. For example, in Statement of Standards for Tax Services ("SSTS") #1, tax confidence levels of "reasonable basis" and "realistic possibility of success on the merits" are set forth as applicable to CPA members. Circular 230, likewise, references tax confidence levels in its rules. So, we know that these tax confidence levels are embedded in the Code, Circular 230 and SSTS. What do these terms mean?

The "reasonable basis" threshold is not precisely defined by Treasury regulations. However, Treas. Reg. §1.6662-3(b), provides that "a reasonable basis is a relatively high standard of tax reporting, that is, significantly higher than not frivolous or not patently improper."

"Substantial authority," as defined in Treas. Reg. §1.6662-4(d), is an "objective standard" involving an analysis of the law and its application to relevant facts. The regulation provides that the substantial authority standard is less stringent than the more-likely-than-not standard, but more stringent than the "reasonable-basis" standard.

Under Circular 230, a "realistic possibility" exists when a reasonable and well-informed analysis by a person knowledgeable in the tax law concludes there is at least an approximately one-in-three (33%) likelihood the position would be upheld on its merits. Under subpart (a) of section 10.34, practitioners should not prepare or sign a return that they are aware takes a position that does not meet the realistic-possibility standard, unless the position is not frivolous and is appropriately disclosed in the tax return.

Below is a summary of the levels of tax confidence and the *approximate* mathematical conversion of these terms. For each tax confidence level, the tax professional has conducted necessary research and determined through a comprehensive review of these authorities as applied to the client's facts that if the IRS audits the tax return position or a court considers the taxpayer's return position that – the tax return position:

- "will" be sustained as correctly reported on the tax return as filed.
- "should" be sustained as correctly reported on the tax return as filed.
- has "substantial authority" to warrant being sustained as correctly reported on the tax return as filed.

- has "a realistic possibility of being sustained on the merits" as correctly reported on the tax return as filed.
- has "reasonable basis" to warrant being sustained as correctly reported on the tax return as filed.
- is "not frivolous" and "not patently improper" as filed.
- is "frivolous" and "patently improper" as filed.

Percentage of Tax Confidence	Confidence Level Standard
>= 90%	"Will"/"Should"
>50%	"More likely than not"
40-50%	"Substantial authority" tax confidence level – the "substantial authority" standard is more stringent than the "reasonable basis" standard as defined in Treas. Reg. § 1.6662-3(b)(3), Treas. Reg. § 1.6662-4(d)(2). In order to satisfy the "substantial authority" standard of section 6662(d)(2)(B)(i), a taxpayer must show that the weight of the authorities supporting the tax return treatment of an item is substantial in relation to the weight of authorities supporting contrary treatment. Antonides v. Commissioner, 91 T.C. 686 T.C. 686, 702 (1988), aff'd 893 F.2d 656 (4th Cir. 1990); Treas. Reg. §1.6662-4(d)(3)(i).
>=33%	"Realistic possibility of being sustained on the merits" tax confidence level – this standard may be met by a well-reasoned construction of the statute. This standard is less stringent than the "substantial authority" standard and stricter than the "reasonable basis" standard. Treas. Reg. §1.6662-3(a).
25%	"Reasonable Basis" tax confidence level – a relatively high standard of tax reporting that is significantly higher than not frivolous or not patently improper. A return position generally has a "reasonable basis" if it is reasonably based on one or more of the following authorities, among others: the IRC and other statutory provisions; proposed, temporary and final regulations construing the statutes; court cases; and congressional intent as reflected in committee reports. Treas. Reg. §1.6662-4(d)(3)(iii). The "reasonable basis" standard is not satisfied by a return position that is merely arguable or is merely a colorable claim. Treas. Reg. §1.6662-3(b)(3).
5-10%	"Not Frivolous/Not Patently Improper" tax confidence level
<5%	"Frivolous/Patently Improper" tax confidence level – a position without supporting tax authority knowingly advanced in bad faith

Why do **taxpayers** need tax confidence levels? Various statutory penalties in Title 26 impose penalties upon taxpayers unless a certain minimum tax confidence level is reached. For example, in section 6662, a taxpayer will be subject to a 20% of the underpayment of tax required to be shown on a return unless the return position is a disclosed item and there exists "reasonable basis" for its tax treatment. I.R.C. § 6662(d)(2)(B).

Why do **tax return preparers** need to determine tax confidence levels? For federal "tax return preparers" as defined in section 7701(a)(36), section 6694 imposes a penalty if the preparer does not determine a specific tax confidence level given various circumstances and transaction involved.[29] In section 6694, Congress sets out three tax confidence levels for tax return preparers to meet in order to prepare/sign such return(s): reasonable basis, substantial authority and more likely than not. In addition to the code, the American Institute of Certified Public Accountants ("AICPA") issues SSTS that reflect the AICPA's standards of tax practice and delineate members' responsibilities to taxpayers, the public, the government, and the profession. Similar to the tax code, these SSTS standards of professional practice set forth tax confidence levels that CPAs must meet in order to conduct their practice.

Whether return preparers or advisors, tax professionals in general need to determine tax confidence levels in order to assess the strength (or weakness) of a tax position to effectively engage in decision-making analysis for their clients. A tax professional's need to obtain a level of confidence to proceed with decision-making is no different than in other disciplines. Psychologists are responsible for making optimal judgments about their client problems, course of treatment, and future behavior among several other decisions based on their degree of confidence in their diagnosis.[30] Financial advisors issue recommendations to clients regarding stocks and bonds, such as "Buy," "Strong Buy," "Hold," etc. These financial sector professionals utilize objective data and subjective information to reach their final recommendations in their specific industry. Similarly, tax confidence levels present professional determinations of judgment based on research to present the overall strength of a specific tax position. As you become more familiar with the types of primary source authorities that can influence your perspective of tax positions, you will develop a much greater comfort level of understanding between various tax confidence levels.

To give the reader a better understanding of tax confidence levels and how it serves to protect the tax system, let's consider two scenarios:

Scenario 1: Client A has engaged in a tax transaction that reduces her overall federal tax liability in tax year 2017. Client A hires Charlie as to prepare her federal tax return. He confirms that the tax transaction employed by Client A in 2017 is not an aggressive tax transaction. The transaction is neither a tax shelter or reportable transaction as provided under section 6694(a)(2)(C). Charlie asks Client A if she would like to disclose the transaction on her return. Client A tells Charlie, "No." So, under section 6694, what level of tax confidence level must Charlie reach to avoid a penalty under section 6694?

Answer: First, the transaction is not a "tax shelter or reportable transaction." So, Charlie doesn't need to reach the "more likely than not" tax confidence level to avoid a penalty. Second, since there is no disclosure, Charlie is not allowed to apply the "reasonable basis" level of confidence to prepare the return. So, Charlie is left with

---

[29] Section 7701(a)(36)(A) defines a "tax return preparer" as "any person who prepares for compensation, or who employs one or more persons to prepare for compensation, any return of tax imposed by this title or any claim for refund of tax imposed by this title."

[30] "A Meta-Analysis of Confidence and Judgment Accuracy in Clinical Decision Making," Journal of Counseling Pschology, 2015, Vo. 62, No. 4, 553-567, by Deborah J. Miller, Elliot S. Spengler and Paul M. Spengler.

the statutory duty to obtain a tax confidence of "substantial authority" in order to avoid a penalty.

Scenario 2: Same facts as Scenario 1, except Client A tells Charlie that he can disclose the transaction. So, under section 6694, what level of tax confidence level must Charlie reach to avoid a penalty under section 6694?

Answer: Due to the disclosure, Charlie can reach a tax confidence level of "reasonable basis" to fulfill his statutory duty under section 6694.

Let's consider how section 6694 provides a partnership between the IRS and Charlie, the tax return preparer. If there is disclosure on the return of the transaction, then the IRS has more information than just the numbers reported on the return to be able to determine the merits of the transaction. Because the disclosure provides the IRS with more information, Charlie is allowed to reach a lower level of confidence to prepare the return – reasonable basis. However, if there is no disclosure, the statute imposes a higher statutory duty on Charlie to conduct more research to reach a higher level of confidence (substantial authority) to ensure that the filed federal return is correct. Make sense?[31]

---

[31] What constitutes "adequate disclosure?" See Rev. Proc. 2010-15. See also CNT Investors, LLC v. Commissioner, 144 T.C. 161 (2015)("....for an alleged disclosure to qualify as adequate, the return need not recite every underlying fact but must provide a clue more substantial than one that would intrigue the likes of Sherlock Holmes. [internal citations omitted]. A disclosure need only be ''sufficiently detailed to alert the Commissioner and his agents as to the nature of the transaction so that the decision as to whether to select the return for audit may be a reasonably informed one.'").

Chapter 1 - Questions

1. The Internal Revenue Code as drafted presents complexity in tax law. Why does the IRS seek to provide guidance in order to promote certainty in tax law?

2. Which tax confidence level is higher – "substantial authority" or "reasonable basis"? Provide the citation to primary source authority that supports your answer.

3. An individual volunteers at a non-profit community center to provide senior citizens free tax preparation services. Is this individual a "tax return preparer" subject to penalties as set forth under section 6694?

4. Provide two statutory sources that refer to tax confidence levels.

5. Provide three executive source authorities that refer to tax confidence levels.

6. Tax law provides a rule on how various transactions either trigger or do not trigger realization and/or recognition of taxable income. But, tax law often requires guidance for taxpayers, the government and practitioners to properly apply. Consider a common situation that touches virtually all of us: frequent flier miles or point award programs. When a person receives and redeems reward miles or loyalty points, does that person receive taxable income that must be reported on their federal tax return? To address this question, consider the following sources: (1) statutory authority from Congress; (2) executive guidance on the issue (or part of the issue) – Exhibit 1, below; and (3) correspondence from a U.S. Senator addressing a bank's award program – Exhibit 2, below; (4) a court decision on the issue – Exhibit 3, below. After you consider the information and exhibits, below, provide your view on whether you have sufficient information to answer this question: if a person receives and redeems award reward miles or loyalty points to obtain something of value (say, a roundtrip flight which normally costs $300), then is that person required to report the value received on their federal income tax return as taxable income in that year?

Part I – Consider Sources That Address This Tax Issue

IRS – <u>See</u> Exhibit 1, below. The IRS published IRS Announcement 2002-18 (Frequent Flier Miles Attributable to Business or Official Travel). In this document, the IRS stated that "it will not assert that any taxpayer has understated his federal tax liability by reason of the receipt or personal use of frequent flier miles or other in-kind promotional benefits attributable to the taxpayer's business or official travel." First, why didn't the IRS simply state that receipt of frequent flier mileage benefits is <u>not</u> gross income under section 61? Well, under the broad definition of "gross income" enacted by Congress, can the IRS take a position that runs counter to clearly broad language set forth in the code? No. However, the IRS provided guidance to taxpayers that if they did not report such receipt of mileage benefits in a tax year received as a result of official or business travel, then the administrative agency in charge of ferreting out the accuracy of filed tax returns would not proceed with any action on such items, e.g., "the IRS will not assert that any taxpayer has understated his federal tax liability......" Second, consider the specific limitation of this IRS guidance addressing frequent flier miles – applicable only to miles attributable to a taxpayer's business or official travel. So, if you earn miles from a non-business or non-official promotional mileage or points program, then this IRS announcement does not apply. How difficult is reading tax code? Well, even Congress encounters challenges in properly interpreting tax law that it enacts. For example, in 2012, Senator Sherrod Brown issued a letter to Citibank objecting to the bank's view that providing customers with points constituted gross income requiring the institution to issue Form 1099 to comply with tax law.

Congress – <u>See</u> Exhibit 2, below. Under I.R.C. §61, Congress provided a very broad definition for the term "gross income" – to mean all income from whatever source derived. Now, under various circumstances, taxpayers may be understandably confused whether they must report as "gross income" certain items that they receive in the course of their daily activities. Without guidance, taxpayers confront a difficult situation in understanding how to comply with their tax obligation in this scenario. Who should provide taxpayers with guidance? Read the letter issued by a U.S. Senator on this issue. This Senator's letter provides an interpretation of IRS Announcement 2002-18. Do you agree with the Senator's understanding of IRS Announcement 2002-18?

The Courts – <u>See</u> Exhibit 3, below. In <u>Shankar v. Commissioner</u>, 143 T.C. No. 5 (2014), the U.S. Tax Court addressed the issue of whether the value of points received by a taxpayer from a non-business, non-official context constitutes gross income under section 61. In holding that a taxpayer's receipt of such benefit did fall within the definition of gross income under section 61, the court explained that IRS Announcement 2002-18 did not fit this situation. Is the U.S. Tax Court's reading of IRS Announcement 2002-18 different or the same as the Senator's view?

Read Exhibits 1, 2, and 3. Then, address questions that follow from the reading material.

Exhibit 1 – Chapter 1, Practical Example of Tax Guidance

Part IV

Items of General Interest

Frequent Flyer Miles Attributable to Business or Official Travel

Announcement 2002-18

Most major airlines offer frequent flyer programs under which passengers accumulate miles for each flight. Individuals may also earn frequent flyer miles or other promotional benefits, for example, through rental cars or hotels. These promotional benefits may generally be exchanged for upgraded seating, free travel, discounted travel, travel-related services, or other services or benefits.

Questions have been raised concerning the taxability of frequent flyer miles or other promotional items that are received as the result of business travel and used for personal purposes. There are numerous technical and administrative issues relating to these benefits on which no official guidance has been provided, including issues relating to the timing and valuation of income inclusions and the basis for identifying personal use benefits attributable to business (or official) expenditures versus those attributable to personal expenditures. Because of these unresolved issues, the IRS has not pursued a tax enforcement program with respect to promotional benefits such as frequent flyer miles.

Consistent with prior practice, the IRS will not assert that any taxpayer has understated his federal tax liability by reason of the receipt or personal use of frequent flyer miles or other in-kind promotional benefits attributable to the taxpayer's business or official travel. Any future guidance on the taxability of these benefits will be applied prospectively.

This relief does not apply to travel or other promotional benefits that are converted to cash, to compensation that is paid in the form of travel or other promotional benefits, or in other circumstances where these benefits are used for tax avoidance purposes.

For information regarding this announcement, call (202) 622-4606 (not a toll-free number). Alternatively, taxpayers may transmit comments electronically via the following e-mail address: Notice.Comments@irscounsel.treas.gov. Please include "Announcement 2002-18" in the subject line of any electronic communications.

Exhibit 2 – Chapter 1, Practical Example of Tax Guidance

SHERROD BROWN
OHIO

COMMITTEES
AGRICULTURE, NUTRITION
AND FORESTRY
APPROPRIATIONS
BANKING, HOUSING,
AND URBAN AFFAIRS
VETERANS AFFAIRS
SELECT COMMITTEE ON ETHICS

United States Senate

WASHINGTON, DC 20510

January 30, 2012

Mr. Vikram Pandit
Citibank
399 Park Avenue
New York, NY 10043

Dear Mr. Pandit:

As Chairman of the Senate Banking Subcommittee on Financial Institutions and Consumer Protection, I write to express my concern regarding recent reports that Citibank is sending 1099 tax forms to customers who received frequent-flier miles as a reward for opening a checking or savings account.

During these challenging economic times, middle-class families are pinching pennies to help pay for the cost of a flight to fly home from college, visit an ailing relative, or see friends. To some, signing up for a bank account in exchange for frequent-flier miles to help make a trip more affordable is an offer that is too good to resist. However, your actions are leaving working families with the seemingly incorrect impression that when they rack up miles, they are hiking up their taxes, too.

Citibank arbitrarily calculates the value of each frequent-flier mile as 2.5 cents of taxable income. Based upon its incorrect interpretation of a rule requiring individuals to report rewards and prizes as taxable income, Citibank has been sending its customers 1099 tax forms to report their frequent-flier miles. A spokesperson stated that the bank is following instructions from the 2012 Internal Revenue Code, and that income tax must be paid if at least $600 in "prizes and awards" is received. These miles are neither a prize nor an award.

Furthermore, the Internal Revenue Service (IRS) has made clear that frequent-flier miles are not taxable income. In a ruling made in 2002 – which still stands – the IRS highlighted that frequent-flier miles are not subject to income tax due to the "numerous technical and administrative issues relating to these benefits." Furthermore, the IRS stated that it "will not assert that any taxpayer has understated his or her federal tax liability by reason of the receipt or personal use of frequent-flier miles or other in-kind promotional benefits attributable to the taxpayer's business or official travel."

Most importantly, given the IRS's ruling, why is Citibank sending its customers 1099 tax forms? Reporting frequent-flier miles as taxable income is inconvenient to consumers, raises their anxiety unnecessarily, and is not required by law.

I urge Citibank to halt this practice. The last thing Citibank should be doing is creating baseless fear in middle-class families, or placing a nonexistent tax burden on the backs of families who are already struggling to make ends meet.

Thank you for your consideration of this matter.

Sincerely,

Sherrod Brown
United States Senator

Exhibit 3 – Chapter 1, Practical Example of Tax Guidance

PARIMAL H. SHANKAR AND MALTI S. TRIVEDI, PETITIONERS v. COMMISSIONER OF INTERNAL REVENUE, RESPONDENT
Docket No. 24414–12. Filed August 26, 2014.

- Excerpt taken from Shankar v. Commissioner, 143 T.C. No. 5 (2014) on the Citibank "Thank You" Points Issue

HALPERN, Judge: Respondent determined a deficiency of $563 in petitioners' 2009 Federal income tax. The deficiency resulted principally from respondent's making the following adjustments to petitioners' reported 2009 tax. Respondent increased petitioners' gross income by $668 on account of that amount's being reported by Citibank, N.A. (Citibank), as the value of 50,000 "Thank You Points" (thank you points) petitioner husband (Mr. Shankar) redeemed in 2009 to purchase an airline ticket. Respondent disallowed petitioners' deduction of $11,000 reflecting their contributions of that sum under a qualified retirement arrangement (IRA). Respondent disallowed the deduction because petitioners' modified adjusted gross income (modified AGI) for 2009 exceeded the statutorily imposed ceiling for such contributions. Respondent reduced petitioners' alternative minimum tax (AMT) from $2,775 to zero. Respondent did not explain that last adjustment. By amendment to answer, respondent increased his claim of a deficiency to $6,883 on account of his recomputation of petitioners' 2009 AMT.

Petitioners, husband and wife, resided in New Jersey when they filed the petition. Petitioners' Reported Income and Tax Return For 2009, petitioners filed a joint Federal income tax return on Form 1040, U.S. Individual Income Tax Return. During 2009, Mr. Shankar was a self-employed consultant who reported his self-employment income on Schedule C, Profit or Loss From Business, attached to the Form 1040. During 2009, petitioner wife (Ms. Trivedi) was employed by University Group Medical Associates, PC (Associates). In addition to paying her a taxable salary, which she reported, Associates made contributions on her behalf to an annuity purchase plan described in section 403(b), which she was not required to report as an item of gross income. Ms. Trivedi also earned self-employment income, which she reported on a second Schedule C attached to the Form 1040. Petitioners claimed a deduction of $11,000 for IRA contributions made in 2009. They reported AGI of $243,729. They also reported alternative minimum taxable income of $235,487 and AMT of $2,775.

During 2009, Mr. Shankar banked at Citibank. Citibank reported to Mr. Shankar and to the Internal Revenue Service on a 2009 Form 1099–MISC, Miscellaneous Income, "Other income" of $668. Petitioners did not report the income shown on the 2009 Form 1099–MISC on the Form 1040. At trial, in order to show that the 2009 Form 1099–MISC properly and accurately reported the income shown thereon, respondent introduced into evidence as a business record the affidavit of Marilyn Kennedy, a duly authorized custodian of records for Citibank. Attached to the affidavit are documents and computer transcripts from Citibank showing that Mr. Shankar redeemed 50,000 thank you points on February 27, 2009, to purchase a restricted coach class airline ticket for travel in the lower 48 United States, Alaska, and Canada. Also, attached to the affidavit is a letter from Ms. Kennedy, in which she, as the custodian of records for Citibank, represents that the fair market value of the airline ticket was $668. Respondent provided the affidavit and attachments to petitioners on September 9, 2013. Trial in this case was held on December 2, 2013.

………………..

II. Unreported Income Respondent increased petitioners' gross income by $668 on account of that amount's being reported as "Other income" on the 2009 Form 1099–MISC. Petitioners deny receipt of the income shown on the 2009 Form 1099–MISC. In general, the taxpayer bears the burden of proving facts to support his assignments of error to the Commissioner's determination of a deficiency. See Rule 142(a). Pursuant to section 6201(d), however, if, in any court proceeding, a taxpayer asserts a reasonable dispute with respect to the income reported on an information return and the taxpayer has fully cooperated with the Commissioner, then the Commissioner has the burden of producing reasonable and probative information in addition to the information return. Because respondent has by way of Ms. Kennedy's affidavit and its attachments provided reasonable and probative information in addition to the information reported on the 2009 Form 1099–MISC that, during 2009, Mr. Shankar received from Citibank other income of $668, we need not consider whether he reasonably disputes that report or that he has fully cooperated with respondent. Respondent has carried any burden imposed on him by section 6201(d). Indeed, in carrying that burden, respondent has provided us with evidence in the form of Citibank records (i.e., computer transcripts) showing that, on February 27, 2009, Mr. Shankar redeemed 50,000 thank you points to purchase a restricted coach class airline ticket. Contradicting that evidence we have only Mr. Shankar's testimony that, in effect, he knows nothing about any thank you points and received no award. Petitioners had ample time between their receipt of the Citibank records on September 9, 2013, and the trial of this case on December 2, 2013, to investigate the information provided in the Citibank records and to show to us that it was in error. They did not do so. Ms. Trivedi did not appear at trial, so we do not have the benefit of her view of whether Mr. Shankar received the award. On balance, we give more weight to Citibank's records showing Mr. Shankar's receipt of an award than we do to his testimony to the contrary, and we find that he did in 2009 receive from Citibank in redemption of 50,000 thank you points a restricted coach class airline ticket.

There are still the questions of whether receipt of the airline ticket constituted receipt of an item of gross income and, if so, its value. Section 61(a) defines the term "gross income" to include "all income from whatever source derived". The term has been broadly interpreted. See, e.g., Commissioner v. Glenshaw Glass Co., 348 U.S. 426, 431 (1955) (gross income includes "instances of undeniable accessions to wealth, clearly realized, and over which the taxpayers have complete dominion"). We are not here dealing with the taxability of frequent flyer miles attributable to business or official travel, with respect to which the Commissioner stated in Announcement 2002–18, 2002–1 C.B. 621, he would not assert that a taxpayer has gross income because he received or used frequent flyer miles attributable to business travel. Petitioners have provided us with no information concerning the reason Citibank awarded Mr. Shankar thank you points. Mr. Shankar did not object when, at the start of the trial in this case, respondent's counsel answered in the affirmative the Court's question as to whether, besides the IRA contribution, the other item in dispute, i.e., "Other income", involved the omission from the Form 1040 of interest. Respondent's counsel added that the omitted income was a noncash award for opening a bank account. We proceed on the assumption that we are dealing here with a premium for making a deposit into, or maintaining a balance in, a bank account. In other words, something given in exchange for the use (deposit) of Mr. Shankar's money; i.e., something in the nature of interest. In general, the receipt of interest constitutes the receipt of an item of gross income. See sec. 61(a)(4). Receipt of the airline ticket constituted receipt of an item of gross income, and petitioners have failed to show that it was worth any less than $668, which Citibank, which had purchased the ticket, said was its fair market value. But cf. Turner v. Commissioner, T.C. Memo. 1954–38 (in which we determined that the "proper fair figure" to be included in the taxpayers' gross income on account of the taxpayer husband's winning steamship tickets on a radio quiz show was substantially less than the tickets' retail price because the tickets' value to the taxpayers was not equal to their retail cost). On account of Mr. Shankar's receipt of the airline ticket, petitioners omitted $668 of gross income from the Form 1040.

7. See parts (a), (b) and (c) to Question 7, below:

(a) Re: IRS Announcement 2002-18 -- The IRS stated that numerous difficulties on the issue of the taxability of frequent flier miles or promotional benefits received from official business travel and used for personal benefits have left this area with no official guidance to assist the public. As such, the IRS provided relief: "….the IRS will not assert that any taxpayer has understated his federal tax liability by reason of the receipt or personal use of frequent flyer miles or other in-kind promotional benefits attributable to the taxpayer's business or official travel." Why didn't the IRS simply state that a person's receipt or personal use of frequent flier miles or other loyalty points benefits did not constitute the receipt of gross income under section 61?

(b) Re: The U.S. Senator's Letter Addressing Award Points -- In the U.S. Senator's letter, he stated: "…the IRS has made clear that frequent flier miles are not taxable income." Is the Senator's reading of IRS Announcement 2002-18 correct?

(c) In Shankar, why did the Tax Court determine that IRS Announcement 2002-18 did not apply to provide relief for Mr. Shankar?

8. What is the difference between primary source authorities and second sources?

9. What is the value of secondary source material?

CHAPTER 2 – TAX PRACTICE

☑   Understand the distinction between tax return preparer and tax practitioners
☑   Understand the requirements to practice before the IRS
☑   Understand the entity that regulations tax practitioners
☑   Understand the basic forms used by tax practitioners

1. Federal Tax Return Preparers
2. Federal Tax Practitioners
3. The Entity that Regulates Federal Tax Practitioners
4. Circular 230 and AICPA Statement on Standards for Tax Services ("SSTS")
5. Basic Forms Used by Tax Practitioners
6. Frequently Asked Questions About Circular 230
7. Tax Practice Considerations

1. Federal Tax Return Preparers

Tax law is an exceptionally difficult discipline to understand and apply as either a lay person as well as a professional. A famous jurist once said, "In my own case the words of such an act as the Income Tax, for example, merely dance before my eyes in a meaningless procession….leave in my mind only a confused sense of some vitally important, but successfully concealed purpose, which it is my duty to extract, but which is within my power, if at all, only after the most inordinate expenditure of time."[32] Despite universal agreement of the incredible complexity inherent in tax law, there is no regulation currently in place that governs federal tax return preparers.

---

[32] Justice Learned Hand, *Thomas Walter Swan*, <u>Yale L.J.</u> 167, 169 (1947).

So, how does Congress define a federal "tax return preparer?" Code section 7701(a)(36) defines a "tax return preparer" to mean any person who prepares for compensation, or who employs one or more persons to prepare for compensation, any return of tax imposed by this title or any claim for refund of tax imposed by this title. Anyone who prepares a substantial portion of a return or claim for refund is treated as if he/she prepared the return. Section 6694 imposes a statutory duty upon "tax return preparers" by imposing a penalty if a tax return prepared by them includes an "unreasonable position." Beyond the statutory definition for "tax return preparer" and the Congressional penalty statute of section 6694, no other tax provision applies to this field of practice.

Taxpayer reliance on paid tax return preparers is inextricably linked to quality return preparation. As such, the IRS attempted to regulate federal tax return preparers by establishing a certification program involving registration, testing and continuing legal education requirements. In or around 2012, the IRS initiated a requirement for all Federal tax return preparers to submit to registration, competency testing and continuing education. However, a few return preparers sued the IRS arguing that the agency's attempt to regulate tax return preparers fell outside any authorization specifically enacted by Congress. And, in Loving v. Commissioner, 742 F.3d 1013 (D.C. Cir. 2014), the District of Columbia Court of Appeals held against the IRS. So, while the regulation of federal tax return preparers to ensure their competency is a worthy goal, there is no such requirement in place today.

After Loving, the IRS was pulled into court, again, this time for its requirement that federal tax return preparers use preparer tax identification numbers (or, "PTINs") to prepare returns for their clients. In Steele, et al. v. United States, 2017-1 U.S.T.C. ¶50,238 (USDC, District of Columbia), tax return preparers sued the IRS alleging that they had been wrongfully required to pay PTIN fees set by the IRS in 2010 at approximately $63. On June 1, 2017, the District Court granted the Plaintiffs' Motion for Summary Judgment in part, ruling that the IRS may continue to require PTINs, but may not charge fees for the issuance or renewal of PTINs. The District Court judge also enjoined the IRS from charging those fees in the future, and ordered the government to refund all PTIN fees paid to date. Thus, while the IRS can continue to require use of PTINs by federal tax return preparers, it cannot charge fees for these PTINs.

2. Federal Tax Practitioners

So, what is the difference between a federal tax return preparer as defined under section 7701(a)(36) and a federal tax practitioner? Whereas the Code defines "federal tax return preparer," Circular 230 defines "federal tax practitioners."[33]

---

[33] Go to https://www.irs.gov/tax-professionals/circular-230-tax-professionals to obtain the current version of Circular 230. See also Appendix B in this textbook.

41

Chapter 2: Tax Practice

Let's start with the definition of "practice" before the IRS as set out in Circular 230, the rules that establish practitioners' conduct in representing taxpayers before the tax agency. "Practice" before the IRS "comprehends all matters connected with a presentation to the Internal Revenue Service or any of its officers or employees relating to a taxpayer's rights, privileges, or liabilities under laws or regulations administered by the Internal Revenue Service. Such presentations include, but are not limited to, preparing documents; filing documents; corresponding and communicating with the Internal Revenue Service; rendering written advice with respect to any entity, transaction, plan or arrangement, or other plan or arrangement having a potential for tax avoidance or evasion; and representing a client at conferences, hearings, and meetings."

"Practitioners" are those specifically identified categories of individuals who are authorized to engage in "practice" before the IRS. What categories of individuals are authorized to "practice?" Section 10.3 provides the following recognized categories who may "practice":

- Attorneys
- Certified public accountants
- Enrolled agents
- Enrolled actuaries
- Enrolled retirement plan agents
- Registered tax return preparers
- Others
  - An individual who is granted *temporary* recognition to practice by the Commissioner pending a determination under a recognized status
  - An individual who decides to self-represent, i.e., representing oneself
- Government officers and employees, i.e., employees of any of the three branches of the federal government
- State officers and employees

Separately, Circular 230, section 10.7, provides "limited practice" for those individuals who are not qualified "practitioners" in any of the recognized categories if they are any of the following:
- A member of the taxpayer's immediate family
- A regular full-time employee of an individual employer
- A general partner or regular full-time employee of a partnership
- A bona fide officer or a regular full-time employee of a corporation
- A regular full-time employee of a trust, receivership, guardianship, or estate may represent the trust, receivership, guardianship, or estate
- An officer or a regular employee of a governmental unit, agency or authority may represent the governmental unit agency or authority
- An individual may represent any individual or entity, who is outside the United States, when such representation takes place outside the United States

Circular 230 defines "registered tax return preparers" and how an individual may qualify for this designation. Under Circular 230, Sec. 10.3(f), practice as a "registered tax return preparer" is limited to preparing and signing tax returns and claims for refund, and other documents for submission to the IRS. Thus, it appears that "practice" under Circular 230 includes the task of preparing federal tax returns at least with respect to "registered tax return preparers." But, in the decision of <u>Loving v. Commissioner</u>, 742 F.3d 1013 (D.C. Cir. 2014), the District of Columbia Court of Appeals held that the IRS is prohibited from regulating tax return preparers because such regulation falls outside any authorization specifically enacted by Congress. However, apart from this limited category of "registered tax return preparers," Circular 230 still provides rules for other designated "practitioners" to follow with respect to their work on tax returns in addition to representing taxpayers before the IRS related to tax issues. <u>See</u> Circular 230, Sec. 10.34 (Standards with respect to tax returns and documents, affidavits and other papers).

3. The Entity that Regulates Federal Tax Practitioners

The Office of Professional Responsibility ("OPR") administers and enforces the provisions set forth under Circular 230. <u>See</u> Cir. 230, Sec. 10.1(a)-(c). What are the types of disciplinary sanctions that may be imposed for violation of the applicable standards under Circular 230?

- Disbarred from practice before the IRS—An individual who is disbarred is not eligible to practice before the IRS as defined at 31 C.F.R. § 10.2(a)(4) for a minimum period of five (5) years.
- Suspended from practice before the IRS—An individual who is suspended is not eligible to practice before the IRS as defined at 31 C.F.R. § 10.2(a)(4) during the term of the suspension.
- Censured in practice before the IRS—Censure is a public reprimand. Unlike disbarment or suspension, censure does not affect an individual's eligibility to practice before the IRS, but OPR may subject the individual's future practice rights to conditions designed to promote high standards of conduct.
- Monetary penalty—A monetary penalty may be imposed on an individual who engages in conduct subject to sanction, or on an employer, firm, or entity if the individual was acting on its behalf and it knew, or reasonably should have known, of the individual's conduct.
- Disqualification of appraiser—An appraiser who is disqualified is barred from presenting evidence or testimony in any administrative proceeding before the Department of the Treasury or the IRS.
- Ineligible for limited practice—An unenrolled/unlicensed return preparer who fails to comply with the requirements in Revenue Procedure 81–38 or to comply with Circular 230 as required by Revenue Procedure 2014 – 42 may be determined ineligible to engage in limited practice as a representative of any taxpayer. Under the regulations, individuals subject to Circular 230 may not assist, or accept assistance from, individuals who are suspended or disbarred with respect to matters constituting practice (i.e., representation) before the IRS, and they

may not aid or abet suspended or disbarred individuals to practice before the IRS.

Disciplinary sanctions are described in these terms: Disbarred by decision, Suspended by decision, Censured by decision, Monetary penalty imposed by decision, and Disqualified after hearing. How are these disciplinary decisions carried out? An administrative law judge ("ALJ") may issue a decision imposing one of these sanctions after the ALJ either (1) grants the government's summary judgment motion or (2) conducts an evidentiary hearing upon OPR's complaint alleging violation of the regulations. After 30 days from the issuance of the decision, in the absence of an appeal, the ALJ's decision becomes the final agency decision and may result in one of the following: Disbarred by default decision, Suspended by default decision, Censured by default decision, Monetary penalty imposed by default decision, and Disqualified by default decision.

Consider excerpts from a 2013 administrative law decision, below, entered against a Federal tax practitioner to understand the application of Circular 230 provisions against a practitioner who failed to follow rules of practice[34]:

UNITED STATES OF AMERICA
THE DEPARTMENT OF THE TREASURY
WASHINGTON, D.C.

KAREN L. HAWKINS,	)	
DIRECTOR,	)	
OFFICE OF PROFESSIONAL	)	Complaint No. IRS 2012-000061
RESPONSIBILITY,	)	
INTERNAL REVENUE SERVICE,	)	
	)	ORDER GRANTING COMPLAINANT'S
Complainant,	)	MOTION TO AMEND THE
	)	COMPLAINT MOTION FOR DEFAULT
v.	)	DECISION
	)	
ANTHONY A. TIONGSON	)	
	)	
Respondent.	)	

PRELIMINARY STATEMENT

On September 5, 2012, the Director, Office of Professional Responsibility (OPR), Internal Revenue Service (IRS), Department of the Treasury issued a Complaint pursuant to 31 C.F.R. §§ 10.60 and 10.91 and 31 U.S.C. § 330. Respondent Anthony A. Tiongson is a Certified Public Accountant (CPA) who practiced before the IRS.

The Complaint sought Respondent's disbarment from practice before the IRS because of Respondent's alleged incompetence and disreputable conduct as defined by 31 C.F.R. § 10.51. The disbarment would prevent Respondent from practicing before the IRS without the explicit

---

[34] https://www.irs.gov/pub/irs-utl/Tiongson%20-%20IRS_Decision%20on%20Tiongson%20Motion%20for%20Default%20(FINAL)%20-%204-3-13.pdf.

approval of OPR. In order to obtain reinstatement, the practitioner needs to demonstrate (at a minimum) that he is likely to conduct himself in accordance with the requirements of 31 C.F.R. Part 10 and that his reinstatement would not be contrary to the public interest. Any such reinstatement would be at the sole discretion of OPR.

****

PRINCIPLES OF LAW

OPR's Ability to Discipline IRS Practitioners

Under 31 U.S.C. § 330(a), the Secretary of the Treasury holds authority to "regulate the practice of representatives of persons before the Department of the Treasury," including the power to suspend or disbar an individual from practice for a number of reasons as long as the individual is first provided with "notice and opportunity" for hearing before an administrative law judge. Id. at § 330(b).

Circular 230 and Delegation Order No. 25-16 (2012) delegates the Director of OPR the authority to bring proceedings to suspend or disbar practitioners before the IRS. See 31 C.F.R. § 10.50(a). Under 31 C.F.R. § 10.50(e), any sanctions imposed "shall take into account all relevant facts and circumstances."

****

FINDINGS OF FACT

1. At all material times, Respondent has been a CPA engaged in practice before the IRS.

2. On March 19, 2009, Respondent and the United States of America filed a Plea Agreement with the United States District Court (Plea Agreement), pleading guilty to one count of: (1) willfully filing a tax return knowing that it contained false information as to any material matter; and (2) acting for the purpose of evading tax laws and not as a result of accident or negligence.

3. By that Plea Agreement, Respondent admitted he was in fact guilty of the offense as described in Count 1 of the Indictment.

4. Respondent stipulated in the Plea Agreement that "beginning in 1999, [he] submitted tax returns to the IRS for clients who lived and worked in California . . . in which he reported that the income was foreign earned income, claiming that California was not part of the United States . . . and therefore not subject to taxation . . . [Respondent] aided and assisted in the preparation and presentation to the Internal Revenue Service of materially false and fraudulent . . .tax returns for [Taxpayers in Count 1 of the Indictment]. As [Respondent] well knew, the IRS considered California part of the United States for tax purposes." ("Form 2555 Position").

5. On April 01, 2009, the United States District Court for the Central District of California issued an Order finding a factual basis for the Plea Agreement. Respondent was convicted of one count of filing a false tax return in violation of 26 U.S.C. § 7207 for the Taxpayers described in Count 1 of the Indictment.

6. On July 30, 2009, Complainant served Respondent with the Notice of Expedited Proceeding and Complaint No. 2006-15646-XP proposing his suspension from practice before the Internal Revenue Service pursuant to 31 C.F.R. § 10.82(b)(2).

7. On or about September 02, 2009, Respondent answered the Notice of Expedited Proceeding and Complaint No. 2006-15646-XP with a response dated August 26, 2009 ("Answer") and requested a conference with the Director, Office of Professional Responsibility.

8. On July 8, 2011, the California Board of Accountancy (CBA) brought an Accusation against Respondent. The CBA found six causes for discipline and concluded that Respondent's conduct was serious.

9. On August 02, 2012, the CBA suspended Respondent's license for one year, effective September 01, 2012, and set a probationary period of five years.

10. On August 06, 2012, Respondent requested pursuant to 31 C.F.R. §10.82(g) that Complainant issue a complaint under 31 C.F.R. §10.60.

11. On September 4, 2012, Complainant sent Respondent a supplemental allegation letter raising additional allegations of misconduct under Circular 230 and requested a response within 10 days, pursuant to § 10.20(a)(3).

12. Allegations contained in the September 4, 2012 letter were incorporated by reference into Complainant's Amended Complaint.

13. Respondent failed to respond to specific requests for information included in the September 4, 2012 supplemental allegation letter.

14. Respondent used a contingent fee structure based upon the expected income tax refunds for client returns prepared using the Form 2555 Position.

15. Respondent charged unconscionable fees for preparation of tax returns using the Form 2555 Position.

16. Respondent represented to IRS Criminal Investigation Special Agents that he charged a "little flat fee" for the preparation of Forms 1040 for clients using the Form 2555 Position and denied charging a contingent, or percentage, fee based on the anticipated refund for preparing a Form 1040 return using the Form 2555 Position.

17. Respondent represented to the CBA that he ceased using Form 2555 after he became aware of the first IRS audit.

18. Contrary to his representation to the CBA, Respondent continued preparing tax returns for clients using the Form 2555 Position, in the 2002 and 2003 tax filing seasons, after learning of an IRS audit for a client using the Form 2555 Position.

19. Respondent advised at least fifty-two clients to include the Form 2555 Position on federal income tax returns for tax years 1998 through 2002, for which the IRS originally assessed $52,000 in civil penalties against Respondent.

20. Respondent obstructed the IRS examination and collection activities for clients whose returns were prepared with the Form 2555 Position, for the IRS civil penalty investigation of Respondent, for the IRS examination of Respondent's personal Form 1040 for 2001, and for a 2006 IRS collection matter for clients who had not used the Form 2555 Position, by repeatedly raising numerous frivolous arguments, aside from the Form 2555 Position, that have been long-rejected by both the IRS, case law, and the Internal Revenue Code (IRC).

21. Respondent threatened lawsuits for damages, and lawsuits against IRS employees, personally, for unauthorized collection actions that Respondent alleged would be avoided if the IRS accepted the taxpayer's settlement offer to pay 20% of the assessed tax.

22. Respondent signed and submitted to the IRS, a Power of Attorney ("Form 2848") for taxpayer clients that listed both the Respondent and an un-enrolled individual as the two representatives.

23. An un-enrolled return preparer is not authorized to represent taxpayers before the IRS in collection matters.

****

CONCLUSIONS OF LAW
****

1. At all relevant times, Respondent engaged in practice before the IRS and is subject to the disciplinary authority of the OPR Director under the rules and regulations contained in 31 C.F.R. Part 10.

2. Respondent's preparation and submission of tax returns on behalf of clients who lived and worked in California in which he reported that the income was foreign earned income because

California was not part of the United States and therefore not subject to taxation and Respondent's aid and assistance in the preparation and presentation to the IRS of materially false and fraudulent tax returns, as evidenced by the Plea Agreement, constitutes disreputable conduct under 31 C.F.R. § 10.51, (2002 1994).

3. Respondent's conviction of one count of filing a false tax return in violation of 26 U.S.C. § 7207 constitutes disreputable conduct pursuant to 31 C.F.R. § 51(a)(1) (2007).

4. Respondent's failure to respond to specific requests for information included in the September 4, 2012 Supplemental Allegation Letter is a violation of 31 C.F.R. § 10.20(a)(3) (2011).

5. Respondent's use of a contingent fee structure based upon the expected income from tax refunds constitutes incompetent and disreputable conduct under 31 C.F.R. § 10.27(b)(1) (2007) (previously enacted as § 10.27(b)(2) (2002) and § 10.28(b) (1994)).

6. Respondent charged unconscionable fees for preparation of tax returns using the Form 2555 Position, which constitutes disreputable conduct under 31 C.F.R. § 10.27(b)(1) (2007) (previously enacted as §10.27(b)(2)(2002) and § 10.28(a) (1994)).

7. Respondent's representations to Special Agents of IRS Criminal Investigation that Respondent charged a "little flat fee" for the preparation of Forms 1040 for clients using the Form 2555 Position and that Respondent denied charging a contingent, or percentage, fee based on the anticipated refund for preparing a Form 1040 return with the Form 2555 Position constitute disreputable conduct under 31 C.F.R. § 10.51(a)(4) (2007) (previously enacted as § 10.51(d) (2002) (1994)).

8. Respondent's false representation to the CBA that he ceased using the Form 2555 Position after he became aware of the first IRS audit, when Respondent continued preparing tax returns for clients using the Form 2555 Position after learning of an IRS audit for a client with the Form 2555 Position, constitutes disreputable conduct under 31 C.F.R. § 10.51(a)(4) (2011).

9. Respondent's advice, with respect to at least fifty-two tax returns for tax years 1998 through 2002, to include the Form 2555 Position on federal income tax returns, constitutes participating in evading or attempting to evade any Federal tax, or knowingly counseling or suggesting to a client an illegal plan to evade Federal taxes in violation of 31 C.F.R. § 10.51(f) (2002) (previously enacted as §10.51(d)(1994)).

10. Respondent's advocacy of positions that have been determined to be frivolous by the IRS, case law, and a reading of the definition of the term United States in IRC § 7701, constitutes giving a false opinion, knowingly, recklessly, or through gross incompetence, including an opinion which is intentionally or recklessly misleading, or engaging in a pattern of providing incompetent opinions on questions arising under the Federal tax laws in violation of 31 C.F.R. § 10.51(l) (2002) (previously enacted as 10.51(j) (1994)).

11. Respondent's lack of outside research into the Form 2555 Position constitutes disreputable conduct for which a practitioner may be sanctioned as such conduct does not meet the due diligence standard in preparing or assisting in the preparation of, approving, and filing tax returns, documents, affidavits, and other papers relating to IRS matters in violation of 31 C.F.R. §10.22(a)(1) (2007) (2002) (previously enacted as § 10.22(a) (1994)).

12. Respondent's preparation of at least fifty-two tax returns for tax years 1998 through 2002 with the Form 2555 Position constitutes disreputable conduct as the Form 2555 Position does not meet the realistic possibility of success standard of being sustained on its merits and so constitutes a violation of 31 C.F.R. §10.34(a)(1) (2002) (previously enacted as § 10.34(a)(1)(i) (1994)).

13. Respondent's pattern of obstructing IRS examination and collection activities by repeatedly raising numerous frivolous arguments, aside from the Form 2555 Position, all of which have been long-rejected by both the IRS, case law, and the IRC: (1) for clients whose returns were prepared with the Form 2555 Position; (2) for himself during the IRS civil penalty investigation of the Form 2555 Position and during the IRS examination of Respondent's personal Form 1040 for 2001, and (3) for the 2006 IRS collection matter of Respondent's clients who had not used the Form 2555 Position constitutes disreputable conduct in that Respondent unreasonably delayed the prompt disposition of matters before the IRS in violation of 31 C.F.R. §10.23 (2002) (1994).

14. This pattern of obstruction constitutes a lack of due diligence in preparing or assisting in the preparation of documents relating to IRS matters and in determining the correctness of written representations to the Department of the Treasury in violation of 31 C.F.R. § 10.22(a)(1) (2002) (previously enacted as §10.22(a) (1994)) and 31 C.F.R. § 10.22(a)(2) (2002) (previously enacted as § 10.22(b) (1994)) and constitutes a pattern of giving false opinions, knowingly, recklessly, or through gross incompetence in violation of 31 C.F.R. § 10.51(a)(13) (2007) (previously enacted as §10.51(l) (2002) and §10.51(j) (1994)).

15. Respondent's threats of lawsuits for damages, and lawsuits against IRS employees personally for unauthorized collection actions that would be avoided if the IRS accepted the taxpayer's settlement offer constitute incompetence or disreputable conduct by directly or indirectly attempting to influence the official action of any officer or employee of the IRS by the use of threats, false accusations, duress or coercion in violation of 31 C.F.R. § 10.51(a)(9) (2011).

16. Respondent's submission to the IRS of a signed Form 2848 listing Respondent as the second representative in an IRS collection matter with an un-enrolled individual constitutes knowingly aiding an un-enrolled individual, during a period of ineligibility of such person, to practice before the IRS in violation of 31 C.F.R. § 10.51(j) (2002) (previously enacted as § 10.51(h) (1994)).

17. Complainant has proven by clear and convincing evidence Respondent's abovedescribed conduct warrants Respondent's disbarment from practice before the IRS.

WHEREFORE:

ORDER

IT IS HEREBY ORDERED Complainant's Motion to Amend the Complaint is **GRANTED.**

IT IS HEREBY FURTHER ORDERED that Complainant's Motion for a Decision by Default is GRANTED and that Anthony A. Tiongson is disbarred from practice before the Internal Revenue Service from the date of this decision and order, reinstatement thereafter being pursuant to the provisions contained in 31 C.F.R. Part 10, section 10.81 and at minimum requiring the practitioner to demonstrate that he is likely to conduct himself in accordance with the requirements of 31 C.F.R. Part 10 and that his reinstatement would not be contrary to the public interest.

IT IS SO ORDERED.

/s/ Parlen L. McKenna
Hon. Parlen L. McKenna
Acting Chief Administrative Law Judge

Dated: March 1, 2013
Alameda, CA

****

Are OPR disciplinary decisions published? Yes, OPR disciplinary decisions are published in the Internal Revenue Bulletin. See an example from IRB 2016-49 (Dec. 5, 2016), below, listing OPR disciplinary proceedings.

City & State	Name	Professional Designation	Disciplinary Sanction	Effective Date(s)
California				
San Mateo	Miyabara, Morris	Enrolled Agent	Disbarred by ALJ default decision	July 8, 2016
Corona Del Mar	Cassidy, Carl R.	CPA	Disbarred by decision on appeal by Treasury Appellate Authority	April 20, 2015
Florida				
Boynton Beach	Merl, Eric L.	Attorney	Suspended by default decision in expedited proceeding under 31 C.F.R. § 10.82(b)	Indefinite from August 4, 2016
Illinois				
Homer Glen	Bujan, Jr., Frank M.	CPA		Reinstated to practice before the IRS September 12, 2016
Kentucky				
Lexington	Cushny, Lillian B.	CPA	Suspended by decision in expedited proceeding under 31 C.F.R. § 10.82(b)	Indefinite from August 26, 2016
New Jersey				
Morris Plains	Fraser, Carlyle F.	CPA	Suspended by decision in expedited proceeding under 31 C.F.R. § 10.82(b)	Indefinite from July 19, 2016
Hasbrouck Heights	Pinto, Steven W.	CPA	Suspended by default decision in expedited proceeding under 31 C.F.R. § 10.82(b)	Indefinite from June 24, 2016
Tennessee				
Murfreesboro	Riddle, Mark S.	CPA		Reinstated to practice before the IRS September 27, 2016
Texas				
Plano	O'Laughlin, Frederick J.	Attorney	Suspended by decision in expedited proceeding under 31 C.F.R. § 10.82(b)	Indefinite from August 8, 2016
Virginia				
Reston	Hartke, Wayne R.	Attorney	Suspended by default decision in expedited proceeding under 31 C.F.R. § 10.82(b)	Indefinite from August 5, 2016

4. Circular 230 and AICPA Statement on Standards for Tax Services ("SSTS")

Treasury Circular 230 and the AICPA SSTSs are crucial guidelines for tax professionals. They set standards for daily tax position decisions, workpaper documentation, document scrutiny, client communication, and practicing before the IRS. These documents are essential for tax practice and practitioners should refer to them as frequently as technical guides when confirming a tax position or treatment of a deduction. Becoming intimately familiar with a CPA's professional responsibilities may ultimately save the CPA from costly litigation or disciplinary proceedings.

The IRS most recently updated Circular 230 in June 2014. These guidelines not only inform a tax practitioner on what "must" or "should" be done in professional tax activities but also provide recommendations for how to maintain the highest-quality service that can be offered. Following Circular 230 will help tax professionals avoid statutory tax preparer penalties and/or administrative sanctions.

Having the relevant Circular 230 section on hand to share with the client has proved to be a helpful tool when convincing a potentially noncompliant client to cooperate by providing all relevant tax information. Informing tax clients that professional practitioners are subject to sanctions and must follow certain rules and guidelines takes some pressure off tax professionals; this compels more clients to be forthcoming and cooperative. The guidance helps to separate the taxpayer's responsibilities from the tax professional's. Additionally, it can remind practitioners of their ethical responsibility to provide a high-quality service/product and that severe consequences may be imposed for failure to follow professional guidelines.

Section 10.22, *Diligence as to Accuracy*, is short but packed with requirements, presumptions, and expectations of a practitioner's actions when preparing tax returns and engaging in other matters involving the IRS. Due diligence is a major theme in this section. For instance, Section 10.22 explains when a practitioner can reasonably rely on others and when the practitioner would be presumed to have exercised due diligence when relying on others. This can help a tax practitioner set his or her bar for how much to scrutinize the advice or opinion of others, including another tax professional.

Another helpful section is Section 10.33, *Best Practices for Tax Advisors*. This section seems to acknowledge that not every situation comes with a clear-cut or perfect answer. Section 10.33 provides suggestions for how to most effectively provide the highest-quality representation concerning federal tax issues, including communication with clients.

The AICPA's Standards contain enforceable tax ethical standards that apply to its members - CPAs. The current version of the SSTSs was released in January 2010 and comprises seven statements, including explanations and interpretations. The good news is much of the guidance from the AICPA is aligned with that from the IRS, so practitioners are not following conflicting advice.

The Standards include: SSTS No. 1, *Tax Return Positions*; SSTS No. 2, *Answers to Questions on Returns*; SSTS No. 3, *Certain Procedural Aspects of Preparing Returns*; SSTS No. 4, *Use of Estimates*; SSTS No. 5, *Departure From a Position Previously Concluded in an Administrative Proceeding or Court Decision*; and SSTS No. 6, *Knowledge of Error: Return Preparation and Administrative Proceedings*. Below is an excerpt from SSTS No. 1:

9

Statement on Standards for Tax Services No. 1, Tax Return Positions

Introduction

1. This statement sets forth the applicable standards for members when recommending tax return positions, or preparing or signing tax returns (including amended returns, claims for refund, and information returns) filed with any taxing authority. For purposes of these standards

    a. a *tax return position* is (i) a position reflected on a tax return on which a member has specifically advised a taxpayer or (ii) a position about which a member has knowledge of all material facts and, on the basis of those facts, has concluded whether the position is appropriate.

    b. a *taxpayer* is a client, a member's employer, or any other third-party recipient of tax services.

2. This statement also addresses a member's obligation to advise a taxpayer of relevant tax return disclosure responsibilities and potential penalties.

3. In addition to the AICPA, various taxing authorities, at the federal, state, and local levels, may impose specific reporting and disclosure standards with regard to recommending tax return positions or preparing or signing tax returns.[1] These standards can vary between taxing authorities and by type of tax.

---

[1] A member should refer to the current version of Internal Revenue Code Section 6694, Understatement of taxpayer's liability by tax return preparer, and other relevant federal, state, and jurisdictional authorities to determine the reporting and disclosure standards that are applicable to preparers of tax returns.

Statement

4. A member should determine and comply with the standards, if any, that are imposed by the applicable taxing authority with respect to recommending a tax return position, or preparing or signing a tax return.

5. If the applicable taxing authority has no written standards with respect to recommending a tax return position or preparing or signing a tax return, or if its standards are lower than the standards set forth in this paragraph, the following standards will apply:

    a. A member should not recommend a tax return position or prepare or sign a tax return taking a position unless the member has a good-faith belief that the position has at least a realistic possibility of being sustained administratively or judicially on its merits if challenged.

    b. Notwithstanding paragraph 5(a), a member may *recommend a tax return position* if the member (i) concludes that there is a reasonable basis for the position and (ii) advises the taxpayer to appropriately disclose that position. Notwithstanding paragraph 5(a), a member may *prepare or sign a tax return* that reflects a position if (i) the member concludes there is a reasonable basis for the position and (ii) the position is appropriately disclosed.

6. When recommending a tax return position or when preparing or signing a tax return on which a position is taken, a member should, when relevant, advise the taxpayer regarding potential penalty consequences of such tax return position and the opportunity, if any, to avoid such penalties through disclosure.

7. A member should not recommend a tax return position or prepare or sign a tax return reflecting a position that the member knows

    a. exploits the audit selection process of a taxing authority, or

    b. serves as a mere arguing position advanced solely to obtain leverage in a negotiation with a taxing authority.

8. When recommending a tax return position, a member has both the right and the responsibility to be an advocate for the taxpayer with respect to any position satisfying the aforementioned standards.

Explanation

9. The AICPA and various taxing authorities impose specific reporting and disclosure standards with respect to tax return positions and preparing or signing tax returns. In a given situation, the standards, if any, imposed by the applicable taxing authority may be higher or lower than the standards set forth in paragraph 5. A member is to comply with the standards, if any, of the applicable taxing authority; if the applicable taxing authority has no standards or if its standards are lower than the standards set forth in paragraph 5, the standards set forth in paragraph 5 will apply.

10. Our self-assessment tax system can function effectively only if taxpayers file tax returns that are true, correct, and complete. A tax return is prepared based on a taxpayer's representation of facts, and the taxpayer has the final responsibility for positions taken on the return. The standards that apply to a taxpayer may differ from those that apply to a member.

11. In addition to a duty to the taxpayer, a member has a duty to the tax system. However, it is well established that the taxpayer has no obligation to pay more taxes than are legally owed, and a member has a duty to the taxpayer to assist in achieving that result. The standards contained in paragraphs 4–8 recognize a member's responsibilities to both the taxpayer and the tax system.

12. In reaching a conclusion concerning whether a given standard in paragraph 4 or 5 has been satisfied, a member may consider a well-reasoned construction of the applicable statute, well-reasoned articles or treatises, or pronouncements issued by the applicable taxing authority, regardless of whether such sources would be treated as *authority* under Internal Revenue Code Section 6662, *Imposition of accuracy-related penalty on underpayments*, and the regulations thereunder. A position would not fail to meet these standards merely because it is later abandoned for practical or procedural considerations during an administrative hearing or in the litigation process.

13. If a member has a good-faith belief that more than one tax return position meets the standards set forth in paragraphs 4–5, a member's advice concerning alternative acceptable positions may include a discussion of the likelihood that each such position might or might not cause the taxpayer's tax return to be examined and whether the position would be challenged in an examination. In such circumstances, such advice is not a violation of paragraph 7.

14. A member's determination of whether information is appropriately disclosed by the taxpayer should be based on the facts and circumstances of the particular case and the disclosure requirements of the applicable taxing authority. If a member recommending a position, but not engaged to prepare or sign the related tax return, advises the taxpayer concerning appropriate disclosure of the position, then the member shall be deemed to meet the disclosure requirements of these standards.

15. If particular facts and circumstances lead a member to believe that a taxpayer penalty might be asserted, the member should so advise the taxpayer and should discuss with the taxpayer the opportunity, if any, to avoid such penalty by disclosing the position on the tax return. Although a member should advise the taxpayer with respect to disclosure, it is the taxpayer's responsibility to decide whether and how to disclose.

16. For purposes of this statement, preparation of a tax return includes giving advice on events that have occurred at the time the advice is given if the advice is directly relevant to determining the existence, character, or amount of a schedule, entry, or other portion of a tax return.

Tax preparers will want to carefully note the auxiliary verbs, such as "should," "must," or "might." These indicators are important guideposts and can make the difference in litigation in determining whether a practitioner followed the applicable standards. Members are expected to comply with the guidelines, or they may later have to explain the deviation in litigation proceedings. A "must" directive *requires* a practitioner to follow the guidance, and any deviation from the guidance ought to have a compelling explanation and be properly documented.

A "should" directive indicates a practitioner is not unconditionally required to follow the guidance and may have a reason for not following the directive, but, again, the practitioner ought to strongly consider the guidance before implementing other methods. During litigation proceedings and disciplinary proceedings, a pattern of not following the guidelines will indicate the practitioner's lack of due care and can cast a negative light on the practitioner's professional performance, even if the departure is not directly related to the alleged damage.

It is important to note that Circular 230 and the AICPA Standards complement each other and often overlap, but practitioners should refer to *both* documents when making decisions regarding a particular engagement. And when there is a variance in the guidance, the higher level of due diligence should be followed. In some instances only one guide may address a specific topic. Also, it is important to understand that these required guides do not provide tax technical advice; they provide guidance on research, documentation, taking a tax position, conveying information to clients, and representing clients before the IRS. Practitioners unfamiliar with the rules on what to do with their technical knowledge are meeting only part of their client responsibilities.

5. Basic Forms Used by Practitioners

Form 2848 is a "Power of Attorney" permitting the designee (the authorized agent for the taxpayer) to receive all tax return information from the IRS regarding the taxpayer and to advance any arguments, positions of law, statements of fact and signatures on behalf of the taxpayer. Because of the incredible scope of authority delegated to the designee via Form 2848, only certain qualified individuals are permitted to become designees under this form. See Circular 230. Form 2848 relieves the IRS from the statutory limitation set forth under Section 6013, which restricts the IRS's ability to release tax return information. Thus, the execution of Form 2848 allows the IRS to freely communicate with the authorized agent on all tax matters as specifically or generally designated by the taxpayer on the form. See pages 1 and 2 of Form 2848, below.

Form **2848**

(Rev. Dec. 2015)
Department of the Treasury
Internal Revenue Service

Power of Attorney
and Declaration of Representative

▶ Information about Form 2848 and its instructions is at www.irs.gov/form2848.

OMB No. 1545-0150

For IRS Use Only

Received by:

Name _____

Telephone _____

Function _____

Date ___/___/___

Part I **Power of Attorney**

Caution: A separate Form 2848 must be completed for each taxpayer. Form 2848 will not be honored for any purpose other than representation before the IRS.

1 **Taxpayer information.** Taxpayer must sign and date this form on page 2, line 7.

Taxpayer name and address	Taxpayer identification number(s)
	Daytime telephone number / Plan number (if applicable)

hereby appoints the following representative(s) as attorney(s)-in-fact:

2 **Representative(s)** must sign and date this form on page 2, Part II.

Name and address	CAF No. _____ PTIN _____ Telephone No. _____ Fax No. _____
Check if to be sent copies of notices and communications ☐	Check if new: Address ☐ Telephone No. ☐ Fax No. ☐
Name and address	CAF No. _____ PTIN _____ Telephone No. _____ Fax No. _____
Check if to be sent copies of notices and communications ☐	Check if new: Address ☐ Telephone No. ☐ Fax No. ☐
Name and address	CAF No. _____ PTIN _____ Telephone No. _____ Fax No. _____
(**Note:** IRS sends notices and communications to only two representatives.)	Check if new: Address ☐ Telephone No. ☐ Fax No. ☐
Name and address	CAF No. _____ PTIN _____ Telephone No. _____ Fax No. _____
(**Note:** IRS sends notices and communications to only two representatives.)	Check if new: Address ☐ Telephone No. ☐ Fax No. ☐

to represent the taxpayer before the Internal Revenue Service and perform the following acts:

3 **Acts authorized (you are required to complete this line 3).** With the exception of the acts described in line 5b, I authorize my representative(s) to receive and inspect my confidential tax information and to perform acts that I can perform with respect to the tax matters described below. For example, my representative(s) shall have the authority to sign any agreements, consents, or similar documents (see instructions for line 5a for authorizing a representative to sign a return).

Description of Matter (Income, Employment, Payroll, Excise, Estate, Gift, Whistleblower, Practitioner Discipline, PLR, FOIA, Civil Penalty, Sec. 5000A Shared Responsibility Payment, Sec. 4980H Shared Responsibility Payment, etc.) (see instructions)	Tax Form Number (1040, 941, 720, etc.) (if applicable)	Year(s) or Period(s) (if applicable) (see instructions)

4 **Specific use not recorded on Centralized Authorization File (CAF).** If the power of attorney is for a specific use not recorded on CAF, check this box. See the instructions for **Line 4. Specific Use Not Recorded on CAF** . . . . ▶ ☐

5a **Additional acts authorized.** In addition to the acts listed on line 3 above, I authorize my representative(s) to perform the following acts (see instructions for line 5a for more information):

☐ Authorize disclosure to third parties; ☐ Substitute or add representative(s); ☐ Sign a return; _____

☐ Other acts authorized: _____

For Privacy Act and Paperwork Reduction Act Notice, see the instructions.　Cat. No. 11980J　Form **2848** (Rev. 12-2015)

b **Specific acts not authorized.** My representative(s) is (are) not authorized to endorse or otherwise negotiate any check (including directing or accepting payment by any means, electronic or otherwise, into an account owned or controlled by the representative(s) or any firm or other entity with whom the representative(s) is (are) associated) issued by the government in respect of a federal tax liability.
List any other specific deletions to the acts otherwise authorized in this power of attorney (see instructions for line 5b): _____

6 **Retention/revocation of prior power(s) of attorney.** The filing of this power of attorney automatically revokes all earlier power(s) of attorney on file with the Internal Revenue Service for the same matters and years or periods covered by this document. If you **do not** want to revoke a prior power of attorney, check here . . . . ▶ ☐
YOU MUST ATTACH A COPY OF ANY POWER OF ATTORNEY YOU WANT TO REMAIN IN EFFECT.

7 **Signature of taxpayer.** If a tax matter concerns a year in which a joint return was filed, each spouse must file a separate power of attorney even if they are appointing the same representative(s). If signed by a corporate officer, partner, guardian, tax matters partner, executor, receiver, administrator, or trustee on behalf of the taxpayer, I certify that I have the legal authority to execute this form on behalf of the taxpayer.
▶ **IF NOT COMPLETED, SIGNED, AND DATED, THE IRS WILL RETURN THIS POWER OF ATTORNEY TO THE TAXPAYER.**

_____	_____	_____
Signature	Date	Title (if applicable)

_____	_____
Print Name	Print name of taxpayer from line 1 if other than individual

Part II **Declaration of Representative**

Under penalties of perjury, by my signature below I declare that:

• I am not currently suspended or disbarred from practice, or ineligible for practice, before the Internal Revenue Service;
• I am subject to regulations contained in Circular 230 (31 CFR, Subtitle A, Part 10), as amended, governing practice before the Internal Revenue Service;
• I am authorized to represent the taxpayer identified in Part I for the matter(s) specified there; and
• I am one of the following:

a Attorney—a member in good standing of the bar of the highest court of the jurisdiction shown below.
b Certified Public Accountant—licensed to practice as a certified public accountant is active in the jurisdiction shown below.
c Enrolled Agent—enrolled as an agent by the Internal Revenue Service per the requirements of Circular 230.
d Officer—a bona fide officer of the taxpayer organization.
e Full-Time Employee—a full-time employee of the taxpayer.
f Family Member—a member of the taxpayer's immediate family (spouse, parent, child, grandparent, grandchild, step-parent, step-child, brother, or sister).
g Enrolled Actuary—enrolled as an actuary by the Joint Board for the Enrollment of Actuaries under 29 U.S.C. 1242 (the authority to practice before the Internal Revenue Service is limited by section 10.3(d) of Circular 230).
h Unenrolled Return Preparer—Authority to practice before the IRS is limited. An unenrolled return preparer may represent, provided the preparer (1) prepared and signed the return or claim for refund (or prepared if there is no signature space on the form); (2) was eligible to sign the return or claim for refund; (3) has a valid PTIN; and (4) possesses the required Annual Filing Season Program Record of Completion(s). **See Special Rules and Requirements for Unenrolled Return Preparers in the instructions for additional information.**
k Student Attorney or CPA—receives permission to represent taxpayers before the IRS by virtue of his/her status as a law, business, or accounting student working in an LITC or STCP. See instructions for Part II for additional information and requirements.
r Enrolled Retirement Plan Agent—enrolled as a retirement plan agent under the requirements of Circular 230 (the authority to practice before the Internal Revenue Service is limited by section 10.3(e)).

▶ **IF THIS DECLARATION OF REPRESENTATIVE IS NOT COMPLETED, SIGNED, AND DATED, THE IRS WILL RETURN THE POWER OF ATTORNEY. REPRESENTATIVES MUST SIGN IN THE ORDER LISTED IN PART I, LINE 2.**

Note: For designations d-f, enter your title, position, or relationship to the taxpayer in the "Licensing jurisdiction" column.

Designation— Insert above letter (a–r).	Licensing jurisdiction (State) or other licensing authority (if applicable).	Bar, license, certification, registration, or enrollment number (if applicable).	Signature	Date

Form 8821 is fundamentally different from Form 2848 in that a designee under Form 8821 may receive tax return information of the taxpayer but the designee may not advocate a position on behalf of a taxpayer. So, a designee on Form 8821 can attend meetings with the IRS and receive tax return information from the IRS but is not authorized to advance legal positions, or offer statements of fact. Why not? First, Form 8821 doesn't require any professional competence as Form 2848 mandates for designees. Second, Form 8821 was signed by the taxpayer specifically to authorize release by the IRS of tax return information but not advocacy by the designee. So, the IRS should respect the specific limitation as designated by the taxpayer who signed the form. See Form 8821, as follows:

Form 8821

(Rev. March 2015)

Department of the Treasury
Internal Revenue Service

Tax Information Authorization

▶ Information about Form 8821 and its instructions is at *www.irs.gov/form8821*.
▶ **Do not sign this form unless all applicable lines have been completed.**
▶ **Do not use Form 8821 to request copies of your tax returns**
or to authorize someone to represent you.

OMB No. 1545-1165

For IRS Use Only

Received by:
Name _____
Telephone _____
Function _____
Date _____

1 Taxpayer information. Taxpayer must sign and date this form on line 7.

Taxpayer name and address	Taxpayer identification number(s)
	Daytime telephone number Plan number (if applicable)

2 Appointee. If you wish to name more than one appointee, attach a list to this form. **Check here if a list of additional appointees is attached ▶** ☐

Name and address	CAF No. _____
	PTIN _____
	Telephone No. _____
	Fax No. _____
	Check if new: Address ☐ Telephone No. ☐ Fax No. ☐

3 Tax Information. Appointee is authorized to inspect and/or receive confidential tax information for the type of tax, forms, periods, and specific matters you list below. See the line 3 instructions.

(a) Type of Tax Information (Income, Employment, Payroll, Excise, Estate, Gift, Civil Penalty, Sec. 4980H Payments, etc.)	(b) Tax Form Number (1040, 941, 720, etc.)	(c) Year(s) or Period(s)	(d) Specific Tax Matters

4 Specific use not recorded on Centralized Authorization File (CAF). If the tax information authorization is for a specific use not recorded on CAF, check this box. See the instructions. If you check this box, skip lines 5 and 6 . . . . ▶ ☐

5 Disclosure of tax information (you **must** check a box on line 5a or 5b unless the box on line 4 is checked):

a If you want copies of tax information, notices, and other written communications sent to the appointee on an ongoing basis, check this box . . . . ▶ ☐

Note. Appointees will no longer receive forms, publications, and other related materials with the notices.

b If you do not want any copies of notices or communications sent to your appointee, check this box . . . . ▶ ☐

6 Retention/revocation of prior tax information authorizations. If the line 4 box is checked, skip this line. If the line 4 box is not checked, the IRS will automatically revoke all prior Tax Information Authorizations on file unless you check the line 6 box and attach a copy of the Tax Information Authorization(s) that you want to retain. . . . . ▶ ☐

To revoke a prior tax information authorization(s) without submitting a new authorization, see the line 6 instructions.

7 Signature of taxpayer. If signed by a corporate officer, partner, guardian, executor, receiver, administrator, trustee, or party other than the taxpayer, I certify that I have the authority to execute this form with respect to the tax matters and tax periods shown on line 3 above.

▶ **IF NOT COMPLETE, SIGNED, AND DATED, THIS TAX INFORMATION AUTHORIZATION WILL BE RETURNED.**

▶ **DO NOT SIGN THIS FORM IF IT IS BLANK OR INCOMPLETE.**

Signature	Date
Print Name	Title (if applicable)

For Privacy Act and Paperwork Reduction Act Notice, see instructions.   Cat. No. 11596P   Form **8821** (Rev. 3-2015)

6. Frequently Asked Questions About Circular 230

What is the Office of Professional Responsibility (OPR)?

OPR supports the IRS's strategy to enhance enforcement of the tax law by ensuring that tax professionals adhere to tax practice standards and follow the law. OPR is the governing body responsible for interpreting and applying the *Regulations Governing Practice before the Internal Revenue Service* (Treasury Department Circular 230). OPR has exclusive responsibility for practitioner conduct and discipline, including instituting disciplinary proceedings and pursuing sanctions. It functions independently of the Title 26 enforcement components of the IRS.

What is Circular 230?

Circular 230 is a document containing the statute and regulations detailing a tax professional's duties and obligations while practicing before the IRS; authorizing specific sanctions for violations of the duties and obligations; and, describing the procedures that apply to administrative proceedings for discipline. Circular 230 is the common name given to the body of regulations promulgated from the enabling statute found at Title 31, United States Code § 330. This statute and the body of regulations are the source of OPR's authority. Title 31 seeks to ensure tax professionals possess the requisite character, reputation, qualifications and competency to provide valuable service to clients in presenting their cases to the IRS. In short, Circular 230 consists of the "rules of engagement" for tax practice. The underlying issue in all Circular 230 cases is the tax professional's "fitness to practice" before the IRS.

How is OPR organized?

OPR completed a significant organizational and operational reorganization effective February 13, 2012. OPR now includes three major segments: Office of the Director, Legal Analysis Branch (LAB), and Operations and Management Branch (O&M). The Director, who reports jointly to the Commissioner and the Deputy Commissioner, Services and Enforcement, has primary supervisory responsibility for OPR, including oversight and control of all policy decisions and implementation. The Director is the final decision-maker on all disciplinary recommendations. The LAB interprets and applies the standards of practice for tax professionals in a fair and equitable manner and applies the principles of due process to the analysis, investigation and disciplinary process involving allegations of practitioner misconduct. O&M manages all of OPR's administrative, communications, budgetary and personnel functions.

What does "practice before the IRS" entail?

"Practice before the IRS" comprehends all matters connected with a presentation to the IRS, or any of its officers or employees, relating to a taxpayer's rights, privileges, or liabilities under laws or regulations administered by the IRS. Such presentations include, but are not limited to, preparing documents; filing documents; corresponding and communicating with the IRS; rendering oral and written advice with respect to any entity, transaction, plan or arrangement, or other plan or arrangement having a potential for tax avoidance or evasion; and representing a client at conferences, hearings and meetings.

Who is subject to Circular 230 jurisdiction?

- State licensed Attorneys and Certified Public Accountants authorized and in good standing with their state licensing authority who interact with tax administrative at any level and in any capacity.
- Persons enrolled to practice before the IRS- Enrolled Agents, Enrolled Retirement Plan Agents, and Enrolled Actuaries.
- Persons providing appraisals used in connection with tax matters (e.g., charitable contributions; estate and gift assets; fair market value for sales gain, etc.).
- Unlicensed individuals who represent taxpayers before the examination, customer service and the Taxpayer Advocate Service in connection with returns they prepared and signed.
- Licensed and unlicensed individuals who give written advice with respect to any entity, transaction, plan or arrangement; or other plan or arrangement, which is of a type the IRS determines as having a potential for tax avoidance or evasion. For this purposes "written advice" contemplates all forms of written material, including the content of an email, given in connection with any law or regulation administered by the IRS.
- Any person submitting a power of attorney in connection with limited representation or special authorization to represent before the IRS with respect to a specific matter before the Agency.

What is the extent of OPR's authority?

OPR's oversight of the conduct of tax practice extends to all individuals who make a presentation to the IRS relating to a taxpayer's rights, privileges, or liabilities under laws or regulations administered by the IRS. Generally speaking, this includes any individual who interacts with Federal tax administration, whether in person, orally, in writing or by the preparation and submission of documents.

What sanctions are authorized by Circular 230 and to whom do they apply?

OPR has oversight of practitioner conduct and exclusive responsibility with respect to practitioner discipline, including disciplinary proceedings and sanctions. OPR may, after notice and an opportunity for a conference, negotiate an appropriate level of discipline with a practitioner; or, initiate an administrative proceeding to Censure (a public reprimand), Suspend (one to fifty-nine months), or Disbar (five years) the practitioner. OPR may also, after notice and an opportunity for a conference, disqualify an appraiser from further submissions in connection with tax matters. OPR also may, after notice and an opportunity for a conference, propose a monetary penalty on any practitioner who engages in conduct subject to sanction. The monetary penalty may be proposed against the individual or a firm, or both, and can be in addition to any Censure, Suspension or Disbarment. The penalty may be up to the gross income derived or to be derived from the conduct giving rise to the penalty.

How does the disciplinary process work?

OPR's authority and case determinations are independent of the enforcement functions performed by the general IRS population. Referrals to OPR alleging violations of Circular 230 are received from a variety of sources both internal and external. Only rarely does OPR initiate its own projects to identify specific issues for investigation. When a referral is received, OPR independently determines, based on all available facts and circumstances, if a violation has occurred, whether the violation is one which calls into question a practitioner's fitness to continue to practice, and if so, what an appropriate sanction for the conduct is.

Following a preliminary investigation, OPR renders an independent determination as to the likelihood that a violation of Circular 230 has occurred. If a violation is identified, OPR communicates with the practitioner. This is done using a "Pre-Allegation Notice." The notice consists of correspondence providing the practitioner with information regarding the conduct alleged, and the fact that OPR has initiated a disciplinary investigation. The notice gives the practitioner an opportunity to provide any evidence or documentation s/he believes is relevant to OPR's determination. After a thorough investigation of the facts and an analysis/consideration of aggravating and mitigating circumstances, OPR determines the lowest level of discipline warranted for the violation(s).

Due process protections are incorporated throughout the disciplinary process. If OPR fails to reach agreement with the practitioner as to an appropriate sanction, a complaint is drafted and the case is referred to the Office of Chief Counsel, General Legal Services (GLS). GLS sends a letter to the practitioner offering a final opportunity to resolve the matter without hearing. If settlement is not reached, GLS files the complaint to commence a proceeding before an Administrative Law Judge (ALJ). The ALJ proceeding is a civil hearing during which the government and respondent present their evidence. The proceeding is conducted according to the provisions of the Administrative Procedures Act (5 USC § 500 et seq.). The case may be settled by concurrence of both parties at any time prior to the hearing.

If a hearing is conducted, and after post-hearing briefs are submitted, the ALJ issues an Initial Decision and Order as to the alleged misconduct and the appropriateness of OPR's proposed sanction. The ALJ may accept OPR's recommendations as to the fact of violation and as to the proposed sanction; may accept the fact of violation but increase or reduce the recommended sanction; or, may reject OPR's recommendations both as to facts and sanctions, and thus dismiss the case.

Following the ALJ's Decision and Order, either party may appeal the case to the Treasury Appellate Authority who will, after receiving briefs from both parties, render the Final Agency Decision. For OPR, a decision by the Appellate Authority is a final determination in the case. In addition, if neither party appeals within 30 days, the ALJ's Initial Decision and Order becomes the Final Agency Decision.

A practitioner who wishes may file a complaint in U.S. District Court to contest the Final Agency Decision when rendered by the Treasury Appellate Authority. This proceeding is also conducted according to the Administrative Procedures Act during which the Federal district judge will review findings of facts based only on the administrative record and will set aside agency action only if arbitrary or capricious, contrary to law, or an abuse of discretion. The proceeding is not a trial de novo.

What documents are required for practitioners electing to be represented during a Circular 230 Investigation?

If you receive an allegation, or other investigative, letter from OPR, you may decide that you want to use a representative to interface with OPR. If so, then you must provide some form of documentation authorizing that representation. The type of documentation needed will depend on what allegations are being raised in the correspondence from OPR.

a. Tax Compliance

If the OPR correspondence only discusses your personal tax compliance issues, for example, not filing a return, or not paying the taxes applicable to a return, then the correct representation documentation is a Form 2848. A separate Form 2848 is required for each person/entity referenced in the correspondence from OPR.

For example, assume you receive correspondence from OPR that states you have failed to file your personal returns for tax years 2010, 2011, and 2012, and you have failed to file S Corporation returns for your 2011 and 2012 tax years. Under this example, OPR would require two separate Forms 2848. The first Form 2848 would be for your 2010, 2011, and 2012 Forms 1040 returns. The second Form 2848 would be for the 2011 and 2012 S Corporation returns.

b. Conduct

If the OPR correspondence only discusses different types of alleged misconduct, such as failure to exercise due diligence, loss of state license, or false/misleading advertising, then the correct representation documentation is a letter of representation from the person you wish to represent you.

The letter of representation must include the following:

i. An affirmation that the representative is authorized to represent people before the IRS;
ii. An affirmation that the representative has the appropriate state or federal license, such as an attorney, CPA, or EA;
iii. A statement that the representative has been authorized by you to represent you; and
iv. A statement of where to send correspondence, i.e. solely to the representative, or to you and the representative. (Note that in some instances OPR will send certain

correspondence directly to you with a copy to your representative regardless of any other instruction.)

c. Both Tax Compliance and Conduct Cases

If the OPR correspondence refers to both tax compliance and conduct, as referenced above, then you must submit both Forms 2848 and a letter of representation. The same rules apply for each Form 2848, where you must submit one for each entity that the correspondence discusses. The same rules also apply for the requirements in a letter of representation, listed above.

Are there any restrictions on practitioners once they are disciplined by OPR?

Yes. See "Restrictions on Practitioners Disciplined by OPR" **on IRS.gov.**

Can Disciplined Practitioners represent clients before IRS?

No. They can submit Form 8821 to obtain tax returns and transcripts from the IRS. If a taxpayer wants the disciplined practitioner to accompany him/her to a conference or meeting with the Service, s/he may do so. However, the practitioner may only respond to questions and provide facts and/or documents; the practitioner may not advocate for the taxpayer or argue the merits of any issue raised.

Are IRS employees required to refer suspected practitioner misconduct to OPR?

Yes. Any IRS employee who believes a practitioner has violated any provision in Circular 230 is required to make a written report to OPR (31 C.F.R. Section 10.53(a)).

What Preparer Penalties require a referral to OPR?

Referrals are mandatory following the assessment of any IRC 6694(b) penalty, e.g. a willful attempt to understate the liability for tax. The referral should be made to OPR **regardless** of any appeal taken by the practitioner.

A referral to OPR should also be made when any of the following penalties or sanctions are imposed:
- Section 6700   - Promoting abusive tax shelters
- Section 6701(a) - Aiding and abetting understatement of a tax liability
- Section 7407   - Injunction of a tax return preparer
- Section 7408   - Injunction of specified conduct relating to tax shelters and reportable transactions

What Preparer Penalties are discretionary referrals to OPR?

- Section 6662   - Accuracy related penalty
- Section 6694(a) - Understatement of liability due to an unreasonable position
- Section 6695   - (a) Failure to furnish copy of return; (b) Failure to sign return; (d) Failure to keep a copy of tax return or list of taxpayer

- Section 6702   - Frivolous tax returns or submissions

Note: If any of the above penalties appear to become a pattern across taxpayers, tax issues or tax years, a referral to OPR should be made.

What are other examples of misconduct typically referred to OPR?

Other circumstances for referral include, but are not limited to:
- Inaccurate or unreasonable entries/omissions on tax returns, financial statements and other documents.
- A lack of due diligence exercised by the practitioner.
- A willful attempt by the practitioner to evade the payment/assessment of any Federal tax.
- Cashing, diverting or splitting a taxpayer's refund by any means, electronic or otherwise.
- "Patterns" of misconduct involving multiple years, multiple clients or inappropriate/unprofessional conduct demonstrated to multiple IRS employees.
- Potential conflict of interest situations, such as representation of both spouses who have a joint liability or when representation is affected by competing interests of the practitioner.
- Any willful violation of Circular 230 provisions.

What is OPR's burden of proof?

For OPR to prevail in a disciplinary proceeding, OPR must prove by "clear and convincing evidence" that the practitioner willfully violated one or more provision of Circular 230. Willful is defined as a voluntary, intentional violation of a known legal duty.

How can I learn more about OPR and Circular 230?

The IRS video portal provides webinars about OPR and Circular 230.

How can I contact OPR if I have questions?

You may contact OPR by fax at (202) 317-6338, or by mail at:

Internal Revenue Service
Office of Professional Responsibility
SE:OPR - Room 7238/IR
1111 Constitution Avenue NW
Washington, DC 20224

7. Tax Practice Considerations

Tax practice involves understanding and integrating multiple sources of applicable professional rules and statutory sources. Consider the following diagram and then a hypothetical fact pattern.

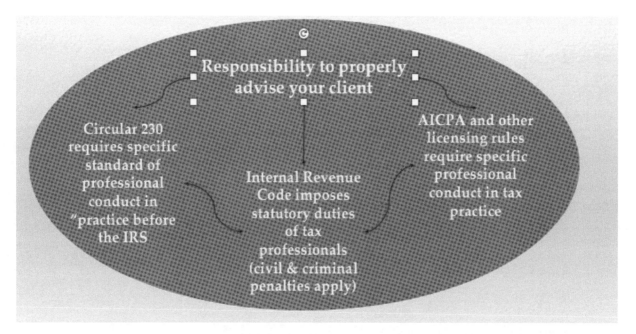

Fact pattern: Apex Accounting Services ("Apex") prepared Client Joe's Federal tax return for tax year 2016. Client Joe calls Apex and requests that the firm forward all of his/her tax records used to prepare his 2016 Federal tax return to another practitioner.

- Question: What must Apex Accounting Services consider before deciding how to proceed with the client's request?
    - Guidance and Statutory Authority to Consider:
        - Circular 230 – Section 10.28 provides, in part, that "a practitioner must, at the request of a client, promptly return any and all records of the client that are necessary for the client to comply with his or her Federal tax obligations."
        - I.R.C. § 6107 – tax return preparer shall furnish a completed copy of such return to the taxpayer not later than the time such return is presented for such taxpayer's signature.
        - I.R.C. § 7216 – provides, in part, that any person who is engaged in the business of preparing returns of tax who knowingly or recklessly discloses any furnished to him for, or in connection with, the preparation of any such return, shall be guilty of a misdemeanor, and upon conviction thereof, shall be fined not more than $1,000, or imprisoned not more than 1 year, or both.

- <u>Suggested Next Steps</u>:
    - o <u>Option 1</u>: Secure a written consent from Client Joe that authorizes Apex to disclose tax return information to his designated recipient, a third party.[35] After securing this written consent from Client Joe, then Apex can forward the information to a third party. Section 7216 presents statutory authority that requires a cautious approach by Apex, a Federal "tax return preparer," on how to handle tax return information.[36] Circular 230, section 10.28 and section 6107 only address scenarios when the tax return preparer returns or furnishes tax records back to the taxpayer, not to third parties.
    - o <u>Option 2</u>: Advise Client Joe that Apex can promptly return all of his tax information back to him as required by Cir. 230 and section 6107. However, Apex cannot forward his Federal tax return information to a third party without his written consent.

The above fact pattern, sources of guidance and suggested next steps illustrate that "practice" as a Federal "tax return preparer" requires review of multiple authorities before a practitioner can proceed even with basic tasks, such as forwarding documents. Weigh carefully the various professional guidelines, governmental regulations and statutory authorities that impact tax practice.

---

[35] The AICPA provides sample client consent forms for review and use by practitioners considering the facts as presented here. See http://www.aicpa.org/InterestAreas/Tax/Resources/StandardsEthics/Pages/Section7216.aspx.

[36] Still concerned about problems with section 7216? Check out the IRS' FAQs addressing section 7216 at: https://www.irs.gov/tax-professionals/section-7216-frequently-asked-questions.

Chapter 2 - Questions

1. You are federal tax return preparer. Are you subject to regulation under Circular 230? Yes or No. Provide a citation to the case that supports your response.

2. The client signs Form 2848 with respect to the accounting firm's partner, Jill. Separately, the client signs Form 8821 with respect to the accounting firm's senior associate, Harry. Both the partner and senior associate (both certified public accountants) attend a meeting with IRS revenue agents conducting an audit of the client. Can the senior associate, Harry, provide responses to IRS requests for facts and authority to support the client's tax position on various audited issues during the meeting?

3. What is the problem with permitting a tax professional who is not designated on Form 2848 from communicating with the IRS? Wouldn't the IRS be able to assemble more information and work its cases faster if it works with more tax professionals?

4. Our firm's client, Outside the Box, Inc., asks that our firm prepare its 2016 federal tax return. Our client has engaged in various tax transactions during 2016 but none which are aggressive to be considered either "tax shelters" as defined under section 6662(d)(2)(C)(ii) or a reportable transaction to which section 6662A applies. However, the client is adamant that our firm should not include any attachments to the return disclosing the nature of any of tax transactions that Outside the Box, Inc. engaged in during 2016. All of our firm's employees <u>are CPAs</u>. As such, we need to know what tax confidence level we must reach to be: (1) in compliance with SSTS; and (2) within the statutory requirements under 6694 to avoid any tax return preparer penalty. So, what tax confidence level is our firm required to reach under these facts for our client's 2016 federal tax return? Explain your answer by comparing SSTS #1 and section 6694.

5. You are a CPA employed with GGU, a mid-sized accounting firm located in San Francisco, California. John Smith, a partner with GGU, provides you with your first

assignment – to assist in providing tax advice to Norcal Associates, one of GGU's best clients. The firm partner, Mr. Smith, sets up a meeting for you to meet Norcal Associates' CFO, David Black. During the meeting with Mr. Black, he tells you that the IRS is interested in a sale/leaseback transaction that NORCAL engaged in during the tax year 2016 which is under audit. The IRS requested any and all documents related to this "sale/leaseback" transaction. Mr. Black stated: "Yeah, I've heard from our internal tax folks that we entered in a sale/lease-back transaction There was some tax advantage in going forward with this deal. I don't have any problems giving the IRS all of the documents related to this deal. But, we did get a tax advisory memo from a CPA firm that provided us with a "green light" on this transaction. This CPA firm never prepared our tax returns. It just served as our tax advisor.

After the meeting, your tax partner (John Smith) sends you the following email:

> *From:*　　*John Smith*
> *To:*　　　*Tax Senior (You are the recipient)*
> *Date:*　　*12/12/20XX*
> *Subject:*　*Meeting with NORCAL Regarding Sale-Leaseback Transaction*
>
> *Please read Cir. 230, Sec. 10.20 and let me know what you think we need to do in response to CFO David Black's question – whether NORCAL has to produce the CPA firm's tax advisory letter issued to NORCAL on the sale-leaseback transaction. Also, take a look at section 7525 as well and add that to your response to me. Please send me a concise memo. I'm busy and need to understand our firm's position with respect to NORCAL quickly. Thanks!*

Draft a memo that is no longer than 1 page responding to your partner's email.

6. You are a licensed CPA. A client's filed Federal tax return is being audited by the IRS. The IRS has focused on one specific transaction reported on the return under audit. You have been engaged by your client to represent her before the IRS. As you conduct research in your client's case, you find two arguments that can be used to support your client's tax position that is the focus of the IRS' inquiry. You determine that the the first argument is supported by several cases and thus, there exists substantial authority for this argument. However, the second position is very weak and is "arguable" at best. You have a meeting coming up with the IRS revenue agent who is examing your client's return. Another partner at your accounting firm suggests that you advance the second, weak position (even though it is arguable, at best) to gain leverage in your meeting with the IRS. The partner notes that if that first weak argument fails to sway the IRS agent, then you can quickly proceed to your stronger second argument. How do you proceed under these facts?

CHAPTER 3 – ELECTRONIC TAX RESEARCH

Learning Objectives:

☑ Understand why tax practitioners utilize fee-based research databases to conduct tax research

☑ Develop tax research strategies in order to develop confidence and efficiency

In this Chapter:

1. Introduction to Electronic Research
2. Free Tax Research Sites
3. Fee Based Tax Research Sites
4. Basics of Electronic Research

1. Introduction to Electronic Research

The picture, above, illustrates electronic tax research – in your author's perspective. This is a photo of a professional golf caddie conducting measurements before the beginning of a PGA golf tournament. In order to give his employer, the professional golfer, the optimal chance of succeeding in the event, the golf caddie takes time to conduct research of the landscape. The caddie identifies hazards, yardages from various points on each hole, and the contour of the green. All of this research does not ensure that the caddie and golf player will be able to correctly utilize the data. But, the research does provide the data points so that the professional caddie and player can engage in logical decision-making to give them the best opportunity for success. Similarly, in electronic tax research, the tax practitioner engages in conducting measurements of the tax landscape in order to reach logical conclusions on tax issues confronting their clients.

The common question when it comes to electronic tax research is: "why do I need to use a fee-based research system when everything is available on the internet for free?" The answer presents itself clearly when you see the number of results of any "Google" search - billions of results. A fee-based legal research system provides two key elements that are essential to a tax professional who must work efficiently to understand complex material and locate applicable primary source material: (1) summaries of tax topics that can provide the user the most effective means to comprehend material quickly; and (2) database management tools to employ a search strategy so the user can limit their search to specific types of material.

There are several comprehensive online tax research databases (free and fee based sources) which collect and organize materials and have sophisticated searching capabilities. These databases are primarily developed for use by experienced tax professionals.

2. Free Tax Research Sites

✓ **Google Scholar** - This is one of the best "free" on-line research sites for case law. Google Scholar (GS) provides an excellent database of court opinions (Supreme Court, Court of Appeals, District court, tax court, etc.). With its full text search engine your likely to get good results to start your tax research project. The advantage of GS is the Google search engine which allows you to search by text rather than using a legal citation or docket number. GS includes law journals, in-addition to State supreme court and intermediate appellate opinions for all 50 states from 1950 to the present. GS will find, rank and link relevant cases better than most other free tax research sites. Its main drawback is it does not yet provide the ability to determine if your tax case is still good law (such as Shepard's or KeyCite) which is crucial any tax research. GS also lacks any federal or state statutes though Google continues to update this site.

✓ **Casetext** - is a free legal research and writing platform that lets researchers search millions of cases, statutes, and regulations annotated with analysis contributed by the members of the legal community. The Casetext library includes federal published and unpublished cases (Supreme Court, appellate, and district court) since 1925, as well as appellate cases for all 50 states, updated daily to include recently issued opinions. Users can also search federal statutes and regulations, and state statutes from California, Delaware, Florida, New Jersey, and New York.

3. Fee Based Tax Research Sites

The advantage offered from fee based tax research sites are well-organized databases along with value-added material summarizing common to difficult areas of tax practice. There are strategic methodologies available that permit users to restrict results. For instance, if you want just Second Circuit cases, you can restrict your results to search just that one circuit court of appeals.

The disadvantage with fee-based services is, well, the cost. Services offer various plans, by hour, by the number of users, by the number of databases selected for access. In addition, fee-based services may require customers to sign a contract to commit to yearly or multi-year agreements with early termination fees. The value offered by fee-based services vary by company. But, there is value in these fee-based companies for tax researchers. And, to secure the best value, practitioners must clearly understand the value proposition for the service selected.

✓ **WestLaw** – a comprehensive full text research system for legal materials, including cases, statutes, regulations, news, treatises, articles, etc. Very similar case law, statue, code, regulation, and secondary source ability and search results to LexisNexis.

✓ **Lexis Nexis** – a comprehensive full text research system for legal materials, including cases, statutes, regulations, news, treatises, articles, etc. Very similar case law, statue, code, regulation, and secondary source ability and search results to Westlaw.

✓ **CCH Tax Research Network** – a system that provides access to federal and state tax codes and cases. The database includes Letter Rulings, IRS Positions (including TAMs and FSAs) and IRS Publications. It also contains the Standard Federal Income Tax Reporter and the Tax Treaties Reporter. Additionally, the database offers Tax Tracker News, a collection of daily journals, which can be customized by subject and jurisdiction and received as an email alert.

✓ **RIA Checkpoint** – a system that offers access to federal, state, and local tax laws and regulations, IRS rulings and releases, IRS forms and publications, and much more. It contains the Federal Tax Coordinator 2d, United States Tax Reporter, Internal Revenue Bulletin, and has selected Warren Gorham & Lamont tax journals and treatises. Checkpoint also provides access to tax news via daily updates from RIA Daily Updates, BNA Daily Tax Report, IBFD Tax News Service, and WG&L Journal Previews.

✓ **Bloomberg Law** – Unlike Westlaw or Lexis, this premium legal research service has no natural/plain language search ability and instead uses the Boolean searching technique instead. In addition, only some cases have headnotes and topic classifications. One advantage though is its extensive federal and state docket search ability compared to the other premium legal research services. Also its citation (Bcite) does not include references to statutes or secondary sources. Its statute, codes and regulations are text only not un-annotated code and provides no historical versions of state codes. Some other differences noted include its secondary source coverage which provides little law review coverage, its extensive BNA material which is an excellent secondary source only available with this service, its excellent law firm "articles" research feature, its lack of legal encyclopedias and ALRs, etc. The quality of this service is improving and should be reviewed annually for added advancements and enhancements.

✓ **Public Access to Court Electronic Records "PACER** - Pacer is a low cost legal research tool providing public access to court electronic records. It is a service that allows users to obtain case and docket information from federal appellate, district and bankruptcy courts, and the PACER Case Locator. It is provided by the federal Judiciary in keeping with its commitment to providing public access to court information via a centralized service. Access includes access to U.S. District, Bankruptcy, and Appellate court records. PACER currently charges $0.10 per page retrieved. This applies to both the pages of search results and the pages of documents you retrieve.

✓ **CaseMaker** - a low cost legal research tool with a powerful search engine providing access to a combination of state and federal materials including historic to current cases, statutes, and regulations. The site provides unlimited access to the members of bar associations that join the Casemaker Consortium. Most state bar associations are members.

✓ **FastCase** - a low cost legal research tool with a powerful search engine providing access to a combination of state and federal materials including historic to current cases, statutes, and regulations. It offers access to its appellate case law library, as well as state and federal codes and regulations. The premium plan also includes U.S. district court opinions, while the national plan does not. Subscriptions for attorneys are free through many state bar associations. It currently provides iPhone/iPad and Android apps with free access to all case law and statutes. FastCase offers two subscription plans: a premium subscription ($95/month or $995/year) and an appellate subscription ($65/month and $695/year). Both plans offer access to the Fastcase appellate case law library, as well as state and federal codes and regulations. The premium plan also includes trial level opinions, while the appellate plan does not. FastCase also offers a free 24-hour trial and 30-day money-back guarantee. Subscriptions are included in 25 state bar associations.

✓ **LoisLaw** – a low cost legal tax research tool with coverage of all types of primary legal materials from all 50 states and federal jurisdictions. It also provides access to treatises organized by subject or jurisdiction. Several different subscription plans are offered, with very reasonable prices.

✓ **VersusLaw** - a low cost legal tax research tool which offers three pricing plans – standard, premium, and professional – which range in price per month. Coverage of materials varies widely by jurisdiction, but the library directory LibCatProfessional provides detailed coverage.

✓ **Proquest Law** - a low cost legal tax research tool for comprehensive legislative history information. Formerly LexisNexis Congressional; this service indexes key federal legislative history materials, including the U.S. Serial Set and the CIS Index. Selected full text includes committee reports from 1995-present and committee hearings from 1824-present. It indexes more than 2 million dissertations (1637-present) on all subject areas, including law; full text in PDF provided where available. It provides compiled legislative history materials for federal laws, mostly from 1929 to the present but with selected additional documents dating back to the 1890s. It also provides index and full-text of statistical reports from federal and state governments, as well as private organizations. The fee for this site is reasonable if you require legislative history tax research.

✓ **Heinonline** – a low cost legal tax research tool with coverage of over a hundred million pages of legal history available in an online, fully-searchable, image-based format. What makes it unique aside from its image-based PDF content is its historical value and the availability of titles back to their inception. It is the world's largest image-based legal research collection and contains more than nine centuries of legal history.

✓ **BNA Tax and Accounting Center** - The BNA Tax and Accounting Center provides access to primary sources, including the Internal Revenue Code, Treasury Regulations, IRS Proposed Regulations, and federal tax cases and treaties. It also includes U.S. Income Portfolios, Estate, Gifts & Trusts Portfolios, Foreign Income Portfolios, the Daily Tax Report, and journal articles. The database contains similar resources for state tax materials, and some international tax resources.

4. Basics of Electronic Research

As recently as a few years ago, if you wanted to be considered a cutting-edge expert in computer-assisted-legal-research ("CALR") you only had to learn to use Lexis and Westlaw. While Lexis and Westlaw are still the major CALR vendors, you must be able to make use of other electronic databases as well as the Internet to do minimally competent research.

Electronic information resources come in two basic levels of completeness: either full text records or abstract/index records. There are two basic linguistic difficulties in finding information: synonymy and ambiguity. There are two basic approaches for overcoming those difficulties in finding information: either subject or keyword search methods. And there are two basic tools for improving search efficiency: Boolean searching and field searching.

a. Completeness

Electronic resources have varying levels of completeness. Some resources are full-text databases, for example, newspaper articles on the Baltimore Sun's web site at http://www.baltimoresun.com. Other resources are abstracts or indexes; a common example is an online library catalog. This type of resource does not provide the full text of the item, but provides varying levels of detail about the item, and citations for retrieving the full text. Some vendors provide databases of both types -- Lexis and Westlaw both have databases that are full-text and databases that are indexes only. The level of completeness is a factor to consider when you choose a certain resource.

b. Structure

Databases also come with varying degrees of structure. For example, a library's catalog has limited records, but the information is in a highly structured format that makes it easy to search for items by subject heading, author, or title. The Internet can be considered a database with virtually unlimited records and with virtually no structure. The nature of the database dictates the methods that should be used to most efficiently search it. One of the first steps in successful electronic research is selecting the appropriate database and learning enough about the database to pick an efficient search method.

c. Linguistic Difficulties

In all research the searcher combats some basic linguistic difficulties: ambiguity and synonymy. Electronic research, especially full text, compounds these difficulties. When searching, you are normally looking for a concept, not a particular set of words. But one of the major tenets of "good" writing is to vary your words and find creative, new ways of expressing your ideas. Synonymy is the problem of there being many ways to express a single concept. For example, "sentenced to die," "death penalty," and "capital punishment" all express essentially the same concept. Electronic research deals only with words, not concepts. To do comprehensive research, the searcher must account for the possible synonyms for the concept being sought. The flip side of the problem is ambiguity. Ambiguity is the problem of multiple concepts all being expressed by the same words. If you were to search one of the case law databases for "release" you would find criminal cases where the sentence was life without release, cases where a plaintiff signed a liability release, and cases about faulty auto brake releases. A counselor could mean an attorney, but it could also mean a social worker; a solicitor could mean an attorney, but it could also mean a salesperson. Overcoming synonymy and ambiguity is a first step in effective research.

d. Efficiency Measures

There are two ways to measure effectiveness of your search. The first measure is precision, which means finding only what you want to find. A precise search for documents about attorneys would include the documents where "counselor" means attorney but exclude all the documents where it meant a social worker. The second measure is recall. Essentially this means finding everything that you want to find. A search for documents about attorneys with good recall would find articles that use any of the words barrister, counselor, lawyer, or litigator. No one but the searcher can determine how precise a search needs to be or how comprehensive the search needs to be. At times a quick and dirty search that retrieves a few examples is all that is needed. At other times the research has to be as comprehensive as possible to retrieve every single case or item on point.

Two major tools exist in electronic research for increasing search efficiency. The first is **Boolean** searching. You have most likely used this at least occasionally when doing research on the Internet. This tool is also available in a much more sophisticated fashion on Lexis and Westlaw and on many other electronic resources. The second is **field searching**. This technique takes advantage of the structure of the database. It is available to a degree on the Internet, but is much more helpful in the more highly structured databases like Westlaw and Lexis.

e. Search Approaches

There are two basic ways you can approach finding information in electronic format: a subject approach or a keyword approach. A common example of a subject approach is the old library card catalog. (Modern online library catalogs offer both the option to search by subject and the option to search by keyword.) A classic example on the Internet is Yahoo, the directory approach. When you search by subject, you search subject headings that have been assigned to an item as descriptive of the item's contents. Another example of the subject approach specific to legal research is the West Topic and Key Number system. The important thing to remember about the subject approach is that someone (or even a program) has analyzed the item and assigned a subject descriptor to it. This means that some of the work is done for you.

For example, by doing a subject search for the heading "homicide" you would find items dealing with that subject even if the item uses the words "murder," "stab," "kill," or "fatally wound" without using the term homicide. Also, a subject search for the heading "homicide" would not retrieve an item about the filming of Homicide: Life on the Street. The subject approach is one way to compensate for the problems of synonymy and ambiguity. While some of the work is done for you, subject searching also means that you are depending on the work having been done correctly, and you are limited to subject headings assigned by somebody else.

When you search using the keyword approach, you are searching for any appearance of your search term. In full text databases this method searches for your term in the title field of the item, the text field, the assigned subject headings, and any other field in the item. The important thing to remember about the keyword approach is that it searches for character strings only, and does not search for concepts. This means that for whatever information you seek, you must decide what terms best describe it. Keyword searching is particularly helpful when the concept you seek is very new and has not yet had a chance to be incorporated into subject headings.

f. Boolean Searching

Boolean logic is used to construct search statements using logical connectors. This kind of searching allows you to relate multiple search terms together to more accurately express the concept you are seeking.

The three basic logical operators are

> **AND** terms on both sides of the connector must be present somewhere in the document in order to be retrieved (Some search engines use the plus symbol (+),

some use the ampersand symbol (&) while others require that the connector be spelled out.)

OR if one of the terms connected by the OR connector appears in a document, that document will be retrieved. (Some search engines spell out the OR connector while some interpret a space as an OR connector.)

NOT documents containing the term after the NOT operator will not be retrieved. (Some search engines call this connector BUT NOT, some call it AND NOT, others use simply NOT or a minus sign.) The NOT connector can be a very tricky connector to use effectively. It takes only one instance of a word to eliminate a document from your results set.

These three connectors are available in just about any electronic research tool. More sophisticated connectors are available on Lexis and Westlaw, and are also becoming more prevalent in Internet search engines as well. One limitation to the basic connectors is that they work on the entire document. If you want to find cases about attorneys committing malpractice, the search attorney AND malpractice is too broad. It will find cases that are about medical malpractice, but have the word "attorney" anywhere in the document - even if it is just a sentence saying "the plaintiff's attorney objected to the evidence."

Proximity connectors help with this difficulty. Common proximity operators are

WITHIN – search terms must be within a specified number of words of each other. There is a great deal of variation among the search engines with this connector. Some search engines call it NEAR, some allow "w/n" where n is the number of words, some offer "w/s" for within the same sentence, and some offer "w/p" for within the same paragraph.

PRE – the first term must precede the second term. Some search engines call it BEFORE, and some allow specifying the maximum number of words in between the search terms, e.g. attorney pre/5 malpractice.

ADJ – adjacency or phrase searching requires the terms to appear directly adjacent to one another and in the specified order. Some search engines use quotation marks to indicate phrase searching.

Most search engines have some methods for dealing with word variations.

. 1) A root expander (often the ! symbol, but different engines may use different symbols) substitutes for any number of characters, e.g., depreciat! will search for depreciate, depreciated, depreciating, depreciation.

. 2) The universal character * stands for one character, e.g. advis*r will search for advisor or adviser. You can use more than one universal character in one word, e.g. bl**d will retrieve blood and bleed.

. 3) Many search engines, including both Lexis and Westlaw, automatically search for both the singular and regular plural forms of a word when you enter the singular form. Keep in mind that while Westlaw searches for both regular plurals - those formed by simply adding the letter "s" to the end of the word - and irregular plurals - for example, woman/women - Lexis searches only for regular plurals. When in doubt, enter both the singular and irregular plural, or use the root expander to pick up the different endings.

In all search engines, certain very common words such as on, under, with, will not be searched. Such words are called stop words, and each database has its own set of stop words. For example, the word "law" might be a useful term in a medical database, but it is so common that it might be a stop word in a legal database. For databases you use frequently, learn the stop words and avoid using those words in your searches.

Again, in all search engines, the order of connectors will dramatically affect your search results. A search in a job listing database for attorney AND (Chicago OR New York) is quite different than a search for (attorney AND Chicago) or New York.

The first search will retrieve job listings for attorneys in Chicago and for attorneys in New York. The second search will retrieve job listings for attorneys in Chicago, and all job listings in New York.

Every search engine, including those for Lexis and Westlaw, has its own "order of processing," the order in which it processes the connectors if you don't explicitly set the order. For the multitude of general search engines, the best strategy is to explicitly set the order of processing by using parentheses and to avoid combining too many different kinds of connectors.

g. Field and Segment Searching

In most databases the records or items are divided into parts that reflect the divisions in the documents themselves. The more highly structured the database, the more parts each record will have. Westlaw and Lexis both have divided their documents into extensive fields or segments and a search using them could, for example, find all the Maryland opinions written by Judge Marvin H. Smith. Without being able to specify a field or segment, a search for such a common word as Smith would make the search very difficult. With field or segment searching, a document is only retrieved if Smith is located in the designated field. This type of searching also can be very helpful in law review databases by giving searchers the option of running keyword searches only in the titles of articles.

h. Lexis and Westlaw Basics

Lexis and Westlaw are established components of legal research. It is no longer cutting-edge to be proficient in using these databases; it is mandatory. The good news is that both Lexis and Westlaw provide extensive, highly structured law-focused databases, and offer sophisticated research mechanisms.

Some advantages to searching Lexis or Westlaw rather than the Internet:

☑ Focused, reliable content. Information on Lexis and Westlaw is focused on primary law and secondary materials that are helpful to the attorney. If you run a search on "habeas corpus" you won't be inundated with retrieved items (hits) that are postings from inmates requesting assistance, or advertisements from attorneys who specialize in habeas corpus matters.

☑ Search engines that index the entire database. Unlike the Internet, where even the best search engines index far less than all of its contents, every document in these commercial databases is indexed.

☑ Search mechanisms that remain consistent. With Westlaw you will always need to put a phrase in quotes, and in Lexis a string of words will always be treated as a phrase. While there are differences between the two vendors, only two systems need to be remembered, not the multitude of search mechanisms available on the Internet.

☑ Highly structured format. Both these vendors provide organization to the document collection as a whole (sources or databases) and detailed organization within each document (segments or fields).

To take best advantage of these features it is essential to become familiar both with the organization schemes used by each vendor and with their respective search mechanisms. Before searching by topic or issue on Westlaw or Lexis, you must identify and select the subset of the documents in the system most likely to contain the sources you want. Selection of the appropriate pool of documents in which to run your search or searches can greatly enhance your research efficiency.

o WESTLAW

On Westlaw, documents are organized by general categories of materials into databases: federal materials (cases, statutes, legislative materials, administrative regulations and other sources); state materials (the same types of materials on the state level, with the user's state listed first); "topical practice areas" which arranges documents by areas such as environmental law, bankruptcy and the like; law reviews, legal periodicals, and current awareness, which includes various secondary sources; and several other categories. Each main category is divided into many subcategories that correspond to individual databases. Clicking on a category at each stage of the menu screen leads you further into the database directory until you reach the point of selecting the database you wish to search. For any database, detailed coverage information, along with helpful search tips, can be obtained by accessing the "Scope" service. Once in the database, click on the "i" (information) button next to the database name in order to access "Scope."

A screen shot from a Westlaw search is provided, below.

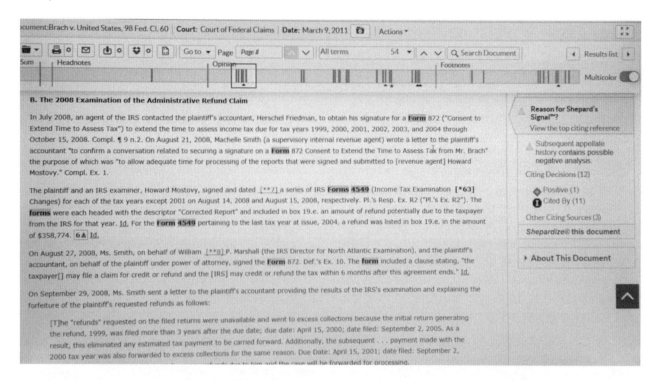

The database selected was limited to "federal tax authorities." And, the search terms were "Form 4549." Each time the first word of the search, "Form" is located, the results page tags the result in the text by highlighting the word green. The second term "4549" is highlighted in orange. Then, the results of both search terms are summarized in the top rectangular box by color to show the researcher the location within the search result where each term – green or orange – is located. Westlaw considers this picture of the location of search terms a time-savings vehicle so that the researcher can move efficiently to the specific search term. As a research, you may or may not find value in this type of search term presentation. What is notable is that every research database strives to provide an "edge" for its clients to value the services it can offer in allowing researchers to become more efficient.

○ LEXIS

Lexis organizes its "Sources" similarly to Westlaw. From the homescreen you may choose to use one of the last sources you have previously used or to "Look for a Source" by browsing through the content types. Broad categories of materials are displayed that can be narrowed by clicking on subcategories until the desired set of materials is reached. For search tips and scope information specific to each source, use the support box on the home screen.

i. Selecting Databases/Sources

The database/source you select for a search is dependent on a number of variables. A rule of thumb that is often heard is to initially select the smallest database containing the type of documents you're looking for, but this is dependent upon the circumstances. However, researchers now often conduct a broad search and then post-filter results using facets such as jurisdiction, type of material, and date. The following tips may provide guidance:

If you are doing secondary source research at the beginning of a project, it might make sense to run a search in one of the combined secondary source databases that combine materials from journals, treatises, and A.L.R. rather than searching separate sources/databases for this information. Depending on your fee arrangement with the vendor, however, note that higher rates might be charged for searching in the larger, combined sources (see below).

On the other hand, if you are researching a problem that is controlled by the law of a particular jurisdiction, it would be more reasonable to search for case or statutory law in a database that contains only materials from that jurisdiction, at least until you determine whether your research will necessitate an examination of persuasive authorities.

Both systems provide databases of materials for specialized areas of law. Often these databases include portions of statutory or regulatory codes, or of reporters, that are relevant to a particular specialty area. These specialized databases can improve search efficiency, but should be used with caution to ensure that relevant materials are not being overlooked because they do not appear in the selected database.

When doing statutory research, you can sometimes opt to use either an annotated (including references to cases and other materials as well as the statutory language) or unannotated (including the statutory language only) version of the code. Often the annotated code is a better choice because the terms actually used in the statute may not be those generally used when discussing a topic. For example, a particular term may not actually appear in the statute but the term may appear in the case annotations, so your search will retrieve the statute you seek. In other situations, the annotations may be so voluminous or the topic so broad that searching the annotated version creates a large retrieval of irrelevant items.

Probably the most difficult selection decision is among the case law databases. Both Lexis and Westlaw provide numerous databases/sources containing cases from various combinations of courts.

Make certain you are familiar with your institution or firm's billing arrangement with Lexis or Westlaw. Unless you have a flat fee arrangement, you may be billed at a higher rate for use of some large combined databases. (Even if a flat fee contract is in place, however, searching in a larger-than-necessary database/source may slow you down considerably due to the need to sort through superfluous documents. Also, frequent use of the larger databases/sources may be the basis for fee increases the next time your institution negotiates its contract.

> j.   Composing Lexis and Westlaw Searches

There are two basic approaches to searching for documents on Lexis and Westlaw.

- <u>Terms and Connectors searching</u>, which you can access from the advanced search link, combines search terms that describe your issue into a query using Boolean logic. The Boolean search mechanisms available on both services give a sophisticated set of proximity connectors beyond the standard AND, OR, and NOT. Conventional wisdom is that this is usually the preferred method of searching if comprehensive results are desired, that is, if your goal is to find all the cases or other sources on a topic.

- <u>Natural language searching</u> allows you to enter your query as an ordinary sentence or phrase and is the default method for searching in Lexis and Westlaw. Natural language searching is usually regarded as more appropriate if you are looking for a sample of relevant cases or secondary sources as part of more general preliminary research. Some studies are showing that the two methods of searching produce comparable results.

Both Lexis and Westlaw publish manuals, some written expressly for law students, which provide extensive explanations and examples of techniques for online research. Copies of current editions of these manuals are usually available from the vendors' student representatives, or ask your instructor about availability.

   o Define your issues

Just as with general electronic searching, you must first determine the issues raised by your problem. If you generate your Internet search on-the-fly, the only cost is your time and perhaps your connect charges. If you generate your Lexis or Westlaw searches on- the-fly you are incurring significant charges from the vendor as well. Identifying the legal issues involved may require some background reading and research. It is very difficult to formulate an effective terms and connectors search if you are unclear about what your issues are. Sometimes a natural language search can help you to find some background information.

   o Select search terms

Once you have a reasonably clear idea what your issues are, list the key terms, including synonyms, antonyms, and related concepts that could appear in an opinion or other document discussing your issue. For example, a medical doctor could be referred to as a doctor, physician, surgeon, or M.D. An opinion discussing the constitutionality of a statute could use "constitutional," "unconstitutional," or both.

When you input a terms and connectors search into Lexis or Westlaw, you should: 1) spell terms correctly; 2) anticipate alternative terms; 3) write your search to pick up different word forms of your search terms. Natural language searching, on the other hand, will automatically look for alternative forms of words you have included as part of your search.

Inclusion of a particular word or phrase within a terms and connectors search mandates that the word appear within a retrieved document unless that word is coupled with another in the search by the "or" connector or the rarely used "and not" of Lexis or "but not" of Westlaw. On the other hand, words and phrases included in a natural language search do not have to appear in every document retrieved. Rather, the documents retrieved are presented in order of statistical relevance, with those documents containing the greatest number of the least common words or phrases from the search being presented first. However, both Lexis and Westlaw allow the researcher to make particular words and phrases mandatory in a natural language search. Both systems recommend that this feature be used with great caution.

In terms and connectors searching on both Lexis and Westlaw, use root expanders and universal characters to include words with variant endings or spellings. On both Lexis and Westlaw, the root expander is the exclamation mark (!) while the universal character is star (*). Neither system allows the use of these characters in natural language searching.

In both systems, certain very common words will not be searched, including a, an, as, on, under, with. Avoid using these words in your terms and connectors searches. In your natural language searches these words will be automatically excluded from your search.

To search for phrases using terms and connectors searching:

- On Westlaw, place the phrase in quotes: "summary judgment" or "blood alcohol"

- On Lexis, simply type the phrase: last clear chance

- In natural language searching on both Lexis and Westlaw many, but not all, phrases will be automatically recognized and searched. However, to insure that a phrase is recognized, you should place it within quotation marks on both systems.

- The two systems treat compound (hyphenated) words and acronyms (such as E.P.A.) somewhat differently. For detailed discussions, consult the manuals for the services. A useful strategy is to enter alternative versions of the term (e.g., EPA or E.P.A. or "Environmental Protection Agency").

    o Relate your terms logically

The next step with terms and connectors searching is to use logical connectors to arrange your terms into ideas and concepts. The basic connectors OR and AND function the same on Lexis and Westlaw as on the Internet.

There are several other connectors that allow you to search for terms occurring in some proximity - and therefore presumably in some logical relationship - to one another in the documents.

    o Order the connectors properly

Both systems process search terms and connectors in a specified order depending upon which connectors are used. Failure to understand the order in which connectors are processed by the computer can lead to unintended results and missing important documents. Following is the basic order of processing:

* OR is always processed first;

* proximity operators are processed next;

* AND is processed next, and;

* AND NOT or BUT NOT processed last.
Evaluate your search
Beginning online researchers often write searches that are long and complex and contain unnecessary or non-specific terms. Usually simpler searches are better, provided they contain the terms most likely to be used in the documents dealing with the issues. As noted above, if you are having trouble even getting started because of unfamiliarity with the topic to be researched, do some background reading, perhaps coupled with a natural language search.

When should you edit your search? Sometimes the cases you retrieve with your first query suggest other terms that should be incorporated in your search query. If your original search was too broad (retrieved too many citations or irrelevant citations), you can modify it by adding other terms after an "AND" or a proximity connector. If your original search was too narrow (few or no citations), you can add terms (synonyms, antonyms, concepts) after an "OR" connector.

It takes practice to compose searches that are both effective (high recall of relevant documents) and efficient (minimal retrieval of irrelevant documents). School is the best time to gain this experience. Because terms and connectors searches are literal, they will not pick up documents with spelling errors, unanticipated variations in language, or that discuss concepts and facts analogous but not identical to your issues.

Natural language searching will sometimes overcome some of these limitations. However, it does much less than many researchers realize in automatically searching for synonyms and related concepts. Nonetheless, a natural language search can often be a good starting point in an area unfamiliar to the researcher, especially if followed by a well-crafted terms and connectors search. More than that, however, most experienced researchers rely on a combination of online and manual research techniques to ensure comprehensive results.

k. Quick Tip for Constructing Online Search Terms

• Terms and connectors searching - select terms & connectors searching when you are familiar with the topic and its language/jargon and/or when you want a comprehensive search (e.g., case research).

• Select natural language searching when you are beginning a research project and are not yet familiar with the vocabulary, or when you need only a sampling of relevant documents. For example, natural language searching can be useful in locating secondary source materials that provide background on the subject of your research. Run a natural language search first if unsure what search terms would create a successful terms and connectors search.

- Select search terms. Identify key terms, along with alternative forms, synonyms, antonyms, and related concepts; Make sure all terms are spelled correctly; Truncate terms appropriately with the "!" or "*" symbol to pick up variations in endings; On Westlaw, place a phrase in quotes; on Lexis, simply type the phrase; If you need help, use a legal dictionary or the online thesaurus.

- Relate terms logically and order connectors properly. Use the logical connectors to arrange your terms into ideas and concepts. The most commonly used connectors are essentially the same on Lexis and Westlaw and include, in order of processing

- Search efficiency may be greatly improved by limiting your searches to particular segments or fields of the documents in the source/database you are searching, or by specifying a date or time period for your search result.

- Browse the documents you have retrieved by looking for highlighted search terms in the text of the documents. Terms are automatically highlighted on Westlaw and one may move easily to points in documents at which search terms appear by clicking on the "Term" arrows at the bottom of the document screen.

- Select your source or database - You must have already determined the controlling jurisdiction. Usually it is most efficient to begin searching in the smallest database containing mandatory authorities.

l. Newer Subscription Databases for Online Tax Research

While Lexis and Westlaw dominated the electronic legal research landscape for many years, new competitors have recently emerged. Alternative electronic legal research databases including Bloomberg Law, Casemaker, Fastcase, VersusLaw, Loislaw, and HeinOnline are continuously expanding their content and features and are providing a challenge to the traditional vendors in an increasingly competitive market. While this Guide cannot individually address each one, the basic principles of electronic research apply: utilize the Help features and tutorials available on the various systems before conducting research in order to educate yourself about how to maximize the effectiveness and efficiency of your research.

m. Internet Research

The Internet as a research tool is both an astoundingly rich resource and an astoundingly frustrating one. The Internet cannot be ignored as a research tool, however. It falls to the searcher to be aware of its limitations.

The Internet is not nearly as structured as the databases from commercial vendors such as Westlaw and Lexis. Most Internet searchers use one of the many search engines as a means of finding information. Each search engine works a little differently, however, and those differences can affect search results. It is easy to think that when you've run a search in a couple of search engines that you've done a fairly thorough search. However, a comprehensive search is impossible on the Internet.

Probably the biggest difficulty with search engines is their lack of standardization. One search engine may treat a search for attorney malpractice as a phrase search, another one may treat it as a search for attorney OR malpractice, and a third may treat it as attorney AND malpractice. Again, there are too many search engines to spend time learning the peculiarities of each one. To learn how to maximize the effectiveness of a search on a particular search engine, click on the Help link, search tips, or advanced search instructions.

With all these negatives, why should a legal researcher use the Internet at all? The Internet can be a cheap alternative to the use of commercial databases such as Lexis and Westlaw for finding primary legal materials such as U.S. federal and state statutes, bills, cases, and regulations. Depending on the topic, some materials can be available more quickly on the Internet than on Lexis and Westlaw. The Internet can augment an average law library's resources by providing alternate copies of print materials, and information that cannot be found in the law library in print or electronic format.

This text can't go into an exhaustive list of Internet legal resources, but a sampling of what is available would include:

http://www.findlaw.com/

FindLaw, a Web portal focused on law and government, provides access to an online library of legal resources for use by legal professionals, consumers and small businesses. FindLaw's mission is to make legal information on the Internet easy to find.

http://www.fdsys.gov

The Federal Digital System disseminates official information from all three branches of the Federal Government. This site includes regulations, the United States Code and Presidential Documents.

http://thomas.loc.gov/

Extensive federal legislative information. The Library of Congress is migrating the content on THOMAS to a new site, Congress.gov. Currently in beta, Congress.gov provides legislative text, Congressional Record, and Committee Reports, and will be continuing to add content over the next several years.

http://www.law.cornell.edu/

The Legal Information Institute offers extensive holdings of case and statutory law, and some administrative sources. Materials are arranged both by jurisdiction and by topic. Most of the case law is fairly recent - there are not full runs of court decisions.

http://www.plol.org/Pages/Search.aspx

The Public Library of Law provides free access to primary sources including federal and state cases, statutes, regulations, and constitutions, as well as legal forms.

http://www.asil.org/resource/home.htm

The American Society of International Law Guide to Electronic Resources for International Law.

http://www.oyez.org/

This site includes U. S. Supreme Court cases as well as a collection of audio recordings of oral arguments from 1981 - present, and arguments from selected earlier cases.

http://scholar.google.com/

The Google Scholar search engine covers scholarly articles (some full text, some abstracts only) as well as case law.

n. Strategies for Internet Research

1. Learn how your favorite research engines operate. There are a number of major Internet search engines. None of them use the same syntax for organizing search requests. Serious researchers are advised to select several, and familiarize themselves with their syntax.

2. Use more than one search engine for important projects. The various search engines do not index the Internet the same way and they do not rank the results of their findings the same way and as previously pointed out, no one engine covers more than a fraction of all the web pages. For this reason, you will want to use more than one. There are "meta search engines" that will send your search request to more than one search engine simultaneously.

3. Plan your searches. There is no surer way to waste time on Internet legal research than to cast about without a plan. Just as you would with Lexis or Westlaw make sure you:

    .   1) define your issues;

    .   2) analyze your facts;

    .   3) decide how to express your search;

    .   4) select the most relevant electronic resources to search; and

    .   5) run your search and evaluate your results.

4. Evaluate reliability. In drafting a brief, would you cite and rely on the National Enquirer or a high school student's essay to support an important point? It's not that

hard to identify and avoid the Internet equivalents. To evaluate the quality of an Internet site as a research tool, consider objectivity, expediency, timeliness, accuracy, authenticity, and scope.

5. Some considerations: Is the site free or fee-based? If it costs, are there any guarantees of quality control? Who is the author/publisher - government agency, university, organization, company, law firm, a good-hearted individual? What is the source of the data - who provided it and in what format? Was the original pagination of paper versions retained? Is there an electronic signature to confirm authorship? What is the date of the web site/document? When was it last modified/updated? Is the document full text, index or abstracts? Is it complete or excerpted? Is the content of the electronic version as accurate as the print? Are there archives? How long is data retained at the web site? Broken links? Ease of navigation? Search mechanisms? How easy is the web site to access? Slow connections? Is information on the site stable? Is there a contact person? Are broken links quickly fixed? If you have a choice of publishers for a document, choose the originator of the document such as a government agency, international organization or similar source. Rely on documents only where it is possible to verify date, authorship, and other indicia of authenticity.

o. Strategies for Fee-Based Database System Research

Years ago, when legal research database systems were first available, the database providers charged the users for each and every executed search. For example, here is how I conducted research as a junior legal researcher working for a major legal publisher:

- First - after reviewing an area of law that I was assigned to update, I would complete a form that asked me to: (1) select the database(s) for search; and (2) draft the precise search words or terms in Boolean format.

- Second - I would present my completed search form for review by my supervisor.

- Third - If approved, I would execute my search on the database system. If the search results provided 10,000 hits (or some number that was too large), then I would have to prepare another search form for approval - embarrassing. If I mis-typed the search in the dialogue box, then I'd have no results since no legal documents in the database matched my mis-typed word "dedutcion" when I meant to type "deduction." Again, if I mis-typed a search term, then I'd have to return to my supervisor with another search form for approval along with an explanation that my shoddy work required another attempt at the same search. Each "executed" search cost the firm $5.00.

The benefit of this system was that it forced the researcher to pause and think about the database selection process as well as the precise search terms. The downside of this system was that it was awkwardly slow. Today, the database systems do not charge per search. And, firms do not require new associates to present their research strategies in written form for pre-review before each search is executed. But, the downside within today's system is that researchers seldom "pause" to craft a search strategy of database and search term selection. With this background, consider the following five step process to conduct searches in fee-based systems today:

1. Database selection - Select secondary source databases only with the goal of finding summaries that can provide you with a quick synopsis of the topic you are searching.

2. Search word selection - Input search words that are relevant to your tax topic (roughly 5-8 words only). The goal should be to get results in the 10-20 range of secondary sources for your search.

3. Invest your time in reviewing the secondary source results - Review the results and select the top items that you believe present the best choices to devote additional time. Open these items and begin your initial analysis.

4. Invest your time in reviewing the primary source results - Once you determine which results present you with the applicable summaries, conduct your second level research by reading the primary source links that are presented as part of the secondary sources that you found and read. Verify that these primary source authorities accurately support the summaries presented in your initial inquiry. Remember - it is possible that the summaries prepared by the legal database provider are either incorrect or not updated to reflect the current law.

5. End your research because you have sufficient confidence from the results of your research or return to Step 1 and begin the process again. After reviewing the primary source materials located, determine whether you need additional or higher level primary source materials to gain more confidence of your position with respect to your client's tax issue.

Chapter 3 Questions

1. Why do we need to use a fee-based research system when everything is available on the internet for free?

2. What are the two basic electronic approaches to search for documents on Lexis and Westlaw?

3. When should a tax professional stop conducting research?

4. Facts: Our firm's clients, Joe and Wanda Smith, reside and work in San Francisco, California. They own a vacation property in South Carolina. They've heard in news reports that Hurricane Florence will be heading towards their vacation property in South Carolina. Several years ago, they purchased their vacation home for $500,000. They've fully paid off their mortgage on the South Carolina property and own it outright. Currently, it's valued at $500,000. Their adjusted cost basis is $500,000. Joe and Wanda have basic insurance on the property but no flood insurance. Joe and Wanda are concerned about partial or full loss of their vacation property due to Hurricane Florence and ask for our firm's advice on possible tax consequences if they suffer any casualty loss from the storm in 2018. W must determine ho to proceed as their tax advisors.   Conduct research and address the following questions:
   - What is the tax issue statement?
   - Based on your research, what tax law/guidance applies in this case?
   - What additional facts, if any, do we need to provide tax advice to our clients?

5. Grandma Jones was a widower in 2011 who received $7,200 in social security benefit (Form SSA-1099). She had saved $105,000 from her many years of work and deposited all of her savings in a foreign bank account in Spain last year (2011). She doesn't seem to trust U.S. banks. A teller in California was rude to her back in 2010. So, she traveled to Spain on vacation in 2011 and placed all of her savings in that foreign account. Grandma Jones asks you for tax advice for her federal tax obligations for 2011.

CHAPTER 4 – THE LEGISLATIVE BRANCH

☑ Understand the role of the legislative branch in tax
☑ Learn about legislative sources of tax law that affect tax administration

1. Introduction to the Legislative Branch
2. The Legislative Process
3. Powers of Congress
4. Government Oversight
5. Staying Current with Tax Law

1. Introduction to the Legislative Branch

Established by Article I of the Constitution, the Legislative Branch consists of the House of Representatives and the Senate, which together form the United States Congress. The Constitution grants Congress the sole authority to enact legislation[37] and declare war, the right to confirm or reject many Presidential appointments, and substantial investigative powers. Specifically, with respect to Federal taxes, Art. I, Sec. 8, of the U.S. Constitution provides in part, "The Congress shall have Power To lay and collect Taxes, Duties, Imposts and Excises, to pay the Debts and provide for the common Defense and general Welfare of the United States...." Later, the Sixteenth Amendment provided, "The Congress shall have power to lay and collect taxes on incomes, from whatever source derived, without apportionment among the several States, and without regard to any census or enumeration."

---

[37] "All Legislative Powers herein granted shall be vested in a Congress of the United States, which shall consist of a Senate and House of Representatives." Art. I, Sec. 1, U.S. Constitution.

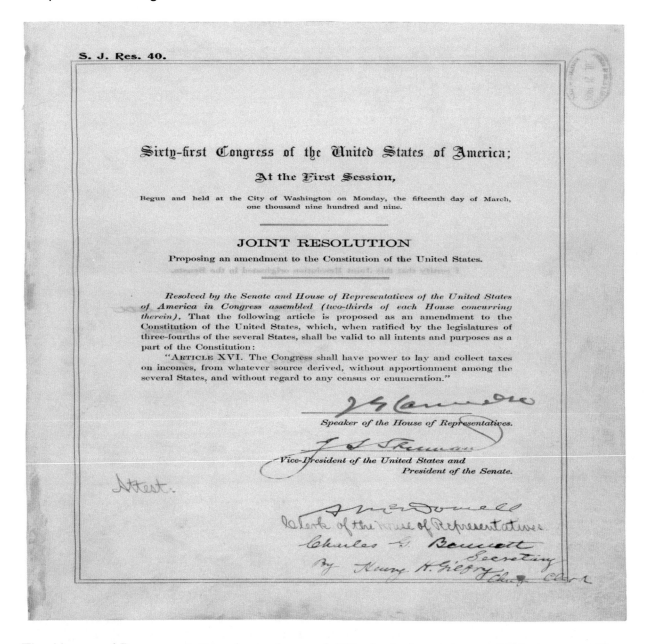

The House of Representatives is made up of 435 elected members, divided among the 50 states in proportion to their total population. In addition, there are 6 non-voting members, representing the District of Columbia, the Commonwealth of Puerto Rico, and four other territories of the United States. The presiding officer of the chamber is the Speaker of the House, elected by the Representatives. He or she is third in the line of succession to the Presidency.

Members of the House are elected every two years and must be 25 years of age, a U.S. citizen for at least seven years, and a resident of the state (but not necessarily the district) they represent.

The House has several powers assigned exclusively to it, including the power to initiate revenue bills, impeach federal officials, and elect the President in the case of an electoral college tie.

The Senate is composed of 100 Senators, 2 for each state. Until the ratification of the 17th Amendment in 1913, Senators were chosen by state legislatures, not by popular vote. Since then, they have been elected to six-year terms by the people of each state. Senator's terms are staggered so that about one-third of the Senate is up for reelection every two years. Senators must be 30 years of age, U.S. citizens for at least nine years, and residents of the state they represent.

The Vice President of the United States serves as President of the Senate and may cast the decisive vote in the event of a tie in the Senate.

The Senate has the sole power to confirm those of the President's appointments that require consent, and to ratify treaties. There are, however, two exceptions to this rule: the House must also approve appointments to the Vice Presidency and any treaty that involves foreign trade. The Senate also tries impeachment cases for federal officials referred to it by the House.

In order to pass legislation and send it to the President for his signature, both the House and the Senate must pass the same bill by majority vote. If the President vetoes a bill, they may override his veto by passing the bill again in each chamber with at least two-thirds of each body voting in favor.

2. The Legislative Process

The legislative process in a nutshell is as follows:
* First, a Representative sponsors a bill.
* The bill is then assigned to a committee for study.
* If released by the committee, the bill is put on a calendar to be voted on, debated or amended.
* If the bill passes by simple majority (218 of 435), the bill moves to the Senate.
* In the Senate, the bill is assigned to another committee and, if released, debated and voted on.
* If the Senate makes changes, the bill must return to the House for concurrence.

* The resulting bill returns to the House and Senate for final approval.
* The President then has 10 days to veto the final bill or sign it into law.

The first step in the legislative process is the introduction of a bill to Congress.38 Anyone can write it, but only members of Congress can introduce legislation. Any Member in the House of Representatives may introduce a bill at any time while the House is in session by simply placing it in the "hopper" at the side of the Clerk's desk in

---

38 Short video summaries of the legislative process is available at: https://www.congress.gov/legislative-process.

the House Chamber. The sponsor's signature must appear on the bill, which may have an unlimited number of cosponsoring Members. The bill is assigned its legislative number by the Clerk and referred to the committee of jurisdiction, which is the committee charged with review of the bill. Some important bills are traditionally introduced at the request of the President, such as the annual federal budget.39 During the legislative process, however, the initial bill can undergo drastic changes.

After being introduced, a bill is referred to the appropriate committee for review. There are 17 Senate committees, with 70 subcommittees, and 23 House committees, with 104 subcommittees. The committees are not set in stone, but change in number and form with each new Congress as required for the efficient consideration of legislation. Each committee oversees a specific policy area, and the subcommittees take on more specialized policy areas. For example, the House Committee on Ways and Means includes subcommittees on Social Security and Trade.

A bill is first considered in a subcommittee, where it may be accepted, amended, or rejected entirely. Usually, the first step in this process is a public hearing where the committee or subcommittee members hear witnesses representing various viewpoints on the measure. After hearings are completed, the bill is considered in a session that is popularly known as the "mark-up" session. At this point, amendments may be offered to the bill, and the committee or subcommittee Members vote to accept or reject these changes. At the conclusion of deliberation, a vote of committee or subcommittee Members is taken to determine what action to take on the measure. It can be reported, with or without amendment, or tabled, which means no further action on it will occur. Tabling effectively "kills" the measure. If the committee has approved extensive amendments, they may decide to report a new bill incorporating all the amendments. This is known as a "clean bill," which will have a new number.

If the members of the subcommittee agree to move a bill forward, it is reported to the full committee, where the process is repeated again. Throughout this stage of the process, the committees and subcommittees call hearings to investigate the merits and flaws of the bill. They invite experts, advocates, and opponents to appear before the committee and provide testimony, and can compel people to appear using subpoena power if necessary. If the full committee votes to approve the bill, it is reported to the floor of the House or Senate, and the majority party leadership decides when to place the bill on the calendar for consideration. If a bill is particularly pressing, it may be considered right away. Others may wait for months or never be scheduled at all. When the bill comes up for consideration, the House has a very structured debate process. Each member who wishes to speak only has a few minutes, and the number and kind of amendments are usually limited. Consideration of a measure by the full House can be a simple or very complex operation. Sometimes, consideration may be governed by a "rule." A rule is itself a simple resolution, which must be passed by the House and that sets out the particular rules of debate for a specific bill (i.e. how much

---

39 More detailed information on the Congressional budget process is available at: https://www.congress.gov/resources/display/content/How+Our+Laws+Are+Made+-+Learn+About+the+Legislative+Process#HowOurLawsAreMade-LearnAbouttheLegislativeProcess-UnitedStatesCode, Sec. XII.

time will be allowed for debate, whether amendments can be offered, and other matters). Debate time for a measure is normally divided between proponents and opponents. Each side yields time to those Members who wish to speak on the bill. When amendments are offered, these are also debated and voted upon. After all debate is concluded and amendments decided upon, the House votes on final passage. In some cases, a vote to "recommit" the bill to committee is requested. This is usually an effort by opponents to change some portion or table the measure. If the attempt to recommit fails, a vote on final passage is ordered. Votes may be taken by the electronic voting system, which registers each individual Member's response. These are referred to as recorded votes, and are available in the record of roll call votes. Votes in the House may also be by voice vote; in that instance, no record of individual responses is available.

In the Senate, debate on most bills is unlimited — Senators may speak to issues other than the bill under consideration during their speeches, and any amendment can be introduced. Senators can use this to filibuster bills under consideration, a procedure by which a Senator delays a vote on a bill — and by extension its passage — by refusing to stand down. A supermajority of 60 Senators can break a filibuster by invoking cloture, or the cession of debate on the bill, and forcing a vote. Once debate is over, the votes of a simple majority passes the bill.

A bill must pass both houses of Congress before it goes to the President for consideration. Though the Constitution requires that the two bills have the exact same wording, this rarely happens in practice. And, the ideal legislative process as presented, above, does not always align with the realities of the political process. Most recently during Congress' deliberations of a major overhaul of the tax code as passed in Pub. Law. No. 115-97, U.S. Senator Jon Tester (Montana) expressed his frustration on Twitter that he was not afforded sufficient time and/or an opportunity to adequately consider the substance of the tax bill. See Senator Tester's Twitter post during the legislative process involving Pub. Law. No. 115-97, at the bottom right of this page:

 Senator Jon Tester ✓ @Senato... ·5h ⌄
I was just handed a 479-page tax bill a few hours before the vote. One page literally has hand scribbled policy changes on it that can't be read. This is Washington, D.C. at its worst. Montanans deserve so much better.

0:45 ▮▮

On the other side of this recent legislative commentary were comments that applauded how the government process finally accomplished tax reform. In House Speaker Paul Ryan's website, he stated "With the economy booming, historic reform continues to deliver on its promises, directly improving the lives of America's workers and families….."[40] Clearly, there are different views on the passage of legislation. Beyond the scrum of politics, students should understand the basics of this legislative process and also appreciate the realities involved as well. Let's head back to the legislative process.

To bring the bills into alignment, a Conference Committee is convened, consisting of members from both chambers. A Conference Committee resolves any differences between the House and Senate versions of the bill and issues its own report intended as the final version of the bill.[41] Each chamber then votes again to approve the conference report. Committee Reports are published in full in the Congressional Record and in part in the Internal Revenue Bulletin and Cumulative Bulletin. Selected reports are found in many commercial tax services.[42]

Depending on where the bill originated, the final text is then enrolled by either the Clerk of the House or the Secretary of the Senate, and presented to the Speaker of the House and the President of the Senate for their signatures. The bill is then sent to the President.

When receiving a bill from Congress, the President has several options. If the President agrees substantially with the bill, he or she may sign it into law, and the bill is then printed in the Statutes at Large. If the President believes the law to be bad policy, he may veto it and send it back to Congress. Congress may override the veto with a two-thirds vote of each chamber, at which point the bill becomes law and is printed.

There are two other options that the President may exercise. If Congress is in session and the President takes no action within 10 days, the bill becomes law. If Congress adjourns before 10 days are up and the President takes no action, then the bill dies and Congress may not vote to override. This is called a pocket veto, and if Congress still wants to pass the legislation, they must begin the entire process anew.[43]

One of the important steps in the enactment of a valid law is the requirement that it shall be made known to the people who are to be bound by it. There would be no justice if the state were to hold its people responsible for their conduct before it made known to them the unlawfulness of such behavior. In practice, our laws are published immediately upon their enactment so that the public will be aware of them.

    Publication - If the President approves a bill, or allows it to become law without signing it, the original enrolled bill is sent from the White House to the Archivist of the United States for publication. If a bill is passed by both Houses over the objections of the President, the body that last overrides the veto transmits it. It is then assigned a public law number, and paginated for the Statutes at Large volume covering that

---

[40] https://www.speaker.gov/general/better-now-tax-reform-stories-keep-coming-plus-armageddon-update.

[41] See IRM 4.10.7.2.2(2).

[42] See IRM 4.10.7.2.2.1(1).

[43] Go to https://www.house.gov/content/learn/legislative_process/ for a more detailed presentation of the legislative process.

session of Congress. The public and private law numbers run in sequence starting anew at the beginning of each Congress and are prefixed for ready identification by the number of the Congress. For example, the first public law of the 110th Congress is designated Public Law 110–1 and the first private law of the 110th Congress is designated Private Law 110–1.

Slip Laws - The first official publication of the statute is in the form generally known as the "slip law." In this form, each law is published separately as an unbound pamphlet. The heading indicates the public or private law number, the date of approval, and the bill number. The heading of a slip law for a public law also indicates the United States Statutes at Large citation. If the statute has been passed over the veto of the President, or has become law without the President's signature because he did not return it with objections, an appropriate statement is inserted instead of the usual notation of approval. The Office of the Federal Register, National Archives and Records Administration, prepares the slip laws and provides marginal editorial notes giving the citations to laws mentioned in the text and other explanatory details. The marginal notes also give the United States Code classifications, enabling the reader immediately to determine where the statute will appear in the Code. Each slip law also includes an informative guide to the legislative history of the law consisting of the committee report number, the name of the committee in each House, as well as the date of consideration and passage in each House, with a reference to the Congressional Record by volume, year, and date. A reference to presidential statements relating to the approval of a bill or the veto of a bill when the veto was overridden and the bill becomes law is included in the legislative history as a citation to the Weekly Compilation of Presidential Documents. Copies of the slip laws are delivered to the document rooms of both Houses where they are available to officials and the public. They may also be obtained by annual subscription or individual purchase from the Government Printing Office and are available in electronic form. Section 113 of title 1 of the United States Code provides that slip laws are competent evidence in all the federal and state courts, tribunals, and public offices.

Statutes at Large - The United States Statutes at Large, prepared by the Office of the Federal Register, National Archives and Records Administration, provide a permanent collection of the laws of each session of Congress in bound volumes. The latest volume containing the laws of the first session of the 109th Congress is number 119 in the series. Each volume contains a complete index and a table of contents. A legislative history appears at the end of each law. There are also marginal notes referring to laws in earlier volumes and to earlier and later matters in the same volume. Under the provisions of a statute enacted in 1895, these volumes are legal evidence of the laws contained in them and will be accepted as proof of those laws in any court in the United States. The Statutes at Large are a chronological arrangement of the laws exactly as they have been enacted. The laws are not arranged according to subject matter and do not reflect the present status of an earlier law that has been amended.

U.S. Code - The United States Code contains a consolidation and codification of the general and permanent laws of the United States arranged according to subject matter under title headings, largely in alphabetical order. It sets out the current status of the laws, as amended, without repeating all the language of the amendatory acts except where necessary. The Code is declared to be prima facie evidence of those laws. Its purpose is to present the laws in a concise and usable form without requiring recourse to the many volumes of the Statutes at Large containing the individual amendments.

On December 22, 2017, H.R. 115-97 became law when the president signed major tax legislation presented to him by Congress. Even though the effective date of this new tax law was set to begin in 2018, most if not all publishers were unable to print the text of this new tax law in their versions of the tax code that set for publication in January, 2018. There just wasn't sufficient time to include all of the changes to the code in such a short amount of time. So, where can practitioners find text of new tax law such as Pub. Law. No. 115-97? You can go online to the following government website address which provides the text of legislation, including Pub. Law. No. 115-97: https://www.congress.gov/bill/115th-congress/house-bill/1/titles.

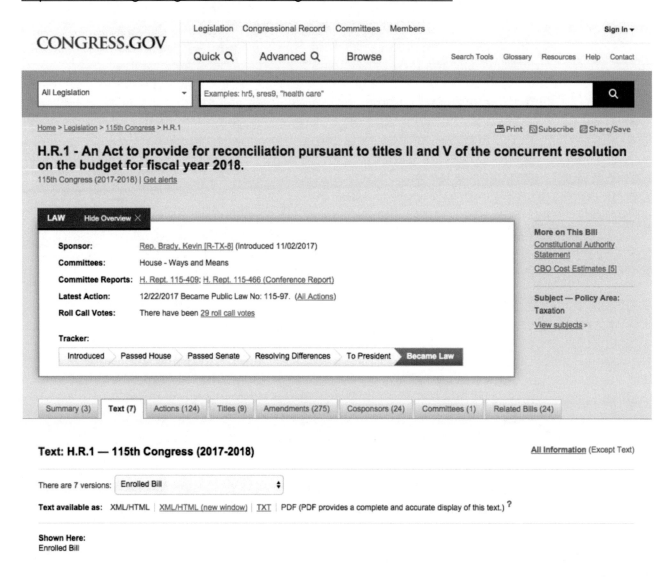

The Congressional website provides the history of legislation as shown for Public Law 115-97, in part by clicking the tab for "Action", as follows:

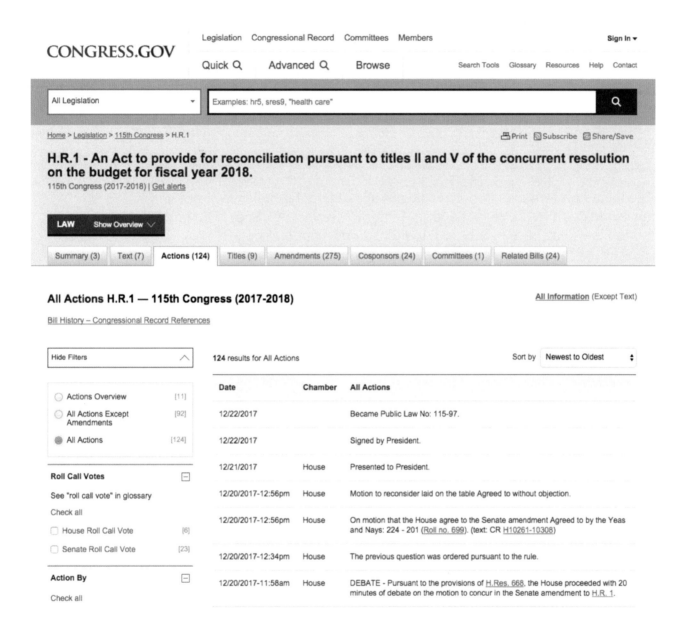

Consider just one section of Public Law 115-97 that changes the tax treatment for moving expenses.

SEC. 11049. SUSPENSION OF DEDUCTION FOR MOVING EXPENSES.

(a) IN GENERAL.—Section 217 is amended by adding at the end the following new subsection:

"(k) SUSPENSION OF DEDUCTION FOR TAXABLE YEARS 2018 THROUGH 2025.— Except in the case of an individual to whom subsection (g) applies, this section shall not apply to any taxable year beginning after December 31, 2017, and before January 1, 2026.".

(b) EFFECTIVE DATE.—The amendment made by this section shall apply to taxable years beginning after December 31, 2017.

- The section references in public law are specific to the public law, not correlated to tax law under Title 26 (the title for the Internal Revenue Code). So, section 11049 relates to Public Law 115-97, not to the tax code under Title 26.
- Public Law 115-97 provides that section 217 will include just one change – an addition of sub-section (k) at provided in section 11049.
- Note that the change in law is effective beginning on January 1, 2018 but is temporary, applicable only for the years 2018 thru 2025.

   a. Legislative History

Reference to legislative history provides tax practitioners the source to understand the purpose of the statute and to resolve any ambiguity in the words contained in the text of the statute.[44] Congressional legislative history is readily available online at www.Congress.gov and at www.gpo.gov/fdsys/browse/collection.action?collectionCode=BILLS. While locating legislative history is not difficult, understanding the process and legislative intent from the House to the Senate to Conference Committee to determine the true intent of Congress is an exceptionally labor intensive exercise. A good place to find a summary of the legislative history for code provisions is with the Joint Committee on Taxation.[45] The Joint Committee on Taxation is a nonpartisan committee of the United States Congress.[46] The Joint Committee Staff is closely involved with every aspect of the tax legislative process. Generally, at the end of each Congress, the Joint Committee on Taxation staff prepare explanations of the enacted tax legislation called the "Blue Book"

---

[44] Landgraf v. USI Film Prods, 511 U.S. 244 (1994); Commissioner v. Soliman, 506 U.S. 168, 174 (1993).

[45] https://www.jct.gov/about-us/overview.html.

[46] Under Internal Revenue Code section 8021, the Joint Committee is empowered to: (1) obtain and inspect tax returns and return information as specified in sec. 6103(f); (2) hold hearings, require attendance of witnesses and production of books, administer oaths, and take testimony; (3) procure printing and binding; (4) make necessary expenditures. In addition, section 8023 authorizes the Joint Committee (or the Chief of Staff), upon approval of the Chairman or Vice-Chairman, to secure tax returns, tax return information or data directly from the IRS or any other executive agency for the purpose of making investigations, reports, and studies relating to internal revenue tax matters, including investigations of the IRS's administration of the tax laws.

which often contains comprehensive analysis and explanation of legislation. Although the Blue Book is not technically legislative history (since it is written post-enactment of legislation), it is often considered in determining legislative intent at the time of enactment.[47] The explanation follows the chronological order of the tax legislation as signed into law. For each provision, the document includes a description of present law, explanation of the provision, and effective date.

Admittedly, understanding the legislative process is tedious. So, let's pause to consider the practical application of the legislative process and how understanding this process can allow us to become better tax practitioners. What follows, below, is one basic code section initially mis-interpreted but ultimately correctly determined that involved two circuit courts of appeals and three case decisions. The question presented in all three cases involved just one sentence of section 165(a) as follows: "There shall be allowed as a deduction any loss sustained during the taxable year and not compensated for by insurance or otherwise." In a basic scenario, where a taxpayer suffers a loss totaling $10,000 in 2016 but received $4,000 from his insurance policy that covered the loss, the taxpayer has $6,000 as an allowable loss deduction in that same year under section 165. But, what is the tax result if the taxpayer has insurance coverage but decides not to pursue payment for either some or all of the loss that is covered by the insurance policy?

You may ask why any taxpayer would decide not to seek insurance proceeds if he/she had loss coverage in place? In Kentucky Utilities Co. v. Glenn, 394 F.2d 631 (6th Cir. 1968), a steam generator was damaged in an accident. The generator was originally sold to Kentucky Utilities ("K.U.") by Westinghouse Electric Corporation and was under warranty at the time of the accident. Based on an independent investigation, K.U. concluded that Westinghouse was responsible for the loss. Rather than jeopardize a valued business relationship by pursuing a claim against Westinghouse, K.U. sought indemnification from its insurance company, Lloyds of London. The insurance carrier did not dispute either its liability or the amount necessary to indemnify the loss. In fact, Lloyds offered to indemnify K.U. for the full amount of the damage. Because Lloyds insisted upon its right of subrogation against Westinghouse, however, K.U. refused to accept any insurance proceeds. Instead, K.U., Westinghouse, and Lloyds entered into a settlement agreement whereby Westinghouse and Lloyds agreed to compensate K.U. in the amount of $65,550.93 and $37,500.00, respectively. Pursuant to this settlement, K.U. agreed to absorb the remaining cost of repairs and proceeded to deduct the $44,486.77 on its corporate income tax return, either as a section 165 loss or as a section 162 "ordinary and necessary" business expense. The district court held that K.U.'s failure reasonably to pursue indemnification from Lloyds barred any casualty loss deduction under section 23(f) of the 1939 I.R.C. (now, section 165), except to the extent of the $10,000 deductible provision in its insurance policy. Likewise, the district

---

[47] See, e.g., Robinson v. Commissioner, 119 T.C. No. 4 (2002)("Consideration of the 1986 Blue Book (where, as here, it does not conflict with the enacted statutory language and does not conflict with what we have referred to as the conference committee sentence (supra F.(4) Thirdly)), in combination with the Joint Committee staff summary and the relevant portion of the Joint Statement of Managers portion of the conference committee report points toward a conclusion that section 1.163-9T(b)(2)(i)(A), Temporary Income, Tax Regs., *supra*, is a permissible construction of section 163(h)(2)(A).")

court held that K.U.'s expenditures did not constitute ordinary or necessary business expenses under section 23(e) of the 1939 I.R.C., similar to section 162 of the 1954 Code. The Sixth Circuit Court of Appeals affirmed the decision of the lower district court - that K.U.'s failure reasonably to pursue indemnification from Lloyds barred any casualty loss deduction under 165.

The Eleventh Circuit addressed a very similar set of facts involving the proper interpretation of section 165 in Hills v. Commissioner, 691 F.2d 997 (11th Cir. 1982). In Hills, the husband and wife owned a vacation home in Georgia that was robbed. The taxpayers suffered loss of $760 from the theft **but chose not to file a claim under their insurance policy** apparently because they had previously filed three other theft claims and feared that a fourth filed claim would result in cancellation of their policy. So, the taxpayers claimed the casualty loss on their 1976 federal income tax return. At the lower trial level proceeding, the IRS argued that if a taxpayer is covered by insurance but *elects not to seek compensation from its insurance policy*, then section 165 denies any claimed loss by the taxpayer. The IRS' view was that the statutory text of "not compensated for by insurance" was functionally equivalent to reading the statute as if it said "not covered by insurance." However, the U.S. Tax Court rejected the IRS' view of section 165 holding that the taxpayers' loss was not compensated for by insurance despite the fact that the taxpayers had insurance coverage. In affirming the decision of the Tax Court, the Sixth Circuit in Hills v. Commissioner, 691 F.2d 997 (6th Cir. 1982), delved into legislative history to reach its conclusion noting:

> The initial House Ways and Means Committee language was "losses ... not covered by insurance or otherwise and compensated for." The Senate Finance Committee amended the language to its final and enacted form of "losses ... not compensated for by insurance or otherwise." [] This change makes clear the fact that Congress was aware of the difference between "covered" and "compensated" and intended to enact what it in fact enacted.

(emphasis added to original text). Thus, the Sixth Circuit applied its understanding of the legislative process to conclude Congressional intent to reach its decision on how to properly interpret statute.

Recognizing that the Sixth Circuit's decision in Kentucky Utilities Co. v. Glenn, 394 F.2d 631 (6th Cir. 1968), reached an opposite statutory interpretation to its decision in Hills, the Eleventh Circuit took pains to attempt to explain why the Sixth Circuit decision in Kentucky Utilities was not contradictory to its own circuit interpretation of section 165:

> Our view of Kentucky Utilities is that the Sixth Circuit agrees with us that section 165 calls for a two-part inquiry, first into loss, then into compensation. They, unlike us, were interested in the loss half of the transaction, [] and were directly addressing the scope of the duty reasonably to pursue the principal to a loss transaction. [] K-U chose not to pursue Westinghouse directly; K-U also chose not to claim under its insurance with Lloyds because it did not want to pursue Westinghouse indirectly either. The holding of Kentucky Utilities, then, is that the duty reasonably to pursue a principal to a loss transaction also extends to

indirect pursuit. [] **This result regarding the loss half of a transaction is not inconsistent with our holding today regarding the compensation half of a transaction.**

(emphasis added to original text). However, in a later decision, Miller v. Commissioner, 733 F.2d 399 (6th Cir. 1984), the Sixth Circuit Court of Appeals addressed a similar set of facts as in Kentucky Utilities. In Miller, a taxpayer did not file a claim for recovery of damage to his boat with his insurance company. The taxpayer's decision not to collect insurance proceeds was motivated by his fear that the submission of another claim would result in the cancellation of his insurance policies.[3] Taxpayer was able to collect $200.00 from his friend, reducing taxpayer's actual loss to $642.55. After taking into account the $100.00 limitation under section 165(c)(3),[4] taxpayer claimed a $542.22 casualty loss deduction on his 1976 return. The IRS disallowed the deduction. Relying on Kentucky Utilities Co. v. Glenn, 394 F.2d 631 (6th Cir.1968), the Tax Court concluded that the taxpayer's failure to pursue insurance proceeds barred the casualty loss deduction. The Tax Court, however, reconsidered its decision in light of Hills v. Commissioner, 76 T.C. 484 (1981), aff'd., 691 F.2d 997 (11th Cir.1982), and allowed the deduction. So, 16 years after its decision in Kentucky Utilties, the Sixth Circuit was asked, again, the same legal question - whether a voluntary election not to file an insurance claim for a casualty loss precludes the insured-taxpayer from taking a casualty loss deduction under section 165. And, with the benefit of reading the Eleventh Circuit's analysis of legislative history in Hills, the Sixth Circuit changed its view with respect to section 165 as stated in its 1984 Miller decision. In Miller, 733 F.2d 399 (6th Cir. 1984), 16 years after its decision in Kentucky Utilties, the Sixth Circuit stated:

> We are not able significantly to distinguish the issue presented in this case from that presented in Kentucky Utilities, and, to the extent it is contrary to our holding in this case, we overrule that decision and AFFIRM the holding of the Tax Court below.

> After our holding in Kentucky Utilities, the Eleventh Circuit handed down its decision in Hills, supra. The Hills court attempted to distinguish, rather than to reject, the holding of Kentucky Utilities. We have been unable to distinguish, however, Kentucky Utilities in any meaningful manner. It is true that Kentucky Utilities deals with a corporation and a claimed business loss akin to a Sec. 165(c)(1) loss, while Hills, as well as the instant case, deal with subsection 165(c)(3) casualty loss claims by individual taxpayers (theft and shipwreck, respectively). Each situation is subject, nevertheless, to the general overriding requirement of Sec. 165(a), whether business or individual, that a loss be "sustained ... and not compensated for by insurance or otherwise." An interpretation of the code subsection under consideration, Sec. 165(c)(3), as it pertains to a claimed individual loss, is therefore closely related to the interpretation given in Kentucky Utilities to the claimed business loss.

The Sixth Circuit pointed specifically to the analysis of the legislative history conducted by the Eleventh Circuit in Hills that was missed by the Sixth Circuit earlier in Kentucky Utilities:

> Absent unusual circumstances, we are bound to apply the plain meaning of a statute. Hills, 691 F.2d at 1000. Moreover, legislative history, scant though it is, does not support an interpretation of Sec. 165 that equates "not compensated by" with "not covered by." As the court in Hills noted: "The initial House Ways and Means Committee language was 'losses ... not covered by insurance or otherwise and compensated for.' The Senate Finance Committee amended the language to its final and enacted form of "losses ... not compensated for by insurance or otherwise."

> The Eleventh Circuit's observation in Hills that "[t]he disposition the Commissioner favore[d] in this case would deny a section 165 deduction any time a loss is covered by insurance," 691 F.2d at 1000, would apply equally here. Such a disposition, that of the Kentucky Utilities case that there was no "insured loss," does not comport with the plain and clear meaning of this section of the Internal Revenue Code **in light of the legislative history pointed out**. We agree with the Hills court in its ultimate holding: "Section 165(a) allows a deduction for an economic detriment that (1) is a loss, and (2) is not compensated for by insurance or otherwise." Id.

(emphasis added to original text). The Circuit Courts of Appeal decisions in Kentucky Utilities Co. v. Glenn, 394 F.2d 631 (6th Cir. 1968) and Hills v. Commissioner, 691 F.2d 997 (11th Cir. 1982), both addressed the proper interpretation of section 165 on the same issue - whether a voluntary election not to file an insurance claim for a casualty loss precludes the insured-taxpayer from taking a casualty loss deduction under section 165. However, the courts reached different views of how section 165 should be interpreted and applied. In Kentucky Utilities, the Sixth Circuit held that a taxpayer's failure to pursue insurance coverage that is available bars any casualty loss deduction under section 165. In contrast, the Eleventh Circuit In Hills held that even if a taxpayer had insurance coverage, the taxpayer was not required to pursue an insurance claim to be allowed a casualty deduction under section 165 since Congress specifically removed the word "coverage" from the text of section 165 and left "not compensated by insurance." In Hills, the Sixth Circuit took its lumps and admitted that it failed to conduct review of legislative history as required to reach a proper interpretation of section 165 as performed by the Eleventh Circuit in Miller. Understand the legislative process and don't make the same mistake in your tax practice.

Let's review another example of using legislative history to properly understand tax law. Retirement accounts are a vital part (or should be) of everyone's long-term financial security. What happens when we are lucky enough to have multiple retirement accounts, say individual retirement accounts ("IRA"), and want to move the funds between accounts or consolidate the accounts? Section 408(d) governs distributions from qualified retirement plans. Generally, section 408(d)(1) provides that any amount distributed from an individual retirement plan is includible in gross income by the payee or distributee. Section 408(d)(3)(A) allows a payee or distributee of an IRA distribution to exclude from gross income any amount paid or distributed from an IRA if the entire amount is subsequently paid into a qualifying IRA, individual retirement annuity, or retirement plan not later than the 60th day after the day on which the payee or distributee receives the distribution.[48] Such distributions and repayments are commonly referred to as "rollover contributions".[49]

But, the tax code limits rollover contributions. Section 408(d)(3)(B) limits a taxpayer from performing more than one nontaxable rollover in a one-year period with regard to IRAs and individual retirement annuities. Specifically, section 408(d)(3)(B) provides:

> This paragraph [regarding tax-free rollovers] does not apply to any amount described in subparagraph (A)(i) received by an individual from an individual retirement account or individual retirement annuity if at any time during the 1-year period ending on the day of such receipt such individual received any other amount described in that subparagraph from an individual retirement account or an individual retirement annuity which was not includible in his gross income because of the application of this paragraph.

The one-year limitation period begins on the date on which a taxpayer withdraws funds from an IRA or individual retirement annuity and has no relation to the calendar year. Thus, for example, a taxpayer may not make a nontaxable rollover on December 31 in one calendar year and make another nontaxable rollover on January 1 in the next calendar year.

If a taxpayer has multiple IRAs, then can a taxpayer exclude from gross income rollover distributions from multiple IRAs in the same 1-year period? The IRS answered, "yes." As discussed in Announcement 2014-15, Proposed Regulation § 1.408-4(b)(4)(ii) and IRS Publication 590, Individual Retirement Arrangements (IRAs), the IRS provided that the one-rollover-per-year limitation under section 408 was applied on an **IRA-by-IRA basis**. IRS Pub. 590 (published January 5, 2014) provided the following example to explain the view of the IRS on rollovers:

> ***Example.*** You have two traditional IRAs, IRA-1 and IRA-2. You make a tax-free rollover of a distribution from IRA-1 into a new traditional IRA (IRA-3). You cannot, within 1 year of the distribution from IRA-1, make a tax-free rollover of any distribution from either IRA-1 or IRA-3 into another traditional IRA.
>
> However, the rollover from IRA-1 into IRA-3 does not prevent you from making a tax-free rollover from IRA-2 into any other traditional IRA. This is because you have not, within the last year, rolled over, tax free, any distribution from IRA-2 or made a tax-free rollover into IRA-2.

---

[48] I.R.C. § 408(d)(3)(A)(i).
[49] I.R.C. § 408(d)(3).

However, the Tax Court in <u>Bobrow v. Commissioner</u>, T.C. Memo. 2014–21, held that the limitation applies on an aggregate basis, meaning that an individual could not make more than one nontaxable 60-day rollover within each 1-year period even if the rollovers involved different IRAs. Critical for us is understanding how the Tax Court reached its interpretation of section that differed from the IRS' view.

In <u>Bobrow v. Commissioner</u>, T.C. Memo. 2014–21, the court focused on the legislative history of section 408:

> Section 408 was enacted as part of the Employee Retirement Income Security Act of 1974, Pub. L. No. 93-406, sec. 2002(b), 88 Stat. at 958. Recognizing that the American workforce had become much more mobile than in previous years, Congress enacted the section 408(d)(3)(A) exemption as a way of providing employees with some measure of flexibility with regard to their retirement planning. **However, Congress added the section 408(d)(3)(B) limitation as a way to ensure that taxpayers did not take advantage of section 408(d)(3)(A) to repeatedly shift nontaxable income in and out of retirement accounts. See, e.g., H.R. Rept. No. 93-779, at 139 (1974), 1974-3 C.B. 244, 382 ("To prevent too much shifting of investments under * * * [section 408(d)(3)(A)(i)], the bill provides that an individual can transfer amounts between individual retirement accounts only once every three years.");** H.R. Conf. 6 Rept. No. 93-1280, at 342 (1974), 1974-3 C.B. 415, 503 ("Tax-free rollovers between individual retirement accounts may occur only once every three years."). **Had Congress intended to allow individuals to take nontaxable distributions from multiple IRAs per year, we believe section 408(d)(3)(B) would have been worded differently. Our conclusion is confirmed by the legislative history, which also refers to the limitation as a general limitation that applies across all of a taxpayer's retirement accounts.**

(emphasis added to original text). The court noted that although Congress had originally imposed a three-year limitation period in section 408 for rollovers, it reduced the limitation from three years to one year in 1978.[50] Based on its review of legislative history, the Tax Court concluded: "Regardless of how many IRAs he or she maintains, a taxpayer may make only one nontaxable rollover contribution within each one-year period."[51] Again, the lesson from a review of section 408 and <u>Bobrow</u> is that practitioners must review legislative history to properly interpret and apply the tax code.[52]

---

[50] <u>Bobrow v. Commissioner</u>, T.C. Memo. 2014–21, *14, fn. 6, citing Revenue Act of 1978, Pub. L. No. 95-600, sec. 157(h)(2), 92 Stat. at 2808.

[51] <u>Id.</u>

[52] Following the Tax Court's decision in <u>Bobrow v. Commissioner</u>, T.C. Memo. 2014–21, the IRS issued Announcement 2014-15 and Announcement 2014-32. In Announcement 2014-32, the IRS stated that it "will apply the <u>Bobrow</u> interpretation of § 408(d)(3)(B) for distributions that occur on or after January 1, 2015. This means that an individual receiving an IRA distribution on or after January 1, 2015, cannot roll over any portion of the distribution into an IRA if the individual has received a distribution from any IRA in the preceding 1-year period that was rolled over into an IRA."

3. Powers of Congress

Congress, as one of the three coequal branches of government, is ascribed significant powers by the Constitution. All legislative power in the government is vested in Congress, meaning that it is the only part of the government that can make new laws or change existing laws. Executive Branch agencies issue regulations with the full force of law, but these are only under the authority of laws enacted by Congress. The President may veto bills Congress passes, but Congress may also override a veto by a two-thirds vote in both the Senate and the House of Representatives.

Article I of the Constitution enumerates the powers of Congress and the specific areas in which it may legislate. Congress is also empowered to enact laws deemed "necessary and proper" for the execution of the powers given to any part of the government under the Constitution.

Part of Congress's exercise of legislative authority is the establishment of an annual budget for the government. To this end, Congress levies taxes and tariffs to provide funding for essential government services. If enough money cannot be raised to fund the government, then Congress may also authorize borrowing to make up the difference. Congress can also mandate spending on specific items: legislatively directed spending, commonly known as "earmarks," specifies funds for a particular project, rather than for a government agency.

Both chambers of Congress have extensive investigative powers, and may compel the production of evidence or testimony toward whatever end they deem necessary. Members of Congress spend much of their time holding hearings and investigations in committee. Refusal to cooperate with a Congressional subpoena can result in charges of contempt of Congress, which could result in a prison term.

The Senate maintains several powers to itself: it ratifies treaties by a two-thirds supermajority vote and confirms the appointments of the President by a majority vote. The consent of the House of Representatives is also necessary for the ratification of trade agreements and the confirmation of the Vice President. Congress also holds the sole power to declare war.

4. Government Oversight

Oversight of the executive branch is an important Congressional check on the President's power and a balance against his discretion in implementing laws and making regulations. A major way that Congress conducts oversight is through hearings. The House Committee on Oversight and Government Reform and the Senate Committee on Homeland Security and Government Affairs are both devoted to overseeing and reforming government operations, and each committee conducts oversight in its policy area.

Congress also maintains an investigative organization, the Government Accountability Office ("GAO"). Founded in 1921 as the General Accounting Office, its original mission was to audit the budgets and financial statements sent to Congress by the Secretary of the Treasury and the Director of the Office of Management and Budget. Today, the GAO audits and generates reports on every aspect of the government, ensuring that taxpayer dollars are spent with the effectiveness and efficiency that the American people deserve.

The executive branch also polices itself: 64 Inspectors General, each responsible for a different agency, regularly audit and report on the agencies to which they are attached.

5. Staying Current with Tax Law

Congress enacts legislation that amends, repeals, extends or adds to Title 26. Given the constant flux of the tax code, it is essential for tax practitioners to keep pace with both proposed (for planning purposes) and enacted changes (to implement new law). As part of a practitioner's daily routine, tax professionals should dedicate time in their day to keep up with tax proposals and changes.

For example, on February 9, 2018, the Bipartison Budget Act of 2018, P.L. 115-123, was signed by the President and became law. P.L. 115-123 provided various extensions of law that had already expired under existing law. Thus, in some instances, taxpayers who may have filed returns for the 2017 tax year prior to February 9, 2018 may have taken positions applying old law before the enactment of P.L. 115-123.

Optimally, taxpayers would want to know applicable tax law impacting in advance so that they are aware of how to comply and report before the year is completed. However, extender provisions such as P.L. 115-123 are not unusual. And, as such, tax practitioners must constantly keep up-to-date with new tax legislation issued in order to provide correct tax advice and tax return services.

Consider the exclusion from gross income resulting from the discharge of indebtedness of a qualified real property residence under section 108(a)(1)(E). Prior to P.L. 115-123, section 108(a)(1)(E) provided that any indebtedness of a qualified real property indebtedness that is discharged before January 1, 2017 is **not** includible as gross income. In other words, say a taxpayer who owned their principal residence owed the bank $100,000 on the mortgage for the home with a fair market value of $50,000 could not pay the bank. If the bank forclosed on the property and forgave the taxpayer's loan in March of 2017, that foregiveness of debt triggered gross income to the taxpayer under section 61(a)(12). For all of 2017, section 108(a)(1)(E) provided that any such discharge of debt related to a taxpayer's qualified real property indebtedness had to be discharged before January 1, 2017. It was not until Februrary 9, 2018 when the President signed P.L. 115-123 into law that the taxpayer knew that the discharge that occurred in April, 2017 would not constitute gross income for his/her 2017 tax year. See section 40201 of P.L. 115-123, below:

SEC. 40201. EXTENSION OF EXCLUSION FROM GROSS INCOME OF DISCHARGE OF QUALIFIED PRINCIPAL RESIDENCE INDEBTEDNESS.

(a) In General.—Section 108(a)(1)(E) is amended by striking "January 1, 2017" each place it appears and inserting "January 1, 2018".

(b) Effective Date.—The amendments made by this section shall apply to discharges of indebtedness after December 31, 2016.

The recent change to section 164 offers another example of the critical need for tax practitioners to keep pace with tax law changes in **both** the Federal and State tax areas. Prior to the Tax Cuts and Jobs Act ("TCJA"), section 164(a) allowed individual taxpayers an itemized deduction for state and local income, real property, and personal property taxes. For tax years from 2018 through 2025, the TCJA created Sec. 164(b)(6), which prohibits individual taxpayers from deducting more than $10,000 in state and local taxes ($5,000 in the case of a married taxpayer filing separately). Subsequently, the California legislature proposed bill SB-227. See https://leginfo.legislature.ca.gov/faces/billTextClient.xhtml?bill_id=201720180SB227. The bill would allow a credit to be applied against an individual's state income tax in an amount equal to 85% of the amount contributed to the "Local Schools and Colleges Voluntary Contribution Fund" as identified in SB-227. As of August 16, 2018, SB-227 is in committee hearing.

So what's the federal tax impact from this pending California bill? A state tax paid by a resident is limited by section 164 to $10,000. However, a charitable contribution is deductible for Federal tax purposes with a much higher limitation. As such, a California taxpayer who "contributes" to the under SB-227 could deduct the amount on his/her Federal tax under section 170, not under section 164 (subject to the $10,000 limitation). Sec. 170(c)(1) allows a federal deduction for charitable contributions, which include donations to a state, a possession of the United States, or any political subdivision of any of the foregoing, or the US or the District of Columbia, but only if the contribution or gift is made for exclusively public purposes. Generally, the amount of the federal deduction available is limited to the amount of cash paid and the fair market value (FMV) of any property (other than cash) transferred by the taxpayer, reduced by the FMV of any goods or services the taxpayer receives in return. However, if a charitable contribution lacks "charitable intent" (e.g., the contribution was made to obtain something of value in return), then the amount is not deductible under section 170.

The IRS issued Notice 2018-54 (Guidance on Certain Payments Made in Exchange for State and Local Tax Credits). The text of this short IRS notice is as follows:

SECTION 1. PURPOSE This notice informs taxpayers that the Department of the Treasury (Treasury Department) and the Internal Revenue Service (IRS) intend to propose regulations addressing the federal income tax treatment of certain payments made by taxpayers for which taxpayers receive a credit against their state and local taxes.

SECTION 2. BACKGROUND Section 11042 of "The Tax Cuts and Jobs Act," Pub. L. No. 115-97, limits an individual's deduction under § 164 for the aggregate amount of state and local taxes paid during the calendar year to $10,000 ($5,000 in the case of a married individual filing a separate return). State and local tax payments in excess of those amounts are not deductible. This new limitation applies to taxable years beginning after December 31, 2017, and before January 1, 2026. In response to this new limitation, some state legislatures are considering or have adopted legislative proposals that would allow taxpayers to make transfers to funds controlled by state or local governments, or other transferees specified by the state, in exchange for credits against the state or local taxes that the taxpayer is required to pay. The aim of these proposals is to allow taxpayers to characterize such transfers as fully deductible charitable contributions for federal income tax purposes, while using the same transfers to satisfy state or local tax liabilities. Despite these state efforts to circumvent the new statutory limitation on state and local tax deductions, taxpayers should be mindful that federal law controls the proper characterization of payments for federal income tax purposes.

SECTION 3. GUIDANCE TO BE ISSUED The Treasury Department and the IRS intend to propose regulations addressing the federal income tax treatment of transfers to funds controlled by state and local governments (or other state-specified transferees) that the transferor can treat in whole or in part as satisfying state and local tax obligations. The proposed regulations will make clear that the requirements of the Internal Revenue Code, informed by substance over-form principles, govern the federal income tax treatment of such transfers. The proposed regulations will assist taxpayers in understanding the relationship between the federal charitable contribution deduction and the new statutory limitation on the deduction for state and local tax payments.

Based on the above, what can we learn? First, practitioners have a continuous responsibility to keep up-to-date with tax law changes.[53] It is critical for a tax practitioner to sign up for regular, daily tax updates with a tax service and devote at minimum the first 30 minutes each morning to scan tax news – both Federal and State. Second, practitioners must understand the interplay of state and federal tax law. Finally, practitioners must appreciate the importance of executive branch issued guidance in interpreting and applying tax law.

There are various sources that provide great tools for practitioners to keep informed of tax news tax pr:

- CCH

---

[53] If California enacts SB-227 into law, then what do you advise your tax clients on the issue of whether they can donate $100 under this new law, claim a Federal tax deduction as a charitable donation for this amount and claim on their State tax return tax credit for $85 for state tax paid as provided under California law (pending under SB-227)? Despite the fact that this State legislative proposal is pending (as of the date of this publication), it remains a practitioner's responsibility to keep informed of pending changes to tax law and the repercussions to their clients.

- o Federal Tax Daily, Federal Tax Weekly, Taxes – The Tax Magazine
- Bloomberg BNA
  - o Daily Tax Report
  - o Weekly Report
  - o IRS Practice Adviser Report
- RIA
  - o RIA Tax Watch
  - o Federal Taxes Weekly Alert Newsletter
- Tax Analysts
  - o Tax Notes
  - o Tax Notes Today
  - o Tax Practice
- IRS Website
  - o IRS Guidewire
  - o IRS IRB, CB

In addition, national newspaper publications such as the New York Times or the Wall Street Journal provide frequent updates on tax developments. These publications are great daily sources to keep current with federal tax developments.

Chapter 4 Questions

1. In what three scenarios will the text of the Internal Revenue Code not reflect applicable law for the tax year at issue?

2. What non-legislative committee report can tax practitioners use to assist them in understanding tax legislation?

3. What legislative committee is convened to bring differing versions of bills (House version vs. Senate version) into alignment?

4. Explain the basis for the Eleventh Circuit's holding in Hills v. Commissioner, 691 F.2d 997 (11th Cir. 1982), interpreting section 165(a) that differed from the Sixth Circuit's holding in Kentucky Utilities Co. v. Glenn, 394 F.2d 631 (6th Cir. 1968) of the same code section.

CHAPTER 5 – HOW TO READ THE TAX CODE

Learning Objectives:

☑ Understand the organization of the Internal Revenue Code
☑ Understand the unique aspects regarding the statutory construction of the Internal Revenue Code

In this Chapter:

1. The Organization & Numbering System of the Code
2. Limiting Language
3. Pinballing
4. Measuring Words
5. Terms of Art
6. Sunset Provisions
7. Historical Amendments
8. The Text of the Internal Revenue Code May Not Always Provide the Applicable Law

For some, the task of reading and understanding the tax code must be akin to aerial refueling – the incredibly difficult task of refueling a jet traveling at a speed of up to 350 miiles per hour. See the picture, above. Pick up the tax code, thumb through its seemingly endless pages and you should be sufficiently awed at the challenge confronting you. Take some deep breaths and let's tackle the code together step-by-step.

The Internal Revenue Code is the statutory foundation of all federal tax authority, except for occasional uncodified provisions and certain international issues covered in tax treaties with foreign countries. Prior to 1939, each individual revenue act passed by Congress amounted to a complete re-enactment of the entire tax law. In 1939, however, all federal tax law was consolidated into Title 26 of the United States Code as the Internal Revenue Code of 1939, and subsequent revenue acts were used to amend the 1939 Code. By 1954, the growth of federal taxation led Congress to completely revise the 1939 Code. The Internal Revenue Code of 1954 was that revision. Despite frequent amendments, the designation "1954" remained fixed with the Code until the Tax Reform Act of 1986 replaced it with "1986."

When we refer to the tax code as consolidated and provided within Title 26, it is useful to understand that this tax title exists as part of the United States Code made up of smaller units called titles. "The United States Code is the official codification of the general and permanent laws of the United States."[54] The Code was created in 1926 to address the need for an updated, authoritative, and useful consolidation of Federal laws. The Code does not include all the general and permanent laws of the United States. Temporary laws, such as appropriation acts, and special laws, such as naming a post office, are not included in the Code.[55]

The United States Code currently consists of 54 titles and five appendices. The 54 titles are as follows:

Title 1 – General Provisions
Title 2 – The Congress
Title 3 – The President
Title 4 – Flag and Seal, Seat of Government, and The States
Title 5 – Government Organization and Employees
Title 6 – Domestic Security
Title 7 – Agriculture
Title 8 – Aliens and Nationality
Title 9 – Arbitration
Title 10 – Armed Forces
Title 11 – Bankruptcy
Title 12 – Banks and Banking
Title 13 – Census
Title 14 – Coast Guard
Title 15 – Commerce and Trade
Title 16 – Conservation
Title 17 – Copyrights
Title 18 – Crimes and Criminal Procedure
Title 19 – Customs Duties
Title 20 – Education
Title 21 – Food and Drugs
Title 22 – Foreign Relations
Title 23 – Highways
Title 24 – Hospitals and Asylums
Title 25 – Indians

---

[54] Preface of the 2012 Edition of the United States Code.
[55] http://uscode.house.gov/faq.xhtml;jsessionid=8726A3F826B8F1CEFD0A82D798AF3DD3.

<u>Title 26 – Internal Revenue Code</u>
Title 27 – Intoxicating Liquors
Title 28 – Judicicary and Judicial Procedure
Title 29 – Labor
Title 30 – Mineral Lands and Mining
Title 31 – Money and Finance
Title 32 – National Guard
Title 33 – Navigation and Navigable Waters
Title 34 – Crime Control and Law Enforcement
Title 35 – Patents
Title 36 – Patriotic and National Observances, Ceremonies, and
　　　　　Organizations
Title 37 – Pay and Allowances of the Uniformed Services
Title 38 – Veterans' Benefits
Title 39 – Postal Service
Title 40 – Public Buildings, Property, and Works
Title 41 – Public Contracts
Title 42 – The Public Health and Welfare
Title 43 – Public Lands
Title 44 – Public Printing and Documents
Title 45 – Railroads
Title 46 – Shipping
Title 47 – Telecommunications
Title 48 – Territories and Insular Possessions
Title 49 – Transportation
Title 50 – War and National Defense
Title 51 – National and Commerical Space Programs
Title 52 – Voting and Elections
Title 53 – [Reserved]
Title 54 – National Park Service and Related Programs

As the text of various provisions contained in the United States Code is updated by Congress, the Office of the Law of Revision Counsel is responsible for maintaining and publishing these changes.[56] The latest laws affecting the Code can be found at: http://uscode.house.gov/currency/currency.shtml.

A 2001 study published by the Joint Committee on Taxation put the number of words in the Code at that time at 1,395,000. Seven years later, a search of the Code conducted in the course of preparing the 2008 Annual Report to Congress by the National Taxpayer Advocate turned up 3.7 million words.[57] The voluminous text of Title 26 offers direct, unequivocal answers to many tax questions. _However, the IRC does not always offer the same certainty from its text alone given subjective language included

---

[56] http://uscode.house.gov/editorialreclassification/reclassification.html.
[57] As you consider the increase of the text of the tax code, consider that Congress has likewise increased the overall body of law throughout the United States Code as well. "During the past 20 years, each Congress has enacted an average of over 6,900 pages of new public laws." http://uscode.house.gov/about_classification.xhtml.

in its provisions.[58] Rather, the tax answer requires additional research beyond the IRC coupled with professional judgment based upon a review of primary source authorities to reach a professional tax conclusion. But, as a start, tax practitioners must first gain solid footing with the IRC. So, let's begin.

1. The Organization & Numbering System of the Code

Reading the Code can, on occasion, become difficult because of references to "subsections," "paragraphs," "subparagraphs," etc. The various Code divisions of the tax code are set forth below:

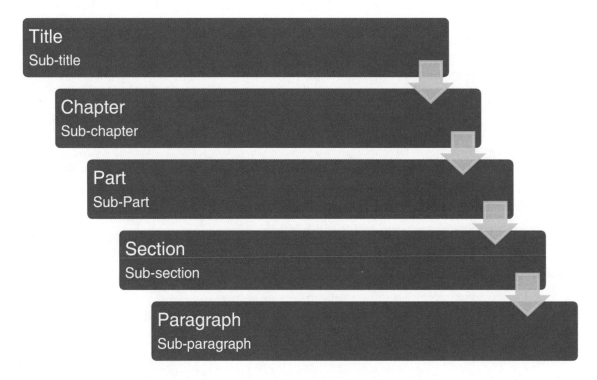

And, below, sub-paragraph, there is "clause," then "sub-clause." Section numbers are of particular importance since they run consecutively through the entire Code, thus allowing a particular provision to be identified by section number alone.

Generally, sections of the Code provide a series of numbers designating each statutory topic. Occassionally, however, you will see that code sections that include capital letters after the number. Why? In 1954, Congress, after extended study, completely overhauled and recodified the Internal Revenue Code.[59] Congress organized the IRC

---

[58] Section 162 provides that "there shall be allowed as a deduction all the ordinary and necessary expenses paid or incurred......" (emphasis added to original text). We must conduct additional research to determine what constitutes "ordinary and necessary expenses....." for purposes of section 162. Section 41(a) provides research credit for "qualified research expenses......" Section 41(d) later defines "qualified research" as research undertaken for the purpose of discovering information "which is technological in nature" and "the application of which is intended to be useful in the development of a new or improved business component of the taxpayer....." (emphasis added to original text). As you can see from the highlighted language from sections 162 and 41, these statutory provisions require research beyond the original text of Title 26 to determine their proper interpretation and application.

by specific categories. Sub-title A deals only with the topic of income taxes whereas sub-title C addresses employment taxes. When Congress seeks to add a provision, say to employment taxes in sub-title C, it must assign this new statutory provision to within the designated sections that already comprise sub-title C. If it did not follow this organizational scheme, the subject-matter organization of the IRC would become completely askew. For example, employment taxes within sub-title C falls within sections 3101 thru 3512. If Congress decided in the future to add another provision to address a taxing matter impacting self-employment, then it would need to adhere to the organizational system of code numbering already established. And, it could and does accomplish this adherence to the organizational numbering system of the IRC by adding a capital letter to a code section when it decides to add another statute to maintain the numbering scheme of the IRC.

For example, Part IV (Credits Against Tax), of Subchapter A (Determination of Tax Liability), of Chapter 1 (Normal Taxes and Surtaxes), of Sub-title A (Income Taxes), in composed of sections 21 thru 54AA. Section 55 is the first section of Part VI which addresses another topic – the alternative minimum tax. So, if Congress decides to add another credit against tax, then in must insert that provision within Part IV, which is composed of section 21 thru 54AA. And, Congress accomplishes this organizational objective by adding a number to a new provision. Examples include:

- Part IV – comprised of Subparts A thru J. These sub-parts are comprised of sections 21 thru 54AA
    - Sub-part H (deals with Non-refundable Credit to Holders of Clean Renewable Energy Bonds) – only section 54
    - Sub-part I (deals with the topic of Qualified Tax Credit Bonds) – assigned section 54A thru 54F
    - Sub-part J (deals with Build America Bonds) designated as section 54AA
        - Congress decided that it may add additional provisions for Qualified Tax Credit Bonds under section 54G etc. So, it adopts 54AA for another credit against tax under Part IV. And, it cannot use section 55 since it is within Part V for another topic (Alternative Minimum Tax)

Under the numbering system, it is recommended that when a practitioner discusses, for exemple, section 54A, you refer to the provision as "54 CAP A." Otherwise, if you state the section as "54a", the listener is led erroneously to understand that you are referring to section 54(a).

2. Limiting Language

---

[59] James v. United States, 366 U.S. 213, 231 (1961).

The language of the Internal Revenue Code implements the will of the people. But, language can be difficult to harness with the level of precision that both provides the intent of the legislative branch who drafts the Code and avoids unintended consequences. A mechanism used in the Code to minimize unintended consequences is commonly referred to as "limiting language." Take for example, part of the text of section 62(a), highlighted below.

> **GENERAL RULE.** For purposes of this subtitle, the term "adjusted gross income" means, in the case of an individual, gross income minus the following deductions:......

The highlighted text, "For purposes of this subtitle" limits the reader to apply the term "adjusted gross income" only within one of 11 subtitles with Title 26. When introduced to limiting language, the reader must then determine the context of this limiting instruction. In our example, section 62 falls within which subtitle? Let's look to the table of contents that is presented in the front of Title 26.

- Subtitle A – Income Taxes (§§1 to 1564)
- Subtitle B – Estate and Gift Taxes (§§2001 to 2801)
- Subtitle C – Employment Taxes (§§3101 to 3512)
- Subtitle D – Miscellaneous Excise Taxes (§§4001 to 5000C)
- Subtitle E – Alcohol, Tobacco, and Certain Other Excise Taxes (§§5001 to 5891)
- Subtitle F – Procedure and Administration (§§6001 to 7874)
- Subtitle G – The Joint Committee on Taxation (§§8001 to 8023)
- Subtitle H – Financing of Presidential Election Campaigns (§§9001 to 9042)
- Subtitle I - Trust Fund Codes (§§9500 to 9602)
- Subtitle J – Coal Industry Health Benefits (§§9701 to 9722)
- Subtitle K – Group Health Plan Requirements (§§9801 to 9834)

Section 62 fits within sub-title A (Income Taxes) comprised of sections 1 thru 1564. Accordingly, Congress has limited the application of the term "adjusted gross income" as defined in section 62 only to be used within sections 1 thru 1564. So, if there is a question posed as to whether the term "adjusted gross income" can be applied for purposes of section 2517, the answer is no since section 2517 is is sub-title B, not sub-title A.

3. Pinballing

In contrast to limiting language (in which Congress drafted language to minimize the impact of statutory language from one section to a defined area within Title 26), another mechanism of statutory construction serves to expand the reach of text for tax purposes. This mechanism whereby designated text within Title 26 applies text from other statutory provisions is commonly referred to as "pinballing." This is a tool that Congress employs as a means of efficiency in drafting and applying its statutory intent.

- *Pinballing Within Title 26* – Consider section 66 as an example where Congress utilizes pinballing to apply a provision:

     (a) Treatment of community income where spouses live apart. If —
          (1) 2 individuals are married to each other at any time during a calendar year;
          (2) such individuals—
               (A) live apart at all times during the calendar year, and
               (B) do not file a joint return under section 6013 with each other for a taxable year beginning or ending in the calendar year;
          (3) one or both of such individuals have earned income for the calendar year which is community income; and
          (4) no portion of such earned income is transferred (directly or indirectly) between such individuals before the close of the calendar year, then, for purposes of this title, any community income of such individuals for the calendar year shall be treated in accordance with the rules provided by section 879(a).

     Within section 66, Congress requires the reader to look to, and apply, two other sections to implement this one provision.

- *Pinballing Outside of Title 26* – Consider section 112(d) as an example where Congress utilizes pinballing to apply a provision:

     (d) Prisoners of War, Etc.
          (1) Members of the Armed Forces
          Gross income does not include compensation received for active service as a member of the Armed Forces of the United States for any month during any part of which such member is in a missing status (as defined in section 551(2) of title 37, United States Code) during the Vietnam conflict as a result of such conflict other than a period with respect to which it is officially determined under section 552© of such title 37 that he is officially absent from his post of duty without authority.

In applying section 112(d), Congress utilizes the definition of "missing status" for "active service as a member of the Armed Forces of the United States" within Title 37 rather than defining the definition anew in Title 36. And this makes practical sense if Congress later decided to alter the definition of "missing status" later. In that case, Congress would only need to change the definition for this term in Title 36, rather than in two different Titles of the United States Code. And, to the extent Congress employs this same mechanism of efficiency in statutory construction, consider how many Titles of the U.S. Code may be impacted.

4. Measuring Words

In some instances, Congress weighs the application of a specific tax result by balancing specific factors. This weighing of factors within statutory text in the Code is commonly referred to as "measuring words." See, for example, section 6662(d):

> (d) Substantial Understatement of Income tax
>> (1) Substantial Understatement
>>> (A) In general. For purposes of this section, there is a substantial understatement of income tax for any taxale year if the amount of the understatement for the taxable year exceeds the greater of—
>>>> (i) 10 percent of the tax required to be shown on the return for the taxable year, or
>>>> (ii) $5,000.

In section 6662(d), Congress establishes a balancing test through its use of measuring words:

Substantial
Understatement Exists **IF**   Understatement > Greater of: (i) 10% of tax required to be shown; or
(ii) $5,000

Reading and understanding measuring words can be frustrating. One method to overcome any difficulties that you may encounter with applying measuring words in Title 26 is to draw a flow chart of the equation, as presented above, to guide you.

5. Terms of Art

Within Title 26, Congress will define specific words or terms with exacting precision. And, regardless of common sense, Webster's dictionary, your uncle's expertise, Wikipedia, nothing can operate to overturn the definition enacted into law for "terms of art" within Title 26. If Congress defines a "dog" to be a "cat" under Title 26, then that is the law for tax purposes. Consider the definition of a "tax return preparer" as defined under section 7701(a)(36):

> The term "tax return preparer" means any person who prepares for compensation, or who employs one or more persons to prepare for compensation, any return of tax imposed by this title or any claim for refund of tax imposed by this title. For purposes of the preceding sentence, the preparation of a substantial portion of a return or claim for refund shall be treated as if it were the preparation of such return or claim for refund.

Thus, a person who prepares a tax return as a community volunteer is not a "tax return preparer" because he/she did not receive compensation.

Some other examples of "terms of art" in the tax code include:

- "medical care" as defined under section 213(d)(1)
- "small business corporation" as defined under section 1361(b)(1)
- "subchapter S item" as defined under section 6037(c)(4)

6. Sunset Provisions

Sometimes, a tax section will include a clause that provides for an automatic expiration or "sunset" of the statute. Once the specified date of the sunset provision is reached, the statutory provision no longer applies. The statute can only continue as law if Congress decides to enact an extension to the previously established expiration date. An example of a tax section set for sunset was section 45 (electricitiy produced from certain renewable resources, etc.). As originally enacted, Congress had set the expiration date of this credit not to extend beyond 2014. But, in 2015, Congress enacted an extension thru 2019 for section 45.[60]

7. Historical Amendments

Below statutory text, historical amendments follow. The history of prior Congressional action related to a specific code section provides critical information on prior law and the effective date for subsequent revisions, if any. Reading the current text of a code section in tandem with the history of prior amendments related to the text is vital because the year at issue for a practitioner's engagement on behalf of a client may involve application of prior law, not current law.

Consider the allowance of medical expense deductions under section 213(a):

> (a) Allowance of Deduction
> There shall be allowed as a deduction the expenses paid during the taxable year, not compensated for by insurance or otherwise, for medical care of the taxpayer, his spouse, or a dependent (as defined in section 152, determined without regard to subsections (b)(1), (b)(2), and (d)(1)(B) thereof), to the extent such expenses exceed 10 percent of adjusted gross income.

Below the text of current law under section 213(a), the underlying history of this code sub-section follows:

---

[60] See Pub.L. 111401113, Sec. 301(a)(1). Under section 45(d)(1), the beginning date for construction of a "qualified facility" necessary to obtain renewable electricity production credit was extended from 2014 to 2019. See "Fading into the sunset: Solar and Wind Energy Get Five More Years of Tax Credits with a Phase-Down," American Bar Association Trends, Vol. 47, No. 5 (May/June 2016), by Felix Mormann.

AMENDMENTS

2010—Subsec. (a). Pub. L. 111–148, § 9013(a), substituted "10 percent" for "7.5 percent".

Subsec. (f). Pub. L. 111–148, § 9013(b), added subsec. (f).

2004—Subsec. (a). Pub. L. 108–311, § 207(17), inserted ", determined without regard to subsections (b)(1), (b)(2), and (d)(1)(B) thereof" after "section 152".

Subsec. (d)(11). Pub. L. 108–311, § 207(18), substituted "subparagraphs (A) through (G) of section 152(d)(2)" for "paragraphs (1) through (8) of section 152(a)" in concluding provisions.

1996—Subsec. (d)(1). Pub. L. 104–191, § 322(b)(2)(A), inserted concluding provisions "In the case of a qualified long-term care insurance contract (as defined in section 7702B(b)), only eligible long-term care premiums (as defined in paragraph (10)) shall be taken into account under subparagraph (D)."

Subsec. (d)(1)(B). Pub. L. 104–191, § 322(a), struck out "or" at end.

Subsec. (d)(1)(C). Pub. L. 104–191, § 322(a), added subpar. (C). Former subpar. (C) redesignated (D).

Subsec. (d)(1)(D). Pub. L. 104–191, § 322(b)(1), inserted before period "or for any qualified long-term care insurance contract (as defined in section 7702B(b))".

Pub. L. 104–191, § 322(a), redesignated subpar. (C) as (D).

Subsec. (d)(6). Pub. L. 104–191, § 322(b)(3)(A), substituted "subparagraphs (A), (B), and (C)" for "subparagraphs (A) and (B)" in introductory provisions.

Subsec. (d)(6)(A). Pub. L. 104–191, § 322(b)(3)(B), substituted "paragraph (1)(D)" for "paragraph (1)(C)".

Subsec. (d)(7). Pub. L. 104–191, § 322(b)(4), substituted "subparagraphs (A), (B), and (C)" for "subparagraphs (A) and (B)".

Subsec. (d)(10), (11). Pub. L. 104–191, § 322(b)(2)(C), added pars. (10) and (11).

1993—Subsec. (f). Pub. L. 103–66 struck out heading and text of subsec. (f). Text read as follows: "The amount otherwise taken into account under subsection (a) as expenses paid for medical care shall be reduced by the amount (if any) of the health insurance credit allowable to the taxpayer for the taxable year under section 32."

1990—Subsec. (d)(9). Pub. L. 101–508, § 11342(a), added par. (9).

Subsec. (f). Pub. L. 101–508, § 11111(d)(1), added subsec. (f).

1986—Subsec. (a). Pub. L. 99–514 substituted "7.5 percent" for "5 percent".

The current text of section 213(a) generally allows a deduction for qualified "medical expenses" to the extent the expenses exceed 10% of adjusted gross income. However, the current AGI percentage limitation of 10% was 7.5% in prior years, and 5% in years before that. The text of the historical amendment for section 213(a), above, tracks the legislative changes to sub-section as enacted by Congress through references to Public Law. So, the change of the AGI limitation from 7.5% to 10% was enacted under Public Law 111-148. Not shown, above, is the effective date that is associated with Public Law 111-148, at section 9013 (of the Public Law, not Title 26). Information on the effective date is included in the text of the historical amendment. As you can see, the text of each code section's historical amendment is lengthy and cumbersome to track. But, the information contained in each code section's history is an essential part of a tax practitioner's responsibilities in properly analyzing tax law.

For various reasons, clients may seek your advice on earlier tax years. If the client requests your analysis of the deductible of medical expenses, then you must: (1) determine the applicable tax year in which the cost was incurred and paid; (2) determine the applicable code text that applies to that year—10%, 7.5% or 5%.

Let's try a practice example.

- Facts: Temp. Treas. Reg. 100Z-1T was issued on November 20, 1988. The underlying code section 100Z was enacted by Congress on January 12, 1975.
- Question: Is this Temporary Treasury regulation effective today?
- Answer: After reading the code section, you search for applicable historical amendments. P.L. 100-647, Sec. 6232(a) provides that Congress added subsection (e) of section 7805 effective for any regulation issued after the date which is 10 days after 11/10/88 (11/20/88). Temp. Treas. Reg. 100Z-1T was issued on November 20, 1988, not after 11/20/88. Therefore, section 7805(e) does not apply since it is not covered by the effective date. Since the terms of 7805(e) do not apply, the temporary regulation is still effective.

Sometimes, the historical amendments included with specific code sections are very lengthy. In practice, how can you effectively sift through long text of historical amendments? Consider the following practice example and recommended steps:

Hypothetical Facts: Client A is a high technology company that was formed as a C corporation in 1997. It suffered a $20 million loss in tax year 1997, its first year of operation. The company has always operated on a calendar year basis, i.e., its tax year begins on January 1 and ends on December 31 each year. Client A has had losses for every year since its formation until 2013 when it finally earned a substantial profit of $30 million. Client A wants to use is loss from 1997 and carry it forward to 2013 to offset its profit in that year. The answer is located in section 172(b)(1)(A)(i) and 172(b)(1)(A)(ii). Look at the applicable code section and determine whether Client A can forward its 1997 loss to offset its 2013 profit.

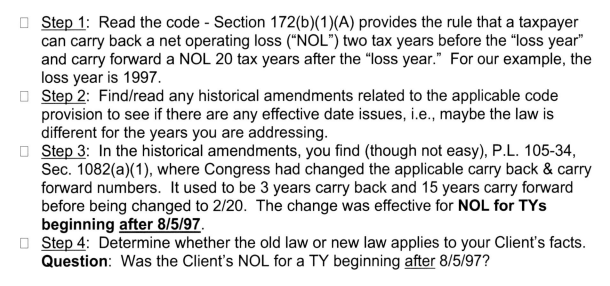

- ☐ Step 1: Read the code - Section 172(b)(1)(A) provides the rule that a taxpayer can carry back a net operating loss ("NOL") two tax years before the "loss year" and carry forward a NOL 20 tax years after the "loss year." For our example, the loss year is 1997.
- ☐ Step 2: Find/read any historical amendments related to the applicable code provision to see if there are any effective date issues, i.e., maybe the law is different for the years you are addressing.
- ☐ Step 3: In the historical amendments, you find (though not easy), P.L. 105-34, Sec. 1082(a)(1), where Congress had changed the applicable carry back & carry forward numbers. It used to be 3 years carry back and 15 years carry forward before being changed to 2/20. The change was effective for **NOL for TYs beginning after 8/5/97**.
- ☐ Step 4: Determine whether the old law or new law applies to your Client's facts. **Question**: Was the Client's NOL for a TY beginning after 8/5/97?

☐ Answer: No. The Client's NOL was for a TY beginning 1/1/97, not beginning after 8/5/97. So, the OLD tax law applies to Client - 3 carryback/15 carryforward for NOLs.

☐ Step 5: Apply law to facts. The loss year was 1997. Apply the old law, which provides that a taxpayer can carry back the NOL 3 years or carry forward the loss 15 years. Under the applicable old law, Client A can carry forward its 1997 loss 15 years, to 2012. **Thus, Client A cannot use the TY 1997 loss to offset profit in 2012**.

Most importantly, in Step 3, when you scan historical amendments under section 172(b)(1), look specifically for changes to **sub-paragraph (A) only**, since that is the operative provision that impacts your analysis – section 172(b)(1)**(A)**. Everytime you see historical amendments that reflect statutory changes to other sub-paragraphs, i.e., section 172(b)(1)**(F)** or 172(b)(1)**(G)**, skim over that part and move on to locate the relevant sub-paragraph. For example, see the text of historical amendments in 2014 and then 2009 that reference sub-paragraphs to section 172(b)(1) other than sub-paragraph (A):

Amendments

2014—Subsec. (b)(1)(D). Pub. L. 113-295, §221(a)(30)(A)(i), redesignated subpar. (E) as (D) and struck out former subpar. (D). Prior to amendment, text of subpar. (D) read as follows: "In the case of any bank (as defined in section 585(a)(2)), the portion of the net operating loss for any taxable year beginning after December 31, 1986, and before January 1, 1994, which is attributable to the deduction allowed under section 166(a) shall be a net operating loss carryback to each of the 10 taxable years preceding the taxable year of the loss and a net operating loss carryover to each of the 5 taxable years following the taxable year of such loss."

Subsec. (b)(1)(D)(i)(II). Pub. L. 113-295, §221(a)(30)(B)(i), struck out "ending after August 2, 1989" after "loss limitation year".

Subsec. (b)(1)(D)(ii). Pub. L. 113-295, §221(a)(30)(B)(ii), substituted "subsection (g)" for "subsection (h)".

Subsec. (b)(1)(E). Pub. L. 113-295, §221(a)(30)(A)(i), redesignated subpar. (F) as (E). Former subpar. (E) redesignated (D).

Subsec. (b)(1)(E)(ii). Pub. L. 113-295, §221(a)(30)(B)(iv), substituted "subsection (h))." for "subsection (i)) or qualified disaster loss (as defined in subsection (j))." in concluding provisions.

2009—Subsec. (b)(1)(H). Pub. L. 111-92 amended subpar. (H) generally. Prior to amendment, subpar. (H) provided for carryback for 2008 net operating losses of small businesses.

Pub. L. 111-5, §1211(a), amended subpar. (H) generally. Prior to amendment, subpar. (H) read as follows: "In the case of a net operating loss for any taxable year ending during 2001 or 2002, subparagraph (A)(i) shall be applied by substituting '5' for '2' and subparagraph (F) shall not apply."

Later, as you skim the historical amendments for section 172(b), you will see for the first time Congressional change to sub-paragraph (A) as follows:

1997—Subsec. (b)(1)(A)(i). Pub. L. 105-34, §☐1082(a)(1), substituted "2" for "3".
Subsec. (b)(1)(A)(ii). Pub. L. 105-34, §1082(a)(2), substituted "20" for "15".

And, the effective date for this statutory change to section 172(b)(1)(A) enacted under Pub. L. 105-34 is provided in the historical amendments as follows:

Effective Date of 1997 Amendment

Pub. L. 105-34, Title X, §1082(c), Aug. 5, 1997, 111 Stat. 951, provided that: "The amendments made by this section [amending this section] shall apply to net operating losses for taxable years beginning after the date of the enactment of this Act [Aug. 5, 1997]."

Go through the steps, above, skim past the non-applicable historical amendments and focus your attention on the applicable sub-paragraph only. Repeat these steps until you feel comfortable with skimming historical amendments.

In addition to understanding how to read statutory text with historical amendments, it is helpful to recognize that various publishers and sources of the internal revenue code present historical amendments differently.

- CCH – organizes the presentation of historical amendments below each affected sub-section.
- RIA – presents historical amendments at the end of the entire section rather than at the end of each impacted sub-section. If there is a particularly long code section, then reviewing an early sub-section with the related historical amendments presented at the very end of the section can be rather cumbersome.
- Electronic IRC – if you use an electronic source for the IRC, for example, https://www.law.cornell.edu/uscode/text/26, each section will include multiple tabs. A window from an electronic view of section 1 is presented, below:

U.S. Code > Title 26 > Subtitle A > Chapter 1 > Subchapter A > Part I > § 1

26 U.S. Code § 1 - Tax imposed

| US Code | Notes | IRS Rulings | Authorities (CFR) |

prev | next

(a) MARRIED INDIVIDUALS FILING JOINT RETURNS AND SURVIVING SPOUSES There is hereby imposed on the taxable income of—

(1) every married individual (as defined in section 7703) who makes a single return jointly with his spouse under section 6013, and

(2) every surviving spouse (as defined in section 2(a)),

a tax determined in accordance with the following table:

If taxable income is:	The tax is:
Not over $36,900	15% of taxable income.
Over $36,900 but not over $89,150	$5,535, plus 28% of the excess over $36,900.
Over $89,150 but not over $140,000	$20,165, plus 31% of the excess over $89,150.
Over $140,000 but not over $250,000	$35,928.50, plus 36% of the excess over $140,000.
Over $250,000	$75,528.50, plus 39.6% of the excess over $250,000.

(b) HEADS OF HOUSEHOLDS

There is hereby imposed on the taxable income of every head of a household (as defined in section 2(b)) a tax determined in accordance with the following table:

If taxable income is:	The tax is:
Not over $29,600	15% of taxable income.
Over $29,600 but not over $76,400	$4,440, plus 28% of the excess over $29,600.
Over $76,400 but not over $127,500	$17,544, plus 31% of the excess over $76,400.
Over $127,500 but not over $250,000	$33,385, plus 36% of the excess over $127,500.
Over $250,000	$77,485, plus 39.6% of the excess over $250,000.

There are certain advantages to using electronic sources for the IRC in tax practice. However, electronic IRC sources require practitioners to open multiple windows on the computer and toggle between one window (IRC) and a second window (historical amendments). Given the lengthy code sections and historical amendments that confront tax practitioners in most cases, it can be quite cumbersome to scroll through multiple windows on a computer screen. In my view, the most efficient tax practice involves the use of paper code publications, specifically CCH versions of Title 26, for day-to-day application. Ultimately, consider each option and choose the presentation of the code and historical amendments that you find most effective.

8. The Text of the Internal Revenue Code May Not Always Provide the Applicable Law

Three scenarios exist in which the text that you read in your brand new IRC book may not reflect applicable law: (1) where Congress has delegated authority to the Secretary of the Treasury to update specific figures in the Code; (2) other sub-sections trigger different law in subsequent years; and (3) historical amendments establish that prior language of the Code applies.

The best way to explain these three scenarios is with a basic example. John Doe is single, unmarried, with no children or dependents (so not a "head of household") nor a surviving spouse. In 2016, John Doe has taxable income of $50,000. What his John Doe's federal tax liability in 2016?

(1) <u>Congress has delegated authority to the Secretary of the Treasury to update specific figures in the Code</u>

Let's look to text of section 1(c), below:

(c) UNMARRIED INDIVIDUALS (OTHER THAN SURVIVING SPOUSES AND HEADS OF HOUSEHOLDS) There is hereby imposed on the taxable income of every individual (other than a surviving spouse as defined in section 2(a) or the head of a household as defined in section 2(b)) who is not a married individual (as defined in section 7703) a tax determined in accordance with the following table:

If taxable income is:	The tax is:
Not over $22,100	15% of taxable income.
Over $22,100 but not over $53,500	$3,315, plus 28% of the excess over $22,100.
Over $53,500 but not over $115,000	$12,107, plus 31% of the excess over $53,500.
Over $115,000 but not over $250,000	$31,172, plus 36% of the excess over $115,000.
Over $250,000	$79,772, plus 39.6% of the excess over $250,000.

Applying the IRC, John Doe's federal tax liability is as follows:

$3,315
+ $7,812   (28% x [$50,000-$22,100])
$11,127

By applying the code as written, $11,127 is the correct answer under tax law, right? Well, no it's not. Let's dig a bit deeper into section 1.

Under section 1(f) we see some additional statutory instructions from Congress to the Secretary of the Treasury:

(f) PHASEOUT OF MARRIAGE PENALTY IN **15**-PERCENT BRACKET; ADJUSTMENTS IN TAX TABLES SO THAT INFLATION WILL NOT RESULT IN TAX INCREASES

(1) IN GENERAL
Not later than December 15 of 1993, and each subsequent calendar year, the Secretary shall prescribe tables which shall apply in lieu of the tables contained in subsections (a), (b), (c), (d), and (e) with respect to taxable years beginning in the succeeding calendar year.

(2) METHOD OF PRESCRIBING TABLES The table which under paragraph (1) is to apply in lieu of the table contained in subsection (a), (b), (c), (d), or (e), as the case may be, with respect to taxable years beginning in any calendar year shall be prescribed—

(A) except as provided in paragraph (8), by increasing the minimum and maximum dollar amounts for each rate bracket for which a tax is imposed under such table by the cost-of-living adjustment for such calendar year,

(B) by not changing the rate applicable to any rate bracket as adjusted under subparagraph (A), and

(C) by adjusting the amounts setting forth the tax to the extent necessary to reflect the adjustments in the rate brackets.

(3) COST-OF-LIVING ADJUSTMENT For purposes of paragraph (2), the cost-of-living adjustment for any calendar year is the percentage (if any) by which—

(A) the CPI for the preceding calendar year, exceeds

(B) the CPI for the calendar year 1992.

(4) CPI FOR ANY CALENDAR YEAR
For purposes of paragraph (3), the CPI for any calendar year is the average of the Consumer Price Index as of the close of the 12-month period ending on August 31 of such calendar year.

(5) CONSUMER PRICE INDEX
For purposes of paragraph (4), the term "Consumer Price Index" means the last Consumer Price Index for all-urban consumers published by the Department of Labor. For purposes of the preceding sentence, the revision of the Consumer Price Index which is most consistent with the Consumer Price Index for calendar year 1986 shall be used.

Here, we see that Congress has delegated the responsibility to update the tables set out in section 1, including the table under section 1(c). See I.R.C. §1(f)(1)-(2). If Congress did not delegate such authority to update the figures set forth in the tax table in section 1, then Congress would have to pass legislative every year if it wanted to continually update the figures to account for inflation.

The IRS carries out the responsibility as delegated by Congress to the Secretary of the Treasury by issuing an annual publication reflecting all required statutory updates. For tax year 2016, the IRS issued Rev. Proc. 2015-53 to fulfill the statutory responsibility as provided under I.R.C. §1(f)(1)-(2) and for all other sections with similar delegations[61]. See the first page of Rev. Proc. 2015-53, below:

Rev. Proc. 2015-53

Table of Contents

SECTION 1. PURPOSE

SECTION 2. CHANGES

SECTION 3. 2016 ADJUSTED ITEMS

	Code Section
.01 Tax Rate Tables	1(a)-(e)
.02 Unearned Income of Minor Children Taxed as if Parent's Income ("Kiddie Tax").	1(g)
.03 Adoption Credit	23
.04 Child Tax Credit	24
.05 Hope Scholarship, American Opportunity, and Lifetime Learning Credits	25A
.06 Earned Income Credit	32
.07 Refundable Credit for Coverage Under a Qualified Health Plan	36B(f)(2)(B)
.08 Rehabilitation Expenditures Treated as Separate New Building	42(e)
.09 Low-Income Housing Credit	42(h)

Now, let's return to the question facing John Doe. What does Rev. Proc. 2015-53, Section 3.01, provide to help with his federal tax liability for 2016?

---

[61] The annual update issued by the IRS of statutory adjustments as required by statute is published in the form of a "Revenue Procedure." However, the number of the applicable revenue procedure will not always be the same number. For example, for tax year 2017, the applicable guidance is Rev. Proc. 2016-55.

TABLE 3 - Section 1(c) – Unmarried Individuals (other than Surviving Spouses and Heads of Households)

If Taxable Income Is:	The Tax Is:
Not over $9,275	10% of the taxable income
Over $9,275 but not over $37,650	$927.50 plus 15% of the excess over $9,275
Over $37,650 but not over $91,150	$5,183.75 plus 25% of the excess over $37,650
Over $91,150 but not over $190,150	$18,558.75 plus 28% of the excess over $91,150
Over $190,150 but	$46,278.75 plus 33% of

Applying Rev. Proc. 2015-53, John Doe's federal tax liability is as follows:

$5,183.75
+ $3,087.50   (25% x [$50,000-$37,650])
$8,271.25

By applying the code as written under both section 1(c) and section 1(f), $8,271 is the correct answer under tax law, not $11,127 as we determined earlier.

(2) Other Sub-Sections of the Code Trigger Different Law in Subsequent Years

If you compare the table for "unmarried individuals" (other than Surviving Spouse and Heads of Households) under section 1(c) and Rev. Proc. 2015-53, the rates of tax are different. Why? Let's look to another sub-section of section 1. This time rather than delegating an inflation adjustment to the Treasury Secretary to update a figure, Congress provides for an automatic trigger in time where the rate changes automatically later. See section 1(i), below.

(i) RATE REDUCTIONS AFTER 2000

(1) 10-PERCENT RATE BRACKET

(A) In general In the case of taxable years beginning after December 31, 2000—

(i) the rate of tax under subsections (a), (b), (c), and (d) on taxable income not over the initial bracket amount shall be 10 percent, and

(ii) the 15 percent rate of tax shall apply only to taxable income over the initial bracket amount but not over the maximum dollar amount for the 15-percent rate bracket.

(B) Initial bracket amount For purposes of this paragraph, the initial bracket amount is—

(i) $14,000 in the case of subsection (a),

(ii) $10,000 in the case of subsection (b), and

(iii) ½ the amount applicable under clause (i) (after adjustment, if any, under subparagraph (C)) in the case of subsections (c) and (d).

(C) Inflation adjustment In prescribing the tables under subsection (f) which apply with respect to taxable years beginning in calendar years after 2003—

(i) the cost-of-living adjustment shall be determined under subsection (f)(3) by substituting "2002" for "1992" in subparagraph (B) thereof, and

(ii) the adjustments under clause (i) shall not apply to the amount referred to in subparagraph (B)(iii).

If any amount after adjustment under the preceding sentence is not a multiple of $50, such amount shall be rounded to the next lowest multiple of $50.

(2) 25-, 28-, AND 33-PERCENT RATE BRACKETS The tables under subsections (a), (b), (c), (d), and (e) shall be applied—

(A) by substituting "25%" for "28%" each place it appears (before the application of subparagraph (B)),

(B) by substituting "28%" for "31%" each place it appears, and

(C) by substituting "33%" for "36%" each place it appears.

(3) MODIFICATIONS TO INCOME TAX BRACKETS FOR HIGH-INCOME TAXPAYERS

(A) 35-percent rate bracket In the case of taxable years beginning after December 31, 2012—

(3) Historical Amendments Establish That Prior Language of the Code Applies

Below the text of a code section, publishers (such as CCH or RIA) provide the history of each code section, commonly referred to as "historical amendments." These historical amendments provide two important pieces of information: (1) the old statutory provisions; and (2) the effective date of the new statutory provisions. With this critical information, the tax practitioner can determine on what date the new statutory provision applies and when the old statutory provision applies. Thus, depending on the tax year at issue for the practitioner, the current text of the code section you are reading may not always provide the applicable law. Look at the historical amendments for the answer.

Chapter 5 Questions

1. Several years ago, Peter Client sued his former employer under the Age Discrimination in Employment Act of 1967 (Title 29 of the U.S. Code). On September 15, 2004, Peter had reached settlement of his age discrimination suit with his former employer. It took years for the settlement payment to finally arrive. On November 18, 2012, Peter received a check for $2,000,000 resulting from his settlement. Peter must pay his attorneys $800,000 for their legal services in representing him in his age discrimination suit. Peter asks our firm whether the payment of $800,000 to his attorneys is allowed as a deduction from gross income to reach his "adjusted gross income" under section 62. Yes or No. Explain your answer.

2. For tax year 2014, Judy estimates that she will have adjusted gross income of $85,000 and tax due of $30,000. Since 1995, Judy has been married but always filed separately from her husband. In 2013, Judy correctly reported federal tax in the amount of $25,000 based on adjusted gross income in the amount of $75,000. What is the required installment amount for Judy to avoid a penalty for failure by an individual to pay estimated income tax in 2014?

3. In Rev. Proc. 2010-36, the IRS issued guidance to individuals regarding the federal income tax treatment of amounts paid to repair damage to their personal residences resulting from corrosive drywall building materials. The text of Rev. Proc. 2010-36 is provided, below. Subsequently, Congress enacted new tax law applicable to personal casualty losses beginning in tax year 2018. The text of the new tax law from P.L. 115-97, section 11044, is provided below. Read both Rev. Proc. 2010-36 and P.L. 115-97, section 11044. In tax year 2018, your clients suffered a loss to their personal residence that is covered under Rev. Proc. 2010-36. Normally, a casualty loss that is progressive is not an allowable, deductible loss but for the limited relief provided under Rev. Proc. 2010-36 ("A casualty is damage, destruction, or loss of property that results from an identifiable event that is sudden, unexpected, and unusual. Rev. Rul 75-592, 1972-2 C.B. 101. Damage or loss resulting from progressive detioration of property through a steadily operating cause is not a casualty loss. See Matheson v. Commissioner, 54 F.2d 537 (2d Cir.

1931)"). In 2018, can your clients claim a personal casualty loss that is covered under the safe-harbor as provided under Rev. Proc. 2010-36? Yes or No. Explain your answer.

4. Let's try an exercise to better understand how tax law changes require us to focus on tracking the precise changes to the code and its application. Sally works as a sales representative for a software company in California. She regularly goes to meetings with prospective clients. When she hosts her clients, Sally will pay for meals and/or entertainment costs. Her software company requires that Sally submit all her sales business meal and entertainment receipts to their accounting department at the end of each week. All of Sally's receipts must include the date, name of client(s) who received the meal and/or entertainment outing, and business reason for the expenditure. It is the software company's policy that no meal or entertainment expense with a client can be lavish. You work for the software company's accounting department. The director of the accounting department asks that you research the new Federal tax law that went into effect beginning in 2018 for two specific types of expenses: (1) the cost of meals when the company's sales department employees pay such expenses as part of their sales work; and (2) the cost of entertainment expenses incurred by the company's sales staff as part of their regular duties taking clients out for various events. The company's president has indicted that regardless of the change in Federal tax law treatment relating to meal and entertainment expenses, that the company's sales staff will continue with business as usual. However, the president has directed the director of the accounting department to update the sales staff on recent tax law changes affecting these sales expenses. The accounting department director asks that you conduct research on the Federal tax treatment of business meals and entertainment expenses and provide the relevant authorities to address these expenses.

5. Julie is a single taxpayer, with no dependents. In 2017, Julie's taxable income was $40,000. In 2017, what was Julie's marginal tax rate? [Marginal tax rate is the percentage of tax applied to the taxpayer's final dollar of taxable income].

6. Same facts as in Question 5, except the tax year is 2018. What is Julie's marginal tax rate in 2018?

7. Same facts as in Question 5, except the tax year is 2026. What is Julie's marginal tax rate in 2026?

8. Larry works as an Uber driver. Larry parked his car in San Francisco while he waited for a customer. He noticed that his customer was across the street looking for Larry. So, Larry exited his car, ran down the street to get his customer's attention. After just a few minutes, Larry and his customer returned to his car. On his car windshield, Larry found a parking citation with a fine of $250. Larry contacts you, his tax advisor, and asks you if his parking ticket is deductible for Federal tax purposes. Conduct a search of the Internal Revenue Code and find the applicable code section to answer Larry's tax question.

Part III

Administrative, Procedural, and Miscellaneous

26 CFR 601.105: Examination of returns and claims for refund, credit or abatement; determination of correct tax liability.
  (Also Part I, §§ 165; 1.165-7(a)(2), 1.165-7(b).)

Rev. Proc. 2010-36

SECTION 1. PURPOSE

This revenue procedure provides guidance to individuals regarding the federal income tax treatment of amounts paid to repair damage to their personal residences resulting from corrosive drywall building materials.

SECTION 2. BACKGROUND

.01 Reported problems have occurred with certain imported drywall installed in homes between 2001 and 2008. Homeowners have reported blackening or corrosion of copper electrical wiring and copper components of household appliances, as well as the presence of sulfur gas odors. In November 2009, the Consumer Product Safety Commission (CPSC) reported that an indoor air study of a sample of 51 homes found a

2

strong association between the problem drywall and levels of hydrogen sulfide in those

homes and corrosion of metals in those homes. See the Commission's Drywall

Information Center website, http://www.cpsc.gov/info/drywall. On January 28, 2010, the

CPSC and the Department of Housing and Urban Development released interim

guidance advising interested parties how to identify homes with problem drywall. See

http://www.cpsc.gov/info/drywall/InterimIDGuidance012810.pdf.

.02 The Internal Revenue Service has received numerous inquiries from

taxpayers about whether a loss resulting from corrosive drywall constitutes a deductible

casualty loss within the meaning of § 165 of the Internal Revenue Code, the taxable

year any such loss would be deductible, and how the amount of the loss would be

computed.

.03 Section 165(a) of the Internal Revenue Code generally allows taxpayers to

deduct losses sustained during the taxable year that are not compensated by insurance

or otherwise. For personal-use property (such as a taxpayer's personal residence and

household appliances), § 165(c)(3) limits an individual's deduction to losses arising from

fire, storm, shipwreck, or other casualty, or from theft. A casualty is damage,

destruction, or loss of property that results from an identifiable event that is sudden,

unexpected, and unusual. Rev. Rul. 72-592, 1972-2 C.B. 101. Damage or loss

resulting from progressive deterioration of property through a steadily operating cause is

not a casualty loss. See Matheson v. Commissioner, 54 F.2d 537 (2d Cir. 1931).

.04 A casualty loss is allowed as a deduction only for the taxable year in which

the loss is sustained. However, if the taxpayer has a claim for reimbursement of the

3

loss (from insurance or otherwise) for which there is a reasonable prospect of recovery, no portion of the loss is deductible until it can be ascertained with reasonable certainty whether or not such reimbursement will be received. See § 1.165–1(c)(4) of the Income Tax Regulations.

.05 The amount of a taxpayer's casualty loss generally is the decrease in the fair market value of the property as a result of the casualty, limited to the taxpayer's adjusted basis in the property. See § 1.165-7(b). To simplify the computation of a casualty loss deduction, existing regulations permit taxpayers to use the cost to repair the damaged property as evidence of the decrease in value of the property. See § 1.165-7(a)(2)(ii).

.06 Section 165(h)(1)-(2) imposes two limitations on casualty loss deductions for personal use property. First, a casualty loss deduction is allowable only for the amount of the loss that exceeds $100 per casualty ($500 for taxable years beginning in 2009 only). Second, the net amount of all of a taxpayer's casualty losses (in excess of casualty gains, if any) is allowable only for the amount of the losses that exceed 10 percent of the taxpayer's adjusted gross income (AGI) for the year.

.07 In view of the unique circumstances surrounding damage resulting from corrosive drywall, the Service and Treasury Department conclude that it is appropriate to provide a safe harbor method that treats certain damage resulting from corrosive drywall as a casualty loss and provides a formula for determining the amount of the loss. Accordingly, for an individual within the scope of this revenue procedure, the Service will not challenge the individual's treatment of damage resulting from corrosive

4

drywall as a casualty loss if the loss is determined and reported as provided in this revenue procedure.

SECTION 3. SCOPE

This revenue procedure applies to any individual who pays to repair damage to that individual's personal residence or household appliances that results from corrosive drywall.

SECTION 4. APPLICATION

.01 An individual who pays to repair damage to that individual's personal residence or household appliances that results from corrosive drywall may treat the amount paid as a casualty loss in the year of payment. For purposes of this revenue procedure, the term "corrosive drywall" means drywall that is identified as problem drywall under the two-step identification method published by the CPSC and the Department of Housing and Urban Development in their interim guidance dated January 28, 2010. As of the date of publication of this revenue procedure, the interim guidance can be found at http://www.cpsc.gov/info/drywall/InterimIDGuidance012810.pdf.

.02 The amount of a loss resulting from corrosive drywall may be limited depending on whether the taxpayer has a pending claim for reimbursement (or intends to pursue reimbursement) of the loss through property insurance, litigation, or otherwise. A taxpayer who does not have a pending claim for reimbursement (and does not intend to pursue reimbursement) may claim as a loss all unreimbursed amounts paid during the taxable year to repair damage to the taxpayer's personal residence and household appliances that results from corrosive drywall. A taxpayer who has a

5

pending claim for reimbursement (or intends to pursue reimbursement) may claim a loss for 75 percent of the unreimbursed amounts paid during the taxable year to repair damage to the taxpayer's personal residence and household appliances that resulted from corrosive drywall. A taxpayer who has been fully reimbursed before filing a return for the year the loss was sustained may not claim a loss. A taxpayer who has a pending claim for reimbursement (or intends to pursue reimbursement) may have income or an additional deduction in subsequent taxable years depending on the actual amount of reimbursement received. See § 1.165-1(d).

.03 Amounts paid for improvements or additions that increase the value of the taxpayer's personal residence above its pre-loss value are not allowed as a casualty loss. Only amounts paid to restore the taxpayer's personal residence to the condition existing immediately prior to the damage qualify for loss treatment.

.04 Where a household appliance is replaced rather than repaired, the amount of the loss attributable to the appliance is the lesser of the current cost to replace the original appliance or the basis of the original appliance (generally its cost).

.05 A taxpayer claiming a casualty loss under this revenue procedure must report the amount of the loss on Form 4684 ("Casualties and Thefts") and must mark "Revenue Procedure 2010-36" at the top of that form. Taxpayers are subject to the $100 ($500 for taxable years beginning in 2009 only) limitation imposed by § 165(h)(1) and the 10-percent-of-AGI limitation imposed by § 165(h)(2).

.06 Taxpayers who choose not to apply the safe harbor treatment provided by this revenue procedure are subject to all of the generally applicable provisions

6

governing the deductibility of losses under § 165. Accordingly, these taxpayers must establish that the damage, destruction, or loss of property resulted from an identifiable event that is sudden, unexpected, and unusual, and was not the result of progressive deterioration through a steadily operating cause. See Rev. Rul. 72-592, 1972-2 C.B. 101; Matheson v. Commissioner, 54 F.2d 537 (2d Cir. 1931). These taxpayers also must prove that the loss is properly deductible in the taxable year claimed by the taxpayer and not in some other year. Further, these taxpayers must prove the amount of the claimed loss and must prove that no claim for reimbursement of any portion of the loss exists for which there is a reasonable prospect of recovery.

SECTION 5. EFFECTIVE DATE

This revenue procedure is effective for federal income tax returns (including amended federal income tax returns) filed after September 29, 2010.

SECTION 6. DRAFTING INFORMATION

The principal author of this revenue procedure is Alan S. Williams of the Office of Associate Chief Counsel (Income Tax & Accounting). For further information regarding this revenue procedure contact Alan S. Williams at 202-622-4950 (not a toll free call).

Public Law 115-97

SEC. 11044. MODIFICATION OF DEDUCTION FOR PERSONAL CASUALTY LOSSES.

(a) IN GENERAL.—Subsection (h) of section 165 is amended by adding at the end the following new paragraph:

"(5) LIMITATION FOR TAXABLE YEARS 2018 THROUGH 2025.—

"(A) IN GENERAL.—In the case of an individual, except as provided in subparagraph (B), any personal casualty loss which (but for this paragraph) would be deductible in a taxable year beginning after December 31, 2017, and before January 1, 2026, shall be allowed as a deduction under subsection (a) only to the extent it is attributable to a Federally declared disaster (as defined in subsection (i)(5)).

"(B) EXCEPTION RELATED TO PERSONAL CASUALTY GAINS.—If a taxpayer has personal casualty gains for any taxable year to which subparagraph (A) applies—

"(i) subparagraph (A) shall not apply to the portion of the personal casualty loss not attributable to a Federally declared disaster (as so defined) to the extent such loss does not exceed such gains, and

"(ii) in applying paragraph (2) for purposes of subparagraph (A) to the portion of personal casualty loss which is so attributable to such a disaster, the amount of personal casualty gains taken into account under paragraph (2)(A) shall be reduced by the portion of such gains taken into account under clause (i).".

(b) EFFECTIVE DATE.—The amendment made by this section shall apply to losses incurred in taxable years beginning after December 31, 2017.

CHAPTER 6 – THE EXECUTIVE BRANCH

☑ Understand the role of the Internal Revenue Service in interpreting and enforcing Title 26

☑ Learn about the organizations of the Executive Branch that affect tax administration

☑ Understand the various types of published guidance issued by the executive branch and their impact upon tax administration

1. Introduction - Overview of the Executive Branch
2. The Internal Revenue Service
   a. Organization of the IRS
   b. Published Guidance Issued By the IRS
3. Treasury Regulations
4. The Problem of Outdated Regulations
5. Other Published Guidance
6. Utilizing Published Guidance - Examples

- End of Chapter Practice Example - Evolving IRS Guidance
- Examples of Executive Branch Tax Documents

1. Introduction - Overview of the Executive Branch

The power of the Executive Branch is vested in the President of the United States, who also acts as head of state and Commander-in-Chief of the armed forces. The President is responsible for implementing and enforcing the laws written by Congress and, to that end, appoints the heads of the federal agencies, including the Cabinet. The Vice President is also part of the Executive Branch, ready to assume the Presidency should the need arise.

The Cabinet and independent federal agencies are responsible for the day-to-day enforcement and administration of federal laws. These departments and agencies have missions and responsibilities as widely divergent as those of the Department of Defense and the Environmental Protection Agency, the Social Security Administration and the Securities and Exchange Commission. Including members of the armed forces, the Executive Branch employs more than 4 million Americans.

Fully understanding the Executive branch's responsibility and limitations to implement and enforce the laws written by Congress may be best understood through one example when it did not enforce federal law. The Defense of Marriage Act ("DOMA") (Pub.L. 104–199, 110 Stat. 2419, enacted September 21, 1996, 1 U.S.C. § 7 and 28 U.S.C. § 1738C), was a federal statute that, prior to being ruled unconstitutional, defined marriage for federal purposes as the union of one man and one woman, and allowed states to refuse to recognize same-sex marriages granted under the laws of other states. Until Section 3 of the Act was struck down in 2013 (United States v. Windsor[62]) by the U.S. Supreme Court, DOMA, in conjunction with other statutes, had barred same-sex married couples from being recognized as "spouses" for purposes of federal laws, effectively barring them from receiving federal marriage benefits. Prior to the Supreme Court decision in United States v. Windsor, the question for the Executive was whether it would continue to defend DOMA. And, in 2011, two years before the Supreme Court ruled DOMA unconstitutional, the Executive (through a statement by Attorney General Eric Holder) announced that it would not continue to defend the DOMA federal statute because it had determined it was unconstitutional. Thus, in this example, we see the interaction of all three branches: legislative (enact laws), executive (interpret and enforce these laws), and judicial (resolve controversies, including determining whether federal statutes violate the Constitution, as in the case involving DOMA).

---

[62] 133 S.Ct. 2675 (2013). The United States v. Windsor opinion is available at: https://www.supremecourt.gov/opinions/12pdf/12-307_6j37.pdf.

The 2011 statement of Attorney General Eric Holder discussing DOMA is set forth, below.[63]

Department of Justice
Office of Public Affairs

FOR IMMEDIATE RELEASE
Wednesday, February 23, 2011

Statement of the Attorney General on Litigation Involving the Defense of Marriage Act

WASHINGTON – The Attorney General made the following statement today about the Department's course of action in two lawsuits, Pedersen v. OPM and Windsor v. United States, challenging Section 3 of the Defense of Marriage Act (DOMA), which defines marriage for federal purposes as only between a man and a woman.

In the two years since this Administration took office, the Department of Justice has defended Section 3 of the Defense of Marriage Act on several occasions in federal court. Each of those cases evaluating Section 3 was considered in jurisdictions in which binding circuit court precedents hold that laws singling out people based on sexual orientation, as DOMA does, are constitutional if there is a rational basis for their enactment. While the President opposes DOMA and believes it should be repealed, the Department has defended it in court because we were able to advance reasonable arguments under that rational basis standard.

Section 3 of DOMA has now been challenged in the Second Circuit, however, which has no established or binding standard for how laws concerning sexual orientation should be treated. In these cases, the Administration faces for the first time the question of whether laws regarding sexual orientation are subject to the more permissive standard of review or whether a more rigorous standard, under which laws targeting minority groups with a history of discrimination are viewed with suspicion by the courts, should apply.

After careful consideration, including a review of my recommendation, the President has concluded that given a number of factors, including a documented history of discrimination, classifications based on sexual orientation should be subject to a more heightened standard of scrutiny. The President has also concluded that Section 3 of DOMA, as applied to legally married same-sex couples, fails to meet that standard and is therefore unconstitutional. Given that conclusion, the President has instructed the Department not to defend the statute in such cases. I fully concur with the President's determination.

Consequently, the Department will not defend the constitutionality of Section 3 of DOMA as applied to same-sex married couples in the two cases filed in the Second

---

[63] Attorney General Eric Holder served in his position from February 2009 through September 25, 2014. See https://obamawhitehouse.archives.gov/blog/2014/09/25/us-attorney-general-eric-holder-stepping-down-after-six-year-tenure.

Circuit. We will, however, remain parties to the cases and continue to represent the interests of the United States throughout the litigation. I have informed Members of Congress of this decision, so Members who wish to defend the statute may pursue that option. The Department will also work closely with the courts to ensure that Congress has a full and fair opportunity to participate in pending litigation.

Furthermore, pursuant to the President's instructions, and upon further notification to Congress, I will instruct Department attorneys to advise courts in other pending DOMA litigation of the President's and my conclusions that a heightened standard should apply, that Section 3 is unconstitutional under that standard and that the Department will cease defense of Section 3.

The Department has a longstanding practice of defending the constitutionality of duly-enacted statutes if reasonable arguments can be made in their defense. At the same time, the Department in the past has declined to defend statutes despite the availability of professionally responsible arguments, in part because – as here – the Department does not consider every such argument to be a "reasonable" one. Moreover, the Department has declined to defend a statute in cases, like this one, where the President has concluded that the statute is unconstitutional.

Much of the legal landscape has changed in the 15 years since Congress passed DOMA. The Supreme Court has ruled that laws criminalizing homosexual conduct are unconstitutional. Congress has repealed the military's Don't Ask, Don't Tell policy. Several lower courts have ruled DOMA itself to be unconstitutional. Section 3 of DOMA will continue to remain in effect unless Congress repeals it or there is a final judicial finding that strikes it down, and the President has informed me that the Executive Branch will continue to enforce the law. But while both the wisdom and the legality of Section 3 of DOMA will continue to be the subject of both extensive litigation and public debate, this Administration will no longer assert its constitutionality in court.

Congress' enactment of DOMA, the Executive's decision not to defend a statute if it is determined to be unconstitutional, and the Judicial branch's holding in <u>Windsor v. United States</u> holding that DOMA is unconstitutional offer a glimpse of our government working independently, with each part functioning within its constitutional authority to strengthen the whole while keeping each in check.

Understanding how government functions and the breadth of federal government programs and responsibilities empowers tax professionals to be far more effective advocates because you can begin to understand the need for tax revenue to fund these essential services. Consider details of the executive branch, below.

The President - The President is both the head of state and head of government of the United States of America, and Commander-in-Chief of the armed forces. Under Article II of the Constitution, the President is responsible for the execution and enforcement of the laws created by Congress. Fifteen executive departments — each led by an appointed member of the President's Cabinet — carry out the day-to-day administration of the federal government. They are joined in this by other executive agencies such as the CIA and Environmental Protection Agency, the heads of which are not part of the Cabinet, but who are under the full authority of the President. The President also appoints the heads of more than 50 independent federal commissions, such as the Federal Reserve Board or the Securities and Exchange Commission, as well as federal judges, ambassadors, and other federal offices. The Executive Office of the President (EOP) consists of the immediate staff to the President, along with entities such as the Office of Management and Budget and the Office of the United States Trade Representative.

The President has the power either to sign legislation into law or to veto bills enacted by Congress, although Congress may override a veto with a two-thirds vote of both houses. The Executive Branch conducts diplomacy with other nations, and the President has the power to negotiate and sign treaties, which also must be ratified by two-thirds of the Senate. The President can issue executive orders, which direct executive officers or clarify and further existing laws.

The Cabinet - The Cabinet is an advisory body made up of the heads of the executive departments. Appointed by the President and confirmed by the Senate, the members of the Cabinet are often the President's closest confidants. In addition to running major federal agencies, they play an important role in the Presidential line of succession — after the Vice President, Speaker of the House, and Senate President pro tempore, the line of succession continues with the Cabinet offices in the order in which the departments were created. All the members of the Cabinet take the title Secretary, except the head of the Justice Department, who is Attorney General.

Departments Within the Executive Branch

(1) **Department of Agriculture** - The U.S. Department of Agriculture (USDA) develops and executes policy on farming, agriculture, and food. Its aims include meeting the needs of farmers and ranchers, promoting agricultural trade and production, assuring food safety, protecting natural resources, fostering rural communities, and ending hunger in America and abroad. The USDA employs more than 100,000 employees and has an annual budget of approximately $95 billion. It consists of 17 agencies, including the Animal and Plant Health Inspection Service, the Food and Nutrition Service, and the Forest Service. The bulk of the department's budget goes towards mandatory programs that provide services required by law, such as programs designed to provide nutrition assistance, promote agricultural exports, and conserve our environment. The USDA also plays an important role in overseas aid programs by providing surplus foods to developing countries. The United States Secretary of Agriculture administers the USDA.

(2) **Department of Commerce** - The Department of Commerce is the government agency tasked with improving living standards for all Americans by promoting economic development and technological innovation. The department supports U.S. business and industry through a number of services, including gathering economic and

demographic data, issuing patents and trademarks, improving understanding of the environment and oceanic life, and ensuring the effective use of scientific and technical resources. The agency also formulates telecommunications and technology policy, and promotes U.S. exports by assisting and enforcing international trade agreements. The Secretary of Commerce oversees a $6.5 billion budget and approximately 38,000 employees.

(3) **Department of Defense** - The mission of the Department of Defense (DOD) is to provide the military forces needed to deter war and to protect the security of our country. The department's headquarters is at the Pentagon. The DOD consists of the Departments of the Army, Navy, and Air Force, as well as many agencies, offices, and commands, including the Joint Chiefs of Staff, the Pentagon Force Protection Agency, the National Security Agency, and the Defense Intelligence Agency. The DOD occupies the vast majority of the Pentagon building in Arlington, VA.

The Department of Defense is the largest government agency, with more than 1.3 million men and women on active duty, nearly 700,000 civilian personnel, and 1.1 million citizens who serve in the National Guard and Reserve forces. Together, the military and civilian arms of DOD protect national interests through war-fighting, providing humanitarian aid, and performing peacekeeping and disaster relief services.

(4) **Department of Education** - The mission of the Department of Education is to promote student achievement and preparation for competition in a global economy by fostering educational excellence and ensuring equal access to educational opportunity. The Department administers federal financial aid for education, collects data on America's schools to guide improvements in education quality, and works to complement the efforts of state and local governments, parents, and students. The U.S. Secretary of Education oversees the Department's 4,200 employees and $68.6 billion budget.

(5) **Department of Energy** - The mission of the Department of Energy (DOE) is to advance the national, economic, and energy security of the United States. The DOE promotes America's energy security by encouraging the development of reliable, clean, and affordable energy. It administers federal funding for scientific research to further the goal of discovery and innovation — ensuring American economic competitiveness and improving the quality of life for Americans. The DOE is also tasked with ensuring America's nuclear security, and with protecting the environment by providing a responsible resolution to the legacy of nuclear weapons production. The United States Secretary of Energy oversees a budget of approximately $23 billion and more than 100,000 federal and contract employees.

(6) **Department of Health and Human Services** - The Department of Health and Human Services (HHS) is the United States government's principal agency for protecting the health of all Americans and providing essential human services, especially for those who are least able to help themselves. Agencies of HHS conduct health and social science research, work to prevent disease outbreaks, assure food and drug safety, and provide health insurance. In addition to administering Medicare

and Medicaid, which together provide health insurance to one in four Americans, HHS also oversees the National Institutes of Health, the Food and Drug Administration, and the Centers for Disease Control. The Secretary of Health and Human Services oversees a budget of approximately $700 billion and approximately 65,000 employees. The Department's programs are administered by 11 operating divisions, including 8 agencies in the U.S. Public Health Service and 3 human services agencies.

(7) Department of Homeland Security - The missions of the Department of Homeland Security are to prevent and disrupt terrorist attacks; protect the American people, our critical infrastructure, and key resources; and respond to and recover from incidents that do occur. The third largest Cabinet department, DHS was established by the Homeland Security Act of 2002, largely in response to the terrorist attacks on September 11, 2001. The new department consolidated 22 executive branch agencies, including the U.S. Customs Service, the U.S. Coast Guard, the U.S. Secret Service, the Transportation Security Administration, and the Federal Emergency Management Agency. DHS employs 216,000 people in its mission to patrol borders, protect travelers and our transportation infrastructure, enforce immigration laws, and respond to disasters and emergencies. The agency also promotes preparedness and emergency prevention among citizens. Policy is coordinated by the Homeland Security Council at the White House, in cooperation with other defense and intelligence agencies, and led by the Assistant to the President for Homeland Security.

(8) Department of Housing and Urban Development - The Department of Housing and Urban Development (HUD) is the federal agency responsible for national policies and programs that address America's housing needs, that improve and develop the nation's communities, and that enforce fair housing laws. The Department plays a major role in supporting homeownership for lower- and moderate-income families through its mortgage insurance and rent subsidy programs. Offices within HUD include the Federal Housing Administration, which provides mortgage and loan insurance; the Office of Fair Housing and Equal Opportunity, which ensures all Americans equal access to the housing of their choice; and the Community Development Block Grant Program, which helps communities with economic development, job opportunities, and housing rehabilitation. HUD also administers public housing and homeless assistance. The Secretary of Housing and Urban Development oversees approximately 9,000 employees on a budget of approximately $40 billion.

(9) Department of the Interior - The Department of the Interior (DOI) is the nation's principal conservation agency. Its mission is to protect America's natural resources, offer recreation opportunities, conduct scientific research, conserve and protect fish and wildlife, and honor our trust responsibilities to American Indians, Alaskan Natives, and our responsibilities to island communities. DOI manages 500 million acres of surface land, or about one-fifth of the land in the United States, and manages hundreds of dams and reservoirs. Agencies within the DOI include the Bureau of Indian Affairs, the Minerals Management Service, and the U.S. Geological Survey. The DOI manages the national parks and is tasked with protecting endangered species. The Secretary of the Interior oversees about 70,000 employees and 200,000 volunteers on a budget of approximately $16 billion. Every year it raises billions in revenue from energy, mineral, grazing, and timber leases, as well as recreational permits and land sales.

(10) Department of Justice - The mission of the Department of Justice (DOJ) is to enforce the law and defend the interests of the United States according to the law; to ensure public safety against threats foreign and domestic; to provide federal leadership in preventing and controlling crime; to seek just punishment for those guilty of unlawful behavior; and to ensure fair and impartial administration of justice for all Americans. The DOJ is comprised of 40 component organizations, including the Drug Enforcement Administration, the Federal Bureau of Investigation, the U.S. Marshals, and the Federal Bureau of Prisons. The Attorney General is the head of the DOJ and chief law enforcement officer of the federal government. The Attorney General represents the United States in legal matters, advises the President and the heads of the executive departments of the government, and occasionally appears in person before the Supreme Court. With a budget of approximately $25 billion, the DOJ is the world's largest law office and the central agency for the enforcement of federal laws.

(11) Department of Labor - The Department of Labor oversees federal programs for ensuring a strong American workforce. These programs address job training, safe working conditions, minimum hourly wage and overtime pay, employment discrimination, and unemployment insurance. The Department of Labor's mission is to foster and promote the welfare of the job seekers, wage earners, and retirees of the United States by improving their working conditions, advancing their opportunities for profitable employment, protecting their retirement and health care benefits, helping employers find workers, strengthening free collective bargaining, and tracking changes in employment, prices, and other national economic measurements. Offices within the Department of Labor include the Bureau of Labor Statistics, the federal government's principal statistics agency for labor economics, and the Occupational Safety & Health Administration, which promotes the safety and health of America's working men and women. The Secretary of Labor oversees 15,000 employees on a budget of approximately $50 billion.

(12) Department of State - The Department of State plays the lead role in developing and implementing the President's foreign policy. Major responsibilities include United States representation abroad, foreign assistance, foreign military training programs, countering international crime, and a wide assortment of services to U.S. citizens and foreign nationals seeking entrance to the U.S. The U.S. maintains diplomatic relations with approximately 180 countries — each posted by civilian U.S. Foreign Service employees — as well as with international organizations. At home, more than 5,000 civil employees carry out the mission of the Department. The Secretary of State serves as the President's top foreign policy adviser, and oversees 30,000 employees and a budget of approximately $35 billion.

(13) Department of Transportation - The mission of the Department of Transportation (DOT) is to ensure a fast, safe, efficient, accessible and convenient transportation system that meets our vital national interests and enhances the quality of life of the American people. Organizations within the DOT include the Federal Highway Administration, the Federal Aviation Administration, the National Highway Traffic Safety Administration, the Federal Transit Administration, the Federal Railroad Administration and the Maritime Administration. The U.S. Secretary of Transportation oversees **approximately 55,000 employees** and a budget of approximately $70 billion.

(14) Department of the Treasury - The Department of the Treasury is responsible for promoting economic prosperity and ensuring the soundness and security of the U.S. and international financial systems. The Department operates and maintains systems that are critical to the nation's financial infrastructure, such as the production of coin and currency, the disbursement of payments to the American public, the collection of taxes, and the borrowing of funds necessary to run the federal government. The Department works with other federal agencies, foreign governments, and international financial institutions to encourage global economic growth, raise standards of living, and, to the extent possible, predict and prevent economic and financial crises. The Treasury Department also performs a critical and far-reaching role in enhancing national security by improving the safeguards of our financial systems, implementing economic sanctions against foreign threats to the U.S., and identifying and targeting the financial support networks of national security threats. The Secretary of the Treasury oversees a budget of approximately $13 billion and a **staff of more than 100,000 employees.**

(15) Department of Veterans Affairs - The Department of Veterans Affairs is responsible for administering benefit programs for veterans, their families, and their survivors. These benefits include pension, education, disability compensation, home loans, life insurance, vocational rehabilitation, survivor support, medical care, and burial benefits. Veterans Affairs became a cabinet-level department in 1989. Of the 25 million veterans currently alive, nearly three of every four served during a war or an official period of hostility. About a quarter of the nation's population — approximately 70 million people — are potentially eligible for V.A. benefits and services because they are veterans, family members, or survivors of veterans. The Secretary of Veterans Affairs oversees a budget of approximately $90 billion and a **staff of approximately 235,000 employees.**

The number of employees within the Federal departments vary year to year. The United States Office of Personnel Management ("OPM") releases an annual document that reports the size of the Executive Branch of the Federal government. Below is a snapshot from the 2017 OPM fiscal year report that provides information on the size of the Federal civilian workforce from FY 2008 through FY 2017.[64]

---

[64] https://www.opm.gov/policy-data-oversight/data-analysis-documentation/federal-employment-reports/reports-publications/sizing-up-the-executive-branch-2016.pdf. The Federal government operates on a fiscal year that begins on October 1 and ends on September 30.

AGENCY	FY2008	FY2009	FY2010	FY2011	FY2012	FY2013	FY2014	FY2015	FY2016	FY2017
DEPARTMENT OF EDUCATION	3,825	3,769	4,010	4,066	3,899	3,865	3,815	3,862	3,973	3,842
DEPARTMENT OF HOUSING AND URBAN DEVELOPMENT	9,445	9,147	9,397	9,269	8,982	8,547	8,255	8,059	7,883	7,697
DEPARTMENT OF STATE	8,428	8,622	8,959	9,443	9,761	10,142	10,068	10,121	10,500	10166
DEPARTMENT OF ENERGY	14,803	15,134	15,757	15,548	15,041	14,739	14,341	14,443	14,499	14,249
DEPARTMENT OF LABOR	14,322	14,762	15,387	15,190	15,705	15,354	15,077	15,086	14,996	14,424
DEPARTMENT OF COMMERCE	32,924	33,642	33,711	34,501	35,013	34,550	34,857	35,249	35,661	35,757
DEPARTMENT OF THE INTERIOR	51,828	52,796	53,460	53,393	53,156	50,959	49,082	48,798	49,679	49,721
DEPARTMENT OF TRANSPORTATION	53,549	55,433	56,151	56,092	55,614	54,374	53,684	53,822	53,992	53,568
DEPARTMENT OF HEALTH AND HUMAN SERVICES	53,325	56,124	58,946	60,303	61,168	62,086	62,099	63,324	65,431	65,866
DEPARTMENT OF AGRICULTURE	78,369	78,962	80,510	79,899	76,785	74,117	72,889	73,663	74,465	73,231
DEPARTMENT OF DEFENSE	72,133	76,622	81,179	85,818	86,135	85,579	89,547	89,521	86,662	90,054
DEPARTMENT OF THE TREASURY	93,961	98,361	99,868	96,232	92,397	89,852	86,049	84,050	82,556	78,734
DEPARTMENT OF JUSTICE	104,282	108,349	112,688	112,867	113,358	112,342	110,427	111,010	112,900	111,778
DEPARTMENT OF THE AIR FORCE	142,957	148,133	158,039	166,338	161,574	159,499	156,195	156,594	158,270	157,418
DEPARTMENT OF HOMELAND SECURITY	147,533	157,573	161,273	166,210	169,116	168,348	167,422	166,777	169,547	173,326
DEPARTMENT OF THE NAVY	172,392	180,913	189,389	191,975	192,500	188,599	187,723	195,815	201,543	201,127
DEPARTMENT OF THE ARMY	225,881	241,329	257,947	255,487	251,257	241,609	235,951	233,035	230,765	228,241
DEPARTMENT OF VETERANS AFFAIRS	236,761	255,012	268,187	277,461	285,436	297,528	308,176	324,639	333,264	342,111
ALL OTHER AGENCIES	156,531	162,422	166,861	166,488	163,414	159,634	160,105	160,626	161,441	158,676
ALL	1,673,249	1,757,105	1,831,719	1,856,580	1,850,311	1,831,723	1,825,762	1,848,494	1,868,027	1,869,986

2. The Internal Revenue Service

The IRS is organized to carry out the responsibilities of the secretary of the Treasury under section 7801 of the Internal Revenue Code. The secretary has full authority to administer and enforce the internal revenue laws and has the power to create an agency to enforce these laws. The IRS was created based on this legislative grant. Section 7803 of the Internal Revenue Code provides for the appointment of a commissioner of Internal Revenue to administer and supervise the execution and application of the internal revenue laws.

"The public's confidence in our tax system rests, in significant part, on their perception of fairness in the administration of the tax laws. This begins with government first." Hartman, et. al. v. Commissioner, T.C. Memo 2008-124 (quoting a former IRS Chief Counsel's address to the annual meeting of the New York State Bar Association Tax Section in January, 2003). The face of the Federal government in tax administration is the IRS. The stated mission of the IRS is to: "Provide America's taxpayers top quality service by helping them understand and meet their tax responsibilities and enforce the law with integrity and fairness to all."

The IRS is a bureau of the Department of the Treasury and one of the world's most efficient tax administrators as the statistics/data that follow illustrate:

- At the end of its fiscal year 2009 (FY begins October 1 each year), the IRS had 93,337 employee, with 14,264 serving as revenue agents - employees who call on taxpayers and conduct face-to-face audits.[65]

151

- In fiscal year 2010, the IRS collected more than $2.3 trillion in revenue and processed more than 230 million tax returns.[66]

- For fiscal year 2012, Congress provided the IRS with funding of $11.8 billion to carry out its responsibilities as the nation's tax authority. With this funding, the IRS spent 48 cents for each $100 that it collected.[67] In FY 2012, the IRS processed more than 239 million tax returns and collected $2.524 trillion in taxes

Type of return	Number of returns	Gross collections (millions of $)
Individual income tax	146,243,886	1,371,402
Corporation income tax	2,262,961[2]	280,965
Employment taxes	29,589,891	784,397
Excise taxes	1,196,789	56,175
Gift tax	249,451	2,110
Estate tax	26,859	12,341

(gross receipts before tax refunds)[68]:

- In fiscal year 2015, the IRS collected almost $3.3 trillion in revenue and processed almost 240 million tax returns. In fiscal year 2015, the IRS spent just 35 cents for each $100 it collected in tax revenue.[69]

a. Organization of the IRS

The IRS is composed of various functional divisions each with a separate mission to support tax administration. The four primary IRS operating divisions are wage & investment, large business & international, small business/self-employed, and tax exempt government entities.

- Wage & Investment Division - The Wage and Investment Division supports the IRS' strategic goals and objectives through initiatives that address the increasing demand for timely, accurate service, and reducing taxpayer burden, address the increasing demand for electronic products and services, improve enforcement

---

[65] www.factcheck.org/2010/03/irs-expansion/.

[66] *www.irs.gov*

[67] IRS 2012 Data Book, Table 29.

[68] http://www.irs.gov/pub/irs-soi/13taxstatscard.pdf. Are you interested in "tax expenditures"? Tax expenditures are defined by law as "revenue losses attributable to provisions of the Federal tax laws which allow a special exclusion, exemption, or deduction from gross income or which provide a special credit, a preferential rate of tax, or a deferral of tax liability." These exceptions may be viewed as alternatives to other policy instruments, such as spending or regulatory programs. For date on tax expenditures, go to: (1) https://www.cbo.gov/publication/52493; or (2) https://www.treasury.gov/resource-center/tax-policy/Pages/Tax-Expenditures.aspx. Additionally, look at: https://www.cbpp.org/research/federal-budget/policy-basics-where-do-our-federal-tax-dollars-go.

[69] 2105 IRS Databook accessible at: https://www.irs.gov/pub/irs-soi/15databk.pdf.

programs to reduce the risks of non-compliance, leverage new technology and reengineer business processes to maximize delivery of new business services, evaluate the tax administration support needs of individual taxpayers as part of its overall management of their portfolio of services and delivery channels, and increase preventive and corrective actions to reduce vulnerability to identity theft.

- Large Business & International Division - serves corporations, subchapter S corporations, and partnerships with assets greater than $10 million. These businesses typically employ large numbers of employees, deal with complicated issues involving tax law and accounting principles, and conduct business in an expanding global environment. LB&I is organized along six domestic industries and four International functions.

- Small Business/Self-Employed Division - serves small businesses with assets of less than $10 million, self-employed persons, and filers of employment, excise, estate and gift tax returns.

- Tax Exempt Government Entities Division - The division is designed to serve the needs of three very distinct customer segments: Employee Plans; Exempt Organizations; and Government Entities. The customers range from small local community organizations and municipalities to major universities, huge pension funds, state governments, Indian tribal governments and participants of complex tax exempt bond transactions. These organizations represent a large economic sector with unique needs. Although generally paying no income tax, this sector does pay over $220 billion in employment taxes and income tax withholding and controls approximately $14 trillion in assets. Governed by complex, highly specialized provisions of the tax law, this sector is not designed to generate revenue, but rather to ensure that the entities fulfill the policy goals that their tax exemption was designed to achieve. The TE/GE Division was created to address four basic key customer needs: education and communication; rulings and agreements; examination; and customer account services.

Examination Function by Operating Divisions - The basic function of auditing tax returns is conducted by revenue agents assigned to each operating division. Revenue agents examine returns to apply the law to the facts in order to determine whether the taxpayer reported the correct tax return position. Revenue agents must apply their judgment and experience in weighing the taxpayer's and government's tax position, based on the applicable law. In conducting their duties, revenue agents (with appropriate managerial approval) have the broad authority to resolve issues based upon the application of tax law to the facts.[70] Examination supports the mission of the Service by maintaining an enforcement presence and encouraging the correct reporting by taxpayers of income, deduction and credit, estate, gift, employment, and certain excise taxes in order to instill the highest degree of public confidence in the tax system's integrity, fairness, and efficiency.71

---

[70] IRM 4.46.5.3(1).
[71] IRM 4.19.10.1(1).

You may wonder how the IRS decides to select a Federal tax return for examination. The IRS selects returns using a variety of methods, including72:

- Potential participants in abusive tax avoidance transactions — Some returns are selected based on information obtained by the IRS through efforts to identify promoters and participants of abusive tax avoidance transactions. Examples include information received from "John Doe" summonses issued to credit card companies and businesses and participant lists from promoters ordered by the courts to be turned over to the IRS.
- Computer Scoring — Some returns are selected for examination on the basis of computer scoring. Computer programs give each return numeric "scores". The Discriminant Function System (DIF) score rates the potential for change, based on past IRS experience with similar returns. The Unreported Income DIF (UIDIF) score rates the return for the potential of unreported income. IRS personnel screen the highest-scoring returns, selecting some for audit and identifying the items on these returns that are most likely to need review.
- Large Corporations — The IRS examines many large corporate returns annually.
- Information Matching — Some returns are examined because payer reports, such as Forms W-2 from employers or Form 1099 interest statements from banks, do not match the income reported on the tax return.
- Related Examinations — Returns may be selected for audit when they involve issues or transactions with other taxpayers, such as business partners or investors, whose returns were selected for examination.
- Other — Area offices may identify returns for examination in connection with local compliance projects. These projects require higher level management approval and deal with areas such as local compliance initiatives, return preparers or specific market segments.

Once a return is selected for examination, there are three different audit methods employed:

1. Correspondence audit – examination of the tax return is conducted solely by mail.
2. Office audit – the taxpayer will be invited to meet with the IRS revenue agent in an IRS field office.
3. Field audit – the examination will be set for a location that is not at an IRS location but rather at the taxpayer's site (home, place of business or taxpayer's representative's office)

In addition to the four operating divisions of the IRS that serve distinct taxpayers, groups and organizations, there are other principal offices within the IRS that provide specific tax support and functional capabilities.

---

72 https://www.irs.gov/newsroom/the-examination-audit-process.

- <u>IRS Office of Appeals</u> - The tax decision reached by the examiner may be appealed to a local Appeals Office, which is separate and independent of the operating division revenue agent who conducted the examination.[73] An Appeals Office is the only level of appeal within the IRS. Conferences with Appeals Office personnel may be conducted in person, through correspondence, or by telephone with the taxpayer or its authorized representative. The mission of Appeals is to "resolve tax controversies, without litigation, on a basis which is fair and impartial to both the government and the taxpayer, and in a manner that will enhance voluntary compliance and public confidence in the integrity and efficiency of the Service." IRM 8.1.1.1(2). Though staffed by IRS employees, Appeals Officers do not take sides in a tax dispute; rather these government officials take an objective point of view on each individual case with the goal of avoiding unnecessary litigation that is wasteful for both taxpayers and the government. Appeals has the authority to settle cases based upon hazards of litigation. For example, when there is uncertainty in the event of litigation, as to how a Court would interpret and apply the law or weigh the facts, Appeals utilizes techniques such as "mutual concession" and "split issue" settlements. Exam is not authorized to use these settlement techniques.[74]

  There is no requirement for a taxpayer to pursue Appeals settlement consideration. However, it behooves a taxpayer to proceed with this administrative opportunity to resolve an unagreed case. First, the function of the Office of Appeals (to resolve tax controversies, without litigation, on a basis which is fair and impartial to both the government and the taxpayer....) is fundamentally different than the Examination Division.   Second, requesting an Appeals conference in response to a 30-day letter is particularly important if the taxpayer later seeks the recovery of litigation costs under section 7430 (requiring taxpayer to "exhaust[] the administrative remedies available to such party within the Internal Revenue Service.")

  How important is a taxpayer's opportunity to pursue settlement consideration with the IRS Office of Appeals? In one recent case set in California where the IRS denied a taxpayer's request to proceed to the Office of Appeals, the taxpayer sued in U.S. District Court demanding Appeals' consideration. The complaint filed by the taxpayer raised two main arguments: (1) Revenue Procedure 2016-22, which permits the IRS to deny taxpayers access to Appeals in docketed cases for "sound tax administration," is invalid under the Administrative Procedure Act; and (2) because the IRS denied the taxpayer access to an independent administrative forum, the taxpayer is entitled to "Mandamus-Like Relief" and the district court must order the IRS to provide the taxpayer the opportunity to present its case at IRS Appeals. On May 14, 2018, the U.S. District Court for the Northern District of California sided with the IRS holding that taxpayers have no legally enforceable right to compel the IRS to

---

[73] https://www.irs.gov/government-entities/federal-state-local-governments/appeals-process.
[74] IRM 4.46.5.3(2).

refer cases to the Office of Appeals. Accordingly, the Court dismissed the taxpayer's complaint.75

- <u>IRS Taxpayer Advocate Service</u> - As an independent organization within the IRS, the Taxpayer Advocate Service helps taxpayers resolve problems and recommends changes that will prevent the problems. There is at least one TAS office in every state, the District of Columbia and Puerto Rico and at every IRS campus.

- <u>Return Preparer Office</u> - works to improve taxpayer compliance by providing comprehensive oversight and support of tax professionals. Specific goals of this office include efforts to register and promote a qualified tax professional community, improving the compliance and accuracy of tax returns prepared by tax preparers, engaging stakeholders to create an environment that fosters compliance and program improvement.

- <u>The Office of Professional Responsibility</u> - works to ensure that all tax practitioners, tax preparers, and other third parties in the tax system adhere to professional standards and follow the law. OPR's goals include the following: (1) Increase awareness and understanding of Circular 230 and OPR through outreach activities, and (2) Apply the principles of due process to the investigation, analysis, enforcement and litigation of Circular 230 cases. OPR's organizational structure includes three major segments: Office of the Director, Legal Analysis Branch, and Operations and Management Branch.

- <u>Criminal Investigation</u> - investigates potential criminal violations of the Internal Revenue Code and related financial crimes in a manner that fosters confidence in the tax system and compliance with the law. CI is comprised of approximately 3,700 employees worldwide, approximately 2,600 of whom are special agents whose investigative jurisdiction includes tax, money laundering and Bank Secrecy Act laws. While other federal agencies also have investigative jurisdiction for money laundering and some bank secrecy act violations, IRS is

---

[75] See <u>Facebook, Inc. & Subs., v. Internal Revenue Service</u>, 2018-U.S.T.C. ¶50,248 (USDC, ND CA). Earlier court decisions have all agreed that there is no general right for taxpayers to take tax cases to IRS Appeals. <u>Swanson v. Comm'r</u>, 106 T.C. 76, 99–100 (1996) (holding that no right exists to an IRS Appeals conference once a taxpayer's case is docketed in the Tax Court); <u>Estate of Weiss v. Comm'r</u>, 90 T.C.M. (CCH) 566, 2005 WL 3418160, at *1–2 (2005) (holding after enactment of the Restructuring and Reform Act of 1998 that taxpayers did not have a substantive right to take their case to IRS Appeals and that there was no statutory basis for such a right). <u>New Hope Servs., Inc. v. United States</u>, 285 F.3d 568, 572 (7th Cir. 2002) ("there is no provision in the procedural rules for a taxpayer request for an Appeals Office conference" for a case docketed in Tax Court) (citing <u>Swanson</u>, 106 T.C. at 99–100); <u>Vosters v. United States</u>, No. C-88-20458-WAI, 1989 WL 90554, at *2 (N.D. Cal. June 2, 1989) (rejecting claim that "the IRS violated its own procedural rules by denying the taxpayer an administrative hearing before the Appellant Review Division" because the IRS's "procedural rules are directory rather than mandatory") (citing <u>Rosenberg v. Comm'r</u>, 450 F.2d 529, 533 (10th Cir. 1971)).

the only federal agency that can investigate potential criminal violations of the Internal Revenue Code.

- Whistleblower Office - The IRS Whistleblower Office, which was established by the Tax Relief and Health Care Act of 2006, will process tips received from individuals who spot tax problems in their workplace, while conducting day-to-day personal business or anywhere else they may be encountered. An award worth between 15 and 30 percent of the total proceeds that IRS collects could be paid, if the IRS moves ahead based on the information provided. Under the law, these awards will be paid when the amount identified by the whistleblower (including taxes, penalties and interest) is more than $2 million. If the taxpayer is an individual, they must have at least $200,000 in gross income. The Whistleblower Office will be responsible for assessing and analyzing incoming tips. After determining their degree of credibility, the case will be assigned to the appropriate IRS office for further investigation.

- The Office of Chief Counsel - The Chief Counsel for the Internal Revenue Service provides advice to the IRS Commissioner on all matters pertaining to the interpretation, administration and enforcement of the Internal Revenue laws, represents the IRS in litigation, and provides all other legal support needed by the IRS to carry out its mission of serving America's taxpayers. In carrying out these responsibilities, Counsel must interpret the law with complete impartiality so that the American pubic will have confidence that the tax law is being applied with integrity and fairness.

Of all of these specific units within the IRS, the general flow of a case moves through just three of these units:

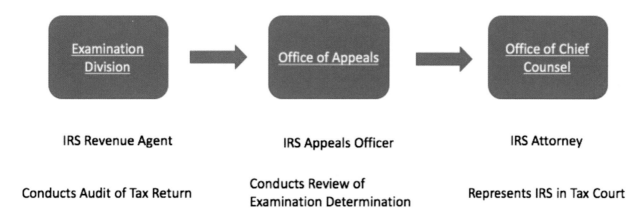

Examination Division	Office of Appeals	Office of Chief Counsel
IRS Revenue Agent	IRS Appeals Officer	IRS Attorney
Conducts Audit of Tax Return	Conducts Review of Examination Determination	Represents IRS in Tax Court

If an IRS examination remains unagreed after the conclusion of an audit, then the taxpayer will receive a "30-day letter." In this letter, the taxpayer is presented with an opportunity to request Appeals consideration of their case. If the taxpayer decides to pursue this option, then the taxpayer submits a "protest letter" in response to the IRS 30-day letter. However, if the taxpayer elects not to pursue Appeals consideration of their case, then the IRS Examination function will issue a "90-day letter" also known as a statutory notice of deficiency. See I.R.C. § 6212. Thereafter, if the taxpayer files a petition with the U.S. Tax Court in response to the notice of deficiency, Counsel for the IRS will answer the case and forward the case for Appeals consideration. Rev. Proc. 87-24; Notice 2015-72, Sec. 3. Below is a slightly more in-depth flowchart of how an audit proceeds forward to Appeals and to courts for review.

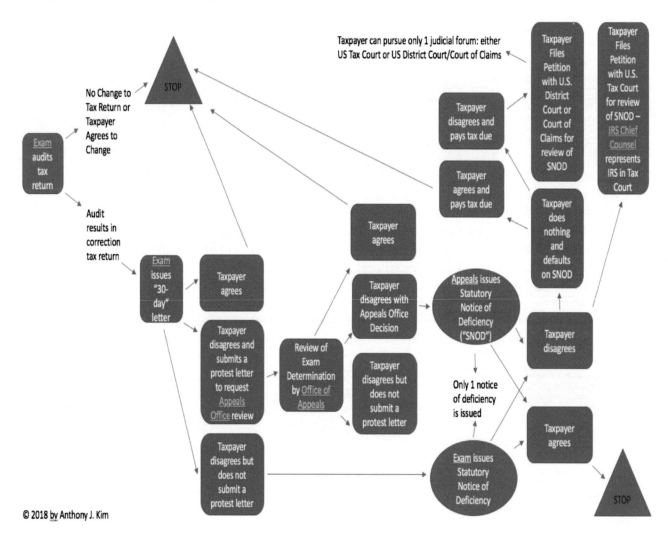

© 2018 by Anthony J. Kim

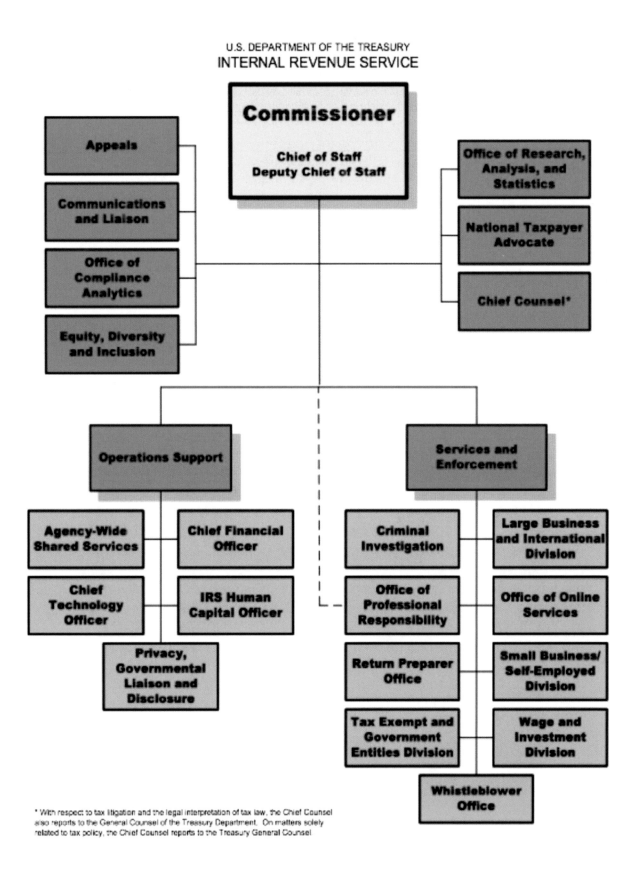

U.S. DEPARTMENT OF THE TREASURY
INTERNAL REVENUE SERVICE

Commissioner

Chief of Staff
Deputy Chief of Staff

Appeals

Communications and Liaison

Office of Compliance Analytics

Equity, Diversity and Inclusion

Office of Research, Analysis, and Statistics

National Taxpayer Advocate

Chief Counsel*

Operations Support

Agency-Wide Shared Services

Chief Financial Officer

Chief Technology Officer

IRS Human Capital Officer

Privacy, Governmental Liaison and Disclosure

Services and Enforcement

Criminal Investigation

Large Business and International Division

Office of Professional Responsibility

Office of Online Services

Return Preparer Office

Small Business/ Self-Employed Division

Tax Exempt and Government Entities Division

Wage and Investment Division

Whistleblower Office

* With respect to tax litigation and the legal interpretation of tax law, the Chief Counsel also reports to the General Counsel of the Treasury Department. On matters solely related to tax policy, the Chief Counsel reports to the Treasury General Counsel

b.Published Guidance Issued by the IRS

In order to fully grasp the various types of published guidance issued by the executive function delegated the responsibility over Title 26, tax practitioners must understand the role of the IRS. The mission of the IRS is to provide America's taxpayers top quality service by helping them understand and meet their tax responsibilities and by applying the tax law with integrity and fairness to all. It is the duty of the IRS to correctly apply the laws enacted by Congress; to determine the reasonable meaning of various Internal Revenue Code provisions in light of the Congressional purpose in enacting them; and to perform this work in a fair and impartial manner, with neither a government nor a taxpayer point of view.[76] At the heart of sound tax administration is interpretation of the Code. It is the responsibility of each person in the IRS charged with the duty of interpreting tax law to try to find the proper interpretation of the statutory provision and not to adopt a strained construction in the belief that he or she is "protecting the revenue." The revenue is properly protected only when the IRS can ascertain and apply the proper interpretation of the statute.[77]

By providing published guidance, the IRS executes its mission to assist taxpayers undertand and apply tax law. What is the process involved when the IRS issues published guidance? Each year the IRS and Treasury develop a Guidance Priority List (GPL), which is also sometimes referred to as the Priority Guidance Plan (or "business plan").[78] The GPL identifies the issues that will be addressed in published guidance during the business plan year. The IRS and Treasury solicit recommendations from the public for items that should be included on the GPL. The IRS and Treasury also consider recommendations from within the Service, the Office of Chief Counsel, and other government agencies. Interested parties may submit recommendations for guidance at any time during the year. When selecting projects for the GPL, the IRS and Treasury consider the following:

- Whether the recommended guidance resolves significant issues relevant to many taxpayers
- Whether the guidance may be appropriate for enhanced public involvement through the process described in Notice 2007-17, 2007-12 I.R.B. 748
- Whether the recommended guidance promotes sound tax administration
- Whether the recommended guidance can be drafted in a manner that will enable taxpayers to understand and apply the guidance easily
- Whether the IRS can enforce the recommended guidance on a uniform basis
- Whether the recommended guidance reduces controversy or lessens the burden on taxpayers or the IRS

In addition to the factors described above, the IRS and Treasury consider whether the guidance is required by statute, the number of taxpayers affected by the proposed

---

[76] IRM 32.1.1.1(1) (8-11-2004). See Rev. Proc. 64-22, 1964-1 C.B. 689; 1964 IRB LEXIS 361; REV. PROC. 64-22 (January, 1964).
[77] IRM 32.1.1.1(2) (8-11-2004).
[78] CCDM 32.2.2.6.2 (09-16-2011).

guidance, and the resources available to complete all the guidance projects proposed for a particular year.79 The IRS and Treasury strive to include the most important suggestions for guidance on the GPL each year.[80]

So, what are the sources for these guidance project issues? Issues to be published are identified from many sources, including, but not limited to:

- Issues in various types of cases, such as technical advice and letter rulings
- Comments and suggestions from the Commissioner and other Service personnel
- Comments and suggestions from taxpayers, practitioners, outside organizations (including issues raised through the industry issues resolution program), tax publications and periodicals, continuing legal education programs for tax professionals, and other comments on tax law directed at professionals or the taxpaying public
- Comments and suggestions from the Chief Counsel, Deputy Chief Counsel, Associate Chief Counsel, and Division Counsel (and their staffs), and from Treasury personnel
- Announcements of acquiescence or nonacquiescence on Tax Court opinions
- Chief Counsel Notices bearing the title "CHANGE IN LITIGATION POSITION" ("CLP")
- Recently enacted legislation
- Common issues in private letter ruling requests (Associate Chief Counsel offices should annually review the uniform issue list codes related to private letter rulings issued during the past year to determine whether the issuance of published guidance may be appropriate for any of the common issues in these requests).[81]

Despite the duty to provide clear and consistent tax guidance, it remains a reality of tax administration that the IRS may issue *evolving* guidance over time. Consider, for example, the question of whether the costs associated with breast feeding are deductible. For many years, the IRS's position was that such costs did not fall within Section 213 that allowed medical expense deductions. See the June 9, 2004 letter from Acting Assistant Secretary for Tax Policy, below.

---

[79] The amount of IRS resources that are available to devote for guidance projects depends in large part on the budget allotted by Congress to the IRS each year.
[80] CCDM 32.2.2.6.2 (04-28-2009).
[81] CCDM 32.2.2.6.1 (09-16-2011).

DEPARTMENT OF THE TREASURY
WASHINGTON, D.C. 20220
JUN 08 2004

Dear

Thank you for the letter addressed to Internal Revenue Service Commissioner Mark W. Everson about breastfeeding equipment and services. I am responding because the letter concerns a matter of tax policy.

The letter expresses concern that funds from a tax-favored health care flexible spending account (FSA) may not be used for the rental of an electric breast pump. Generally, FSA funds are for medical care. The Internal Revenue Code defines medical care to include the diagnosis, cure, mitigation, treatment, or prevention of disease. Consequently, medical care would not include goods or services that are merely beneficial to general health, but are not for the purpose of affecting any structure or function of the body. Under current law, therefore, the cost of an electric breast pump, although it may have many benefits as mentioned in your letter, would not come within the definition of a medical care expense for FSA purposes. It is not within the power of the IRS to classify breastfeeding equipment or services as medical care in contravention of current law. A change to the Internal Revenue Code must be made by Congress.

The Breastfeeding Promotion bill (H.R. 2790), introduced in the House of Representatives on July 18, 2003, would amend the Civil Rights Act of 1964 and the Federal Food, Drug, and Cosmetic Act, as well as the Internal Revenue Code. The amendments would include a tax credit for employer expenses for breast pumps, or other equipment or tangible personal property, and consultation services, to assist employed mothers to breastfeed or express milk for their children, along with an expansion of the definition of medical care to include breastfeeding equipment and services.

Your letter asserts that most women who have children incur reduced earnings, in addition to numerous child-care costs. The tax law already includes several provisions for the benefit of parents and children, such as the dependency exemption and the dependent care credit. In particular, this Administration has championed an increase in the child tax credit. As a tax policy question, we will review the legislative proposal with a view to why breastfeeding would represent a particular expense separable from other child-care costs, why breastfeeding would be subsidized most effectively through the tax system, and the consequences of treating the costs of breastfeeding equipment in the same manner as costs for medical care.

Thank you for writing on this important matter.

Sincerely,

Gregory F. Jenner
Acting Assistant Secretary (Tax Policy)

Later, after receiving numerous reports from Senators, Congressman and medical professionals pointing out the mounting research in support of the medical benefits from breast feeding, the IRS reversed its position and issued guidance stating its new position in Announcement 2011-14 that such costs are deductible. See IRS Announcement 2011-14, below.

Part IV – Items of General Interest

Lactation Expenses as Medical Expenses

Announcement 2011-14

The Internal Revenue Service has concluded that breast pumps and supplies that assist lactation are medical care under § 213(d) of the Internal Revenue Code because, like obstetric care, they are for the purpose of affecting a structure or function of the body of the lactating woman. Therefore, if the remaining requirements of § 213(a) are met (for example, the taxpayer's total medical expenses exceed 7.5 percent of adjusted gross income), expenses paid for breast pumps and supplies that assist lactation are deductible medical expenses.

Amounts reimbursed for these expenses under flexible spending arrangements, Archer medical savings accounts, health reimbursement arrangements, or health savings accounts are not income to the taxpayer.

The Service will revise Publication 502, Medical and Dental Expenses, to include this information.

Reviewing Code section 213, readers will note that Congress did not include specific statutory language to address breast pumps or related costs. Nor did Congress amend the Code between 2004 (when the Treasury's letter was issued expressing the non-deductibility of electric breast pump costs) and 2011 when the IRS issued Announcement 2011-14. The IRS filled this statutory gap in the Code by applying its understanding of Congressional intent specifically related to the medical benefits from breast feeding. Later, with additional medical research presented to the agency, the IRS updated its position with respect to costs related to breast feeding reversing its prior stance. Additional facts and medical evidence tipped the scale resulting in a change of administrative position, interpretation and guidance.

One side may view the IRS as having issued erroneous guidance initially with respect to the deductibility of breast feeding costs. As the agency accumulated a better understanding of the facts, it updated its tax position. Another side may view the IRS as having issued erroneous guidance in Announcement 2011-14 creating another tax deduction where none existed before for such costs. If, for a moment, we concede that there is no perfect answer under these facts, then do you think that the IRS carried out its responsibility by providing the best determination under the facts at each point in time? Or, should Congress have addressed the answer head-on by enacting a change in the code? But, if Congress decides to change the code to address each new situation that arises over time, what will result with the tax code? How will Congress reasonably keep pace with changes arising every year? How voluminous will the Internal Revenue Code become if Congress added to the tax code every time a new fact pattern arises calling for an answer?

Consider two additional examples of whether specific costs qualify as "medical care" under section 213 and, therefore, qualify as allowed deductions under the tax code:

- Can costs for tuition and boarding at a "special school" qualify as deductible "medical care" expenses?

    Answer: Yes. Again, the code establishes only basic language that costs for "medical care" qualify as deductible expenses. Specific guidance is provided in Treas. Reg. § 1.213-1(e)(1)(v) to address the precise question of whether "special school" costs can qualify as "medical care." Court decisions offer additional authority on this issue on how specific facts (present and/or absent) will lead to a specific tax result. See, e.g., Fay v. Commissioner, 76 T.C. 408 (1981); Greisdorf v. Commissioner, 54 T.C. 1684 (1970).

    Note: *Congress did not include additional statutory language to address these whether these expenses qualify as "medical care" after the Treasury issued guidance through regulations or the courts rendered decisions on these costs. Can Congress enact specific changes to the tax code to specifically address the deductibility of these costs? Absolutely, but it chose not to amend the code to specifically address these costs.*

- Whether hormone therapy and sex re-assignment surgery constitute "medical care" within the meaning of section 213?

    Answer: Yes. In O'Donnabhain v. Commissioner, 134 T.C. 34, 52 (2010), the U.S. Tax Court rejected the government's position that such costs related to gender re-assignment were nondeductible "cosmetic surgery or other similar procedures" under section 213(d)(9) because they were directed at improving petitioner's appearance and did not treat an illness or disease, meaningfully promote the proper function of the body, or ameliorate a deformity. The Court rejected the government's position and held that such costs qualified as "medical care" under section 213. After the government lost the case, it issued AOD 2011-03 with a recommendation of "Acquiescence" to the court decision in O'Donnabhain and stated that it will no longer take the position that hormone therapy and sex reassignment surgery do not treat a medically recognized disease or promote the proper function of the body.

    Note: *Congress did not include additional statutory language to address these* *whether these expenses qualify as "medical care" after the court rendered its decision on these costs or the government issued is AOD. Can Congress enact specific changes to code to specifically address the deductibility of these costs? Yes, but it chose not to amend the code to specifically address these costs.*

The point of reviewing these additional examples is to understand that the myriad facts that arise in life to test the application of static law cannot always lead to statutory answers. Rather, administrative or judicial responses present expedient (hopefully) guidance for taxpayers on how to comply with tax law. But, for any set of facts or situation, Congress always maintains the final word on whether to amend the statute to specifically address application of a tax result if it so chooses.

Congress - the Final Word on the Tax Code

The IRS strives to correctly interpret and apply the Code. But, what happens if IRS guidance is determined by Congress to conflict with the legislative intent of the drafters of the statute? Consider the issuance of IRS Notice 2008-83. Congress enacted Section 382 to prevent tax-motivated acquisitions where companies were purchased just to sweep up existing losses for tax advantage. On September 30, 2008, the IRS issued Notice 2008-83 in an effort to provide guidance for the struggling banking sector by allowing acquiring banks the ability to deduct built-in losses of any banks they acquired that possessed a portfolio of loans that had fallen in value.
In response to IRS Notice 2008-83, Congress enacted The American Recovery and Reinvestment Act of 2009, also called "ARRA," signed into law revoking Notice 2008-83. On February 17, 2009, ARRA was signed into federal law. ARRA provides that the IRS is not authorized under federal law to provide exemptions or special rules that are restricted to particular industries or classes of taxpayer, and that Notice 2008-83 is inconsistent with the Congressional intent of federal law. In addition, ARRA provided that although IRS's legal authority to prescribe Notice 2008-83 is doubtful, for taxpayers who have already relied upon its guidance, it is effective only for ownership changes occurring on or before January 16, 2009.

In another example, Congress enacted a statutory amendment in response to the IRS' interpretation of statute that it determined could not be allowed to stand. Back in 1999, a taxpayer requested assistance from the IRS in determining the proper application of claiming a dependency exemption on their federal tax return. Section 151(a) of the Internal Revenue Code allows a deduction for the dependency exemption provided by section 151(c). Under section 152 (a) of the Internal Revenue Code, generally, the term "dependent" includes a child of a taxpayer **if the taxpayer provided over half of the child's support for the calendar year** in which the taxable year of the taxpayer begins. Treas. Reg. § 1.152-1(a)(2)(i) defines the term "support" by example. It states that support "includes food, shelter, clothing, medical and dental care, education, and the like." Can parents claim their child as a dependent, who otherwise qualifies as a "dependent," but for the fact that the child is not living at home, thus, leaving the parents unable to establish that they provide "over half of the child's support" in that year? <u>Section 152 provided clear authority to address this question.</u> And, the IRS likewise provided clear administrative guidance to reflect guidance in applying the relevant facts to law in a Chief Counsel Advice ("CCA"), below. One fact in the specific taxpayer's situation that was not addressed in the statute was critical – **the taxpayer's child had been kidnapped.** But, the IRS could not point to any clear language or legislative history to address the situation of a kidnapped child any differently for purposes of issuing guidance. And, so, the following CCA was issued in July, 2000:

DEPARTMENT OF THE TREASURY
INTERNAL REVENUE SERVICE
WASHINGTON, D.C. 20224

OFFICE OF
CHIEF COUNSEL

July 25, 2000   CC:IT&A:2
                       WTA-N-108040-00

Number: **200034029**
Release Date: 8/25/2000
UIL: 152.06-00

MEMORANDUM FOR RICHARD POPRICK, CUSTOMER SERVICE DIVISION

FROM: George Baker, Assistant to the Branch Chief CC:IT&A:2

SUBJECT: Support for Kidnapped Child
               WTA-N-108040-00

This Chief Counsel advice is in response to your memorandum dated April 6, 2000. Chief Counsel advice is not binding on Examination or Appeals and is not a final case determination. Under section 6110(k)(3) of the Internal Revenue Code, this document is not to be used or cited as precedent.

Your memorandum raises the following issues: (1) Do the parents of a minor child who was kidnapped by a person not related to the child meet the support test for taking a dependency exemption for the child in the year of the kidnapping, if the parents provided the sole support for the child before the kidnapping, and the child is missing at the end of the year. (2) If the parents meet the support test for the year of the kidnapping, do the parents meet the support test in later years if the parents continue to maintain a room for the child and incur expenses to search for the child.

Section 151(a) of the Internal Revenue Code allows a deduction for the dependency exemption provided by section 151(c).

Under section 152 (a) of the Internal Revenue Code, generally, the term "dependent" includes a child of a taxpayer if the taxpayer provided over half of the child's support for the calendar year in which the taxable year of the taxpayer begins.

Section 1.152-1(a)(2)(i) of the Income Tax Regulations defines the term "support" by example. It states that support "includes food, shelter, clothing, medical and dental care, education, and the like."

In the absence of any legal authority directly on point, we conclude that in the circumstances described in the statement of the issue, the parents should be presumed to meet the support test of section 152(a) if, before the kidnapping, the parents provided over half of the support for the child. Under the circumstances described in the statement of the issue, proof of total support for the period before

2

the kidnapping and proof that the parents provided over half of that support should suffice. In favor of this presumption, we note that on the facts presented, no other person would be entitled to the dependency exemption for the child. See section 152(a), which requires that a dependent be related to the taxpayer or be a member of the taxpayer's household for the entire year.

For taxable years after the year of the kidnapping, although the issue is not free from doubt, we do not think that the parents meet the support test of section 152(a), even if the parents continue to maintain a room for the child and continue to expend funds searching for the child. We do not think that under these circumstances, these expenses constitute support. Cf. Otmishi v. Commissioner, T.C.M. 1980-472. In Otmishi, the court stated that the taxpayer did not provide any support for his child in the year in issue, although he expended amounts to locate his child who had been taken by the child's mother.

If you have any questions, please call George Baker at (202) 622-4920.

News coverage of this administrative guidance impacting the parents of kidnapped children came out quickly. The New York Times reported, "Several tax experts said….that they agreed with the lawyer's advisory opinion – though not all were confident how long it would stand."[82]

In response to this unpopular administrative guidance, Congress enacted the Working Families Tax Relief Act of 2004, Pub. L. 108-311, Sec. 201, to amend section 152(f), by adding the following language effective for tax years beginning in 2005:

> (6) Treatment of missing children
> > (A) In general. Solely for the purposes referred to in subparagraph (B), a child of the taxpayer—
> > > (i) who is presumed by law enforcement authorities to have been kidnapped by someone who is not a member of the family of such child or the taxpayer, and
> > > (ii) who had, for the taxable year in which the kidnapping occurred, the same principal place of abode as the taxpayer for more than one-half of the portion of such year before the date of the kidnapping,

shall be treated as meeting the requirement of subsection (c)(1)(B) with respect to a taxpayer for all taxable years ending during the period that the child is kidnapped.

---

[82] "I.R.S. Rules That Kidnapped Child Earns One-Year Exemption," The New York Times, August 31, 2000, by David Cay Johnston.

(B) Purposes. Subparagraph (A) shall apply solely for purposes of determining—
    (i) the deduction under section 151(c),
    (ii) the credit under section 24 (relating to child tax credit),
    (iii) whether an individual is a surviving spouse or a head of a household (as such terms are defined in section 2), and
    (iv) the earned income credit under section 32.

Congress can, and will in specific instances, enact legislation to specifically address unique facts to make clear how it wants tax law to apply. But, practically, it is more expedient for the executive branch to issue administrative guidance on the multitude of tax issues that arise year after year than it is for Congress to constantly amend the tax code to address every factual scenario that requires a direct answer.

Consider as an example the recent surge of data system breaches that has resulted in the potential for widespread identify theft. What happens when a customer's private information stored by a company is stolen? The company responds by providing identify theft protection services for its customers who may later suffer harm from their identity being stolen. But, this tax question arises: if Customer A receives $300 value of identity theft protection services from Company X in tax year 201X as a result of a data breach at Company X, then has Customer A received taxable gross income in tax year 201X that he/she must report?

Let's begin our analysis by looking to the applicable code section that address gross income. Section 61 provides a very broad definition for "gross income" to mean "all income from whatever source derived….." Unless Congress provides an exception, the default statutory result is that everything constitutes gross income. Well, Customer A received identity theft services paid for by Company X. The value of the identify theft protection service was $300. Under section 61, Customer A received $300 of gross income.

Under the unusual circumstances presented by data breaches and the resulting identity theft dilemma, the IRS provided guidance in Announcement 2015-22. This guidance stated, in part:

> Questions have been raised concerning the taxability of identity protection services provided at no cost to customers, employees, or other individuals whose personal information may have been compromised in a data breach. Existing guidance does not specifically address these questions.
>
> **The IRS will not assert that an individual whose personal information may have been compromised in a data breach must include in gross income the value of the identity protection services provided by the organization that experienced the data breach.** Additionally, the IRS will not assert that an employer providing identity protection services to employees whose personal information may have been compromised in a data breach of the employer's (or employer's agent or service provider's) recordkeeping system must include the

value of the identity protection services in the employees' gross income and wages. The IRS will also not assert that these amounts must be reported on an information return (such as Form W–2 or Form 1099–MISC) filed with respect to such individuals.

(emphasis added to original text). Given the broad statutory definition for gross income under section 61, the IRS could not take a guidance position stating that value received by a customer/taxpayer was NOT income. Such a statement would be contrary to statute. Rather, the IRS stated that it "**will not assert that**..." such value received by the customer whose personal information may have been compromised in a data breach must be included in gross income. Through Announcement 2015-22, the executive tax agency provided guidance on how it would enforce section 61 in the context of the receipt identify protection services provided to data breach victims. This guidance promotes tax compliance because taxpayers clearly understand how to fulfill their tax reporting requirements under these facts.

As we can see from the examples, above, in very limited circumstances, Congress can take direct action to confirm its statutory intent and to limit the exercise of the executive's function, as in the case involving Notice 2008-83. In other instances, Congress may advocate for the IRS to change its existing interpretation as in the case of breast feeding equipment costs and avoid adding more text to the tax code. Congress can enact changes to the Code or decide to do nothing and allow the IRS to issue guidance as in the case involving identity protection services.

3. Treasury Regulations

To fulfill its mission, the Treasury and the Internal Revenue Service promulgate interpretations of the Internal Revenue Code using two primary formats: (1) Treasury regulations, which can be adopted pursuant to specific or general authority and which Treasury issues in proposed, temporary, and final form; and (2) a collection of rulings, procedures and notices that the IRS issues and publishes in the Internal Revenue Bulletin each week and the Cumulative Bulletin annually.

Regulations are issued by the Internal Revenue Service and Treasury Department to provide guidance for new legislation and to address issues that arise with respect to existing Code sections, (e.g., a court decision that invalidates part of a regulation, a new financial product, or an abusive business transaction). Some Treasury regulations are issued pursuant to specific legislative grants contained in substantive provisions of the Code to fill acknowledged statutory gaps.[83] Most, however, are adopted under the general authority provided by IRC §7805(a) to the Secretary of the Treasury to "prescribe all needful rules and regulations for the enforcement of" the Code.[84] The Treasury, the IRS, taxpayers, and the courts all operate with the understanding that both specific and general authority Treasury regulations are legally binding. The government routinely asserts, and the circuit courts generally concur, that legal

---

[83] See, e.g., I.R.C. §§ 1502, 6014(b), 6015(h).
[84] I.R.C. § 7805(a).

interpretations advanced in both specific and general authority Treasury regulations carry the force of law for purposes of judicial deference.[85] The Treasury and the IRS purport to comply with Administrative Procedures Act (5 U.S.C. §551) rulemaking requirements in promulgating Treasury regulations.[86] Treasury usually publishes a notice of proposed rulemaking in the Federal Register and offers the opportunity for public comment at some point for most of its regulation projects.

Two types of notices provide information to the public about the government's work on regulations: (1) an advance notice of proposed rulemaking, aka "ANPRM"; and (2) a notice of proposed rulemaking, aka "NPRM."

- ANPRM – the ANPRM describes a problem or situation, announces that the agency is considering regulatory action, describes the agency's anticipated regulatory approach, and seeks input from the public about the issues, the need for regulation, and the adequacy of the agency's proposed regulatory action. When an ANPRM is issued, it is typically issued early in the rulemaking process, but can be issued at any time in the regulatory process it becomes clear that an ANPRM would be the most appropriate form of guidance.[87]

- NPRM – An NPRM announces to the public that an agency is considering modifying regulations as published in the Code of Federal Regulations (CFR) or issuing rules on matters not addressed in existing regulations. In either circumstance, an NPRM sets out the proposed regulatory text. NPRMs contain a preamble that explains the rules and requests public comments on the suggested changes. NPRMs may also contain a Notice of Hearing. Unlike Treasury Decisions (TDs), NPRMs do not have full force and legal effect unless and until they are adopted as final regulations. Prior to adoption, proposed regulations may be withdrawn or modified at any time.Taxpayers generally may not rely on proposed regulations for planning purposes, except if there are no applicable final or temporary regulations in force and there is an express statement in the proposed regulations that taxpayers may rely on them currently.[88] If there are applicable final or temporary regulations in

---

[85] United States v. Mead Corp., 533 U.S. 218, 226-27 (2001); Chevron U.S.A. Inc. v. Natural Resources Defense Council, Inc., 467 U.S. 837, 842-43 (1984).

[86] See, e.g., Treas. Reg. § 601.601(a)(2) (2007) ("Where required by 5 U.S.C. [§] 553 and in such other instances as may be desirable, the Commissioner publishes in the *Federal Register* general notice of proposed rules.").

[87] CCDM 32.1.1.2.

[88] See IRM 32.1.1.2.2(2) (8-2-2018)("Taxpayers generally may not rely on proposed regulations for planning purposes, except if there are no applicable final or temporary regulations in force and there is an express statement in the preamble to the proposed regulations that taxpayers may rely on them currently.")

For example, the preamble to proposed Treasury Regulations issued on August 16, 2018 relating to new code section 199A enacted on December 22, 2017 by section 11011 of P.L. 115-97 provided, in part, as follows:

> "....proposed §§ 1.199A-1 through 1.199A-6 generally are proposed to apply to taxable years ending after the date of publication of a Treasury decision adopting these rules as final regulations. However, **taxpayers may rely on the rules set forth in**

force, taxpayers may only rely on proposed regulations for planning purposes in the limited circumstance if the proposed regulations contain an express statement permitting taxpayers to rely on them currently, notwithstanding the existence of the final or temporary regulations. If there are no final or temporary regulations currently in force addressing a particular matter, but there are proposed regulations on point, the Office of Chief Counsel generally should look to the proposed regulations to determine the office's position on the issue. The Office of Chief Counsel ordinarily should not take any position in litigation or advice that would yield a result that would be harsher to the taxpayer than what the taxpayer would be allowed under the proposed regulations.

Regulations are written by the Office of Chief Counsel, Internal Revenue Service, and are approved by the Department of the Treasury.[89] There are three classes of regulations: proposed, temporary, and final.[90]

- Proposed Regulations — Proposed regulations provide guidance concerning Treasury's interpretation of a Code section. The public is given an opportunity to comment on a proposed regulation and a public hearing may be held if a sufficient number of requests to speak at a hearing are received. Generally, Taxpayers may rely on a proposed regulation, although they are not required to do so.[91] Examiners, however, should follow proposed regulations, unless the proposed regulation is in conflict with an existing final or temporary regulation.

- Temporary Regulations — Temporary regulations are often issued soon after a major change in the law to provide guidance for the public and Internal Revenue Service employees with respect to procedural and computational matters. Temporary regulations are authoritative and have the same weight as final regulations.

- Final Regulations — Final regulations supersede both temporary and proposed regulations. A final regulation is effective, unless stated otherwise, the day that it is published as a Treasury Decision in the Federal Register. Final regulations are published as Treasury Decisions (T.D.'s) in the Federal Register, and the I.R.B. They are then codified into Title 26 of the Code of Federal Regulations. Regulations are numbered with a prefix or "part number" identifying the general area to which they are related. The prefix "1." is for income tax regulations; "20." is for estate tax regulations; "53." is for foundation and similar excise taxes; etc., the first group of numbers

---

proposed §§ 1.199A-1 through 1.199A-6, in their entirety, until the date a Treasury decision adopting these regulations as final regulations is published in the Federal Register." \

[89] A preamble, which provides an introduction of the regulation, may be used as an aid to interpret the regulation it accompanies. Krokowski v. Commissioner, 114 T.C. 366, 392 (2000); see, e.g., DHL v. Commissioner, 285 F. 3d 1210, 1222 (9th Cir. 2002)(relying on preamble to interpret Treas. Reg. §1.482-2(d)); cf. Armco, Inc. v. Commissioner, 87 T.C. 865, 868-869 (1986) (determining that a preamble can assist in interpreting a regulation but that a post-hoc statement by one involved in the drafting process is of no consequence).
[90] IRM 4.10.7.2.3.3.
[91] See the discussion of proposed Treasury regulations in the discussion of NPRM, above, for more specific guidance.

following the decimal indicates the section of the Code that the regulation interprets. The last group represents the sequence of the regulation but does not correlate directly with the sequence designation of the Code.

What is the difference between a Temporary regulation and a Final regulation? Final regulations are issued after considering the public comments on the proposed regulations whereas Temporary regulations are issued without public review or comments due to the urgency of issuing immediate guidance.[92] The preamble of a final rule also cites to the underlying NPRM and other rulemaking history (for example, an ANPRM), discusses and analyzes public comments received and explains the agency's final decision. A final regulation is almost always preceded by an NPRM.

Treasury Regulations follow the same numbering convention as the *Internal Revenue Code*, so that the Regulations for Section 121 will be numbered 1.121. The prefix indicates the type of regulation represented -- here, the prefix "1" indicates that these are final regulations issued under an income tax statute. A prefix of "301" indicates that a regulation is a final procedural or administrative regulation. A prefix between 5 and 18 indicates that the regulation is a "temporary" regulation (discussed later in this exercise). Regulations are also issued under other titles of the United States Code -- for example, regulations are issued under the Bankruptcy Code and the Federal Criminal Code. These regulations will have different prefixes than regs issued under the Internal Revenue Code (Title 26 of the U.S. Code).

Regulations often have suffixes as well as prefixes. For example, the regulations under §162 (Itemized Deductions for Individuals and Corporations) are numbered §1.162-1 through §1.162-29. These suffixes do *not* correspond to any particular sequence of subsections of the Internal Revenue Code. (For example, §162 itself, while relatively lengthy, only has 16 subsections). The suffixes merely represent different topics within the regulations for a particular statute. For example, Treas. Reg. §1.162-1 addresses the general rule for allowance of deductions, while Treas. Reg. §1.162-8 addresses the proper treatment of excessive compensation payments (not addressed in the Code itself), and Treas. Reg. §1.162-29 governs the tax treatment of expenditures incurred to influence legislation.

---

[92] CCDM 32.1.1.2.4.

4. The Problem of Outdated Regulations

The rapid change of the Internal Revenue Code by Congress many times leave regulations limping behind to keep pace. As the IRS and Treasury attempt to keep pace by issuing new regulations in response to changes to existing code sections and entirely new code sections, the problem arises with respect to existing regulations that do not reflect recent changes to the Code.[93]

This problem of outdated regulations is sometimes reflected by the publisher of Treasury regulations in the paragraph heading or symbols when accessed via electronic tax law research or printed text. It remains the responsibility of the tax researcher to determine whether published regulations remain effective or have become outdated.

CCH, RIA and other secondary sources provide readers with blanket warnings that a regulation may be outdated. For example, if you are reading Treas. Reg. §1.162-7, Congress amended some part or perhaps all of the underlying Internal Revenue Code section 162. If Congress amended some other part of Section 162, it may not have any impact on Treas. Reg. §1.162-7. However, there **may** be an impact. *E.g.*, all or part of this regulation may be outdated and no longer effective after change to the underlying code section. So, what **must** a practitioner do when presented with such a warning?

- **Step 1** – Look at the warning provided. There is a P.L. citation next to the warning. Search the IRC and find the exact P.L. section in the historical amendments under the affected code section.
- **Step 2** – Determine exactly what Congress changed in this P.L. for the affected code section.
- **Step 3** – Review the Treasury Regulation you believe provides guidance impacting your issue/analysis.
- **Step 4** – Compare the P.L. changes to the Treasury Regulation. If Congress changed the law and this change presents a conflict with the Treasury Regulation as currently published, then you have an "OUTDATED" regulation. You cannot rely on this Treasury Regulation with respect the amended statutory provision(s) as of the effective date of the new provision. Alternatively, if you determine that the change made by Congress in the identified P.L. does not impact the Treasury regulation, then the guidance still has the "force and effect of law."

As noted above, a change of the code by Congress may create an outdated Treasury regulation. However, a new or modified interpretation of a code section by the Treasury may also create an outdated, or limited effective period for, Treasury regulations.

To better understand how regulations may work in work in real practice, let's consider the following example:

---

[93] See IRM 4.10.7.2.3.7 (1-1-2006).

- Section 6404(e)(1) authorizes the Comissioner to abate (e.g., reverse) assessed interest attributable to error or delay in an IRS officer or employee's performance of a ministerial act. However, section 6404(e) does not define the term "ministerial act."
- Temp. Treas. Reg. §301.6404-2T(b), 52 Fed. Reg. 30163 (Aug. 13, 1987), defines "ministerial act."
- "Ministerial act" was later defined under Treas. Reg. §301.6404-2(d)(1) as well. This final Treasury regulation was issued on December 18, 1998, effective for interest accruing on deficiencies or payments of tax described in section 6212(a) for tax years beginning after July 30, 1996.
- Section 6404(h) authorizes the Tax Court to determine whether the IRS's failure to abate interest is an abuse of discretion and, if so, then to order an abatement.
- A taxpayer argues that an IRS officer committed error in performing a ministerial act and, therefore, requests that the IRS abate assessed interest as authorized under section 6404(e)(1). The IRS officer's alleged error in performing a "ministerial act" occurred during the period December 2, 1993 through October 26, 1994.

Question 1: Which definition of "ministerial act" applies to the period December 2, 1993 through October 26, 1994 to apply section 6404(e)(1)?
- o Temp. Treas. Reg. §301.6404-2T(b); or
- o Treas. Reg. §301.6404-2(d)(1)

- The period at issue: December 2, 1993 through October 26, 1994
- Temp. Treas. Reg. §301.6404-2T(b) was issued on August 13, 1987. We must consider how long this "Temporary" regulations remains effective.
  - o Sec. 6232(a) of the Technical and Miscellaneous Revenue Act of 1988 (TAMRA 1988), Pub. L. 100-647, 102 Stat. 3342, 3734-3735, added subsec. (e) to sec. 7805. Sec. 7805(e)(2) provides that "Any temporary regulation shall expire within 3 years after the date of issuance of such regulation." Sec. 7805(e)(2) applies to any temporary regulation issued **after Nov. 20, 1988**. TAMRA 1988 sec. 6232(b), 102 Stat. at 3735. The regulation herein involved was issued before August 13, 1987 (so, on or before Nov. 20, 1988), and thus the "sunset" provision of sec. 7805(e)(2) does not apply to this regulation. Temp. Treas. Reg. §301.6404-2T(b) applies for the period at issue.
- Final Treas. Reg. §301.6404-2(d)(1) was issued on December 18, 1998, effective for interest accruing on deficiencies or payments of tax described in section 6212(a) for tax years **beginning after July 30, 1996**.

Answer to Question 1: Temp. Treas. Reg. §301.6404-2T(b) provides the applicable definition of "ministerial act" by the IRS applies through July 30, 1996. The normal 3-year effective period of a temporary regulation is extended for Temp. Treas. Reg. §301.6404-2T(b) because it was issued on August 13, 1987, before the effective date (after Nov. 20, 1988) of section 7805(e). However, the new definition of "ministerial act" as defined under Treas. Reg. §301.6404-2(d)(1) applies beginning July 31, 1996 based on the effective date of this final Treasury regulation. So, for the period December 2,

1993 through October 26, 1994, the definition of "ministerial act" under Temp. Treas. Reg. §301.6404-2T(b) applies.[94]

5. Other Published Guidance

Revenue Rulings, Revenue Procedures, and Notices are less formal than Treasury regulations but are all nevertheless official and authoritative pronouncements of the IRS. All of these documents inform the public about the decision making of the IRS regardless of any limitation that they may not be cited as precedent.[95]

The IRS will occasionally solicit public comments with respect to Revenue Rulings, Revenue Procedures, and Notices. See, e.g., IRS Notice 2008-80, 2008-40 I.R.B. 820 (seeking comments on proposed Revenue Procedure); IRS Notice 2007-59, 2007-30 I.R.B. 135 (same).

(1) Revenue Rulings - The Internal Revenue Manual defines a revenue ruling as "an official interpretation by the IRS of the tax laws, related statutes, treaties, and regulations published in the Internal Revenue Bulletin. It is the conclusion of the IRS on how the law is applied to a specific set of facts."[96] The IRS acknowledges in the IRM that revenue rulings do not have the force and effect of Treasury Regulations, but still may be used as precedents.[97] The Treasury regulations warn that reliance on a revenue ruling is appropriate only if the ruling has been unaffected by subsequent legislation, regulations, cases or other revenue rulings. Treas. Reg. §601.601(d)-(e) (2001). Absent a change in the underlying law cited in a revenue ruling, IRS employees must follow revenue rulings.[98]

How do courts view revenue rulings? Historically, courts treated revenue rulings as non-binding on taxpayers. See, e.g., Dixon v. United States, 381 U.S. 68, 73 (1965) (declaring that Congress had not given IRS rulings the "force of law"). The United States Tax Court in Rauenhorst v. Commissioner, 119 T.C. No. 9 (2002), stated the Tax Court's view regarding the limited effect of revenue rulings:

> We agree with respondent [IRS] that revenue rulings are not binding on this Court, or other Federal courts for that matter. See Frazier v. Comm'r, 111 T.C. 243, 248 (1998); N. Ind. Pub. Serv. Co. v. Comm'r, 105 T.C. 341, 350 (1995), aff'd. 115 F.3d 506 (7th Cir. 1997).

---

[94] See Goettee v. Commissioner, T.C. Memo. 2003-43.
[95] See Chapter 7, supra, for a discussion of "precedent" or "precedential authority." If you would like to receive emails from the IRS when new revenue rulings, revenue procedures, notices and announcements are issued, then you can subscribe to IRS Guidewire to automatically receive links to the latest released published guidance. Go to: https://www.irs.gov/newsroom/subscribe-to-irs-guidewire and click the "Subscribe" hyperlink. Please make sure **not** to go to: www.irs.com.
[96] IRM 8.6.3.1(1) (10-26-2007); IRM 4.10.7.2.6(1).
[97] IRM 8.6.3.1(2) (10-26-2007).
[98] IRM 4.10.7.2.6(3) (1-1-2006).

The general view is that a revenue ruling presents guidance but does not possess the force and effect of law.[99] That said, the IRS is not free to argue against its own guidance in court.[100]

(2) Revenue Procedures - A revenue procedure is issued to assist taxpayers in complying with procedural issues that deal with tax return preparation and compliance.[101] As with revenue rulings, revenue procedures promote uniform application of the tax laws.

- Terminology affecting revenue rulings and revenue procedures

Revenue Rulings and Revenue Procedures that have an effect on previous rulings use the following defined terms to describe the effect[102]:

a. **Amplified** describes a situation where no change is being made in a prior published position, but the prior position is being extended to apply to a variation of the original fact situation.

b. **Clarified** is used in those instances where the language in a prior ruling is being made clear because the language has caused, or may cause, confusion. It is not used where a position in a prior ruling is being changed.

c. **Distinguished** describes a situation where a ruling mentions a previously published ruling and points out an essential difference between them.

d. **Modified** is used where the substance of a previously published position is being changed.

e. **Obsoleted** describes a previously published ruling that is not considered determinative with respect to future transactions. The term is most commonly used in a ruling that lists previously published rulings that are obsoleted because of changes in law or regulations. A ruling may also be obsoleted because the substance has been included in regulations subsequently adopted.

f. **Revoked** describes situations where the position in the previously published ruling is not correct and the correct position is being stated in a new ruling.

g. **Superseded** describes a situation where the new ruling does nothing more than restate the substance and situation of a previously published ruling (or rulings). Thus, the term is used to republish under the 1986 Code and regulations the same position published under the 1939 Code and regulations. The term is also used when it is desirable to republish in a single ruling a series of situations, names, etc., that were previously published over a period of time in separate rulings. If the new ruling does more than restate the substance of a prior ruling, a combination of terms is used. For example, modified and superseded describes a situation where the substance of previously published ruling is being changed in part and is continued without change in

---

[99] IRM 4.10.7.2.6.1(1) (1-1-2006).

[100] Rauenhorst v. Commissioner, 119 T.C. No. 9 (2002) ("However, we cannot agree that the Commissioner is not bound to follow his revenue rulings in Tax Court proceedings. Indeed, we have on several occasions treated revenue rulings as concessions by the Commissioner where those rulings are relevant to our disposition of the case. Walker v. Commissioner, 101 T.C. 537, 550-551 (1993); Burleson v. Commissioner, T.C. Memo. 1994-364.")

[101] IRM 4.10.7.2.6(3) (1-1-2006).

[102] IRM 4.10.7.2.6(4) (1-1-2006).

part and it is desired to restate the valid portion of the previously published ruling in a new ruling that is self contained. In this case the previously published ruling is first modified and then, as modified, is superseded.

h. **Supplemented** is used in situations in which a list, such as a list of the name of countries, is published in a ruling and that list is expanded by adding further names in subsequent rulings. After the original ruling has been supplemented several times, a new ruling may be published that includes the list in the original ruling and the additions, and supersedes all prior rulings in the series.

i. **Suspended** is used in rare situations to show that the previously published ruling will not be applied pending some future action such as the issuance of new or amended regulations, the outcome of cases in litigation, or the outcome of a Service study.

Consider an example of the use of some of the terminology, above. Every year, the IRS issues inflation-adjusted items for various provisions of the tax code. For tax year 2018, the annual inflation-adjusted guidance was provided on November 6, 2017 in Rev. Proc. 2017-58, which noted that it reflected the code as of October 19, 2017.[103] On December 22, 2017, H.R. 115-97 was enacted into law, which provided in part new individual tax rates beginning in 2018.[104] These new individual tax rates were not reflected in Rev. Proc. 2017-58, which was issued by the IRS approximately a month and half before enactment of Pub. Law. No. 115-97. Since IRS guidance may be updated, as in the case of Rev. Proc. 2017-58 due tax code changes, practitioners must utilize secondary source tools, such as CCH's "citator" to confirm whether various IRS guidance remain current.[105] Using CCH's citator for "Rev. Proc. 2017-58" results in the following:

*"Rev. Proc. 2017-58 **modified and superseded** by: Rev. Proc. 2018-18"*

Rev. Proc. 2018-18 was issued on March 2, 2018 in IRB 2018-10. From the definitions of the terminology, above, "modified and superseded" describes "a situation where the substance of previously published ruling is being changed in part and is continued without change in part and it is desired to restate the valid portion of the previously published ruling in a new ruling that is self contained."

What is the distinction between revenue rulings and revenue procedures? The revenue ruling series is used to set forth statements of Service position or to interpret the law

---

[103] In Section 3.01, Rev. Proc. 2017-58, provided tax rates for "married filing joint returns and surviving spouses" in part as follows: "If taxable income is over $77,400 but not over $156,150, the tax is "$10,657.50 plus **25%** of the excess over $77,400."

[104] In Section 3.01, Rev. Proc. 2018-18, provided tax rates for "married filing joint returns and surviving spouses" in part as follows: "If taxable income is over $77,400 but not over $165,000, the tax is "$8,907 plus **22%** of the excess over $77,400." The updated IRS procedure included the new marginal tax rate applicable of 22%.

[105] A discussion of "citator", aka "sheperdizing" a case is discussed in detail in Chapter 7. The authority in certain administrative guidance, such as revenue rulings and revenue procedures, change over time. And, it is incumbent upon tax professionals to use "citator" to check whether the authority presents current admistrative guidance or is stale, i.e., no longer the current administrative position of the government.

with respect to particular tax issues.106 The revenue procedure series is used to announce statements of procedure or general instructional information. A holding on a substantive tax issue to the effect that taxpayers must meet some procedural requirement is a statement of Service position and is not the proper subject for a revenue procedure. Generally, a revenue ruling states a Service position, whereas a revenue procedure provides instructions concerning a Service position that enable taxpayers to achieve a particular result. For example, a revenue ruling may hold that taxpayers may deduct certain automobile expenses, and a revenue procedure may provide the procedures that eligible taxpayers must follow to compute the amount of the deduction by using certain mileage rates in lieu of determining actual operating expenses.107 A revenue ruling does not ordinarily include a statement of Service practice or procedure, and a revenue procedure does not ordinarily include a statement of Service position on a substantive tax issue. When a matter involves both a statement of Service position on a substantive tax issue and a statement of practice or procedure, it normally requires the issuance of both a revenue ruling and a revenue procedure. They should be issued simultaneously and should be cross-referenced.108

(3) Private Letter Ruling - A "private letter ruling" or "PLR" is a written determination issued to a taxpayer by an Associate office109 in response to the taxpayer's written inquiry, filed prior to the filing of returns or reports that are required by the tax laws, about its status for tax purposes or the tax effects of its acts or transactions.110 A PLR interprets the tax laws and applies them to the taxpayer's specific set of facts. Once a ruling (favorable or adverse to the requestor) is issued by the IRS, a copy of the ruling is sent to the appropriate Service official in the operating division having examination jurisdiction of the taxpayer's return.111 Once the IRS issues its letter ruling, the taxpayer who requested the ruling must attach it to the applicable tax return.112

The IRS provides instructions on the process involved for the public to request a private letter ruling in annually re-issued guidance under Revenue Procedure 2017-1 and 2017-3. PLRs can help taxpayers confirm the tax treatment of proposed

---

106 IRM 32.2.2.4(2).

107 Id.

108 Id.

109 The term "Associate office" refers to the Office of Associate Chief Counsel (Corporate), the Office of Associate Chief Counsel (Financial Institutions and Products), the Office of Associate Chief Counsel (Income Tax and Accounting), the Office of Associate Chief Counsel (International), the Office of Associate Chief Counsel (Passthroughs and Special Industries), the Office of Associate Chief Counsel (Procedure and Administration), or the Office of Division Counsel/Associate Chief Counsel (Tax Exempt and Government Entities), as appropriate. Rev. Proc. 2010-1, Sec. 1.01(2).

110 Rev. Proc. 2010-1, Sec. 2.01.

111 IRM 32.3.2.3.2(12); IRM 32.3.2.7.

112 "A taxpayer who, before filing a return, receives a letter ruling or determination letter about any transaction that has been consummated and that is relevant to the return being filed must attach to the return a copy of the letter ruling or determination letter. Taxpayers filing their returns electronically may satisfy this requirement by attaching a statement to their return that provides the date and control number of the letter ruling or determination letter." Rev. Proc. 2010-1, Sec. 7.05.

transactions before they are undertaken, so the timeliness of advice is important. In general, taxpayers requesting a letter ruling are required to pay the IRS a user fee to receive advice. The amount of the user fee depends on the tax issue, but generally ranges from $625 to $11,500 per request. A PLR can be relied upon only by the specific taxpayer receiving the ruling; however, the general facts of the ruling are made available to the public. The number of PLR cases closed has decreased from 1,330 cases in Fiscal Year (FY) 2003 to 1,000 cases in FY 2009.[113] However, PLRs remain a popular mechanism with taxpayers and their representatives.

How long does it take to for the IRS to issue a PLR in response to a request filed by a taxpayer? A government audit of the PLR process determined that in a sample of 65 cases that the IRS issued PLRs within 120 to 180 days of receiving the request in 54 percent of the cases.[114] The other cases in the sample population took longer than 180 days for the PLR to be issued. Obtaining certainty through a PLR issued by the IRS is valuable. However, before beginning the process of preparing a request for a PLR from the IRS, one should consider: (1) whether the issue is on the "No Rule" list issued by the IRS on an annual revenue procedure; (2) whether the PLR is cost effective; and (3) the timeframe for obtaining a responsive PLR.

A few notable considerations with respect to Private Letter Rulings:

- An involved process that will take a good deal of effort to assemble information, structure arguments and follow the procedures to submit a request.
- Normally, the ruling issued will bind the IRS unless there has been a misstatement or omission of controlling facts by the requestor of the ruling.[115] However, if a closing agreement was not executed by the requesting taxpayer and the IRS as part of the ruling process, the ruling may be revoked or modified if it is found to be in error or not in accord with the current views of the Service.[116]
- A fee is charged by the IRS to proceed with a request for a letter ruling.
- If the taxpayer requesting the ruling receives an adverse answer, the taxpayer is not bound to the IRS ruling. But, the applicable revenue procedure addressing private letter rulings require that the taxpayer attach the ruling to the related tax return.[117]
- Subject to the deletion of certain information, letter rulings are required to be open to public inspection under section 6110.[118] I.R.C. §6110, enacted as part of the Tax Reform Act of 1976, allows private letter rulings and relevant background information to be open for public inspection once the material has been "sanitized" to remove information that could be used to identify the taxpayer. (Disclosure of exemption applications, rulings, and related documents is governed by I.R.C. §6104.) IRC §6110 requires the Service to make each ruling available to the public no later than 90 days after issuing it to the requesting taxpayer. Moreover, disclosure is not limited to the

---

[113] Treasury Inspector General for Tax Administration Report dated September 10, 2010, reference number 2010-10-106, http://www.treas.gov/tigta/auditreports/2010reports/201010106fr.pdf.
[114] Id.
[115] Rev. Proc. 2010-1, Sec. 11.05.
[116] Rev. Proc. 2010-1, Sec. 11.04.
[117] Rev. Proc. 2010-1, Sec. 7.05.
[118] I.R.C. § 6110; IRM 32.3.1.14.3(1) (8-11-2004).

ruling itself. Anyone who wishes to examine the background file can do so after paying charges for the Service's search, deletion of identifying details and duplication.
• The legal effect of a letter ruling is limited. So, while the requesting taxpayer may rely on the ruling (absent misrepresentation of material facts), other taxpayers may not use the ruling as a basis to secure the same result from the IRS. In every PLR issued, the IRS will cite to section 6110(k)(3) which warns "**Precedential Status**.— Unless the Secretary otherwise establishes by regulations, a written determination may not be used or cited as precedent."

PLRs, like certain other written determinations issued by the IRS, "may not be used or cited as precedent."[119] Most courts, therefore, do not find PLRs, issued to other taxpayers, to be of precedential value in deciding the tax claims before them.[120]

(4) Determination Letter - A "determination letter" is a written determination issued by a Director that applies the principles and precedents previously announced by the Service to a specific set of facts.[121] It is issued only when a determination can be made based on clearly established rules in a statute, a tax treaty, the regulations, a conclusion in a revenue ruling, or an opinion or court decision that represents the position of the Service. A taxpayer can complete a request for a determination letter by following Rev. Proc. 2017-4. This procedural document is re-issued at the beginning of every year and re-numbered. Thus, in 2018, this procedural guide would be re-issued as Rev. Proc. 2018-4.

(5) Information Letter - An "information letter" is a statement issued by an Associate office or Director that calls attention to a well-established interpretation or principle of tax law (including a tax treaty) without applying it to a specific set of facts.[122] An information letter may be issued if the taxpayer's inquiry indicates a need for general information or if the taxpayer's request does not meet the requirements of this revenue procedure and the Service concludes that general information will help the taxpayer. An information letter is advisory only and has no binding effect on the Service.

---

[119] 26 U.S.C. § 6110(k)(3) (2006)

[120] See, e.g., Lucky Stores, Inc. & Subsidiaries v. Commissioner, 153 F.3d 964, 966 n.5 (9th Cir. 1998) ("Taxpayers other than those to whom such rulings or memoranda were issued are not entitled to rely on them.") (citations omitted); Liberty Nat. Bank & Trust Co. v. United States, 867 F.2d 302, 304-05 (6th Cir. 1989) (noting that "private letter rulings are directed only to the taxpayer who requested the ruling [and] . . . may not be used or cited to as precedent"); Fla. Power & Light Co. v. United States, 56 Fed. Cl. 328, 332 (2003) (stating that "private letter rulings have no precedential value in that they do not represent the IRS's position as to taxpayers generally and thus are irrelevant in the context of litigation brought by other taxpayers") (citations omitted), aff'd, 375 F.3d 1119 (Fed. Cir. 2004). But see Glass v. Commissioner, 471 F.3d 698, 709 (6th Cir. 2006) (acknowledging that under section "6110(k)(3), a Private Letter Ruling cannot be used as precedent," but nonetheless commenting that "a recent [private letter] ruling provides persuasive authority for refuting the Commissioner's argument" in that case); Thom v. United States, 283 F.3d 939, 943 n.6 (8th Cir. 2002) ("Although private letter rulings have no precedential value and do not in any way bind this court, 26 U.S.C. § 6110(k)(3), we believe they are an instructive tool that we have at our disposal."). See Chapter 7, supra, for a discussion of "precedent" or "precedential authority."

[121] Rev. Proc. 2010-1, Sec. 2.03.

[122] Rev. Proc. 2010-1, Sec. 2.04.

(6) The Internal Revenue Bulletin - The Internal Revenue Bulletin (I.R.B.) is the authoritative instrument of the Commissioner of Internal Revenue for announcing official IRS rulings and procedures and for publishing Treasury Decisions, Executive Orders, Tax Conventions, legislation, court decisions, and other items of general interest. It is published on a weekly basis by the Government Printing Office.[123] It is the policy of the Service to publish in the Bulletin all substantive rulings necessary to promote a uniform application of the tax laws, including rulings that supersede, revoke, modify, or amend any of those previously published in the Bulletin. All published rulings apply retroactively unless otherwise indicated. As an example, the first page of I.R.B. 2018-10 follows:

---

[123] IRM 4.10.7.2.4 (1-1-2006).

 **INTERNAL REVENUE BULLETIN**

 IRS

HIGHLIGHTS
OF THIS ISSUE

Bulletin No. 2018–10
March 05, 2018

These synopses are intended only as aids to the reader in identifying the subject matter covered. They may not be relied upon as authoritative interpretations.

ADMINISTRATIVE

Announcement 2018–04, page 401.
The Office of Professional Responsibility (OPR) announces recent disciplinary sanctions involving attorneys, certified public accountants, enrolled agents, enrolled actuaries, enrolled retirement plan agents, and appraisers. These individuals are subject to the regulations governing practice before the Internal Revenue Service (IRS), which are set out in Title 31, Code of Federal Regulations, Part 10, and which are published in pamphlet form as Treasury Department Circular No. 230. The regulations prescribe the duties and restrictions relating to such practice and prescribe the disciplinary sanctions for violating the regulations.

REG-132197–17, page 404.
Pursuant to the policies stated in Executive Orders 13777 and 13789, the Treasury Department and the IRS conducted a review of existing regulations, with the goal of reducing regulatory burden for taxpayers by revoking or revising existing tax regulations that meet the criteria set forth in the executive orders. This notice of proposed rulemaking proposes to streamline IRS regulations by removing 298 regulations that are no longer necessary because they do not have any current or future applicability under the Internal Revenue Code and by amending 79 regulations to reflect the proposed removal of the 298 regulations. The proposed removal and amendment of these regulations may affect various categories of taxpayers.

Rev. Proc. 2018–18, page 392.
This procedure modifies certain 2018 cost-of-living adjustments set forth in Rev. Proc. 2017–58, 2017–45 I.R.B. 489, and Rev. Proc. 2017–37, 2017–21 I.R.B. 1252, to reflect statutory amendments made by An Act to provide for reconciliation pursuant to titles II and V of the concurrent resolution on the budget for fiscal year 2018.

EMPLOYEE PLANS

Notice 2018-16, page 390.
This notice sets forth updates on the corporate bond monthly yield curve, the corresponding spot segment rates for February 2018 used under § 417(e)(3)(D), the 24-month average segment rates applicable for February 2018, and the 30-year Treasury rates. These rates reflect the application of § 430(h)(2)(C)(iv), which was added by the Moving Ahead for Progress in the 21st Century Act, Public Law 112-141 (MAP-21) and amended by section 2003 of the Highway and Transportation Funding Act of 2014 (HATFA).

REG-132197–17, page 404.
Pursuant to the policies stated in Executive Orders 13777 and 13789, the Treasury Department and the IRS conducted a review of existing regulations, with the goal of reducing regulatory burden for taxpayers by revoking or revising existing tax regulations that meet the criteria set forth in the executive orders. This notice of proposed rulemaking proposes to streamline IRS regulations by removing 298 regulations that are no longer necessary because they do not have any current or future applicability under the Internal Revenue Code and by amending 79 regulations to reflect the proposed removal of the 298 regulations. The proposed removal and amendment of these regulations may affect various categories of taxpayers.

EMPLOYMENT TAX

REG-132197–17, page 404.
Pursuant to the policies stated in Executive Orders 13777 and 13789, the Treasury Department and the IRS conducted a review of existing regulations, with the goal of reducing regulatory burden for taxpayers by revoking or revising existing tax regulations that meet the criteria set forth in the executive orders. This notice of proposed rulemaking proposes to

Finding Lists begin on page ii.

(7) The Cumulative Bulletin - The Cumulative Bulletin is a consolidation of items published in the weekly Internal Revenue Bulletin.[124] The Cumulative Bulletin is issued on a semiannual basis. The Cumulative Bulletin is number 1 to 5, inclusive (April 1919 to December 31, 1921); and I–1 and I–2 to XV–1 and XV–2, inclusive (January 1, 1922, to December 31, 1936) . Each Cumulative Bulletin number thereafter bears the particular year covered, for example, 1963–1 (January 1 to June 30, 1963).

---

[124] IRM 4.10.7.2.5(1) (1-1-2006).

(8) Announcements - Announcements are public pronouncements on matters of general interest, such as effective dates of temporary regulations, clarification of rulings and form instructions.[125] They are issued when guidance of a substantive or procedural nature is needed quickly. An announcement is a public pronouncement that has only immediate or short-term value.[126] Announcements can be relied on to the same extent as revenue rulings and revenue procedures. Announcements are identified by a two digit number representing the year and a sequence number.

> *Example:* Announcement 96-124, 1996-49 I.R.B. 22. This announcement is found in Internal Revenue Bulletin No. 1996-49, issued December 2, 1996, at page 22.

(9) Notices - Notices are public announcements issued by the Internal Revenue Service.[127] Notices may be used in circumstances in which a revenue ruling or revenue procedure would not be appropriate. In addition, notices may be used to solicit public comments on issues under consideration, in connection with non-regulatory guidance, such as a proposed revenue procedure. A notice also can be used to relate what regulations will say in situations in which the regulations may not be published in the immediate future.[128] Notices appear in the Internal Revenue Bulletin and are included in the bound Cumulative Bulletin. Notices are identified by a two digit number representing the year and a sequence number. Consider Notice 2010-33 as an example of the impact of one such notice. Section 407 of the Tax Relief and Health Care Act of 2006, Pub. L. No. 109-432, amended section 6702 to increase the amount of the penalty for frivolous tax returns from $500 to $5,000 on any person who submits a "specified frivolous submission." Congress amended Section 6702 by adding subsection (c) requiring the Secretary to prescribe, and periodically revise, a list of positions identified as frivolous. Notice 2007-30 contained the prescribed list, followed by Notice 2008-14, then modified and superseded by Notice 2010-33. What is an example of a "frivolous submission" listed in Notice 2010-33 that would subject a taxpayer to penalty under Section 6702? It is a frivolous submission to argue that "[m]andatory or compelled compliance with the internal revenue laws is a form of involuntary servitude prohibited by the Thirteenth Amendment."

(10) Technical Advice Memoranda - A Technical Advice Memorandum ("TAM") is a final determination of the Service's position for a specific case.[129] A TAM is requested only when the facts have been fully developed and the issue is novel, complex or is not governed by established Service position.[130] Guidance regarding the process for requesting TAMs are provided by the IRS annually in the second Revenue Procedure issued each year. E.g., Rev. Proc. 2010-2. Unlike a PLR or CCA, the Associate Office assigned to the TAM will consider both parties' submission of facts

---

[125] IRM 4.10.7.2.4.1(1)a (1-1-2006).
[126] IRM 32.2.2.3.4(1)(8-11-2004).
[127] IRM 4.10.7.2.4.1(1)b. (1-1-2006).
[128] IRM 32.2.2.3.3(a)(8-11-2004).
[129] IRM 4.8.8.12.4(2) (10-1-2003).
[130] IRM 4.8.8.12.4.1(1) (10-1-2003).

rather than just the facts submitted by the requestor – either the taxpayer in the case of a PLR or the Examination Division in the case of a CCA.[131] Conferences are held by all interested parties with the Associate Office attorney assigned to the TAM to clarify issues, facts and timeline of actions items to complete the request. And, given the additional consideration of facts and conferences held, the timeframe for completion of a TAM can become lengthy. The targeted time frame to complete a TAM is between 120 to 180 days.[132] A Technical Advice Memorandum is intended to establish the proper interpretation and application of the Internal Revenue laws to the facts of a specific case. A Technical Advice Memorandum is a final determination of the Service's position for a specific case.[133] The examiner must follow the Technical Advice Memorandum in preparing the report and closing the case. The IRS Area Director determines whether to request technical advice on any issue being considered. The taxpayer may request technical advice on the grounds that a lack of uniformity exists regarding an issue, or that the issue is so unusual or complex that it warrants consideration by Headquarters. (See Policy Statement P-4-82 in IRM 1.2.1.4.23). Each request for a Technical Advice Memorandum is forwarded through the Area Technical Coordinator in Technical Services (Exam). The Technical Coordinator reviews and processes the requests for technical advice. (See IRM 4.8.8.14).

(11) Chief Counsel Advice - Chief Counsel advice ("CCA") means written advice or instruction prepared by any national office component of the Office of Chief Counsel which is issued to the field or service center employees of the IRS or Chief Counsel and conveys: (1) any legal interpretation of a revenue provision, (2) any position or policy concerning a revenue position; or (3) any legal interpretation of state law, foreign law or other federal law relating to the assessment or collection of any federal tax liability.[134] Although legal advice is not an official ruling or position of the Service, Field Counsel or Service employees, including Appeals officers, may use, as appropriate, the advice in the development, settlement, or other resolution of the case in which the advice was issued.[135]

CCAs and PLRs are very similar in that both documents provide legal conclusions from the IRS National Office to the requestor - either the IRS field component (CCA) or a taxpayer (PLR) - based on only one version of the facts submitted by the requestor. In contrast, a TAM involves the submission of both parties' versions of relevant facts that are reviewed by the IRS National Office in determining its conclusion on the issue(s) presented for decision.

(12) Field Service Advice - Field Service Advice ("FSA") memoranda are prepared by attorneys employed in the Office of Chief Counsel for the IRS, located in Washington, D.C., and issued to, among others, IRS field attorneys, revenue agents and appeals officers. FSAs are issued in response to requests for advice, guidance

---

[131] IRM 4.46.3.9.9(5) (3-1-2006).
[132] IRM 4.46.3.9.9(5) (3-1-2006).
[133] IRM 4.2.3.4(2) (10-1-2003).
[134] I.R.C. § 6110(i)(1)(A); IRM 33.1.2.2.3.4(1) (8-11-2004).
[135] IRM 33.1.2.2.3.5(1) (8-11-2004).

and analysis on difficult or significant tax issues. They are taxpayer-specific documents, written in particular cases, with reference to particular taxpayers. FSAs provide advice on docketed (meaning a tax controversy that is before a court for disposition) or non-docketed cases, or, alternatively, may provide advice on industry-wide issues, or in response to hypothetical questions; and may address substantive and procedural matters. FSAs deal with "significant" tax issues, and one of their purposes is the "promotion of uniformity" in IRS assertions of positions on tax law. FSAs are advisory; they are not binding on either the taxpayers to whom they pertain or the IRS. Whether they are followed is determined on a case-by-case basis by IRS field personnel. FSAs and CCAs are identical forms of guidance. CCAs now take over the realm of FSAs. However, since a tax researcher's work may bring up both FSAs and CCAs, it is important to know both terms.

(13) Treasury Decision - A Treasury Decision ("TD") is a document that contains the text of a final or temporary regulation. The TD adds new text to, removes, or revises text already published in the Code of Federal Regulations (CFR).[136] It contains a preamble that explains the rule. It must state the effective date for the change made to the CFR. A TD is cited as legal authority and is binding on taxpayers as well as the IRS, unless invalidated.

(14) IRS Publication - Publications are guides published by the IRS to provide assistance to taxpayers. Though informative, informal publications issued by the IRS do not present sources of authoritative law in the area of Federal taxation.[137] In other words, reliance on an informal IRS publication may not be used to justify a reporting position that is inconsistent with the operative law.[138]

(15) General Counsel Memorandum - A general counsel memorandum ("GCM") is a legal opinion from one division of the Commissioner's Office of Chief Counsel to another and is not binding on courts.[139] GCMs are internal documents written by the Service's Office of Chief Counsel in connection with the review of proposed private letter rulings, proposed technical advice memorandums to field offices,

---

[136] IRM 32.1.1.2.5(1) (8-11-2004).

[137] See Zimmerman v. Commissioner, 71 T.C. 367, 371 (1978), aff'd. without published opinion 614 F.2d 1294 (2d Cir. 1979); Green v. Commissioner, 59 T.C. 456, 458 (1972); see also Dixon v. United States, 381 U.S. 68, 73-75 (1965); Adler v. Commissioner, 330 F.2d 91, 93 (9th Cir. 1964), aff'g T.C. Memo. 1963-196; Carter v. Commissioner, 51 T.C. 932, 935 n.3 (1969).

[138] See, e.g., Johnson v. Commissioner, 620 F.2d 153, 155 (7th Cir. 1980), aff'g T.C. Memo. 1978-426; Jones v. Commissioner, T.C. Memo. 1993-358. Publications cannot provide adequate protection for taxpayers who may rely on incorrect tax positions published by the IRS. What about erroneous statements made by IRS agents or other employees that are relied upon by taxpayers? An agent's oral statement does not constitute authority that a taxpayer may rely on. Generally, a misstatement of law by a Government agent, by itself, is not sufficient to support a claim that a taxpayer can rely on such statement to support his/her tax position. See Schweiker v. Hansen, 450 U.S. 785 (1981); see also Henry v. United States, 870 F.2d 634, 637 (Fed. Cir. 1989) (erroneous advice of IRS agent not sufficient misconduct to estop IRS from raising statute of limitations where advice caused taxpayer to file claim after limitations period had run).

[139] See Old Harbor Native Corp. v. Commissioner, 104 T.C. 191, 207 (1995).

proposed revenue rulings, and other legal questions posed within the Service. The GCMs set forth the legal issues considered and the conclusions reached along with a summary of the pertinent facts in the particular case and, usually, a detailed legal analysis. Like private letter rulings, "sanitized" GCMs are released to the general public after the lapse of specified time periods. While the discussion and analyses of the legal issues contained in a GCM may be utilized, the GCM itself may not be cited as authority by the Service or taxpayers.

(16) Generic Legal Advice Memorandum - The authoritative force of a "GLAM" exceeds a PLR or CCA because of the level of government official who executes this form of guidance. While it remains true that these documents may not serve as precedential authority, GLAMs provide significant administrative force since they are signed by executives in the National Office of the Office of Chief Counsel and issued to Internal Revenue Service personnel who are national program executives and managers. They are issued to assist Service personnel in administering their programs by providing authoritative legal opinions on certain matters, such as industry-wide issues. See CCDM 33.1.2, Chief Counsel's Legal Advice Program. An up-to-date list of GLAMs issued may be found at http://www.irs.gov/uac/Legal-Advice-Issued-by-Associate-Chief-Counsel.

(17) The Internal Revenue Manual - Published guidance issued by the Treasury and the IRS present various levels of authoritative value. Many practitioners acknowledge the existence of the Internal Revenue Manual ("IRM") but don't fully appreciate the value of this resource. So, what is the IRM? The provisions of the IRM provide guidelines to be followed by IRS employees in the course of their work. The IRM is designed to serve as the single official compilation of policies, procedures, instructions and guidelines relating to the organization, functions, administration, and operations of the Service and is divided into parts based upon Service function. These provisions govern only the internal affairs of the IRS; they do not have the force and effect of law.[140] As such, the IRM does not present published guidance. Procedures in the IRM do not confer rights on taxpayers.[141] Instances where taxpayers have alleged that substantive violations resulted from the IRS not following the IRM have been lost in court.[142] Despite the apparent limitations of the IRM, the provisions of the IRM provide useful information on how the IRS goes about its business. The IRM is designed to serve as the single official compilation of policies, procedures, instructions and

---

[140] Valen Manufacturing Co. v. United States, 90 F.3d 1190, 1194 (6th Cir. 1996); United States v. Horne, 714 F.2d 206, 207 (1st Cir. 1983). See generally Reich v. Manganas, 70 F.3d 434, 437 (6th Cir. 1995) ("Internal operating manuals * * * do not carry the force of law, bind the agency, or confer rights upon the regulated entity.").

[141] United States v. Horne, supra; United States v. Mapp, 561 F.2d 685, 690 (7th Cir. 1977).

[142] Respondent's failure to comply with the IRM does not invalidate a notice of deficiency or confer substantive rights upon taxpayers. Cf. Vallone v. Commissioner, 88 T.C. 794, 808 (1987) (failure to comply with IRM procedure for obtaining extension of period of limitation did not necessitate suppression of evidence obtained after extension obtained); Epstein v. Commissioner, T.C. Memo. 1989-498 (failure to follow IRM procedure did not invalidate the notice of deficiency). IRM procedures are directory and not mandatory. Stone v. Commissioner, T.C. Memo. 1994-314.

guidelines relating to the organization, functions, administration, and operations of the Service and is divided into parts based upon Service function. Part VII deals exclusively with employee plans and exempt organizations. The following examples of chapter headings that are indicative of the material contained in Part VII.

> 7200 Authorities and Standards
> 7300 Administrative Procedures
> 7400 Field Organization and Functions
> 7500 Program Planning and Management
> 7600 Processing and Grading of Applications
> 7700 Rulings, Determination Letters, Opinion Letters, and Information Letters
> 7800 Master Files
> 7900 Classification and Selection of Returns, Claims and Information Items
> 7(10)00 Examination Procedures
> 7(11)00 Closing Procedures
> 7(12)00 Post Review Program
> 7(13)00 Technical Advice and Appeals
> 7(14)00 National Office Projects
> 7(15)00 Other Programs
> 7(16)00 Publicity and Limitations of EP/EO Material

(18) Audit Technique Guide ("ATG") - ATGs are non-precedential IRS documents that assist revenue agents who conduct audits by providing insight into issues and accounting methods unique to specific industries. While ATGs are designed to provide guidance for IRS employees, they're also useful to small business owners and tax professionals who prepare returns. ATGs explain industry-specific examination techniques and include common, as well as, unique industry issues, business practices and terminology.

6. Utilizing Published Guidance – Examples

Depending on the type of administrative guidance located during tax research, you will reach various levels of confidence regarding your view of a particular code section or what to expect when working with the IRS. For example, would it be useful if you knew in advance of a meeting with the IRS what types of questions may be asked of the taxpayer on a particular audited issue? Recall the reference, above, to ATGs. Within ATGs, guidance may include interview techniques and evaluation of evidence.[143] Specifically, in the ATG developed to assist revenue agents pursue the application of section 183 (activities not engaged in for profit, sometimes referred to as the "hobby loss rule"), a part of the publicly available guide provides an extensive list of suggested taxpayer interview questions all nine factors contained in Treas. Reg. 1.183-2(b) that may be used by agents to establish if an activity is or is not engaged in for profit. Consider Appendix B from the ATG for section 183, below, that suggests questions for agents to pose during an interview of a taxpayer on this issue:

---

[143] https://www.irs.gov/businesses/small-businesses-self-employed/audit-techniques-guides-atgs.

Appendix B - Suggested Interview Questions for Each of 9 Relevant Factors

The following are suggested possible interview questions for each of the nine factors contained in Treas. Regs. §1.183-2(b)(1) through (9) which may be used by examiners to establish if an activity is or is not for profit. Other factors not listed may also need to be considered.

These questions should not be considered all-inclusive. The interview should be tailored to each specific taxpayer. The questions should be asked of the taxpayer in an interview and not be given to the taxpayer and/or authorized representative to complete.

1.183-2(b)(1) Manner in which the taxpayer carries on the activity

- Background and general description of the business.
  - When did the taxpayer first include (first Schedule C, F. 1120S, 1065, etc.) this business for tax purposes?
  - General industry, what specialized niche?
  - Where is business conducted?
  - What geographical area?
  - Specific demographic target population?
  - Is the business seasonal?
  - Did the taxpayer have a business plan?
  - Was the plan followed?
  - How did the taxpayer propose to compete with similar businesses?
  - When/how did the idea for the business activity originate?
  - Was a business plan written-up?
  - What were the financial requirements to start the business?
  - How were the funds obtained?
  - Bank loans, investors, personal savings, family, etc.?
  - What documentation is available?
  - How is the business currently being financed?
  - What financial risks are involved in this type of business?
  - Is any type of business insurance carried?
  - Are policies in the business name?

Although these ATGs provide useful tools for IRS agents to conduct audits, they can serve as important sources of information for taxpayer and researchers to become similarly informed on specific issues to better plan and prepare tax positions.

As another example, consider the question of appellate venue under section 7482(b)(1)(B). When a party loses a dispute reviewed by the U.S. Tax Court, Congress enacted section 7482 to provide the specific venue for the losing party to appeal their case. For a corporate taxpayer, section 7482(b)(1)(B) provides that such decisions may be reviewed by the United States court of appeals for the circuit in which is located—

> (B) in the case of a corporation seeking redetermination of tax liability, the principal place of business or principal office or agency of the corporation, or, if it has no principal place of business or principal office or agency in any judicial circuit, then the office to which was made the return of the tax in respect of which the liability arises......

A corporate taxpayer may determine that caselaw in a particular circuit presents a more favorable venue for appeal of their case. So, how would a corporate taxpayer determine their "principal place of business" under section 7482(b)(1)(B) to seek redetermination of it tax liability?

Sometimes, administrative guidance may offer useful clues as to the proper reading of codes sections such as section 7482(b)(1)(B). Executing a search of section "7482(b)(1)" results in a "hit" of a 1999 Field Service Advice ("FSA") that reviewed a different subparagraph of the same code section – 7482(b)(1)(E). Notably, the FSA analyzed the same term in reviewing section 7482(b)(1)(E) as provided in section 7482(b)(1)(B) – "what is the meaning of 'principal place of business'....." See selected excerpts taken from the 1999 FSA, below.

99ARD 204-9, October 20, 1999

CC:FS:P&SI

*****

Date: *****

To: District Counsel, *****

Attn: *****

From: *****, Passthroughs and Special Industries Branch CC:FS:P&SI

Subject: *****

This in response to your request for assistance, dated *****

ISSUE

For purposes of determining appellate venue, what is the meaning of "principal place of business" of a partnership under I.R.C. §7482(b)(1)(E)?

CONCLUSION:

The location of a partnership's principal place of business is a question of fact. The proper test for determining the appellate venue of a partnership is the place where the partnership makes its principal or major business decisions.

FACTS:

****

DISCUSSION:

You have asked that we provide guidance with respect to the definition of the term "principal place of business" under section 7482(b)(1)(B) of the Code.

Development of Venue Provisions:

I.R.C. §7482 as it originally appeared in the Internal Revenue Code of 1954 provided, in pertinent part:

(b) Venue.—

(1) In general.— Except as provided in paragraph (2), such decision may be reviewed by the United States Court of Appeals for the circuit in which is located the office to which was made the return of the tax in respect of which the liability arises, or if no return was made, then by the United States Court of Appeals for the District of Columbia.

This subsection was subsequently amended in 1966 by P.L. 89-713. The amended statute changed the venue provisions and provided that venue should be based upon the status of the taxpayer as either a corporate or noncorporate taxpayer. The revised statute provided as follows:

(b) Venue.—

(1) In general.— Except as otherwise provided in paragraph (2), such decisions may be reviewed by the United States court of appeals for the circuit in which is located—

A. (A) in the case of a petitioner seeking redetermination of tax liability other than a corporation the legal residence of the petitioner,

B. (B) in the case of a corporation seeking redetermination of tax liability, the principal place of business or principal office or agency of the corporation, or, if it has no principal place of business or principal office or agency in any judicial circuit, the office to which was made the return of the tax in respect of which the liability arises.

If for any reason neither subparagraph (A) nor (B) applies, then such decisions may be reviewed by the Court of Appeals for the District of Columbia. For purposes of this paragraph, the legal residence, principal place of business, or principal office or agency referred to herein shall be determined as of the time the petition seeking redetermination of tax liability was filed with the Tax Court.

This subsection of the Code was changed several times between 1966 and 1982. The changes dealt primarily within venue in the case of declaratory judgment actions.

This subsection was again modified in 1982 by P.L. 97-248. With this change, the venue provisions for TEFRA partnerships were added to this subsection.

Section 7482(b) as it appears in the Code today, in relevant part, is as follows:

> (1) **In general.**— Except as provided in paragraphs (2) and (3), such decision may be reviewed by the United States court of appeals for the circuit in which is located—
>
> * * * * *
>
> > (E) in the case of a petition under section 6226 or 6228(a), the principal place of business of the partnership.
>
> If for any reason no subparagraph of the preceding sentence applies, then such decisions may be reviewed by the Court of Appeals for the District of Columbia. For purposes, of this paragraph, the legal residence, principal office or agency referred to herein shall be determined as of the time of the petition seeking redetermination of the tax liability was filed with the Tax Court or as of the time the petition seeking a declaratory decision under section 7428 or 7476 or the petition under section 6226 or 6228(a), was filed with the Tax Court.

Legislative Comments on Venue Provision Revisions:

The meaning of the phrase "principal place of business" was briefly addressed in the House Committee Report to H.R. 6958 explaining the 1966 amendment of section 7482:

> As a result the bill provides that appeals from Tax Court decisions are to be made to the court of appeals for the circuit in which (in the case of a taxpayer other than a corporation) the taxpayer resides. Appeals by corporations are to be made to the court of appeals for the circuit in which they have their principal place of business or principal office or agency. For this purpose the residence, principal place of business, or principal office or agency of the taxpayer is to be determined as of the time he files his petition with the Tax Court. This provision of the bill is modeled after the provision of existing law which prescribes the venue for a refund suit against the United States in the district courts.

Similarly, a statement in the Congressional Record appears to mirror the language contained in the House Report:

> For this purpose the residence, principal place of business, or principal office or agency of the taxpayer is to be determined as of the time he files his petition with the Tax Court. This provision of the bill is modeled after the provision of the

existing law which prescribes the venue for a refund suit against the United States in the district courts.

****

While 28 U.S.C. §1402(a) provides no help in understanding the meaning of "principal place of business" for a partnership, a review of the legislative history with respect to this phrase as it applies to a corporation provides guidance as to the origin of this phrase. ****************************

From this FSA, you get a "window" into the legal perspective of the government and how it interprets "principal place of business" for purposes of section 7482(b)(1)(E), e.g., the government's view is that "the place where the partnership makes its principal or major business decisions constitutes its principal place of business." And, for purposes of section 7482(b)(1)(B), you may follow the same steps of analysis as conducted for section 7482(b)(1)(E) to reach a similar conclusion. While locating and reading this FSA does not provide a definitive answer to answer the question of what "principal place of business" means under section 7482(b)(1)(B), this administrative guidance provides a great start to better understanding the term.[144]

---

[144] Further research leads to <u>John Hancock Life Insurance Company v. Commissioner</u>, 141 T.C. No. 1 (2013), in which the Tax Court held that a corporation's "principal place of business" is a test best read as referring to the place where a corporation's officers direct, control, and coordinate the corporation's activities." <u>Hertz Corp. v. Friend</u>, 559 U.S. 77, 92-93 (2010). Thus, the court decision in <u>John Hancock</u> as to corporations and section 7482(b)(1)(B) aligns with the FSA view of "principal place of business" for partnerships under section 7482(b)(1)(E).

Chapter 6 Questions

1. A colleague at work provides you with the following text from an internal office memo. The colleague asks, "I thought temporary regulations expired after 3 years from the date it's issued. Is Temp. Treas. Reg. §1.469-5T(a) valid authority for our client's 2016 tax year." Temp. Treas. Reg. §1.469-5T(a) was issued on Feb. 25, 1988. Yes or No? Explain your answer.

```
    As pertinent here, temporary regulations relating to when a

taxpayer is to be treated as "materially participating" in an

activity for purposes of section 469(h)(1) provide that in gen-

eral

        an individual shall be treated, for purposes of section
        469 and the regulations thereunder, as materially par-
        ticipating in an activity for the taxable year if and
        only if--

                (1) The individual participates in the activity
        for more than 500 hours during such year * * *

Sec. 1.469-5T(a), Temporary Income Tax Regs., 53 Fed. Reg. 5725

(Feb. 25, 1988).
```

2. Read Rev. Proc. 2007-57. In this published guidance applicable to poker tournament sponsors, the IRS restates the requirements imposed upon them as payers of poker winnings: (1) section 3402(q)(1) provides that every person who makes any payment of winnings which are subject to withholding shall deduct and withhold from the payment; and (2) Treas. Reg. § 31.3402(q)-1(f)(1) provides that every person making a payment of winnings for which withholding is required shall file a Form W-2G with the IRS. Then, later in section 6 of Rev. Proc. 2007-57, the IRS states: "The IRS will not assert any liability for additional tax or additions to tax for violations

of any withholding obligation with respect to amounts paid to winners of poker tournaments under section 3402, provided that the poker tournament sponsor meets all of the requirements for information reporting under section 3402(q) and the regulations thereunder." Why didn't the IRS simply state that sponsors of poker tournaments could disregard Treas. Reg. § 31.3402(q)-1(f)(1) that requires payers of poker winnings to withhold applicable tax?

3. In some instances, the IRM can provide options that are not available from other normal sources of authorities or published guidance as the next example illustrates. Read the hypothetical facts set forth below. Then, read IRM 20.1.1.3.6 as provided, in part, below, and answer these two questions:

   a. Does IRM 20.1.1.3.6.1 provide statutory or administrative relief from penalties?
   b. Why does this IRM matter?

Facts: John Smith has been a diligent taxpayer for many years. He has never filed a late federal tax return or received a tax penalty of any kind. For his tax return filed for tax year 2008, John used a reputable tax return software program to prepare and file his return. Somehow, he input some erroneous data which triggered problems on his return. He received notice from the IRS about the errors. Worse still, the IRS determined that he would be subject to the accuracy related penalty under Section 6662 due to the errors on his return. He acknowledges that he made the errors and did not rely on any professional tax advice in preparing his return. He arrives in your office, explains his situation and asks for your advice. He has no problem paying the extra tax that he owes the IRS. But, he would like to avoid paying the hefty penalty that the IRS has determined applies in his case.
Source : Internal Revenue Manual 20.1.1.3.6 - Reasonable Cause Assistant (RCA)[145]

The Reasonable Cause Assistant (RCA) will be used when considering penalty relief due to reasonable cause. RCA is to be used after normal case research has been performed, (i.e., applying missing deposits/payments, adjusting tax, or researching for missing extensions of time to file, etc.) for the following penalties:

   - IMF - Failure to File (FTF) and Failure to Pay (FTP)

   - BMF - Failure to Deposit (FTD)

RCA is a decision-support interactive software program developed to reach a reasonable cause determination. RCA is accessed through the AMS (Accounts Management Services) *Tools* menu.

   Use of RCA will ensure consistent and equitable administration of penalty relief

---

[145] Go to https://www.irs.gov/pub/foia/ig/tas/tas-13-0212-007.pdf to find the National Taxpayer Advocate's Memorandum on Interim Guidance on Penalty Relief Advocacy, and Using the Reasonable Cause Assistant (RCA).

consideration.

When an employee has determined that a taxpayer has requested penalty relief based on Reasonable Cause, whether the request was made by telephone or in writing, RCA will be accessed to determine if penalty relief will be granted.
<u>Source</u>: IRM 20.1.1.3.6.1 (12-11-2009) First Time Abate (FTA)

RCA provides an option for penalty relief for the FTF, FTP, and/or FTD penalties if the taxpayer has not previously been required to file a return or if no prior penalties (except the Estimated Tax Penalty, TC 17X) have been assessed on the same MFT (see the exception for MFTs 01 and 14 in paragraph (3)(f)) in the prior 3 years. This First-time Abate (FTA) aspect is an Administrative Waiver and does not carry any Oral Statement Authority (OSA) dollar threshold. *See IRM 20.1.1.3.6.3* for additional OSA information. ....

The reasonable cause explanation provided by the taxpayer will be considered after RCA performs the First-time Abate/Clean Compliance History analysis. If FTA criteria does not apply based on reasons shown in (3) below, then the taxpayer's explanation will be used to determine if reasonable cause penalty relief criteria is met. If the RCA determination is to abate the penalty(s), penalty relief can be granted as appropriate per the RCA conclusion (i.e., Reasonable Cause, Official Disaster Relief area, IRS Error, Statutory and Administrative Waivers). Using the First-time Abate/Clean Compliance History analysis up front was based on a request from HQ Customer Accounts Services.

A First Time Abate conclusion <u>WILL NOT</u> apply if any of the following criteria applies:

a. Any tax period in the prior 3 years, for the same MFT (see the exception for MFTs 01 and 14 in paragraph (3)(f)), is in TDI Status 02 or 03, or IMF Status 04

b. An unreversed penalty for a significant amount (See *Caution* for an explanation of significant amount) is present (except the ES penalty) on any tax period in the prior 3 years, for the same MFT (see the exception for MFT's 01 and 14 in paragraph (3)(f)), and a notice was issued showing the assessed penalty(s).

4. Analysis of research results may sometimes require practitioners to understand that various types of tax authories will influence the IRS and courts differently. Consider the following scenario. In 2015, Joe is a full-time student in college entering his second year of post-secondary education at City College. For his English course, the professor requires everyone to purchase a computer either from the school or any outside vendor. During the second week of the semester, Joe's parents purchased a computer for their son's use at City College for his English course from an outside vendor for $1,500. Joe's parents claim him as a dependent on their joint federal income tax return. Joe's parent's AGI is $100,000 in 2015. And, their MAGI

(modified AGI) is the same amount as their AGI in 2015. Joe qualifies for all required elements of the Section 25A American Opportunity Tax credit for tax year 2015. Joe's parents want to know whether the $1,500 paid to purchase their son's computer in 2015 qualifies under Section 25A(i) as "tuition, fees, and course materials" for purposes of receiving the American Opportunity Tax Credit ("AOTC"). *[Note: do not consider the Lifetime Learning Credit].* Conducting research on this factual scenario, you locate the following primary source material: (1) IRS Pub. 970 (Jan. 29, 2016); (2) Mameri v. Comm'r, T.C. Summ. Op. 2016-47; (3) Prop. Treas. Reg. §1.25A-2; (4) I.R.C. §25A. Read this material. Then, after understanding facts and all available authorities, determine with an acceptable level of tax confidence the correct tax position for Joe's parents with respect to their purchase of Joe's computer in 2105. The current IRS publication follows the language of the proposed Treasury regulation regarding "course materials" for the AOTC (American Opportunity Tax Credit) – both sources provide that **students can buy course materials anywhere**. But, a recent Tax Court case (Mameri v. Comm'r, T.C. Summ. Op. 2016-47), follows the definition of "books, supplies and equipment" under the final Treasury regulation for the AOTC – **students must buy course materials directly from the educational institution**. With these primary sources pointing us to opposite conclusions regarding what constitutes allowable "course materials," how do we make sense of all this? What is your professional tax opinion if a client asks, "If I buy a computer from an outside vendor that I need to use in my college course, is that cost eligible for the AOTC under Section 25A(i)?"

    a. How should the IRS proceed under the facts and applicable tax authorities?
    b. How would courts proceed under the facts and applicable tax authorities?

5. Consider the following facts, section 274 and Treas. Reg. 1.274-2 (the relevant text which is provided below) to answer the questions that follow:

FACTS: Sue is a sales employee working for ABC Corporation based in New Jersey. As part of her job, she spent time with her clients, Jane and Jim, entertaining them on a Thursday night in 2017. The cost of her evening out entertaining her clients was $300. Her company's accounting department is unsure if the cost of her outing with her clients qualifies as a deductible business expense. As such, the accounting department conducted tax research and reviewed I.R.C. §274 and Treas. Reg. §1.274-2.

    a. Treas. Reg. §1.274-2(b)(1), which provides a definition of "entertainment" for purposes of section 274, presents applicable tax authority to determine whether Sue's expenses taking her clients out qualifies as a type generally considered to constitute "entertainment" for purposes of section 274. True or False?

    b. Same facts, except the tax year is now 2018, not 2017. Treas. Reg. §1.274-2(b)(1), which provides a definition of "entertainment" for purposes of section 274, presents applicable tax authority to determine whether Sue's expenses taking her clients out qualifies as a type generally considered to constitute "entertainment" for purposes of section 274.   True or False?

c. Based on P.L. 115-97, Treas. Reg. §1.274-2 presents <u>outdated</u> regulations with respect to entertainment expenses incurred or paid before 2018. True or False?

d. Based on P.L. 115-97, Treas. Reg. §1.274-2 presents <u>outdated</u> regulations with respect to entertainment expenses incurred or paid after December 31, 2017. True or False?

e. Section 274(a)(1) provides in part, "No deduction otherwise allowable under this chapter shall be allowed for any item….." The "chapter" referenced in section 274(a)(1) refers to:

    i. Chapter 1
    ii. Chapter 2
    iii. Chapter 2A
    iv. Chapter 3
    v. Chapter 4
    vi. None of the above.

I.R.C. §274

(a) ENTERTAINMENT, AMUSEMENT, RECREATION, OR QUALIFIED TRANSPORTATION FRINGES

    (1) IN GENERAL. No deduction otherwise allowable under this chapter shall be allowed for any item—

        (A) Activity

            With respect to an activity which is of a type generally considered to constitute entertainment, amusement, or recreation, or

        (B) Facility

            With respect to a facility used in connection with an activity referred to in subparagraph (A).

    (2) SPECIAL RULES. For purposes of applying paragraph (1)—

        (A) Dues or fees to any social, athletic, or sporting club

    or organization shall be treated as items with respect to facilities.

        (B) An activity described in section 212 shall be treated as a trade or

business.

(3) DENIAL OF DEDUCTION FOR CLUB DUES

Notwithstanding the preceding provisions of this subsection, no deduction shall be allowed under this chapter for amounts paid or incurred for membership in any club organized for business, pleasure, recreation, or other social purpose.

(4) QUALIFIED TRANSPORTATION FRINGES

No deduction shall be allowed under this chapter for the expense of any qualified transportation fringe (as defined in section 132(f)) provided to an employee of the taxpayer.

Historical Amendments

2017—Subsec. (a). Pub. L. 115–97, §13304(c)(1)(A), substituted "recreation, or qualified transportation fringes" for "or recreation" in section catchline.

Subsec. (a)(1). Pub. L. 115–97, §13304(a)(1)(B), struck out concluding provisions which read as follows: "In the case of an item described in subparagraph (A), the deduction shall in no event exceed the portion of such item which meets the requirements of subparagraph (A)."

Subsec. (a)(1)(A). Pub. L. 115–97, §13304(a)(1)(A), struck out "unless the taxpayer establishes that the item was directly related to, or, in the case of an item directly preceding or following a substantial and bona fide business discussion (including business meetings at a convention or otherwise), that such item was associated with, the active conduct of the taxpayer's trade or business," after "or recreation,".

Effective Date of 2017 Amendment

Pub. L. 115–97, title I, §13304(e), Dec. 22, 2017, 131 Stat. 2126, provided that:

"(1) IN GENERAL.—
Except as provided in paragraph (2), the amendments made by this section [amending this section and section 7701 of this title] shall apply to amounts incurred or paid after December 31, 2017.
"(2) EFFECTIVE DATE FOR ELIMINATION OF DEDUCTION FOR MEALS PROVIDED AT CONVENIENCE OF EMPLOYER.—
The amendments made by subsection (d) [amending this section] shall apply to amounts incurred or paid after December 31, 2025."
Pub. L. 115–97, title I, §13310(b), Dec. 22, 2017, 131 Stat. 2132, provided that:

"The amendments made by this section [amending this section] shall apply to amounts paid or incurred after December 31, 2017."

Treas. Reg. §1.274-2 Disallowance of deductions for certain expenses for entertainment, amusement, recreation, or travel.

(a) General rules -

(1) Entertainment activity. Except as provided in this section, no deduction otherwise allowable under Chapter 1 of the Code shall be allowed for any expenditure with respect to entertainment unless the taxpayer establishes:

(i) That the expenditure was directly related to the active conduct of the taxpayer's trade or business, or

(ii) In the case of an expenditure directly preceding or following a substantial and bona fide business discussion (including business meetings at a convention or otherwise), that the expenditure was associated with the active conduct of the taxpayer's trade or business.

Such deduction shall not exceed the portion of the expenditure directly related to (or in the case of an expenditure described in subdivision (ii) of this subparagraph, the portion of the expenditure associated with) the active conduct of the taxpayer's trade or business.

(2) Entertainment facilities -

(i) Expenditures paid or incurred after December 31, 1978, and not with respect to a club. Except as provided in this section with respect to a club, no deduction otherwise allowable under chapter 1 of the Code shall be allowed for any expenditure paid or incurred after December 31, 1978, with respect to a facility used in connection with entertainment.

(ii) Expenditures paid or incurred before January 1, 1979, with respect to entertainment facilities, or paid or incurred before January 1, 1994, with respect to clubs -

(a) Requirements for deduction. Except as provided in this section, no deduction otherwise allowable under chapter 1 of the Internal Revenue Code shall be allowed for any expenditure paid or incurred before January 1, 1979, with respect to a facility used in connection with entertainment, or for any expenditure paid or incurred before January 1, 1994, with respect to a club used in connection with entertainment, unless the taxpayer establishes -

(1) That the facility or club was used primarily for the furtherance of the taxpayer's trade or business; and

(2) That the expenditure was directly related to the active conduct of that trade or business.

(b)Amount of deduction. The deduction allowable under paragraph (a)(2)(ii)(a) of this section shall not exceed the portion of the expenditure directly related to the active conduct of the taxpayer's trade or business.

(iii) Expenditures paid or incurred after December 31, 1993, with respect to a club -

(a) In general. No deduction otherwise allowable under chapter 1 of the Internal Revenue Code shall be allowed for amounts paid or incurred after December 31, 1993, for membership in any club organized for business, pleasure, recreation, or other social purpose. The purposes and activities of a club, and not its name, determine whether it is organized for business, pleasure, recreation, or other social purpose. Clubs organized for business, pleasure, recreation, or other social purpose include any membership organization if a principal purpose of the organization is to conduct entertainment activities for members of the organization or their guests or to provide members or their guests with access to entertainment facilities within the meaning of paragraph (e)(2) of this section. Clubs organized for business, pleasure, recreation, or other social purpose include, but are not limited to, country clubs, golf and athletic clubs, airline clubs, hotel clubs, and clubs operated to provide meals under circumstances generally considered to be conducive to business discussion.

(b) Exceptions. Unless a principal purpose of the organization is to conduct entertainment activities for members or their guests or to provide members or their guests with access to entertainment facilities, business leagues, trade associations, chambers of commerce, boards of trade, real estate boards, professional organizations (such as bar associations and medical associations), and civic or public service organizations will not be treated as clubs organized for business, pleasure, recreation, or other social purpose.

(3) Cross references. For definition of the term entertainment, see paragraph (b)(1) of this section. For the disallowance of deductions for the cost of admission to a dinner or program any part of the proceeds of which inures to the use of a political party or political candidate, and cost of admission to an inaugural event or similar event identified with any political party or political candidate, see § 1.276-1. For rules and definitions with respect to:

(i) "Directly related entertainment", see paragraph (c) of this section,

(ii) "Associated entertainment", see paragraph (d) of this section,

(iii) "Expenditures paid or incurred before January 1, 1979, with respect to entertainment facilities or before January 1, 1994, with respect to clubs", see paragraph (e) of this section, and

(iv) "Specific exceptions" to the disallowance rules of this section, see paragraph (f) of this section.

(b) Definitions -

(1) Entertainment defined -

(i) In general. For purposes of this section, the term entertainment means any activity which is of a type generally considered to constitute entertainment, amusement, or recreation, such as entertaining at night clubs, cocktail lounges, theaters, country clubs, golf and athletic clubs, sporting events, and on hunting, fishing, vacation and similar trips, including such activity relating solely to the taxpayer or the taxpayer's family. The term entertainment may include an activity, the cost of which is claimed as a business expense by the taxpayer, which satisfies the personal, living, or family needs of any individual, such as providing food and beverages, a hotel suite, or an automobile to a business customer or his family. The term entertainment does not include activities which, although satisfying personal, living, or family needs of an individual, are clearly not regarded as constituting entertainment, such as (a) supper money provided by an employer to his employee working overtime, (b) a hotel room maintained by an employer for lodging of his employees while in business travel status, or (c) an automobile used in the active conduct of trade or business even though used for routine personal purposes such as commuting to and from work. On the other hand, the providing of a hotel room or an automobile by an employer to his employee who is on vacation would constitute entertainment of the employee.

(ii) Objective test. An objective test shall be used to determine whether an activity is of a type generally considered to constitute entertainment. Thus, if an activity is generally considered to be entertainment, it will constitute entertainment for purposes of this section and section 274(a) regardless of whether the expenditure can also be described otherwise, and even though the expenditure relates to the taxpayer alone. This objective test precludes arguments such as that entertainment means only entertainment of others or that an expenditure for entertainment should be characterized as an expenditure for advertising or public relations. However, in applying this test the taxpayer's trade or business shall be considered. Thus, although attending a theatrical performance would generally be considered entertainment, it would not be so considered in the case of a professional theater critic, attending in his professional capacity. Similarly, if a manufacturer of dresses conducts a fashion show to introduce his products to a group of store buyers, the show would not be generally considered to constitute entertainment. However, if an appliance distributor conducts a fashion show for the wives of his retailers, the fashion show would be generally considered to constitute entertainment.

Examples of Executive Branch Tax Documents

⬇ Revenue Ruling

Part I
Section 162 - Trade or Business Expenses
26 CFR 1.162-1: Business Expenses (Also sections 263; 263A; sections 1.162-4, 1.263(a)-1, 1.263A-1)

Rev. Rul. 2001-4

ISSUE
Are costs incurred by a taxpayer to perform work on its aircraft airframe, including the costs of a "heavy maintenance visit," deductible as ordinary and necessary business expenses under 162 of the Internal Revenue Code, or must they be capitalized under 263 and 263A?

FACTS
X is a commercial airline engaged in the business of transporting passengers and freight throughout the United States and abroad. To conduct its business, X owns or leases various types of aircraft. As a condition of maintaining its operating license and airworthiness certification for these aircraft, X is required by the Federal Aviation Administration ("FAA") to establish and adhere to a continuous maintenance program for each aircraft within its fleet. These programs, which are designed by X and the aircraft's manufacturer and approved by the FAA, are incorporated into each aircraft's maintenance manual. The maintenance manuals require a variety of periodic maintenance visits at various intervals during the operating lives of each aircraft. The most extensive of these for X is termed a "heavy maintenance visit" (also known in the industry as a "D check", "heavy C check", or "overhaul"), which is required to be performed by X approximately every eight years of aircraft operation. The purpose of a heavy maintenance visit, according to X's maintenance manual, is to prevent deterioration of the inherent safety and reliability levels of the aircraft equipment and, if such deterioration occurs, to restore the equipment to their inherent levels. In each of the following three situations, X reasonably anticipated at the time the aircraft was placed in service that the aircraft would be useful in its trade or business for up to 25 years, taking into account the repairs and maintenance necessary to keep the aircraft in an ordinarily efficient operating condition. In addition, each of the aircraft in the following three situations is fully depreciated for federal income tax purposes at the time of the heavy maintenance visit.

Situation 1
In 2000, X incurred $2 million for the labor and materials necessary to perform a heavy maintenance visit on the airframe of Aircraft 1, which X acquired in 1984 for $15 million (excluding the cost of engines). To perform the heavy maintenance visit, X extensively disassembled the airframe, removing items such as its engines, landing gear, cabin and

passenger compartment seats, side and ceiling panels, baggage stowage bins, galleys, lavatories, floor boards, cargo loading systems, and flight control surfaces. As specified by X's maintenance manual for Aircraft 1, X then performed certain tasks on the disassembled airframe for the purpose of preventing deterioration of the inherent safety and reliability levels of the airframe. These tasks included lubrication and service; operational and visual checks; inspection and functional checks; restoration of minor parts and components; and removal, discard, and replacement of certain life-limited single cell parts, such as cartridges, canisters, cylinders, and disks.

Whenever the execution of a task revealed cracks, corrosion, excessive wear, or dysfunctional operation, X was required by the maintenance manual to restore the airframe to an acceptable condition. This restoration involved burnishing corrosion; repairing cracks, dents, gouges, punctures, or scratches by burnishing, blending, stopdrilling, or applying skin patches or doublers over the affected area; tightening or replacing loose or missing fasteners, rivets, screws, bolts, nuts, or clamps; repairing or replacing torn or damaged seals, gaskets, or valves; repairing or replacing damaged or missing placards, decals, labels, or stencils; additional cleaning, lubricating, or painting; further inspecting or testing, including the use of sophisticated non-destructive inspection methods; repairing fiberglass or laminated parts; replacing bushings, bearings, hinges, handles, switches, gauges, or indicators; repairing chaffed or damaged wiring; repairing or adjusting various landing gear or flight surface control cables; replacing light bulbs, window panes, lenses, or shields; replacing anti-skid materials and stops on floors, pedals, and stairways; replacing floor boards; and performing minor repairs on ribs, spars, frames, longerons, stringers, beams, and supports. In addition to the tasks described above, X also performed additional work as part of the heavy maintenance visit for Aircraft 1. This work included applying corrosion prevention and control compounds; stripping and repainting the aircraft exterior; and cleaning, repairing, and painting airframe interior items such as seats, carpets, baggage stowage bins, ceiling and sidewall panels, lavatories, galleys, and passenger service units. Other additional work included implementing certain outstanding service bulletins ("SB"s) issued by the aircraft manufacturer and airworthiness directives ("AD"s) issued by the FAA. Implementing these SBs and ADs involved inspecting specific skin locations and applying doublers over the areas where cracks were found; inspecting bolts or fasteners at specific locations, and replacing those found to be broken, worn, or missing; and installing structural reinforcements between body frames in a small area in the lower aft fuselage to reduce skin wrinkling and replacing a small number of the wrinkled skin panels in this area with stronger skin panels. None of the work performed by X as part of the heavy maintenance visit (including the execution of SBs and ADs) for Aircraft 1 resulted in a material upgrade or addition to its airframe or involved the replacement of any (or a significant portion of any) major component or substantial structural part of the airframe. This work maintained the relative value of the aircraft. The value of the aircraft declines as it ages even if the heavy maintenance work is performed. After 45 days, the heavy maintenance visit was completed, and Aircraft 1 was reassembled, tested, and returned to X's fleet. X then continued to use Aircraft 1 for the same purposes and in the same manner that it did prior to the performance of the heavy maintenance visit. The performance of the heavy maintenance visit did not extend the useful life of the airframe beyond the 25-year useful life that X anticipated when it acquired the airframe.

Situation 2

Also in 2000, X incurred costs to perform work in conjunction with a heavy maintenance visit on the airframe of Aircraft 2. The heavy maintenance visit on Aircraft 2 involved all of the same work described in Situation 1. In addition, X found significant wear and corrosion of fuselage skins of Aircraft 2 that necessitated more extensive work than was performed on Aircraft 1. Namely, X decided to remove all of the skin panels on the belly of Aircraft 2's fuselage and replace them with new skin panels. The replaced skin panels represented a significant portion of all of the skin panels of Aircraft 2, and the work performed materially added to the value of the airframe. Because Aircraft 2 was already out of service and its airframe disassembled for the heavy maintenance visit, X also performed certain modifications to the airframe. These modifications involved installing a cabin smoke and fire detection and suppression system, a ground proximity warning system, and an air phone system to enable passengers to send and receive voice calls, faxes, and other electronic data while in flight.

Situation 3

Also in 2000, X decided to make substantial improvements to Aircraft 3, which was 22 years old and nearing the end of its anticipated useful life, for the purpose of increasing its reliability and extending its useful life. X's improvement of Aircraft 3 involved many modifications to the structure, exterior, and interior of the airframe. The modifications included removing all the belly skin panels on the aircraft'/s fuselage and replacing them with new skin panels; replacing the metal supports under the lavatories and galleys; removing the wiring in the leading edges of both wings and replacing it with new wiring; removing the fuel tank bladders, harnesses, wiring systems, and connectors and replacing them with new components; opening every lap joint on the airframe and replacing the epoxy and rivets used to seal the lap joints with a non-corrosive sealant and larger rivets; reconfiguring and upgrading the avionics and the equipment in the cockpit; replacing all the seats, overhead bins, sidewall panels, partitions, carpeting, windows, galleys, lavatories, and ceiling panels with new items; installing a cabin smoke and fire detection system, and a ground proximity warning system; and painting the exterior of the aircraft. The work performed on Aircraft 3 also included modifications necessary to terminate every aging aircraft AD applicable to Aircraft 3. In order to upgrade the airframe to the desired level, X performed much of the same work that would be performed during a heavy maintenance visit (as described in Situation 1). The result of the work performed on Aircraft 3 was to materially increase the value of the airframe and substantially prolong its useful life.

LAW

Section 162 and 1.162-1(a) of the Income Tax Regulations allow a deduction for all the ordinary and necessary expenses paid or incurred during the taxable year in carrying on any trade or business, including "incidental repairs." Section 1.162-4 allows a deduction for the cost of incidental repairs that neither materially add to the value of the property nor appreciably prolong its useful life, but keep it in an ordinarily efficient operating condition. However, 1.162-4 also provides that the cost of repairs in the nature of replacements that arrest deterioration and appreciably prolong the life of the property must be capitalized and depreciated in accordance with 167. Section 263(a) provides that no deduction is allowed for (1) any amount paid out for new buildings or permanent improvements or betterments made to increase the value of any property or estate or (2) any amount expended in restoring property or in making good the exhaustion thereof for which an allowance has been made. See also 1.263(a)-1(a).

Section 1.263(a)-1(b) provides that capital expenditures include amounts paid or incurred to (1) add to the value, or substantially prolong the useful life, of property owned by the taxpayer, or (2) adapt property to a new or different use. However, that regulation also provides that amounts paid or incurred for incidental repairs and maintenance of property within the meaning of 162 and 1.162-4 are not capital expenditures under 1.263(a)-1. Section 263A provides that the direct and indirect costs properly allocable to real or tangible personal property produced by the taxpayer must be capitalized. Section 263A(g)(1) provides that, for purposes of 263A, the term produce includes construct, build, install, manufacture, develop, or improve. The United States Supreme Court has specifically recognized that the "decisive distinctions" [between capital and ordinary expenditures] are those of degree and not of kind, and a careful examination of the particular facts of each case is required. Deputy v. du Pont, 308 U.S. 488, 496 (1940), quoting Welch v. Helvering, 290 U.S. 111, 114 (1933). To determine whether certain costs should be classified as capital expenditures or as repair and maintenance expenses, "it is appropriate to consider the purpose, the physical nature, and the effect of the work for which the expenditures were made." American Bemberg Corp. v. Commissioner, 10 T.C. 361, 376 (1948), aff'd, 177 F.2d 200 (6th Cir. 1949). Any properly performed repair, no matter how routine, could be considered to prolong the useful life and increase the value of the property if it is compared with the situation existing immediately prior to that repair. Consequently, courts have articulated a number of ways to distinguish between deductible repairs and non-deductible capital improvements. For example, in Illinois Merchants Trust Co. v. Commissioner, 4 B.T.A. 103, 106 (1926), acq., V-2 C.B. 2, the court explained that repair and maintenance expenses are incurred for the purpose of keeping the property in an ordinarily efficient operating condition over its probable useful life for the uses for which the property was acquired. Capital expenditures, in contrast, are for replacements, alterations, improvements, or additions that appreciably prolong the life of the property, materially increase its value, or make it adaptable to a different use. In Estate of Walling v. Commissioner, 373 F.2d 190, 192-193 (3rd Cir. 1966), the court explained that the relevant distinction between capital improvements and repairs is whether the expenditures were made to "put" or "keep" property in ordinary efficient operating condition. In Plainfield-Union Water Co. v. Commissioner, 39 T.C. 333, 338 (1962), nonacq. on other grounds, 1964-2 C.B. 8., the court stated that if the expenditure merely restores the property to the state it was in before the situation prompting the expenditure arose and does not make the property more valuable, more useful, or longer-lived, then such an expenditure is usually considered a deductible repair. In contrast, a capital expenditure is generally considered to be a more permanent increment in the longevity, utility, or worth of the property. The Supreme Court's decision in INDOPCO Inc. v. Commissioner, 503 U.S. 79 (1992) does not affect these general principles. See Rev. Rul. 94-12, 1994-1 C.B. 36; Ingram Industries, Inc. v. Commissioner, T.C.M. 2000-323. Even if the expenditures include the replacement of numerous parts of an asset, if the replacements are a relatively minor portion of the physical structure of the asset, or of any of its major parts, such that the asset as whole has not gained materially in value or useful life, then the costs incurred may be deducted as incidental repairs or maintenance expenses. See Buckland v. United States, 66 F.Supp. 681, 683 (D. Conn. 1946) (costs to replace all window sills in factory building were deductible repairs). See also, e.g., Libby & Blouin Ltd. v. Commissioner, 4 B.T.A. 910 (1926) (costs to replace all the tubing in sugar evaporator, which were small parts in a large machine, were deductible repairs). The same conclusion is true even if such minor portion of the asset is replaced with new and improved materials. See, e.g., Badger Pipeline v. Commissioner, T.C.M. 1997-457 (costs to replace 1,000 feet of pipeline in a 25-mile section of pipeline were deductible repairs, regardless of whether the new pipe was of better quality or has a longer life). If, however, a major component or a substantial structural part of the asset is replaced and, as a result, the asset as a whole has increased in value, life expectancy, or use then the costs of the replacement must be capitalized. See, e.g., Denver & Rio Grande Western R.R. Co. v. Commissioner, 279 F.2d 368 (10th Cir. 1960) (costs to replace major portion of a viaduct - all of the floor planks and 85-90% of the stringers - were capital expenditures); P. Dougherty Co. v. Commissioner, 159 F.2d 269, 272 (4th Cir. 1946) (costs to replace entire stern section of barge with new materials were capital expenditures); Vanalco Inc. v. Commissioner, T.C.M. 1999-265 (cost to replace the cell lining, an essential and substantial component of the cell, was required to be capitalized); Stark v. Commissioner, T.C.M. 1999-1 (cost to replace building roof were capital expenditures); Rev. Rul. 88-57, 1988-2 C.B. 36, modified by Rev. Rul. 94-38, 1994-1 C.B. 35 (costs to perform major cyclical rehabilitations on railroad freight train cars as part of a plan of rehabilitation in which all of the structural components were either reconditioned or replaced were capital expenditures). In addition, although the high cost of the work performed may be considered in determining whether an expenditure is capital in nature, cost alone is not dispositive. Compare R.R. Hensler, Inc. v. Commissioner, 73 T.C. 168, 177 (1979), acq. in result, 1980-2 C.B. 1 (the fact that taxpayer's expense was large does not change its character as ordinary); Buckland at 683 (replacements of relatively minor proportions of the entire physical asset constitute repairs even where high in cost); and American Bemberg, 10 T.C. 361 (1948) (deduction allowed for drilling and grouting to prevent cave-ins even though the total cost of the expenditures exceeded $1.1 million), with Wolfsen Land & Cattle Co. v. Commissioner, 72 T.C. 1, 17 (1979) (costs to dragline an irrigation ditch were capital expenditures, in part, because they could be as high as the cost to construct a new ditch); and Stoeltzing v. Commissioner, 266 F.2d 374, 376 (3d Cir. 1959) (expenditures could not be incidental repairs because they exceeded by almost 200% the cost of the building). Similarly, the fact that a taxpayer is required by a regulatory authority to make certain repairs or to perform certain maintenance on an asset in order to continue operating the asset in its business does not mean that the work performed materially increases the value of such asset, substantially prolongs its useful life, or adapts it to a new use. See, e.g., Midland

Empire Packing Co. v. Commissioner, 14 T.C. 635 (1950), acq., 1950-2 C.B. 3 (costs of applying concrete liner to basement walls and floors in order to satisfy federal meat inspectors were deductible repairs); L&L Marine Service Inc. v. Commissioner, T.C.M. 1987-428 (work performed on barges that was necessary to enable the barges to continue to qualify for sea duty was deductible repair). The characterization of any cost as a deductible repair or capital improvement depends on the context in which the cost is incurred. Specifically, where an expenditure is made as part of a general plan of rehabilitation, modernization, and improvement of the property, the expenditure must be capitalized, even though, standing alone, the item may be classified as one of repair or maintenance. United States v. Wehrli, 400 F.2d 686, 689 (10th Cir. 1968). Whether a general plan of rehabilitation exists, and whether a particular repair or maintenance item is part of it, are questions of fact to be determined based upon all the surrounding facts and circumstances, including, but not limited to, the purpose, nature, extent, and value of the work done. Id. at 690. The existence of a written plan, by itself, is not sufficient to trigger the plan of rehabilitation doctrine. See Moss v. Commissioner, 831 F.2d 833, 842 (9th Cir. 1987); Vanalco v. Commissioner, T.C.M. 1999-265. In general, the courts have applied the plan of rehabilitation doctrine to require a taxpayer to capitalize otherwise deductible repair and maintenance costs where the taxpayer has a plan to make substantial capital improvements to property and the repairs are incidental to that plan. See, e.g., California Casket Co. v. Commissioner, 19 T.C. 32 (1952), acq., 1953-1 C.B. 3 (costs of repairing the foundation although not in the original plan became, when undertaken, incidental to and involved in the plan of completely renovating and remodeling an old warehouse building); Stoeltzing at 377 (costs to renovate old building by shoring up floors; constructing steps, landing and new driveway; replacing wiring and plumbing; installing new roof; plastering; insulating; performing carpentry work; patching the gutters; and removing rubbish must be capitalized as part of plan of rehabilitation); Bank of Houston v. Commissioner, T.C.M. 1960-110 (costs incurred for various repairs incident to the reconstruction and renovation of a bank building must be capitalized as part of a general plan of rehabilitation). On the other hand, the courts and the Service have not applied the plan of rehabilitation doctrine to situations where the plan did not include substantial capital improvements and repairs to the same asset, the plan primarily involved repair and maintenance items, or the work was performed merely to keep the property in an ordinarily efficient operating condition. See, e.g., Moss at 840 (repairs incurred in conjunction with a hotel remodeling project not required to be capitalized as part of a plan of rehabilitation because the project's capital expenditures were not of the nature or scope necessary to trigger the plan of rehabilitation doctrine); Schroeder v. Commissioner, T.C.M. 1996-336 (costs of renovating barns were not required to be capitalized as part of a plan of rehabilitation where most of the renovation costs were repairs and maintenance to keep the barns in an efficient operating condition); Rev. Rul. 70-392, 1970-2 C.B. 33 (costs incurred to relocate existing capital assets in order to install new assets intended to increase a utility's distribution voltage were not required to be capitalized as part of a general plan of rehabilitation because the relocation merely kept the existing assets in an ordinarily efficient operating condition).

ANALYSIS

In Situation 1, the heavy maintenance visit on Aircraft 1 primarily involved inspecting, testing, servicing, repairing, reconditioning, cleaning, stripping, and repainting numerous airframe parts and components. The heavy maintenance visit did not involve replacements, alterations, improvements, or additions to the airframe that appreciably prolonged its useful life, materially increased its value, or adapted it to a new or different use. Rather, the heavy maintenance visit merely kept the airframe in an ordinarily efficient operating condition over its anticipated useful life for the uses for which the property was acquired. See Illinois Merchant Trust Co. at 106; Estate of Walling at 192-193; Ingram Industries, Inc. at 538-539. The fact that the taxpayer was required to perform the heavy maintenance visit to maintain its airworthiness certificate does not affect this determination. See Midland Empire Packing at 642. Although the heavy maintenance visit did involve the replacement of numerous airframe parts with new parts, none of these replacements required the substitution of any (or a significant portion of any) major components or substantial structural parts of the airframe so that the airframe as a whole increased in value, life expectancy, or use. Compare Buckland at 683 with P. Dougherty at 272. Thus, the facts in Situation 1 are distinguishable from those in Rev. Rul. 88-57 in which all of the structural components of a railroad freight car were either reconditioned or replaced so that the car was restored to a "like new" condition with a new, additional service life of 12 to 14 years. Moreover, the heavy maintenance visit also did not restore the airframe, or make good exhaustion for which an allowance had been made, within the meaning of 263(a)(2). In order to have a restoration under 263(a)(2), much more extensive work would have to be done so as to substantially prolong the useful life of the airframe. See Denver & Rio Grande at 373. Thus, the costs of the heavy maintenance visit constitute expenses for incidental repairs and maintenance under 1.162-4.

Finally, the costs of the heavy maintenance visit are not required to be capitalized under 263 or 263A as part of a plan of rehabilitation, modernization, or improvement to the airframe. Because the heavy maintenance visit involved only repairs for the purpose of keeping the airframe in an ordinarily efficient operating condition, it did not include the type of substantial capital improvements necessary to trigger the plan of rehabilitation doctrine. See Schroeder v. Commissioner, T.C.M. 1996-336; Moss at 842. Accordingly, the costs incurred by X for the heavy maintenance visit in Situation 1 may be deducted as ordinary and necessary business expenses under 162.

In Situation 2, in addition to performing all of the work described in Situation 1 on Aircraft 2, X replaced all of the skin panels on the belly of the fuselage and installed a cabin smoke and fire detection and suppression system, a ground proximity warning system and an air phone system. Because the replacement of the skin panels involved replacing a significant portion of the airframe's skin panels (which in the aggregate represented a substantial structural part of the airframe) thereby materially adding to the value of and improving the airframe, the cost of replacing the skin panels must be capitalized. See Vanalco, T.C.M. 1999-265; P. Dougherty at 272. In addition, the additions and upgrades to Aircraft 2 in the form of the fire protection, air phone, and ground proximity warning systems must be capitalized because they materially improved the airframe. See Phillips and Easton Supply Co. v. Commissioner, 20 T.C 455, 460 (1953). Accordingly, the costs incurred by X for labor and materials allocable to these capital improvements must be treated as capital expenditures under 263. Moreover, because the improvement of property constitutes production within the meaning of 263A(g)(1), X is required to capitalize under 263A the direct costs and a proper share of the allocable indirect costs associated with these improvements.

Further, the mere fact that these capital improvements were made at the same time that the work described in Situation 1 was performed on Aircraft 2 does not require capitalization of the cost of the heavy maintenance visit under the plan of rehabilitation doctrine. Whether a general plan of rehabilitation exists is a question of fact to be determined based on all the facts and circumstances. See Wehrli at 690. X's plan in Situation 2 was not to rehabilitate Aircraft 2, but merely to perform discrete capital improvements to the airframe. See Moss at 839; Schroeder v. Commissioner, T.C.M. 1996-336; Rev. Rul. 70-392. For this reason, the facts of Situation 2 are distinguishable from Rev. Rul. 88-57, which involved a major rehabilitation that constituted a plan of rehabilitation undertaken near the end of the freight car's life for the purpose of restoring it to a "like new" condition. Accordingly, the costs of the work described in Situation 1 are not part of a general plan of rehabilitation, modernization, or improvement to the airframe. The costs incurred by X for the work performed on Aircraft 2 must be allocated between capital improvements, which must be capitalized under 263 and 263A, and repairs and maintenance, which may be deducted under 162.

In Situation 3, X is required to capitalize under 263 the costs of all the work performed on Aircraft 3. The work in Situation 3 involved replacements of major components and significant portions of substantial structural parts that materially increased the value and substantially prolonged the useful life of the airframe. See P. Dougherty at 272 and Rev. Rul. 88-57. In addition, the value of Aircraft 3 was materially increased as a result of material additions, alterations and upgrades that enabled X to operate Aircraft 3 in an improved way. See Dominion Resources, 48 F. Supp. 2d 527, 553. In contrast to Situation 1, the extensiveness of the work performed on Aircraft 3 constitutes a restoration within the meaning of 263(a)(2). See, e.g. Denver & Rio Grande at 373.

X performed much of the same work on Aircraft 3 that would be performed during a heavy maintenance visit (as described in Situation 1) ("Situation 1"-type work). Although these costs, standing alone, generally are deductible expenses under 162, in this context, they are incurred as part of a general plan of rehabilitation, modernization, and improvement to the airframe of Aircraft 3 and X is required to capitalize under 263 and 263A the costs of that work. See Wehrli at 689-90. In this situation, X planned to perform substantial capital improvements to upgrade the airframe of Aircraft 3 for the purpose of increasing its reliability and extending its useful life. See Rev. Rul. 88-57. The Situation 1-type work was incidental to X's plan to upgrade Aircraft 3. See California Casket at 38. The effect of all the work performed on Aircraft 3, including the inspection, repair, and maintenance items, is to materially increase the value of the airframe and substantially prolong its useful life. Thus, all the work performed by X on Aircraft 3 is part of a general plan of rehabilitation, modernization, and improvement to the airframe and the costs associated with this work must be capitalized under 263. Further, because the improvement of the airframe constitutes production of property within the meaning of 263A(g)(1), X is required to capitalize under 263A the direct costs and a proper share of the allocable indirect costs associated with this improvement plan.

The conclusions in this ruling would be the same whether X transported only freight or only passengers.

HOLDINGS

Costs incurred by a taxpayer to perform work on its aircraft airframe as part of a heavy maintenance visit generally are deductible as ordinary and necessary business expenses under 162. However, costs incurred in conjunction with a heavy maintenance visit must be capitalized to the extent they materially add to the value of, substantially prolong the useful life of, or adapt the airframe to a new or different use. In addition, costs incurred as part of a plan of rehabilitation, modernization, or improvement must be capitalized.

APPLICATION

Any change in a taxpayer's method of accounting to conform with this revenue ruling is a change in method of accounting to which the provisions of 446 and 481 and the regulations thereunder apply. A taxpayer wanting to change its method of accounting to conform with the holding in this revenue ruling must follow the automatic change in accounting method provisions of Rev. Proc. 99-49, 1999-52 I.R.B. 725, provided the change is made for the first taxable year ending after January 16, 2001. However, the scope limitations in section 4.02 of Rev. Proc. 99-49 do not apply unless the taxpayer's method of accounting for costs incurred to perform work on its aircraft airframes is an issue pending, within the meaning of section 6.01(6) of Rev. Proc. 2000- 38, 2000-40 I.R.B. 310, at the time the Form 3115 is filed with the national office. If the taxpayer is under examination, before an appeals office, or before a federal court with respect to any income tax issue, the taxpayer must provide a copy of the Form 3115, Application for Change in Accounting Method, to the examining agent, appeals officer, or counsel for the government, as appropriate, at the same time that it files the copy of the Form 3115 with the national office. The Form 3115 must contain the name(s) and telephone number(s) of the examining agent(s), appeals officer, or counsel for the government, as appropriate.

EFFECT ON OTHER DOCUMENTS

Rev. Proc. 99-49 is modified and amplified to include the prospective change in accounting method in the APPENDIX. Rev. Rul. 88-57 is distinguished.

DRAFTING INFORMATION

The principal author of this revenue ruling is Merrill D. Feldstein of the Office of Associate Chief Counsel (Income Tax and Accounting). For further information regarding this revenue ruling, contact Ms. Feldstein or Beverly Katz on (202) 622-4950 (not a toll-free call).

+ Revenue Procedure

Internal Revenue Bulletin: 2007-36
September 4, 2007
Rev. Proc. 2007-57

Table of Contents
SECTION 1. PURPOSE

This revenue procedure informs taxpayers of their obligations under section 3402(q) pertaining to withholding and information reporting applicable to certain amounts paid to winners of poker tournaments. It further sets forth procedures to be used to comply with the relevant requirements of the Internal Revenue Code and Treasury Regulations thereunder.

SECTION 2. FACTUAL BACKGROUND

A business taxpayer ("poker tournament sponsor") may sponsor a poker tournament, charging an entry fee and a "buy-in" fee for each participant. In exchange for the fees, each participant receives a set of poker chips with a nominal face value for use in the specific poker tournament. The poker tournament sponsor pays amounts, which exceed a participant's fees by $5,000, to a certain number of tournament winner(s), out of a pool comprised of all the participants' fees.

SECTION 3. LEGAL BACKGROUND

.01. *Withholding under section 3402.* Section 3402(q)(1) provides that every person who makes any payment of winnings which are subject to withholding shall deduct and withhold from the payment an amount equal to the product of the third lowest rate of tax applicable under section 1(c) and such payment. Section 3402(q)(3) provides that the term "winnings which are subject to withholding" means, in part, proceeds from a wagering transaction, if the proceeds are more than $5,000 from a wager placed in any sweepstakes, wagering pool, or lottery. The term "wagering pool" includes "all pari-mutuel betting pools, including on- and off-track racing pools, and similar types of betting pools." H.R. Conf. Rep. No. 94-1515, at 488 (1976) (relating to the enactment of § 3402(q)). "In common usage the term 'pool' connotes a particular gambling practice, an arrangement whereby all bets constitute a common fund to be taken by the winner or winners." *United States v. Berent*, 523 F.2d 1360, 1361 (9th Cir. 1975). Section 3402(q)(4)(A) provides that proceeds from a wager shall be determined by reducing the amount received by the amount of the wager.

.02. *Information reporting under section 31.3402(q)-1(e)*. Section 31.3402(q)-1(e) of the Employment Tax Regulations provides that each person who is to receive a payment of winnings subject to withholding shall furnish to the payer a statement on Form W-2G or Form 5754 (whichever is applicable) made under the penalties of perjury containing certain required information, including the name, address, and Taxpayer Identification Number of the winning payee. Section 31.3402(q)-1(f)(1) provides that every person making a payment of winnings for which withholding is required shall file a Form W-2G with the IRS on or before February 28 (March 31 if filed electronically) of the calendar year following the calendar year in which the payment of winnings is made and shall furnish a copy of the Form to the payee.

SECTION 4. APPLICATION

A poker tournament sponsor is required to withhold and report on payments of more than $5,000 made to a winning payee in a taxable year by filing an information return with the IRS as prescribed by section 3402(q). The poker tournament sponsor must furnish a copy of the information return to the IRS on or before February 28 (March 31 if filed electronically) of the calendar year following the calendar year in which the payment is made, as prescribed by section 31.3402(q) of the regulations.

SECTION 5. SCOPE

This revenue procedure applies to poker tournament sponsors, including casinos, which pay amounts to winners in a manner substantially similar to that described in section 2 of this revenue procedure.

SECTION 6. WAIVER OF LIABILITY UNDER SECTION 3402 AND WAIVER OF OTHER PENALTIES OR ADDITIONS TO TAX

The IRS will not assert any liability for additional tax or additions to tax for violations of any withholding obligation with respect to amounts paid to winners of poker tournaments under section 3402, provided that the poker tournament sponsor meets all of the requirements for information reporting under section 3402(q) and the regulations thereunder.

SECTION 7. EFFECTIVE DATE

This revenue procedure is effective for payments made on or after March 4, 2008.

SECTION 8. DRAFTING INFORMATION

The principal author of this revenue procedure is Blaise G. Dusenberry of the Office of Associate Chief Counsel (Procedure and Administration). For further information regarding this revenue procedure, contact Cynthia McGreevy at (202) 622-4910 (not a toll-free call).

↓ <u>Private Letter Ruling</u>

Internal Revenue Service

Number: **201726008**
Release Date: 6/30/2017

Index Numbers: 9100.00-00, 9100.10-00,
9100.10-01

Department of the Treasury
Washington, DC 20224

Third Party Communication: None
Date of Communication: Not Applicable

Person To Contact:
, ID No.

Telephone Number/Fax Number:

Refer Reply To:
CC:ITA:B7
PLR-134191-16
Date: April 5, 2017

In re: Request For An Extension Of Time To
File a Form 3115, *Application for Change in
Accounting Method*

LEGEND

Parent =
S1 =
S2 =
S3 =
S4 =
S5 =
S6 =
Firm =
Date1 =
Date2 =
Date3 =
Date4 =

Dear   :

This ruling letter responds to a letter dated October 18, 2016, submitted on behalf of Parent, S1, S2, S3, S4, S5, and S6 (hereinafter, collectively referred to as Taxpayer). Taxpayer is requesting an extension of time pursuant to §§ 301.9100-1 and 301.9100-3 of the Procedure and Administration Regulations to file an original Form 3115, Application for Change in Accounting Method, pursuant to section 6.03(1)(a)(i)(A) of Rev. Proc. 2015-13, 2015-5 I.R.B. 419, 432, with Parent's timely filed (including extension) consolidated federal income tax return for the taxable year ending Date1.

PLR-134191-16   2

FACTS

Taxpayer represents that the facts are as follows:

Parent was the common parent of an affiliated group of corporations, including S1, S2, S3, S4, S5 and S6, that filed consolidated federal income tax returns on a calendar year basis.

In Date2, Taxpayer engaged Firm to evaluate Taxpayer's method of accounting for certain costs attributable to the development of computer software and provided Firm with all the relevant facts. Based on Firm's recommendation, Taxpayer decided to request permission from the Commissioner of Internal Revenue to change its method of accounting for expenditures properly attributable to the development of computer software to treat those costs in accordance with Rev. Proc. 2000-50, as modified by Rev. Proc. 2007-16, 2007-1 C.B. 358, beginning with the taxable year ending Date1.

Taxpayer instructed Firm to take the appropriate steps necessary to make the accounting method change, including attaching the original Form 3115 to Parent's consolidated federal income tax return. Taxpayer relied on Firm to advise it as to all filings relating to the accounting method change. Taxpayer believed and understood that Firm had extensive experience in assisting clients in matters relating to changes in accounting methods.

Prior to Date3, Firm prepared the Form 3115 application request for permission to make the accounting method change under section 9.01 of Rev. Proc. 2016-29, 2016-21 I.R.B. 880, 920 (designated automatic method change number (DCN) 18). Firm timely filed the return and the required copy of the Form 3115 with the appropriate office of the Internal Revenue Service prior to the due date (including extension) of the relevant tax return, Date3. *See*, section 6.03(1)(a)(i)(B) of Rev. Proc. 2015-13.

Firm reflected the desired accounting method change on Parent's consolidated federal income tax return for the taxable year ending Date1, but inadvertently failed to attach the original of the required Form 3115 to that return. On Date4, Firm discovered its error and informed Taxpayer of the missing filing. Subsequently, Firm submitted this request for an extension of time to file the original of Taxpayer's Form 3115.

RULING REQUESTED

Taxpayer requests an extension of time pursuant to §§ 301.9100-1 and 301.9100-3 to file the original Form 3115 that is required by Rev. Proc. 2015-13 with its consolidated federal income tax return to obtain the consent of the Commissioner of Internal Revenue to change to the previously described accounting method (DCN 18) for the taxable year ending Date1.

PLR-134191-16   3

LAW AND ANALYSIS

Rev. Proc. 2015-13 provides the procedures by which a taxpayer may obtain automatic consent to change certain accounting methods. Section 9 of Rev. Proc. 2015-13 provides that consent of the Commissioner to change its accounting method under § 446(e) of the Internal Revenue Code and § 1.446-1(e) of the Income Tax Regulations is granted only if the taxpayer complies with all the applicable provisions of the revenue procedure and implements the change in method on its federal income tax return for the requested year of change to which the original Form 3115 is attached pursuant to section 6.03.

Section 6.03(1)(a)(i) of Rev. Proc. 2015-13 provides that a taxpayer changing an accounting method pursuant to Rev. Proc. 2015-13 must complete and file a Form 3115 in duplicate. The original Form 3115 must be attached to the taxpayer's timely filed (including any extension) original federal income tax return for the year of change, and a copy (with signature) of the Form 3115 must be filed with the appropriate office of the Service no earlier than the first day of the year of change and no later than when the original is filed with the federal income tax return for the year of change.

Sections 301.9100-1 through 301.9100-3 provide the standards the Commissioner will use to determine whether to grant an extension of time to make an election. Section 301.9100-2 provides automatic extensions of time for making certain elections. Section 301.9100-3 provides extensions of time for making elections that do not meet the requirements of § 301.9100-2.

Section 301.9100-1(b) defines a regulatory election as an election whose due date is prescribed by a regulation published in the Federal Register, or a revenue ruling, revenue procedure, notice, or announcement published in the Internal Revenue Bulletin.

Section 301.9100-1(c) provides that the Commissioner has discretion to grant a reasonable extension of time under the rules set forth in §§ 301.9100-2 and 301.9100-3 to make certain regulatory elections.

Section 301.9100-3(a) provides that requests for relief subject to § 301.9100-3 will be granted when the taxpayer provides evidence to establish to the satisfaction of the Commissioner that the taxpayer acted reasonably and in good faith and that the granting of relief will not prejudice the interests of the Government.

Section 301.9100-3(c)(2) imposes special rules for accounting method regulatory elections. This section provides, in relevant part, that the interests of the Government are deemed to be prejudiced except in unusual and compelling circumstances when the accounting method regulatory election for which relief is requested is subject to the procedure described in § 1.446-1(e)(3)(i) or the relief requires an adjustment under § 481(a) (or would require an adjustment under § 481(a) if the taxpayer changed to the accounting method for which relief is requested in a taxable year subsequent to the

PLR-134191-16   4

taxable year the election should have been made).

CONCLUSION

Based solely on the facts and representations submitted, we conclude that the requirements of §§ 301.9100-1 and 301.9100-3 have been satisfied in Taxpayer's case. Accordingly, Taxpayer is granted 60 calendar days from the date of this letter to file the required original of the Form 3115 pertaining to the previously described accounting change for the taxable year ending Date1. This filing must be made by Parent filing an amended consolidated federal income tax return for that year, and attaching a copy of this letter ruling to the amended return. A copy of this letter ruling is enclosed for that purpose. Alternatively, a taxpayer filing its federal income tax return electronically may satisfy this requirement by attaching a statement to the return that provides the date and control number of the letter ruling.

Except as expressly set forth above, we express no opinion concerning the federal tax consequences of the facts described above under any other provision of the Code or regulations. Specifically, no opinion is expressed or implied, concerning whether (1) the accounting method change Taxpayer has made is eligible to be made under section 9.01 of Rev. Proc. 2016-29 and Rev. Proc. 2015-13, (2) Taxpayer otherwise meets the requirements of Rev. Proc. 2015-13 to make its accounting method change using the procedures of Rev. Proc. 2015-13, (3) Taxpayer's costs of computer software are eligible for a method of accounting described in Rev. Proc. 2000-50, (4) Taxpayer's method of accounting for computer software costs is correct.

The ruling contained in this letter ruling is based upon information and representations submitted on behalf of Taxpayer, with accompanying penalty of perjury statements executed by appropriate parties. While this office has not verified any of the material submitted in support of this request for an extension of time to file the required Form 3115, all material is subject to verification on examination.

This letter ruling is directed only to the taxpayer requesting it. Section 6110(k)(3) provides that this ruling may not be used or cited as precedent.

PLR-134191-16   5

In accordance with the Power of Attorney on file with this office, we are sending a copy of this letter to Parent's authorized representatives. We also are sending a copy of this letter ruling to the appropriate operating division director.

Sincerely,

DEENA M. DEVEREUX
Assistant to the Branch Chief, Branch 7
Office of Associate Chief Counsel
(Income Tax & Accounting)

Enclosures (2):
   copy of this letter
   copy for section 6110 purposes

⬇ Generic Legal Advice Memorandum

Office of Chief Counsel
Internal Revenue Service
Memorandum

Number: **AM 2007-0012**

Release Date: 6/8/07

UILC: 9999.00-00

date: March 22, 2007

to: Deborah M. Nolan
Commissioner, Large and Mid-Size Business Division

from: Donald L. Korb
Chief Counsel

---

subject: FIN 48 & Tax Accrual Workpapers

This memorandum addresses the issue of whether documents produced by the taxpayer and/or its auditors to substantiate the taxpayer's uncertain tax positions in compliance with FIN 48 are included within the Service's interpretation of Tax Accrual Workpapers (TAW) as provided in IRM Section 4.10.20.2 (2). As discussed below, FIN 48 and the other Financial Accounting Standards Board (FASB) pronouncements articulate financial accounting and reporting requirements. However, neither FIN 48, nor other relevant FASB pronouncements, prescribe documentation requirements. Rather, the documentation requirements that taxpayers and their auditors must follow are established by the Securities and Exchange Commission (SEC), the Public Company Accounting Oversight Board (PCAOB), and the American Institute of Certified Public Accountants (AICPA), and these documentation requirements remain unchanged by the issuance of FIN 48. Consequently, it is our conclusion that documentation resulting from the issuance of FIN 48 is considered tax accrual workpapers for purposes of IRM Section 4.10.20.2(2).

IRM Section 4.10.20.2(2) defines tax accrual workpapers as "those audit workpapers, whether prepared by the taxpayer, the taxpayer's accountant or the independent auditor, that relate to the tax reserve for current, deferred and potential or contingent tax liabilities, however classified or reported on audited financial statements, and to footnotes disclosing those tax reserves on audited financial statements." These

219

workpapers reflect an estimate of a company's tax liabilities and may also be referred to as the tax pool analysis, tax liability contingency analysis, tax cushion analysis, or tax contingency reserve analysis. The name given the workpapers by the taxpayer, the taxpayer's accountant, or the independent auditor is not determinative. Tax accrual workpapers typically include determinations and related documentation of estimates of potential or contingent tax liabilities related to tax positions taken by the taxpayer on certain transactions. In addition, there may be an audit trail and/or complete explanation of the transactions. There may also be information on whether there was reliance on outside legal advice; an assessment of the taxpayer's position and potential for sustention; references to promotional materials; and comments on unwritten agreements, confidentiality agreements, restitution agreements, contingency fees, expectations, and other material facts surrounding the transactions. The workpapers may include documents written by the taxpayer's employees and officers describing or evaluating the tax strategies. The scope and quality of the workpapers will vary.[1]

FASB Statement No. 109 (Accounting for Income Taxes, effective 1992) established financial accounting and reporting standards for the effects of income taxes that result from an enterprise's activities during the current and preceding years. It requires an

---

[1] IRM Section 4.10.20.2(2) also provides that the total amount of the reserve established on a company's general ledger for all contingent tax liabilities of the company for a specific reporting period is not considered a part of the company's tax accrual workpapers. An examiner may ask a taxpayer about the existence and the total amount of a reserve for all contingent tax liabilities as a matter of routine examination procedure, without a showing of unusual circumstances and without seeking executive approval for the request. In addition, it provides that a request to reveal the existence or amount of a tax reserve established for any specific known or unknown transaction, however, is the same as asking for a description of a portion of the contents of the tax accrual workpapers. Requests for a description of the contents of the tax accrual workpapers are covered by the same policy of restraint as requests for the actual documents that make up the tax accrual workpapers.

IRM Section 4.10.20.2(1) defines Audit Workpapers as workpapers created by or for the independent auditor. They are retained by the independent auditor and may be shared with the taxpayer. These workpapers include information about the procedures followed, the tests performed, the information obtained, and the conclusions reached pertinent to the independent auditor's review of a taxpayer's financial statements. Audit workpapers may include work programs, analyses, memoranda, letters of confirmation and representation, abstracts of company documents, and schedules or commentaries prepared or obtained by the auditor. These workpapers provide important support for the independent auditor's opinion as to the fairness of the presentation of the financial statements, in conformity with generally accepted auditing standards and generally accepted accounting principles.

IRM Section 4.10.20.2(3) defines Tax Reconciliation Workpapers as workpapers are used in assembling and compiling financial data preparatory to placement on a tax return. These papers typically include final trial balances for each entity and a schedule of consolidating and adjusting entries. They include information used to trace financial information to the tax return. Any tax return preparation documents that reconcile net income per books or financial statements to taxable income are also tax reconciliation workpapers. Tax reconciliation workpapers do not become tax accrual workpapers when they are used in the preparation of tax accrual workpapers or are attached to tax accrual workpapers. Preexisting documents that a taxpayer, the taxpayer's accountant, or the taxpayer's independent auditor consults, refers to, or relies upon in making evaluations or decisions regarding the tax reserves or in performing an audit are not themselves considered tax accrual workpapers or audit workpapers, even though the taxpayer, the taxpayer's accountant, or independent auditor may store such documents with the tax accrual workpapers or audit workpapers.

asset and liability approach to financial accounting and reporting for income taxes. The objectives of accounting for income taxes are to recognize (a) the amount of taxes payable or refundable for the current year and (b) deferred tax liabilities and assets for the future tax consequences of events that have been recognized in an enterprise's financial statements or tax returns. FASB No. 109 established procedures to (i) measure deferred tax liabilities and assets using a tax rate convention and (ii) assess whether a valuation allowance should be established. All available evidence, both positive and negative, is considered to determine whether, based on the weight of that evidence, a valuation allowance is needed for some portion or all of a deferred tax asset. Judgment must be used in considering the relative impact of negative and positive evidence. The weight given to the potential effect of negative and positive evidence should be commensurate with the extent to which it can be objectively verified.

FASB Interpretation No. 48 (FIN 48) (Accounting for Uncertainty in Income Taxes, effective December 15, 2006) interprets FASB Statement No. 109 and clarifies the accounting for uncertainty in income taxes. It is intended to provide a more consistent approach to accounting for income taxes. The interpretation prescribes a recognition threshold and a measurement attribute. It requires a two step analysis. First, the enterprise determines whether it is more-likely-than-not that a tax position will be sustained upon examination, including resolution of any related appeals or litigation processes, based on the technical merits of the position. In evaluating whether a tax position has met the more-likely-than-not recognition threshold, the enterprise should assume that the position will be examined by the appropriate taxing authority that has full knowledge of all relevant information. If a tax position meets the more-likely-than-not threshold, the second step is to measure the amount of benefit to recognize in the financial statement. The tax position is measured at the largest amount of benefit that is greater than 50 percent likely of being realized upon settlement (cumulative 50% test). FIN 48 requires an enterprise to make certain disclosures at the end of each annual reporting period.[2]

Documentation Considerations

FASB No. 5, FASB No. 109 and FIN 48 articulate accounting and reporting principles with respect to accounting for contingent liabilities, income taxes and contingent tax liabilities. While they provide different standards for accounting for such items (i.e. different thresholds for recognizing the liabilities and calculating the amount of such liability), none of those provisions set forth specific record keeping or documentation requirements necessary to comply with those provisions.[3] Rather, the documentation requirements for the auditors are set forth by the SEC, PCAOB and AICPA.

---

[2] FIN 48 requires the disclosure of a tabular reconciliation of the total amounts of unrecognized tax benefits, the total amount of unrecognized tax benefits that, if recognized, would affect the effective tax rate, total amounts of interest and penalties, positions for which there is a reasonable possibility that the total amounts of unrecognized tax benefits will significantly increase of decrease within 12 months of the reporting date, and a description of the tax years that remain subject to examination by major tax jurisdiction.
[3] See December 13, 2006, Speech by SEC Staff Regarding Remarks before the 2006 AICPA National Conference on Current SEC and PCAOB Developments at www.sec.gov/news/speech/2006

4

<u>SEC Reg. S-X, Article 2, 210.2-06</u> (attached) requires that auditors retain for a period of seven years records relevant to the audit or review, including workpapers and other documents that form the basis of the audit or review of the issuer's financial statements, and memoranda, correspondence, communications, other documents, and records (including electronic records), which are created, sent or received in connection with the audit or review and contain conclusions, opinions, analyses, or financial data related to the audit or review.

The PCAOB established auditing standards that require registered public accounting firms to prepare and maintain, for at least seven years, audit documentation "in sufficient detail to support the conclusions reached" in the auditor's report.[4] The PCAOB adopted as interim standards <u>AICPA Auditing Standard No. 95</u>, (attached) which sets forth auditor documentation requirements. <u>Auditing Standard No. 95</u> provides that the auditors must obtain sufficient competent evidential matter through inspection, observation, inquiries, and confirmations to afford a reasonable basis for an opinion regarding the financial statements under audit.

The PCAOB also adopted <u>AU Section 9326, Evidential Matter: Auditing Interpretations of Section 326</u> (attached).   <u>AU Section 9326</u> specifically addresses the audit of tax liability contingency analysis. It provides that auditor's documents should include sufficient competent evidential matter about the significant elements of the client's tax liability contingency analysis, including "copies of the client's documents, schedules, or analyses (or auditor-prepared summaries thereof) to enable the auditor to support his or her conclusions regarding the appropriateness of the client's accounting and disclosure of significant tax-related contingency matters…The audit documentation should include the significant elements of the client's analysis of tax contingencies or reserves, including roll-forward of material changes to such reserves. In addition, the documentation should provide the client's position and support for income tax related disclosures."[5]

<u>Conclusion</u>

None of the relevant FASB pronouncements, including <u>FIN 48</u>, prescribe documentation that the taxpayer and/or its auditors must produce, maintain or rely upon in evaluating uncertain tax positions. Rather, the documentation requirements that taxpayers and their auditors must follow are established by the SEC, PCAOB, and the AICPA and are unaffected by the issuance of <u>FIN 48</u>. Moreover, these documentation requirements have not been changed since the issuance of <u>FIN 48</u>. Accordingly, the issuance of <u>FIN 48</u> does not change whether a document is considered to be a tax accrual workpaper as defined by <u>IRM Section 4.10.20.2(2).</u>

<u>/spch121306jmg.htm.</u>
[4] See PCAOB Auditing Standards No. 1 & 3 (attached).
[5] The relevant portions of <u>AU Section 9326</u> were issued in March, 1981, and amended April 9, 2003, and also discuss the concern over the IRS's access to tax accrual workpapers and its potential effect on taxpayers to not prepare or maintain appropriate documentation of the calculation or contents of the accrual for income taxes. See Section 2.06-2.09.

＋ IRS Notice

Part III - Administrative, Procedural, and Miscellaneous

Notice 2014-7

PURPOSE

This notice provides that certain payments received by an individual care provider under a state Medicaid Home and Community-Based Services Waiver (Medicaid waiver) program, described in this notice, are difficulty of care payments excludable under § 131 of the Internal Revenue Code.

BACKGROUND

Qualified foster care payments

Section 131(a) excludes qualified foster care payments from the gross income of a foster care provider. Section 131(b)(1) defines a qualified foster care payment, in part, as any payment under a foster care program of a state or a political subdivision that is either (1) paid to the foster care provider for caring for a qualified foster individual in the foster care provider's home, or (2) a difficulty of care payment. Section 131(b)(2) defines a qualified foster individual as any individual who is living in a foster family home in which the individual was placed by an agency of a state or political subdivision or by a qualified foster care placement agency. Section 131(b)(3) defines a qualified foster care placement agency, in part, as a placement agency that is licensed or certified for the foster care program of a state or political subdivision of a state.

Section 131(c) defines a difficulty of care payment as compensation to a foster care provider for the additional care required because the qualified foster individual has a physical, mental, or emotional handicap. The provider must provide the care in the provider's foster family home, a state must determine the need for this compensation, and the payor must designate the compensation for this purpose. In the case of any foster home, difficulty of care payments are not excludable to the extent that the payments are for more than 10 qualified foster individuals who have not attained age 19 or 5 qualified foster individuals who have attained age 19. See § 131(c)(2).

State Medicaid waiver programs

Under § 1915(c) of the Social Security Act (42 U.S.C. § 1396n(c)), a state may obtain a Medicaid waiver that allows the state to include in the state's Medicaid program the cost of home or community-based services (other than room and board) provided to individuals who otherwise would require care in a hospital, nursing facility, or intermediate care facility (eligible individuals). Home or community-based services include personal care services, habilitation services, and other services that are "cost effective and necessary to avoid institutionalization." See 42 C.F.R. § 440.180. Personal care services are defined under rules of the Centers for Medicare and Medicaid

Services to include assistance with eating, bathing, dressing, toileting, transferring, maintaining continence, personal hygiene, light housework, laundry, meal preparation, transportation, grocery shopping, using the telephone, medication management, and money management. Skilled services that only a health professional may perform are not personal care services. Habilitation services, defined in 42 U.S.C. § 1396n(c)(5)(A), assist individuals in acquiring, retaining, and improving the self-help, socialization, and adaptive skills necessary to reside successfully in home and community-based settings. Medicaid waiver programs generally do not compensate a family member for providing personal care services to an eligible individual if the family member is legally responsible for the individual (for example, a minor child). See 42 C.F.R. § 440.167(a)(2) and (b). Some states compensate family members, as well as unrelated individual care providers, for residential habilitation, foster/companion care, or transportation services provided as a part of an eligible individual's plan of care. A plan of care is a term defined by the state, but generally means an individualized plan of treatment, services, and/or providers. A state, directly or indirectly through an agency under contract with the state, certifies individuals and entities as Medicaid providers to provide services to eligible individuals. An entity that is a certified Medicaid provider may contract with an individual care provider to care for an eligible individual in the care provider's home. A state or an agency under contract with the state approves the plan of care for the eligible individual in the provider's home and monitors the eligible individual's care. State agencies, certified Medicaid provider entities, and individual care providers have asked whether Medicaid waiver payments for the care of eligible individuals, who are related or unrelated to the individual care provider, in the individual care provider's home may be treated as difficulty of care payments excludable under § 131.

Current treatment of government-funded payments for home care
The Service historically has challenged the excludability of payments to individual care providers caring for related individuals in the provider's home. See Alexander v. Commissioner, T.C. Summary Opinion 2011-48, filed April 12, 2011 (Medicaid waiver payments to taxpayers caring for a taxpayer's parents residing in the taxpayers' home are not excludable under § 131 because the taxpayers did not show that they operated a "foster family home" under state law and the parents were not "placed" in the taxpayers' home by the state). See also Bannon v. Commissioner, 99 T.C. 59 (1992) (payments received by the taxpayer for caring for her adult disabled daughter residing in the taxpayer's home under a state program for in-home supportive services are not excludable under the general welfare exclusion) and Harper v. Commissioner, T.C. Summary Opinion 2011-56, filed May 2, 2011 (following Bannon). Similarly, Program Manager Technical Advice (PMTA 2010-007) concludes that a biological parent of a disabled child may not exclude payments under § 131 because the ordinary meaning of foster care excludes care by a biological parent. Section 131 does not explicitly address whether payments under Medicaid waiver programs are qualified foster care payments. Medicaid waiver programs and state foster care programs, however, share similar oversight and purposes. The purpose of Medicaid waiver programs and the legislative history of § 131 reflect the fact that home care programs prevent the institutionalization of individuals with physical, mental, or emotional handicaps. See 128 Cong. Rec. 26905

(1982) (stating that "[difficulty of care payments] are not income to the [foster] parents, regardless of whether they, dollar for dollar only cover expenses. [These] parents are saving the taxpayers' money by preventing institutionalization of these children."); S. Rep. No. 97- 139 at 481 (1981) (describing the purpose of the amendment to 42 U.S.C. section 1396n, allowing Medicaid waivers for home and community-based services, as "[permitting] the Secretary to waive the current definition of covered [M]edicaid services to include certain nonmedical support services, other than room and board, which are provided pursuant to a plan of care to an individual otherwise at risk of being institutionalized and who would, in the absence of such services be institutionalized"). Both programs require state approval and oversight of the care of the individual in the provider's home. The programs share the objective of enabling individuals who otherwise would be institutionalized to live in a family home setting rather than in an institution, and both difficulty of care payments and Medicaid waiver payments compensate for the additional care required.

GUIDANCE
Treatment of qualified Medicaid waiver payments under § 131
To achieve consistent federal tax treatment of Medicaid waiver payments among the states and individual care providers, this notice provides that as of January 3, 2014, the Service will treat qualified Medicaid waiver payments as difficulty of care payments under § 131(c) that are excludable under § 131, and this treatment will apply whether the care provider is related or unrelated to the eligible individual. Accordingly, as of January 3, 2014, the Service will no longer assert the position in PMTA 2010-007, or apply Alexander, Bannon, or Harper, to conclude that a caregiver of a biological relative receiving qualified Medicaid waiver payments may not qualify as a foster care provider under § 131. For purposes of this notice, qualified Medicaid waiver payments are payments made by a state or political subdivision thereof, or an entity that is a certified Medicaid provider, under a Medicaid waiver program to an individual care provider for nonmedical support services provided under a plan of care to an eligible individual (whether related or unrelated) living in the individual care provider's home. Section 131(c) defines a difficulty of care payment as compensation to a foster care provider for the additional care required because the qualified foster individual has a physical, mental, or emotional handicap. Qualified Medicaid waiver payments compensate a care provider for providing the additional care required because of an eligible individual's physical, mental, or emotional handicap for which a state has determined that there is a need for additional compensation. Thus, the treatment of qualified Medicaid waiver payments as "difficulty of care payments" is consistent with the definition under § 131(c). Under § 131, payments are excludable as difficulty of care payments only if the care is provided to a "qualified foster individual," meaning any individual who is living in a "foster family home" in which the individual was "placed" by an agency of a state or a political subdivision thereof, or a qualified foster care placement agency. Section 131(b)(2). The term "foster family home" is not defined under § 131. However, the Tax Court has concluded that, for purposes of § 131, "a person's 'home' is where he resides." See Stromme v. Commissioner, 138 T.C. 213, 218 (2012), citing Dobra v. Commissioner, 111 T.C. 339 (1998). Therefore, an eligible individual receiving care under a Medicaid waiver program lives in a "foster family home" because the eligible

individual is a qualified "foster" individual who receives care in a "family home" setting, as opposed to an institution, where the individual care provider also resides. Medicaid waiver payments made to a provider for care outside of the home where the provider resides are not qualified Medicaid waiver payments and are not excludable under § 131.

Similarly, the term "placed" is not defined in § 131. Under state foster care programs, a state or political subdivision thereof, or a qualified foster care placement agency, may assist in locating a home that meets the qualified foster individual's needs, negotiate or approve the foster care payment rates, and contract with the foster care providers for the provision of foster care. The Tax Court has determined that these activities constitute "placement" for purposes of § 131(b)(2). <u>Micorescu v. Commissioner</u>, T.C. Memo 1998-398. States perform similar activities with respect to individuals participating in Medicaid waiver programs. Under a Medicaid waiver program, a state, an agency of a state or political subdivision thereof, or a certified Medicaid provider may assist in locating a home for an eligible individual or approve the eligible individual's choice to reside in the individual care provider's home, approve an eligible individual's plan of care, assess the suitability of the home for fulfilling the eligible individual's plan of care, and enter into a contract or other arrangement with the individual care provider for services provided to the eligible individual. Thus, an eligible individual receiving care in the home of the individual care provider under the Medicaid waiver program will be treated as "placed" by an agency of a state or political subdivision thereof, or a qualified foster care placement agency, for purposes of § 131. Accordingly, an eligible individual receiving care in the individual care provider's home under a Medicaid waiver program is a "qualified foster individual" under § 131(b)(2).

Section 131(d)(2) provides that a provider may not exclude payments for the care of more than 10 eligible individuals under age 19 or more than five eligible individuals who are age 19 or over. Because qualified Medicaid waiver payments are difficulty of care payments, they are subject to these limits.

This notice does not address whether qualified Medicaid waiver payments excluded from income under this notice may be subject to tax under the Federal Insurance Contributions Act (FICA) or the Federal Unemployment Tax Act (FUTA) in certain circumstances.

EFFECTIVE DATE
This notice is effective for payments received on or after January 3, 2014. Taxpayers may apply this notice in taxable years for which the period of limitation on claims for a credit or refund under § 6511 has not expired.

DRAFTING INFORMATION
The principal author of this notice is Victoria J. Driscoll of the Office of Associate Chief Counsel (Income Tax & Accounting). For further information regarding this notice, contact Ms. Driscoll at (202) 317-4718 (not a toll-free call).

⬇ <u>IRS Announcement</u>

Internal Revenue

Bulletin No. 2002–10
March 11, 2002

HIGHLIGHTS
OF THIS ISSUE
These synopses are intended only as aids to the reader in identifying the subject matter covered. They may not be relied upon as authoritative interpretations.

SPECIAL ANNOUNCEMENT

Announcement 2002–18, page 621.
The IRS will not assert that any taxpayer has understated his federal tax liability by reason of the receipt or personal use of frequent flyer miles or other in-kind promotional benefits attributable to the taxpayer's business or official travel. Any future guidance on the taxability of these benefits will be applied prospectively. The relief provided by this announcement does not apply to travel or other promotional benefits that are converted to cash, to compensation that is paid in the form of travel or other promotional benefits, or in other circumstances where these benefits are used for tax avoidance purposes.

INCOME TAX

Rev. Rul. 2002–9, page 614.
Impact fees. This ruling provides that impact fees incurred by a taxpayer in connection with the construction of a new residential rental building are capitalized costs allocable to the building. Rev. Proc. 2002–9 modified and amplified.

Rev. Rul. 2002–10, page 616.
Federal rates; adjusted federal rates; adjusted federal long-term rate and the long-term exempt rate. For purposes of sections 382, 1274, 1288, and other sections of the Code, tables set forth the rates for March 2002.

Rev. Rul. 2002–11, page 608.
Election in respect of losses attributable to a disaster. This ruling lists the areas declared by the President to qualify as major disaster or emergency areas during 2001 under the Disaster Relief and Emergency Assistance Act.

Notice 2002–19, page 619.
The "differential earnings rate" under section 809 of the Code is tentatively determined for 2001 together with the "recomputed differential earnings rate" for 2000.

EXEMPT ORGANIZATIONS

Announcement 2002–25, page 621.
A list is provided of organizations now classified as private foundations.

Announcement 2002–18

Most major airlines offer frequent flyer programs under which passengers accumulate miles for each flight. Individuals may also earn frequent flyer miles or other promotional benefits, for example, through rental cars or hotels. These promotional benefits may generally be exchanged for upgraded seating, free travel, discounted travel, travel-related services, or other services or benefits. Questions have been raised concerning the taxability of frequent flyer miles or other promotional items that are received as the result of business travel and used for personal purposes. There are numerous technical and administrative issues relating to these benefits on which no official guidance has been provided, including issues relating to the timing and valuation of income inclusions and the basis for identifying personal use benefits attributable to business (or official) expenditures versus those attributable to personal expenditures. Because of these unresolved issues, the IRS has not pursued a tax enforcement program with respect to promotional benefits such as frequent flyer miles. Consistent with prior practice, the IRS will not assert that any taxpayer has understated his federal tax liability by reason of the receipt or personal use of frequent flyer miles or other in-kind promotional benefits attributable to the taxpayer's business or official travel. Any future guidance on the taxability of these benefits will be applied prospectively. This relief does not apply to travel or other promotional benefits that are converted to cash, to compensation that is paid in the form of travel or other promotional benefits, or in other circumstances where these benefits are used for tax avoidance purposes.

For information regarding this announcement, call (202) 622–4606 (not a toll-free number). Alternatively, taxpayers may transmit comments electronically via the following e-mail address:
Notice.Comments@irscounsel.treas.gov. Please include "Announcement 2002–18" in the subject line of any electronic communications.

⬇ Action on Decision

IRB 2016-31
August 1, 2016

ACTION ON DECISION

Subject: <u>Voss v. Commissioner</u>, 796 F.3d 1051 (9th Cir. 2015), rev'g <u>Sophy v. Commissioner</u>, 138 T.C. 204 (2012)

Issue: Whether the § 163(h)(3) debt limitations on deductions for qualified residence interest apply on a per-taxpayer basis, rather than on a per-residence basis.

Discussion: Section 163(h)(2)(D) of the Internal Revenue Code allows taxpayers to deduct a limited amount of personal interest paid on residential mortgages. The mortgage must be secured by a "qualified residence," defined by § 163(h)(4)(A) to include the taxpayer's principal residence plus one other residence. Section 163(h)(3) limits the amount of deductible interest to interest paid on $1 million of acquisition indebtedness (or refinanced acquisition indebtedness, up to the amount of the original loan's balance), plus interest paid on $100,000 of home equity indebtedness.

Mr. Voss and Mr. Sophy, unmarried co-owners of two residences, each filed an individual tax return claiming a deduction for qualified residence interest paid on acquisition indebtedness and home equity indebtedness in excess of $1.1 million (for a combined amount in excess of $2.2 million). The IRS disallowed portions of each taxpayer's deduction for qualified residence interest on the grounds that § 163(h)(2) and (3) limit the aggregate amount of indebtedness to $1 million and $100,000, respectively, on any qualified residence, allocated among all taxpayers entitled to an interest expense deduction for that qualified residence.

Mr. Voss and Mr. Sophy petitioned the Tax Court, challenging the Service's determinations. The Tax Court agreed with the IRS, finding that the language of the statute limits the total amount of indebtedness with respect to acquisition indebtedness and home equity indebtedness that may be claimed in relation to the qualified residence, rather than in relation to an individual taxpayer. The taxpayers appealed to the United States Court of Appeals for the Ninth Circuit.

The Ninth Circuit reversed the Tax Court decision, agreeing with the taxpayers that the statutory limitations apply to unmarried co-owners of a qualified residence on a per-taxpayer basis. The court based its conclusion largely on its interpretation of the language of the statute that expressly provides that married individuals filing separate returns are entitled to deduct interest on up to $500,000 of acquisition indebtedness and $50,000 of home equity indebtedness. By providing lower debt limits for married

CHAPTER 7 – THE JUDICIAL BRANCH

☑ Learn about the various courts that comprise the Judicial Branch
☑ Understand the role of courts in the tax system
☑ Understand the doctrine of *stare decisis* and the <u>Golsen Rule</u>
☑ Understand the different levels of precedential authority for caselaw
☑ Understand the steps required to determine whether a court case can be cited as primary source authority to support a tax position

9. Privacy Concerns in Judicial Opinions

> • End of Chapter Example - Conflict of Court Case and IRS Guidance

1. Introduction

When statutory or administrative authority alone fails to resolve a particular research problem, it may be necessary to consult judicial authority. To assess the relative weight of authority to be given court decisions it is necessary to have a basic familiarity with the various federal courts that hear tax cases.

As discussed earlier, the Constitution provides Congress with the authority to enact law with respect to taxes. Similarly, Article III of the Constitution invests the judicial power of the United States in the federal court system. Article III, Section 1 specifically creates the U.S. Supreme Court and gives Congress the authority to create the lower federal courts. Congress has used this power to establish 13 U.S. courts of appeals, 94 U.S. district courts, the U.S. Court of Claims, and the U.S. Court of International Trade. Congress created several Article I or legislative courts that do not have full judicial power. Judicial power is the authority to be the final decider in all questions of Constitutional law, all questions of federal law and to hear claims at the core of habeas corpus issues. Article I courts are the U.S. Court of Veteran's Appeals, the U.S. Court of Military Appeals and the U.S. Tax Court.

2. The Federal Court Structure

The federal judiciary operates separately from the executive and legislative branches, but often works with them as the Constitution requires. Federal laws are passed by Congress and signed by the President. The judicial branch decides the constitutionality of federal laws and resolves other disputes about federal laws. On an issue involving a constitutional decision, the judiciary presents the final word. For example, in Dickerson v. United States, 530 U.S. 428 (2000), the Supreme Court confronted a Congressional statutory provision that would overrule a prior decision of the Court. In Miranda v. Arizona, 384 U.S. 436 (1966), the Supreme Court held that to adequately protect an individual's constitutional right as provided under the Fifth Amendment against self-incrimination certain warnings must be given before a suspect's statement during custodial interrogation could be admitted in evidence. After the Miranda decision, Congress enacted 18 U.S.C. §3501, which in essence laid down a rule that the admissibility of such statements should turn only on whether they were voluntarily made, not whether the statement was made after the required Miranda warning was provided. In Dickerson, 530 U.S. 428, 444, the Supreme Court concluded "that Miranda announced a constitutional rule that Congress may not supersede legislatively."[146]

---

[146] Judge Scalia in dissent noted that the limits of Congressional statutory authority over court decisions was settled back in 1803: "Marbury v. Madison, 1 Cranch 137 (1803), held that an Act of Congress will not be enforced by the courts if what it prescribes violates the Constitution of the United States. That was the basis on which Miranda was decided."

So, what's the plain-speak role of courts? Two parties come into court and perhaps have three different sides to their dispute. Courts decide what really happened and what should be done about it. They decide whether a person committed a crime and what the punishment should be. They also provide a peaceful way to decide private disputes that people can't resolve themselves. Depending on the dispute or crime, some cases end up in the federal courts and some end up in state courts. The United States Supreme Court is the highest court in the federal Judiciary. Congress has established two levels of federal courts under the Supreme Court: the trial courts and the appellate courts.

a. Trial Level Courts

i. The U.S. Tax Court

Congress established the United States Tax Court effective December 30, 1969. I.R.C. §7441. Prior to the amendment of Section 7441 creating the U.S. Tax Court, the Board of Tax Appeals ("BTA") reviewed IRS determinations. The BTA served as an independent agency in the Executive Branch. Congress established the U.S. Tax Court under Article I of the U.S. Constitution because it deemed it "anomalous to continue to classify" the Tax Court with executive agencies and questioned whether it was "appropriate for one executive agency to be sitting in judgment on the determinations of another executive agency [the IRS]."[147] The clear intent of Congress was to transform the Tax Court from an independent agency in the Executive Branch into an Article I legislative court.[148] Under Article I, Section 8, Congress possesses the power "[t]o constitute tribunals inferior to the Supreme Court..." Through its amendment of Section 7441, Congress created a legislative Tax Court – a court of law.[149]

The Tax Court interprets the Internal Revenue Code in disputes between taxpayers and the Government.[150] By resolving these disputes, the court exercises a portion of the judicial power of the United States.[151] The Tax Court exercises judicial power to the exclusion of any other function.[152] It is neither advocate nor rulemaker.[153] As an adjudicative body, it construes statutes passed by Congress and regulations promulgated by the IRS.[154] It does not make political decisions.[155] The Tax Court remains independent of the Executive and Legislative branches.[156] Its decisions are not subject to review by either the Congress or the President. Nor has Congress made Tax Court decisions subject to review in the federal district courts.[157] Rather, like the

---

[147] S. Rep. No. 91-552, p. 303 (1969).
[148] Freytag, et. al. v. Commissioner, 501 U.S. 868, 888 (1991).
[149] Id. at 909.
[150] Id. at 891.
[151] Id. While the Supreme Court in Freytag held that the Tax Court exercises "judicial" power, Justice Scalia dissented from this view stating "that the Tax Court, like the Internal Revenue Service, the FCC and the NLRB, exercises executive power." Id. at 912.
[152] Id.
[153] Id.
[154] Id.
[155] Id.
[156] Id.

judgments of the district courts, the decisions of the Tax Court are appealable only to the regional United States courts of appeal, with ultimate review in the Supreme Court of the United States.[158]

The U.S. Tax Court is a unique trial level forum.[159] Though established under Article I, the Tax Court exercises judicial, rather than executive, legislative, or administrative power.[160] "The Tax Court's function and role in the federal judicial scheme closely resemble those of the federal district courts. Furthermore, the Tax Court exercises its judicial power in much the same way as the federal district courts exercise theirs. It has authority to punish contempts by fine or imprisonment, 26 U.S.C. 7456(c); to grant certain injunctive relief, 6213(a); to order the Secretary of the Treasury to refund an overpayment determined by the court, 6512(b)(2); and to subpoena and examine witnesses, order production of documents, and administer oaths, 7456(a). All these powers are quintessentially judicial in nature."[161]

Below is an example of the first page from a Tax Court decision.

---

[157] Id.
[158] I.R.C. §7482(a).
[159] See, e.g., Ballard v. Commissioner, 544 U.S. 40 (2005) (holding that the Tax Court, like other decision-making tribunals, must follow its own rules – in this case Rule 183(b)).
[160] Freytag v. Commissioner, 501 U.S. 868 (1991).
[161] Id. at 891.

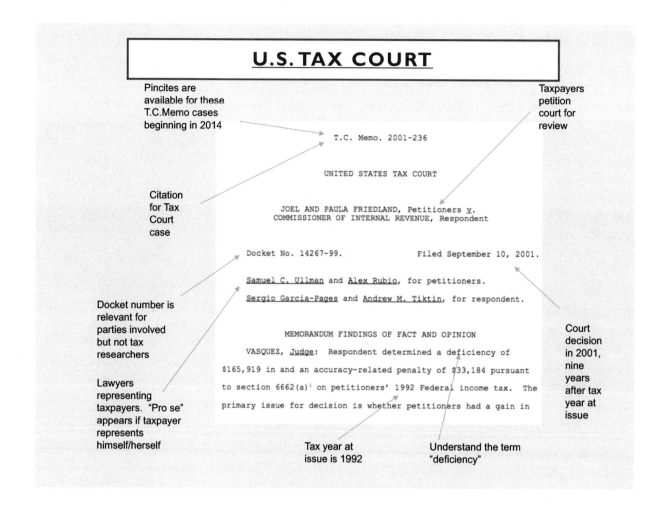

U.S. TAX COURT

Pincites are available for these T.C.Memo cases beginning in 2014

Taxpayers petition court for review

T.C. Memo. 2001-236

UNITED STATES TAX COURT

Citation for Tax Court case

JOEL AND PAULA FRIEDLAND, Petitioners v. COMMISSIONER OF INTERNAL REVENUE, Respondent

Docket No. 14267-99.   Filed September 10, 2001.

Samuel C. Ullman and Alex Rubio, for petitioners.

Sergio Garcia-Pages and Andrew M. Tiktin, for respondent.

Docket number is relevant for parties involved but not tax researchers

MEMORANDUM FINDINGS OF FACT AND OPINION

Court decision in 2001, nine years after tax year at issue

VASQUEZ, Judge: Respondent determined a deficiency of

$165,919 in and an accuracy-related penalty of $33,184 pursuant

Lawyers representing taxpayers. "Pro se" appears if taxpayer represents himself/herself

to section 6662(a)[1] on petitioners' 1992 Federal income tax. The

primary issue for decision is whether petitioners had a gain in

Tax year at issue is 1992

Understand the term "deficiency"

Though taxpayers may choose to litigate tax matters in a variety of legal settings, the Tax Court is the only forum in which taxpayers outside of bankruptcy may do so without having first paid the disputed tax in full. Parties who contest the imposition of a tax may also bring an action in District Court, or in the Court of Federal Claims; however these venues require that the tax be paid first, and that the party then file a lawsuit to recover the contested amount paid.

The Tax Court consists of 19 judges, each appointed by the President for a 15-year term.[162] Although the principal office of the Tax Court is located in Washington, D.C., the court conducts hearings in most large cities in the United States, usually with only a single judge present. See the picture, below, of one such U.S. Tax Court setting

located in a city outside of Washington, DC.

After hearing a case, the assigned judge submits the findings of fact and an opinion, in writing, to the Chief Judge who then decides whether the case should be reviewed by the full court. If sufficient facts are stipulated, the assigned judge may render an opinion without a formal trial. Juries are not used in the Tax Court.

In most cases, the Chief Judge will decide that a full review by all 19 judges ("en banc" review) is not necessary. In that event, the opinion will stand and be issued as either a "regular" or "memorandum" decision of the Tax Court.

- "T.C." Opinion - A "regular" decision of the Tax Court reported as a "T.C." opinion is issued when the Court believes it is addressing a sufficiently important legal issue or principle.[163] A regular decision is cited as [Name of Petitioner/Taxpayer] v. Commissioner, [Volume # of Tax Court Reports] T.C. [page of volume] (year issued). Regular decisions constitute precedential authority of the U.S. Tax Court for the specific Federal tax issues addressed in each opinion.

- Memorandum Opinions - A "memo" opinion is issued in a case that does not involve a novel legal issue but rather delves into settled well-established principles of law that, in the opinion of the Chief Judge, present only a variation of the facts.[164] A memorandum opinion is cited as [Name of Petitioner] v. Commissioner, T.C. Memo. [year issued - #]. Technically, a memorandum decision does not rise to the level of precedent since the court is merely applying well-settled law to different facts in the case. However, memorandum decisions serve as persuasive authority.

---

[162] I.R.C. §§ 7443, 7443A.
[163] https://www.ustaxcourt.gov/taxpayer_info_after.htm.
[164] Id.

- Summary Opinions - The Tax Court issues "small case" or "S" case opinions involving an expedited litigation process enacted by Congress under Section 7463. Subject to a taxpayer's election, a case may be an "S" case if it meets the dollar limitations under section 7463(a) and (f) and section 7436(c)(1) as to the amount of the deficiency in dispute. A taxpayer may elect small tax case status in any case in which the amount of the deficiency placed in dispute (including any additions to tax, additional amounts and penalties) or claimed overpayment does not exceed $50,000 for any one taxable year in an income tax case; $50,000 in an estate tax case; $50,000 for any one calendar year in a gift tax case; $50,000 in employment taxes for each calendar quarter involved in a worker classification case under section 7436; $50,000 for any one taxable period or, if there is no taxable period, for any taxable event in the case of excise taxes under Code chapters 41, 42, 43, or 44 or under chapter 45 (windfall profit tax); claim for relief under section 6015(e) not in excess of $50,000; or an appeal under section 6330 in which the unpaid tax does not exceed $50,000.

Under Section 7463, Congress sought to provide taxpayers with efficient access to judicial review of IRS determinations. However, in order to balance the risks associated with an expedited judicial process, Congress placed restrictions on "S" cases. "S" case decisions are not subject to appeal and do not constitute precedential authority as set forth under section 7463.

Why choose small "S" Case status? Taxpayers receive relaxed rules of evidence and procedure, a longer list of cities from which to choose a place of trial, and usually a faster decision.[165] Each of these features makes access to the court system easier and less costly for taxpayers with small claims. For example, Tax Court Rule 174 provides, "[t]he Court will make reasonable efforts to conduct the trial at the location most convenient to that requested where suitable facilities are available." The U.S. Tax Court's Form 5 ("Request for Place of Trial") dated as of September 2010 provides 15 additional locations in the country where the Tax Court will allow an "S" case to be designated for trial but not a regular case.

However, there are drawbacks in pursuing "S" case designation. Depending on the result of the case, the major hazard from an "S" case designation is that the losing party cannot appeal the decision. Another problem recognized by the Tax Court from these proceedings is that complicated questions of tax law may be decided incorrectly since these small cases will often be advanced by taxpayers without professional assistance.[166]

In this unique, fast-track forum for tax litigation, additional questions remain unsettled with respect to "S" cases[167]:

[165] Mitchell v. Comm'r, 131 T.C. No. 15, at 17 (2008) (citing S.Rept. 91-552, at 302-304 (1969), 1969-3 C.B. 423, 614-15.

[166] Mitchell v. Comm'r, 131 T.C. No. 15, at 18 (2008).

[167] In Estate of Burton W. Kanter, et al. v. Commissioner, 544 U.S. 40 (2005), the U.S. Supreme Court resolved the issue of whether the Tax Court could exclude from the record on appeal Tax Court Rule 183(b) reports submitted by Special Trial Judges. In a 7-2 opinion, the Supreme Court held that no statute authorized the concealment of the report issued by the Special Trial Judge.

- What does the statutory limitation of "S" cases not being treated as "precedent for any other case" really mean for practical purposes? This question was raised in <u>Mitchell v. Comm'r</u>, 131 T.C. No. 15, at 24 (2008), by Judge Holmes in his concurring opinion. He noted that "S" cases *can be* cited, **but not as precedent**, i.e., as stating a point or principle of law or as furnishing a rule or authority for the determination of an identical or similar case afterwards arising, or of a similar question of law.

- Does the Tax Court's decision in an "S" case collaterally estop the losing party in later litigation? Collateral estoppel is a doctrine by which an earlier decision rendered by a court in a lawsuit between parties is conclusive as to the issues or controverted points so that they cannot be re-litigated in subsequent proceedings involving the same parties. The potential application of collateral estoppel involving "S" cases was raised in <u>Mitchell v. Comm'r</u>, 131 T.C. No. 15, at 24 (2008), by Judge Holmes in his concurring opinion. He noted the majority sidestepped the potential collateral estoppel effect involving "S" cases. So, if a taxpayer loses an "S" case involving his tax return for year 2012 and pursues the exact same facts for the next year, 2013, can the IRS point to the prior "S" case decision for 2012 to estop the taxpayer from re-litigating the same tax issues?

- Will the Tax Court follow the <u>Golsen</u> Rule in "S" cases or its own body of law? In <u>Amundson v. Comm'r</u>, Dkt. No. 24594-10 "S", the Tax Court issued an Order in which it stated "[i]n general, we follow the rule of law in the U.S. Circuit Court of Appeals to which our decisions are appealable, <u>see</u> <u>Golsen</u>...even if as here, the decision is not appealable." However, given that this Order was issued in a "small" case matter that cannot be cited as precedent, the issue of how the Tax Court will proceed in applying caselaw for taxpayers who elect "S" case status residing in various jurisdictions remains unsettled. A more thorough discussion of the <u>Golsen</u> Rule is set forth, below.

Prior to 1943, the the Board of Tax Appeals' decisions, both regular and memorandum, were reported in volumes cited as the United States Board of Tax Appeals Reports (B.T.A.). Since the latter part of 1942, regular Tax Court decisions have been published by the Government Printing Office as the Tax Court of the United States Reports (T.C.). The government provides only unbound copies of the memorandum decisions. However, CCH publishes bound volumes of memorandum decisions under the title Tax Court Memorandum Decisions (T.C.M.) and Prentice-Hall makes them available as the Prentice-Hall T.C. Memorandum Decisions (P-H T.C. Memo.).

Type of Opinion	Level of Authoritative Value	Unique Aspects of Tax Court Decisions

Type of Opinion	Level of Authoritative Value	Unique Aspects of Tax Court Decisions
T.C. En Banc	Greatest Weight	All judges review and participate in decision
T.C. Regular	High	One judge opines on a "novel or significant" tax issue
T.C. Memorandum	Medium	One judge opines on a well-settled matter of tax law that is applied to a variation of facts
Summary Opinion	None	One judge issues decision but without any precedential authority

It is important to remember that citations containing the letters "U.S.T.C." do not refer to Tax Court cases. U.S.T.C. refers to United States Tax Cases which is a special reporter service published by CCH containing all of the tax cases decided by all federal courts other than the Tax Court. Both CCH and PrenticeHall publish such reporters with the Prentice-Hall service being called American Federal Tax Reports (A.F.T.R.) for years prior to 1958 and American Federal Tax Reports, 2nd Series (A.F.T.R. 2d) for years after 1957.

1. The Golsen Rule

Section 7482(b) governs the venue for appeal from a decision of the U.S. Tax Court. Section 7482(b)(1) provides, in part, that Tax Court decisions may be reviewed by the U.S. court of appeals for the circuit which is located:

> (A) in the case of a petitioner seeking redetermination of tax liability other than a corporation, the legal residence of the petitioner,
> (B) in the case of a corporation seeking redetermination of tax liability, the principal place of business or principal office or agency of the corporation, or, if it has no principal place of business or principal office or agency in any judicial circuit, then the office to which was made the return of the tax in respect of which the liability arises……

(emphasis added to original text). The text of section 7482(b) does not provide clear statutory direction on venue, at least with respect to corporate litigants. The Supreme Court recently determined that a corporation's "principal place of business" is "best read as referring to the place where a corporation's officers direct, control, and coordinate the corporation's activities."[168] This is often referred to as the "nerve center" test, and it normally refers to where a corporation maintains its headquarters, provided that the headquarters is the actual center of direction, control, and coordination.[169] Thus, in John Hancock Life Insurance Company v. Comssioner, 141 T.C. 1 (2013), the Tax Court held that the corporation's "nerve center" existed where six of nine of its corporate officer and all three of its directors work, not the state where it was incorporated.

Upon determining the proper venue for appeal of its decision, the Tax Court will apply that circuit court's jurisprudence governing issues to be determined at the trial level under the "Golsen" rule. Under the rule of Golsen v. Commissioner, 54 T.C. 742, 757 (1970), aff'd, 445 F.2d 985 (10th Cir. 1971), the U.S. Tax Court will "follow a Court of Appeals decision which is squarely in point where appeal from our decision lies to that Court of Appeals." This rule aims to promote efficient and harmonious judicial administration of Tax Court decisions.[170] In Lardas v. Comm'r, 99 T.C. 490, 495 (1992), the Tax Court stated: "The logic behind the Golsen doctrine is not that we lack the authority to render a decision inconsistent with any Court of Appeals….but that it would be futile and wasteful to do so where we would surely be reversed." The reach of the Golsen rule is construed narrowly by the U.S. Tax Court and applied only if "a reversal would appear inevitable, due to the clearly established position of the Court of Appeals to which an appeal would lie".[171]. If the Tax Court finds that the circuit law to which its decision would proceed for review, if appealed, does not substantively differ, then the court will determine the Golsen rule inapplicable.[172] Thus, as a court of national jurisdiction with expertise in the area of Federal taxes, the Tax Court will follow its own body of law.[173]

ii.United States District Courts

The United States district courts are the trial courts of the federal court system. Within limits set by Congress and the Constitution, the district courts have jurisdiction to hear nearly all categories of federal cases, including both civil and criminal matters. District courts are called "Article III" courts, since their judicial power is derived from Article III of the Constitution, together with Acts of Congress. District courts have jurisdiction, in law and equity, over cases under the laws of the United States—including most tax cases. There are 94 federal judicial districts, including at least one district in each state, the District of Columbia and Puerto Rico. Each district includes a United States bankruptcy court as a unit of the district court. Three territories of the United States — the Virgin Islands, Guam, and the Northern Mariana Islands — have district courts that hear federal cases, including bankruptcy cases. Decisions of U.S. District Court are

---

[168] Hertz Corp. v. Friend, 559 U.S. 77, 92–93 (2010).

[169] Id.

[170] Id.

[171] Lardas v. Commissioner, 99 T.C. 490, 494-495 (1992).

[172] See Ad Investment 2000 Fund LLC v. Commissioner, T.C. Memo. 2015-223.

[173] See, e.g., Estate of Willis Edward Clack, Deceased v. Commissioner, 106 T.C. No. 6 (1996)(Halpern, J., in dissent stating, "Because we are a trial court of national jurisdiction, we enjoy an autonomy not enjoyed generally by Federal trial courts. Because I am jealous of that autonomy, I would be slow to give it up.").

appealable to the court of appeals for the circuit "embracing the circuit."[174] Thus, a decision of the U.S. District Court of the Northern District of California is appeable to the Ninth Circuit Court of Appeals.

Most tax cases proceed to the U.S. Tax Court because taxpayers seek review without the requirement to first pay the disputed amount of tax determined as due by the government. However, there are specific tax matters that are heard only in District Court, including the following partial list:

- §7402(b), §7609   - summons enforcement actions filed by the government

- §7609(b)(2)   - petition to quash third-party summons filed by a taxpayer

- §7403(a)   - action to enforce or discharge liens in favor of the U.S.

- §6334(c)(1)(B)   - judicial approval of principal residence levy filed by U.S.

- §7405(a)   - erroneous refund suit filed by the U.S.

- §7407(a), §7408(a) - tax return preparer and tax shelter injunctions suits

- §7426   - wrongful levy actions

- §7431(a)   - civil disclosure damages actions filed by taxpayers

- §7433(a)   - civil damage actions against U.S. for failure to release liens

Each state has at least one district court in which both tax and nontax litigation is heard. Taxpayers may sue in a federal district court only if they first pay the tax deficiency assessed by the Service and then sue for a refund. Only in a district court can a taxpayer request a jury trial in a tax dispute. Published decisions of the U.S. district courts, including both tax and all other types of litigation are contained in the Federal Supplement (F. Supp.) published by West Publishing Company. The tax decisions of the district courts are also published in U.S.T.C. and A.F.T.R. or A.F.T.R. 2nd.

Unlike Courts of Appeals decisions, district court opinions are not precedential.[175] Thus, trial level opinions issued by district courts provide persuasive primary source authority

---

[174] 28 U.S.C. § 1294.
[175] See Nat'l Union Fire Ins. Co. v. Allfirst Bank, 282 F. Supp. 2d 339, 351 (D.Md. 2003)("Of course, no decision of a district court judge is technically binding on another district court judge, even within the same district.")

but not precedential authority.

iii.United States Claims Courts

Prior to October 1, 1982, some tax cases were heard in a court called the U.S. Court of Claims. Decisions of the Court of Claims could be appealed only to the U.S. Supreme Court. Under the "Federal Courts Improvement Act of 1982," however, the U.S. Court of Claims was merged with the Court of Customs and Patent Appeals and is now called the U.S. Court of Appeals for the Federal Circuit. At the same time a new trial court called the U.S. Claims Court was established. As in a U.S. district court, a taxpayer must first pay the disputed amount before bringing suit before this court, except for IRC 7428 declaratory judgment cases. The Claims Court has nationwide jurisdiction and sits in Washington, D.C. The court consists of 16 judges nominated by the President and confirmed by the Senate for a term of fifteen years. Decisions of the U.S. Claims Court are appealable exclusively to the U.S. Court of Appeals for the Federal Circuit.[176]

The U.S. Claims Court is authorized to hear primarily money claims founded upon the Constitution, federal statutes, executive regulations, or contracts, express or implied in fact, with the United States. Many cases before the court involve tax refund suits, an area in which the court exercises concurrent jurisdiction with the United States district courts. The cases generally involve complex factual and statutory construction issues in tax law. Another aspect of the court's jurisdiction involves government contracts. It was within the public contracts jurisdiction that the court was given new equitable authority in late 1996. In recent years, the court's Fifth Amendment takings jurisdiction has included many cases raising environmental and natural resources issues. Another large category of cases involves civilian and military pay claims. In addition, the court hears intellectual property, Indian tribe, and various statutory claims against the United States by individuals, domestic and foreign corporations, states and localities, Indian tribes and nations, and foreign nationals and governments.

	Tax Court	District Court	Claims Court
Pre-pay	No	Yes	Yes

---

[176] 28 U.S.C. § 1295(a)(3).

	Tax Court	**District Court**	**Claims Court**
Jury	No	Yes	No
Appeal to	Applicable Circuit Court of Appeals *26 U.S.C. § 7482*	Applicable Circuit Court of Appeals *28 U.S.C. § 1294*	U.S. Court of Appeals for the Federal Circuit *28 U.S.C. § 1295(a)(3)*
Specialization in Tax	Yes	No	No

b.Circuit Courts of Appeal

The 94 judicial districts are organized into 12 regional circuits, each of which has a United States court of appeals. A court of appeals hears appeals from the district courts located within its circuit, as well as appeals from decisions of federal administrative agencies. The District of Columbia Circuit Court of Appeals oversees the smallest geographic area of the 12 regional circuits - its jurisdiction extends only to Washington D.C. The D.C. Circuit was created in 1801. In addition, the Court of Appeals for the Federal Circuit (the 13th circuit court of appeals, but not one of the 12 regional circuits) has nationwide jurisdiction to hear appeals in specialized cases.

The Federal Circuit is unique among the 13 Circuit Courts of Appeals. It has nationwide jurisdiction in a variety of subject areas, including international trade, government contracts, patents, certain money claims against the United States government, federal personnel, veterans' benefits, and public safety officers' benefits claims. Appeals to the court come from all federal district courts, the United States Court of Federal Claims, the United States Court of International Trade, and the United States Court of Appeals for Veterans Claims. The court also takes appeals of certain administrative agencies' decisions, including the United States Merit Systems Protection Board, the Boards of Contract Appeals, the Patent Trial and Appeal Board, and the Trademark Trial and Appeal Board. Decisions of the United States International Trade Commission, the Office of Compliance, an independent agency in the legislative branch, the Government Accountability Office Personnel Appeals Board, and the Department of Justice Bureau of Justice Assistance also are reviewed by the court.

The Federal Circuit's jurisdiction consists of administrative law cases (55%), intellectual property cases (31%), and cases involving money damages against the United States government (11%). The administrative law cases consist of personnel and veterans claims. Nearly all of the intellectual property cases involve patents. Suits for money damages against the United States government include government contract cases, tax refund appeals, unlawful takings, and civilian and military pay cases. The jurisdiction of the U.S. Court of Appeals for the Federal Circuit, unlike that of the regional courts of appeal, is defined by subject matter rather than geography. It hears appeals of tax cases only if they arise from decisions of the U.S. Claims Court. Decisions of the U.S. Court of Appeals for the Federal Circuit have nationwide precedential value and, therefore, offer a forum-shopping opportunity to taxpayers living in circuits where courts

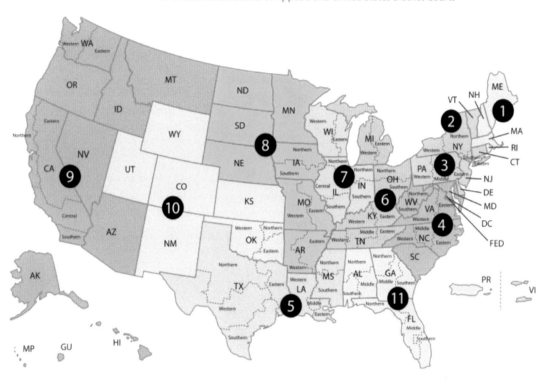

Geographic Boundaries
of United States Courts of Appeals and United States District Courts

of appeals decisions involving similar issues are adverse.

Decisions of the Tax Court and the district courts may be appealed either by the Service or the taxpayer to the U.S. circuit court of appeals with jurisdiction. Jurisdiction is based on the location of the taxpayer's residence. Each circuit court must follow the decisions of the Supreme Court but not those of the other circuits. However, the Eleventh Circuit has announced that it will follow the case precedent of the Fifth Circuit for those cases decided prior to its creation on October 1, 1981. The Eleventh Circuit is composed of three states (Alabama, Georgia, and Florida) previously included in the Fifth Circuit. When conflicts develop between the circuits, district courts of each individual circuit are required to follow precedents set by the appellate court of their own circuit.

District courts must follow the decisions of the court of appeals for the circuit in which they are located. For example, the District Court for the Eastern District of Missouri must follow decisions of the Court of Appeals for the Eight Circuit. If the Eighth Circuit has not rendered a decision on a particular issue, the district court may reach its own conclusion on the issue or follow the decision of another circuit or district court that has reviewed the issue. Under the rule of Golsen v. Commissioner, 54 T.C. at 757, the U.S. Tax Court will "follow a Court of Appeals decision which is squarely in point where appeal from our decision lies to that Court of Appeals."

All decisions of the various circuit courts are published by West Publishing Company in the Federal Reporter - 2nd series (F.2d). The tax decisions are also contained in U.S.T.C. and A.F.T.R. or A.F.T.R. 2d.

i.Procedure to Appeal a Trial Level Decision to a Court of Appeal

A litigant who files an appeal, known as an "appellant" or "petitioner" must show that the trial court or administrative agency made a legal error that affected the decision in the case. The other side that comes to court to respond and argue against the petitioner's case is the "respondent" or "appellee."

How are appellate courts different from trial courts? At a trial in a U.S. District Court or U.S. Tax Court, witnesses give testimony and a judge or jury decides who is guilty or not guilty — or who is liable or not liable. The appellate courts do not retry cases or hear new evidence. They do not hear witnesses testify. There is no jury. Appellate courts review the procedures and the decisions in the trial court to make sure that the proceedings were fair and that the proper law was applied correctly. The court of appeals makes its decision based on the record of the case established by the trial court or agency. The court of appeals also may review the factual findings of the trial court or agency, but typically may only overturn a decision on factual grounds if the findings were "clearly erroneous."[177]

Appeals are decided by panels of three judges working together. The appellant presents legal arguments to the panel, in writing, in a document called a "brief." In the brief, the appellant tries to persuade the judges that the trial court made an error, and that its decision should be reversed. On the other hand, the party defending against the appeal, known as the "appellee," tries in its brief to show why the trial court decision was correct, or why any error made by the trial court was not significant enough to affect the outcome of the case. Because any case may be decided without oral argument, all

---

[177] For example, in Medtronic, Inc. & Consolidated Subsidiaries v Commissioner, 2018-2 USTC ¶50,379 (August 16, 2018), the Eighth Circuit Court of Appeals vacated the U.S. Tax Court's decision, T.C.Memo. 2016-112 (Jan. 25, 2017),

determined that the lower court had failed to reach findings as to various elements required under applicable Treasury guidelines for the appellate court to conclude whether the correct transfer pricing method was applied by the lower court. https://www.justice.gov/opa/press-release/file/1087916/download. Reading the Medtronic opinion is instructive for students to understand how appellate courts can serve as a check on the decision-making of lower courts. Likewise, the U.S. Supreme Court serves as another level of check upon the judicial opinions rendered by Courts of Appeal.

major arguments are typically fully developed in the briefs by the litigants. However, the parties may include in their briefs a statement setting forth the reasons why, in their opinion, oral argument should be heard.[178]

The court of appeals decision usually will be the final word in the case, unless it sends the case back to the trial court for additional proceedings, or the parties ask the U.S. Supreme Court to review the case. In some cases the decision may be reviewed *en banc*, that is, by a larger group of judges (usually all) of the court of appeals for the circuit.

ii. Procedure to Appeal a Court of Appeals Decision to the U.S. Supreme Court

A litigant who loses in a federal court of appeals, or in the highest court of a state, may file a petition for a "writ of certiorari," which is a document asking the Supreme Court to review the case. The Supreme Court, however, does not have to grant review. The Court typically will agree to hear a case only when it involves an unusually important legal principle, or when two or more federal appellate courts have interpreted a law differently. There are also a small number of special circumstances in which the Supreme Court is required by law to hear an appeal. When the Supreme Court hears a case, the parties are required to file written briefs and the Court may hear oral argument.

c. The U.S. Supreme Court

Final appeals from a circuit court of appeals rest with the Supreme Court. Appeal is by "Writ of Certiorari"[179] which may or may not be granted. Refusal to grant the writ (reported as "cert. den.") does not mean that the Supreme Court necessarily agrees with the decision of the lower court, only that the Court did not wish to hear the case. It is the Court's custom and practice to "grant cert" if four of the nine Justices decide that they should hear the case. Of the approximately 7,500 requests for certiorari filed each

---

[178] See, e.g., U.S. Court of Apeeals for the Fourth Circuit, Local Rule 34(a). Interested in viewing oral arguments before a U.S. Court of Appeals? Then, go to: https://www.ca9.uscourts.gov/media/view_video.php?pk_vid=0000014453.

[179] From the Latin *certiorari volumnus*, "we wish to be informed."

year, the Court usually "grants cert" to fewer than 150. [180] These are typically cases that the Court considers sufficiently important to require their review; a common example is the occasion when two or more of the federal courts of appeals have ruled differently on the same question of federal law.

By statute, the annual term of the Supreme Court begins the first Monday in October.[181] By custom, it ends when the year's schedule of cases is finished. In 1941, the Court had 1,302 docketed cases. By the end of the 2015 term, the annual inflow was over 6,475 cases. During the 2015 Term, only 81 cases were taken for oral argument out of all petitions filed. That means the decisions made by the 12 Circuit Courts of Appeals across the country and the Federal Circuit Court are the last word in thousands of cases.

If the Court grants certiorari, Justices accept legal briefs from the parties to the case, as well as from amicus curiae, or "friends of the court." These can include industry trade groups, academics, or even the U.S. government itself. Before issuing a ruling, the Supreme Court usually hears oral arguments, where the various parties to the suit present their arguments and the Justices ask them questions. If the case involves the federal government, the Solicitor General of the United States presents arguments on behalf of the United States. The Justices then hold private conferences, make their decision, and (often after a period of several months) issue the Court's opinion, along with any dissenting arguments that may have been written.

The Constitution does not stipulate the number of Supreme Court Justices; the number is set instead by Congress. There have been as few as six, but since 1869 there have been nine Justices, including one Chief Justice. All Justices are nominated by the President, confirmed by the Senate, and hold their offices under life tenure. Since Justices do not have to run or campaign for re-election, they are thought to be insulated from political pressure when deciding cases. Justices may remain in office until they resign, pass away, or are impeached and convicted by Congress.

---

[180] http://www.uscourts.gov/about-federal-courts/court-role-and-structure/about-us-courts-appeals.
[181] http://supremecourthistory.org/socinfo_home.html.

The Court's caseload is almost entirely appellate in nature, and the Court's decisions cannot be appealed to any authority, as it is the final judicial arbiter in the United States on matters of federal law. However, the Court may consider appeals from the highest state courts or from federal appellate courts. The Court also has original jurisdiction in cases involving ambassadors and other diplomats, and in cases between states. Although the Supreme Court may hear an appeal on any question of law provided it has jurisdiction, it usually does not hold trials. Instead, the Court's task is to interpret the meaning of a law, to decide whether a law is relevant to a particular set of facts, or to rule on how a law should be applied. Lower courts must follow the precedent set by the Supreme Court when rendering decisions.

Supreme Court cases come in three varieties. First, there are original jurisdiction actions – brought by one state against another, or between states and the federal government. Second, there are cases from state courts. If any state tribunal decides a federal question and the litigant has no further remedy within the state, the Supreme Court may consider it. Finally, roughly two-thirds of the total caseload of the Supreme Court are requests for review of decisions of federal appellate or district courts.[182]

All Supreme Court decisions are published by the U.S. Government Printing Office in U.S. Reports (U.S.) and by West Publishing Company the Supreme Court Reporter (S. Ct.). The tax decisions are published in U.S.T.C., A.F.T.R. or A.F.T.R. 2d, and the I.R.B. How important are Supreme Court decisions in the lives of Americans?

3. The Role of Courts in Understanding the Code

The Supreme Court acknowledged that the courts' approach in interpreting the Code is

---

[182] http://supremecourthistory.org/htcw_casesthecourthears.html.

limited. In <u>United States v. Olympic Radio & Television</u>, 349 U.S. 232, 236 (1955), the Supreme Court instructed as follows: "It may be that Congress granted less than some thought or less than was originally intended. We can only take the Code as we find it and give it as great an internal symmetry and consistency as its words permit." "Congress enacts statutes, not purposes, and courts may not depart from the statutory text because they believe some other arrangement would better serve the legislative goals."[183] The legislative history to a statute may sometimes override the statute's plain meaning interpretation and lead to a different result where the statute's history contains unequivocal evidence of a clear legislative intent.[184]

There may well be a distinction between using legislative history to supply the meaning of a particular word or phrase and using legislative history to discern the purpose or goal of the statute in which Congress placed that word or phrase so as to be able to best construe it in a particular case. Judge Easterbrook, in his landmark taxonomy on uses of legislative history, <u>In re Sinclair</u>, 870 F.2d 1340, 1342 (7th Cir. 1989), suggested that legislative history may be used as a dictionary of sorts—to determine Congress's objective rather than subjective intent.[185] Seen in this light, legislative history should be used to discover the statute's "original meaning", rather than the intent of the individual congressman. Id. at 1343 ("An opinion poll revealing the wishes of Congress would not translate to legal rules").

Beyond the role of courts to provide clear guidance as to how statutes enacted by Congress should be properly interpreted and applied, it remains a very difficult task to provide consistency in the judicial arena. Consider the data from just one year – the 2017 October term of the U.S. Supreme Court.[186] In that period, the U.S. Supreme Court decided just 74 cases. And, from these 74 cases, the Supreme Court reversed the decisions rendered by lower Federal circuit courts of appeal and state courts in 74% of these cases.[187] See the table below of the U.S. Supreme Court's October 2017 term:

---

[183] <u>In re Cavanaugh</u>, 306 F.3d 726, 731-732 (9th Cir. 2002).

[184] See <u>Consumer Prod. Safety Commn. v. GTE Sylvania, Inc.</u>, 447 U.S. 102, 108 (1980); <u>see also</u> <u>Allen v. Commissioner</u>, 118 T.C. 1, 17 (2002).

[185] <u>Id.</u> at 1343 ("'we ask, not what this man meant, but what those words would mean in the mouth of a normal speaker of English, using them in the circumstances in which they were used.'" (quoting Holmes, "The Theory of Legal Interpretation", 12 Harv. L. Rev. 417, 417-419 (1899)).

[186] The Term of the Court begins, by law, on the first Monday in October and lasts until the first Monday in October of the next year. 28 U.S.C. §2. Each Term, approximately 7,000-8,000 new cases are filed in the Supreme Court. However, the Court grants and hears oral argument in about 80 cases each term. https://www.supremecourt.gov/about/courtatwork.aspx.

[187] http://www.scotusblog.com/reference/stat-pack/.

	Number	Affirmed	Reversed	Affirmed %	Reversed %
CA 1	1	0	1	0%	100%
CA 2	4	2	2	50%	50%
CA 3	3	0	3	0%	100%
CA 4	-	-	-	-	-
CA 5	4	1	3	25%	75%
CA 6	4	0	4	0%	100%
CA 7	7	3	4	43%	57%
CA 8	3	1	2	33%	67%
CA 9	15	2	12	14%	86%
CA 10	3	2	1	67%	33%
CA 11	6	1	5	17%	83%
CA DC	5	1	4	20%	80%
CA FED	3	1	2	33%	67%
CA AF	1	1	0	100%	0%
State Ct	8	2	6	25%	75%
Dist Ct	4	1	3	25%	75%
Orig	3	N/A	N/A	N/A	N/A
	74	**18**	**52**	**26%**	**74**

The fact that the Supreme Court reversed nearly 3 out of 4 cases that it reviewed in the October 2017 term indicates that the objective of providing consistency of statutes through caselaw is a particularly difficult task. Moreover, this reversal rate indicates that there very likely exists an ample inventory of cases to provide both favorable and unfavorable primary source authority for various tax positions until the disputed issues reach Supreme Court review.

4. The Doctrine of *Stare Decisis*

The doctrine of *stare decisis* generally directs that courts follow the holding of a previously decided case, absent special justification.[188] By adhering to this doctrine, courts provide stability to law by providing predictability of its view of the law given materially similar facts. While different circuits may establish its own view of the same code section, all circuit courts work to provide its body of predictable law within its jurisdiction. "[F]ederal law is for all practical purposes what the Supreme Court says it is. When the Court's view is embodied in a holding, the Court's reluctance to overrule its precedents enables a confident prediction that that holding is 'the law.'"[189] "The rule

---

[188] Sec. State Bank v. Commissioner, 214 F. 3d 1254 (10th Cir. 2000); IRS. v. Osborne, 76 F. 3d 306 (9th Cir. 1996).
[189] Reich v. Continental Cas. Co., 33 F.3d 754, 757 (7th Cir. 1994).

of *stare decisis,* though one tending to consistency and uniformity of decision, is not inflexible. Whether it shall be followed or departed from is a question entirely within the discretion of the court...."[190] In his dissenting opinion in <u>Burnet v. Coronado Oil & Gas Co.</u>, 285 U.S. 393, 406 (1932), Justice Brandeis stated: *"Stare decisis* is usually the wise policy, because, in most matters, it is more important that the applicable rule of law be settled than that it be settled right."

And, specifically related to tax disputes, courts well-understand the importance of maintaining consistency in its decisions. <u>See</u> <u>South Dakota v. Wayfair, Inc.</u>, 138 S.Ct. 2080, 2086 (2018) ("It is essential to public confidence in the tax system that [courts] avoid creating inequitable exceptions.")

5. Relative Weight of Judicial Authorities - The Meaning of Precedential Authority

Court opinions do not carry equal authoritative weight. On the far ends of the spectrum, U.S. Supreme Court opinions carry the highest level of authoritative value whereas U.S. Tax Court summary opinions present the lowest level of value - no precedential authority. In utilizing cases to form the strongest arguments to support a tax position, it is essential to understand the relative weight of various types of court opinions.

<u>Binding or governing authority</u> presents case opinions that parties must follow. All Supreme Court opinions are binding/governing/controlling on parties. Circuit court of appeals decision are binding or governing with respect to parties who fall within its jurisdiction. So, individual taxpayers residing in California would look to Ninth Circuit court of appeals decisions as binding, precedential authority.[191] However, for a California resident, a Sixth Circuit Court of Appeals decision presents persuasive, not binding primary source authority.

In the realm of <u>persuasive or non-governing authorities</u>, there exists a top down ordering of authorities. Supreme Court Justice Antonin Scalia provided a useful list of how a practitioner can view various persuasive primary source authorities[192]:

- *Most persuasive - dicta*[193] in opinions from governing courts (e.g., the U.S.

---

[190] <u>Hertz v. Woodman</u>, 218 U.S. 205, 212 (1910).

[191] It is no easy task to determine whether a case provides "controlling," binding authority. Consider the Ninth Circuit's opinion in <u>Altera Corp. v. Commissioner</u>, 122 AFTR 2d __ (9th Cir. July 24, 2018), <u>withdrawn,</u> [citation omitted] (August 7, 2018), in which the panel of three judges attempted to determine whether the Circuit's prior decision in <u>Xilinx, Inc. v. Comm'r ("Xilinx II")</u>, 598 F.3d 1191 (9th Cir. 2010), presented binding precendential authority that the panel was required to follow. In the majority opinion, Chief Judge Thomas concluded that the Ninth Circuit's prior <u>Xilinx II</u> decision did not present binding precedent because the issue confronted in the prior case was distinguishable from the issue before the current panel of judges. In contrast, Judge O'Malley stated in her dissenting opinion the opposite conclusion: "....I believe that this court's decision in <u>Xilinx II</u> controls....."

[192] <u>Making Your Case, The Art of Persuading Judges</u>, by Antonin Scalia and Bryan A. Garner, pp. 52-55.

[193] "Dicta" in a case opinion is a statement, remark or observation that is not necessarily involved or relevant in the immediate case before the court. Such a statement does not present the reasoning,

Supreme Court or your binding Court of Appeals).

- *More persuasive* - opinions from other non-governing Courts of Appeal

- *Persuasive* - trial court level opinions in your jurisdiction, e.g., District Court and Tax Court decisions appealable in your Circuit

- *Least persuasive* - trial court opinions from other jurisdictions, e.g., District Court or Tax Court decisions appealable to a non-binding Circuit.

Determining which case offers the highest level of authority in support of a tax position is not an easy task. One must determine that the issue addressed by the court is the same and that the facts in your client's matter are materially similar to the facts included in the case opinion. Then, it is critical to determine the value of the cited case - binding/governing/controlling or non-binding/non-governing/non-controlling.

Scholars disagree about what it means to treat a decision of a court as "precedent." In my view, the traditional definition of "precedent" is this: the holding or decision of a case or matter that **must** be either followed, distinguished, or overruled. So, we have these two categories:

- Persuasive authority, aka non-binding authority
                    or
- Binding authority, aka "precedent" or "precedential authority"

Consider the following examples:

- District Court case – persuasive authority, but cannot serve as precedent

- Revenue Ruling – precedent, because it binds the IRS (not courts) to the result as long as the facts are materially the same to the facts in the Revenue Ruling. In other words, revenue rulings present precedential authority for the IRS but not for Courts since the judicial branch is not bound to follow revenue rulings.

- Court of Appeals decision – precedent or binding authority within the same circuit that the decision was issued. Otherwise, for other circuits, decisions from other circuits present persuasive authority

- Supreme Court decision – always binding authority or precedent

6. Action on Decision Issued by the IRS

An action on decision ("AOD") may be prepared by the IRS when a court decides one or more significant issues adversely to the Government.[194] An issue is decided adversely

---

resolution or determination of the court or full consideration of a matter of law presented with all necessary facts being presented and analyzed by the court. Dicta may offer a view of a judge on hypothetical facts not presented in that particular case.

to the Government when the Service's legal position is negatively affected by the court's opinion. An issue may be considered adverse for the purpose of determining whether an AOD should be issued even if neither the case nor the issue is appealable.[195] An AOD expeditiously alerts Service personnel and the public to the current litigating position of the Office of Chief Counsel. An AOD conveys the Office's recommendation on whether the Service will follow a significant adverse opinion.

Generally, an AOD is issued where guidance would be helpful to Service personnel working with the same or similar issues.[196] Unlike a Treasury Regulation or a Revenue Ruling, an AOD is not an affirmative statement of Service position. It is not intended to serve as public guidance and may not be cited as precedent. However, Chief Counsel attorneys are required to follow the litigating positions announced in AODs in future litigation or dispute resolution.[197] An AOD is not prepared for issues that are on appeal, or will be appealed, by the Government. Although rare, an AOD can be prepared and can be issued when the court has sustained the Government's determination as to the amount of the tax liability.

The recommendation in every AOD is summarized as acquiescence, acquiescence in result only, or nonacquiescence. Both "acquiescence " and "acquiescence in result only" mean that the Service accepts the holding of the court in a case and that the Service will follow it in disposing of cases with the same controlling facts. The following differences are noted:

- "Acquiescence" indicates neither approval nor disapproval of the reasons assigned by the court for its conclusions.

- "Acquiescence in result only" indicates disagreement or concern with some or all of those reasons.

Nonacquiescence signifies that, although no further review was sought, the Service does not agree with the holding of the court and generally, will not follow the decision in disposing of cases involving other taxpayers. In reference to an opinion of a circuit court of appeals, a nonacquiescence indicates that the Service will not follow the holding on a nationwide basis. However, the Service will recognize the precedential impact of the opinion on cases arising within the venue of the deciding circuit.

Consider the situation where an AOD is issued announcing that the IRS acquiesces in a case and will follow the holding of a lower court on a tax issue. Chief Counsel attorneys are required to follow the position stated in an AOD. However, the IRM does not require non-Chief Counsel employees, such as IRS revenue agents, to do the same. An AOD cannot serve as precedential authority for courts or for taxpayers.

Below is an AOD acquiescence following an IRS loss in U.S. Tax Court:

---

[194] CCDM 36.3.1.2.
[195] Go to https://apps.irs.gov/app/picklist/list/actionsOnDecisions.html for a list of additional AODs.
[196] IRM 4.10.7.2.9.8.1.
[197] CCDM 36.3.1.1.

ACTION ON DECISION

<u>Ronald Andrew Mayo and Leslie Archer Mayo v. Commissioner</u>, 134 T.C. 81 (2011)

IRB No. 2012-3, January 17, 2012

Issue: Are expenses incurred by a taxpayer in the trade or business of gambling "losses from wagering transactions" subject to the limitation on deductions in § 165(d) of the Internal Revenue Code?

Discussion: Ronald Mayo ("Taxpayer") was in the trade or business of gambling on horse races. In 2001, Taxpayer incurred $10,968 of business expenses. He also had an $11,297 loss from wagering (wagering gains of $120,463 less wagering losses of $131,760). On his Schedule C, Taxpayer deducted both the $11,297 wagering loss and the $10,968 of business expenses ($22,265 total deductions). The Service disallowed the entire $22,265 deduction under § 165(d), which limits deductions for wagering losses to the amount of wagering gains. The Service argued that Taxpayer's business expenses of $10,968, as well as the $11,297 wagering loss, were "losses from wagering transactions" within the meaning of § 165(d). Therefore § 165(d) prevented Taxpayer from deducting both amounts. Taxpayer asserted that the limitation in § 165(d) does not apply to persons engaged in the trade or business of gambling. Alternatively, Taxpayer argued that if § 165(d) applies to persons engaged in the trade or business of gambling, the §165(d) limitation does not apply to gambling related business expenses, because business expenses are not "losses from wagering transactions." The Tax Court held that the limitation in § 165(d) applies to persons engaged in the trade or business of gambling, and therefore taxpayer may not deduct the $11,297 of excess wagering losses over wagering gains. The court further held that a gambler's business expenses are not "losses from wagering transactions" subject to the § 165 deduction limitation. Therefore, the court allowed Taxpayer's deduction under § 162(a) for the $10,968 of gambling related business expenses. The court further announced that it will no longer follow the contrary holding of Offutt v. Commissioner, 16 T.C. 1214 (1951), and other cases applying the § 165(d) deduction limitation to § 162 business expenses.

We agree with the court's analyses. Section 165(d) limits the deduction for the wagering losses of persons engaged in the trade or business of gambling. However, § 165(d) does not limit deductions for expenses incurred to engage in the trade or business of gambling. Those business expenses are deductible under § 162.

Recommendation: Acquiescence

7.   Citator & the Limits of Caselaw as Applicable Primary Source Authority

Much like a family tree or an organizational chart, a court case is linked. If a trial level decision is appealed, then the lower opinion becomes connected to the court of appeals decision and perhaps to a U.S. Supreme Court decision as well. The highest level court decision presents the final decision that stands as precedential authority. Thus, it is essential for a tax practitioner to determine all of the links for each case. But, how?

Citator, or a comparable name for this service such as "Shephards" service used by the Lexis/Nexus tax database, presents a system that provides an update of all court cases so that users can determine: (1) the presence of any prior and subsequent case history; (2) whether any IRS guidance exists that cites to the case as part of the government's analysis; and (3) if other courts cited to the case as part of its judicial analysis. This is an essential, required tool for practitioners to determine the validity and current authoritative value of caselaw. Various fee-based research sites offer citator services under different names:

- CCH – "Citator"

- RIA – "Citator, 2nd"

- Westlaw – "Keycite"

- Lexis – "Shephard's"

What are the limitations of this "citator" system?   First, "citator" does not provide current information on whether the underlying code section addressed by courts in its analysis has been amended or repealed by Congress subsequent to the date of the court's decision. Although citator provides a link to connected authorities, it does not provide up-to-date history of the underlying code section analyzed in the cases. For example, let's start with the hypothetical situation where the Sixth Circuit reverses the decision of the U.S. Tax Court in Jones v. Commissioner in 1987 in which the court addressed the proper interpretation of Code section 162. Subsequent to this court decision, Congress amends Section 162 in 1995 to fundamentally change the intent and language of this tax provision. In 2014, a practitioner locates Jones v. Commissioner in her research and citates the case. Citator will show the trial level U.S. Tax Court decision, the Sixth Circuit Court of Appeals decision, and any other links to IRS guidance or other subsequent cases that reference Jones v. Commissioner as part of its analysis. However, "citator" will not disclose any reference to the fact that the underlying code section analyzed in Jones v. Commissioner has been impacted.

Under this same scenario, the highest level decision in Jones v. Commissioner stands as precedence **but only** for periods prior to the effective date of the change to code section 162 enacted by Congress. On and after the effective date of the new code section, Jones v. Commissioner does not provide valid precedential authority even though citator does not highlight this point. Recall that administrative and judicial authorities provide guidance of the underlying code section. If the underlying code section changes, then any prior analysis of old law is limited to the effective period of that old provision. So, while utilizing citator is essential in tax practice so too is determining the current code section applicable for the year at issue.

So, how must a tax practitioner proceed to ensure that caselaw remains applicable in citing as primary source authority?

Let's work through a practical example to better understand the steps in the diagram, above. A client incurs cell phone costs as part of his business. The client uses the same cell phone for personal calls as well as business calls. The client reports $1,200 for telephone charges as a business expense on Schedule C for tax year 2015. The IRS selects your client's 2015 tax return for audit. During the audit, the IRS questions the telephone expense claimed for $1,200 and requests substantiation. The client produces limited documentation to substantiate his claimed telephone expenses. But, the client states that under Cohan v. Commissioner, 39 F.2d 540 (2d Cir. 1930), when a taxpayer establishes that he or she paid or incurred a deductible expense but does not establish the amount of the expense, courts may estimate the allowable amount (aka, the "Cohan rule"). The IRS states that your client is subject to strict substantiation requirements under section 280F(d)(4)(A) for telephone expenses and cites to Bogue v. Commissioner, T.C. Memo. 2007-150, in support of the argument that the Cohan rule cannot apply to telephone expenses. Bogue v. Commissioner, T.C. Memo. 2007-150, provides, in relevant part, as follows:

> Petitioners claimed $240 of cellular phone expenses for 2003. Cellular phones are included in the definition of "listed property" for purposes of section 274(d)(4) and are thus subject to the strict substantiation requirements. Sec. 280F(d)(4)(A)(v); Gaylord v. Commissioner, T.C. Memo. 2003-273. A taxpayer must establish the amount of business use and the amount of total use for the property to substantiate the amount of expenses for listed property. Nitschke v. Commissioner, T.C. Memo. 2000-230; sec. 1.274-5T(b)(6)(i)(B), Temporary Income Tax Regs., 50 Fed. Reg. 46016 (Nov. 6, 1985). Expenses subject to strict substantiation may not be estimated under the Cohan rule. Sanford v. Commissioner, 50 T.C. at 827.

The court in Bogue held that cell phone expenses are subject to strict substantiation may not be estimated under the Cohan rule. Is this right?

Step 1: Let's assume our research determines that this case is the highest authority that we can locate.

Step 2: We confirm that the facts are materially the same for the cell phone substantiation issue.

Step 3: We citate the case and determine that this case was not subsequently reversed or overruled.

Step 4: We find out after reading <u>Bogue</u> that the court decided how to apply section 280F(d)(4)(A) for tax year 2003. Our client's tax year is 2015. So, we need to determine if Congress changed code section 280F after tax year 2003. Let's look at code section 280F(d)(4)(A), below.

> **(4) LISTED PROPERTY**
>
>> **(A) In general** Except as provided in subparagraph (B), the term "listed property" means—
>>
>>> **(i)** any passenger automobile,
>>>
>>> **(ii)** any other property used as a means of transportation,
>>>
>>> **(iii)** any property of a type generally used for purposes of entertainment, recreation, or amusement,
>>>
>>> **(iv)** any computer or peripheral equipment (as defined in section 168(i)(2)(B)), "and" [1]
>>>
>>> **(v)** any other property of a type specified by the Secretary by regulations.

Next, let's review the historical amendment for this part of section 280F:

In Pub.L. 111-240, §2043(b), Congress enacted the following changes to code section 280F(d)(4)(A) –

> Inserted "'and'" at end of clause (iv), redesignated clause (vi) as (v), and struck out former cl. (v) which read as follows: "any cellular telephone (or other similar telecommunications equipment), and".

(Emphasis added to original text). The effective date for this change is tax years beginning afer December 31, 2009. So, what did we learn?

- Beginning in tax year 2010, cell phone charges are no longer covered under section 280F(d)(4)(A) as "listed property" subject to strict substantiation requirements. The <u>Cohan</u> rule can be applied as long as the taxpayer establishes that he or she paid or incurred a deductible expense but does not establish the amount of the expense.

- <u>Bogue v. Commissioner</u>, T.C. Memo. 2007-150, is **not** applicable judicial authority that we can cite as support for an interpretation of section 280F(d)(4)(F) for years beginning in 2010 because Congress changed the underlying code section addressed in <u>Bogue</u>.

The process is not easy to understand at first. Review the steps, above, a few times and you will become more comfortable with this process soon!

Let's try another more recent example of how practitioners must keep track of caselaw, IRS guidance and statutory changes to understand the proper application of law of a tax issue that impacts every homeowner – the home mortgage interest deduction. Section 163(h)(2)(D) of the Internal Revenue Code allows taxpayers to deduct a limited amount of personal interest paid on residential mortgages. The mortgage must be secured by a "qualified residence," defined by § 163(h)(4)(A) to include the taxpayer's principal residence plus one other residence. Section 163(h)(3) limits the amount of deductible interest to interest paid on $1 million of acquisition indebtedness (or refinanced acquisition indebtedness, up to the amount of the original loan's balance), plus interest paid on $100,000 of home equity indebtedness. The tax issue that spawned litigation was whether the § 163(h)(3) debt limitations on deductions for qualified residence interest apply on a per-taxpayer basis, rather than on a per-residence basis. The IRS argued that the debt limitation under section 163(h)(3) was on a per-residence basis. Taxpayers challenged this interpretation arguing the the limitation applied on a per taxpayer basis, as long as the taxpayers were not married. Litigation, IRS guidance and recent legislation on this issue is summarized in the following diagram:

Timeline of Sec. 163(h)(3)

Section 163(h)(3) limits the amount of deductible interest to interest paid on $1 million of acquisition indebtedness (or refinanced acquisition indebtedness, up to the amount of the original loan's balance), plus interest paid on $100,000 of home equity indebtedness.

IRS Position: IRC § 163(h)(2) and (3) limit the aggregate amount of indebtedness to $1 million and $100,000, respectively, on any qualified residence, allocated among all taxpayers entitled to an interest expense deduction for **that qualified residence.** In other words, the interest deduction limit applies PER RESIDENCE.

2012	2015	2016	2018
Sophy v. Comm'r, 138 T.C. 204 (2012) – U.S. Tax Court decides in favor of IRS position.	In Voss v. Comm'r, 796 F.3d 1051 (9th Cir. 2015), the Ninth Circuit reversed the U.S. Tax Court and decided that the limitation only applies to married taxpayers. An unmarried co-owner filing a separate return is entitled to deduct interest on up to $1,000,000 of acquisition indebtedness and $100,000 of home equity indebtedness.	In 2016, the IRS issues AOD 2016-02 stating that it will follow the Voss opinion and will apply the § 163(h)(2) and (3) limitations on a per-taxpayer basis, allowing each taxpayer to deduct mortgage interest on indebtedness of up to $1 million and $100,000, respectively, on a qualified residence. **Change from § 163(h)(2) and (3) limits applying per residence to per taxpayer.**	P.L. 115-97, sec. 11043, eliminated home equity interest deductions and limited "qualified residence interest deductions to $750,000 beginning in 2018. Added sub-paragraph (F) but nothing else changed that was addressed in Voss.

Not until the Ninth Circuit decision decided in 2015 was there any primary source authority contrary to the IRS position on this issue. And, after the Voss decision, only taxpayers within the jurisdiction of the Ninth Circuit could present governing authority to the IRS that supported a position contradicting the IRS' long-standing view of section 163(h)(3). See I.R.C. § 7482(b)(1); Golsen v. Commissioner, 54 T.C. 742 (1970). Then, in 2016, the IRS issued Action on Decision 2016-02 that it would follow the Voss decision not only as required in the Ninth Circuit, but with respect to every taxpayer in the country regardless of circuit jurisdiction.

Subsequently, effective January 1, 2018, P.L. 115-97, section 11043 reduced the limitation for mortage interest deduction from $1,000,000 to $750,000. See the text of this new tax provision, below:

SEC. 11043. LIMITATION ON DEDUCTION FOR QUALIFIED RESIDENCE INTEREST.

(a) IN GENERAL.—Section 163(h)(3) is amended by adding at the end the following new subparagraph:

"(F) SPECIAL RULES FOR TAXABLE YEARS 2018 THROUGH 2025.—

"(i) IN GENERAL.—In the case of taxable years beginning after December 31, 2017, and before January 1, 2026—

"(I) DISALLOWANCE OF HOME EQUITY INDEBTEDNESS INTEREST.—Subparagraph (A)(ii) shall not apply.

"(II) LIMITATION ON ACQUISITION INDEBTEDNESS.—Subparagraph (B)(ii) shall be applied by substituting '$750,000 ($375,000' for '$1,000,000 ($500,000'.

"(III) TREATMENT OF INDEBTEDNESS INCURRED ON OR BEFORE DECEMBER 15, 2017.—Subclause (II) shall not apply to any indebtedness incurred on or before December 15, 2017, and, in applying such subclause to any indebtedness incurred after such date, the limitation under such subclause shall be reduced (but not below zero) by the amount of any indebtedness incurred on or before December 15, 2017, which is treated as acquisition indebtedness for purposes of this subsection for the taxable year.

"(IV) BINDING CONTRACT EXCEPTION.—In the case of a taxpayer who enters into a written binding contract before December 15, 2017, to close on the purchase of a principal residence before January 1, 2018, and who purchases such residence before April 1, 2018, subclause (III) shall be applied by substituting 'April 1, 2018' for 'December 15, 2017'.

"(ii) TREATMENT OF LIMITATION IN TAXABLE YEARS AFTER DECEMBER 31, 2025.—In the case of taxable years

259

beginning after December 31, 2025, the limitation under subparagraph (B)(ii) shall be applied to the aggregate amount of indebtedness of the taxpayer described in subparagraph (B)(i) without regard to the taxable year in which the indebtedness was incurred.

"(iii) TREATMENT OF REFINANCINGS OF INDEBTEDNESS.—

"(I) IN GENERAL.—In the case of any indebtedness which is incurred to refinance indebtedness, such refinanced indebtedness shall be treated for purposes of clause (i)(III) as incurred on the date that the original indebtedness was incurred to the extent the amount of the indebtedness resulting from such refinancing does not exceed the amount of the refinanced indebtedness.

"(II) LIMITATION ON PERIOD OF REFINANCING.— Subclause (I) shall not apply to any indebtedness after the expiration of the term of the original indebtedness or, if the principal of such original indebtedness is not amortized over its term, the expiration of the term of the 1st refinancing of such indebtedness (or if earlier, the date which is 30 years after the date of such 1st refinancing).

"(iv) COORDINATION WITH EXCLUSION OF INCOME FROM DISCHARGE OF INDEBTEDNESS.—Section 108(h)(2) shall be applied without regard to this subparagraph.".

(b) EFFECTIVE DATE.—The amendments made by this section shall apply to taxable years beginning after December 31, 2017.

However, the text of the new provision under P.L. 115-97 did not alter the language of section 163(h) that was the focus of the Ninth Circuit in <u>Voss</u>. Thus, despite the change to *the amount* of the limitation under section 163, the decision of the <u>Voss</u> court addressing *the application of this dollar limitation* appears to remain the same – "per taxpayer" (as long as taxpayers are not married), not "per residence."

8. Standards of Proof, Evidence in the Internal Revenue Code Addressed by Courts

The Internal Revenue Code includes various terms that impact the manner in which taxpayers, the IRS and courts must proceed in tax matters. Some of these common terms and courts' definitions of these terms follow:

<u>Burden of Production</u> - With respect to Section 7491(c), the burden of production means that the IRS "must come forward with sufficient evidence indicating that it is appropriate to impose the relevant penalty."[198]

---

[198] <u>Higbee v. Commissioner</u>, 116 T.C. 438, 446 (2001).

Burden of Proof - Placement of the burden of proof affects only the obligation to prove facts. The burden of proof does not affect the Court's determination of what the law is.[199] As a general rule, the IRS's determination of a taxpayer's liability is presumed correct; the taxpayer bears the burden of proving that it is incorrect.[200] In certain circumstances, the burden of proof shifts to the IRS if the taxpayer introduces credible evidence with respect to any factual issue relevant to ascertaining the taxpayer's tax liability.[201]

Credible Evidence - Credible evidence is evidence the Court would find sufficient upon which to base a decision on the issue in the taxpayer's favor, absent any contrary evidence.[202]

Preponderance of the Evidence - See Knudsen v. Commissioner, 131 T.C. 185, 189 (2008) ("In a case where the standard of proof is preponderance of the evidence and the preponderance of the evidence favors one party, we may decide the case on the weight of the evidence and not on an allocation of the burden of proof."); see also Estate of Jorgensen v. Commissioner, T.C. Memo. 2009-66, aff'd, 431 Fed. Appx. 544 (9th Cir. 2011).

Clear and Convincing - Clear and convincing evidence is "that measure or degree of proof which will produce in the mind of the trier of facts a firm belief or conviction as to the allegations sought to be established. It is intermediate, being more than a mere preponderance, but not the extent of such certainty as is required beyond a reasonable doubt in criminal cases. It does not mean clear and unequivocal."[203]

9. Privacy Concerns in Judicial Opinions

Individuals should take great comfort in the statutory protection afforded under section 6103 that provides confidentiality for federal tax returns and tax return information filed with the IRS. Unless the statute specifically authorizes disclosure of tax returns or tax return information, civil and criminal penalties apply to any violations of confidentiality of such information.

- Civil Liability – Section 7431 of the Internal Revenue Code provides for a civil remedy against the United States for a taxpayer who has been injured by the unlawful disclosure or inspection of his or her tax information by an employee of the United States. Suit may be brought only against the United States; the individual employee who made the improper disclosure or inspection is neither personally liable nor a proper party to the suit.[204] The United States is not civilly liable for unauthorized disclosures or inspections made by former employees.[205]

---

[199] Shea v. Commissioner, 112 T.C. No. 14 (1999).
[200] Tax Court Rule 142(a); Welch v. Helvering, 290 U.S. 111, 115 (1933).
[201] Sec. 7491(a)(1).
[202] See Higbee v. Commissioner, 116 T.C. 438, 442 (2001).
[203] Ohio v. Akron Ctr. for Reprod. Health, 497 U.S. 502, 516 (1990) (quoting Cross v. Ledford, 161 Ohio St. 469 (1954)); see also Hobson v. Eaton, 399 F.2d 781, 784 n.2 (6th Cir. 1968).
[204] Diamond v. United States, 944 F.2d 431, 435 (8th Cir. 1991).

A two-year statute of limitations, which begins to run at the time the taxpayer discovers the disclosure or inspection, applies to actions brought under Section 7431.[206] In order to make a case for recovery under section 7431, a taxpayer must show (1) that an unauthorized examination or disclosure of return information was made, (2) that the examination or disclosure was knowing or was the result of negligence, and (3) that the examination or disclosure violated 26 U.S.C. § 6103.[207] No liability shall attach, however, if the United States shows either that the disclosure or inspection resulted from a good faith, but erroneous, interpretation of Section 6103, or that the disclosure or inspection was requested by the taxpayer.[208] If successful, the aggrieved taxpayer may recover the greater of actual damages or $1,000 per improper disclosure, plus court costs.[209]

- Criminal Liability - Section 7213 of the Internal Revenue Code provides for criminal penalties for willful violations of Section 6103, and Section 7213A provides for criminal penalties for willfully inspecting any return or return information, except as authorized by the Code. Section 7213 provides that a willful violation of the non-disclosure provisions of section 6103 is a felony, punishable with up to five years in jail, or a fine, or both.[210] In the case of federal employees and officers, Section 7213 also mandates dismissal or discharge upon conviction. The statute of limitations for prosecutions brought under the Section is three years.[211]

   Section 7213A is a misdemeanor offense and governs the unauthorized examination of return information, without regard for whether the "examiner" discloses the information to others. To secure a conviction under Section 7213A, the government must establish that (1) an officer or employee of the United States, any person described in Section 6103(n) of the Code, or any state or other employee described in Section 7213A(a)(2) of the Internal Revenue Code (2) willfully inspected (3) any return or return information (4) in a manner not authorized by the Code. A violation of Section 7213A is punishable by a fine of up to $100,000 (pursuant to 18 U.S.C. § 3571), imprisonment of up to one year, and, if the offender is a federal employee, mandatory discharge from employment.

However, this overarching rule providing privacy of tax return information does not apply once a tax dispute remains unresolved at the administrative level and proceeds to the judicial forum. In Rice v. United States, 166 F.3d 1088, 1092 (10th Cir. 1999), the Tenth

---

[205] See 26 U.S.C. § 7431(a)(1) (referring only to conduct by "any officer or employee of the United States").

[206] 26 U.S.C. § 7431(d).

[207] See 26 U.S.C. § 7431(a).

[208] 26 U.S.C. § 7431(b); see, e.g., Barrett v. United States, 51 F.3d 475, 479 (5th Cir. 1995) (disclosure of taxpayer information not in good faith when IRS employee did not review Section 6103 and did not secure approval of supervisor before circulating taxpayer's return information).

[209] See 26 U.S.C. § 7431(c)(1).

[210] See United States v. Richey, 924 F.2d 857 (9th Cir. 1991).

[211] See 26 U.S.C. § 6531.

Circuit Court of Appeals held that revelation of return information in trial proceedings was proper "under the exception to § 6103 allowing such disclosure in federal court where the taxpayer is a party to the proceedings. 26 U.S.C. § 4."

And, if a court cases requires a written decision by the presiding judge, then publication of the underlying facts of the case including all tax return information heard and presented during the case becomes publicly available. Specifically, for U.S. Tax Court cases, section 7458 provides that "[h]earings before the Tax Court and its divisions shall be open to the public." Section 7461(a) similarly provides that "all evidence received by the Tax Court and its divisions, including a transcript * * * of the hearings, shall be public records open to the inspection of the public." An exception to these general rules is set forth in section 7461(b)(1), captioned "Trade Secrets or Other Confidential Information." It provides that the Court "may make any provision which is necessary to prevent the disclosure of trade secrets or other confidential information, including a provision that any document or information be placed under seal to be opened only as directed by the court.

That a taxpayer's private tax return information becomes a matter of public record available for everyone to see after the matter proceeds to decision in a court case is an important point that must be communicated to clients. For example, once a tax dispute proceeds for disposition by a court, the opinion lays bare an individual's financial situation[212], family issues such as child custody battles and domestic relations including allegations of abuse[213], or the presence of a gambling addiction.[214] For celebrities, sports icons or not, court cases opens up for public viewing information that must by statute remain confidential as long as it does not proceed to the judicial forum.[215] So, although courts provide a final opportunity for taxpayers to continue their tax dispute beyond administrative review before the IRS, be careful what you wish for.

---

[212] See, e.g., W.T. Snipes v. Comm'r, T.C. Memo. 2018-184.

[213] See, e.g., Agudelo v. Comm'r, T.C. Memo. 2015-124.

[214] See, e.g., Yancey v. Comm'r, T.C. Memo. 2017-59.

[215] See, e.g., Estate of Michael J. Jackson, https://www.ustaxcourt.gov/InternetOrders/DocumentViewer.aspx?IndexSearchableOrdersID=247453&Todays=Y; Retief Goosen v. Comm'r, 136 T.C. 547 (2011); Sergio Garcia v. Comm'r, 140 T.C. 140 (2013).

Chapter 7 - Questions

1. Different caselaw has developed on the proper interpretation of code section XX. The Second Circuit has interpreted that code section XX means A. The Fifth Circuit has interpreted that code section XX means B. And, the Federal Circuit Court of Appeals has determined that this same code section means C. Is it possible for your corporate client who is incorporated in California to proceed to litigate code section XX in any one of the three circuit forums? E.g., this is an example of a taxpayer proceeding to the most favorable venue for appeals. In other words, is this type of venue "shopping" possible?

2. Your research on an issue involving Roth IRAs uncovers a case that you find applicable to your client's case – Summa Holdings, Inc. et al. v. Commissioner, T.C. Memo. 2015-119. Citate the case. Is Summa Holdings a case that you can cite as valid legal authority to support your tax argument?

3. Read the selected text, below, from Pau v. Commissioner, T.C. Memo. 1997-43, Counsel Advice Memorandum 200940030 (August 7, 2009) and Rev. Rul. 2010-25 all addressing the issue of whether indebtedness that is incurred by a taxpayer to acquire, construct, or substantially improve a qualified residence can constitute "home equity indebtedness" (within the meaning of §163(h)(3)(C) of the Internal Revenue Code) to the extent it exceeds $1 million. Can the IRS disagree with the position taken by a court on the proper interpretation of a tax statute?

Selected text from *Pau v. Commissioner*, T.C. Memo. 1997-43

****

II. The Mortgage Interest Deduction

Until 1989, petitioners owned a condominium in San Mateo, California, that they used as their primary residence. In 1989, after their move, petitioners reclassified the condominium as rental property. In that year, petitioners also purchased a home in Hillsborough, California, for use as their primary residence and they have since lived there at all times. The purchase price of the residence was $ 1,780,000. Petitioners have a mortgage on the Hillsborough residence, the original principal amount of which was $ 1,330,000.

In 1990, petitioners claimed a home mortgage interest deduction on Schedule A of $ 107,226. Despite having actually paid a greater amount of mortgage interest, petitioners limited their deduction to interest on $ 1.1 million indebtedness based on advice from an accountant. In her notice of deficiency, respondent completely disallowed petitioners' Schedule A deduction for home mortgage interest.

As a result of the October 31, 1995, meeting with petitioner, Clement allowed the Paus a home mortgage interest deduction, but he limited the allowable deduction to the interest on $ 1 million indebtedness. Consequently, he calculated that the allowable deduction is $ 99,040 rather than the $ 107,226 claimed by petitioners, a difference of $ 8,186. Clement also increased the Schedule A deduction for personal interest by $ 819, from $ 4,210 to $ 5,029.

****

Issue 2. Section 163(h)(3) Restriction on Home Mortgage Interest Deduction
Section 163(a) states the general rule for deductions for interest paid or incurred on indebtedness within the taxable year. Other provisions of section 163 limit such deductions. Section 163(h) disallows personal interest deductions unless they fit within certain narrowly prescribed categories. Among these narrow exceptions is the deduction for interest on a qualified residence. Sec. 163(h)(2)(D). The parties agree that the interest paid on the mortgage for petitioners' home was qualified residence interest, because the Paus paid it on acquisition indebtedness pursuant to section 163(h)(3)(A)(i) and (B)(i). The parties dispute only the amount of acquisition indebtedness petitioners may use in computing their deduction.

Section 163(h) restricts home mortgage interest deductions to interest paid on $ 1 million of acquisition indebtedness for debt incurred after October 13, 1987. Acquisition indebtedness is defined as that which is "incurred in acquiring, constructing, or substantially improving any qualified residence of the taxpayer, and * * * is secured by such residence." Sec. 163(h)(3)(B). A taxpayer may be entitled to a greater deduction if he has incurred home equity indebtedness up to $ 100,000, as allowed by section 163(h)(3)(C)(ii). There can be no additional deduction where taxpayers fail to show that they had home equity indebtedness. See Notice 88-74, 1988-2 C.B. 385. Home equity indebtedness is defined as "any indebtedness (other than acquisition indebtedness) secured by a qualified residence". Sec. 163(h)(3)(C) (emphasis added).

Petitioners, who purchased their home in 1989, did not demonstrate that any of their debt was not incurred in acquiring, constructing or substantially improving their residence and thus have failed to carry their burden of proof. We therefore sustain respondent's determination as to the amount petitioners may properly deduct for home mortgage interest.

****

Chief Counsel Advice Memorandum 200940030 (August 7, 2009)

SUBJECT MATTER: Definition of Home Equity Indebtedness under Section 163(h)(3)

TEXT:

to: Samuel Berman
Special Counsel
(Small Business/Self-Employed)

from: Christopher F. Kane, Branch Chief
(Income Tax & Accounting)

This Chief Counsel Advice responds to an issue under your consideration. This advice may not be used or cited as precedent.

ISSUE

Whether indebtedness that is incurred by a taxpayer to acquire, construct, or substantially improve a qualified residence can constitute "home equity indebtedness" (within the meaning of §163(h)(3)(C)) to the extent it exceeds $1 million.

CONCLUSION

Indebtedness incurred by a taxpayer to acquire, construct, or substantially improve a qualified residence can constitute home equity indebtedness to the extent it exceeds $1 million (subject to the $100,000 and fair market value limitations imposed on home equity indebtedness by §163(h)(3)(C)).

BACKGROUND

The law allows taxpayers to deduct interest on two categories of indebtedness secured by their residences: acquisition indebtedness and home equity indebtedness. Acquisition indebtedness is indebtedness to acquire, construct, or substantially improve a residence, but the amount treated as acquisition indebtedness cannot exceed $1 million. Home equity indebtedness is indebtedness other than acquisition indebtedness, but the amount treated as home equity indebtedness cannot exceed $100,000.

You pose the following situation: Taxpayer buys a principal residence for $1,500,000, paying $200,000 in cash and borrowing the remaining $1,300,000 through a loan that is secured by the residence. You ask whether $100,000 of Taxpayer's indebtedness in excess of $1 million can qualify as home equity indebtedness. If so, interest on up to $1.1 million of the debt would be deductible ($1 million of acquisition indebtedness and $100,000 of home equity indebtedness). Because home equity indebtedness is defined in §163(h)(3)(C) as debt other than acquisition indebtedness, the resolution of the issue depends upon the definition of "acquisition indebtedness."

LAW AND ANALYSIS

Statutory provisions

Section 163(h)(1) provides that, in the case of a taxpayer other than a corporation, no deduction shall be allowed for personal interest. Section 163(h)(2) defines personal interest as "any interest allowable as a deduction ... other than ...", inter alia, qualified residence interest (§163(h)(2)(D)). Section 163(h)(3)(A) defines "qualified residence interest" to include interest on "acquisition indebtedness" and "home equity indebtedness."

Section 163(h)(3)(B) and (C) define acquisition indebtedness and home equity indebtedness as follows:

(B)   Acquisition Indebtedness.
    (i)   In general. The term "acquisition indebtedness" means any indebtedness which
    (I) is incurred in acquiring, constructing or substantially improving any qualified residence of the taxpayer, and
    (II) is secured by such residence.
    Such term also includes any indebtedness ... resulting from the refinancing ...
    (ii) $1,000,000 limitation. The aggregate amount treated as acquisition indebtedness for any period shall not exceed $1,000,000 ($500,000 in the case of a married individual filing a separate return).

(C)   Home Equity Indebtedness.
    (i)   In general. The term "home equity indebtedness" means any indebtedness (other than acquisition indebtedness) secured by a qualified residence to the extent the aggregate amount of such indebtedness does not exceed -
    (I)   the fair market value of such qualified residence, reduced by
    (II)   the amount of acquisition indebtedness with respect to such residence.
    (ii)   Limitation. The aggregate amount treated as home equity indebtedness for any period shall not exceed $100,000 ($50,000 in the case of a separate return by a married individual).

We see two possible interpretations of the definition of acquisition indebtedness. Under the first interpretation, acquisition indebtedness means all indebtedness, regardless of amount, incurred to acquire, construct, or substantially improve a qualified residence. That is, under this interpretation, the $1 million limitation in §163(h)(3)(B)(ii) is not an element of the definition of acquisition indebtedness, but is a separate limitation on deductibility. If this interpretation is correct, then a taxpayer who borrows in excess of $1 million to acquire, construct, or substantially improve a qualified residence may not treat the excess above $1 million as home equity indebtedness, because that amount, even though in excess of $1 million, remains acquisition indebtedness.

Under the second interpretation, the $1 million limitation in § 163(h)(3)(B)(ii) is an element of the definition of acquisition indebtedness, so that indebtedness that otherwise qualifies as acquisition indebtedness fails to qualify to the extent it exceeds

$1 million. If this interpretation is correct, then a taxpayer who borrows in excess of $1 million to acquire, construct, or substantially improve a qualified residence may treat the excess above $1 million as home equity indebtedness, because that amount by definition does not constitute acquisition indebtedness.

We think the second interpretation is the better interpretation. We read the definition of "acquisition indebtedness" in §163(h)(3)(B) as including both the §163(h)(3)(B)(i) and §163(h)(3)(B)(ii) elements. As discussed below, we think this interpretation comports with how the term "acquisition indebtedness" is used in other sections of the Code.

Use of the term "acquisition indebtedness" in §163(h)(3)(A)

Section 163(h)(3)(A) defines qualified residence interest as interest paid or accrued during the taxable year on acquisition indebtedness or home equity indebtedness with respect to any qualified residence of the taxpayer. Since qualified residence interest is intended to be interest that is deductible, to define acquisition indebtedness or home equity indebtedness without regard to the $1,000,000 and $100,000 limitations would arguably render the statute meaningless. The term "acquisition indebtedness," as used in §163(h)(3)(A) must mean indebtedness incurred to acquire, construct, or substantially improve the qualified residence that does not exceed the $1,000,000 limitation. Similarly, the term "home equity indebtedness," as used in §163(h)(3)(A) must mean indebtedness that does not exceed the $100,000 limitation.

Use of the term "acquisition indebtedness" in §108

Section 108 adopts a definition of acquisition indebtedness provided by §163(h)(3)(B) that is consistent with defining acquisition indebtedness by reference to both §163(h)(3)(B)(i) and (ii). Sections 108(a)(1)(E) and 108(h) provide an exclusion for the discharge of indebtedness on a taxpayer's qualified principal residence. In doing so, §108(h) adopts and modifies the definition of acquisition indebtedness found in §163(h)(3)(B) to determine what indebtedness qualifies for the exclusion.

Section 108(h)(2) reads as follows:

Qualified principal residence indebtedness. For purposes of this section, the term "qualified principal residence indebtedness" means acquisition indebtedness (within the meaning of §163(h)(3)(B), applied by substituting "$2,000,000 ($1,000,000" for "$1,000,000 ($500,000" in clause (ii) thereof) with respect to the principal residence of the taxpayer.

Importantly, §108(h)(2) does not adopt the definition of acquisition indebtedness provided by §163(h)(3)(B)(i) and then simply apply a $2 million limitation on the exclusion. Instead, recognizing that the $1 million limitation in §163(h)(3)(B)(ii) is incorporated in the definition of the term "acquisition indebtedness," §108(h)(2) modifies the dollar amount defining the term. Therefore, the debt treated as acquisition indebtedness under §163(h)(3)(B) is only the first $1 million of debt used to acquire, construct, or substantially improve a qualified residence. If acquisition indebtedness was instead defined to include all debt used to acquire, construct, or substantially improve a qualified residence, it would not be necessary for §108(h)(2) to modify the definition of acquisition indebtedness. Instead, it would suffice simply to state that acquisition indebtedness, limited to $2 million, is eligible for exclusion.

Use of the term "acquisition indebtedness" in §56 (e)

The alternative minimum tax provisions also refer to §163(h) in §56(e) of the Code, and also suggest that the definition of acquisition indebtedness in §163(h)(3)(B) incorporates the $1 million limitation in §163(h)(3)(B)(ii). Section 56 (b) allows a deduction for qualified housing interest, as defined in §56(e). Section 56(e) defines qualified housing interest as interest which is qualified residence interest under §163(h)(3) (i.e., interest paid on acquisition indebtedness and home equity indebtedness) and is paid or accrued during the taxable year on indebtedness which is incurred in acquiring, constructing, or substantially improving any property which is the principal residence of the taxpayer or is a qualified dwelling which is a qualified residence of the taxpayer.

If the $1 million limitation on acquisition indebtedness is not part of the definition of acquisition indebtedness in §163(h)(3)(B), then arguably interest on acquisition indebtedness is deductible for AMT purposes without limitation. Since that result plainly was not contemplated by Congress, it is more consistent with the statutory scheme to define acquisition indebtedness by reference to both §§163(h)(3)(B)(i) and (ii).

CONCLUSION

Indebtedness that is incurred to acquire, construct or substantially improve a residence, thus satisfying §163(h)(3)(B)(i), but that exceeds $1,000,000, so not satisfying §163(h)(3)(B)(ii), is not acquisition indebtedness. Therefore, home equity indebtedness, as defined in §163(h)(3)(C) includes indebtedness incurred to acquire, construct or substantially improve a qualified residence, to the extent that the indebtedness exceeds the $1 million limit on acquisition indebtedness and to the extent the other requirements of §163(h)(3)(C) are satisfied.

We recognize that the position taken in this memorandum is inconsistent with Pau v. Commissioner, T.C. Memo. 1997-43 and Catalano v. Commissioner, T.C. Memo. 2000-82, regarding the definition of acquisition indebtedness in §163(h)(3)(B). However, we believe that the position in this memorandum is the better interpretation of §163(h)(3)(B) and (C).

After issuing CCA 200940030, the IRS released Rev. Rul. 2010-25 shortly thereafter providing guidance on the same code section. By providing its formal, national position on this one code section, the IRS released definitive guidance with binding authority that taxpayers could rely on and in which the IRS would be bound to follow. In contrast, CCA 200940030 presented non-precedential authority.

Revenue Ruling 2010-25

Rev. Rul. 2010-25; 2010-2 C.B. 571; 2010-44 I.R.B. 571

October 14, 2010

SUMMARY:

An unmarried Taxpayer purchased a principal residence for its fair market value. Taxpayer paid a portion of the price and financed the remainder through a loan secured by the residence. The IRS ruled that debt incurred by a taxpayer to acquire, construct, or substantially improve a qualified residence could constitute home equity debt to the extent it exceeded $1 million (subject to the dollar and fair market value limitations imposed on home equity indebtedness by I.R.C. §163(h)(3)(C)). Thus, Taxpayer could deduct, as interest on acquisition debt under I.R.C. §163(h)(3)(B), interest paid on the debt on up to $1 million of the indebtedness used to acquire the residence. Taxpayer could also deduct, as interest on home equity indebtedness under I.R.C. §163(h)(3)(C), interest on $ 100,000 of the remaining debt. That excess was secured by the qualified residence, was not acquisition debt under I.R.C. §163(h)(3)(B), and did not exceed the fair market value of the residence reduced by the acquisition debt secured by the residence. Thus, $100,000 of the excess was treated as home equity debt under I.R.C. §163(h)(3)(C).

TEXT:

ISSUE

Limitations on qualified residence interest. This ruling holds that indebtedness in excess of $1 million that a taxpayer incurs to acquire, construct, or substantially improve a qualified residence may constitute home equity indebtedness within the meaning of section 163(h)(3)(C) of the Code.

Whether indebtedness that is incurred by a taxpayer to acquire, construct, or substantially improve a qualified residence can constitute "home equity indebtedness" (within the meaning of §163(h)(3)(C) of the Internal Revenue Code) to the extent it exceeds $1 million.

FACTS

In 2009, an unmarried individual (Taxpayer) purchased a principal residence for its fair market value of $1,500,000. Taxpayer paid $300,000 and financed the remainder by borrowing $1,200,000 through a loan that is secured by the residence. In 2009, Taxpayer paid interest that accrued on the indebtedness during that year. Taxpayer has no other debt secured by the residence.

LAW

Section 163(a) allows as a deduction all interest paid or accrued within the taxable year on indebtedness. However, for individuals §163(h)(1) disallows a deduction for personal interest. Under §163(h)(2)(D), qualified residence interest is not personal interest. Section 163(h)(3)(A) defines qualified residence interest as interest paid or accrued during the taxable year on acquisition indebtedness or home equity indebtedness secured by any qualified residence of the taxpayer. Under §163(h)(4)(A), "qualified residence" means a taxpayer's principal residence, within the meaning of § 121, and one other residence selected and used by the taxpayer as a residence.

Section 163(h)(3)(B)(i) provides that acquisition indebtedness is any indebtedness that is incurred in acquiring, constructing, or substantially improving a qualified residence and is secured by the residence. However, §163(h)(3)(B)(ii) limits the amount of indebtedness treated as acquisition indebtedness to $1,000,000 ($500,000 for a married individual filing separately). Accordingly, any indebtedness described in §163(h)(3)(B)(i) in excess of $1,000,000 is, by definition, not acquisition indebtedness for purposes of § 163(h)(3).

Section 163(h)(3)(C)(i) provides that home equity indebtedness is any indebtedness secured by a qualified residence other than acquisition indebtedness, to the extent the fair market value of the qualified residence exceeds the amount of acquisition indebtedness on the residence. However, §163(h)(3)(C)(ii) limits the amount of indebtedness treated as home equity indebtedness to $100,000 ($50,000 for a married individual filing separately). Accordingly, any indebtedness described in §163(h)(3)(C)(i) in excess of $100,000 is, by definition, not home equity indebtedness for purposes of §163(h)(3).

In Pau v. Commissioner, T.C. Memo. 1997-43, the Tax Court limited the taxpayers' deduction for qualified residence interest to the interest paid on $1 million of the $1.33 million indebtedness incurred to purchase their residence. The court stated that §163(h) restricts home mortgage interest deductions to interest paid on $1 million of acquisition indebtedness and $100,000 of home equity indebtedness. Citing §163(h)(3)(B), the court stated that acquisition indebtedness is defined as indebtedness that is incurred in acquiring, constructing, or substantially improving any qualified residence of the taxpayer, and is secured by the residence. Citing §163(h)(3)(C), the court further stated that home equity indebtedness is defined as any indebtedness (other than acquisition indebtedness) secured by a qualified residence. The court concluded that the taxpayers failed to demonstrate that any of their debt was not incurred in acquiring, constructing, or substantially improving their residence and thus was not acquisition indebtedness. However, the court did not   address the effect of the $1 million limitation in §163(h)(3)(B)(ii) on the definition of acquisition indebtedness for purposes of § 163 (h) (3). The Tax Court followed Pau in Catalano v. Commissioner, T.C. Memo. 2000-82.

ANALYSIS

Taxpayer may deduct, as interest on acquisition indebtedness under §163(h)(3)(B), interest paid in 2009 on $1,000,000 of the $1,200,000 indebtedness used to acquire the principal residence. The $1,200,000 indebtedness was incurred in acquiring a qualified residence of Taxpayer and was secured by the residence. Thus, indebtedness of $1,000,000 is treated as acquisition indebtedness under §163(h)(3)(B).

Taxpayer also may deduct, as interest on home equity indebtedness under §163(h)(3)(C), interest paid in 2009 on $100,000 of the remaining indebtedness of $200,000. The $200,000 is secured by the qualified residence, is not acquisition indebtedness under §163(h)(3)(B), and does not exceed the fair market value of the residence reduced by the acquisition indebtedness secured by the residence. Thus, $100,000 of the $200,000 is treated as home equity indebtedness under §163(h)(3)(C).

Under §163(h)(3)(A), the interest on both acquisition indebtedness and home equity indebtedness is qualified residence interest. Therefore, for 2009 Taxpayer may deduct interest paid on indebtedness of $1,100,000 as qualified residence interest. Any interest Taxpayer paid on the remaining indebtedness of $100,000 is nondeductible personal interest under §163(h).

The Internal Revenue Service will not follow the decisions in Pau v. Commissioner and Catalano v. Commissioner. The holding in Pau was based on the incorrect assertion that taxpayers must demonstrate that debt treated as home equity indebtedness "was not incurred in acquiring, constructing or substantially improving their residence." The definition of home equity indebtedness in §163(h)(3)(C) contains no such restrictions, and accordingly the Service will determine home equity indebtedness consistent with the provisions of this revenue ruling, notwithstanding the decisions in Pau and Catalano.

HOLDING

Indebtedness incurred by a taxpayer to acquire, construct, or substantially improve a qualified residence can constitute home equity indebtedness to the extent it exceeds $1 million (subject to the applicable dollar and fair market value limitations imposed on home equity indebtedness by §163(h)(3)(C)).

DRAFTING INFORMATION

The principal author of this revenue ruling is Sharon Hall of the Office of Associate Chief Counsel (Income Tax & Accounting). For further information regarding this revenue ruling, contact Ms. Hall at (202) 622-4950 (not a toll-free call).

CHAPTER 8 – HOW TO READ COURT CASES

☑   Understand how to approach reading court cases
☑   Understand the limitations of the Doctrine of *Stare Decisis*

1. Introduction
2. Court Decisions – The Good, the Bad, the Opaque and Abstruse
3. Similar Facts Applied to the Same Rules Do Not Always Lead to Predictable Results Despite the Doctrine of *Stare Decisis*

1. Introduction

Court decisions, commonly referred to as "case law," provide primary source authority that informs us on how the judiciary interprets statutes. Initially, the executive agency in charge of interpreting and executing the tax code as enacted under Title 26 will provide applicable interpretations and guidance. However, when taxpayers disagree with the IRS' view, courts step in to settle any disputes and issues its decision. Depending on the level of the decision (trial court, Court of Appeals or Supreme Court), the holding of the court can either offer persuasive authority or binding authority.[216] While it is important that we understand the various levels of court decisions, it is vital that we know how to properly read court cases so that we can become properly informed on

---

[216] Persuasive authority is sometimes referred to as "non-governing" authority. Binding authority is sometimes referred to as "governing" authority.

how statutes should be interpreted. This chapter focuses on how to approach reading court decisions.

2. Court Decisions - The Good, the Bad, the Opaque and Abstruse

Yes, there is great value in finding court cases that can serve to support your understanding of a statute and your tax position. But, the problem is that reading a case is often a very difficult undertaking. And, honestly, the difficulty of properly grasping the reasoning in case decisions is not entirely your fault.

Judges who draft court decisions discharge an incredibly important responsibility in not only deciding the fate of the litigants involved in the case but also in adding to the body of caselaw on the tax statute addressed in the opinion for other taxpayers and the government. With all due respect to the judiciary, not all judges write clearly. Supreme Court Justice Roberts appeared to appreciate the need for clearer court decisions at his confirmation hearing, stating: "I hope we haven't gotten to the point where the Supreme Court's opinions are so abstruse that the educated layperson can't pick them up and read them and understand them."

The pinnacle of legal prowess in court decision clarity and precision must come from the Supreme Court, where nine of the finest legal minds in our country decide the most important cases in the land. And, at this apex of the judicial branch, there is evidence that even Supreme Court decisions present difficulties for everyone including the justices.[217]

- *Outside Software Looking at Supreme Court Decisions* - Two political scientists used linguistic software to analyze the complexity of the usage and concepts in some 5,800 Supreme Court opinions from 1983 to 2008. "Unanimous opinions are the most complex," the study, by Ryan J. Owens of Harvard and Justin Wedeking of the University of Kentucky, found, while majority opinions in 5-to-4 decisions are the clearest.[218]
- *Supreme Court Justices Commenting on their Own Decisions* – In Philip Morris USA v. Williams, 549 U.S. 346 (2007), the Court addressed an issue of the proper jury instructions that must be provided for damage awards. In a state negligence and deceit lawsuit, a jury found that Jesse Williams' death was caused by smoking and that petitioner Philip Morris, which manufactured the cigarettes he favored, knowingly and falsely led him to believe that smoking was safe. In respect to deceit, it awarded $821,000 in compensatory damages and $79.5 million in punitive **damages to respondent, the personal representative**

---

[217] See, e.g., Vanessa Stuart v. Alabama, 586 U.S. ___ (2018)(in his dissent of a decision by the Supreme Court denying review of a case addressing the admissibility of blood alcohol tests, Justice Gorsuch noted that "I believe we owe lower courts struggling to abide our holdings more clarity than we have afforded them in this area.") For more detailed guidance on how to read Supreme Court decisions, please go to https://www.americanbar.org/content/dam/aba/images/public_education/Reading-SCOTUS-Opinion.pdf.

[218] Adam Liptak, "Justices are Long on Words but Short on Guidance," The New York Times, Nov. 17, 2010.

of Williams' estate. The trial court reduced the latter award, but it was restored by the Oregon Court of Appeals. The State Supreme Court rejected Philip Morris' arguments that the trial court should have instructed the jury that it could not punish Philip Morris for injury to persons not before the court. In the majority, Justice Breyer wrote that juries may consider evidence concerning harm to people not involved in the case (such as the personal representative of a person's estate) and the assess the reprehensibility of the defendant's conduct **but not** to punish the defendant for harm caused to others. Huh? In the opinion, Just Stevens wrote in a dissent, "This nuance eludes me." And, in a second dissent, Justice Ginsburg joined by Justice Scalia and Thomas asked what a justice was supposed to do with the instructions as presented by the Court's decision drafted by Justice Breyer. Justice Ginsburg wrote, "The answer slips from my grasp."

What's the message to take away? Court decisions are difficult to read. Some decisions are easier to read than others. But, a good start is getting to a basic comfort level of what is involved in this adventure. Before we begin this task, let's look at one of my favorite Tax Court judges who writes succinct and entertaining court decisions – Judge Holmes. A shortened version of his reported opinion, <u>Avrahami v. Commissioner</u>, 149 T.C. No. 7 (2017), follows:

---

149 T.C. No. 7 (2017)

UNITED STATES TAX COURT

BENYAMIN AVRAHAMI AND ORNA AVRAHAMI, Petitioners v. COMMISSIONER OF INTERNAL REVENUE, Respondent

HOLMES, Judge: Benyamin and Orna Avrahami own three shopping centers and three thriving jewelry stores. In 2006 they spent a little more than $150,000 insuring them. In 2009 this insurance bill soared to more than $1.1 million and it flew even higher, to more than $1.3 million, in 2010. The Avrahamis were paying the overwhelming share of these big bills to a new insurance company called Feedback that was wholly owned by Mrs. Avrahami. Yet there were no claims made on any of the Feedback policies until the IRS began an audit of the Avrahamis' and their various entities' returns. With money flooding in and none going back out to pay claims, Feedback accumulated a surplus of more than $3.8 million by the end of 2010, $1.7 million of which ended up back in the Avrahamis' bank account--as loans and loan repayments, say the Avrahamis; as distributions, says the Commissioner. Also included in Feedback's surplus was $720,000 that the Avrahamis' jewelry stores sent down to a Caribbean company for terrorism-risk insurance. The full $720,000 then flew right back to Feedback after--the Avrahamis argue--it distributed enough risk for the whole plan to constitute insurance as that term is commonly understood.

OPINION

I.   Taxation of Insurance

Amounts paid for insurance are deductible under section 162(a) as ordinary and necessary expenses paid or incurred in connection with a trade or business. Sec. 1.162-1(a), Income Tax Regs. But amounts set aside in a loss reserve as a form of self-insurance are not. See Harper Grp. v. Commissioner, 96 T.C. 45, 46 (1991), aff'd, 979 F.2d 1341 (9th Cir. 1992); see also Steere Tank Lines, Inc. v. United States, 577 F.2d 279, 280 (5th Cir. 1978); Spring Canyon Coal Co. v. Commissioner, 43 F.2d 78, 80 (10th Cir. 1930). However, neither the Code nor the regulations define "insurance". Securitas Holdings, Inc. v. Commissioner, T.C. Memo. 2014-225, at *18. Instead we are guided by caselaw when determining whether insurance exists for federal income tax purposes. The Supreme Court has stated that insurance is a transaction that involves "an actual 'insurance risk'" and that "[h]istorically and commonly insurance involves risk-shifting and risk-distributing." Helvering v. Le Gierse, 312 U.S. 531, 539 (1941).

****

Judge Holmes writes directly and efficiently. And, often times, in his opinions, you sense that he clearly understands his duty to present a well-organized, well-reasoned analysis so that it adds to clarify the body of tax law developed by the U.S. Tax Court. As you read more court opinions at all levels, you will find some decisions that elevate your perception of the law and others that may cause you to stare at the pages befuddled. As tax practitioners, we cannot direct jurists to write in plain english. Interestingly, Congress enacted the Plain Writing Act of 2010 to require federal agencies to write "clear Government communication that the public can understand and use."[219] Later, in 2014, Treasury Secretary Lew reminded all employees of their legal requirement to comply with the Plain Writing Act of 2010.

---

[219] Pub.L. 111-274.

DEPARTMENT OF THE TREASURY
WASHINGTON, D.C.

SECRETARY OF THE TREASURY

July 31, 2014

Dear Colleagues,

President Obama and I share the goal of making our government more transparent and more accessible to the general public. Over the course of this Administration, we have made great progress on this front, but our work is far from over. One way we can continue to build upon existing efforts is through our compliance with the Plain Writing Act of 2010. The Plain Writing Act mandates that federal agencies communicate to the public in a clear, concise, and well-organized manner. While the Act's mandate only covers certain outward-facing documents, we should all work to incorporate its principles into our day-to-day writing, as clear communication leads to more efficient decision-making and better outcomes.

We all know that the issues we deal with at Treasury can be complex, but the overuse of technical jargon and acronyms does not convey greater understanding of an issue. We demonstrate our grasp of an issue most clearly when we are able to distill complicated subject matter into simple and straightforward language. It is important that we work every day to make sure that our writing—whether a quick email or detailed analysis—is understandable to an outside reader.

I urge each of you to take a few minutes this week to read about the Plain Writing Act on Treasury's Plain Writing website and to look for opportunities to improve your writing, particularly when it will be public-facing.

While the clarity of our writing may appear to be a minor detail at times, we must remain focused on fulfilling our responsibility to communicate clearly with the people we serve. Thank you for your work on this front—I look forward to the continued progress we will make as we take up this effort together.

Sincerely,

Jacob J. Lew

No comparable "Plain Writing" statute applies for the judicial branch. We can only seek to understand the courts' role and do our best to understand the relevant decisions that we find from our research.

Caselaw Fills the Gap

As noted in Avrahami v. Commissioner, 149 T.C. No. 7 (2017), above, caselaw must fill statutory gaps when necessary, as in the how to define "insurance," when neither the tax code nor the regulations do so. And, when court decisions provide such guidance, tax practitioners must carefully mine the court's decisions to understand the precise rationale presented. Put on your coal miner's hat and let's read Blackman v. Commissioner, 88 T.C. 677 (1987). This case involved a guy who had a bad temper that ultimately led to the destruction of his home. The problem for the IRS was that this ill-tempered man sought to deduct the loss of his home on his return as a casualty loss. The IRS denied his claimed loss. Mr. Blackman didn't like the answer and took the IRS to Tax Court for relief.

---

88 T.C. 677 (1987)
BILTMORE BLACKMAN, PETITIONER
v.
COMMISSIONER OF INTERNAL REVENUE, RESPONDENT

United States Tax Court.

Filed March 24, 1987.

Biltmore Blackman, *pro se.*
C. Ellen Pilsecker, for the respondent.

SIMPSON, Judge:

The Commissioner determined a deficiency of $22,737.38 in the petitioner's Federal income tax for 1980 …….. After concessions, the issues remaining for decision are: (1) Whether the petitioner is entitled to a deduction for the loss of his residence by fire when that fire was started by him……..

FINDINGS OF FACT
Some of the facts have been stipulated, and those facts are so found.
At the time of the filing of the petition in this case, the petitioner, Biltmore Blackman, resided in Billerica, Massachusetts. He and his wife filed their joint Federal income tax return for 1980 on April 28, 1981, with the Internal Revenue Service Center, Atlanta, Georgia.[2]

The petitioner's employer transferred him from Baltimore, Maryland, to South Carolina. The petitioner relocated his wife and children to South Carolina. Mrs. Blackman was dissatisfied with South Carolina and returned, with the couple's five children, to Baltimore. During the 1980 Labor Day weekend, the petitioner returned to Baltimore, hoping to persuade his wife to give South Carolina another chance. When he arrived at his Baltimore home, he discovered that another man was living there with his wife. The neighbors told the petitioner that such man had been there on other occasions when the petitioner had been out of town on business.

On September 1, 1980, the petitioner returned to his former home to speak to his wife. However, Mrs. Blackman was having a party; her guests refused to leave despite the petitioner's request that they do so. He returned to the house several times, repeating his request, and emphasizing it by breaking windows. Mrs. Blackman's guests did not leave the house until about 3 a.m., September 2, 1980.

Later, on September 2, 1980, the petitioner again went to his former home. He wanted to ask his wife whether she wanted a divorce. They quarreled, and Mrs. Blackman left the house. After she left, the petitioner gathered some of Mrs. Blackman's clothes, put them on the stove, and set them on fire. The petitioner claims that he then "took pots of water to dowse the fire, put the fire totally out" and left the house. The fire spread, and the fire department was called. When the firefighters arrived, they found some of the clothing still on the stove. The house and its contents were destroyed.

The petitioner was arrested later that day and charged with one count of Setting Fire while Perpetrating a Crime, a violation of Md. Ann. Code art. 27, sec. 11 (Repl. vol. 1982), and one count of Destruction of Property (Malicious Mischief), a violation of Md. Ann. Code art. 27, sec. 111 (Repl. vol. 1982). The arson charge was based on the allegation that the petitioner "had set fire to and burned * * * [the house] while perpetrating the crime of Destruction of Property" and the malicious destruction charge was based on the allegation that he "did willfully and maliciously destroy, injure, deface and molest clothing, the property of" Mrs. Blackman. The petitioner pleaded not guilty to both charges. On November 5, 1980, by order of the District Court of Baltimore County, the arson charge was placed on the "stet" docket. The petitioner was ordered to serve 24 months unsupervised probation without verdict on the malicious destruction charge.

The petitioner filed a claim for the fire damage with his insurer, State Farm Fire & Casualty Co. of Baltimore, Maryland. The company refused to honor the claim due to the cause of the fire.

On his 1980 Federal income tax return, the petitioner deducted as a casualty loss $97,853 attributable to the destruction of his residence and its contents. In his notice of deficiency, the Commissioner disallowed the deduction and made other adjustments. He now concedes those other adjustments and does not dispute the amount of the casualty loss, if the loss is allowable. ......

OPINION

The primary issue for our decision is whether the petitioner is allowed to deduct the loss resulting from the fire started by him. Section 165(a) allows a deduction for "any loss sustained during the taxable year and not compensated for by insurance or otherwise." Section 165(c)(3) provides, in pertinent part, that in the case of an individual, the deduction allowed in subsection (a) is to be limited to "losses of property not connected with a trade or business, if such losses arise from fire, storm, shipwreck, or other casualty, or from theft." The Commissioner concedes that the petitioner sustained a loss through fire. However, the Commissioner argues that the petitioner intentionally set the fire which destroyed his home in violation of Maryland's public policy, that allowing the deduction would frustrate that public policy, and that, therefore, under the doctrine of Commissioner v. Heininger, 320 U.S. 467 (1943), and subsequent cases, the petitioner is not entitled to a deduction for the damage caused by his fire.

Courts have traditionally disallowed business expense and casualty loss deductions under section 162 or 165 where national or State public policies would be frustrated by the consequences of allowing the deduction. Commissioner v. Heininger, supra. "[T]he test of non-deductibility always is the severity and immediacy of the frustration resulting from allowance of the deduction." Tank Truck Rentals v. Commissioner, 356 U.S. 30, 35 (1958). "From the cases, it is clear that the question of illegality to frustrate public policy is, in the last analysis, one of degree, to be determined from the peculiar facts of each case." Fuller v. Commissioner, 213 F.2d 102, 106 (10th Cir. 1954), aff'g, 20 T.C. 308 (1953); emphasis supplied. In examining the facts of each case, courts have examined both the taxpayer's conduct and the policy his conduct is said to frustrate. See, e.g., Commissioner v. Heininger, supra; Tank Truck Rentals v. Commissioner, supra; Holt v. Commissioner, 69 T.C. 75 (1977), affd. per curiam 611 F.2d 1160 (5th Cir. 1980); Mazzei v. Commissioner, 61 T.C. 497 (1974); Richey v. Commissioner, 33 T.C. 272 (1959).

Conviction of a crime is not essential to a showing that the allowance of a deduction would frustrate public policy. In Richey v. Commissioner, supra, and Mazzei v. Commissioner, supra, we denied theft loss deductions to two different taxpayers who were swindled by their co-conspirators in counterfeiting schemes. In Richey, we said the acts of the taxpayer constituted "an attempt to counterfeit, an actual start in the counterfeiting activity, and overt acts looking to consummation of the counterfeiting scheme." 33 T.C. at 276. In Mazzei, we said "The petitioner conspired with his covictim to commit a criminal act, namely, the counterfeiting of United States currency." 61 T.C. at 502. Neither of the taxpayers in Richey or Mazzei was charged with a crime. In Wagner v. Commissioner, 30 B.T.A. 1099 (1934), the Commissioner disallowed the taxpayer's deduction of losses which resulted from confiscation of the taxpayer's business. The taxpayer was alleged to have violated State usury statutes, but he was not arrested, nor were any charges filed against him. We upheld the disallowance of the loss deduction on the grounds that the taxpayer's business practices violated the policy expressed by the State lending and usury laws. 30 B.T.A. at 1105-1107. Similarly, in Davis v. Commissioner, 17 T.C. 549 (1951), the taxpayer was accused, by the SEC, of a violation of section 16(b) of the Securities Exchange Act of 1934. The SEC ordered the taxpayer to pay a corporation, of which the taxpayer was general counsel, the profits taxpayer had received from sales of the corporation's stock. The taxpayer was not formally charged with any crime. We upheld the Commissioner's disallowance of a deduction of the payment as a loss on the ground that allowing the deduction would frustrate the public policy expressed in section 16(b). 17 T.C. at 556.

Moreover, it is well settled that the negligence of the taxpayer is not a bar to the allowance of the casualty loss deduction. Anderson v. Commissioner, 81 F.2d 457, 460 (10th Cir. 1936); Shearer v. Anderson, 16 F.2d 995, 997 (2d Cir. 1927). On the other hand, gross negligence on the part of the taxpayer will bar a casualty loss deduction. Heyn v. Commissioner, 46 T.C. 302, 308 (1966). "Needless to say, the taxpayer may not knowingly or willfully sit back and allow himself to be damaged in his property or willfully damage the property himself." White v. Commissioner, 48 T.C. 430, 435 (1967).

In our judgment, the petitioner's conduct was grossly negligent, or worse. He admitted that he started the fire. He claims that he attempted to extinguish it by putting water on it. Yet, the firemen found clothing still on the stove, and there is no evidence to corroborate the petitioner's claim that he attempted to dowse the flame. The fact is that the fire spread to the entire house, and we have only vague and not very persuasive evidence concerning the petitioner's attempt to extinguish the fire. Once a person starts a fire, he has an obligation to make extraordinary efforts to be sure that the fire is safely extinguished. The petitioner has failed to demonstrate that he made such extraordinary efforts. The house fire was a foreseeable consequence of the setting of the clothes fire, and a consequence made more likely if the petitioner failed to take adequate precautions to prevent it. We hold that the petitioner's conduct was grossly negligent and that his grossly negligent conduct bars him from deducting the loss claimed by him under section 165(a) and (c)(3).

In addition, allowing the petitioner a deduction would severely and immediately frustrate the articulated public policy of Maryland against arson and burning. Maryland's policy is clearly expressed. Article 27, section 11, of the Maryland Annotated Code (Repl. vol. 1982), makes it a felony to burn a residence while perpetrating a crime. The petitioner admits that he set fire to his wife's clothes, and he has not denied that the residence burned as a result of the fire started by him. The petitioner was charged with violating that section, but that charge was placed on the "stet" docket. As we understand Maryland practice, such action merely postponed any action on the charge. See Maryland Rule 4-248(a); Fuller v. State, 64 Md. App. 339, 495 A.2d 366 (1985); State v. Weaver, 52 Md. App. 728, 451 A.2d 1259 (1982). However, the mere fact that the petitioner was never brought to trial for burning the house does not foreclose a finding by this Court that the petitioner acted in violation of that policy. See Richey v. Commissioner, supra; Mazzei v. Commissioner, supra; Wagner v. Commissioner, supra; Davis v. Commissioner, supra. We are mindful, also, that Maryland has an articulated public policy against domestic violence. We refuse to encourage couples to settle their disputes with fire. We hold that allowing a loss deduction, in this factual setting, would severely and immediately frustrate the articulated public policies of Maryland against arson and burning, and against domestic violence.

. . . .

In <u>Blackman</u>, the court acknowledges that code section 165(a) allows a deduction for "any loss sustained during the taxable year and not compensated for by insurance or otherwise." However, the court addresses the caselaw that traditionally disallowed business expense and casualty loss deductions under section 162 or 165 where national or State public policies would be frustrated by the consequences of allowing the deduction. Commissioner v. Heininger, supra. So, what is the test that the court in Blackman applied to reach its ultimate conclusion to deny Mr. Blackman's claimed loss?

Here's a start to understanding the holding of the court in <u>Blackman</u>:

- **Test:** If allowing a deduction under section 162 or 165 would frustrate national or state public policies, then a taxpayer's claim loss is not allowed.
Source? "Courts have traditionally disallowed business expense and casualty loss deductions under section 162 or 165 where national or State public policies would be frustrated by the consequences of allowing the deduction."

- **Two Factors Analyzed for the Test:** (1) Taxpayer's conduct and (2) Policy his conduct is said to frustrate. *Source?* "In examining the facts of each case, courts have examined both the taxpayer's conduct and the policy his conduct is said to frustrate."
    - o Factor 1 - Taxpayer's Conduct: (1) conviction of a crime not essential; (2) grossly negligent action based on the following: (i) intentional act with loss that was foreseeable from the action taken and which directly caused the loss220; (ii) no persuasive evidence that taxpayer made extraordinary effort to mitigate loss; (iii) failure to take adequate precautions to prevent loss.
        - *Source?* "He admitted that he started the fire. He claims that he attempted to extinguish it by putting water on it. Yet, the firemen found clothing still on the stove, and there is no evidence to corroborate the petitioner's claim that he attempted to dowse the flame. The fact is that the fire spread to the entire house, and we have only vague and not very persuasive evidence concerning the petitioner's attempt to extinguish the fire. Once a person starts a fire, he has an obligation to make extraordinary efforts to be sure that the fire is safely extinguished. The petitioner has failed to demonstrate that he made such extraordinary efforts. The house fire was a foreseeable consequence of the setting of the clothes

---

220 Source: "The petitioner admits that he set fire to his wife's clothes, and he has not denied that <u>the residence burned as a result of the fire started by him.</u>"

fire, and a consequence made more likely if the petitioner failed to take adequate precautions to prevent it."

- o <u>Factor 2</u> – Policy his conduct is said to frustrate: National or state public policy
  - *Source?* "….allowing the petitioner a deduction would severely and immediately frustrate the articulated public policy of Maryland against arson and burning. Maryland's policy is clearly expressed. Article 27, section 11, of the Maryland Annotated Code (Repl. vol. 1982), makes it a felony to burn a residence while perpetrating a crime."

If we properly read and understood this judicial rule disallowing losses where a taxpayer's grossly negligent conduct was involved, then can we apply to a different set of facts involving section 165? In another case, taxpayers decided to build a house deep in the woods of California without the necessary building permits. California deemed the area too hazardous to build homes due to the frequency of wild fires. So, when a fire does eventually destroy the homes that are built in fire zones, should these taxpayers be allowed to claim a casualty loss deduction? Recall <u>Blackman</u> as we consider the analysis and decision in Chief Counsel Advice 201346009, below.

Office of Chief Counsel
Internal Revenue Service Memorandum
Number: 201346009
Release Date: 11/15/2013
CC:ITA:B02 POSTF-152104-12

date: August 01, 2013
to: ********** Attorney, San Francisco, Group 1 (Small Business/Self-Employed)

from: ********** Senior Technician Reviewer, Branch 2 (Income Tax & Accounting)

subject: Deductibility of Claimed Casualty Loss of ****************

This Chief Counsel Advice responds to your request for assistance. This advice may not be used or cited as precedent.

****

ISSUES

Whether Taxpayers may be denied a casualty loss deduction under section 165(c)(3) of the Internal Revenue Code based on public policy considerations for two uninsured structures which were built without the requisite permits and were destroyed in a fire. CONCLUSIONS Based on the facts provided, there are not sufficient grounds to deny Taxpayers a casualty loss deduction based on public policy considerations. Further, Taxpayers have not provided sufficient evidence to substantiate the amount of their casualty loss. We recommend that Exam further develop the issue of whether Taxpayers properly computed and adequately substantiated the casualty loss claimed on the two structures.

FACTS AND BACKGROUND

The facts provided are summarized below. A full statement of the facts is set forth in the incoming request. In Year1, Taxpayers purchased a N1-acre parcel of property jointly with another couple, the A. The property is located in the mountains of County. Taxpayers built a home themselves on the property and lived in the home since the early Year2. Based on statements from Taxpayers' representative, Taxpayers knowingly built the home without the necessary permits because they wanted to live without Government interference. The State Building Code requires building, plumbing, electrical, and mechanical permits to be obtained in order to build a home. There are various remedies available to the State and County to enforce the building code, such as recording a notice of violation on the property, as well as imposing penalties and fines. A also built their own home on the property in the early Year2 and lived in it. In Year 3, Taxpayers bought the A's share of the property including the A's home. Taxpayers claim that they converted the A's home into a timber mill. Taxpayers did not file a Schedule C regarding the sale of timber and did not report income or expenses from the sale of timber on their Year4 return. In Year4, a large fire burned N2 acres of forested land in the County. Both of Taxpayers' structures were totally destroyed in the fire. According to press reports N3 other structures and homes in the area were destroyed, a number of which were built without the required permits. Taxpayers claimed a casualty loss deduction on their Year4 amended return.

Taxpayers computed their adjusted basis in the two structures using statistical data for the cost of building comparable structures in an adjacent county in Year5, which included the cost of labor. Taxpayers did not provide any substantiation of the expenses they incurred in building the home or for converting the purchased home into a timber mill. Exam and field counsel believe that Taxpayers are not entitled to a casualty loss deduction because allowing the deduction would severely and completely frustrate the State policy of obtaining permits before building a home. Field counsel states that the policy reflected in the State and County laws is to protect public safety by ensuring the safety and integrity of the houses and the public. In support of this position, they assert that: first, allowing the deduction would cause the Federal Government to be the insurer of last resort for unpermitted, and thus illegal, homes; second, Taxpayers would have no financial incentive to comply with the State and County statutes if the Federal government effectively insured their loss; third, the loss does not need to be related to the illegal activity; and fourth because Taxpayers knowingly did not get the required permits, they were not legally entitled to incur the costs for building their home, buying the A's home, and making improvements to that home, and they should not get the benefit of a casualty loss deduction.

LAW

Section 165(a) allows a deduction for losses sustained during the taxable year and not compensated for by insurance or otherwise.

Section 165(c) limits a deduction for losses under section 165(a) for individuals to: (1) losses incurred in a trade or business; (2) losses incurred in any transaction entered into for profit, though not connected with a trade or business; and (3) except as provided in section 165(h), losses of property not connected with a trade or business or a transaction entered into for profit, if such losses arise from fire, storm, shipwreck, or other casualty, or from theft.

Section 1.165-7(a)(1) of the Income Tax Regulations provides that any loss arising from fire, storm, shipwreck, or other casualty is allowable as a deduction under section 165(a) for the taxable year in which the loss is sustained.

Section 1.165-7(b)(1) provides that the amount of the loss to be taken into account for purposes of section 165(a) is the lesser of either—(i) The amount which is equal to the fair market value of the property immediately before the casualty reduced by the fair market value of the property immediately after the casualty; or (ii) The amount of the adjusted basis prescribed in section 1.1011-1 for determining the loss from the sale or other disposition of the property involved. However, if business or income-producing property is totally destroyed by casualty, and the fair market value of the property immediately before the casualty was less than the adjusted basis of the property, the adjusted basis is treated as the amount of the loss. A casualty loss deduction for business or income-producing property must be computed based on each single identifiable property damaged or destroyed pursuant to section 1.165-7(b)(2)(i). Therefore, a casualty loss must be computed separately for each improvement (e.g., a building, landscaping) to the property.

Section 1.165-7(a)(2)(i) provides, in part, that in determining the amount of the deductible loss, the fair market value of the property immediately before and immediately after the casualty shall generally be ascertained by competent appraisal. However, section 1.165-7(a)(2)(ii) provides that the cost of repairs to the property damaged is acceptable as evidence of the loss of value if the taxpayer shows that (a) the repairs are necessary to restore the property to its condition immediately before the casualty, (b) the amount spent for the repairs is not excessive, (c) the repairs do not care for more than the damage suffered, and (d) the value of the property after the repairs does not as a result of the repairs exceed the value of the property immediately before the casualty. Section 1.165-7(a)(5) provides, in part, that in the case of property which originally was not used in a trade or business or for income-producing purposes and which is thereafter converted to either of such uses, the fair market value of the property on the date of conversion, if less than the adjusted basis of the property at such time, shall be used, after making proper adjustments in respect of basis, as the basis for determining the amount of loss.

Courts have imposed a limitation on various deductions, including section 165 loss deductions, where allowance of the deduction would severely and immediately frustrate a sharply defined national or state policy. Tank Truck Rentals, Inc. v. Commissioner, 356 U.S. 30, 35 (1958) (the Supreme Court affirmed disallowance of business deductions of fines imposed on truck owners for violations of state maximum truck weight laws based on public policy considerations; case decided before the enactment of section 162(f)); Richey v. Commissioner, 33 T.C. 272, 276 (1959) (theft loss disallowed for money stolen from the taxpayer during his participation in a counterfeiting scheme based on public policy against counterfeiting). "[T]he question of illegality to frustrate public policy is . . . one of degree, to be determined from the peculiar facts of each case." Fuller v. Commissioner, 213 F.2d 102, 106 (10th Cir. 1954) (disallowed the taxpayer's loss for cost of confiscated whiskey as deduction would frustrate state law). The mere fact that an expenditure bears a remote relationship to an illegal act does not make it nondeductible. Commissioner v. Heininger, 320 U.S. 467, 474 (1943).

In analyzing whether the allowance of a deduction would severely and immediately frustrate a sharply defined national or state policy, courts have looked at several factors. One factor is whether the taxpayer's activity directly caused the loss. In Blackman v. Commissioner, 88 T.C. 677 (1987), the taxpayer claimed a casualty loss deduction for his home that was destroyed by a fire the taxpayer started when he intentionally set his wife's clothes on fire. The Tax Court disallowed the loss deduction on the grounds of his grossly negligent conduct and because allowing the deduction would severely and immediately frustrate the public policy of the Maryland statutes against arson and burning and domestic violence. See also Madsen v. Commissioner, T.C. Memo. 1989-431 (citing Blackman, the court noted that if public policy would be frustrated by permitting the deduction, such as for a casualty loss attributable to arson, the loss is not deductible); Rev. Rul. 81-24, 1981-1 C.B. 79 (loss on destruction of taxpayer's building by fire would not qualify as a casualty due to taxpayer's knowing and willful act of arson). But see Hossbach v. Commissioner, T.C. Memo. 1981-291 (the Tax Court allowed the taxpayer a casualty loss deduction for a fire resulting from the taxpayer's illegal drug manufacturing that destroyed taxpayer's building because the taxpayer did not recklessly create a risk of catastrophe in violation of the state statute).

Even if the taxpayer's activity did not directly cause the loss, courts have examined whether a direct relationship exists between the claimed loss and the violation of the public policy. In Mazzei v. Commissioner, 61 T.C. 497 (1974), the Tax Court held that a taxpayer who entered into a conspiracy to counterfeit U.S. currency could not take a theft loss deduction when genuine currency the taxpayer provided for use in the counterfeiting process was stolen by co-conspirators. The Tax Court found that "the loss claimed by the petitioner here had a direct relationship to the purported illegal act which the petitioner conspired to commit" and therefore, the loss should be denied based on a clearly defined public policy against counterfeiting. Mazzei, 61 T.C. at 502. Similarly, in Lincoln v. Commissioner, T.C. Memo. 1985-300, the Tax Court disallowed the taxpayer a theft loss for money that was stolen by co-conspirators during a scheme to purchase stolen currency at a discount because the loss had a direct relationship to the taxpayer's active participation in the scheme. In reaching this conclusion, the Tax Court noted that the "[t]he frustration of policy resulting from the allowance of the deduction must be severe and immediate. The expenditure must be directly related to the violation of the public policy; the fact that the expenditure bears a remote relationship to an illegal act does not make it nondeductible."

The Supreme Court also emphasized the importance of the direct relationship between the deduction and the frustration of public policy in Tank Truck Rentals:

> Certainly the frustration of state policy is most complete and direct when the expenditure for which deduction is sought is itself prohibited by statute. . . . If the expenditure is not itself an illegal act, but rather the payment of a penalty imposed by the State because of such an act, as in the present case, the frustration attendant upon deduction would be only slightly less remote, and would clearly fall within the line of disallowance. Deduction of fines and penalties uniformly has been held to frustrate state policy in severe and direct fashion by reducing the 'sting' of the penalty prescribed by the state legislature.

356 U.S. at 35. See also Hossbach, T.C. Memo. 1981-291 ("where a loss is directly related to conduct proscribed by a legislative body, it would obviously be inconsistent with articulated public policy to permit a tax deduction for that loss").

Another factor is whether allowing the loss would defeat the purpose of the laws that the taxpayer violated and would encourage others to violate those laws. Courts have disallowed deductions for fines, penalties, and forfeitures specifically imposed by the state for the violation of various laws. Courts have held that to allow a deduction for the fines and penalties, and for the value of the goods forfeited, would encourage continued violations of the stated laws by increasing the odds in favor of non-compliance, and would tend to destroy the effectiveness of those laws. See, e.g., Tank Truck Rentals, 356 U.S. at 35 (allowing business expense deduction of fines for violations of state maximum truck weight restrictions would frustrate the purpose of the restrictions); Holt, 69 T.C. 75, 80 (1977), aff'd 611 F.2d 1160 (2d Cir. 1980) (the Tax Court disallowed the taxpayer a loss deduction for assets seized in an illegal drug trafficking business because allowing the deductions would frustrate a sharply defined national policy against illegal drug trafficking). See also Murillo v. Commissioner, T.C. Memo. 1998-13 (denial of a loss deduction for forfeited money that was used in a bank deposit structuring scheme; allowing the deduction would frustrate the clearly defined Federal policy against structuring); Farris v. Commissioner, T.C. Memo. 1985-346 (disallowed loss deduction for cash and gambling equipment was that was seized; allowing the deduction arising out of the illegal activities would undermine the public policy prohibiting certain gambling activities).

Finally, courts have examined whether allowing the loss would alleviate the sting of any punishment imposed on the taxpayer for violation of a statute. See Murillo, T.C. Memo.

1998-13 (allowing loss deduction for forfeited money arising from illegal activities would take the sting out of the forfeiture); Revenue Ruling 77-126, 1977-1 C.B. 47 (deduction denied for losses incurred for the forfeiture of coin-operated gambling devices; deduction would soften the sting of, and thus frustrate, the sanction of the seizure and forfeiture). See also Rohrs v. Commissioner, T.C. Summ. Op. 2009-190 (casualty loss deduction allowed for a truck the taxpayer damaged while driving intoxicated; allowing the loss would not in any way alleviate the sting of the punishment of imprisonment and fines imposed by the state for a DUI offense).

ANALYSIS

Although we recognize that based on the information you provided Taxpayers' failure to obtain permits for the two structures is in violation of State law, we believe that allowing Taxpayers a casualty loss deduction would not severely and immediately frustrate the policy (i.e. promoting public safety) behind the State law requiring building permits. Applying the various factors courts have used to determine whether allowing the taxpayer a deduction would severely and immediately frustrate State's policy of obtaining permits, we do not see a sufficiently direct link between the casualty loss Taxpayers suffered and their failure to obtain permits to deny the loss based on public policy considerations.

The incoming memo cites cases such as Holt and Mazzei to support a finding that the Government should not bear the cost incurred by Taxpayers resulting from Taxpayers' failure to obtain permits. Taxpayers' facts are distinguishable from the cases described above where courts have used the public policy doctrine to deny a deduction. In those cases, such as Tank Truck Rentals, Holt, Lincoln, and Mazzei, the loss claimed by the taxpayers bore a more direct relationship to the purported illegal act which the taxpayer either conspired to commit or actually committed, and based on the language cited above the courts have acknowledged that relationship in deciding to deny the taxpayers a deduction those cases. The Tax Court in Holt stated that "public policy is directly offended by Holt's actions. Holt had no right, constitutional or otherwise, to transport marijuana. He did so at his own risk, and losses inflicted on him by the Government must be borne solely by him, not in part by the Government through a tax benefit." Holt, 69 T.C. at 81. In Holt, however, there is more a direct relationship between the loss incurred by the taxpayer and the taxpayer's illegal activity because the Government seized the taxpayer's money and property that was directly used in or obtained by engaging in the illegal activity. Similarly, in Mazzei, because the taxpayer's money was stolen while the taxpayer was engaged in a conspiracy to counterfeit currency, there was a direct relationship between the theft loss and the illegal act of counterfeiting that the taxpayer conspired to commit. Mazzei, 61 T.C. at 502. Likewise in Lincoln, the taxpayer's money was stolen while the taxpayer was engaged in a conspiracy to purchase stolen money at a discount, and the Tax Court held that allowing a theft loss that was directly related to the taxpayer's active participation in the scheme would severely and immediately frustrate the public policy against purchasing stolen money. Lincoln, T.C. Memo. 1985-300. Here, in contrast, the casualty loss was not directly related to Taxpayers' failure to obtain permits, and the loss would have occurred regardless of whether Taxpayers had obtained the required permits.

We believe that allowing the casualty loss would neither severely frustrate nor defeat the purpose of the State laws requiring permits or lessen the sting of the various punitive measures prescribed by State and County law for failure to obtain proper permits. Additionally, allowing the casualty loss deduction would not necessarily increase the odds in favor of non-compliance and encourage others to build without obtaining the proper permits. State has specific punitive measures for property owners who do not obtain the required permits (e.g. placing a notice of violation on the property, imposing penalties and fines). Allowing Taxpayers' casualty loss deduction here would have no impact on these punitive measures.

CASE DEVELOPMENT, HAZARDS AND OTHER CONSIDERATIONS

****

This writing may contain privileged information. Any unauthorized disclosure of this writing may undermine our ability to protect the privileged information. If disclosure is determined to be necessary, please contact this office for our views. Please call (202) 622-7900 if you have any further questions.

- **Takeaway 1**: Reading cases requires carefully noting the specific factors or elements that the court assigns to reaching its final decision. A general understanding of a case decision doesn't help you to fully grasp the implications of caselaw. You must "mine" decisions by outlining the elements that form the court's rationale.
- **Takeaway 2**: Read subsequent cases that provide other judges' views of case decisions that supplement or reaffirm your own view. While you do have time limitations in how many cases you can research, the more important a case presents to your analysis, the more time you must devote to find additional sources to support your own reading of case opinions. Read subsequent IRS guidance that summarizes important cases to better understand the agency's views. The IRS' view of cases may differ from yours or other judges' views. But, these differing perspectives provide you with useful context to test your own understanding. After reading CCA 201346009, do you have a better understanding of the holding from Blackman? You should.

Next, let's read Rohrs v. Commissioner, T.C. Summ. Op. 2009-190, cited in CCA 201346009. The judge in Rohrs cites to Blackman in support of his ultimate decision in allowing a taxpayer to claim a casualty loss deduction. Read the case and ask yourself, "Did the judge properly summarize the holding from Blackman?

T.C. Summary Opinion 2009-190

JUSTIN M. ROHRS, Petitioner,
v.
COMMISSIONER OF INTERNAL REVENUE, Respondent.

United States Tax Court

Filed December 10, 2009

Justin M. Rohrs, pro se.
Michael A. Skeen and Sarah Sexton (specially recognized), for respondent.

GERBER, Judge.
This case was heard pursuant to the provisions of section 7463 of the Internal Revenue Code in effect when the petition was filed. Pursuant to section 7463(b), the decision to be entered is not reviewable by any other court, and this opinion shall not be treated as precedent for any other case.

For petitioner's 2005 tax year respondent determined a $6,230 income tax deficiency .... The issues for our consideration are: (1) Whether petitioner is entitled to a casualty loss deduction for 2005....................

Background
Some of the facts have been stipulated and are so found. The stipulation of facts and the attached exhibits are incorporated herein by this reference. Petitioner resided in California when his petition was filed.

On August 12, 2005, petitioner purchased a 2006 Ford F-350 pickup truck for $40,210.65. On October 28, 2005, petitioner attended a gathering at a friend's house. Anticipating that he would be drinking alcohol, he arranged for transportation to and from his home. After returning home petitioner decided to drive to his parents' house. On the way there he failed to successfully negotiate a turn, and his truck slid off an embankment. The truck rolled over and was severely damaged. Because his blood-alcohol level was 0.09 percent, he was cited and arrested for driving under the influence of alcohol (DUI). 3*3 The legal threshold for blood-alcohol level in the State of California is 0.08 percent. He was then taken to the hospital.

Petitioner's loss claim filed with his automobile insurance carrier was denied in accordance with the terms of his policy because of his DUI citation and arrest.
On April 13, 2006, petitioner filed his 2005 Form 1040, U.S. Individual Income Tax Return. On that return he claimed a $33,629 casualty loss deduction for the damage to his truck. On March 25, 2008, respondent issued a notice of deficiency disallowing

petitioner's casualty loss deduction and determining a $6,230 income tax deficiency .... for petitioner's 2005 tax year. On June 9, 2008, petitioner filed a timely petition with this Court.

<u>Discussion</u>

Section 165(a) allows a deduction for losses not compensated for by insurance or otherwise. If a loss is not incurred in connection with a trade or business or in a transaction entered into for profit, it may be deducted by an individual if it arises from a fire, storm, shipwreck, or other casualty, or from theft, except as provided in section 165(h). Sec. 165(c)(3). There is no question about whether petitioner's loss generally qualified as a casualty loss under section 165.

Although negligence may not be a bar to a casualty loss deduction, courts have held that gross negligence may be. <u>Heyn v. Commissioner</u>, 46. T.C. 302, 308 (1966). In addition, section 1.165-7(a)(3), Income Tax Regs., provides that an automobile may be the subject of a casualty loss when the damage is not due to the willful act or willful negligence of a taxpayer.

Petitioner concedes that his act of driving while intoxicated constitutes negligence. Petitioner, however, disagrees with respondent's contention that his behavior rose to the level of gross or willful negligence, thereby barring a casualty loss deduction. Neither the Internal Revenue Code nor the underlying regulations define "willful negligence" for purposes of section 1.165-7(a)(3), Income Tax Regs. Respondent argues that the definitions of "willful negligence" and "gross negligence" are supplied by caselaw. Respondent relies upon <u>People v. Bennett</u>, 819 P.2d 849 (Cal. 1991), in support of his position.

In <u>People v. Bennett</u>, <u>supra</u>, a driver was convicted of vehicular manslaughter and gross negligence while driving under the influence of alcohol. Before driving, Mr. Bennett and three friends shared the entire contents of a keg of beer. He was then involved in a single-car accident in which one of his friends died. Mr. Bennett's blood-alcohol level was measured at 0.20 percent 2 hours after the accident. In affirming his conviction, the California Supreme Court defined gross negligence as "the exercise of so slight a degree of care as to raise a presumption of conscious indifference to the consequences." <u>Id.</u> at 852. The court further explained that "The state of mind of a person who acts with conscious indifferences to the consequences is simply, 'I don't care what happens'." <u>Id.</u> (quoting <u>People v. Olivas</u>, 218 Cal. Rptr. 567, 569 (Ct. App. 1985)). The court held that conscious indifference could be inferred from the severity of defendant's intoxication:

> "one who drives with a very high level of intoxication is indeed more negligent, more dangerous, and thus more culpable than one who drives near the legal limit of intoxication, just as one who exceeds the speed limit by 50 miles per hour exhibits greater negligence than one who exceeds the speed limit by 5 miles per hour."

<u>Id.</u> at 853 (quoting <u>People v. Von Staden</u>, 241 Cal. Rptr. 523, 527 (Ct. App. 1987)).

We agree with petitioner that his actions did not amount to willful or gross negligence. While petitioner's decision to drive after drinking was negligent, that alone does not automatically rise to the level of gross negligence. "'[G]ross negligence cannot be shown by the mere fact of driving under the influence and violating the traffic laws.'" Id. at 852 (emphasis added) (quoting People v. Von Staden, supra at 527). The overall circumstances of the defendant's actions, including the level of intoxication and/or the manner in which he drove must be considered. Id. at 853.

The circumstances do not support a holding that petitioner was willfully or grossly negligent. Petitioner's level of intoxication and the manner in which he drove do not suggest that he was consciously indifferent to the hazards of drunk driving. Unlike the defendant in People v. Bennett, supra, petitioner was less impaired and not severely intoxicated when he chose to drive. At the time of the accident petitioner's blood-alcohol level was 0.09 percent, which is slightly over California's legal limit of 0.08 percent. See Cal. Veh. Code sec. 23152 (West 2000). Further and significantly distinguishing petitioner's situation from that in People v. Bennett, supra, petitioner made arrangements not to drive immediately after consuming alcohol. He arranged for transportation home and thus allowed some time for his body to process the alcohol before driving. If petitioner truly did not care what happened, he would not have gone to the trouble to arrange for transportation.

Likewise, there is no evidence in the record that petitioner was aware his actions would result in injury. In addition, there was no evidence that excess speed or alcohol directly caused petitioner's accident. On brief, petitioner claimed he lost control of his vehicle because of the windy conditions on the road, and no evidence was presented at trial as to what the precise cause of petitioner's accident was.

In the alternative, respondent contends that petitioner's casualty loss deduction should not be allowed because to do so would frustrate public policy. Courts have disallowed deductions where national or State public policy would be frustrated by the allowance of a deduction. Commissioner v. Heininger, 320 U.S. 467, 473 (1943). However, this rule is not applied indiscriminately. Tank Truck Rentals, Inc. v. Commissioner, 356 U.S. 30, 35 (1958). "[T]he test of nondeductibility always is the severity and immediacy of the frustration resulting from allowance of the deduction." Id.

California, like most other States, has "a strong public policy against * * * drunk driving." Carrey v. Dept. of Motor Vehicles, 228 Cal. Rptr. 705, 708 (Ct. App. 1986). But the fact that petitioner's loss may have resulted from his drunk driving does not ipso facto mean a casualty loss deduction would severely and immediately frustrate public policy. "It has never been thought * * * that the mere fact that an expenditure bears a remote relation to an illegal act makes it non-deductible." Commissioner v. Heininger, supra at 474.

In cases where a deduction has been denied, the taxpayers typically knew their actions encouraged an illegal activity or were illegal. See Blackman v. Commissioner, 88 T.C. 677 (1987) (arson), affd. without published opinion 867 F.2d 605 (1st Cir. 1988); Holt

v. Commissioner, 69 T.C. 75 (1977) (drug trafficking), affd. per curiam 611 F.2d 1160 (5th Cir. 1980); Mazzei v. Commissioner, 61 T.C. 497 (1974) (counterfeiting); Towers v.Commissioner, 24 T.C. 199 (1955) (extortion payment), affd. 247 F.2d 233 (2d Cir. 1957), affd. on other grounds sub nom. Bonney v. Commissioner, 247 F.2d 237 (2d Cir. 1957); Hackworth v. Commissioner, T.C. Memo. 2004-173 (illegal gambling).

In contrast, petitioner believed that he was no longer impaired or intoxicated at the time he chose to drive. Moreover, he had taken precautions to avoid driving immediately after drinking. There was no evidence that intoxication, high speed, or reckless driving was the ultimate cause of petitioner's accident. Where the taxpayer is reasonably unaware that he is doing something wrong, it is less likely that allowance of a casualty loss deduction would so severely frustrate public policy as to require disallowance.

In Tank Truck Rentals, Inc. v. Commissioner, supra, the taxpayer attempted to deduct as business expenses fines imposed for violations of State maximum weight laws. The Court disallowed the deduction because the "Deduction of fines and penalties uniformly has been held to frustrate state policy in severe and direct fashion by reducing the `sting' of the penalty prescribed by the state legislature." Id. at 35-36.

By contrast, allowing petitioner's casualty loss deduction would not in any way alleviate the "sting" of any punishment imposed by the State of California. In California, a first-time DUI offense is punishable by imprisonment of at least 96 hours and a fine of at least $390. See Cal. Veh. Code sec. 23536 (West Supp. 2009). Petitioner's casualty loss deduction would have no impact on either the sentence or the fine.

This Court is not empowered to judge petitioner's actions from a criminal perspective or to punish him for his actions. In reaching our decision, we do not reflect upon or in any way condone the act of driving under the influence of alcohol. It is our obligation to decide whether petitioner's actions amounted to gross or willful negligence and/or whether the allowance of a casualty loss deduction in the setting of this Federal income tax case would frustrate public policy.

We hold that petitioner is entitled to the claimed casualty loss deduction ………...

To reflect the foregoing,
Decision will be entered for petitioner.

In Rohrs, the Tax Court states, "In cases where a deduction has been denied, the taxpayers typically knew their actions encouraged an illegal activity or were illegal. See Blackman v. Commissioner, 88 T.C. 677 (1987) (arson), affd. without published opinion 867 F.2d 605 (1st Cir. 1988)." This is a pivotal reference to prior caselaw because it is the basis for the court to reach its favorable conclusion for taxpayer Rohrs. In essence, the court in Rohrs summarizes Blackman to stand for the proposition that deductions are disallowed where taxpayers "typically **_knew_** their actions encouraged an illegal activity or were illegal." Re-read Blackman. Now, where in the Blackman opinion did the court's reasoning provide explicitly or implicitly a finding that Mr. Blackman **_knew_** what he was doing (burning his wife's clothes on a stove in his house) encouraged an illegal activity or were illegal? The Tax Court judge found it. Can you? This author couldn't find such a reference in the <u>Blackman</u> case. What's the takeaway? Reading caselaw is a difficult task. Moreover, as Congress tinkers with Internal Revenue Code, practitioners must constantly consider whether these changes impact the continued vitality of court decisions, such as <u>Blackman</u>. Consider the following two examples to better appreciate how changes in the underlying tax code require us to revisit the force of caselaw that interprets the code.

<u>Example 1 Facts</u>: Client Joe Smith, unmarried, had his home completely destroyed by a sudden, unexpected wildfire on December, 2017. Mr. Smith asks you, as his tax advisor, whether he can claim the loss of his home on his 2017 Federal income tax return.

Read section 165 to find the tax answer for your client.

1. The general rule under section 165(a) seems to allow Mr. Smith to claim the loss of his home as a deduction. The text of section 165(a) provides, in part, as follows:

    "There shall be allowed as a deduction any loss sustained during the taxable year and not compensated for by insurance or otherwise."

What fact(s) does our reading of section 165(a) direct us to determine?

- For the loss of his home in 2017, does Mr. Smith have insurance to cover all or part of the loss? And, if he does have insurance, did Mr. Smith receive any compensation for the loss?

2. Moving on to section 165(c) requires us to find another fact. Section 165(c) provides:

    (c) Limitation on losses of individuals. In the case of an individual, the deduction under subsection (a) shall be limited to—
    (1) losses incurred in a trade or business;
    (2) losses incurred in any transaction entered into for profit, though not connected with a trade or business; and
    (3) except as provided in subsection (h), losses of property, not connected with a trade or business or a transaction entered into for profit, if such losses arise from fire, storm, shipwreck, or other casualty, or from theft.

What fact(s) does our reading of section 165(c) direct us to locate?

- For the loss of his home in 2017, was the loss incurred in a trade or business, in a transaction entered into for profit, or not connected with either?

3. Moving on to section 165(h) provides more facts to determine.

> (h)(2)(A) In general. If the personal casualty losses for any taxable year exceed the personal casualty gains for such taxable year, such losses shall be allowed for the taxable year only to the extent of the sum of—
>> (i) the amount of the personal casualty gains for the taxable year, plus
>> (ii) so much of such excess as exceeds 10 percent of the adjusted gross income of the individual.

What fact(s) does our reading of section 165(h)(2)(A) direct us to determine?

- What "personal casualty gains" and other "personal casualty losses" did Mr. Smith have in the year of loss – 2017? The term "personal casualty gains" is defined in section 165(h)(3)(A).
- What is Mr. Smith's adjusted gross income in 2017?

4. Next, moving on to section 165(h)(5), we have even more facts to gather.

> (A) In the case of an individual, except as provided in subparagraph (B), any personal casualty loss which (but for this paragraph) would be deductible in a taxable year beginning after December 31, 2017, and before January 1, 2026, shall be allowed as a deduction under subsection (a) only to the extent it is attributable to a Federally declared disaster (as defined in subsection (i)(5)).

- The loss of Mr. Smith's home in 2017 is deductible despite the limitation under section 165(h)(5)(A) since such loss occurred prior to the change in law that covers losses from 2018 through 2025.

5. Next, moving on to read section 165(i)(1) informs us that we need even more facts.

> (1) Election to Take Deduction for Preceding Year. Notwithstanding the provisions of subsection (a), any loss occurring in a disaster area and attributable to a federally declared disaster may, at the election of the taxpayer, be taken into account for the taxable year immediately preceding the taxable year in which the disaster occurred.

- Did the loss occur in a "disaster area" attributable to a "Federally declared disaster?"
- We must determine whether the loss is more beneficial for Mr. Smith to claim in 2016 or 2017? So, we need to calculate the difference between claiming the loss amount in 2016 versus 2017.

How can you, as a tax practitioner, determine whether Mr. Smith's loss qualifies as a "Federally declared disaster?" Searching for IRS guidance can help pin down the answer. See the following web link for guidance. https://www.irs.gov/individuals/tax-law-provisions-for-disaster-areas. Part of the guidance provided by the IRS follows:

> "Affected taxpayers can also identify themselves to the IRS or ask disaster-related questions by calling the special IRS disaster hotline at 1-866-562-5227. Qualified disaster losses are claimed on Form 4684, Casualties and Thefts."

The table that follows summarizes the facts needed from reviewing section 165 when we apply the facts from Example 1.

#	Source	Needed Facts	Status
1	165(a)	Insurance coverage?	Need to determine
2	165(c)	Loss incurred from business or for profit activity?	Need to determine
3	165(c)	losses arise from fire, storm, shipwreck, or other casualty, or from theft?	Yes, loss arose from fire
4	165(h)(2)(A)	"personal casualty gain" or other "personal casualty loss" in 2017?	Need to determine
5	165(h)(2)(A)	Adjusted gross income in 2017	Need to determine
6	165(h)(5)	Did loss occur before 2018 or after 2025?	Yes, before 2017
7	165(i)(1)	Did loss occur in a "disaster area" and attributable to "Federally declared disaster?	Need to determine . If yes, then Taxpayer can elect to claim loss (if allowable) to one earlier year—2016.

As the table shows, the Internal Revenue Code provides an essential guide that directs us to the facts needed to reach a proper tax conclusion. Certainly, it is not an easy process to read and properly apply the code. We are required to methodically acquire several facts in order to reach a final tax conclusion.

Example 2 Facts: Same as in Example 1, above, except the loss occurred in 2018.

1. Section 165(h)(5) provides us with a fundamental change in law beginning in 2018.

   (A) In the case of an individual, except as provided in subparagraph (B), any personal casualty loss which (but for this paragraph) would be deductible in a taxable year beginning after December 31, 2017, and before January 1, 2026, shall be allowed as a deduction under subsection (a) only to the extent it is attributable to a Federally declared disaster (as defined in subsection (i)(5)).

   • The loss of Mr. Smith's home in 2018 is deductible only to the extent it is attributable to a "Federally declared disaster" as defined in subsection (i)(5).

Unlike in Example 1, the Internal Revenue Code now severely limits "personal casualty losses." For years 2018 thru 2025, section 165 disallows any "personal casualty loss" unless:

- It is a "Federally declared disaster" – remember before there was only a timing benefit for a "Federally declared disaster" where a taxpayer could claim the loss one year earlier; and
- The taxpayer claims a "personal casualty loss" even if not a "Federally declared disaster" only to offset against "personal casualty gains" for that same tax year.

So, before 2018, a taxpayer who suffered a loss from a fire could claim the loss (absent some other unique circumstances) even if the taxpayer had no "personal casualty gains" and the President did not declare the circumstances of the loss to be attributable to a "Federally declared disaster."

2. Section 165(i)(5) defines "Federally Declared Disaster."

   o See discussion, above, in Example 1, regarding "Federally declared disaster."

Given the changes to section 165, does a case like <u>Blackman v. Commissioner</u> remain good caselaw? The answer is YES! Citing to Supreme Court precedent, <u>Blackman</u> reminds us that casualty loss deductions under section 165 are limited where national or State public policies would be frustrated by the consequences of allowing the deduction. More specifically, <u>Blackman</u> establishes caselaw that says if a taxpayer is grossly negligent or worse in his/her conduct, then not casualty loss deduction is allowed.

If a taxpayer suffers a loss of his home from fire in 2018, and that loss is a "Federally declared disaster," then does the loss qualify as an allowable personal casualty loss under section 165? Well, <u>Blackman</u> still applies because we must continue to ask, "Would national or State public policies be frustrated by the consequences of allowing the deduction?" And, we would need to ask, "Was the taxpayer's conduct grossly negligent or worse related to the cause of the loss?"

3. Similar Facts Applied to the Same Rules Do Not Always Lead to Predictable Results Despite the Doctrine of *Stare Decisis*

By adhering to the doctrine *stare decisis*, courts provide stability to law by providing predictability of its view of the law given materially similar facts. While this is an overarching objective, court decisions do not always present such predictability even where the same rule and materially similar facts exist. Recall different circuits may develop inconsistent circuit law. Thus, judges at every level may reach opposite conclusions despite the presence the exact same facts.

To illustrate, let's review two substantially similar cases: (1) <u>Myers v. Commissioner</u>, T.C. Summ. Op. 2007-194; and (2) <u>Hastings v. Commissioner</u>, T.C. Memo. 2009-69. In both cases, the taxpayer argued that she was engaged in the trade or business of gambling which would allow to deducting her wagering losses to the extent allowable in computing adjusted gross income. See sec. 62. If the taxpayer was not in the trade or business of gambling, on the other hand, she could only deduct the wagering losses to the extent allowable as an itemized deduction to compute taxable income.

In both cases, the court started with a review the applicable code section - all ordinary and necessary expenses paid or incurred during the taxable year in carrying on a trade or business are generally deductible. Sec. 162(a). From the code, the court examined whether the taxpayer engaged in the activity with the actual and honest objective of making a profit. And, for this analysis, the court structured its analysis around nine nonexclusive factors as set forth in Treas. Reg. §1.183-2(b): (1) The manner in which the taxpayer carried on the activity; **(2) the expertise of the taxpayer or his or her advisers;** (3) the time and effort expended by the taxpayer in carrying on the activity; (4) the expectation that the assets used in the activity may appreciate in value; (5) the success of the taxpayer in carrying on other similar or dissimilar activities; (6) the taxpayer's history of income or loss with respect to the activity; (7) the amount of occasional profits, if any, which are earned; (8) the financial status of the taxpayer; and (9) whether elements of personal pleasure or recreation are involved.

Focusing on just Factor #2 (the expertise of the taxpayer or his/her advisers), the court was presented with identical facts by the taxpayers in these two cases. Yet, the Tax Court reached opposite conclusions for Factor #2. See the table, below.

Myers v. Comissioner	Hastings v. Commissioner
"The continuity and regularity of her gambling activity strongly suggest that she is an expert at slot machines. **Petitioner also consulted regularly with casino employees to further her gambling strategy and watched other gamblers to understand what she believed to be slot machine payout patterns.** We find that this factor favors petitioner."	"Consulting with experts and developing one's expertise may indicate a profit objective. Sec. 1.183-2(b)(2), Income Tax Regs. Petitioner, however, has not shown that she acquired any gambling expertise. **Petitioner's strategy of observing the casino's slot machines and talking to casino employees and patrons is insufficient.** See Calvao v. Commissioner, T.C. Memo. 2007-57."
Court Determination: Factor Favors Petitioner (Taxpayer)	Court Determination: Factor Favors Respondent (IRS)

What's the lesson from reading Myers and Hastings side-by-side? Judges strive for consistency and predictability in drafting court opinions. But, at times, we must recognize that our research may lead us to opposite tax conclusions even when identical facts are applied to the same code section or Treasury regulation. Welcome to the gray area of tax caselaw.

With all this background, here are my suggestions for you to read tax cases:
1. First, proceed with an <u>initial read</u> to get the background of the story, the parties involved, each parties' position and result. After reading the case this first time, your

goal is to be able to summarize the case to your friend or colleague in just a few minutes.

2. Second, <u>focus on the precise legal issue</u> in dispute in the case. The case ended up in court because the parties couldn't agree on how the law applied to the given facts. What statute was in dispute? What was the precise nature of the parties' divergent views?

3. Third, focus closely on the court's reasoning. This is your <u>second read</u> of the case. Unlike in the first step (where you initially read the case for the overall storyline), in this step you are <u>paying very close attention to the court's analysis of both prior precedent and focus on particular facts</u>. In the "Facts" or "Background" section, the court may list a multitude of facts. But, in the "Analysis" or "Law" section, the court will focus only on the facts that it has determined is relevant as part of its analysis. Write each fact that the court focuses on as part of its analysis and write it down. Write down each precedential authority that the court relies upon as a basis for analogy. The court will point to some cases as distinguishable from the case before it whereas it will point to other cases as materially similar. What facts, present or absent, were identified by the court in its opinion as the reason that it found one or more cases distinguishable or indistinguishable? You should take this list of facts and compare it to the facts present or absent in your client's case.

4. Fourth, <u>verify</u> that the court has properly summarized the cited cases in its opinion for the stated proposition. You cannot assume that a judge has properly recited the properly holding of prior caselaw in his/her case opinion. Recall from Chapter 7 that in the October 2017 term, the U.S. Supreme Court reversed nearly 75% of cases that it reviewed. So, check the stated holding of each case cited in a court opinion to confirm that the judge has accurately summarized that prior precedential authority.

5. Fifth, and finally, <u>read the case a third time</u> to ensure that you have a comfortable understanding of the case facts, issue presented and of the court's analysis.

Chapter 8 - Questions

1. The IRS lost <u>Rohrs v. Commissioner</u>. Why didn't the IRS appeal the <u>Rohrs</u> case and request the Ninth Circuit court of appeals to review the case?

2. You read a case and have a general understanding of the reasoning within the opinion. What can you do to gain a better perspective of this case?

3. Read <u>Californians Helping To Alleviate Medical Problems, Inc. v. Commissioner</u>, 128 T.C. 173 (2007), as provided below. Then answer two questions: (1) whether a company that has as its principal business the retail sale of marijuana may deduct cost of goods sold if such costs are properly substantiated; and (2) whether a medical marijuana dispensary that allows its customers to consume medical marijuana on its premises with similarly situated individuals is a "caregiver" if the dispensary also provides the customers with incidental activities, consultation or advice. After answering these questions, read <u>Olive v. Comissioner</u>, 139 T.C. 19 (2012).

Californians Helping To Alleviate Medical Problems, Inc.
v.
Commissioner of Internal Revenue

Case Citation: 128 T.C. No. 14

Docket No. 20795-05.   Filed May 15, 2007.

LARO, Judge: Respondent determined a $355,056 deficiency in petitioner's 2002 Federal income tax and a $71,011 accuracy-related penalty under section 6662(a). [Footnote 1 omitted]. Following concessions by respondent, including a concession that petitioner is not liable for the determined accuracy-related penalty, we decide whether section 280E precludes petitioner from deducting the ordinary and necessary expenses attributable to its provision of medical marijuana pursuant to the California Compassionate Use Act of 1996, codified at Cal. Health & Safety Code sec. 11362.5 (West Supp. 2007).[2] We hold that those deductions are precluded. We also decide whether section 280E precludes petitioner from deducting the ordinary and necessary expenses attributable to its provision of counseling and other caregiving services (collectively, caregiving services). We hold that those deductions are not precluded.

FINDINGS OF FACT

Certain facts were stipulated and are so found. The stipulation of facts and the exhibits attached thereto are incorporated herein by this reference. When the petition was filed, petitioner was an inactive California corporation whose mailing address was in San Francisco, California. Petitioner was organized on December 24, 1996, pursuant to the California Nonprofit Public Benefit Corporation Law, Cal. Corp. Code secs. 5110-6910.(West 1990).[3]

Its articles of incorporation stated that it "is organized and operated exclusively for charitable, educational and scientific purposes" and "The property of this corporation is

---

[2] At a general election held on Nov. 5, 1996, the California electors approved an initiative statute designated on the ballot as Proposition 215 and entitled "Medical Use of Marijuana". See People v. Mower, 49 P.3d 1067, 1070 (Cal. 2002). The statute, the California Compassionate Use Act of 1996, codified at Cal. Health & Safety Code sec. 11362.5 (West Supp. 2007), was intended

> To ensure that seriously ill Californians have the right to obtain and use marijuana for medical purposes where that medical use is deemed appropriate and has been recommended by a physician who has determined that the person's health would benefit from the use of marijuana in the treatment of * * * any * * * illness for which marijuana provides relief.

Id. sec. 11362.5(b)(1)(A); see also People v. Mower, supra at 1070. We use the term "medical marijuana" to refer to marijuana provided pursuant to the statute. Supp. 2007).

[3] Under California law, public benefit corporations are organized for a public or charitable purpose; they are not operated for the mutual benefit of their members but for a broader good. See Knapp v. Palisades Charter High School, 53 Cal. Rptr. 3d 182, 186 n.5 (Ct. App. 2007).

irrevocably dedicated to charitable purposes". Petitioner did not have Federal tax-exempt status, and it operated as an approximately break-even (i.e., the amount of its income approximated the amount of its expenses) community center for members with debilitating diseases. Approximately 47 percent of petitioner's members suffered from Acquired Immune Deficiency Syndrome (AIDS); the remainder suffered from cancer, multiple sclerosis, and other serious illnesses. Before joining petitioner, petitioner's executive director had 13 years of experience in health services as a coordinator of a statewide program that trained outreach workers in AIDS prevention work.

Petitioner operated with a dual purpose. Its primary purpose was to provide caregiving services to its members. Its secondary purpose was to provide its members with medical marijuana pursuant to the California Compassionate Use Act of 1996 and to instruct those individuals on how to use medical marijuana to benefit their health. Petitioner required that each member have a doctor's letter recommending marijuana as part of his or her therapy and an unexpired photo identification card from the California Department of Public Health verifying the authenticity of the doctor's letter. Petitioner required that its members not resell or redistribute the medical marijuana received from petitioner, and petitioner considered any violation of this requirement to be grounds to expel the violator from membership in petitioner's organization.

Each of petitioner's members paid petitioner a membership fee in consideration for the right to receive caregiving services and medical marijuana from petitioner. Petitioner's caregiving services were extensive. First, petitioner's staff held various weekly or biweekly support group sessions that could be attended only by petitioner's members. The "wellness group" discussed healing techniques and occasionally hosted a guest speaker; the HIV/AIDS group addressed issues of practical and emotional support; the women's group focused on women-specific issues in medical struggles; the "Phoenix" group helped elderly patients with lifelong addiction problems; the "Force" group focused on spiritual and emotional development. Second, petitioner provided its low-income members with daily lunches consisting of salads, fruit, water, soda, and hot food. Petitioner also made available to its members hygiene supplies such as toothbrushes, toothpaste, feminine hygiene products, combs, and bottles of bleach. Third, petitioner allowed its members to consult one-on-one with a counselor about benefits, health, housing, safety, and legal issues. Petitioner also provided its members with biweekly massage services. Fourth, petitioner coordinated for its members weekend social events including a Friday night movie or guest speaker and a Saturday night social with live music and a hot meal. Petitioner also coordinated for its members monthly field trips to locations such as beaches, museums, or parks. Fifth, petitioner instructed its members on yoga and on topics such as how to participate in social services at petitioner's facilities and how to follow member guidelines. Sixth, petitioner provided its members with online computer access and delivered to them informational services through its Web site. Seventh, petitioner encouraged its members to participate in political activities. Petitioner furnished its services at its main facility in San Francisco, California, and at an office in a community church in San Francisco. The main facility was approximately 1,350 square feet and was the site of the daily lunches, distribution of hygiene supplies, benefits counseling, Friday and Saturday night social events and dinners, and computer access. This location also was the site where petitioner's members received their distribution of medical marijuana; the medical marijuana was dispensed at a counter of the main room of the facility, taking up approximately 10 percent of the main facility. The peer group meetings and yoga classes were usually held at the church, where petitioner rented space. Pursuant to the rules of the church, petitioner's members were prohibited from bringing any marijuana into the church. Petitioner also maintained a storage unit at a third location in San Francisco. Petitioner used the storage unit to store confidential medical records; no medical marijuana was distributed or used there. Petitioner paid for the services it provided to its members by charging a membership fee that covered, and in the judgment of petitioner's management approximated, both the cost of petitioner's caregiving services and the cost of the medical marijuana that petitioner supplied to its members. Petitioner notified its members that the membership fee covered both of these costs, and petitioner charged its members no additional fee. Members received from petitioner a set amount of medical marijuana; they were not entitled to unlimited supplies.

On May 6, 2002, petitioner's board of directors decided that petitioner would henceforth discontinue all of its activities. Petitioner thus ceased conducting any activity and filed a "Final Return" (Form 1120, U.S. Corporation Income Tax Return) for 2002.

[text omitted]

In a notice of deficiency mailed to petitioner on August 4, 2005, respondent disallowed all of petitioner's deductions and costs of goods sold, determining that those items were "Expenditures in Connection with the Illegal Sale of Drugs" within the meaning of section 280E. Respondent has since conceded this determination except to the extent that it relates to the "Total deductions" of $212,958.[4] Respondent has also conceded that the expenses underlying the $212,958 of total deductions are substantiated.

The "Total deductions" were ordinary, necessary, and reasonable expenses petitioner incurred in running its operations during the subject year.

[text omitted]

OPINION

The parties agree that during the subject year petitioner had at least one trade or business for purposes of section 280E. According to respondent, petitioner had a single trade or business of trafficking in medical marijuana. Petitioner argues that it engaged in two trades or businesses. Petitioner asserts that its primary trade or business was

---

[4] In other words, respondent concedes that the disallowance of sec. 280E does not apply to costs of goods sold, a concession that is consistent with the caselaw on that subject and the legislative history underlying sec. 280E. See Peyton v. Commissioner, T.C. Memo. 2003-146; Franklin v. Commissioner, T.C. Memo. 1993-184; Vasta v. Commissioner, T.C. Memo. 1989-531; see also S. Rept. 97-494 (Vol. 1), at 309 (1982).

the provision of caregiving services. Petitioner asserts that its secondary trade or business was the supplying of medical marijuana to its members. As to its trades or businesses, petitioner argues, the deductions for those trades or businesses are not precluded by section 280E in that the trades or businesses did not involve "trafficking" in a controlled substance. Respondent argues that section 280E precludes petitioner from benefiting from any of its deductions.

Accrual method taxpayers such as petitioner may generally deduct the ordinary and necessary expenses incurred in carrying on a trade or business. See sec. 162(a). Items specified in section 162(a) are allowed as deductions, subject to exceptions listed in section 261. See sec. 161. Section 261 provides that "no deduction shall in any case be allowed in respect of the items specified in this part." The phrase "this part" refers to part IX of subchapter B of chapter 1, entitled "Items Not Deductible". "Expenditures in Connection With the Illegal Sale of Drugs" is an item specified in part IX. Section 280E provides:

> No deduction or credit shall be allowed for any amount paid or incurred during the taxable year in carrying on any trade or business if such trade or business (or the activities which comprise such trade or business) consists of trafficking in controlled substances (within the meaning of schedule I and II of the Controlled Substances Act) which is prohibited by Federal law or the law of any State in which such trade or business is conducted.

In the context of section 280E, marijuana is a schedule I controlled substance. See, e.g., Sundel v. Commissioner, T.C. Memo. 1998-78, affd. without published opinion 201 F.3d 428 (1st Cir. 1999). Such is so even when the marijuana is medical marijuana recommended by a physician as appropriate to benefit the health of the user. See United States v. Oakland Cannabis Buyers' Coop., 532 U.S. 483 (2001). Respondent argues that petitioner, because it trafficked in a controlled substance, is not permitted by section 280E to deduct any of its expenses. We disagree. Our analysis begins with the text of the statute, which we must apply in accordance with its ordinary, everyday usage. See Conn. Natl. Bank v. Germain, 503 U.S. 249, 253-254 (1992). We interpret that text with reference to its legislative history primarily to learn the purpose of the statute. See Commissioner v. Soliman, 506 U.S. 168, 174 (1993); United States v. Am. Trucking Associations, Inc., 310 U.S. 534, 543-544 (1940); Venture Funding, Ltd. v. Commissioner, 110 T.C. 236, 241-242 (1998), affd. without published opinion 198 F.3d 248 (6th Cir. 1999); Trans City Life Ins. Co. v. Commissioner, 106 T.C. 274, 299 (1996).

Congress enacted section 280E as a direct reaction to the outcome of a case in which this Court allowed a taxpayer to deduct expenses incurred in an illegal drug trade. See S. Rept. 97-494 (Vol. 1), at 309 (1982). In that case, Edmondson v. Commissioner, T.C. Memo. 1981-623, the Court found that the taxpayer was self-employed in a trade or business of selling amphetamines, cocaine, and marijuana. The Court allowed the taxpayer to deduct his business expenses because they "were made in connection with * * * [the taxpayer's] trade or business and were both ordinary and necessary." Id. In discussing the case in the context of the then-current law, the Senate Finance Committee stated in its report:

> Ordinary and necessary trade or business expenses are generally deductible in computing taxable income. A recent U.S. Tax Court case allowed deductions for telephone, auto, and rental expense incurred in the illegal drug trade. In that case, the Internal Revenue Service challenged the amount of the taxpayer's deduction for cost of goods (illegal drugs) sold, but did not challenge the principle that such amounts were deductible.
>
> On public policy grounds, the Code makes certain otherwise ordinary and necessary expenses incurred in a trade or business nondeductible in computing taxable income. These nondeductible expenses include fines, illegal bribes and kickbacks, and certain other illegal payments. [S. Rept. 97-494 (Vol. 1), supra at 309.]

The report then expressed the following reasons the committee intended to change the law:

> There is a sharply defined public policy against drug dealing. To allow drug dealers the benefit of business expense deductions at the same time that the U.S. and its citizens are losing billions of dollars per year to such persons is not compelled by the fact that such deductions are allowed to other, legal, enterprises. Such deductions must be disallowed on public policy grounds. [Id.]

The report explained that the enactment of section 280E has the following effect:

> All deductions and credits for amounts paid or incurred in the illegal trafficking in drugs listed in the Controlled Substances Act are disallowed. To preclude possible challenges on constitutional grounds, the adjustment to gross receipts with respect to effective costs of goods sold is not affected by this provision of the bill. [Id.]

Section 280E and its legislative history express a congressional intent to disallow deductions attributable to a trade or business of trafficking in controlled substances.

They do not express an intent to deny the deduction of all of a taxpayer's business expenses simply because the taxpayer was involved in trafficking in a controlled substance. We hold that section 280E does not preclude petitioner from deducting expenses attributable to a trade or business other than that of illegal trafficking in controlled substances simply because petitioner also is involved in the trafficking in a controlled substance.

Petitioner argues that its supplying of medical marijuana to its members was not "trafficking" within the meaning of section 280E. We disagree. We define and apply the gerund "trafficking" by reference to the verb "traffic", which as relevant herein denotes "to engage in commercial activity: buy and sell regularly". Webster's Third New International Dictionary 2423 (2002). Petitioner's supplying of medical marijuana to its members is within that definition in that petitioner regularly bought and sold the marijuana, such sales occurring when petitioner distributed the medical marijuana to its members in exchange for part of their membership fees.[5] Accord United States v. Oakland Cannabis Buyers' Coop., supra at 489.

We now turn to analyze whether petitioner's furnishing of its caregiving services is a trade or business that is separate from its trade or business of providing medical marijuana. Taxpayers may be involved in more than one trade or business, see, e.g., Hoye v. Commissioner, T.C. Memo. 1990-57, and whether an activity is a trade or business separate from another trade or business is a question of fact that depends on (among other things) the degree of economic interrelationship between the two undertakings, see Collins v. Commissioner, 34 T.C. 592 (1960); sec. 1.183-1(d)(1), Income Tax Regs. The Commissioner generally accepts a taxpayer's characterization of two or more undertakings as separate activities unless the characterization is artificial or unreasonable. See sec. 1.183-1(d)(1), Income Tax Regs. We do not believe it to have been artificial or unreasonable for petitioner to have characterized as separate activities its provision of caregiving services and its provision of medical marijuana. Petitioner was regularly and extensively involved in the provision of caregiving services, and those services are substantially different from petitioner's provision of medical marijuana. By conducting its recurring discussion groups, regularly distributing food and hygiene supplies, advertising and making available the services of personal counselors, coordinating social events and field trips, hosting educational classes, and providing other social services, petitioner's caregiving business stood on its own, separate and apart from petitioner's provision of medical marijuana. On the basis of all of the facts and circumstances of this case, we hold that petitioner's provision of caregiving services was a trade or business separate and apart from its provision of medical marijuana.

---

[5] In support of its position, petitioner relies upon Raich v. Ashcroft, 352 F.3d 1222, 1228 (9th Cir. 2003), vacated and remanded sub nom. Gonzales v. Raich, 545 U.S. 1 (2005), where the Court of Appeals for the Ninth Circuit reasoned that the use of medical marijuana is "different in kind from drug trafficking". Petitioner's reliance on that reasoning is mistaken. The U.S. Supreme Court rejected the reasoning in Gonzales v. Raich, supra at 26-28, 31-33, holding that the Controlled Substances Act applied to individuals within the purview of California's medical marijuana law.

Respondent argues that the "evidence indicates that petitioner's principal purpose was to provide access to marijuana, that petitioner's principal activity was providing access to marijuana, and that the principal service that petitioner provided was access to marijuana * * * and that all of petitioner's activities were merely incidental to petitioner's activity of trafficking in marijuana." We disagree. Petitioner's executive director testified credibly and without contradiction that petitioner's primary purpose was to provide caregiving services for terminally ill patients. He stated: "Right from the start we considered our primary function as being a community center for seriously ill patients in San Francisco. And only secondarily as a place where they could access their medicine." The evidence suggests that petitioner's operations were conducted with that primary function in mind, not with the principal purpose of providing marijuana to members.

As stated by the Board of Tax Appeals in Alverson v. Commissioner, 35 B.T.A. 482, 488 (1937): "The statute is not so restricted as to confine deductions to a single business or principal business of the taxpayer. A taxpayer may carry on more than one trade or business at the same time." Moreover, as the Supreme Court has observed in the context of illegal, nondeductible expenditures: "It has never been thought * * *that the mere fact that an expenditure bears a remote relation to an illegal act makes it non-deductible." Commissioner v. Heininger, 320 U.S. 467, 474 (1943).

Respondent relies heavily on his assertion that "Petitioner's only income was from marijuana-related matters, except for a couple of small donations". The record does not support that assertion, and we decline to find it as a fact. Indeed, the record leads us to make the contrary finding that petitioner's caregiving services generated income attributable to those services. In making this finding, we rely on the testimony of petitioner's executive director, whom we had an opportunity to hear and view at trial. We found his testimony to be coherent and credible, as well as supported by the record. He testified that petitioner's members paid their membership fees as consideration for both caregiving services and medical marijuana, and respondent opted not to challenge the substance of that testimony. While a member may have acquired, in return for his or her payment of a membership fee, access to all of petitioner's goods and services without further charge and without explicit differentiation as to the portion of the fee that was paid for goods versus services, we do not believe that such a fact establishes that petitioner's operations were simply one trade or business. As the record reveals, and as we find as a fact, petitioner's management set the total amount of the membership fees as the amount that management consciously and reasonably judged equaled petitioner's costs of the caregiving services and the costs of the medical marijuana.

Given petitioner's separate trades or businesses, we are required to apportion its overall expenses accordingly. Respondent argues that "petitioner failed to justify any particular allocation and failed to present evidence as to how * * * [petitioner's expenses] should be allocated between marijuana trafficking and other activities." We disagree. Respondent concedes that many of petitioner's activities are legal and unrelated to petitioner's provision of medical marijuana. The evidence at hand permits an allocation of expenses to those activities. Although the record may not lend itself to a perfect allocation with pinpoint accuracy, the record permits us with sufficient confidence to allocate petitioner's expenses between its two trades or businesses on the basis of the number of petitioner's employees and the portion of its facilities devoted to each business. Accordingly, in a manner that is most consistent with petitioner's breakdown of the disputed expenses, we allocate to petitioner's caregiving services 18/25 of the expenses for salaries, wages, payroll taxes, employee benefits, employee development training, meals and entertainment, and parking and tolls (18 of petitioner's 25 employees did not work directly in petitioner's provision of medical marijuana), all expenses incurred in renting facilities at the church (petitioner did not use the church to any extent to provide medical marijuana), all expenses incurred for "truck and auto" and "laundry and cleaning" (those expenses did not relate to any extent to petitioner's provision of medical marijuana), and 9/10 of the remaining expenses (90 percent of the square footage of petitioner's main facility was not used in petitioner's provision of medical marijuana). [6] We disagree with respondent that petitioner must further justify the allocation of its expenses, reluctant to substitute our judgment for the judgment of petitioner's management as to its understanding of the expenses that petitioner incurred as to each of its trades or businesses. Cf. Boyd Gaming Corp. v. Commissioner, 177 F.3d 1096 (9th Cir. 1999), rev'g, T.C. Memo. 1997-445.

All arguments by the parties have been considered. We have rejected those arguments not discussed herein as without merit.

Accordingly,

Decision will be entered
under Rule 155

---

[6] While we apportion most of the $212,958 in "Total deductions" to petitioner's caregiving services, we note that the costs of petitioner's medical marijuana business included the $203,661 in labor and $43,783 in other costs respondent conceded to have been properly reported on petitioner's tax return as attributable to cost of goods sold in the medical marijuana business.

CHAPTER 9 – WORKING EFFECTIVELY WITH THE INTERNAL REVENUE SERVICE

Learning Objectives:

☑ Understand how to work effectively with the IRS
☑ Understand alternative dispute resolution options with the IRS Operating Divisions and the Office of Appeals

In this Chapter:

1. Understand Your Audience to Work Well with the IRS
2. Understand the Manual that Guides IRS Employees' Conduct and Practice
3. Recognize the Statutory Incentives for Practitioners to Work Cooperatively With the IRS
4. Understand that Alternative Dispute Resolution Options are Available When Working with the IRS

1. Understand Your Audience to Work Well with the IRS

Employees of the IRS believe in the mission of the organization - to "provide America's taxpayers top quality service by helping them understand and meet their tax responsibilities and by applying the tax law with integrity and fairness to all." There are no financial or promotion incentives for employees to find new issues, to extend the depth or duration of audits or to inflate adjustments. Any pre-conceived notions of malice or improper motives imputed upon the IRS is not only incorrect but serves to poison the working relationship between practitioner and the IRS. If the practitioner views the IRS as an enemy from the beginning of the engagement, then there is a very high probability that communication will be poor, at best. Therefore, it is critical for the practitioner to understand the IRS.

First, consider as context the oath every IRS employee must take upon entering government service. As Federal civil servants, IRS employees take an oath of office by which they swear to support and defend the Constitution of the United States of America. The Constitution not only establishes our system of government, it actually defines the work role for Federal employees - "to establish Justice, insure domestic tranquility, provide for the common defense, promote the general welfare, and secure the blessings of liberty."

The history of the Oath for Federal employees can be traced to the Constitution, where Article II includes the specific oath the President takes - to "preserve, protect, and defend the Constitution of the United States." Article VI requires an oath by all other government officials from all three branches, the military, and the States. It simply states that they "shall be bound by oath or affirmation to support the Constitution." The very first law passed by the very first Congress implemented Article VI by setting out this simple oath in law: "I do solemnly swear or affirm (as the case may be) that I will support the Constitution of the United States."

The wording used today for Executive Branch employees is now set out in chapter 33 of Title 5, United States Code. The wording dates to the Civil War and what was called the Ironclad Test Oath. Starting in 1862, Congress required a two-part oath. The first part, referred to as a "background check," affirmed that you were not supporting and had not supported the Confederacy. The second part addressed future performance, that is, what you would swear to do in the future. It established a clear, publicly sworn accountability. In 1873, Congress dropped the first part of the Ironclad Test Oath, and in 1884 adopted the wording we use today.

Oath

> *I, [name], do solemnly swear (or affirm) that I will support and defend the Constitution of the United States against all enemies, foreign and domestic; that I will bear true faith and allegiance to the same; that I take this obligation freely, without any mental reservation or purpose of evasion; and that I will well and faithfully discharge the duties of the office on which I am about to enter. So help me God.*

> *5 U.S.C. §3331*

What should you take away from knowing that all IRS employees take this oath of office to begin their Federal employment? These are government officials who strive to make a difference by fulfilling a public service. Do you want to serve the role of assisting these government officials in quickly resolving their inquiries? Or, do you want to consider and treat the government as the "enemy"? Your knowledge of your audience will drive your approach with the IRS. And, a positive, knowledgeable approach with the IRS will provide your client with the most efficient interaction and provide the least burden upon the government.

From IRS Publication 5125, the following points are set forth from the IRS to taxpayers or their representatives to work productively with the IRS:

- Work transparently with the exam team by providing a thorough overview of business activities, operational structure, accounting systems, and a global tax organizational chart
- Identify personnel for each issue with sufficient knowledge who can provide input when establishing initial audit steps, timelines, and actively assist in the development of the issues selected by the exam team

- Follow the Information Document Request ("IDR")[221] procedures by:

  - 1. Reviewing and discussing IDRs with the issue team before issuance to ensure that they are properly focused and identify the issue
  - 2. Working with the issue team to reach a reasonable response date for each IDR

- For issues identified for examination, provide work papers and supporting documents requested, including those the taxpayer relied on when preparing the return

- Collaborate with the issue team to arrive at an acknowledgment of the facts for unagreed issues; provide support for any additional or disputed facts

- To foster early resolution, respond timely to each Form 5701 by providing a written legal position for issues in dispute

- Resolve issues at earliest appropriate point using an issue resolution tool

In reviewing each recommendation, I can summarize the common thread as: "Let's work together in a trust-based relationship so the government can understand the taxpayer's tax return position and we can quickly reach closure." Focus on establishing trust with the IRS at every opportunity and you will achieve the best result for your client and assist the government in fulfilling its mission. Win-win.

When I worked as a private practitioner at Ernst & Young, I had multiple objectives upon being hired to represent a client before the IRS:

For my client: **provide clear messaging** of what to expect from my services. There were no guarantees that I would "win." Rather, I committed to provide cost-effective services and present the strongest positions for my client to reach a quick resolution. Oftentimes, my clients would not timely respond to my requests for information or

---

[221] An IDR (Form 4564) is a initial, informal written information request presented to the taxpayer or taxpayer's representative by the IRS. See IRM 4.71.1.7.3, IRM 4.71.1.7(5). Form 4564 is generally prepared to request additional information after the initial appointment letter.

access to specific employees because they had other pressing matters. One client of a public company candidly admitted, "With limited staff and time, I'm a lot more worried about the SEC than I am of the IRS. I'll get to you when I can." Within the reality of a hectic business environment, my approach was to be firm in my communication with busy clients advising them of risks associated with delay. Regardless of clients' tight schedules and priorities, tax practitioners remain subject to statutory, Circular 230, SSTS and or other professional duties. Communicate clearly and firmly with your clients on your professional responsibilities in every engagement.

For the IRS: **become a trusted partner** who can be viewed as an asset, not an adversary, to the IRS agent or team in order to move the audit quickly and efficiently. Be transparent, exceed the IRS' expectations, never ever take any action that would cause the IRS to second guess your professionalism or motives. Earn the government's trust. When you work with the IRS, think, "How can I help?" Certainly, a practitioner serves as the client's representative. But, what makes you an effective representative? Becoming trusted by the IRS allows you to develop the most effective, efficient relationship with the government and, consequently, you serve your client most efficiently. Your reputation takes a great deal of time and effort to develop. But, that hard earned reputation can be lost in one conversation.

- For the practitioner and practitioner's firm: follow applicable professional guides, such as Cir. 230, and statutes, such as section 6694. Never engage in any conduct that would expose you (practitioner) or your firm to discipline or liability or the potential for loss of your professional license.

2. Understand the Manual that Guides IRS Employees' Conduct and Practice

IRS employees rely on their manual of instructions (referred to as the Internal Revenue Manual or IRM) for guidance on how to conduct their duties. The provisions of the Internal Revenue Manual govern only the internal affairs of the IRS; they do not have the force and effect of law.222 Some language in the IRM is mandatory whereas other parts are merely suggestive. But, it is useful for the practitioner to understand what drives or influences IRS employee processes and/or conduct in various situations. For IRS Chief Counsel attorneys, a comparable employee guidebook is the Chief Counsel Directives Manual or CCDM.

The IRM and CCDM are vast documents that are not easy to navigate and understand. Set forth below is the table of contents for the IRM:

---

[222] Valen Manufacturing Co. v. United States, 90 F.3d 1190, 1194 (6th Cir. 1996); United States v. Horne, 714 F.2d 206, 207 (1st Cir. 1983). See generally Reich v. Manganas, 70 F.3d 434, 437 (6th Cir. 1995) ("Internal operating manuals * * * do not carry the force of law, bind the agency, or confer rights upon the regulated entity."). Procedures in the Internal Revenue Manual do not confer rights on taxpayers. United States v. Horne, supra; United States v. Mapp, 561 F.2d 685, 690 (7th Cir. 1977).

Internal Revenue Manual
Table of Contents

Part 1	Organization, Finance, and Management
Part 2	Information Technology
Part 3	Submission Processing
Part 4	Examining Process
Part 5	Collecting Process
Part 6	Human Resources Management
Part 7	Rulings and Agreements
Part 8	Appeals
Part 9	Criminal Investigation
Part 10	Security, Privacy and Assurance
Part 11	Communications and Liaison
Part 13	Taxpayer Advocate Service
Part 20	Penalty and Interest
Part 21	Customer Account Services
Part 22	Taxpayer Education and Assistance
Part 25	Special Topics
Part 30	Administrative
Part 31	Guiding Principles
Part 32	Published Guidance and Other Guidance to Taxpayers
Part 33	Legal Advice
Part 34	Litigation in District Court, Bankruptcy Court, Court of Federal Claims, and State Court
Part 35	Tax Court Litigation
Part 36	Appellate Litigation and Actions on Decision
Part 37	Disclosure
Part 38	Criminal Tax
Part 39	General Legal Services

For example, audit technique guides (ATGs) are included in the IRM to help IRS examiners during audits by providing insight into issues and accounting methods unique to specific industries. While ATGs are designed to provide guidance for IRS employees, they're also useful to small business owners and tax professionals who prepare returns.

ATGs explain industry-specific examination techniques and include common, as well as, unique industry issues, business practices and terminology. Guidance is also provided on the examination of income, interview techniques and evaluation of evidence. So, ATGs may be helpful for business and tax planning purposes.[223]

Practitioners should devote time to become familiar with the various provisions within the IRM as part of their basic tax practice to become a more informed, effective advocate for clients. The material is publicly available on the internet as well as on every major tax database.

3. Statutory Incentives for Practitioners to Work Cooperatively With the IRS

Practitioners should work cooperatively, cordially and in a profesional manner with the IRS because to do so is in the best interests of their client and promotes efficient tax adminstration.[224] But, in addition, there are statutory incentives for practitioners to work cooperatively with the IRS. Within the tax code, taxpayers generally bear the burden of proving their positions taken on returns. For instance, deductions are a matter of legislative grace, and a taxpayer bears the burden of proving entitlement to any claimed deductions.[225] If a taxpayer's case proceeds to Tax Court, then again the taxpayer bears the burden of proving by a preponderance of the evidence that the determinations of the Commissioner as set forth in a notice of deficiency are incorrect.[226]

However, there are statutory provisions within Title 26 that provide incentives for taxpayers to cooperate with the IRS. For example, under section 7491, the burden of proof that is normally placed on the taxpayer shifts to the IRS if the taxpayer has complied with the basic requirements for substantiation and "has cooperated with reasonable requests by the Secretary for witnesses, information, documents, meetings, and interviews....." Similarly, section 7430 provides that the "prevailing party" is eligible to obtain reasonable administrative costs incurred in connection with an IRS

---

[223] The IRS provides videos to assist taxpayers understand ATGs. See https://www.irsvideos.gov/SmallBusinessTaxpayer/Resources/ATG2011.

[224] Recall that under Circular 230, section 10.51, incompetent and disreputable conduct by a practitioner is subject to sanction. "Incompetent and disreputable" conduct under section 10.51 includes: giving false or misleading information, or participating in any way in the giving of false or misleading information to the Department of the Treasury or any officer or employee thereof, engaging in contemptuous conduct in connection with practice before the Internal Revenue Service, including the use of abusive language, making false accusations or statements, knowing them to be false, or giving a false opinion, knowingly, recklessly, or through gross incompetence, including an opinion which is intentionally or recklessly misleading, or engaging in a pattern of providing incompetent opinions on questions arising under the Federal tax laws.

[225] INDOPCO, Inc. v. Commissioner, 503 U.S. 79, 84 (1992).

[226] Welch v. Helvering, 290 U.S. 111, 115 (1933).

administrative proceeding and reasonable litigation costs incurred in connection with court proceedings, in part, as long as the taxpayer has not "unreasonably protracted such proceeding."

4. Understand that alternative dispute resolution options are available when working with the IRS

Working effectively with the IRS means not only understanding their role and function but also becoming familiar with their internal processes, issue resolution tools when working with the Examination Division and alternative dispute resolution ("ADR") options with Appeals.

a. Examination Division

Revenue agents must apply their judgment and experience in weighing the taxpayer's and government's tax position, based on the applicable laws, to determine the correct tax return position. Exam has broad authority to resolve issues based on the application of tax law to the facts. In addition, Exam can apply other issue resolution tools when appropriate. Using appropriate issue resolution tools can potentially reduce examination time, save resources and lessen the burden on both parties. Practitioners should not assume that all agents are aware of the available resolution tools or when such tools are applicable. Rather, practitioners should be knowledgeable regarding these tools to be able to raise them as possible options in the appropriate situation.

Taxpayer-Specific Pre-filing Resolution Tools

> Pre-Filing Agreements (PFA) permit a taxpayer to request the examination of specific issues relating to a tax return before the return is timely filed. The purpose is to resolve issues involving factual questions under well- settled principles of law. A PFA can often resolve such issues more effectively and efficiently. A PFA also provides the taxpayer with a greater level of certainty regarding the examined issue at an earlier point in time than a post-filing examination. The request is subject to a user fee. For more information see Rev. Proc. 2009-14 and the PFA web page at http://lmsb.irs.gov/hq/pftg/pfts/pfa/preagree.asp.[227]

> Advanced Pricing Agreements (APA) is a process that provides for determining the proper treatment of transfer pricing issues prior to the filing of returns. In some circumstances the agreed application methods for resolving the transfer pricing issue may also be used to resolve issues present on filed returns currently under examination. For more information see Rev. Proc. 2015-41 or successor and the APA web page at http://lmsb.irs.gov/international/dir_treaty/treaty/index.asp.[228]

---

[227] IRM 4.46.5.4.1.1.
[228] IRM 4.46.5.4.1.2.

- ➢ Compliance Assurance Process (CAP) is a method of identifying and resolving tax issues through open, cooperative and transparent interaction between the IRS and LB&I taxpayers prior to the filing of a return.[229] Through the CAP program, the taxpayer should achieve tax certainty sooner and with less administrative burden than conventional examinations. CAP is a voluntary program for taxpayers. Taxpayers must apply and be accepted into CAP. For more information see the CAP web page at *http://lmsb.irs.gov/hq/pftg/CAP/index.asp* and IRM 4.51.8.

- ➢ Industry Issue Resolution Program resolves frequently disputed or burdensome tax issues that affect a significant number of business taxpayers through the issuance of guidance. IRS solicits suggestions for issues from taxpayers, representatives and associations for the IIR Program. For each issue selected for the program, a resolution team of IRS, Chief Counsel and Treasury personnel is assembled to gather and analyze relevant information for the issue and develop and recommend guidance. Selected IIR Program requests may result in published guidance, such as a regulation, revenue ruling, revenue procedure, or notice. Alternatively, selected requests may result in new or revised administrative procedures such as an LB&I Operating Division directive or a revision to an Internal Revenue Manual provision. See Rev. Proc. 2016-19 for more details of the IIR Program.

- ➢ Private Letter Rulings are written rulings issued by National Office Chief Counsel that apply the tax laws to a taxpayer's specific set of facts. A private letter ruling, or PLR, is a written statement issued to a taxpayer that interprets and applies tax laws to the taxpayer's specific set of facts. A PLR is issued to establish with certainty the federal tax consequences of a particular transaction before the transaction is consummated or before the taxpayer's return is filed. A PLR is issued in response to a written request submitted by a taxpayer and is binding on the IRS if the taxpayer fully and accurately described the proposed transaction in the request and carries out the transaction as described. A PLR may not be relied on as precedent by other taxpayers or IRS personnel. PLRs are generally made public after all information has been removed that could identify the taxpayer to whom it was issued.

- ➢ A written ruling is subject to a user fee, issued based on the taxpayer's request, on proposed or completed transactions prior to the filing of the return. The identical issue cannot be on an earlier return that was examined in Appeals or in litigation. For more information see Rev. Proc. 2018-1 or the first revenue procedure of the current year.[230]

Taxpayer-Specific Post-filing Resolution Tools
Technical Advice Memoranda ("TAMs") are written statements issued by National Office Chief Counsel on technical or procedural questions on the proper application of tax law,

---

[229] IRM 4.46.5.4.1.3.
[230] IRM 4.46.5.4.1.4.

treaties, regulations, etc. on a specific set of facts submitted by the IRS and/or taxpayer in a written request. A TAM is guidance furnished by the Office of Chief Counsel upon the request of an IRS director or an area director, appeals, in response to technical or procedural questions that develop during a proceeding. A request for a TAM generally stems from an examination of a taxpayer's return, a consideration of a taxpayer's claim for a refund or credit, or any other matter involving a specific taxpayer under the jurisdiction of the territory manager or the area director, appeals. Technical Advice Memoranda are issued only on closed transactions and provide the interpretation of proper application of tax laws, tax treaties, regulations, revenue rulings or other precedents. The advice rendered represents a final determination of the position of the IRS, but only with respect to the specific issue in the specific case in which the advice is issued. Technical Advice Memoranda are generally made public after all information has been removed that could identify the taxpayer whose circumstances triggered a specific memorandum. See the TAM web page at http://lmsb.irs.gov/hq/pftg/pfts/downloads/tams/tams.asp and Rev. Proc. 2015-2 or the second revenue procedure of the current year.[231]

> Accelerated Issue Resolution (AIR) is an examination process to apply the resolution of the same or similar issues arising for an examination of an LB&I taxpayer from one or more tax periods to other tax periods. Refer to Rev. Proc. 94-67 and Rev. Proc. 68-16 when considering the utilization of AIR procedures.[232]
>   o AIR does not include settlement authority for managers.
>   o AIR does not alter in any way the authority case managers have to resolve issues.
>   o IRS Chief Counsel assistance is mandatory when using AIR.
>   o An AIR agreement is generally limited in scope to issues on filed returns arising from an audit of specific taxpayers under the jurisdiction of the Director of Field Operations. Certain issues are excluded or require additional approvals. See Rev. Proc. 94-67, Sec. 3, Scope of an AIR Agreement.

> Early Referral to Appeals is a process to resolve cases more expeditiously through LB&I and Appeals working simultaneously. Appeals can consider a fully developed unagreed issue while exam is developing other issues. This process is optional and may be requested by the taxpayer or the examiner. An early referral may be requested on one or more unagreed issues. Rev. Proc. 99-28, 1999-2 C.B. 109, sets forth the procedures to request early referral. More information can be found at IRM 8.26.4 , *Early Referral Procedures* or on the Appeals web site at http://appeals.web.irs.gov/tech_services/adr/early-referral.htm.[233]

> Fast Track Settlement - FTS must be considered for all unagreed issues. The program is not right for every situation, but when properly applied, it can save

---

[231] IRM 4.46.5.4.2.1.
[232] IRM 4.46.5.4.2.3.
[233] IRM 4.46.5.4.2.4.

significant time and administrative burden for the service and the taxpayer. Issues should be fully developed prior to consideration of FTS. A fully developed case is one without any significant unresolved factual differences.FTS is a collaborative effort where the taxpayer, the LB&I members of the issue team and Appeals agree to participate and work toward a mutual resolution based on an agreed set of facts. See a fuller explanation of FTS, below, in the discussion of the tool with the IRS Office of Appeals.[234]

b. IRS Office of Appeals

When working with Appeals, there are five ADR options.

- ➢ Arbitration - If settlement negotiations are unsuccessful, taxpayers and Appeals may jointly request binding arbitration for qualifying, factual issues already in the Appeals administrative process after consulting with each other. Arbitration is also available after unsuccessful attempts to enter into a closing agreement under Internal Revenue Code section 7121. However, some of the cases excluded from Appeals arbitration are:
  - ○ Compliance and Appeals Coordinated Issues;
  - ○ Legal issues
  - ○ Collection issues, except for those detailed in Announcement 2011-6, or subsequent guidance issued by the IRS
  - ○ Those not consistent with sound tax administration
  - ○ Frivolous arguments; and
  - ○ Those where the taxpayer(s) did not act in good faith during settlement negotiations. For complete information, see Revenue Procedure 2006- 44. The Model Agreement to Arbitrate in the revenue procedure allows the parties certain flexibility in designing the arbitration process.

- ➢ Fast Track Mediation is designed to help Small Business/Self Employed (SB/SE) taxpayers resolve many disputes resulting from examinations (audits), offers in compromise, trust fund recovery penalties, and other collection actions while your case stays in SB/SE. Appeals personnel trained in mediation assist taxpayers and an IRS representative discuss the issues involved in their disagreement, and possible ways to resolve it. Appeals' goal is to reach a jointly agreeable solution, consistent with relevant law, within 40 days. The mediator will not require either party to accept a certain outcome. The taxpayer and the IRS representative must sign an agreement to mediate, Form 13369, for the case to be considered for mediation. A taxpayer is not required to file a formal protest to request fast track mediation, but must provide a written position with a request for mediation. Most cases, which are not docketed in any court, qualify for fast track mediation. Some of the excluded cases are:
  - ○ Issues with no legal precedent
  - ○ Issues where the courts' decisions differ between jurisdictions
  - ○ Campus and Automated Collection Service cases

---

[234] IRM 4.46.5.4.2.5.

- o Collection Appeals Program cases; and
- o Those with only frivolous arguments

For mediation to succeed, all the decision-makers must be present. Taxpayers may have a representative assist them at the mediation session, or proceed without one. A taxpayer may withdraw from the mediation process anytime. A taxpayer will retain all the usual appeal rights for any issues that do not get resolved through fast track mediation. For complete information, see Publication 3605 and Revenue Procedure 2003-41.

➢ Fast Track Settlement is designed to help other IRS Operating Division taxpayers expeditiously resolve disputes during an examination while their case is still in Examination or Collection. Fast Track Settlement ("FTS") brings Appeals resources to a mutually agreed upon location to resolve the dispute before the 30-day letter is issued. A specially trained Appeals employee facilitates the discussion between a taxpayer and the revenue agent and their team or group manager to reach and execute a settlement with which the parties can agree. A taxpauer may request Fast Track Settlement after Form 5701, Summary of Issues, Examination Re-Engineering Lead Sheets or other similar document has been issued and the taxpayer has provided a written response. FTS may be available for factual and legal issues, including listed transactions, Compliance and Appeals Coordinated Issues, and issues that require consideration of the hazards of litigation.   Benefits with Fast Track Settlement include:
- o A one-page application, Form 14017
- o Consideration of the hazards of litigation
- o An answer within 120 days for Large Business and International (LB&I) cases and within 60 days for Small Business Self Employed (SB/SE) and Tax Exempt Government Entities (TE/GE) cases
- o No 'hot' interest under IRC 6621
- o An option to withdraw from the process at any time
- o Retention of all traditional appeal rights
- o Significantly shorter IRS experience
- o Only one tax computation
- o Taxpayer's case closes agreed in the other Operation Division; and
- o Immediate use of Delegation Order 236 Fast Track Settlement is available for certain LB&I, SB/ SE and TE/GE taxpayers. The program is also available to other IRS Operating Division taxpayers on a case-by-case basis. For complete information see: (1) LB&I - Revenue Procedure 2003-40; (2) SB/SE – Announcement 2011-5; (3) TE/GE – Announcement 2008-105.

➢ Mediation is available when a limited number of legal and factual issues remain unresolved after settlement discussions in Appeals. The mediator's role is to impartially facilitate discussion between the disputing parties to help them reach their own negotiated settlement. A trained Appeals mediator will be assigned to the case at no cost to the taxpayer. Taxpayers may also elect to use a non-IRS co-mediator at their own expense. Taxpayers may request mediation if they are already in the Appeals administrative process with any qualifying issues, and their case is not docketed in any court. It is available for both factual issues, such as valuation and transfer pricing issues, and legal issues. Qualifying issues include Compliance and Appeals Coordinated Issues. It is also available after unsuccessful attempts to enter into a closing agreement under Internal Revenue Code section 7121. There are no dollar limitations. Some of the cases or issues excluded from mediation are:

- o Collection issues except for those detailed in Announcement 2011-6, or subsequent guidance issued by the IRS
- o Those not consistent with sound tax administration
- o Frivolous arguments; and
- o Those where the taxpayer did not act in good faith during settlement negotiations.

Mediation is optional and does not create any special settlement authority for Appeals. Taxpayers and the assigned Appeals officer assigned the case may request mediation after consulting with each other. A taxpayer can initiate mediation by sending a written request to the appropriate Appeals Team Manager, with a copy to the appropriate Area Director and Chief of Appeals. For complete information, see Revenue Procedure 2009-44.

➢ Early Referral - Taxpayers whose returns are under the jurisdiction of Examination or Collection may request the transfer of a developed but unagreed issue to Appeals, while the other issues in the case continue to be developed in Examination or Collection. See the discussion of Early Referral, above, in "Taxpayer-Specific Post-filing Resolution Tools."

Chapter 9 - Questions

1. List two code sections in Title 26 that provide incentives for taxpayers to work cooperatively with the IRS.

2. The Internal Revenue Manual ("IRM") does not carry the force of law, bind the agency or confer rights upon taxpayers who may decide to cite to the IRM. So, why should taxpayers or tax practitioners spend any time researching the IRM?

3. What is the difference between a TAM and a PLR?

CHAPTER 10 – TAX PROCEDURE & PENALTIES

Learning Objectives:

☑ Understand basic tax terms and concepts, including tax assessment, the statute of limitations, "30-Day Letter," "90-Day Letter," what constitutes a "valid tax return" and why that matters for purposes of the statute of limitations

☑ Understand the IRS examination process, including information gathering tools employed by the IRS, and summons enforcement procedures

In this Chapter:

1. Basic Tax Terms & Concepts
2. IRS Audit/Examination Process
3. Penalties Applicable to Taxpayers
4. Penalties Applicable to Tax Return Preparers

Understanding the substantive code provisions in Title 26 establishes the core element of tax practice. However, it is essential to understand the application of procedural rules and penalties in order to be an effective tax practitioner.

First, we need to be grounded with an understanding of basic tax terms and concepts:

1. Basic Tax Terms & Concepts

Tax Assessment – A tax assessment is the statutorily required recording of the tax liability.[235] Assessment is made by recording the taxpayer's name, address, and tax liability.[236] The tax assessment is a predicate to collection of federal tax due. Before the IRS can collect tax from a taxpayer through a levy or lien filing, it must first assess the tax.[237] The IRS has three methods in which it assesses taxes.[238] The first method is the automatic assessment that occurs when a taxpayer files a return without paying the tax due. This is sometimes referred to as self-assessment. The second is the deficiency assessment that occurs after examination and administrative and judicial review. If the taxpayer files a petition to the Tax Court after receipt of a statutory notice of deficiency, assessment is postponed until the Tax Court's final decision. The third method of assessment is the termination or the jeopardy assessment. An example of this kind of assessment may occur when the IRS believes the taxpayer is planning to leave the country in an effort to evade paying the tax liability.

Tax Abatement – An abatement of tax is the reduction or elimination of a tax assessment.[239] In other words, abatement of tax reverses (in part or whole) the previous assessment made. There are several circumstances when a taxpayer may request an abatement. The IRS also has general abatement authority under IRC Section 6404. Section 6404 provides the general abatement authority for the IRS. Section 6404(a) permits the IRS to abate a liability where the liability is improper, either because it is excessive in amount or illegally made. This includes an assessment made after the expiration of the assessment statute of limitations date.[240] Section 6404(c) permits the IRS to abate a liability when the IRS determines that the administration and collection costs involved would not warrant collection of the liability. Sections 6404(e) and (f) provide for the abatement of interest or penalties in certain specified situations.

Statute of Limitations - A statute of limitation ("SOL") is a time period established by law to review, analyze and resolve taxpayer and/or IRS tax related issues.[241] The Internal Revenue Code requires that the Internal Revenue Service will assess, refund, credit, and collect taxes within specific time limits. These limits are known as the SOL. When they expire, the IRS can no longer assess additional tax, allow a claim for refund by the taxpayer, or take collection action.[242] There are two different types of SOL:

- Statute of Limitations on Tax Assessment – Under section 6501(a), the tax code provides a 3-year limitation within which time any additional tax must be assessed by the IRS after a valid return was filed by the taxpayer. This 3-year SOL period

---

[235] IRC § 6203.
[236] See IRM 35.9.2.1(1).
[237] Atkins v. Commissioner, T.C. Memo. 2011-12.
[238] IRC § 6203.
[239] IRM 25.6.1.10.1.1.
[240] IRM 25.6.1.10.1.1(2).
[241] IRM 25.6.1.2(1).
[242] IRM 25.6.1.2(2).

may be extended by agreement between the taxpayer and the IRS prior to the expiration date.

- o Early return filed – if a taxpayer files a return before the last day prescribed by law or by regulations for the filing of such return(s), then the return is deemed to be filed on the last day.[243]

- o False return – if a taxpayer files a false return, then no SOL period applies. IRC § 6501(c)(1). So, if a taxpayer files a federal tax return that includes some item of fraud, but immediately files an amended return to correct the fraud, the SOL remains tied to the original fraudulent return. In other words, the taxpayer will never have the SOL expire for the year in which he filed a fraudulent return even if he later corrects the fraudulent item.[244]

- o Substantial Ommission of Items – if a taxpayer omits from gross income an amount that is greater than 25% of the amount that is reported in gross income on the return, then the SOL period is extended an additional 3 years to a 6-year SOL period for assessment.[245] The 6-year SOL applies because the government is at a disadvantage in discovering an omitted item of income. A taxpayer can overcome the application of the 6-year SOL by establishing that the item of omitted income was disclosed in the return – or in a statement attached to the return – in a manner adequate to put the IRS on notice as to the nature and amount of such item.

- Statute of Limitations on Tax Collection – Under section 6502(a), the tax code provides a 10-year limitation within which time tax that is timely assessed may be collected.

- Suspension of the Statute of Limitations - There are several situations when the SOL for collection is suspended: a Tax Court petition is filed (§ 6503(a)), bankruptcy (§ 6503(h)), offers in compromise (§ 6331(k)).

- Statute of Limitations Does Not Begin to Run – There are several situations when the statute of limitations for assessment never begins to run, thus, there is no consideration for suspension of this time.

  Example 1: Failure to Notify Secretary of Certain Foreign Transfers - Under section 6501(c)(8), if a taxpayer fails to comply with specific statutory requirements to report information as required under sections 1298(f), 6038, 6038A, 6038B, 6038D, 6046, 6046A, or 6048, then the statute of limitations only begins to run after the taxpayer provides the required information. The Foreign Account Tax Compliance Act, enacted in 2010, created new IRC Section 6038D and requires individuals to file a statement with their income tax returns to report interests in specified foreign financial assets if the aggregate value of those

---

[243] IRC § 6501(b)(1).
[244] Badaracco v. Commissioner, 464 U.S. 386, 395-96 (1984).
[245] IRC § 6501(e)(1)(A).

assets exceeds certain thresholds. Reporting thresholds vary based on whether a filer files a joint tax return or resides abroad, and are higher for married couples and taxpayers who qualify for foreign residency.

Example 2: Invalid Return – If a taxpayer submits an invalid return, the statute of limitations on assessment never begins at all.[246] Courts have stated that four criteria are necessary for a valid tax return: (1) there must be sufficient data to calculate a tax liability; (2) the document must purport to be a return; (3) there must be an honest and reasonable attempt to satisfy the requirements of tax law; and (4) the taxpayer must execute the return under penalties of perjury.[247]

"30-Day Letter" - If the IRS and a taxpayer disagree on the treatment of an item following an audit, the taxpayer will receive a letter that contains instructions on how to appeal the IRS proposed deficiency. This letter also is received if the taxpayer ignores the IRS audit. This letter is commonly referred to as the "30-day letter" because it gives the taxpayer 30 days in which to appeal the decision of the examining agent. To appeal the examiner's proposed adjustments, a "Protest" is submitted requesting a conference with the Appeals Office to discuss the disputed issues.

Why submit a protest letter? (1) The taxpayer obtains an additional opportunity to resolve issues with the IRS, before incurring litigation expenses. Unlike Exam, Appeals is able to settle issues on a hazards of litigation basis. I.R.M. § 8.6.4; (2) The taxpayer leaves open options to proceed to all litigation forums; (3) The taxpayer delays payment of proposed tax increases; and (4) The taxpayer can learn more about the IRS's position, continue to develop facts, and refine their own arguments. Why not proceed with submitting a protest letter? (1) The taxpayer may not want any delay, if he/she seeks to litigate as soon as possible; and (2) The taxpayer may not want to give the IRS more time to develop its position.

Because the "30-day letter" is not a statutory letter, extensions may be granted to request an appeals conference. Many practitioners do not recognize the practical effect of a "30-day letter," but it actually has significant implications for appeal rights. A 30-day letter is a letter from the IRS that proposes adjustments to a taxpayer's liability. Upon receiving this letter, a taxpayer has three options: (1) pay the proposed tax liability, (2) contest the findings with the IRS Appeals Division, or (3) do nothing and wait to receive a Statutory Notice of Deficiency (a 90-day letter). If the taxpayer does nothing and receives the Statutory Notice of Deficiency, he or she has lost the immediately opportunity to proceed to the IRS Appeals Office to resolve the dispute. The taxpayer must then file a petition in Tax Court to address the issue. However, it is the practice of

---

[246] IRM 25.6.1.9.4.1(1). For example, taxpayers have attempted to alter returns by striking parts of the federal tax return as part of their submission. Modifications of the federal tax return can lead to a determination that the tax return is invalid, which results in the statute of limitations never beginning to run at all. For a full discussion of various circumstances where a taxpayer has altered the federal tax return that may lead to problems, see Chief Counsel Advice 200107035 (January 16, 2001) and Rev. Rul. 2005-18.

[247] Beard v. Commissioner, 82 T.C. 766, 777 (1984), aff'd per curiam, 793 F.2d 139 (6th Cir. 1986). IRM 25.6.1.9.4.1(1).

attorneys for the IRS to forward cases for Appeals Office consideration where the taxpayer has not yet had the opportunity settlement consideration after the case proceeds to U.S. Tax Court.

Notice of Deficiency, aka, the "90 Day Letter" - A notice of deficiency, also called a "statutory notice of deficiency," "SNOD" or "90 Day Letter," is a legal notice in which the Commissioner determines the taxpayer's tax deficiency. The notice of deficiency is a legal determination that is presumptively correct and consists of:

1. A letter explaining the purpose of the notice, the tax period(s) involved, the amount of the deficiency and the taxpayer's options,

2. An agreement form (waiver) to allow the taxpayer to agree to the additional tax liability,

3. A statement showing the computation of the deficiency and

4. An explanation of the adjustments.

The purpose of a notice of deficiency is: (1) To ensure the taxpayer is formally notified of the IRS's intention to assess a tax deficiency, and (2) To inform the taxpayer of the opportunity and right to petition the Tax Court to dispute the proposed adjustments.[248]

Tax Avoidance – tax minimization through legal techniques.

Tax Evasion – while also aimed at the elimination or reduction of tax, tax evasion connotes the use of subterfuge and/or fraud as a means to achieve the tax objective. Tax evasion constitutes a crime that may give rise to substantial monetary penalties, imprisonment, or both. Section 7201 provides, "Any person who willfully attempts in any manner to evade or defeat any tax imposed by this title or the payment thereof shall, in addition to other penalties provided by law, be guilty of a felony and, upon conviction thereof, shall be fined not more than $100,000 ($500,000 in the case of a corporation), or imprisoned not more than 5 years, or both, together with the costs of prosecution."

2. IRS Audit/Examination Process

Pursuant to section 7601, the IRS is authorized to conduct examinations. Certain limits are imposed, such as the requirement that the time and place of the examination be reasonable under the circumstances and that the taxpayer not be subject to unnecessary examinations or multiple examinations for each taxable year. IRC § 7605(a) and (b). Otherwise, IRS examinations may seek any information that "may be relevant or material."[249]

There are three distinct types of IRS audits:

- *Correspondence audit* – contact with the IRS by written correspondence only.
- *Office audit* – taxpayer meets the IRS at a government office

---

[249] Code § 7602(a).

- *Field audit* – the IRS travels to the taxpayer's location. Travel outside of the IRS office occurs, generally, because it is more convenient to conduct the audit at the taxpayer's site, e.g., the bulk of voluminous document are located off-site.

During the course of an audit, the IRS will first seek tax return information through an informal process.

- Informal Information Gathering Process

The IRS obtains information through the issuance of information document requests ("IDRs") on Form 4564. IDRs must be issue-focused, rather than requests for general information. The issue must be stated in the IDR, and only information relevant to that issue may be requested. Typically, each issue is addressed with a separate IDR. A response date to the IDR will be set, with taxpayer input, as well as a deadline for review by the examiner. If the taxpayer fails to respond or provides an incomplete response, an examiner may grant an extension to a taxpayer for up to 15 business days before the Enforcement Process is triggered.

If the IRS is unsuccessful in gathering necessary information to understand tax issues related to a return subject to examination, then the government officials may proceed to formal information methods.

- Formal Information Gathering Process

What happens if a taxpayer fails to timely respond to an IDR? A delinquency notice (Letter 5077) will be issued. Then, a pre-summons letter (Letter 5078) will be issued if the taxpayer does not provide a complete response to the IDR by the date indicated in the delinquency notice. An administrative summons will be issued if the taxpayer continues to fail to provide a complete response to the IDR by the pre-summons letter response date. The examiner can use a summons to compel testimony and/or the production of relevant books, papers, records, or other data. The information, however, must already be in existence. A summons may not require the creation of documents. Original documents, not just copies, may be summoned. Also, a summons may request more than written materials. Examiners may summon computer tapes, video cassettes, handwriting exemplars, and any other type of information.[250] Where the information is stored on tapes or in a computer format, it may be necessary to summon information about the tape or computer system sufficient to access the information.

IRC § 7602(a) authorizes the Service to use its summons power for the following purposes: (1) to determine if a return is correct; (2) to make a return where there is none; (3) to determine tax liability; (4) to collect taxes; and (5) to inquire into any offense connected with the administration or enforcement of the internal revenue laws. Thus, an examiner can summon any person with information helpful to a tax investigation and direct that person to testify or produce written evidence.[251]

---

[250] See United States v. Campbell, 524 F.2d 604 (8th Cir. 1975).
[251] United States v. Powell, 379 U.S. 48 (1964).

IRC § 7602 permits a summons to be issued to: (1) a person liable for tax, (2) an officer or employee of such person, (3) a person with possession, custody, or care of the business books of a person liable for tax, or (4) any other person that the examiner deems necessary. Below, is a publicly available example of an IRS administrative summons filed in U.S. District Court.[252]

---

[252] This document was available on the internet because it was filed with the U.S. District Court. However, the author redacted (removed) some additional tax information contained in this publicly available document.

Summons

In the matter of   Tax Liability of John Does*

Internal Revenue Service (Division):   Large Business & International Division

Industry/Area (name or number):   Withholding & International Individual Compliance, Offshore Compliance Initiatives

Periods: Years ending _____ through _____

The Commissioner of Internal Revenue

To: _____

At: Attn: CEO, _____, San Franscisco, CA 94563

You are hereby summoned and required to appear before _____ Senior Revenue Agent or Designee

an officer of the Internal Revenue Service, to give testimony and to bring with you and to produce for examination the following books, records, papers, and other data relating to the tax liability or the collection of the tax liability or for the purpose of inquiring into any offense connected with the administration or enforcement of the internal revenue laws concerning the person identified above for the periods shown.

See attachment

Attestation

I hereby certify that I have examined and compared this copy of the summons with the original and that it is a true and correct copy of the original.

Signature   Program Manager-OCI

Signature of IRS officer serving the summons   Title

Business address and telephone number of IRS officer before whom you are to appear:

1818 East Southern Avenue, Mesa, AZ 85204 / 626-927-1237

Place and time for appearance at Internal Revenue Service, 450 Golden Gate Avenue, San Francisco CA 94102

IRS

Department of the Treasury
Internal Revenue Service

www.irs.gov

Form 2039 (Rev. 10-2010)
Catalog Number 21405J

on the _____ 9th _____ day of _____ January _____ 2017 _____ at _____ 09:00 _____ o'clock _____ a. _____ m.

Issued under authority of the Internal Revenue Code this 6th day of December , 2016

Signature
Signature of issuing officer   Senior Revenue Agent
                                                      Title

Signature
Signature of approving officer (if applicable)   Program Manager-OCI
                                                      Title

Part A - to be given to person summoned

If the taxpayer does not respond to the summons, the IRS can proceed to court to judicially enforce the summons. Code § 7402(b). To justify enforcement of the summons, the IRS need only present a prima facie showing that the summons is valid, usually by affidavit.[253] The taxpayer may contest the government's summons in the enforcement proceeding. In order to get a hearing on the issue, the taxpayer must present some credible evidence to support a claim of improper motive for issuing the summons must be presented, rather than bare allegations.

The Service has broad "information-gathering" powers.[254] Its powers are analogous to those of a Grand Jury, which can "investigate merely on suspicion that the law is being violated, or even just because it wants assurance that it is not."[255] Courts are reluctant to restrict these powers. For example, the Supreme Court held in United States v. Arthur Young & Co., 465 U.S. 805, 816 (1984), that except for traditional privileges and limitations, "other restrictions upon the [Service's] summons power should be avoided absent unambiguous directions from Congress."

Although expansive, the Service's summons power is not limitless. To get its summons enforced, the Service must show the court: (1) the investigation has a legitimate purpose; (2) the examiner only seeks information that may be relevant to that purpose; (3) the information is not in the Service's possession; and (4) all required administrative steps have been followed.[256] The Service must also show that the case has not been referred to the Department of Justice.[257] The Service's burden to prove these matters is "slight." An affidavit from the examiner attesting to these facts is sufficient.[258]

After the Service has established these prerequisites to enforcement, the taxpayer can "challenge the summons on any appropriate grounds."[259] To quash the summons, the taxpayer must show: (1) there has already been an examination of his books and records; (2) the tax years under investigation have been closed by the statute of limitations; (3) enforcing the summons will violate the taxpayer's constitutional rights or common law privileges; or (4) the summons has been issued for an improper purpose. An "improper purpose" includes harassing the taxpayer, pressuring the taxpayer to settle a collateral dispute, or any other purpose reflecting negatively on the good faith of the particular investigation. Id.

The tax investigation must have a legitimate purpose. IRC § 7602 authorizes the issuance of a summons for five purposes only: (1) to determine if a return is correct; (2) to make a return where there is none; (3) to determine tax liability; (4) to collect taxes; and (5) to inquire into any offense connected with the administration or enforcement of

---

[253] See United States v. Powell, 379 U.S. 48, 57-58 (1964).

[254] Holifield v. United States, 909 F.2d 201, 205 (7th Cir. 1990).

[255] United States v. Powell, 379 U.S. 48, 57 (1964).

[256] Powell, 379 U.S. at 57-58.

[257] Zoe Christian Leadership, Inc. v. United States, 89-1 USTC (CCH) ¶ 9236 (C.D. Cal. 1988).

[258] United States v. Samuels, Kramer and Co., 712 F.2d 1342, 1345 (9th Cir. 1983).

[259] Powell, 379 U.S. at 58.

the internal revenue laws. The Service may not issue a summons for any other purpose unless specifically authorized by Congress.

Pursuant to IRC § 7602(a), an examiner may summon any information that *may be relevant* to the legitimate purpose of the investigation. The information does not have to be relevant in any "technical, evidentiary sense," rather it is "relevant" if it "might throw light upon the correctness of the return."[260] Congress bestowed upon the Service broad investigatory powers because it realized that the examiner cannot be certain that the documents requested are relevant until he or she sees them.[261] The examiner, however, must have "a realistic expectation rather than an idle hope that something may be discovered" in the summoned information.[262]

IRC § 7604(a) and (b) grant primary jurisdiction over Service summons enforcement to the United States district courts. The Service must seek enforcement in the court for the district in which the summonee resides or is found. If the court determines that the summons should be enforced, it will order the summonee to comply with the summons. The court has inherent power to hold the summonee in contempt for refusing to obey its order.[263] The Service can bring an action against the summonee under either IRC § 7604(a) or (b). Enforcement under IRC § 7604(a) is appropriate where the summonee appears in response to the summons, and refuses, in good faith and on appropriate grounds, to testify or surrender documents.[264] Enforcement under IRC § 7604(b) constitutes a criminal contempt action. It authorizes the government to request the prehearing sanctions of attachment and arrest.[265] The Service rarely, if ever, brings an action under IRC § 7604(b). A summons enforcement proceeding is a limited hearing. The sole reason for such a proceeding is to ensure that the Service has issued the summons for proper investigatory purposes and not for some illegitimate purpose.[266] To obtain enforcement of its summons, the Service must show the court that it met the requirements of Powell and IRC § 7602(c).

After the IRS files a petition[267] with the U.S. District Court to enforce its administrative summons, the Court may issue an "Order Directing Service and Establishing a Response Deadline" to the summonee to explain to the court why the IRS' summons should not be enforced. If the summonee fails to convince the court why the IRS summons should not be enforced (see Powell requirements, above), then the Court will issue an Order of Enforcement of Summons. See below for an example of such a Court enforcement Order. Note that if the summonee fails to comply with the U.S. District

---

[260] United States v. Harrington, 388 F.2d 520, 524 (2d Cir. 1968).

[261] Arthur Young, 465 U.S. at 814.

[262] Id. at 813 n.11.

[263] United States v. Asay, 614 F.2d 655, 659 (9th Cir. 1980).

[264] See United States v. Powell, 379 U.S. 48, 52 (1964).

[265] Id.

[266] United States v. Kis, 658 F.2d 526, 535 (7th Cir. 1981).

[267] An example of a filed petition to enforce an IRS administrative summons is publicly available on the web at: https://assets.documentcloud.org/documents/2942985/01-Main.pdf. Once documents are filed with a federal court, all such documents become a matter of public record unless one of the parties files a request for protective order to seal the record and such request is granted by the court.

Court's Order of Enforcement, then the summonee may be subject to monetary penalty, incarceration, or both.

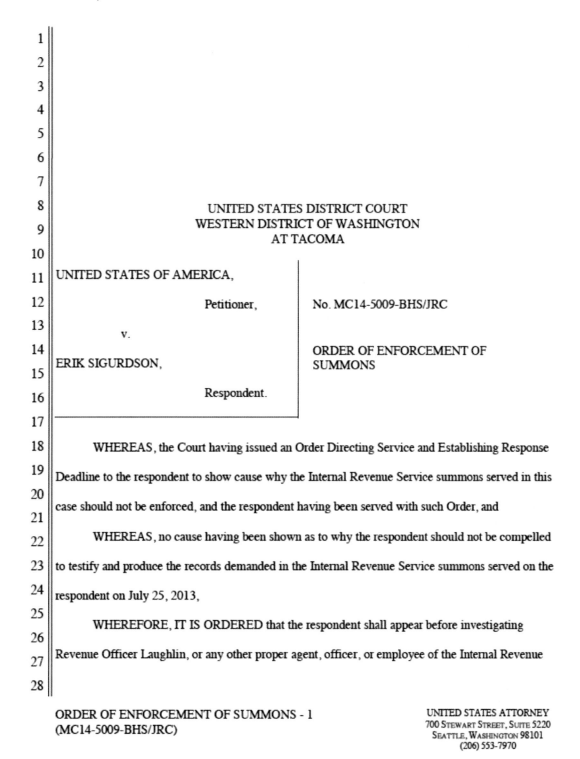

UNITED STATES DISTRICT COURT
WESTERN DISTRICT OF WASHINGTON
AT TACOMA

UNITED STATES OF AMERICA,

               Petitioner,

     v.

ERIK SIGURDSON,

               Respondent.

No. MC14-5009-BHS/JRC

ORDER OF ENFORCEMENT OF SUMMONS

      WHEREAS, the Court having issued an Order Directing Service and Establishing Response Deadline to the respondent to show cause why the Internal Revenue Service summons served in this case should not be enforced, and the respondent having been served with such Order, and

      WHEREAS, no cause having been shown as to why the respondent should not be compelled to testify and produce the records demanded in the Internal Revenue Service summons served on the respondent on July 25, 2013,

      WHEREFORE, IT IS ORDERED that the respondent shall appear before investigating Revenue Officer Laughlin, or any other proper agent, officer, or employee of the Internal Revenue

ORDER OF ENFORCEMENT OF SUMMONS - 1
(MC14-5009-BHS/JRC)

UNITED STATES ATTORNEY
700 STEWART STREET, SUITE 5220
SEATTLE, WASHINGTON 98101
(206) 553-7970

1 Service, not later than twenty (20) workdays following the entry of this Order to testify and produce

2 records as demanded in such summons.

3
4   IT IS FURTHER ORDERED that if the respondent fails to comply with this Order, the

5 respondent can be held in contempt of Court and be subject to imprisonment, fine or both.

6   IT IS FURTHER ORDERED that the Clerk of the Court shall send a copy of this ORDER by

7 certified mail and first-class mail to the respondent, Erik Sigurdson, 3125 NW 20th Cir., Camas,

8 Washington 98607, to the United States Attorney, and to the United States Magistrate Judge to

9 whom this matter is assigned.

10
11   DATED this 24th day of July, 2014.

12

13   _____

14   J. Richard Creatura
   United States Magistrate Judge

15 Presented by:

16

17 /s/ Christina Fogg
   _____
18 Christina Fogg, WSBA #40159
   Assistant United States Attorney
19

20

21

22

23

24

25

26

27

28

ORDER OF ENFORCEMENT OF SUMMONS - 2
(MC14-5009-BHS/JRC)

UNITED STATES ATTORNEY
700 STEWART STREET, SUITE 5220
SEATTLE, WASHINGTON 98101
(206) 553-7970

The IRS can seek to obtain information from "third parties" as well as from the taxpayer being audited. A third-party summons is a summons served on anyone who is not the person or entity under investigation.[268] The following examples illustrate third-party summonses: (1) An examiner, investigating the extent of a taxpayer's income, summons the taxpayer's attorney and requires him to surrender all information about his financial arrangement with the taxpayer; (2) the taxpayer's accountant receives a summons directing him to surrender the taxpayer's financial records in his possession; (3) a financial institution receives a summons directing it to surrender records relating to the taxpayer; and (4) the Service serves a summons on a former officer of an exempt organization ordering him to provide information about his previous employer.

The special procedures contained in IRC § 7609(a) and (b) apply anytime an examiner issues a third-party summons to a third-party recordkeeper. These procedures require the examiner to notify the taxpayers that a third-party recordkeeper summons has been issued and inform them of their right to intervene in any court proceeding brought to enforce the summons. These procedures apply only when the summonee is a third-party recordkeeper. A third-party recordkeeper is specifically defined in IRC § 7609(a)(3) as: (1) any bank, savings institution, or credit union; (2) any consumer reporting agency; (3) a broker; (4) an attorney; (5) an accountant; (6) any barter exchange; and (7) any regulated investment company and its agents. Also included in this group are recordkeepers that extend credit by credit cards or similar devices, such as telephone companies and gambling casinos that extend credit or cashing privileges through credit cards.[269]

A third-party recordkeeper, because it is not the target of the tax investigation, generally does not have a sufficient interest in the summoned records to protect them from governmental intrusion. The third-party recordkeeper may voluntarily surrender the records, whether or not they are relevant to the investigation. Congress did not want the examiner going on a fishing expedition where the summonee is compliant. Thus, Congress established the special notice procedures of IRC § 7609 to prevent the examiner from trampling on the taxpayer's legitimate privacy rights. I

IRM 4022.12(1), which implements IRC §7609, requires that a case manager, group manager, or higher supervisory official pre-authorize the issuance of either a third-party or a third-party recordkeeper summons. The authorizing official should indicate the pre-authorization by signing the face of the original and all copies of the summons. If the examiner receives oral authorization or the authorizing official cannot sign the summons, the examiner should write on the face of the original and all copies of the summons that authorization was received to issue it. This notation should include the title of the authorizing official and the date the authorization was received. Another way of noting this would be for the authorizing official to confirm in a separate document that he or she pre-authorized the summons. This can be done after the summons is issued.

---

[268] Tiffany Fine Arts, Inc. v. United States, 469 U.S. 310, 315-16 (1985).
[269] See United States v. New York Telephone Co., 644 F.2d 953 (2d Cir. 1981).

Pursuant to IRC §7609(a), the examiner must notify the taxpayer within three days of issuing a third-party recordkeeper summons, that a summons was issued. The notice must: (1) be in writing; (2) include an attested copy of the summons; and (3) inform the taxpayer of his or her statutory right to intervene in any court proceeding brought to enforce the summons. The examiner should ensure that the notice is handed to the taxpayer or sent to his (or the fiduciary's) last known address by certified or registered mail. If neither the taxpayer nor the fiduciary has a last known address, the notice should be left with the third-party recordkeeper.

If the Service seeks court enforcement of the summons, it will file suit against the recordkeeper. IRC § 7609(b) gives the taxpayer the absolute right to intervene in any court proceeding brought by the Service to enforce a third-party recordkeeper summons. The taxpayer's right to intervene allows the taxpayer to come to court and protect his or her right to privacy.

It is not always necessary for the Service to go to court to obtain summoned information. The third-party recordkeeper may voluntarily surrender the summoned records to avoid the expense of litigation. In this situation, IRC §7609(b)(2) allows the taxpayer to initiate a court action to quash the summons. If the taxpayer is successful, enforcement is denied and the third-party recordkeeper does not surrender the records.

The taxpayer must file the petition to quash the summons with the court no later than twenty days after the examiner serves the taxpayer with notice of the summons. The taxpayer must then send, by registered or certified mail, a copy of the petition to the third-party recordkeeper and the Service. Although the government and the taxpayer are the principal participants in a proceeding to quash the summons, IRC §7609(b)(2)(C) gives the third-party recordkeeper the right to intervene in the proceeding to protect its interests.

Violate the rules, and penalties follow. In the picture, to the left, everyone knows what happens when you fail to follow posted parking rules. Likewise, the Internal Revenue Code imposes penalties upon taxpayers and tax return preparers for specific violations of tax rules. Let's begin with a discussion of penalties applicable to taxpayers.

3. Penalties Applicable to Taxpayers

The purpose of tax penalties is to "encourage voluntary compliance by supporting the standards of behavior expected by the Internal Revenue Code."[270] Thus, only behavior that falls below the relevant standards of care should be subject to penalty.

- Civil Tax Penalties

The number of civil penalties in the Code has grown from about 14 in 1954 to over 130 today.[271] As a consequence of "penalty creep," some penalties can be obscure. Let's cover some of the more common penalties within Title 26.

The failure to file penalty under section 6651(a)(1) is charged on returns filed after the due date or extended due date, absent a reasonable cause for filing late.
- The combined penalty is 5% (4.5% late filing and 0.5% late payment) for each month or part of a month that your return was late, up to 25%.
- The late filing penalty applies to the tax that remains unpaid after the due date. Unpaid tax is the total tax shown on your return reduced by amounts paid through withholding, estimated tax payments, and allowed refundable credits.
- If after five months you still haven't paid, the failure to file penalty will max out, but the failure to pay penalty continues until the tax is paid, up to 25%.
- The maximum total penalty for failure to file and pay is 47.5% (22.5% late filing and 25% late payment) of the tax.
- However, if your return was over 60 days late, the minimum failure to file penalty is the smaller of $205 or 100% of the tax required to be shown on the return.

The failure to pay penalty under section 6651(a)(2) is charged for failing to pay your tax by the due date.

- The late payment penalty is 0.5% of the tax owed after the due date, for each month or part of a month the tax remains unpaid, up to 25%.
- You won't have to pay the penalty if you can show reasonable cause for the failure to pay on time.
- 10 days after the IRS issues a final notice of intent to levy or seize property, the 0.5% rate increases to 1% per month.

The penalty rate is 0.25% for each month or part of a month in which an installment agreement is in effect. When you file your tax return late, you'll be charged interest on any unpaid balance. Interest accrues on the unpaid balance and compounds daily from the due date of the return (without regard to any extension of time to file) until you pay the balance in full.

---

[271] 2008 Annual Report to Congress by the Taxpayer Advocate Service.

For both the failure to file and failure to pay penalties, a taxpayer may qualify for relief from imposition of the penalty if "reasonable cause" is established. But what constitutes "reasonable cause?"

Reasonable cause is based on all the facts and circumstances in each taxpayer's situation. The IRS will consider any reason which establishes that a taxpayer used all ordinary business care and prudence to meet their Federal tax obligations but were nevertheless unable to do so. The IRS will consider any sound reason for failing to file a tax return, make a deposit, or pay tax when due. Sound reasons, if established, include:

- Fire, casualty, natural disaster or other disturbances
- Inability to obtain records
- Death, serious illness, incapacitation or unavoidable absence of the taxpayer or a member of the taxpayer's immediate family
- Other reason which establishes that a taxpayer used all ordinary business care and prudence to meet their Federal tax obligations but were nevertheless unable to do so

A lack of funds, in and of itself, is not reasonable cause for failure to file or pay on time. However, the reasons for the lack of funds may meet reasonable cause criteria for the failure-to-pay penalty.

What are facts that can serve to establish reasonable cause?

- What happened and when did it happen?
- What facts and circumstances prevented the taxpayer from filing their return or paying their tax during the period of time he/she did not file and/or pay their taxes timely?
- How did the facts and circumstances affect the taxpayer's ability to file and/or pay their taxes or perform their other day-to-day responsibilities?
- Once the facts and circumstances changed, what actions did the taxpayer take to file and/or pay their taxes?
- In the case of a Corporation, Estate or Trust, did the affected person or a member of that individual's immediate family have sole authority to execute the return or make the deposit or payment?

What documents may be useful in establishing "reasonable cause" relief applies? Most reasonable cause explanations require that taxpayers provide documentation to support their claim, such as:

- Hospital or court records or a letter from a physician to establish illness or incapacitation, with specific start and end dates.
- Documentation of natural disasters or other events that prevented compliance.

Is relief from charges for interest on the amount of tax and/or penalties available? Interest cannot be abated for reasonable cause. Interest charged on a penalty will be reduced or removed when that penalty is reduced or removed. If an unpaid balance remains on your account, interest will continue to accrue until the account is full paid. Interest will start on April 15, if a taxpayer's return shows tax is owed. An extension of time to file is NOT an extension of time to pay. If April 15 is on a weekend or holiday, a tax return will be considered timely filed and paid, as long as the taxpayer files and pays by the next business day.

The accuracy-related penalty under section 6662(a) imposes an addition to tax of 20% of the portion of the "underpayment to which [Sec. 6662] applies," which is any underpayment attributable to certain conditions or taxpayer conduct identified in Sec. 6662 itself. Thus, for the section 6662 penalty to apply, a taxpayer must have an underpayment of tax, and the underpayment must be attributable to one of the specific conditions or behaviors identified in section 6662, including:

- Negligence or disregard of rules or regulations;
- Any substantial understatement of income tax;
- Any substantial valuation misstatement under chapter 1 dealing with normal taxes and surtaxes);
- Any substantial overstatement of pension liabilities; and
- Any substantial estate or gift tax valuation understatement.

The amount that is subject to penalty is reduced if the taxpayer has substantial authority for the position that was taken on the return or makes full and adequate disclosure of the position taken where there is a reasonable basis for the position as reported on Form 8275 or 8275-R. See both Forms 8275 and 8275-R, below.

Form 8275

(Rev. August 2013)

Department of the Treasury
Internal Revenue Service

Disclosure Statement

Do not use this form to disclose items or positions that are contrary to Treasury regulations. Instead, use Form 8275-R, Regulation Disclosure Statement.

▶ Information about Form 8275 and its separate instructions is at *www.irs.gov/form8275*.

▶ Attach to your tax return.

OMB No. 1545-0889

Attachment
Sequence No. **92**

Name(s) shown on return	Identifying number shown on return

If Form 8275 relates to an information return for a foreign entity (for example, Form 5471), enter:

Name of foreign entity ▶

Employer identification number, if any ▶

Reference ID number (see instructions) ▶

Part I   **General Information** (see instructions)

	(a) Rev. Rul., Rev. Proc., etc.	(b) Item or Group of Items	(c) Detailed Description of Items	(d) Form or Schedule	(e) Line No.	(f) Amount
1						
2						
3						
4						
5						
6						

Part II   **Detailed Explanation** (see instructions)

1

2

3

4

5

6

Part III   **Information About Pass-Through Entity.** To be completed by partners, shareholders, beneficiaries, or residual interest holders.

Complete this part only if you are making adequate disclosure for a pass-through item.

Note: *A pass-through entity is a partnership, S corporation, estate, trust, regulated investment company (RIC), real estate investment trust (REIT), or real estate mortgage investment conduit (REMIC).*

1 Name, address, and ZIP code of pass-through entity	2 Identifying number of pass-through entity
	3 Tax year of pass-through entity / / to / /
	4 Internal Revenue Service Center where the pass-through entity filed its return

For Paperwork Reduction Act Notice, see separate instructions.   Cat. No. 61935M   Form **8275** (Rev. 8-2013)

Form **8275-R**

(Rev. August 2013)

Department of the Treasury
Internal Revenue Service

Regulation Disclosure Statement

Use this form only to disclose items or positions that are contrary to Treasury regulations. For other disclosures, use Form 8275, Disclosure Statement.

▶ Information about Form 8275-R and its separate instructions is at *www.irs.gov/form8275.*

▶ **Attach to your tax return.**

OMB No. 1545-0889

Attachment
Sequence No. **92A**

Name(s) shown on return

Identifying number shown on return

If Form 8275-R relates to an information return for a foreign entity (for example, Form 5471), enter:

Name of foreign entity ▶

Employer identification number, if any ▶

Reference ID number (see instructions) ▶

Part I   General Information (see instructions)

	(a) Regulation Section	(b) Item or Group of Items	(c) Detailed Description of Items	(d) Form or Schedule	(e) Line No.	(f) Amount
1						
2						
3						
4						
5						
6						

Part II   Detailed Explanation (see instructions)

1

2

3

4

5

6

Part III   **Information About Pass-Through Entity.** To be completed by partners, shareholders, beneficiaries, or residual interest holders.

Complete this part only if you are making adequate disclosure for a pass-through item.

Note: *A pass-through entity is a partnership, S corporation, estate, trust, regulated investment company (RIC), real estate investment trust (REIT), or real estate mortgage investment conduit (REMIC).*

1 Name, address, and ZIP code of pass-through entity	2 Identifying number of pass-through entity
	3 Tax year of pass-through entity / / to / /
	4 Internal Revenue Service Center where the pass-through entity filed its return

For Paperwork Reduction Act Notice, see separate instructions.   Cat. No. 14594X   Form **8275-R** (Rev. 8-2013)

341

The civil fraud penalty is applicable under section 6663. The civil fraud penalty will be asserted when there is clear and convincing evidence to prove that some part of the underpayment of tax was due to fraud. Such evidence must show the taxpayer's intent to evade the assessment of tax, which the taxpayer believed to be owing. Intent is distinguished from inadvertence, reliance on incorrect technical advice, sincerely-held difference of opinion, negligence or carelessness. In the case of a joint return, intent must be established separately for each spouse as required by IRC 6663(c) . The fraud of one spouse cannot be used to impute fraud by the other spouse. Thus, the civil fraud penalty may be asserted only on one spouse, unless there is sufficient evidence that both spouses participated in the fraudulent act(s) resulting in the underpayment reported in their joint return.

Since direct proof of fraudulent intent is rarely available, fraud must be proven by circumstantial evidence and reasonable inferences. Fraud generally involves one or more of the following elements:

- Deception

- Misrepresentation of material facts

- False or altered documents

- Evasion (i.e., diversion or omission)

The courts focus on key badges of fraud in determining whether there was an "intent to evade" tax. A determination of fraud is based on the taxpayer's entire course of conduct, with each badge of fraud given the weight appropriate to a particular case. An evaluation of fraud is based on the weight of the evidence rather than the quantity of the factors. Some of the common "first indicators (or badges) of fraud" include:

- Understatement of income (e.g., omissions of specific items or entire sources of income, failure to report substantial amounts of income received)

- Fictitious or improper deductions (e.g., overstatement of deductions, personal items deducted as business expenses)

- Accounting irregularities (e.g., two sets of books, false entries on documents)

- Obstructive actions of the taxpayer (e.g., false statements, destruction of records, transfer of assets, failure to cooperate with the examiner, concealment of assets)

- A consistent pattern over several years of underreporting taxable income

- Implausible or inconsistent explanations of behavior

- Engaging in illegal activities (e.g., drug dealing), or attempting to conceal illegal activities

- Inadequate records

- Dealing in cash

- Failure to file returns, and

- Education and experience

The penalty for underpayment of estimated tax is provided under section 6654. The United States income tax system is a pay-as-you-go tax system, which means that you must pay income tax as you earn or receive your income during the year. You can do this either through withholding or by making estimated tax payments. If you don't pay your tax or you pay an insufficient amount of tax through withholding, you might also have to pay estimated taxes. If you didn't pay enough tax throughout the year, either through withholding or by making estimated tax payments, you may have to pay a penalty for underpayment of estimated tax. Generally, most taxpayers will avoid this penalty if they either owe less than $1,000 in tax after subtracting their withholding and estimated tax payments, or if they paid at least 90% of the tax for the current year or 100% of the tax shown on the return for the prior year, whichever is smaller. Generally, taxpayers should make estimated tax payments in four equal amounts to avoid a penalty. However, if a taxpayer receives income unevenly during the year, he/she may be able to vary the amounts of the payments to avoid or lower the penalty by using the annualized installment method.

Tax law allows the IRS to waive the penalty if:

1. The taxpayer didn't make a required payment because of a casualty event, disaster, or other unusual circumstance and it would be inequitable to impose the penalty, or
2. The taxpayer retired (after reaching age 62) or became disabled during the tax year or in the preceding tax year for which the taxpayer should have made estimated payments, and the underpayment was due to reasonable cause and not willful neglect.

The failure to deposit penalty ("FTD") is provided under code section 6656. Section 6656 provides for the FTD penalty if a taxpayer does not deposit tax in the correct amount, within the prescribed time period, and/or in the required manner. So, who is required to make timely tax deposits or become subject to penalty? Generally, taxpayers who file Form 941, *Employer's Quarterly Federal Tax Return*, Form 943, *Employer's Annual Tax Return for Agricultural Employees*, Form 944, *Employer's ANNUAL Federal Tax Return*, Form 940, *Employer's Annual Federal Unemployment (FUTA) Tax Return*, Form 945, *Annual Return of Withheld Federal Income Tax*, Form 720, *Quarterly Federal Excise Tax Return*, Form 1042, *Annual Withholding Tax Return for U.S. Source Income of Foreign Persons*, and Form CT-1, *Employer's Annual Railroad Retirement Tax Return* must deposit taxes using an authorized deposit method when the tax liability reaches certain dollar amounts. See *IRM 20.1.4.6, De Minimis Exception to Deposit Requirements*, for additional information. However, Form 720 filers are only liable for deposits of certain excise taxes.

The civil penalty for providing false information with respect to withholding is provided under code section 6682. Where do we see the information that may trigger this penalty? Form W-4.

----------------------------- Separate here and give Form W-4 to your employer. Keep the top part for your records. -----------------------------

Form **W-4** Department of the Treasury Internal Revenue Service	**Employee's Withholding Allowance Certificate** ▶ Whether you are entitled to claim a certain number of allowances or exemption from withholding is subject to review by the IRS. Your employer may be required to send a copy of this form to the IRS.	OMB No. 1545-0074 **2017**

1 Your first name and middle initial	Last name		2 Your social security number

Home address (number and street or rural route)	3 ☐ Single ☐ Married ☐ Married, but withhold at higher Single rate. **Note:** If married, but legally separated, or spouse is a nonresident alien, check the "Single" box.
City or town, state, and ZIP code	4 If your last name differs from that shown on your social security card, check here. You must call 1-800-772-1213 for a replacement card. ▶ ☐

5	Total number of allowances you are claiming (from line H above **or** from the applicable worksheet on page 2)	5	
6	Additional amount, if any, you want withheld from each paycheck	6	$
7	I claim exemption from withholding for 2017, and I certify that I meet **both** of the following conditions for exemption.		

• Last year I had a right to a refund of **all** federal income tax withheld because I had **no** tax liability, **and**
• This year I expect a refund of **all** federal income tax withheld because I expect to have **no** tax liability.
If you meet both conditions, write "Exempt" here . . . . ▶ | 7 |

Under penalties of perjury, I declare that I have examined this certificate and, to the best of my knowledge and belief, it is true, correct, and complete.

Employee's signature
(This form is not valid unless you sign it.) ▶   Date ▶

8 Employer's name and address (Employer: Complete lines 8 and 10 only if sending to the IRS.)	9 Office code (optional)	10 Employer identification number (EIN)

For Privacy Act and Paperwork Reduction Act Notice, see page 2.   Cat. No. 10220Q   Form **W-4** (2017)

All employees are required to give their employer a completed Form W-4 (Employee's Withholding Allowance Certificate). This form notifies the employer of the number of withholding exemptions that the employee is entitled to claim. Based on the employee's submitted Form W-4 information, the employer then calculates the amount of tax that must be withheld from each of the employees. A civil penalty in the amount of $500 applies on any person who gives the employer false information with respect to the withholding status or the number of exemptions to which he/she is entitled.

The penalty for filing a frivolous tax return under section 6702 is $5,000. The penalty is applied to anyone who submits a tax return or other specified submission, if any portion of the submission is based on a position the IRS identifies as frivolous. Section 6702(c) requires the IRS to periodically publish a list of frivolous tax return positions. In IRS Notice 2010-33, the IRS published the following list of positions that qualify as "frivolous" if they are the same or similar to facts set forth:

(1) Compliance with the internal revenue laws is voluntary or optional and not required by law, including arguments that:

(a) Filing a Federal tax or information return or paying tax is purely voluntary under the law, or similar arguments described as frivolous in Rev. Rul. 2007-20, 2007-1 C.B. 863.

(b) Nothing in the Internal Revenue Code imposes a requirement to file a return or pay tax, or that a person is not required to file a tax return or pay a tax unless the Internal Revenue Service responds to the person's questions, correspondence, or a request to identify a provision in the Code requiring the filing of a return or the payment of tax.

(c) There is no legal requirement to file a Federal income tax return because the instructions to Forms 1040, 1040A, or 1040EZ or the Treasury regulations associated with the filing of the forms do not display an OMB control number as required by the Paperwork Reduction Act of 1980, 44 U.S.C. § 3501 *et seq.*, or similar arguments described as frivolous in Rev. Rul. 2006-21, 2006-1 C.B. 745.

(d) Because filing a tax return is not required by law, the Service must prepare a return for a taxpayer who does not file one in order to assess and collect tax.

(e) A taxpayer has an option under the law to file a document or set of documents in lieu of a return or elect to file a tax return reporting zero taxable income and zero tax liability even if the taxpayer received taxable income during the taxable period for which the return is filed, or similar arguments described as frivolous in Rev. Rul. 2004-34, 2004-1 C.B. 619.

(f) An employer is not legally obligated to withhold income or employment taxes on employees' wages.

(g) Only persons who have contracted with the government by applying for a governmental privilege or benefit, such as holding a Social Security number, are subject to tax, and those who have contracted with the government may choose to revoke the contract at will.

(h) A taxpayer may lawfully decline to pay taxes if the taxpayer disagrees with the government's use of tax revenues, or similar arguments described as frivolous in Rev. Rul. 2005-20, 2005-1 C.B. 821.

(i) An administrative summons issued by the Service is *per se* invalid and compliance with a summons is not legally required.

(2) The Internal Revenue Code is not law (or "positive law") or its provisions are ineffective or inoperative, including the sections imposing an income tax or requiring the filing of tax returns, because the provisions have not been implemented by regulations even though the provisions in question either (a) do not expressly require the Secretary to issue implementing regulations to become effective or (b) expressly require implementing regulations which have been issued.

(3) A taxpayer's income is excluded from taxation when the taxpayer rejects or renounces United States citizenship because the taxpayer is a citizen exclusively of a State (sometimes characterized as a "natural-born citizen" of a "sovereign state"), that is claimed to be a separate country or otherwise not subject to the laws of the United States. This position includes the argument that the United States does not include all or a part of the physical territory of the 50 States and instead consists of only places such as the District of Columbia, Commonwealths and Territories (*e.g.*, Puerto Rico), and Federal enclaves (*e.g.*, Native American reservations and military installations), or similar arguments described as frivolous in Rev. Rul. 2004-28, 2004-1 C.B. 624, or Rev. Rul. 2007-22, 2007-1 C.B. 866.

(4) Wages, tips, and other compensation received for the performance of personal services are not taxable income or are offset by an equivalent deduction for the personal services rendered, including an argument that a taxpayer has a "claim of right" to exclude the cost or value of the taxpayer's labor from income or that taxpayers have

a basis in their labor equal to the fair market value of the wages they receive, or similar arguments described as frivolous in Rev. Rul. 2004-29, 2004-1 C.B. 627, or Rev. Rul. 2007-19, 2007-1 C.B. 843.

(5) United States citizens and residents are not subject to tax on their wages or other income derived from sources within the United States, as only foreign-based income or income received by nonresident aliens and foreign corporations from sources within the United States is taxable, and similar arguments described as frivolous in Rev. Rul. 2004-30, 2004-1 C.B. 622.

(6) A taxpayer has been untaxed, detaxed, or removed or redeemed from the Federal tax system though the taxpayer remains a United States citizen or resident, or similar arguments described as frivolous in Rev. Rul. 2004-31, 2004-1 C.B. 617.

(7) Only certain types of taxpayers are subject to income and employment taxes, such as employees of the Federal government, corporations, nonresident aliens, or residents of the District of Columbia or the Federal territories, or similar arguments described as frivolous in Rev. Rul. 2006-18, 2006-1 C.B. 743.

(8) Only certain types of income are taxable, for example, income that results from the sale of alcohol, tobacco, or firearms or from transactions or activities that take place in interstate commerce.

(9) Federal income taxes are unconstitutional or a taxpayer has a constitutional right not to comply with the Federal tax laws for one of the following reasons:

(a) The First Amendment permits a taxpayer to refuse to pay taxes based on religious or moral beliefs.

(b) A taxpayer may withhold payment of taxes or the filing of a tax return until the Service or other government entity responds to a First Amendment petition for redress of grievances.

(c) Mandatory compliance with, or enforcement of, the tax laws invades a taxpayer's right to privacy under the Fourth Amendment.

(d) The requirement to file a tax return is an unreasonable search and seizure contrary to the Fourth Amendment.

(e) Income taxation, tax withholding, or the assessment or collection of tax is a "taking" of property without due process of law or just compensation in violation of the Fifth Amendment.

(f) The Fifth Amendment privilege against self-incrimination grants taxpayers the right not to file returns or the right to withhold all financial information from the Service.

(g) The Ninth Amendment exempts those with religious or other objections to military spending from paying taxes to the extent the taxes will be used for military spending.

(h) Mandatory or compelled compliance with the internal revenue laws is a form of involuntary servitude prohibited by the Thirteenth Amendment.

(i) Individuals may not be taxed unless they are "citizens" within the meaning of the Fourteenth Amendment.

(j) The Sixteenth Amendment was not ratified, has no effect, contradicts the Constitution as originally ratified, lacks an enabling clause, or does not authorize a non-apportioned, direct income tax.

(k) Taxation of income attributed to a trust, which is a form of contract, violates the constitutional prohibition against impairment of contracts.

(l) Similar constitutional arguments described as frivolous in Rev. Rul. 2005-19, 2005-1 C.B. 819.

(10) A taxpayer is not a "person" within the meaning of section 7701(a)(14) or other provisions of the Internal Revenue Code, or similar arguments described as frivolous in Rev. Rul. 2007-22, 2007-1 C.B. 866.

(11) Only fiduciaries are taxpayers, or only persons with a fiduciary relationship to the United States are obligated to pay taxes, and the United States or the Service must prove the fiduciary status or relationship.

(12) Federal Reserve Notes are not taxable income when paid to a taxpayer because they are not gold or silver and may not be redeemed for gold or silver.

(13) In a transaction using gold and silver coins, the value of the coins is excluded from income or the amount realized in the transaction is the face value of the coins and not their fair market value for purposes of determining taxable income.

(14) A taxpayer who is employed on board a ship that provides meals at no cost to the taxpayer as part of the employment may claim a so-called "Mariner's Tax Deduction" (or the like) allowing the taxpayer to deduct from gross income the cost of the meals as an employee business expense.

(15) A taxpayer may purport to operate a home-based business as a basis to deduct as business expenses the taxpayer's personal expenses or the costs of maintaining the taxpayer's household when the maintenance items or amounts as reported do not correspond to a *bona fide* home business, such as when they are grossly excessive in relation to the conceivable costs for some portion of the home being used exclusively and regularly as a business, or similar arguments described as frivolous by Rev. Rul. 2004-32, 2004-1 C.B. 621.

(16) A "reparations" tax credit exists, including arguments that African-American taxpayers may claim a tax credit on their Federal income tax returns as reparations for slavery or other historical mistreatment, that Native Americans are entitled to an analogous credit (or are exempt from Federal income tax on the basis of a treaty), or similar arguments described as frivolous in Rev. Rul. 2004-33, 2004-1 C.B. 628, or Rev. Rul. 2006-20, 2006-1 C.B. 746.

(17) A Native American or other taxpayer who is not an employer engaged in a trade or business may nevertheless claim (for example, in an amount exceeding all reported income) the Indian Employment Credit under section 45A, which explicitly requires, among other criteria, that the taxpayer be an employer engaged in a trade or business to claim the credit.

(18) A taxpayer's wages are excluded from Social Security taxes if the taxpayer waives the right to receive Social Security benefits, or a taxpayer is entitled to a refund of, or may claim a charitable-contribution deduction for, the Social Security taxes that the taxpayer has paid, or similar arguments described as frivolous in Rev. Rul. 2005-17, 2005-1 C.B. 823.

(19) Taxpayers may reduce or eliminate their Federal tax liability by altering a tax return, including striking out the penalty-of-perjury declaration, or attaching documents to the return, such as a disclaimer of liability, or similar arguments described as frivolous in Rev. Rul. 2005-18, 2005-1 C.B. 817.

(20) A taxpayer is not obligated to pay income tax because the government has created an entity separate and distinct from the taxpayer—a "straw man"—that is distinguishable from the taxpayer by some variation of the taxpayer's name, and any tax obligations are exclusively those of the "straw man," or similar arguments described as frivolous in Rev. Rul. 2005-21, 2005-1 C.B. 822.

(21) A taxpayer may use a Form 1099-OID, *Original Issue Discount*, (or another Form 1099 Series information return) as a financial or other instrument to obtain or redeem (under a theory of "redemption" or "commercial redemption") a monetary payment out of the United States Treasury or for a refund of tax, such as by drawing on a "straw man" or similar financial account maintained by the government in the taxpayer's name (see paragraph (20), above); a taxpayer may file a Form 56, *Notice Concerning Fiduciary Relationship*, that names the Secretary of the Treasury or some other government employee as a fiduciary of the taxpayer and requires the Treasury Department to honor a Form 1099-OID as a financial or redemption instrument; or similar arguments described as frivolous in Rev. Rul. 2005-21, 2005-1 C.B. 822, and Rev. Rul. 2004-31, 2004-1 C.B. 617.

(22) A taxpayer may claim on an income tax return or purported return an amount of withheld income tax or other tax that is obviously false because it exceeds the taxpayer's income as reported on the return or is disproportionately high in comparison with the income reported on the return or information on supporting documents filed with the return (such as Form 1099 Series, Form W-2, or Form 2439, *Notice to Shareholder of Undistributed Long-Term Capital Gains*).

(23) Inserting the phrase "nunc pro tunc" on a return or other document filed with or submitted to the Service has a legal effect, such as reducing a taxpayer's tax liability, or similar arguments described as frivolous in Rev. Rul. 2006-17, 2006-1 C.B. 748.

(24) A taxpayer may avoid tax on income by attributing the income to a trust, including the argument that a taxpayer can put all of the taxpayer's assets into a trust to avoid income tax while still retaining substantial powers of ownership and control over those

assets or that a taxpayer may claim an expense deduction for the income attributed to a trust, or similar arguments described as frivolous in Rev. Rul. 2006-19, 2006-1 C.B. 749.

(25) A taxpayer may lawfully avoid income tax by sending income offshore, including depositing income into a foreign bank account.

(26) A taxpayer can claim the section 44 Disabled Access Credit to reduce tax or generate a refund, for example, by purportedly having purchased equipment or services for an inflated price (which may or may not have been actually paid), even though it is apparent that the taxpayer did not operate a small business that purchased the equipment or services to comply with the requirements of the Americans with Disabilities Act.

(27) A taxpayer may claim a refund of tax based on purported advance payments to employees of the Earned Income Tax Credit as reported by the taxpayer on a filed Form 941, *Employer's Quarterly Federal Tax Return*, or other employment tax return that reports an amount of purported wages, tips, or other compensation but leaves other line items on the return blank (or with a zero as the amount).

(28) A taxpayer may claim the section 6421 fuels tax credit (such as on Form 4136, *Credit for Federal Tax Paid on Fuels*; Form 8849, *Claim for Refund of Excise Taxes*; or Form 1040) even though the taxpayer did not buy the gasoline or the gasoline was not used for an off-highway business use during the period for which the credit is claimed. Also, if the taxpayer claims an amount of credit that is so disproportionately excessive to any (including zero) business income reported on the taxpayer's income tax return as to be patently unallowable (*e.g.* , a credit that is 150 percent of business income reported on Form 1040) or facially reflects an impossible quantity of gasoline given the business use, if any, as reported by the taxpayer.

(29) A taxpayer is allowed to buy or sell the right to claim a child as a qualifying child for purposes of the Earned Income Tax Credit.

(30) An IRS Form 23C, *Assessment Certificate — Summary Record of Assessments*, is an invalid record of assessment for purposes of section 6203 and Treas. Reg. § 301.6203-1, the Form 23C must be personally signed by the Secretary of the Treasury for an assessment to be valid, the Service must provide a copy of the Form 23C to a taxpayer if requested before taking collection action, or similar arguments described as frivolous in Rev. Rul. 2007-21, 2007-1 C.B. 865.

(31) A tax assessment is invalid because the assessment was made from a section 6020(b) substitute for return, which is not a valid return.

(32) A statutory notice of deficiency is invalid because the taxpayer to whom the notice was sent did not file an income tax return reporting the deficiency or because the statutory notice of deficiency was unsigned or not signed by the Secretary of the Treasury or by someone with delegated authority.

(33) A Notice of Federal Tax Lien is invalid because it is not signed by a particular official (such as by the Secretary of the Treasury), or because it was filed by someone without delegated authority.

(34) The form or content of a Notice of Federal Tax Lien is controlled by or subject to a state or local law, and a Notice of Federal Tax Lien that does not comply in form or content with a state or local law is invalid.

(35) A collection due process notice under section 6320 or 6330 is invalid if it is not signed by the Secretary of the Treasury or other particular official, or if no certificate of assessment is attached.

(36) Verification under section 6330 that the requirements of any applicable law or administrative procedure have been met may only be based on one or more particular forms or documents (which must be in a certain format), such as a summary record of assessment, or that the particular forms or documents or the ones on which verification was actually determined must be provided to a taxpayer at a collection due process hearing.

(37) A Notice and Demand is invalid because it was not signed, was not on the correct form (*e.g.*, a Form 17), or was not accompanied by a certificate of assessment when mailed.

(38) The United States Tax Court is an illegitimate court or does not, for any purported constitutional or other reason, have the authority to hear and decide matters within its jurisdiction.

(39) Federal courts may not enforce the internal revenue laws because their jurisdiction is limited to admiralty or maritime cases or issues.

(40) Revenue Officers are not authorized to issue levies or Notices of Federal Tax Lien or to seize property in satisfaction of unpaid taxes.

(41) A Service employee lacks the authority to carry out the employee's duties because the employee does not possess a certain type of identification or credential, for example, a pocket commission or a badge, or it is not in the correct form or on the right medium.

(42) A person may represent a taxpayer before the Service or in court proceedings even if the person does not have a power of attorney from the taxpayer, has not been enrolled to practice before the Service, or has not been admitted to practice before the court.

(43) A civil action to collect unpaid taxes or penalties must be personally authorized by the Secretary of the Treasury and the Attorney General.

(44) A taxpayer's income is not taxable if the taxpayer assigns or attributes the income to a religious organization (a "corporation sole" or ministerial trust) claimed to be tax-exempt under section 501(c)(3), or similar arguments described as frivolous in Rev. Rul. 2004-27, 2004-1 C.B. 625.

(45) The Service is not an agency of the United States government but rather a private-sector corporation or an agency of a State or Territory without authority to administer the internal revenue laws.

(46) Any position described as frivolous in any revenue ruling or other published guidance in existence when the return adopting the position is filed with or the specified submission adopting the position is submitted to the Service.

Returns or submissions that contain positions not listed above, which on their face have no basis for validity in existing law, or which have been deemed frivolous in a published opinion of the United States Tax Court or other court of competent jurisdiction, may be determined to reflect a desire to delay or impede the administration of Federal tax laws and thereby subject to the $5,000 penalty.

The Tax Relief Health Care Act of 2006 amended section 6702 to allow imposition of a $5,000 penalty for frivolous tax returns and for specified frivolous submissions other than returns, if the purported returns or specified submissions are either based upon a position identified as frivolous by the IRS in a published list or reflect a desire to delay or impede tax administration.[272] The term "specified submission" means: a request for a hearing under section 6320 (relating to notice and opportunity for hearing on filing of a notice of lien), a request for hearing under section 6330 (relating to notice and opportunity for hearing before levy), an application under section 6159 (relating to agreements for payment of tax liability in installments), an application under section 7122 (relating to compromises), or an application under section 7811 (relating to taxpayer assistance orders).

- Criminal Tax Penalties

Penalty for attempting to evade or defeat tax - Taxpayers who rely on frivolous arguments may be subject to criminal prosecution under section 7201. These taxpayers may be convicted of a felony for attempting to evade or defeat tax.[273] Section 7201 provides as a penalty a fine of up to $100,000 ($500,000 in the case of a corporation) and imprisonment for up to 5 years.

Section 7201 creates two offenses: (a) the willful attempt to evade or defeat the assessment of a tax, and (b) the willful attempt to evade or defeat the payment of a tax.[274]

[a] Evasion of assessment. The most common attempt to evade or defeat a tax is the affirmative act of filing a false return that omits income and/or claims deductions to which the taxpayer is not entitled. The tax reported on the return is falsely understated

---

[272] Pub. L. No. 109-432, § 407(a), 120 Stat. 2922 (2006).

[273] I.R.C. § 7201.

[274] Sansone v. United States, 380 U.S. 343, 354 (1965). See also United States v. Shoppert, 362 F.3d 451, 454 (8th Cir.), cert. denied, 543 U.S. 911 (2004); United States v. Mal, 942 F. 2d 682, 687-88 (9th Cir. 1991) (if a defendant transfers assets to prevent the I.R.S. from determining his true tax liability, he has attempted to evade assessment; if he does so after a tax liability has become due and owing, he has attempted to evade payment).

and creates a deficiency. Consequently, such willful under reporting constitutes an attempt to evade or defeat tax by evading the correct assessment of the tax.

[b] Evasion of payment. This offense generally occurs after the existence of a tax due and owing has been established (either by the taxpayer reporting the amount of tax or by the I.R.S. assessing the amount of tax deemed to be due and owing) and almost always involves an affirmative act of concealment of money or assets from which the tax could be paid. It is not essential that the I.R.S. have made a formal assessment of taxes owed and a demand for payment in order for tax evasion charges to be brought. Tax deficiency can arise by operation of law when there is a failure to file and the government later determines the tax liability.[275]

Note: These two offenses share the same basic elements necessary to prove a violation of I.R.C. § 7201.

Penalty for willfully making and signing a false return - Taxpayers may be convicted of a felony for willfully making and signing under penalties of perjury any return, statement, or other document that the person does not believe to be true and correct as to every material matter.[276] The penalty for violating section 7206 is a fine of up to $100,000 ($500,000 in the case of a corporation) and imprisonment for up to 3 years. Any individual found guilty of either offense may be subject to an increased fine of up to $250,000.[277] The United States Attorney's Office for the Northern District of California issued a press release in 2018, below, summarizing a recent conviction of an individual for violation of section 7206(2) for aiding and abetting the filing of a false tax return.[278]

---

[275] United States v. Daniel, 956 F.2d 540, 542 (6th Cir. 1992).
[276] I.R.C. § 7206(1).
[277] 18 U.S.C. § 3571(b)(3).
[278] https://www.justice.gov/usao-ndca/pr/bay-area-cpa-convicted-tax-fraud.

THE UNITED STATES ATTORNEY'S OFFICE

NORTHERN DISTRICT *of* CALIFORNIA

| HOME | ABOUT | NEWS | U.S. ATTORNEY | NOTIFICATIONS | PROGRAMS |

U.S. Attorneys » Northern District of California » News

Department of Justice

SHARE

U.S. Attorney's Office

Northern District of California

FOR IMMEDIATE RELEASE   Wednesday, July 18, 2018

Bay Area CPA Convicted Of Tax Fraud

SAN FRANCISCO – A federal jury convicted Marc Howard Berger today of three counts of aiding and abetting the filing of a false tax return announced Acting United States Attorney Alex G. Tse; Principal Deputy Assistant Attorney General Richard E. Zuckerman of the Justice Department's Tax Division; Internal Revenue Service, Criminal Investigation (IRS-CI), Acting Special Agent in Charge Tara Sullivan; and Federal Bureau of Investigation (FBI) Special Agent in Charge John F. Bennett.

The jury found that Berger willfully assisted in the preparation of three false Form 1040s for codefendant G. Steven Burrill for 2011, 2012, and 2013. The guilty verdict followed a three-week jury trial before the Honorable Richard Seeborg, U.S. District Court Judge.

"We commend today's jury verdict," said Acting United States Attorney Alex G. Tse. "Tax preparers must know that they cannot willfully assist clients in defrauding the IRS and failing to pay their fair share."

Evidence at trial showed that Berger, 67, of Walnut Creek, Calif., was a Certified Public Accountant and partner with a regional tax preparation firm, Burr Pilger Mayer. Berger's client, Burrill, was the owner and CEO of Burrill & Company, Burrill Capital, and a number of related entities. Through the entities, Burrill managed venture capital funds, including Burrill Life Sciences Capital Fund III, L.P. (the Fund), a $283 million investment fund focused on the life sciences industry. Between December 2007 and September 2013, Burrill transferred more than $18 million from the Fund to his management companies in excess of the management fees that were due and allowable under the agreements that governed the Fund. Berger intentionally prepared and filed false income tax returns for Burrill that failed to report more than $18 million in income, resulting in unpaid taxes of more than $4.7 million. With Berger's assistance, Burrill paid no individual income taxes for the years 2009 through 2013.

Berger and Burrill were indicted by a federal grand jury on September 14, 2017. Berger was charged with three counts of aiding and assisting in the preparation of a false tax return, in violation of 26 U.S.C. § 7206(2).

Berger is currently free on bond. The maximum statutory penalty for each count in violation of 26 U.S.C. § 7206(2) is three years in prison and a fine of $100,000. However, any sentence will be imposed by the court after consideration of the U.S. Sentencing Guidelines and the federal statute governing the imposition of a sentence, 18 U.S.C. § 3553. Berger's sentencing hearing has not yet been scheduled.

Willful Failure to Collect or Pay Over Tax under Section 7202 - This statute describes two offenses: (1) a willful failure to collect; and (2) a willful failure to truthfully account for and pay over tax. It was designed primarily to assure compliance by third parties obligated to collect excise taxes and to deduct from wages paid to employees the employees' share of Federal Insurance Contribution Act (FICA) taxes and the withholding tax on wages applicable to individual income taxes. The withheld sums are commonly referred to as "trust fund taxes."[279] To establish a violation of I.R.C. § 7202, the following elements must be proved beyond a reasonable doubt:

> 1. Duty to collect, and/or to truthfully account for and pay over;
> 2. Failure to collect, or truthfully account for and pay over; and
> 3. Willfulness.

[1] Duty to collect, and/or to truthfully account for and pay over taxes. The duty of employers to truthfully account for and pay over is created by I.R.C. §§ 3102(s), 3111(a), and 3402 (1986).[280] Specifically, it is the individual with the duty to truthfully account for and pay over who is culpable when there is a failure to perform this duty. For an example of the criteria used to determine the individual with the duty to truthfully account for and pay over, see Datlof v. United States, 252 F. Supp. 11, 32 (E.D. Pa.), aff'd., 370 F.2d 655, 656 (3d Cir. 1966), cert. denied, 387 U.S. 906 (1967), involving a civil penalty under 26 U.S.C. § 6672 for unpaid federal withholding and employment taxes.

[2] Failure to collect, or truthfully account for and pay over. The Department of Justice Tax Division's position historically has been that a willful failure to truthfully to account for and pay over is a "breach of an inseparable dual obligation." 2008 Criminal Tax Manual, United States Department of Justice, Tax Division, Criminal Section, p. 9-4. Under this theory, a willful failure to pay after a truthful accounting is made, by filing a return, would still leave "the duty as a whole unfulfilled and the responsible person subject to prosecution." Some defendants have argued § 7202 is a conjunctive statute requiring the government to prove both a failure to account for and a failure to pay withholding tax to establish a violation of the statute.[281] In Evangelista, the Second Circuit held a violation of § 7202 can result from either a failure to account for withholding taxes and FICA contributions or a failure to pay over such taxes, but the statute does not require both to sustain a conviction.[282] In Thayer, the defendant argued the statute was conjunctive; therefore, if both requirements of § 7202 were not met, he could not be convicted. The Third Circuit disagreed and relied on the decision in Brennick: "A conjunctive interpretation of § 7202 would result in a greater penalty for one who simply failed to collect trust fund taxes than for one who

---

[279] See Slodov v. United States, 436 U.S. 238, 242-249 (1978).
[280] See United States v. Porth, 426 F.2d 519, 522 (10th Cir.), cert. denied, 400 U.S. 824 (1970).
[281] See also United States v. Thayer, 201 F.3d 214, 219-22 (3d Cir. 1999), cert. denied, 530 U.S. 1244 (2000); United States v. Evangelista, 122 F.3d 112, 120-22 (2d Cir. 1997); United States v. Brennick, 908 F. Supp. 1004, 1011 (D. Mass. 1995).
[282] See United States v. Thayer, 201 F.3d 214, 219-22 (3d Cir. 1999), cert. denied, 530 U.S. 1244 (2000)); United States v. Brennick, 908 F. Supp. 1004, 1007 (D. Mass. 1995).

collected them. . . [t]hat Congress intended to make such a distinction is simply inconceivable." United States v. Brennick, 908 F. Supp. 1004, 1017 (D. Mass. 1995). The Third Circuit affirmed Thayer's conviction, stating the defendant's argument did not convincingly answer the Brennick court's Congressional intent analysis. In United States v. Gilbert, 266 F.3d 1180, 1183-85 (9th Cir. 2001), the Ninth Circuit relied on the decisions in Evangelista and Thayer in arriving at the same holding.

[3] Willfulness. The requisite element of willfulness under section 7202 is the same as in other offenses under Title 26. It must be shown that a defendant voluntarily and intentionally acted in violation of a known legal duty.[283]

Failure to File Return, Supply Information, or Pay Tax Under Section 7203 -

There are four separate offenses described in I.R.C. § 7203:

[a] Failure to pay an estimated tax or tax. This element is predicated on the requirement imposed on taxpayers under I.R.C. § 6151(a) that: "Except as otherwise provided in this subchapter, when a return of tax is required under this title or regulations, the person required to make such return shall, without assessment or notice and demand from the Secretary, pay such tax to the internal revenue officer with whom the return is filed, and shall pay such tax at the time and place fixed for filing the return ...."[284] The difference between an attempted evasion of payment in violation of I.R.C. § 7201 and a failure to pay a tax in violation of I.R.C. § 7203 is the existence of an affirmative act required to make out the evasion of payment offense, e.g., the concealment of assets or use of nominees;

[b] Failure to make (file) a return. Various Code provisions (and regulations thereunder) specify the events which trigger the obligation to file a return. I.R.C. § 6012 lists the persons and entities required to make returns with respect to income taxes. [b] The government need not prove that any taxes are due, but only that gross income requirements have been met so as to trigger the filing requirement.[285] But proof of taxes due will help to establish willfulness;

[c] Failure to keep records. As a general rule, invocation of this criminal sanction entails the practical difficulty of defining what books and records were required to be maintained. By regulation the Secretary requires taxpayers to "keep such permanent books of account or records, including inventories, as are sufficient to establish the amount of gross income, deductions, credits, or other matters required to be shown by such person in any return of such tax or information." Treas. Reg. 1.6001-1(a). The

---

[283] Cheek v. United States, 498 U.S. 192, 201 (1991); United States v. Pomponio, 429 U.S. 10, 12 (1976); United States v. Bishop, 412 U.S. 346, 360 (1973); United States v. Simkanin, 420 F.3d 397, 404 (5th Cir. 2005), cert. denied, 547 U.S. 1111 (2006).

[284] See United States v. Drefke, 707 F.2d 978, 981 (8th Cir.), cert. denied, 464 U.S. 359 (1983).

[285] United States v. Bell, 734 F.2d 1315, 1316 (8th Cir. 1984); United States v. Wade, 585 F.2d 573, 574 (5th Cir. 1978), cert. denied, 440 U.S. 928 (1979).

regulation does not mandate any form of record keeping but simply requires that such records be accurate and sufficient to enable the district director to ascertain whether liability for tax is incurred and, if so, the amount thereof. District Directors are empowered to require any person (by notice served upon him) to keep specific records which will enable the District Director to ascertain if such person is liable for tax. Treas. Reg. 1.6001-1(d); and,

[d] Failure to supply information. In general, an individual return is to be filed either in the internal revenue district where the taxpayer resides or has his/her principal place of business; or at the Service Center serving the internal revenue district where the taxpayer resides or has his/her principal place of business. In those instances where the Internal Revenue Code does not provide for the place of filing, the Secretary "shall by regulations" prescribe the place for filing.

Fraudulent Withholding Exemption or Failure to Supply Information Penalty Under Section 7205 - Of the two offenses contained in this section, those committed in violation of § 7205(a) are far more common. Section 7205(a) applies to Form W-4 and Form W-4E. Some common fact patterns involving section 7205 are as follows:

1. An employee falsely claims exemption from withholding, certifying no tax liability incurred for preceding year and none anticipated for current year. The section 7205 charge is based on the falsity of the employee's certification regarding the preceding year.[286]

2. An employee falsely inflates the number of "allowances" claimed, thereby reducing or eliminating taxes withheld.[287] Because the allowances for credits and itemized deductions are difficult to compute, prosecution on this fact pattern will probably be confined to overstated allowances for dependents. The problem is that allowances for dependents were lumped together with other allowances on the face of the old W-4, so it was difficult to prove which allowances were falsely stated unless the employee provided agents with his worksheet or made admissions.

What are the elements of the offense under section 7205(a)?

[a] The individual had a duty to supply information to employer under I.R.C. § 3402. The employee's duty to supply an employer with information relating to the number of withholding exemptions claimed is contained in I.R.C. § 3402(f)(2)(A), as follows: "On or before the date of commencement of employment with an employer, the employee shall furnish the employer with a signed withholding exemption certificate relating to the number of withholding exemptions which he claims, which shall in no event exceed the number to which he is entitled." The taxpayer's status as an employee is an essential element of the offense which the government must establish beyond a reasonable doubt.[288]

---

[286] United States v. Echols, 677 F.2d 498, 499 (5th Cir. 1982).
[287] United States v. Herzog, 632 F.2d 469, 472 (5th Cir. 1980).
[288] United States v. Bass, 784 F.2d 1282, 1284 (5th Cir. 1986); United States v. Herzog, 632 F.2d 469,

[b] The individual supplied false or fraudulent information or failed to supply information which would require increase in tax withheld. Most courts have rejected the argument that the information provided must be either deceptive or provided with the intent to deceive.[289] The Fourth Circuit has refused to equate "false" with "untrue" and has required, for a Section 7205 conviction, that the information be either provided with the intent to deceive or deceptive enough to possible change the amount withheld.[290]

[c] The act or failure to act was willful.[291] Willfulness in a section 7205 prosecution is the same as it is in all specific intent criminal tax offenses -- "a voluntary, intentional violation of a known legal duty."[292] Examples: 1. Evidence that the defendant had a tax liability in a prior year and then filed a Form W-4 in which 99 exemptions were claimed and a document that falsely declared he had no tax liability in the prior year and anticipated none in the year in issue.[293] Defendant's filing of "Affidavits of Revocation" stating that she was not required to file returns or pay taxes, and letters to I.R.S. stating that wages are not income is evidence of willfulness.[294] Evidence of prior tax paying history and of attempts by the defendant's employer and the Internal Revenue Service to explain legal requirements to the defendant is sufficient to sustain the jury's finding that the defendant was aware of his legal obligations and intentionally chose not to comply.[295]

4. Penalties Applicable to Tax Return Preparers

Tax Return Preparer Penalty - A tax return preparer, as defined by section 7701(a)(36), who prepares any return or claim of refund with respect to which any part of an understatement of liability is due to an unreasonable position, including any frivolous position discussed in this outline, and who knew or reasonably should have known of the position, may be required to pay a penalty equal to the greater of $1,000 or 50 percent of the income derived by the tax return preparer with respect to preparing the return or claim for refund.[296] The minimum penalty amount increases to $5,000 for willful or reckless conduct of the tax return preparer.[297]

Penalty for Assisting in Preparing a Return that Result in Understatement - The IRS may impose a penalty of $1,000 for aiding or assisting in the preparation or

---

472 (5th Cir. 1980).

[289] United States v. Lawson, 670 F.2d 923, 928 (10th Cir. 1982); United States v. Hinderman, 528 F.2d 100, 102 (8th Cir. 1976); United States v. Malinowski, 347 F. Supp. 347 (E.D. Pa. 1972), aff'd, 472 F.2d 850, 852-853 (3d Cir.), cert. denied, 411 U.S. 1970 (1973).

[290] United States v. Snider, 502 F.2d 645 (4th Cir. 1974).

[291] United States v. Herzog, 632 F.2d 469, 471-72 (5th Cir. 1980); United States v. Olson, 576 F.2d 1267 (8th Cir.), cert. denied, 439 U.S. 896 (1978).

[292] Cheek v. United States, 498 U.S. 192, 194 (1991).

[293] United States v. Grumka, 728 F.2d 794, 797 (6th Cir. 1984).

[294] United States v. Ferguson, 793 F.2d 828, 831 (7th Cir. 1986), cert. denied, 479 U.S. 933 (1987).

[295] United States v. Foster, 789 F.2d 457, 460 (7th Cir. 1986).

[296] I.R.C. § 6694(a).

[297] I.R.C. § 6694(b).

presentation of any portion of a return with knowledge that it will result in an understatement of tax liability.[298]

In addition to statutory penalties, Federal tax return preparers who engage in misconduct may be thwarted by court injunction. The Justice Department's Tax Division and the Internal Revenue Service work hard to shut down fraudulent tax return preparers and tax-fraud promoters, using both civil and criminal enforcement tools. Under the civil injunction program, the Division sues preparers and promoters seeking a court order, called an injunction, that bars a person or business from engaging in specified misconduct or from preparing tax returns for others. An alphabetical list of such civil tax injunctions can be found at: https://www.justice.gov/tax/program-shut-down-schemes-and-scams.

---

[298] I.R.C. § 6701(a).

IRS 30-Day Letter

Internal Revenue Service
District Director

Department of the Treasury

Date:

Taxpayer Identification Number:

Form:

Tax Period(s) Ended:

Person to Contact:

Contact Telephone Number:

Employee Identification Number:

Refer Reply to:

Last Date to Respond to this Letter:

Dear

We have enclosed two copies of our examination report showing the changes we made to your tax for the period(s) shown above. Please read the report and let us know whether you agree or disagree with the changes. (Our report may not reflect the results of later examinations of partnerships, S Corporations, trusts, etc., in which you have an interest. Changes made to their tax returns could affect your tax.

IF YOU AGREE with the changes in the report, please sign, date, and return one copy to us by the response date shown above. If you filed a joint return, both taxpayers must sign the report. If you owe more tax, please include payment for the full amount to limit penalty and interest charges.

IF YOU CAN'T PAY the full amount you owe now, pay as much as you can. If you want us to consider an installment agreement, please complete and return the enclosed Form 9465, *Installment Agreement Request*. If we approve your request, we will charge a $43 fee to help offset the cost of providing this service. We will continue to charge penalties and interest until you pay the full amount you owe.

IF YOU DON'T AGREE with the changes shown in the report, you should do one of the following by the response date shown above:

- Mail us any additional information you'd like us to consider
- Discuss the report with the examiner
- Discuss your position with the examiner's supervisor
- Request a conference with an Appeals Officer, as explained in the enclosed Publication 5, *Your Appeal Rights and How to Prepare a Protest If You Don't Agree*

Letter 915 (DO) (Rev. 4-2000)
Catalog Number 62712V

Letter 915(DO) - 30-Day Letter from District Office

IF YOU DON'T TAKE ANY ACTION by the response date shown above, we will process your case based on the information shown in the report. We will send you a statutory notice of deficiency that allows you 90 days to petition the United States Tax Court. If you allow the 90-day period to expire without petitioning the tax court, we will bill you for any additional tax, interest, and penalties.

We have enclosed Publication 1, *Your Rights as a Taxpayer*. If additional tax is due, we have also enclosed Publication 594, *The IRS Collection Process*, for your information.

If you have any questions, please contact the person whose name and telephone number are shown in the heading of this letter. If you write, please include your telephone number and the best time for us to call in case we need more information. We have enclosed an envelope for your convenience.

Thank you for your cooperation.

Sincerely yours,

District Director

Enclosures:
Examination Report (2)
☐ Form 9465
Publication 1
Publication 5
☐ Publication 594
Envelope

Letter 915 (DO) (Rev. 4-2000)
Catalog Number 62712V

Letter 894(RO) – Notice of Deficiency from Appeals Office (with Waiver Form 4089-A)

Department of the Treasury
Internal Revenue Service

Letter Number: 894 (RO)
Letter Date:

Taxpayer Identifying Number:

Form:

Person to Contact:

Telephone Numbers:

Contact Person Identification Number:

Refer Reply To:

In Re:

Last Day to File a Petition With
the United States Tax Court:

NOTICE OF DEFICIENCY

<u>Tax Year(s) Ended</u>

Tax

Dear

   We have determined that you owe additional tax or other amounts, or both, for the tax year(s) identified above. This letter is your **NOTICE OF DEFICIENCY** as required by law. The enclosed statement shows how we figured the deficiency.

   If you want to contest this determination in court before making any payment, you have 90 days from the date of this letter (150 days if this letter is addressed to you outside of the United States) to file a petition with the United States (U.S.) Tax Court for a redetermination of the deficiency. You can get a copy of the rules for filing a petition and a petition form you can use by writing to the address below:

> United States Tax Court
> 400 Second Street, NW
> Washington, DC 20217

   The Tax Court has a simplified procedure for small cases when the amount in dispute is $50,000 or less for any one tax year. You also can get information about this procedure by writing to the Tax Court. You should write promptly if you intend to file a petition with the Tax Court.

(over)

Letter 894 (RO) (Rev. 3-1999)
Cat. No. 40356H

Letter 894(RO) – Notice of Deficiency from Appeals Office (with Waiver Form 4089-A) (p. 2)

Send the completed petition form, a copy of this letter, and copies of all statements and/or schedules you received with this letter to the Tax Court at the above address. The court cannot consider your case if you file the petition late. The petition is considered timely filed if the postmark date falls within the prescribed 90 or 150 day period and the envelope containing the petition is properly addressed with the correct postage.

The time you have to file a petition with the court is set by law and cannot be extended or suspended. Thus, contacting the Internal Revenue Service (IRS) for more information, or receiving other correspondence from the IRS won't change the allowable period for filing a petition with the Tax Court.

As required by law, separate notices are sent to husbands and wives. If this letter is addressed to both husband and wife, and both want to petition the Tax Court, both must sign and file the petition or each must file a separate, signed petition. If only one spouse petitions the Tax Court, the full amount of the deficiency will be assessed against the non-petitioning spouse. If more than one tax year is shown above, you may file one petition form showing all of the years you are contesting.

You may represent yourself before the Tax Court, or you may be represented by anyone admitted to practice before the Tax Court.

If you decide not to file a petition with the Tax Court, please sign the enclosed waiver form and return it to us at the IRS address on the top of the front of this letter. This will permit us to assess the deficiency quickly and can help limit the accumulation of interest. The enclosed envelope is for your convenience.

If you decide not to sign and return the waiver, and you don't file a petition with the Tax Court within the time limit, the law requires us to assess and bill you for the deficiency after 90 days from the date of this letter (150 days if this letter is addressed to you outside the United States).

If you are a C corporation, under Internal Revenue Code Section 6621 ©, large corporate underpayments may be subject to a higher rate of interest than the normal rate of interest for underpayments.

If you have questions about this letter, you may write to or call the contact person whose name, telephone number, and IRS address are shown on the front of this letter. If you write, please include your telephone number, the best time for us to call you if we need more information, and a copy of this letter to help us identify your account. Keep the original letter for your records. If you prefer to call and the telephone number is outside your local calling area, there will be a long distance charge to you.

Thank you for your cooperation.

Sincerely,

Commissioner
By

Enclosures:

Letter 894 (RO) (Rev. 3-1999)
Cat. No. 40356H

Chapter 10 - Questions

1. What occurs first – a tax assessment or collection of tax due?

2. Married taxpayers Jon and Jane Doe fail to file Form 8938 as required by section 6038D for tax year 2015. When does the statute of limitations for assessment expire with respect to their tax year 2015 federal tax return?

3. Your client states to you his belief that a taxpayer may lawfully decline to pay taxes if the taxpayer disagrees with the government's use of tax revenues. Your client asks for you for your view of his belief. You disagree with your client. What statutory penalty applies if your client decides not to pay his Federal taxes under his stated view?

CHAPTER 11 – EFFECTIVELY COMMUNICATING TAX RESEARCH

1. Introduction

The ultimate goal of a tax professional is to effectively and concisely communicate the tax analysis to your intended audience. Central to becoming successful in communicating your tax results is understanding that you MUST ALWAYS RESPECT YOUR AUDIENCE'S TIME. Presenting 10 pages of analysis when five pages is sufficient causes your audience to labor through reading unnecessary material. Citing to three similar primary source authorities when one will do wastes your audience's time. Failing to take time to carefully edit your analysis to refine your points wastes your audience's time. Adding latin terms, taking a pedantic[299] approach to communicating your analysis or including volume to dazzle the reader serves your ego or billing statement but not your reader. In short, the tax professional is tasked to present complex tax law in a simple, comprehensible manner so that the audience (co-worker, supervisor, client or government official) is better informed on the subject matter as quickly as possible. Thus, a successful tax practitioner should view their tax communication abilities as a core skill set.

2. Core Elements of Every Written Tax Communication

In every written tax communication, there are four core elements: (1) issue statement; (2) relevant facts; (3) tax analysis; and (4) conclusion/recommendation. Most written communication will include waiver language at the beginning the document, which is addressed later in this chapter. Regardless of whether the tax document is an internal memo, IRS analysis or a court opinion, all of these documents share the same core aspects.

- **Issue Statement** – an issue statement focuses the reader's attention to the precise tax matter being addressed. There *should* be three parts included in every good tax issue statement: (i) the code section in dispute; (ii) the unique facts involved; and (iii) the tax year at issue. As an illustrative example, take a look at the case, below, Samsung Electronics Co., Ltd., et al. v. Apple, 580 U.S. ___ (2016). For tax issues, we want to include the tax year at issue because the applicable law for various years may be different. However, for legal questions outside of Title 26, the issue statement may leave out the year in dispute. For example, in Samsung Electronics Co., Ltd., et al. v. Apple, 579 U.S. ___ (2016), the Supreme Court framed the issue through multiple statements, not just one statement which is the common form for a tax issue statement. Whether a tax practitioner drafts one statement or multiple statements, the objective is to inform the reader of the precise nature of the tax question.

---

[299] The Cambridge Oxford Dictionary defines the adjective "pedantic" as "caring too much about unimportant rules or details and not enough about understanding or appreciating a subject."

Cite as: 580 U. S. ____ (2016)   1

Opinion of the Court

NOTICE: This opinion is subject to formal revision before publication in the preliminary print of the United States Reports. Readers are requested to notify the Reporter of Decisions, Supreme Court of the United States, Washington, D. C. 20543, of any typographical or other formal errors, in order that corrections may be made before the preliminary print goes to press.

SUPREME COURT OF THE UNITED STATES

No. 15—777

SAMSUNG ELECTRONICS CO., LTD., ET AL., PETITIONERS v. APPLE INC.

ON WRIT OF CERTIORARI TO THE UNITED STATES COURT OF APPEALS FOR THE FEDERAL CIRCUIT

[December 6, 2016]

JUSTICE SOTOMAYOR delivered the opinion of the Court.

Section 289 of the Patent Act provides a damages remedy specific to design patent infringement. A person who manufactures or sells "any article of manufacture to which [a patented] design or colorable imitation has been applied shall be liable to the owner to the extent of his total profit." 35 U. S. C. §289. In the case of a design for a single-component product, such as a dinner plate, the product is the "article of manufacture" to which the design has been applied. In the case of a design for a multicomponent product, such as a kitchen oven, identifying the "article of manufacture" to which the design has been applied is a more difficult task.

This case involves the infringement of designs for smartphones. The United States Court of Appeals for the Federal Circuit identified the entire smartphone as the only permissible "article of manufacture" for the purpose of calculating §289 damages because consumers could not separately purchase components of the smartphones. The question before us is whether that reading is consistent with §289. We hold that it is not.

Another example of how to frame an issue statement comes from Stephen L. Vosine and William E. Armstrong v. United States, 579 U.S. ___ (2016), below:

Cite as: 579 U. S. ____ (2016)   1

Opinion of the Court

NOTICE: This opinion is subject to formal revision before publication in the preliminary print of the United States Reports. Readers are requested to notify the Reporter of Decisions, Supreme Court of the United States, Washington, D. C. 20543, of any typographical or other formal errors, in order that corrections may be made before the preliminary print goes to press.

SUPREME COURT OF THE UNITED STATES

No. 14–10154

STEPHEN L. VOISINE AND WILLIAM E. ARMSTRONG, III, PETITIONERS *v.* UNITED STATES

ON WRIT OF CERTIORARI TO THE UNITED STATES COURT OF APPEALS FOR THE FIRST CIRCUIT

[June 27, 2016]

JUSTICE KAGAN delivered the opinion of the Court.

Federal law prohibits any person convicted of a "misdemeanor crime of domestic violence" from possessing a firearm. 18 U. S. C. §922(g)(9). That phrase is defined to include any misdemeanor committed against a domestic relation that necessarily involves the "use . . . of physical force." §921(a)(33)(A). The question presented here is whether misdemeanor assault convictions for reckless (as contrasted to knowing or intentional) conduct trigger the statutory firearms ban. We hold that they do.

Justice Kagan introduced two foundational statements of law before presenting the precise issue for decision by the Supreme Court. A good issue statment focuses the reader to the specific matter of concern – what is the controversy about?

Drafting an effective issue statement is an evolving process that relies upon an input of facts from the client as well as continuous refinement from legal research. Consider the follow example.

- Stage 1: Your Client has a business providing technology services to hundreds of clients. Client asks, "I want to buy a gift for my customers this year to thank them for their continued patronage of my business. What are the tax aspects that I need to think about when I buy gifts for my clients?" Start by drafting a generic issue statement.
    - o Issue Statement #1: "What are the tax requirements for deducting gifts by a business to a client?"
    - o Initial Tax Research: Now, conduct tax research on this issue to help craft a more precise issue statement.

- Internal Revenue Code – section 274(b)(1) provides a limit of $25 each year as a deductible gift that is allowed as a business deduction under section 162.
    - Two items are excluded from this annual limitation amount: (1) a sign, display rack or other promotional material to be used on the business premises of the recipient; or(2) an item that has the name of the Client's business permanently imprinted, which is identical to items generally distributed by the Client and which costs the Client $4.00 or less.
    - Application to different types of taxpayers
        - In the case of a partnership, the annual $25 limitation applies to the partnership as well as to each member
        - In the case of a husband and wife, the couple is treated as one taxpayer.
- Stage 2: Based on your initial tax research results, you ask your Client additional questions:
    - Question 1: How is your business organized? E.g., as a corporation, partnership, sole proprietorship owned by husband and wife?
        - Answer 1: Client tells you that it is formed as a C corporation.
    - Question 2: Do you have an idea of what type of gift that you'd like to provide your clients?
        - Answer 2: Clients tells you that it is open to provide any type of gift to their clients.
    - Issue Statement #2: Our tax firm's Client (a C corporation) provides one gift each year to its customers in order to promote its business. The tax question is whether Client may deduct under section 162 a gift of _____ costing $25 or less that it expends to promote its business?
- Stage 3: You conduct additional research. The results of your second round of tax research and additional facts provided by your Client produce a more refined issue statement.
    - Additional Research: Treas. Reg. §1.274-3(c) provides that incidental costs such as "for customary engraving on jewelry, or for packaging, insurance, and mailing or other delivery" are no considered an expense for a "gift" under section 274.
    - Issue Statement #3: Our tax firm's Client provides one gift each year to its customers in order to promote its business. Whether Client may deduct under section 162 a gift of _____ costing $25 or less (excluding related packaging, insurance and/or mailing costs) that it plans to expend in tax year _____ to promote its business?

Drafting issue statements requires recognition that this is your first opportunity to focus your audience's attention to the precise tax question presented. Take adequate time to understand that an effective issue statement results from a development of interaction with the client as well as ongoing tax research.

- **<u>Relevant facts</u>** – a practitioner must include facts against which tax law is applied. However, the facts should include only "relevant" facts – facts which present or absent would change the tax conclusion. Different practitioners may dispute whether certain facts are, indeed, relevant or not. As a guide to define what is "relevant," let's rely upon how the Federal Rules of Evidence ("FRE") defines this word. Under FRE Rule 401, evidence is relevant if: "(a) it has any tendency to make a fact more or less probable than it would be without the evidence; and (b) the fact is of consequence in determining the action." So, on a tax question involving depreciation, the cost basis of the automobile presents a relevant fact, but not the color of the car. Reducing unnecessary facts in tax communication streamlines the document allowing the reader to be free of the burden of reading bloated text.

- **<u>Analysis/Law/Discussion</u>** – The legal analysis section presents the reader with the applicable authorities that should serve as the source material to guide them to the correct tax conclusion. The presentation of tax authorities should always begin with the highest level tax authority to the lowest level.

    IRC→Treas. Reg.→Caselaw (S.Ct→Ct.of App→Trial Level)→Admin. Guidance

In the opinion below from <u>U.S. v. Nosal</u>, the court begins its analysis with the applicable statute before going on to discuss any other authority.

UNITED STATES V. NOSAL   13

---

assessment and approximately $828,000 in restitution to Korn/Ferry.

ANALYSIS

I. CONVICTIONS UNDER THE COMPUTER FRAUD AND ABUSE ACT

A. Background of the CFAA

The CFAA was originally enacted in 1984 as the Counterfeit Access Device and Computer Fraud and Abuse Act, Pub. L. No. 98-473, § 2102(a), 98 Stat. 2190 (1984). The act was aimed at "hackers who accessed computers to steal information or to disrupt or destroy computer functionality." *Brekka*, 581 F.3d at 1130–31 (citing H.R. Rep. No. 98-894, at 8–9 (1984), *reprinted in* 1984 U.S.C.C.A.N. 3689, 3694). The original legislation protected government and financial institution computers,[2] and made it a felony to access classified information in a computer "without authorization." Counterfeit Access Device and Computer Fraud and Abuse Act § 2102(a).

---

[2] A computer is defined broadly as "an electronic . . . data processing device performing logical, arithmetic, or storage functions, and includes any data storage facility or communications facility directly related to or operating in conjunction with such device." 18 U.S.C. § 1030(e)(1). The CFAA's restrictions have been applied to computer networks, databases and cell phones. *See, e.g., United States v. Valle*, 807 F.3d 508, 513 (2d Cir. 2015) (restricted police databases); *United States v. Barrington*, 648 F.3d 1178, 1184 (11th Cir. 2011) (a university's Internet-based grading system); *United States v. Kramer*, 631 F.3d 900, 903 (8th Cir. 2011) (cell phones); *United States v. Shea*, 493 F.3d 1110, 1115–16 (9th Cir. 2007) (computer network).

- **Conclusion/Recommendation** – For a court, the final conclusion in its published opinion is referred to as its "holding." A court's holding is its final decision that it reaches in favor of one side or the other. Likewise, in an office memo, client letter or correspondence submitted to the IRS, tax communication includes a tax professional's ultimate assessment/conclusion as to the merits of the issue presented. What is an example of a tax professional's conclusion in a client letter? Consider the following: "Based on application of tax authorities as noted in this letter, our firm concludes that there exists substantial authority that the return position with respect to the "XYZ Transaction" would be sustained in the event the client's tax return position is audited by the IRS."

These fundamental elements are followed by practitioners, courts and government attorneys. For example, the Chief Counsel Directives Manual (an employee guide applicable to IRS attorneys provides the following instructions on how to prepare legal advice[300]:

---

[300] CCDM 33.1.2.2.3.3 (04-12-2013). The CCDM for this citation is publicly available online at

1. **Issue** headings should be used as appropriate. If there is more than one issue, each issue is stated in a separate paragraph, and each paragraph is numbered. State the issues in clear, precise language. Whenever appropriate, state any additional issues that have been identified but were not specifically raised in the incoming request for advice.

2. A **Conclusion** heading should be used if an issue heading is appropriate. There should be a specific statement of the conclusion reached with respect to each issue. This conclusion must be written to leave no doubt as to its meaning and to make it clear it is based solely on the facts presented.

3. A **Statement of Facts** heading should normally be used. It should contain those facts necessary to understand the analysis of the issues. The facts should be set out concisely, but without sacrificing clarity. Generic facts may be used if they do not sacrifice clarity.

4. A **Law and Analysis** heading should normally be used. The analysis portion of the advice sets forth clearly and concisely the pertinent law, regulations, published rulings of the Service, and case law or other precedent and the rationale to bridge between the issue, facts, law, and conclusion.

With the four core elements identified, above, what is an example of good tax communication? Consider Chief Counsel Advice 201310029, below, drafted by the National Office of the Office of Chief Counsel to Field Counsel for the IRS.[301]

---

https://www.irs.gov/irm/part33/irm_33-001-002.html#d0e391.

[301] In Chief Counsel Advice 201310029, you will notice blank spaces where normally text should appear. These sections are redacted (edited) to remove personally identifiable information prior to the document being released to the public.

**Office of Chief Counsel
Internal Revenue Service**

Memorandum

Number: **201310029**
Release Date: 3/8/2013

CC:ITA:B03: |
POSTS-153214-12

UILC: 164.01-00, 164.09-00

date: January 14, 2013

to:

(Chief Counsel)

from:

(Income Tax & Accounting)

---

subject: Real Property Tax Deduction for Fire Prevention Fees

This Chief Counsel Advice responds to your request for assistance. This advice may
not be used or cited as precedent

ISSUE

May California residents deduct the Fire Prevention Fee they may pay on their federal
income tax returns as a real property tax deduction under section 164 of the Internal
Revenue Code and § 1.164-4 of the Income Tax Regulations?

CONCLUSION

California residents may not deduct the Fire Prevention Fee as a real property tax
deduction because (i) the fee is not a tax under California or federal law (ii) the fee is
not levied at a like rate, (iii) the fee is not imposed throughout the taxing authority's
jurisdiction, and (iv) the fee is assessed only against specific property to provide a local
benefit.

FACTS

In 2011, California enacted legislation requiring the State Board of Equalization to
charge an amount not to exceed $150 as a fire prevention fee (the fire fee) on each

POSTS-153214-12   2

structure within a state responsibility area. Cal. Pub. Res. Code § 4212(a)(1). A state responsibility area is an area of the state "in which the financial responsibility of preventing and suppressing fires has been determined by the [Board of Forestry and Fire Protection]... to be primarily the responsibility of the state." Cal. Pub. Res. Code § 4102. The legislature gave the following reasons for enacting the legislation:

(a) Fire protection of the public trust resources on lands in the state responsibility areas remains a vital interest to California. Lands that are covered in whole or in part by a diverse plant community prevent excessive erosion, retard runoff, reduce sedimentation, and accelerate water percolation to assist in the maintenance of critical sources of water for environmental, irrigation, domestic, or industrial uses.

(b) The presence of structures within state responsibility areas can pose an increased risk of fire ignition and an increased potential for fire damage within the state's wildlands and watersheds. The presence of structures within state responsibility areas can also impair wild land firefighting techniques and could result in greater damage to state lands caused by wildfires.

(c) The costs of fire prevention activities aimed at reducing the effects of structures in state responsibility areas should be borne by the owners of these structures.

(d) Individual owners of structures within state responsibility areas receive a disproportionately larger benefit from fire prevention activities than that realized by the state's citizens generally.

(e) It is the intent of the Legislature that the economic burden of fire prevention activities that are associated with structures in state responsibility areas shall be equitably distributed among the citizens of the state who generally benefit from those activities and those owners of structures in the state responsibility areas who receive a specific benefit other than that general benefit.

(f) It is necessary to impose a fire prevention fee to pay for fire prevention activities in the state responsibility areas that specifically benefit owners of structures in the state responsibility areas.

Cal. Pub. Res. Code § 4210.

The legislation requires the State Department of Forestry and Fire Prevention to submit the names and addresses of those liable for the fee, and the amount of the fee, within 30 days of the legislation's effective date and each January 1 thereafter. Cal. Pub. Res. Code § 4213(c). It empowers the State Board of Equalization to collect the fee pursuant to the Fee Collection Procedures Law in Part 30 of Division 2 of the California Revenue and Taxation Code. Cal. Pub. Res. Code § 4213(a)(1). The legislation requires an appeals process separate and distinct from that in the Fee Collection Procedures Law in which the Department of Forestry and Fire Prevention, not the State Board of Equalization, determines whether the feepayer is liable for the fee. Cal. Pub. Res. Code §§ 4213(2), 4220. Thus, a feepayer may not file a petition for redetermination of the fee with the State Board under the Fee Collection Procedures Law as the feepayer might for other fees.

LAW AND ANALYSIS

Section 164(a)(1) of the Internal Revenue Code ("Code") permits a deduction for real property taxes, but does not define what constitutes a real property tax. Personal property taxes may also be deductible under § 164(a), but § 164(b)(1) requires a personal property tax be an ad valorem tax to be deductible. The Code does not explicitly require the same for real property taxes. Section 1.164-4(a) of the Income Tax Regulations explains that to be deductible, a real property tax must be levied for the general public welfare at a like rate against all real property in the taxing authority's jurisdiction. In general, an amount that is assessed only on specific property benefitted by a local benefit (such as for streets, sidewalks, and like improvements) cannot be deducted as a real property tax.

Revenue Ruling 80-121, 1980-1 C.B. 43, notes that a characteristic common to many real property taxes is that the tax is measured by the value of the real property. However, there is no statutory or regulatory requirement that a real property tax be an ad valorem tax to be deductible for federal income tax purposes. Assessments on real property owners, based other than on the assessed value of the property, may be deductible if they are levied for the general public welfare by a proper taxing authority at a like rate on owners of all properties in the taxing authority's jurisdiction, and if the assessments are not for local benefits (unless for maintenance, repair, or interest charges).

The fire fee does not qualify as a deductible real property tax under the Code and the regulations. First, the fire fee is not a tax under California or federal law:

> A tax is an enforced contribution, exacted pursuant to legislative authority in the exercise of the taxing power, and imposed and collected for the purpose of raising revenue to be used for public or governmental purposes. Taxes are not payments for some special privilege granted or service rendered and are, therefore, distinguishable from various other charges imposed for particular purposes under particular powers or functions of government.

Rev. Rul. 77-29, 197-1 C.B. 44 citing Rev. Rul. 61-152, 1961-2 C.B. 42 and Rev. Rul. 71-49, 1971-1 C.B. 103; see also Rev. Rul. 58-141, 1958-1 C.B. 101.

Article 13A, § 3(a) of the California Constitution requires a two-thirds vote of both houses of the California legislature to raise taxes, and it forbids new ad valorem taxes and sales or transactions taxes on real property. Regulatory fees require only a simple majority to be enacted into law. California Farm Bureau Federation v. State Water Resources Control Bd., 51 Cal. 4th 421, 428 (Cal. 2011). The bill enacting the fire fee into law, Assembly Bill 29 in the 2011-2012 session of the legislature, did not pass with a two-thirds vote.[1] Thus, the fire fee only has force of law as a regulatory fee.

Article 13A, § 3(b)(1) states that a tax does not include "a charge imposed for a specific benefit conferred or privilege granted directly to the payor that is not provided to those not charged, and which does not exceed the reasonable costs to the State of conferring the benefit or granting the privilege to the payor." The charge § 3(b)(1) refers to is a regulatory fee. In California, "a fee may be charged by a government entity so long as it does not exceed the reasonable cost of providing services necessary to regulate the activity for which the fee is charged." Id. at 437, citing Sinclair Paint Co. v. State Bd. of Equalization, 15 Cal. 4th 866, 876 (Cal. 1997). Regulatory fees are imposed under the police power, rather than the taxing power. Id. at 875. The fire fee was imposed to "to pay for fire prevention activities in the state responsibility areas that specifically benefit owners of structures in the state responsibility areas." Cal. Pub. Res. Code § 4210. It was not imposed to collect revenue for general governmental purposes, but to provide the specific benefit of fire prevention for certain structures in the state. It is thus a regulatory fee, like the fees assessed on manufacturers and other persons contributing to environmental lead contamination that the Supreme Court of California in Sinclair ruled were regulatory fees. Sinclair Paint Co., supra at 874-875.

Regulatory fees in California are also collected according to a different procedure than are taxes. Ad valorem real property taxes are collected under the provisions of Part 5 of Division 1 of the Revenue and Tax Code, entitled Collection of Taxes. Mello-Roos special taxes are collected under the same procedures. Cal. Gov. Code 53340(3).[2] But all fees charged in California under the state's regulatory power, including the fire fee, are collected pursuant to the Fee Collection Procedures Law, Part 30 of Division 1 of the Revenue and Tax Code. See also Cal. Pub. Res. Code § 4213(a)(1); California Farm Bureau Federation, supra at 432 (fee collected according to Fee Collection Procedures Law). As noted above, the appeals process for the fire prevention fee is separate and distinct from that provided for in the Fee Collection Procedures Law, which further differentiates the fire fee from a tax. See Cal. Pub. Res. Code §§ 4213(2),

---

[1] The vote in the California Assembly was 52-26 in favor of the legislation and the vote in the California Senate was 23-16 (less than two-thirds voted for passage in the Senate). See http://www.leginfo.ca.gov/cgi-bin/postquery?bill_number=abx1_29&sess=PREV&house=B&author=blumenfield.

[2] "The special tax shall be collected in the same manner as ordinary ad valorem property taxes are collected and shall be subject to the same penalties and the same procedure, sale, and lien priority in case of delinquency as is provided for ad valorem taxes, unless another procedure has been authorized in the resolution of formation establishing the district and adopted by the legislative body."

POSTS-153214-12   5

4220. The supermajority requirement and this disparate collection treatment for fees in California indicate that the fire fee is an ordinary regulatory fee rather than a tax.

Second, the fire fee is not levied at a like rate as § 1.164-4(a) requires. Although neither the Code nor the regulations define "like rate", we believe that the term requires that the rate must uniformly apply based upon an independent variable, such as property value or parcel or structure size, to be considered similar or "like." A charge of $150 against each structure no matter how large or small is not levied at a "like" rate.

Third, the fire fee is not imposed against all real property throughout the taxing authority's jurisdiction as § 1.164-4(a) requires. First, It is imposed only against real property containing structures, not all real property within the state. Second, it is imposed only within state responsibility areas as designated by the state Board of Forestry and Fire Prevention, not all real property throughout the taxing authority's jurisdiction. These areas are geographically limited and do not cover the entire state of California or the entirety of the territory over which the appropriate taxing authority within the state has jurisdiction.

Fourth, the fire fee is assessed only against specific property to provide a local benefit. § 1.164-4(a) requires that a real property tax be levied for the general public welfare and not for a local benefit to be deductible. In its statement of findings, the California legislature stated that the presence of structures within state responsibility areas poses an increased risk of fire ignition and an increased potential for fire damage within the state's wildlands and watersheds, and also impairs wild land firefighting techniques. Cal. Pub. Res. Code § 4210. It noted that "individual owners of structures within state responsibility areas receive a disproportionately larger benefit from fire prevention activities than that realized by the state's citizens generally." Id. It concluded that "[t]he costs of fire prevention activities aimed at reducing the effects of structures in state responsibility areas should be borne by the owners of these structures". Id. Thus, the legislature decided that "[i]t is necessary to impose a fire prevention fee to pay for fire prevention activities in the state responsibility areas that specifically benefit owners of structures in the state responsibility areas." Id. The legislature was explicit that the fee be levied against specific property to provide a distinctly local benefit to these properties within state responsibility areas. Thus, the fire fee fails the general public welfare requirement of § 1.164-4(a) and it is not a deductible real property tax.

I hope this information is helpful. If you have any questions, please contact me or
          at

What is an example of a "bad" tax opinion letter? A stinging decision in <u>Canal Corp. v. Commissioner</u>, 135 T.C. No. 9 (2010), presents an illustration of what not to do when preparing a tax opinion letter for a client. In <u>Canal Corp.</u>, the client sought a tax opinion from PriceWaterhouseCoopers on the merits of a transaction. PWC provided its opinion, the IRS determined that the transaction did not have sufficient merit and disallowed it. However, the IRS determined that the transaction warranted the imposition of the accuracy-related penalty under section 6662. In response to the taxpayer's argument that it reasonably relied upon the professional tax opinion on the transaction from PWC, the IRS and the Court both agreed that the PWC opinion was so far from an acceptable tax opinion that the taxpayer could not reasonably rely on it to avoid penalty.

The Court in <u>Canal</u> began with the basics on how a taxpayer may avoid tax penalty when it relies upon a tax professional's opinion:

> Reasonable cause has been found when a taxpayer selects a competent tax adviser, supplies the adviser with all relevant information and, in a manner consistent with ordinary business care and prudence, relies on the adviser's professional judgment as to the taxpayer's tax obligations. Sec. 6664(c); <u>United States v. Boyle</u>, 469 U.S. 241, 250–251 (1985); sec. 1.6664–4(b)(1), Income Tax Regs. A taxpayer may rely on the advice of any tax adviser, lawyer or accountant. <u>United States v. Boyle</u>, <u>supra</u> at 251.

The Court pointed to fundamental deficiencies underlying the tax opinion letter and the odd responses from the tax partner (Mr. Miller) responsible for the opinion letter.

> Chesapeake paid PWC an $800,000 flat fee for the opinion, not based on time devoted to preparing the opinion. Mr. Miller testified that he and his team spent hours on the opinion. We find this testimony inconsistent with the opinion that was admitted into evidence. The Court questions how much time could have been devoted to the draft opinion because it is littered with typographical errors, disorganized and incomplete. Moreover, Mr. Miller failed to recognize several parts of the opinion. The Court doubts that any firm would have had such a cavalier approach if the firm was being compensated solely for time devoted to rendering the opinion. In addition, the opinion was riddled with questionable conclusions and unreasonable assumptions. Mr. Miller based his opinion on WISCO maintaining 20 percent of the LLC debt. Mr. Miller had no case law or Code authority to support this percentage, however. He instead relied on an irrelevant revenue procedure as the basis for issuing the "should" opinion. A "should" opinion is the highest level of comfort PWC offers to a client regarding whether the position taken by the client will succeed on the merits. We find it unreasonable that anyone, let alone an attorney, would issue the highest level opinion a firm offers on such dubious legal reasoning. We are also nonplused by Mr. Miller's failure to give an understandable response when asked at trial how PWC could issue a "should" opinion <u>if no authority on point existed</u>.

We are also troubled by the number of times the draft opinion uses "it appears." For example, it states: "[i]n focusing on the language of the 752 regs, it appears that such regulation adopts an all or nothing approach."…..We find that Chesapeake's tax position did not warrant a "should" opinion because of the numerous assumptions and dubious legal conclusions in the haphazard draft opinion that has been admitted into the record. Further, we find it inherently unreasonable for Chesapeake to have relied on an analysis based on the specious legal assumptions.

So, what can we learn from Canal Corp.? Avoid including the following in your written tax communication:

(1) typographical errors, grammatical errors
(2) disorganized material
(3) incomplete sections
(4) unreasonable assumptions
(5) questionable conclusions
(6) presenting analysis that does not include citations to applicable authorities
(7) equivocal language, such as "it appears" or "it seems"

All of the above elements are obviously problems that any basic tax practitioner can agree as avoidable and unacceptable in our work. Now, make sure to keep such hazards far away from written correspondence authored by you!

Another aspect of effective written communication is understanding that you must organize your document to present your main issue with the highest level authority first, not last. In other words, don't confuse your reader by presenting ancilliary issues first but rather begin by presenting your best and highest level authority first. To illustrate this point, consider the following example of a student's written office memo submission to the following fact pattern:

Class Writing Assignment: Your client, Sue Jones, is president of NORCAL, a C corporation with headquarters and operations located in California. NORCAL is a small, privately held company. Ms. Jones wants our firm's advice to her plan to recommend to NORCAL's board of directors that key employees receive year-end bonuses at the end of 2017 that is equal to their anual salaries. The key employees that Ms. Jones has identified to receive bonuses are: the CFO, VP, Executive Assistant and Ms. Jones. Each of these key employess own shares of NORCAL. Ms. Jones owns 51% of NORCAL while the other three employees each own 5% of NORCAL shares. There are 9 other shareholders of NORCAL in addition to the key employees. The annual salaries of these key employees are: $500,000 for Ms. Jones, $300,000 for the CFO, $250,000 for the VP and $100,000 for the Executive Assistant. NORCAL is an accrual taxpayer that operates on calendar year rather than fiscal year. NORCAL is successful with net revenues of $10 million in 2016. Your tax firm's partner has asked you to draft an office memo to address Ms. Jones' question seeking our firm's advice on her plan to pay bonuses to key employees in 2017.

Now, review the first page of a student's writing submission, below. The student does a good job of setting out specific elements necessary in a tax document: Issue Statement, Facts section, Analysis etc. However, in the "Analysis" section, the student defers addressing the main issue and proceeds to discuss an ancillary issue – the potential application of section 280G ("golden parachute" payments). Regardless of whether this section applies to the facts in the hypothetical problem – it doesn't, it is not the best method of presenting tax analysis.

What are the lessons to take away from this student's submission? Present the highest level primary source authority for your main issue first. Don't start with secondary issues or lower level authorities in order to lead up to the best authority that supports your analysis. Here, the student identified section 162 as the main statutory source to analyze the client's tax situation. And, then, the student proceeds to address to other sections (280G and 267) before discussing the main statutory provision. This presents disorganized analysis that does not offer the best method to capture your reader's attention. Lead with your main issue and the highest primary source authority that addresses the main issue. Proceed with strength, not leading up to it. Because if you take the approach of leading with tertiary issues first, you may have lost your reader's attention and patience by the time they reach your main issue discussion.

Based on your issue statement, you have correctly identified that section 162 is the primary code section to address. But, you address: ① §280G & ② §267 before your main code section. Don't do that. Place the most important issue + code section FIRST

From: Jonathan

Re: NORCAL Bonus payments to officer – shareholders

Date: 7/26/2017

Primary Issue:

Whether bonus payments made by a closely held C corporation to its president and shareholders qualify as reasonable compensation and are fully deductible under Section 162(a)(1) for tax year 2016.

lower case

Facts:

Norcal is a privately held C corporation that operates in Northern California. It is a calendar year taxpayer and its net operating revenue was $10,000,000 in 2016. It is owned by 9 unrelated shareholders. Mrs. Jones, the president of Norcal, owns 51% of all shares and no other shareholder holds more than 10% of the remaining shares. The CFO, VP, and EA each own 5% of shares. The salaries of the President, CFO, VP, and EA are 500k, 300k, 250k, and 100k respectively. The corporation regularly pays dividends to shareholders and will continue to do so. The corporation is on the accrual basis and the employees, as individuals, are on the cash basis. Mrs. Jones has engaged our firm to provide her with tax guidance as to the level of exposure, if any, the corporation may face if it makes bonus payments equal to the salaries of the mentioned executives.

Get right to your main point

Analysis:

ORGANIZATIONAL Problem

Before moving on the primary issue at hand, which is the definition of reasonable compensation under Section 162(a)(1), there are few other code sections that should be touched upon. First is section 280G(a), which defines excess golden parachute payments. If a payment is made to an officer or shareholder that contingent to a change in ownership, and if that amount exceeds a base amount which is three times the average compensation of the office or shareholder over the last five years, then a special excise tax of 20% will be assessed on the excess of the payment over the base amount. Although the facts given to us by Mrs. Jones do not make reference to any of these described circumstances, it would be in our best interest to confirm that no changes of ownership will take place contingent on any of the payments the Corporation will make. If this is the case, then we will need to gather salary information for the officer-shareholders for the four years previous to 2016 to confirm that the tentative bonus payments do not exceed their base amounts.

Be efficient and avoid this type of filler language ↓ shorter is better in tax communication

The second code section that we must address before Section 162 is Section 267(a)(2), which provides that payments between related parties are only deductible to the payor at the time they are included in the gross income of the payee. Though the 9 shareholders of Norcal Corporation may be unrelated to one another as individuals, under section 267(b)(2), Mrs. Jones and Norcal Corporation are in fact related parties because Mrs. Jones owns more than 50% of the stock of the corporation. Because of this fact, it is Mrs. Jones's accounting method as a cash basis taxpayer that determines the timing of

you always want to address the issue directly presented before you dive into the unknown. If your client/partner told you to address a ... directly

3. Citing to Source Authorities

The central function of a legal citation is to allow the reader to efficiently locate the cited source.[302] "Persuasive [writing] allows the [reader] to draw favorable conclusions from accurate descriptions of your authorites."[303] Written tax communication must provide citations to primary source authorities to support tax analysis, conclusions and recommendations. Without these citations, the reader is unable to verify that a code, a Treasury regulation, a case, or IRS guidance rightly persuades or requires us to reach a specific result. And, without specific source reference in your tax document, there is no supporting basis to reach a tax confidence level.

The main reference tool to properly cite to legal authority is --- *The Blue Book: A Uniform System of Citation.* The Blue Book instructs that a proper full case citation includes five basic components: (1) name of case; (2) published source in which the case may be found; (3) a parenthetical indicating the court and year of decision; (4) other parenthetical information, if any; and (5) the subsequent case history, if any.[304]

Rather than restate the elements provided in the Blue Book, I urge all students to purchase this essential reference guide because it will serve you well throughout your entire career. However, I offer the following points:

Q1: **Why** do tax professionals need to cite to primary source tax authorities?
   A1: Your professional value derives from your ability to locate the highest level of tax authority that is most similar factually to your client's case. Then, you must weigh the level of authoritative value of this primary source authority to guide your client on how to proceed properly under tax law. Weak tax authority provides risk for your client to engage in a specific tax transaction or report an item in a certain manner. However, strong tax authority presents a great measure of certainty that your client can proceed in a specific way and that, if audited, the tax position taken will withstand IRS scrutiny. Strength of position, confidence that you and your client are proceeding correctly under tax law, begins and ends with citation to tax authority. So, always remember to cite to tax authority.

Q2: **Where** should I cite to tax authority?
   A2: Provide your citation within a sentence or at the end of a sentence. As long as the reader knows how to find the referenced tax authority, then you have properly informed your reader. For example, consider the following sentence: "In Johnson v. Commissioner, the Tax Court held that taxpayers who provide documents that establish [xxxxx] qualify under section 162....." The author has properly referenced the source tax authority (Johnson v. Commissioner) in the sentence. However, since there is no citation included with the name of the case, the reader cannot readily locate the case. Consider another example: "Recently, a Tax Court held that taxpayers who engage in a 'covered transaction" will be permitted a current deduction of termination fees

---

[302] The Blue Book: A Uniform System of Citations, Nineteenth Edition, page 1.
[303] Managing Your Case, The Art of Persuading Judges, Antonin Scalia and Bryan Garner, page 123.
[304] The Blue Book: A Uniform System of Citations, Nineteenth Edition, Rule 8.4.1.2.

where.......Jones v. Commissioner, 147 T.C. 55 (1999)." Here, the author provides the reader with the source authority - Jones v. Commissioner, 147 T.C. 55 (1999) – at the end of the sentence. This citation allows the reader to understand the source tax authority, the weight of the source and how to locate the source.

Q3: **What** is the proper format to cite to tax authorities?

A3: There are various sources of tax authorities. So, the answer to this question is best left to citation manuals, such as the Blue Book on Citations. But, for a basic court case, an example of proper citation format is as follows: - Kirkwood v. Commissioner, 120 F.3d 78, 109 (9th Cir. 1990). Always differentiate the name of cases by either underlining or italicizing the name. Note that the first number (**120** F.3d 78, 109) references the volume of the case reporter – in this case the reporter is the Federal reporter, third series or "F.3d" for short. The second number (120 F.3d **78**, 109), provides the first page of the opinion within the case reporter. The third number (120 F.3d 78, **109**), provides the spot citation to the precise page of the court opinion that directly supports the reasoning or conclusion of the court that you are highlighting to the audience. So, for example, if you cited to Housley v. Commissioner, 697 F.Supp. 3 (D.D.C. 1988), the reader would pull volume "697" from the library. Then, the reader would turn to the first page listed in the citation – page 3. See the picture to the below. With all caselaw so easily accessible via online database searches, virtually no one visits the law library to physically locate cases. These days, all cases are retrieved online. Still, the function of guiding your audience through properly formatted citaitons remains the same. Volume – Reporter – First Page – Spot Citation.

Q4: **How** should I cite to a case if the court's decision includes a citation to another case?

A4: First, recognize that a judge who issues a decision will cite to other, earlier cases because he/she is attempting to follow earlier precedential authority to provide predictability to law. Formally, courts abide by the doctrine of stare decisis – latin for "to stand by things decided." Second, how should a tax professional cite to a case decision (say, Goeke v. Commissioner, 66 T.C. 868 (1990)), where the decision cites to an earlier precedent (say, Pearson v. Commissioner, 85 T.C. Memo. 1998 (1956))? The Blue Book offers two options: (1) Goeke v. Commissioner, 66 T.C. 868, 877 (1990) (internal citations omitted); or (2) Goeke v. Commissioner, 66 T.C. 868, 877 (1990), citing Pearson v. Commissioner, 85 T.C. Memo. 1998 (1956). With each option, the author is providing specific information to the reader.

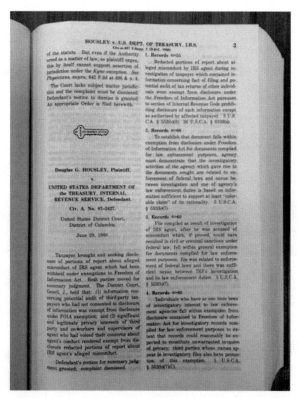

Q5: **When** should I cite to primary source authorities? It seems that I'm citing to tax authority in almost every sentence within my document.

A5: Include a citation every time you refer to tax authority as the source of the sentence. Unless your sentence presents a statement of fact, provide the source authority either within the sentence or at the end of the sentence. The Blue Book provides short cuts to reduce the visual but necessary "clutter" of frequent citations. Also, some professionals recommend that authors provide citations in footnotes to offer some relief to readers who are deluged with too many citations.

4. The Different Types of Written Client Tax Communication

- Comfort Opinion letter – this type of written tax communication provides the client with assurance that the contemplated transaction is viewed by a professional with specfic expected tax consequences. With such assurance, then the client knows with a measure of certainty how it can proceed.

- Penalty Protection Opinion letter – A professional's tax opinion can, but not always, serve as an effective defense against the imposition of a penalty. Recall in the case of Canal Corporation v. Commissioner that there are limitations to when a tax opinion letter can serve to protect the client/recipient from imposition of a penalty by the IRS. Below are summaries from select cases that provide useful context in considering the limits of protection provided by tax professional opinions.

  o Rovakat, LLC v. Comm'r, T.C. Memo 2011-225 aff'd 529 Fed.Appx. 124 (3d. Cir. 2013): "The mere fact that a taxpayer purchases an 'opinion' from a self-professed expert does not necessarily mean that the taxpayer relied on the 'expert' in good faith. An individual who blindly relies on a professional opinion to support a facially too good to be true transaction such as we have here does so at his or her own peril."
  o Murfam Farms LLC v. United States, 94 Fed. Cl. 235 (2010): Cannot rely on opinion for penalty protection where opinion provider also had a financial interest in the tax savings; fee was % of tax loss. Court found client could not reasonably have expected unbiased advice.
  o Michael H. Stough v Comm'r, 144 T.C. No. 16 (June 2, 2015). Taxpayer relied on CPA that prepared return and reported a deduction. Court concluded the CPA was a competent professional with sufficient experience, and with complete information. However, taxpayer did not discuss the deduction with the CPA before signing return. The court believed that discussion with the preparer would have revealed the error, and states that reliance on a preparer "and choosing to not adequately review the contents" of the tax return is not enough to avoid penalty
  o Palm Canyon X Investments, LLC v. Comm'r, T.C. Memo. 2009-288: Court held that any reliance on an opinion was misplaced because (1) the drafter was part of the promoter team and had a conflict of interest; (2) the taxpayer failed to provide signed representations, which were an express condition of

reliance; (3) the taxpayer and its advisers did not provide the opinion drafter with necessary facts that would have affected the drafter's conclusions.

o <u>CNT Investors v. Comm'r</u>, 144 T.C. No. 11 (March 23, 2015). Son of boss transaction. Reasonable reliance on a professional, even though taxpayer did not review the returns before signing. Also, while government claimed result was too good to be true, taxpayer was not knowledgeable enough to know that. Also, taxpayer's failure to review return is "troubling, but not fatal", because advisor was a long term advisor and review of return would not have indicated the real problem (a sham partnership that tax advisor was not aware of).

In providing tax opinion letters to clients, tax professionals must always be aware of their responsibilities to both their clients and applicable civil and criminal statutes when drafting tax opinions. Consider the tortured history of one accounting firm that did not keep its tax opinion communication within the bounds of legal limits. In <u>Blum v. Commissioner</u>, T.C. Memo. 2012-16, the U.S. Tax Court addressed whether taxpayers were entitled to deduct certain capital losses claims from their participation in an "Offshore Portofio Investment Strategy" ("OPIS") transaction and whether the taxpayers were liable for penalties for engaging in the transaction. In the court opinion, the Tax Court noted that a major accounting firm had promoted the OPIS transaction and provided the taxpayers with a tax opinion representing the firm's view that the transaction was "more likely than not" to be sustained. The court described the mechanics of the OPIS transaction in its opinion and then recounted the devasting aftermath to the accounting firm from its tax opinion issued to clients regarding OPIS: (1) government interest and rejection of the opinion; (2) focus by the U.S. Senate Permanent Subcommittee on Investigations of OPIS as an abusive tax shelter; (3) the accounting firm entering into a deferred prosecution agreement with the federal government; (4) admission that certain accounting partners engaged in unlawful and fraudulent conduct, including issuing tax opinions they knew relied on false facts and representations; (5) the accounting firm's agreement to pay the govenrment $456 million; and (6) numerous indictments obtained by Federal prosecutors against accounting firm employees and partners. Read the full court case, <u>Blum v. Commissioner</u>, T.C. Memo. 2012-16, to consider the potential consequences when civil and criminal requirements imposed upon tax professionals are not met.

- <u>FIN 48 Opinion letter</u> – A tax professional may be asked to render an opinion to satisfy a client's "FIN 48" analysis on a particular tax issue. The Financial Accounting Standards Board issued Interpretation Number 48, Accounting for Uncertainty in Income Taxes ("FIN 48"), which provides guidance on when a company that issues GAAP financial statements can recognize, for financial accounting purposes, a tax benefit where there is some uncertainty as to whether the benefit would ultimately be sustained. FIN 48 requires a company to undertake a two-part analysis with respect to each uncertain tax position. The first step of the analysis determines whether any portion of the claimed tax benefit can be recognized at all. The standard here is "more likely than not"; that is, in order to recognize, for financial statement purposes, a tax benefit with respect to which there is some legal or factual uncertainty, the company must conclude that, on its merits, the position would "more likely than not" be sustained. In making this determination, the company is required to assume that the position will be examined by the relevant taxing authority and that such taxing authority has full knowledge of all relevant facts. If the "more likely than not" standard is not satisfied, the inquiry ends; however, the company cannot report any portion of the uncertain item. If the company concludes that the item is "more likely than not" to be sustained, however, that does not necessarily mean that the company can book the entire amount. Instead, the analysis proceeds on to the second stage, which determines the amount of the tax benefit that can be recognized.

In addition to correspondence with clients, tax practitioners may be asked to prepare a "protest letter." What is a protest letter? If a taxpayer fails to reach an agreeable resolution with a revenue agent who is conducting an audit, then the taxpayer may request an appeal of the revenue agent's determination by submitting a written "protest" with the Office of Appeals. The protest letter should be completed and mailed to the IRS revenue agent, not to the Office of Appeals.

What should be included in a formal written protest letter? Include all of the following:

1. Taxpayer's name, address, and a daytime telephone number.
2. A statement that the taxpayer wants to appeal the IRS findings to the Office of Appeals.
3. A copy of the letter the taxpayer received that shows the proposed change(s).
4. The tax period(s) or year(s) involved.
5. A list of each proposed item with which the taxpayer disagrees.
6. The reason(s) the taxpayer disagrees with each item.
7. The facts that support the taxpayer's position on each item.
8. The law or authority, if any, that supports the taxpayer's position on each item.
9. The penalties of perjury statement as follows: "Under the penalties of perjury, I declare that the facts stated in this protest and any accompanying documents are true, correct, and complete to the best of my knowledge and belief."
10. The taxpayer's signature under the penalties of perjury statement.

If the taxpayer's representative prepares and signs the protest on behalf of the taxpayer, he or she must substitute a declaration for the penalties of perjury statement that includes:

1. That he or she submitted the protest and any accompanying documents, and
2. Whether he or she knows personally that the facts stated in the protest and any accompanying documents are true and correct.

The taxpayer must send the formal written protest within the time limit specified in the letter that offers the taxpayer the right to appeal the proposed changes. Generally, the time limit is 30 days from the date of the letter.

What does an example of a protest letter look like? See below:

_____

February 10, 2015

Group Manager
Internal Revenue Service
San Francisco, CA

       Re: Mr. & Mrs. Smith
               Soc. Sec. # ***_**_**** and ***_**_****
               Reference # 123ABC

Dear Sir/Madam,

Reference is made to your 30-Day Letter (Letter 915(DO)) dated January 15, 2015 enclosed herewith regarding the proposed adjustment to the casualty loss deduction in the amount of $250,000 claimed by the taxpayers.

The taxpayers respectfully protest the proposed adjustment and reserve the right to file one or more supplements to this protest. The following information is submitted in support of this protest:

1. Taxpayers' name, address and identification number
    Mr. & Mrs. Smith

    _____
    Soc. Sec. # ***_**_**** and ***_**_****

2. Date of the 30-Day Letter: January 15, 2015

3. Taxable Year at issue: Year ended December 31, 2012

4. Request for conference: Taxpayers request a conference with the Internal Revenue Office of Appeals in the San Francisco, CA office with respect to the findings of the examining Revenue Agent.

5. Facts - In 2000, the taxpayers, Mr. & Mrs. Smith decided to build a house in Northern California. The house was constructed without securing building permits required by the relevant county. In 2012, a fire swept through taxpayers' neighborhood completely destroying their home. While officials are still investigating the cause of the fire, there is no dispute that the taxpayers had no involvement with the fire.

    The taxpayers claimed a casualty loss deduction of $250,000 on their 2012 tax return.

6. Applicable Law

Section 165(a) allows a deduction for "any loss sustained during the taxable year and not compensated for by insurance or otherwise." Section 165(c)(3) provides that in the case of an individual, the deduction allowed in subsection (a) is to be limited to "losses of property not connected with a trade or business, if such losses arise from fire, storm, shipwreck, or other casualty, or from theft."

The taxpayers' claim clearly falls within the scope of deduction under section 165 as:
(i)   they sustained a loss of $250,000 during the taxable year;
(ii)   it was not compensated by insurance or otherwise; and
(iii)   the taxpayers, as individuals, satisfy the requirements of section 165(c)(3) since the property (their home) was not connected with a trade or business, and the cause of the loss was fire.

Admittedly, courts have disallowed casualty loss deductions, where allowance of the deduction would severely and immediately frustrate a sharply defined national or State policy. Tank Truck Rentals, Inc. v. Commissioner, 356 U.S. 30, 35 (1958) (affirmed disallowance of deductions of fines imposed on truck owners for violations of state maximum truck weight laws); Richey v. Commissioner, 33 T.C. 272, 276 (1959) (theft loss disallowed for money stolen from taxpayer during his participation in a counterfeiting scheme).

In analyzing whether the allowance of a deduction would severely and immediately frustrate a sharply defined national or state policy, courts have looked at various factors. One key factor is whether the taxpayer's activity directly caused the loss. Blackman v. Commissioner, 88 T.C. 677, 682 (1987), aff'd, without published opinion, 867 F.2d 605 (1st Cir. 1988); Holt v. Commissioner, 69 T.C. 75, 81 (1977), aff'd 611 F.2d 1160 (2d Cir. 1980).

With respect to the taxpayers' claim, the following aspects are relevant (i) there is no dispute that taxpayers had no involvement with the fire (unlike Blackman, where the taxpayer intentionally started the fire); and (ii) casualty loss was not directly related to taxpayers' failure to obtain permits, and the loss would have occurred regardless of whether taxpayers had obtained the required permits. The mere fact that an expenditure bears a remote relation to an illegal act does not make it nondeductible. Commissioner v. Heininger, 320 U.S. 467, 474 (1943).

Courts have also examined whether allowing the loss would defeat the purpose of the laws that the taxpayer violated or alleviate the sting of any punishment imposed on the taxpayer for violation of the statute. Murillo v. Commissioner, T.C. Memo. 1998-13 (allowing loss deduction for forfeited money arising from illegal activities would take the sting out of the forfeiture).

The taxpayers' facts are distinguishable as State has specific punitive measures for property owners who do not obtain the required building permits. Allowing taxpayers' casualty loss deduction would have no impact on these punitive measures. See Rohrs v. Commissioner, T.C. Summ. Op. 2009-190 (casualty loss deduction allowed for a truck the taxpayer damaged while driving intoxicated; allowing the loss would not in any way alleviate the sting of the punishment of imprisonment and fines imposed by the state for a DUI offense).

Apart from the above, in facts that were substantially similar to the taxpayers', the IRS has also provided favorable guidance on casualty loss deduction. See CCA 201346009. The issue under consideration was whether taxpayers may be denied a casualty loss deduction under section 165(c)(3) for two uninsured structures which were built without the requisite permits and were destroyed in a fire. The IRS concluded that there were not sufficient grounds to deny taxpayers a casualty loss deduction based on public policy considerations.

In conclusion, the taxpayers' claim for casualty loss deduction is clearly covered under section 165. The casualty loss was not directly related to taxpayers' failure to obtain permits, a key factor considered by the courts. See Blackman and Holt. Also, since the State has specific punitive measures for property owners who do not obtain the required building permits, allowing the loss would not defeat the purpose of the laws that the taxpayers violated or alleviate the sting of any punishment imposed on the taxpayers for violation of the statute. See Murillo and Rohrs. Lastly, the claim for casualty loss deduction is consistent with IRS guidance on the issue. See CCA 201346009.

The attached protest was prepared by the taxpayers' representative, CPA _____ (Form 2848 enclosed) on the basis of information available to him. All statements contained therein are true to the best of his knowledge and belief.

Sincerely,

_____, CPA

Encl:
30-Day Letter (Letter 915(DO)
Form 2848

---

5. Waiver Language

Waiver language is often included in a tax opinion to define the limits of the written communication. From the perspective of the drafter, inclusion of waiver language limits the author's liability in the event the opinion is incorrect or subject to dispute. From the perspective of the client, waiver language is an unwelcome barrage of legalese but acknowledged as part of the tax professional's manner of limiting liability. Here are some examples of waiver language that may be included in tax opinion letters:

- This Opinion is limited to the tax issues specifically addressed in the Opinion. Additional issues exist that could affect the tax treatment of the transaction or matter that is the subject of this Opinion and the Opinion does not consider or provide a conclusion with respect to any additional issues.
- The conclusions reached in this Opinion represent and are based upon the Firm's best judgement regarding the application of the U.S. Federal income tax laws arising under the Internal Revenue Code, judicial decisions, administrative regulations, published rulings and other tax authorities existing as of the date of this Opinion. This Opinion is not binding upon the Internal Revenue Service or the courts and there is no guarantee that the Internal Revenue Service will not successfully assert a contrary position. Furthermore, no assurance can be given that future legislative or administrative changes, on either a prospective or retroactive basis, would not adversely affect the accuracy of the conclusions stated herein.

- The Opinion set forth in paragraph III above is based upon the Internal Revenue Code and its legislative history, Treasury Regulations, judicial decisions, and current administrative rulings and practices of the IRS, all as in effect on the date of this Opinion letter. These authorities may be amended or revoked at any time. Any changes may or may not be retroactive with respect to the transactions entered into or contemplated prior to the date thereof and could cause the Opinion to be or become incorrect, in whole or in part, with respect to the U.S. federal income tax consequences described herein. The Firm has assumed that all court cases have been properly litigated. There is and can be no assurance that such legislative, judicial or administrative changes will not occur in the future. The Firm assumes no obligation to update or modify this Opinion letter to reflect any developments that may impact the Opinion from and after the date of the Opinion letter.

- This Opinion does not address any federal tax consequences of the transactions set forth herein, or transactions related or proximate to such transactions, except as set forth herein. This Opinion does not address any state, local, foreign, or other tax consequences that may result from any of the transactions. This Opinion is addressed solely to C&C and Colonial BancGroup and may not be relied upon by any other party to this transaction or in any other transaction without our prior written consent.

- This Opinion is based upon the representations, documents, facts, and assumptions that have been included or referenced herein and the assumptions that such information is accurate, true, and authentic. This Opinion does not address any transactions other than those described herein. This Opinion does not address any transactions whatsoever if all the transactions described herein are not consummated as described herein without waiver or breach of any material provision thereof or if the assumptions set forth herein are not true and accurate at all relevant times. In the event any one of the facts or assumptions is incorrect, in whole or in part, the conclusions reached in this Opinion might be adversely affected.

6. Are Tax Opinions and Related Communication Between Client and Tax Professional Subject Protection as Privileged Communication?

For communications on after after July 22, 1998, section 7525 specifically extends the common law attorney-client privilege for communcations to "federally authorized tax practitioners." Section 7525 provides that, for "tax advice," the same common-law protections of confidentiality which apply to a communication between a taxpayer and an attorney also apply to a communication between a taxpayer and any federally authorized tax practitioner to the extent the communication would be considered a privileged communication if it were between a taxpayer and an attorney. However, this privilege may only be asserted in any noncriminal tax matter before the Internal Revenue Service, and any noncriminal tax proceeding in Federal court brought by or against the United States. IRC § 7525(a)(2). Communication between a tax return preparer (CPA, who is a federally authorized tax practitioner) and a taxpayer related to the preparation and filing of a federal tax return would not be subject to privilege under section 7525 because there was no confidential communication between the parties. The expectation from this engagement was that the material submitted to the CPA would be used to disclose on the filed federal tax return. This example illustrates the point that applying section 7525 to withhold information from the IRS is not an easy task and should be carefully reviewed before a tax practitioner asserts its application.[305]

7. Shorter Written Communication

Whether long or short, every written tax communication must focus on one objective – educate the reader on the tax issue addressed. Sometimes, a tax professional is called upon to draft a shorter length tax document. Internally, this type of document may be referred to as a "case summary" or "case memo." An example of a short case summary is provided, below, in an Action on Decision ("AOD"). An AOD is a formal memorandum prepared by the IRS Office of Chief Counsel that announces the future litigation position the IRS will take with regard to the court decision addressed by the AOD.[306] After reading the AOD that follows, which addresses the limits of claiming the home mortgage

---

[305]Cir. 230, Section 10.20(a)(1) provides, "A practitioner must, on a proper and lawful request by a duly authorized officer or employee of the Internal Revenue Service, promptly submit records or information in any matter before the Internal Revenue Service unless the practitioner believes in good faith and on reasonable grounds that the records or information are privileged." (emphasis added). Thus, if a practitioner refuses to promptly submit records in response to an IRS request without determining "in good faith and on reasonable grounds that the records or information are privileged" then, the practitioner is violating Circular 230. IRM 4.11.55.2.2 provides that a referral to the Office of Professional Responsibility should be made when "in matters involving non-willful conduct.....it can be established that the preparer has a pattern of failing to meet the required standards of Circular 230."
[306]AODs are accessible at: https://apps.irs.gov/app/picklist/list/actionsOnDecisions.html.

interest deduction, consider whether this short case summary has adequately informed you of the holding of the reported case – <u>Voss v. Commissioner</u>, 796 F.3d 1051 (9th Cir. 2015).

IRB 2016-31
August 1, 2016

ACTION ON DECISION

Subject: <u>Voss v. Commissioner</u>, 796 F.3d 1051 (9th Cir. 2015), <u>rev'g</u> <u>Sophy v. Commissioner</u>, 138 T.C. 204 (2012)

Issue: Whether the § 163(h)(3) debt limitations on deductions for qualified residence interest apply on a per-taxpayer basis, rather than on a per-residence basis.

Discussion: Section 163(h)(2)(D) of the Internal Revenue Code allows taxpayers to deduct a limited amount of personal interest paid on residential mortgages. The mortgage must be secured by a "qualified residence," defined by § 163(h)(4)(A) to include the taxpayer's principal residence plus one other residence. Section 163(h)(3) limits the amount of deductible interest to interest paid on $1 million of acquisition indebtedness (or refinanced acquisition indebtedness, up to the amount of the original loan's balance), plus interest paid on $100,000 of home equity indebtedness.

Mr. Voss and Mr. Sophy, unmarried co-owners of two residences, each filed an individual tax return claiming a deduction for qualified residence interest paid on acquisition indebtedness and home equity indebtedness in excess of $1.1 million (for a combined amount in excess of $2.2 million). The IRS disallowed portions of each taxpayer's deduction for qualified residence interest on the grounds that § 163(h)(2) and (3) limit the aggregate amount of indebtedness to $1 million and $100,000, respectively, on any qualified residence, allocated among all taxpayers entitled to an interest expense deduction for that qualified residence.

Mr. Voss and Mr. Sophy petitioned the Tax Court, challenging the Service's determinations. The Tax Court agreed with the IRS, finding that the language of the statute limits the total amount of indebtedness with respect to acquisition indebtedness and home equity indebtedness that may be claimed in relation to the qualified residence, rather than in relation to an individual taxpayer. The taxpayers appealed to the United States Court of Appeals for the Ninth Circuit.

The Ninth Circuit reversed the Tax Court decision, agreeing with the taxpayers that the statutory limitations apply to unmarried co-owners of a qualified residence on a per-taxpayer basis. The court based its conclusion largely on its interpretation of the language of the statute that expressly provides that married individuals filing separate returns are entitled to deduct interest on up to $500,000 of acquisition indebtedness and $50,000 of home equity indebtedness. By providing lower debt limits for married

2

couples, and not for unmarried co-owners, Congress singled out married couples for specific treatment, implying that an unmarried co-owner filing a separate return is entitled to deduct interest on up to $1,000,000 of acquisition indebtedness and $100,000 of home equity indebtedness.

The Internal Revenue Service will follow the <u>Voss</u> opinion and will apply the § 163(h)(2) and (3) limitations on a per-taxpayer basis, allowing each taxpayer to deduct mortgage interest on indebtedness of up to $1 million and $100,000, respectively, on a qualified residence.

Recommendation: Acquiescence

Elizabeth R. Binder
General Attorney, Branch 1
(Income Tax & Accounting)

Reviewers:

Approved:

WILLIAM J. WILKINS
Chief Counsel
Internal Revenue Service

By:

Scott K. Dinwiddie
Associate Chief Counsel
(Income Tax & Accounting)

THIS DOCUMENT IS NOT TO BE RELIED UPON OR
OTHERWISE CITED AS PRECEDENT BY TAXPAYERS

Shorter length tax documents are more difficult to draft than longer documents. In the modern age, think about drafting a Twitter message. Twitter forces users to keep track of the 140 character limit in this forum. Brevity, conciseness and directness in each and every message is the cardinal rule. Tax involves synthesizing a vast amount of technical material, citing to primary authorities as a basis for analysis and carefully guiding the reader through every point. This laborious tax process takes time and a great deal of space on paper. Imposing a Twitter-like focus on written tax communication poses a difficulties. But, the type of filtering approach will reward you with a clearer, sharper document for your audience. Shorten your tax documents, make critical choices on what to include/exclude and elevate the effectiveness of your written communication.

8. The Ultimate Goal of Tax Communication - Educate

While there are core elements that should be included in tax communication, the ultimate goal of every tax communication (in written form or oral briefing) should be to educate the audience. Present the authorities that support your position, cite to these authorities properly, present the relevant facts and your legal position in a clear fashion, and guide the audience in a succinct presentation. This prescription seems plain but it is effective.

Oftentimes, students will avoid presenting the basic reasons underlying a code section because they feel that it is unnecessary particularly since the audience is too sophisticated. However, tax communication is at every level an opportunity to educate the reader in the simplest of terms. Effective tax communication should build a strong foundation of information from the ground up.

Consider, for example, a recent 2018 decision by the Ninth Circuit Court of Appeals addressing the complicated issue of transfer pricing.[307] In the initial section of the Ninth Circuit's opinion provided below, note how the Court carefully guides the audience along through this complex topic.

---

[307] Altera Corp. v. Commissioner, 122 AFTR 2d __ (9th Cir. July 24, 2018), withdrawn, [citation omitted] (August 7, 2018). This court opinion offers a wonderful example of tax analysis that is presented clearly, informatively and interestingly. Note, however, that this opinion of the Ninth Circuit issued on July 24, 2018 was withdrawn for a reconstituted panel to confer on the decision. Regardless of the ultimate disposition of this case, the lesson to be drawn from this opinion is how to draft tax material in an educational format.

OPINION

THOMAS, Chief Judge:

In this case, we consider the validity of 26 C.F.R. § 1.482-7A(d)(2),[1] under which related entities must share the cost of employee stock compensation in order for their cost-sharing arrangements to be classified as qualified cost-sharing arrangements ("QCSA") and thus avoid an IRS adjustment. We conclude that the regulations withstand scrutiny under general administrative law principles, and we therefore reverse the decision of the Tax Court.

I

Corporations often elect to conduct business through international subsidiaries. Transactions between related companies can provide opportunities for minimizing or avoiding taxes, particularly when a foreign subsidiary is located in a low tax jurisdiction. For example, a parent company in a high tax jurisdiction can sell property to its subsidiary in a low tax jurisdiction and have its subsidiary sell the property for profit. The profits from those sales are thus taxed in a lower tax jurisdiction, resulting in significant tax savings for the parent. This practice, known as "transfer pricing" can result in United States companies shifting profits that would be subject to tax in America offshore to avoid tax. Similarly, related companies can identify and shift costs

---

[1] The 2003 amendments to Treasury's cost-sharing regulations are at issue. Although they are still in effect, the Code has been reorganized, and what was § 1.482-7 in 2003 is now numbered § 1.482-7A. To minimize confusion, our citations are to the current version of the regulations unless otherwise specified.

between American and foreign jurisdictions to minimize tax exposure. In recent years, United States corporations have used these techniques to develop intangible property with their foreign subsidiaries, and to share the cost of development between the companies. Under these arrangements, a U.S. corporation might enter into a research and development ("R&D") cost-sharing agreement with its foreign subsidiary located in a low tax jurisdiction and grant the offshore company rights to exploit the property internationally. The interplay of cost and income allocation between the two companies in such a transaction can result in significantly reduced taxes for the United States parent.

To address the risk of multinational corporation tax avoidance, Congress passed legislation granting the United States Department of the Treasury the authority to allocate income and costs between such related parties. 26 U.S.C. § 482. In turn, the Secretary of the Treasury promulgated regulations authorizing the Commissioner of the Internal Revenue Service to allocate income and costs among these related entities. 26 C.F.R. §§ 1.482-0 through 1.482-9.

At issue before us are employee stock options, the cost of which the companies in this case elected not to share, resulting in substantial tax savings for the parent—here, the tax associated with over $80 million in income. The Commissioner contends that allocation of stock compensation costs between the companies is appropriate to reflect economic reality; Altera Corporation ("Altera") and its subsidiaries contend that any cost allocation exceeds the Commissioner's authority.

Fundamental to resolution of this dispute is an understanding of the arm's length standard, a tool that

Treasury developed in the mid-twentieth century to ensure that controlled taxpayers were taxed similarly to uncontrolled taxpayers. The arm's length standard is results-oriented, meaning that its goal is parity in taxable income rather than parity in the method of allocation itself. 26 C.F.R. § 1.482-1(b)(1) ("A controlled transaction meets the arm's length standard if the results of the transaction are consistent with the results that would have been realized if uncontrolled taxpayers had engaged in the same transaction under the same circumstances (arm's length result)."). A traditional arm's length analysis looks to comparable transactions among non-related parties to achieve an arm's length result. The issue in this case is whether Treasury can permissibly allocate between related parties a cost that unrelated parties do not agree to share.

Altera asserts that the arm's length standard always demands a comparability analysis, meaning that the Commissioner cannot allocate costs between related parties in the absence of evidence that unrelated parties share the same costs when dealing at arm's length. Altera argues that, because uncontrolled taxpayers do not share the cost of employee stock options, the Commissioner cannot require related parties to share that cost.

The Commissioner argues that he may, consistent with the arm's length standard, apply a purely internal method of allocation, distributing the costs of employee stock options in proportion to the income enjoyed by each controlled taxpayer. This "commensurate with income" method analyzes the income generated by intangible property in comparison with the amount paid (usually as royalty) to the parent. In the Commissioner's view, the commensurate with income method is consistent with the arm's length standard

8	ALTERA CORP. V. CIR

because controlled cost-sharing arrangements have no equivalent in uncontrolled arrangements, and Congress has provided that the Commissioner may dispense with a comparability analysis where comparable transactions do not exist in order to achieve an arm's length result.

Because this case involves a challenge to regulations, the ultimate issue is not what the arm's length standard should mean but rather whether Treasury may define the standard as it has. We conclude that the challenged regulations are not arbitrary and capricious but rather a reasonable execution of the authority delegated by Congress to Treasury.

Emulate the Ninth Circuit as in Altera Corporation opinion, above. Educate your reader.

In addition to providing an effective discussion of the tax issue, practitioners should avoid engaging in coarse behavior in how you communicate with the opposing side, whether the opposing side is the government or any other party. It seems that as years pass, cordial discussions have given way to unfiltered attacks. Rather than written tax communication serving as a means to educate the reader, more and more tax communication seems to focus on berating or denigrating the opposing side. If you communicate in a professional, cordial, and respectful manner, then are you more or less likely to have your document reviewed with an open mind? In contrast, if you denigrate the reader for being ill-informed, uneducated, a lackey or political operative, then have you laid the foundation for open communication or shut down any possibility for a meeting of the minds? When the objective is to find the proper interpretation and application of tax law, it serves you and your client best when you conduct yourself in written communication professionally and nobly.

In my classes, students appreciate learning about the core elements that should be included in every written tax communication and the objective of these documents. But, students always want to see examples that illustrate these learning concepts. These examples are reflected in court cases, AODs, and CCAs included in this publication. Look to these examples to see the common elements that are embedded in each written document.

9. Oral Tax Communication

What is the difference between oral and written tax communication? The answer – time. It is sometimes said that a written memo or letter often benefits the author more than the recipient because written tax communication <u>documents</u> the advice and primarily serves to establish evidence to support the author if a dispute arises later between advisor and client. Because of this aspect of written communication, the typical written product is often lengthy (more facts and analysis than perhaps necessary) and includes waiver language. In contrast, oral communication of tax serves just one pristine function – inform/educate the audience.

Success as tax practitioners begins when we conduct efficient tax research and culminates when we are able to present our findings and views effectively in either oral or written form. Below is a checklist of basic elements that can help you successfully communicate tax results in non-written form:

1. **Respect your audience's time** - how much time should you allocate to complete an oral briefing? Target no more than 5 minutes to present your views. Questions that arise during or after the briefing my extend the length of your presentation. But, for your part, refine the points of your discussion to last no more than 5 minutes.
2. **Focus on the specific issue and critical facts** – present the bare bones facts (not just relevant facts, but "critical" facts) and focus your audience on the precise issue. Drilling down to the most essential facts and issue statement is a difficult task, and much more difficult than how you would present such material in written form because there is no time to progressively develop a sequence of facts or legal analysis.
3. **Define the ultimate message that you want your audience to take away after the briefing** – clearly understand at the beginning of your oral presentation the message that you want your audience to appreciate at the end of your presentation. For example,
   a. I want the audience to understand that this tax issue is novel, a matter of first impression for the Tax Court, and warrants our highest attention;
   b. I want the audience to understand that this tax issue is not novel but rather turns on one critical fact that is absent/present in this case.
4. Recognize that **non-verbal communication** affects your message – what is this? Have you ever spoken to someone who has their arms crossed, or continues to look at their watch, or taps their feet, or continues to look at a document while you talk? Just as the listener can present cues and messages through their body/facial movements, you as the presenter can enhance or distract from your message. So, consider some of the following non-verbal types of communication as you prepare to orally present your tax views:

   a. <u>Body language</u> – posture, body gestures, facial expressions

b. <u>Proxemics</u> – consider how much space is necessary to set between you and your listener

c. <u>Appearance</u> – your attire provides a visual message to your audience. Let's consider extreme examples to make the point that your attire matters for the effectiveness of your oral presentation. In one scenario, you attend a meeting and orally brief the audience wearing a T-shirt with the message, "I'm with Stupid!" In another scenario, you arrive at the meeting in a suit. Which version of these two scenarios presents the most effective non-verbal cue to enhance, or at least to not-distract, from your message?

5. **Rehearse** – What you believe will occur during an oral presentation is far different than what actually happens. Below are a list of things to "Do" and "Avoid" as you rehearse:

a. **Things to Do**
   i. *Focus on providing a concise, organized presentation. When we are nervous, we may tend to ramble from point to point. Jot down the main points* on a legal pad or index card to remind you of the sequence of your presentation and speak slowly.[308]
   ii. If the tax transaction involves complicated entities or transactions, then *prepare a flowchart* to assist in guiding the audience.
   iii. Tax is inherently complicated. Reduce complicated tax jargon and present material in the most direct, straightforward language possible.[309]
   iv. *Keep eye contact* with the audience to look for cues of interest or confusion. If you spot that what you have said appears to have confused your audience, then address that point immediately. "I think that I may have confused you on that point. In other words......"
   v. If you have one main primary source authority, then discuss the one pivotal case that supports your tax view, *bring a copy with you*, highlight and tab the specific part of the case that you determine critical in the event your audience asks for the source document.

---

[308] The American Medical Association and health literacy experts recommend using 17 communication techniques to improve patient-provider communication, including its recommendation for medical practitioners to speak slowly to promote more effective communication. *Schwartzberg JG, Cowett A, VanGeest J, Wolf MS, American Journal of Health Behavior, Sept-Oct. 2007, 31 Suppl 1: S96-104. Am J Health Behav. 2007 Sep-Oct; 31 Suppl 1():S96-104.* Yes, the medical and tax professions are different. But, effective oral communication is strongly driven by how we communicate, not principally what we communicate.

[309] <u>Id.</u> The American Medical Association recommends that medical practitioners communicate using simple "living room" language, or plain language, that provides clear, straightforward communication which avoids complicated vocabulary and sentence structure so that the audience can understand the message the first time that they hear it.

       vi.   Videotape your presentation to rehearse your presentation to confirm your organization, substantive message and time. Over the course of a year, it's likely that you may have a dozen or fewer opportunities to orally brief your supervisor or client. These limited opportunities should be treated with an appropriate amount of preparation. If you think you need more practice, then join "Toastmasters" or some other public speaking group to become more comfortable with your oral communication abilities.

b. **Things to Avoid**
       i.   Don't take a long script and read directly off a prepared statement.
       ii.   Avoid trying to present tax jargon or acronyms. This is not about establishing your credentials. Focus on educating the listener. It's not about you.
       iii.   Don't stare into your notes/script or gaze away from your audience. Maintain eye contact and engage your listener(s). You can't have an engaged audience if you're focusing on your notes and not at your target audience.
       iv.   Don't rush through your presentation because you've packed 10 minutes of material to a 5-minute discussion. Organize your material so that you can present streamlined material in 5 minutes of normal speech.
       v.   Reduce repetitive fillers, such as "um," "like," "uh."
       vi.   If your audience interrupts you with questions, address the questions and don't talk over the listener. The audience always has the "right of way" in an oral briefing.
       vii.   Leave your cell phone behind or turn it to "silent mode." Yes, this is an obvious point but still worth a reminder.

There are two ways to become better at oral communication: (1) preparation; and (2) practice. Preparation just takes good old fashioned hard work. You can log in structured oral communication sessions by joining organizations such as Toastmasters.[310] Additionally, it may help to watch others provide oral presentations. For a good source to view oral presentations, go to the Ninth Circuit Court of Appeals government website that provides a database of oral arguments. See a snapshot of the government website, below.

---

[310] https://www.toastmasters.org/membership/facts-for-first-timers.

10. Email Communication

Email correspondence presents the main form of communication in the workplace. As such, I believe that it is critical for you understand some basic guidelines on email use beyond the rules that may be mandated in a workplace manual. I offer three points for your consideration:

(1) Always remember that workplace email communication is <u>official correspondence</u>. Emails present formal communication akin to a written letter mailed out by your organization. Do not treat emails as text messages or Snapchats. This type of communication is a reflection of you and your organization.

(2) <u>Assume that your emails will be released</u> to the public-at-large. Email communication is always preserved and subject to release outside of the

intended audience unless some type of privilege applies. When drafting emails, operate under the assumption that your drafted emails will be released to both individuals within your organization who are not included in the intended distribution chain and to those outside of your organization.

(3) <u>Note the nuances of email communication:</u>

- How quickly should you respond to an email?
  - o Suggestion – respond no later than within 24 hours from the receipt of an email. This also means that whenever you are out of the office for more than 24 hours, you must initiate an "out of office" auto response.
- Should you respond in a formal or informal tone?
  - o Suggestion – always respond in a formal tone, unless you have developed a trusted, informal relationship. And, avoid using emojis in your communication.
- Draft a long or short response?
  - o Suggestion – when in doubt, default to a shorter version. Drafting a shorter message always takes more work. Devote the extra time to prepare a concise, informative response.
- Proof-read your emails?
  - o Suggestion – yes, you should respond to email messages quickly. But, it's always best practice to pause before hitting the "Send" button to check for typographical, grammatical errors. Take an extra few minutes to conduct a basic review of the text of your message.
- Copy yourself or select "blind copy"?
  - o Suggestion – think about the message you are sending to the recipient when you copy yourself on an email. E.g., "I may need this email as proof later. So, I'm copying myself." Your email is automatically in the "Sent" folder. Avoid copying yourself. And, always avoid blind copying others. Inevitably, someone you blind copy will forget that you've selected that feature and will end up forwarding your message on to someone you did not intend to see the email.
- Basic format
  - o Suggestion – (1) always type an informative "Subject" line; (2) If you are forwarding a long cascade of earlier emails, assist the reader by providing a quick summary of the prior correspondence; (3) do not include your favorite quote as part of your signature line. Keep the work email short and professional.

Chapter 11 - Questions

1. List the four core elements of every written tax communication.

2. Define what constitutes a "relevant" fact.

3. Why did the court in <u>Canal Corp. v. Commissioner</u> determine that the written tax advice issued by the tax advisor could not be reasonably relied upon by the taxpayer to avoid imposition of a penalty?

4. You are an associate of an accounting firm. Follow the instructions below and draft a client letter after conducting tax research.

   Date: March 15, 2018
   From: Anthony Kim, Partner (GGU Accountants, LLP)
   To: Firm Associate (GGU Accountants, LLP)
   Subject: Ebay Sales by Our Client Jillian Smith

   Discussion
   Our longtime client Jillian Smith has requested our firm's assistance with a tax matter. Ms. Smith and the firm have agreed to provide her with tax advice on her specific question for a fixed fee of $2,500. The issue and basic factual summary follows: Jilliam received clothes, both new and used, from her auth Rosey Pittsubrgh on or about January, 2017. The clothes had labels from Tony Burch, Ann Taylor, Lululemon etc. No original cost data such as receipts were provided with the gifts to Ms. Smith by Ms. Pittsburgh. The items varied in retail price from $50-$300. Jilliam established an account on eBay and sold these items that she received from Ms. Pittsburgh in 2017 and used the proceeds from her sales to pay for her daughter's college expenses. The tax question is whether the proceeds from Jilliam Smith's eBay sales of items received as a gift from donor Rosey Pittsburg constitute gross income to Jilliam, the donee?

   Your assignment is as follows:

A. provide **a client letter** for my review addressed to Ms. Smith on the tax question presented to our firm for tax year 2017. The client letter should be no longer than 3 pages, single-spaced that provides citations to all primary source authorities supporting your analysis. Remember that the letter will be provided to tax novices. So, please make sure to guide the reader through each step of your analysis; and

B. provide a separate page listing:

   i. your total hours devoted to research;

   ii. your total hours devoted to writing; and

   iii. your bill rate. Our firm charges clients $200/hr for your time.

Total the total research and writing hours, multiply your bill rate and provide me with the total cost to charge our client for your work. Remember that the firm has already agreed to a fixed fee of $2,500. So, please try to be efficient with your time on this project.

CHAPTER 12 – TAX PLANNING

Learning Objectives:

☑ Understand the definition of tax planning
☑ Understand how to recognize tax planning opportunities

In this Chapter:

1. Tax Planning
2. Examples of Tax Planning
   a. Example #1 – The Struggling Couple
   b. Example #2 – New Qualified Plug-in Electric Drive Motor Vehicles

3. The Limits of Lawful Tax Planning

1. Tax Planning

What is tax planning? Some people refer to tax planning as the *art* of arranging a person's tax affairs to maximize tax deferral or avoidance. I don't subscribe to this view of tax planning. There is no *art* involved in tax planning. Instead, effective tax planning involves careful, critical reading of the tax code and understanding how facts can trigger its application or non-application in the future to maximize tax deferral or avoidance. Moreover, tax planning is not restricted to tax deferral or avoidance.[311] If a sole proprietor is required to comply with federal estimated tax payments during the year,

---

[311] In providing tax planning advice, the practitioner must recognize the difference between tax avoidance and tax evasion. <u>See</u> definitions, above, in Chapter 11.

then planning ahead for these required payments averts a penalty but does not either defer or avoid tax.[312] Where there are opportunities to plan tax minimization strategies, tax practitioners must consider the applicable tax sections, professional and ethical guidelines, the intent of Congress in enacting these statutes and how to clearly lay out the steps in implementing the tax strategy for their clients.

To gain a better sense of tax planning, let's consider the difference between tax reporting and tax planning. On the one hand, "tax reporting" involves reaching the proper tax determination after applying completed facts to applicable tax law and passing along the information to the tax authority.   On the other hand, "tax planning" involves situations where some or all facts are not yet completed leaving opportunities to implement or avoid certaing facts that are relevant to reach a desired tax outcome. From slightly different angle, let's look at the difference between tax planning and tax evasion. Tax planning is aimed at the elimination or reduction of tax and/or penalty through legitimate means whereas tax evasion connotes the use of subterfuge and/or fraud as a means to achieve the tax objective. If tax planning is still somewhat confusing, then let's review a few examples to reach a better understanding.

2. Examples of Tax Planning

Understanding the definition of tax planning is far removed from becoming comfortable with how it's applied in practice. And, the best approach to understanding tax planning is through examples. 313 So let's go through some sample scenarios!

a. Tax Planning Example #1 – The Struggling Couple

o **Factual Scenario** – It's July, 2018. Husband and wife reside in California. One spouse has an annual salary of $300,000 while the other spouse does not work. On their Federal income tax return, it is more beneficial for the couple to claim the standard deduction. Husband and wife are struggling to make their marriage work. Both spouses are hopeful that they will improve their relationship. Still, they arrive at your tax office to discuss the Federal tax impact if they should proceed with a divorce.

o **Tax Law** – Your basic tax research points you to two code sections that may be applicable to your clients' situation in the event divorce occurs – sections 71 and 215. Read each code section and the associated historical amendments.

o Section 215

---

[312] For a very insightful summary of considerations in providing tax planning advice, read Heather M. English, Giving Useful Planning Advice, 134 Tax Notes 1299 (2012) at http://repository.uchastings.edu/faculty_scholarship.

[313] Nothing in these tax planning scenarios states or implies that the analyses are recommended, proper or improper. Rather, the scenarios and analyses provide material for students' review and consideration only.

General Rule. In the case of an individual, there shall be allowed as a deduction an amount equal to the alimony or separate maintenance payments during such individual's taxable year…..[the remaining subsections are omitted]

Historical Amendments - Pub. L. 115-97, Title I, §11051(a), (c), Dec. 22, 2017, 131 Stat. 2089, 2090, provided that, applicable to any divorce or separation instrument (as defined in former section 71(b)(2) of this title as in effect before Dec. 22, 2017) executed after Dec. 31, 2018, and to such instruments executed on or before Dec. 31, 2018, and modified after Dec. 31, 2018, if the modification expressly provides that the amendment made by section 11051 of Pub. L. 115-97 applies to such modification, this section is repealed.

o   Section 71
General Rule. Gross income includes amounts received as alimony or separate maintenance payments…..[the remaining subsections are omitted]

Historical Amendments - Pub. L. 115-97, Title I, §11051(b)(1)(B), (c), Dec. 22, 2017, 131 Stat. 2089, 2090, provided that, applicable to any divorce or separation instrument (as defined in former subsec. (b)(2) of this section as in effect before Dec. 22, 2017) executed after Dec. 31, 2018, and to such instruments executed on or before Dec. 31, 2018, and modified after Dec. 31, 2018, if the modification expressly provides that the amendment made by section 11051 of Pub. L. 115-97 applies to such modification, this section is repealed.

o   **Identify the Tax Planning Scenarios** – Based on your reading of sections 71 and 215, consider the application of tax law to your clients' facts:
   o   Scenario 1: No divorce – neither section 71 nor section 215 apply since no alimony or separate maintenance payments arise.
   o   Scenario 2: The couple's divorce or separation instrument is executed on or before December 31, 2018. The payor is allowed a deduction of the alimony or separate maintenance payments that are made following the divorce. The recipient of the alimony or separate maintenance payments must include as gross income the amount received from the payor. Assume that the payor is the spouse who earns an annual salary of $300,000. Assume that the alimony payment is $3,000/month
      ▪ Payor of Alimony
         • Adjusted Gross Income = $300,000
         • Standard Deduction = ($12,000)
         • Alimony = ($36,000)
         • Taxable Income = $252,000
         • Tax = $63,889.50 (35% marginal rate)
         • Recipient of Alimony
         • Adjusted Gross Income = $36,000 (alimony)
         • Standard Deduction = (12,000)
         • Taxable Income = $24,000
         • Tax = $2,689.50 (12% marginal rate)

- Combined tax = $66,579

- Scenario 3: The couple's divorce or separation instrument is executed after December 31, 2018. The payor is not allowed a deduction of the alimony or separate maintenance payments that are made following the divorce. The recipient of the alimony or separate maintenance payments does not include as gross income the amount received from the payor.
  - Payor of Alimony
    - Adjusted Gross Income = $300,000
    - Standard Deduction = ($12,000)
    - Alimony = ($0)
    - Taxable Income = $288,000
    - Tax = $76,489.50 (35% marginal rate)
  - Recipient of Alimony
    - Adjusted Gross Income = $0 (alimony)
    - Standard Deduction = (12,000)
    - Taxable Income = $0
    - Tax = $0
    - **Combined tax = $76,489.50**

Analysis: If the couple executes a divorce on or before December 31, 2018, then they will pay $9,910.50 less Federal tax combined. If they divorce after December 31, 2018, then they will pay more combined tax. Consider the analysis from each client's perspective:

- Payor of Alimony – there is a significant additional cost of greater Federal tax incurred if the divorce is delayed after December 31, 2018. Any additional tax will likely impact the payor's financial ability to pay more alimony.

- Recipient of Alimony – there is an advantage to executing divorce after December 31, 2018 since that would result in no income from the receipt of alimony and, therefore, no Federal tax liability. However, this scenario would increase the Federal tax burden on the payor and may result in less financial ability for the payor to increase the final agreed amount of alimony.

In this example, tax planning involves understanding how tax law applies to given facts and educating clients on the potential tax impact. Ultimately, it is the client who is left to make his/her decision on how to proceed given the analysis provided.

b. Tax Planning Scenario #2 – New Qualified Plug-in Electric Drive Motor Vehicles

- **Factual Scenario** – You are a member of the tax department of a large U.S. automaker ("Car Maker Y") that manufactures gas and electric drive motor vehicles. The head of the company's tax department instructs you to read section 30D of the Internal Revenue Code and provide your view on what the company should consider as it continues to manufacture electric motor vehicles. From January 2017 to date, the company sold over 80,000 electric vehicles that meet the definition of "Qualified Plug-in Electric Motor Vehicles" under section 30D. It is now July 2018. For the remainder of 2018, the company expects to sell another 120,000 "Qualified Plug-in Electric Motor Vehicles." Read section 30D and report back to the head of the company's tax department with your tax planning ideas.

- **Tax Law** – Your basic tax research points you to section 30D. Read section 30D and the associated historical amendments.

Section 30D

(a) Allowance of credit. There shall be allowed as a credit against the tax imposed by this chapter for the taxable year an amount equal to the sum of the credit amounts determined under subsection (b) with respect to each new qualified plug-in electric drive motor vehicle placed in service by the taxpayer during the taxable year.

(b) Per vehicle dollar limitation.
    (1) The amount determined under this subsection with respect to any new qualified plug-in electric drive motor vehicle is the sum of the amounts determined under paragraphs (2) and (3) with respect to such vehicle.
    (2) Base amount. The amount determined under this paragraph is $2,500.
    (3) Battery capacity. In the case of a vehicle which draws propulsion energy from a battery with not less than 5 kilowatt hours of capacity, the amount determined under this paragraph is $417, plus $417 for each kilowatt hour of capacity in excess of 5 kilowatt hours. The amount determined under this paragraph shall not exceed $5,000.
(c) Application with other credits
    (1) Business credit treated as part of general business credit. So much of the credit which would be allowed under subsection (a) for any taxable year (determined without regard to this subsection) that is attributable to property of a character subject to an allowance for depreciation shall be treated as a credit listed in section 38(b) for such taxable year (and not allowed under subsection (a))
    (2) Personal credit. For purposes of this title, the credit allowed under subsection (a) for any taxable year (determined after application of paragraph (1)) shall be treated as a credit allowable under subpart A for such taxable year.

(d) New qualified plug-in electric drive motor vehicle. For purposes of this section—
    (1) In general. The term "new qualified plug-in electric drive motor vehicle" means a motor vehicle—
        (A) the original use of which commences with the taxpayer,
        (B) which is acquired for use or lease by the taxpayer and not for resale,
        (C) which is made by a manufacturer,

(D) which is treated as a motor vehicle for purposes of title II of the Clean Air Act,

(E) which has a gross vehicle weight rating of less than 14,000 pounds, and

(F) which is propelled to a significant extent by an electric motor which draws electricity from a battery which—

(i) has a capacity of not less than 4 kilowatt hours, and

(ii) is capable of being recharged from an external source of electricity.

(2) Motor vehicle. The term "motor vehicle" means any vehicle which is manufactured primarily for use on public streets, roads, and highways (not including a vehicle operated exclusively on a rail or rails) and which has at least 4 wheels.

(3) Manufacturer. The term "manufacturer" has the meaning given such term in regulations prescribed by the Administrator of the Environmental Protection Agency for purposes of the administration of title II of the Clean Air Act (42 U.S.C. 7521 et seq.).

(4) Battery capacity. The term "capacity" means, with respect to any battery, the quantity of electricity which the battery is capable of storing, expressed in kilowatt hours, as measured from a 100 percent state of charge to a 0 percent state of charge.

(e) Limitation on number of new qualified plug-in electric drive motor vehicles eligible for credit.

(1) In general. In the case of a new qualified plug-in electric drive motor vehicle sold during the phaseout period, only the applicable percentage of the credit otherwise allowable under subsection (a) shall be allowed.

(2) Phaseout period. For purposes of this subsection, the phaseout period is the period beginning with the second calendar quarter following the calendar quarter which includes the first date on which the number of new qualified plug-in electric drive motor vehicles manufactured by the manufacturer of the vehicle referred to in paragraph (1) sold for use in the United States after December 31, 2009, is at least 200,000.

(3) Applicable percentage. For purposes of paragraph (1), the applicable percentage is—

(A) 50 percent for the first 2 calendar quarters of the phaseout period,

(B) 25 percent for the 3d and 4th calendar quarters of the phaseout period, and

(C) 0 percent for each calendar quarter thereafter.

(4) Controlled groups. Rules similar to the rules of section 30B(f)(4) shall apply for purposes of this subsection.

(f) Special rules

(1) Basis reduction. For purposes of this subtitle, the basis of any property for which a credit is allowable under subsection (a) shall be reduced by the amount of such credit so allowed (determined without regard to subsection (c)).

(2) No double benefit. The amount of any deduction or other credit allowable under this chapter for a vehicle for which a credit is allowable under subsection

(a) shall be reduced by the amount of credit allowed under such subsection for such vehicle (determined without regard to subsection (c)).

(3) Property used by tax-exempt entity. In the case of a vehicle the use of which is described in paragraph (3) or (4) of section 50(b) and which is not subject to a lease, the person who sold such vehicle to the person or entity using such vehicle shall be treated as the taxpayer that placed such vehicle in service, but only if such person clearly discloses to such person or entity in a document the amount of any credit allowable under subsection (a) with respect to such vehicle (determined without regard to subsection (c)). For purposes of subsection (c), property to which this paragraph applies shall be treated as of a character subject to an allowance for depreciation.

(4) Property used outside United States not qualified. No credit shall be allowable under subsection (a) with respect to any property referred to in section 50(b)(1).

(5) Recapture. The Secretary shall, by regulations, provide for recapturing the benefit of any credit allowable under subsection (a) with respect to any property which ceases to be property eligible for such credit.

(6) Election not to take credit. No credit shall be allowed under subsection (a) for any vehicle if the taxpayer elects to not have this section apply to such vehicle.

(7) Interaction with air quality and motor vehicle safety standards. A vehicle shall not be considered eligible for a credit under this section unless such vehicle is in compliance with—

    (A) the applicable provisions of the Clean Air Act for the applicable make and model year of the vehicle (or applicable air quality provisions of State law in the case of a State which has adopted such provision under a waiver under section 209(b) of the Clean Air Act), and

    (B) the motor vehicle safety provisions of sections 30101 through 30169 of title 49, United States Code.

(g) Credit allowed for 2- and 3-wheeled plug-in electric vehicles

    (1) In general. In the case of a qualified 2- or 3-wheeled plug-in electric vehicle—

        (A) there shall be allowed as a credit against the tax imposed by this chapter for the taxable year an amount equal to the sum of the applicable amount with respect to each such qualified 2- or 3-wheeled plug-in electric vehicle placed in service by the taxpayer during the taxable year, and

        (B) the amount of the credit allowed under subparagraph (A) shall be treated as a credit allowed under subsection (a).

    (2) Applicable amount. For purposes of paragraph (1), the applicable amount is an amount equal to the lesser of—

        (A) 10 percent of the cost of the qualified 2- or 3-wheeled plug-in electric vehicle, or

        (B) $2,500.

    (3) Qualified 2- or 3-wheeled plug-in electric vehicle. The term "qualified 2- or 3-wheeled plug-in electric vehicle" means any vehicle which—

        (A) has 2 or 3 wheels,

(B) meets the requirements of subparagraphs (A), (B), (C), (E), and (F) of subsection (d)(1) (determined by substituting "2.5 kilowatt hours" for "4 kilowatt hours" in subparagraph (F)(i)),
(C) is manufactured primarily for use on public streets, roads, and highways,
(D) is capable of achieving a speed of 45 miles per hour or greater, and
(E) is acquired—
> (i) after December 31, 2011, and before January 1, 2014, or
> (ii) in the case of a vehicle that has 2 wheels, after December 31, 2014, and before January 1, 2017.

- **Identify the Tax Planning Scenarios** – Based on your reading of section 30D, consider the application of tax law to your client's facts:

  o Scenario 1: The qualified plug-in electric drive motor vehicle credit phases out for a manufacturer's vehicles over the one-year period beginning with the second calendar quarter after the calendar quarter in which at least 200,000 qualifying vehicles manufactured by that manufacturer have been sold for use in the United States (determined on a cumulative basis for sales after December 31, 2009) ("phase-out period"). Qualifying vehicles manufactured by that manufacturer are eligible for 50 percent of the credit if acquired in the first two quarters of the phase-out period and 25 percent of the credit if acquired in the third or fourth quarter of the phase-out period. Vehicles manufactured by that manufacturer are not eligible for a credit if acquired after the phase-out period. If Car Maker Y sells 200,000 qualifying vehicles in the last calendar quarter in 2018 (Sept, Oct, Nov, Dec), then the full credit allowed under section 30D will begin to phase out to 50% beginning the second calendar quarter in 2019 (Apr, May, June) and thru the third quarter (July, Aug, Sept). Thereafter, the phase will be reduced to 25% of the maximum credit allowed under section 30D in the third and fourth quarters after the phase out begins – Oct, Nov, Dec of 2019 and Jan, Feb, Mar of 2010.

  o Scenario 2: What if Car Maker Y reaches 200,000 qualifying vehicles sold later than the last calendar quarter in 2018, say the first calendar quarter in 2019? Then, the second calendar quarter after the calendar quarter in which at least 200,000 qualifying vehicles manufactured by that manufacturer have been sold for use in the United States would be Apr, May, June of 2010. Thus, by reaching the 200,000 milestone of sales later by just one quarter (first calendar quarter of 2019, rather than last calendar quarter of 2018), Car Maker Y can delay the start of the phase out period of the section 30D electric car credit by one full year -- from Apr, May, June of 2019 to Apr, May, June of 2010.

3. The Limits of Lawful Tax Planning

Beyond the limits of lawful tax planning, there exists the realm of tax abuse. Given the difficulties of constructing a bright line to separate lawful from unlawful tax planning, Congress enacted various statutory guidelines including the definition of "tax shelter" to denote the general boundary. In section 6662(d)(2)(C)(ii), "tax shelter" is defined as a "partnership or other entity, any investment plan or arrangement, or any other plan or arrangement if a significant purpose of such partnership, entity, plan or arrangement is the avoidance of evasion of Federal income tax." This definition of a tax plan that may involve something beyond a lawful tax arrangement provides a start to understanding the legal limits of proper tax planning.

Why would someone engage in, or promote, illegal tax shelters? The answer to this question is not surprisingly the same as allegedly provided by a famous bank robber, Willie Sutton, when he was asked by a reporter why he robbed banks – "Because that's where the money is." Promoters of tax shelters often attempt to take advantage of highly technical tax rules to obtain tax benefits not intended by Congress.[314] However, as noted in the official website of the Department of the Treasury, the government applies its regulatory authority to stop abusive transactions and eliminate potential opportunities for abuse.[315] A review of some the types of abusive tax transactions summarized by the Department of Jusice on its official website offers an initial understanding of the types of transactions that fall on the wrong side of the legal limit.[316]

o **Abusive Partnership Intercompany Financing Arrangements** – These arrangements involve a corporation's use of a partnership to obtain inappropriate interest deductions for payments to related entities. The Treasury Department and the IRS issued Notice 2004-31 to shut down these abusive arrangements.

o **Abusive S Corporation Income Shifting Arrangements** – These arrangements are structured to eliminate tax on S corporation shareholders by inappropriately shifting income to a tax-exempt organization through the use of nonvoting stock. The Treasury Department and the IRS issued Notice 2004-30 to shut down these abusive arrangements. The Treasury Department and the IRS also, for the first time, designated any tax-exempt party to these arrangements as a "participant" in a tax avoidance transaction under the tax shelter regulations and will require the disclosure of the names of tax-exempt parties facilitating these arrangements.

o **Abusive Foreign Tax Credit Transactions** – These transactions involve a domestic corporation's transitory ownership of a foreign target corporation when, pursuant to a prearranged plan, the domestic corporation acquires the stock of the

---

[314] See BCP Trading and Investments, LLC v. Commissioner, T.C. Memo. 2017-151, if you would like to read a detailed description of a tax scheme that attempted to manipulate the technicalities of the tax code for tax benefit.

[315] https://www.justice.gov/tax/program-shut-down-schemes-and-scams.

[316] Id.

target corporation and then all or substantially all of the target corporation's assets are sold in a transaction that gives rise to foreign tax without a corresponding inclusion of income for U.S. tax purposes. The Treasury Department and the IRS issued Notice 2004-20 to shut down these transactions. The Treasury Department and the IRS at the same time also issued Notice 2004-19, which details the legislative and regulatory approaches that the Treasury Department and the IRS are using to address other abusive foreign tax credit transactions.

o **Abusive Excess Life Insurance in Defined Benefit Pension Plans** – These arrangements involve specially designed life insurance policies intended primarily to benefit highly-compensated employees through a retirement plan. The Treasury Department and the IRS issued Rev. Rul. 2004-20 to shut down abusive excess life insurance arrangements.

o **Abusive S Corporation ESOP Arrangements**– These arrangements are intended to assist companies in avoiding tax rules designed to protect rank-and file participants in employee stock ownership plans ("ESOPs"). The Treasury Department and the IRS issued Rev. Rul. 2003-6 and Rev. Rul. 2004-4 to stop these abuses and protect rank-and-file participants in S corporation ESOPs.

o **Abusive Roth IRA Transactions** – These arrangements involve the contribution of property to an IRA through a transaction that disguises the value of the contribution to circumvent Roth IRA contribution limits. The Treasury Department and the IRS issued Notice 2004-8 to stop abusive structures designed to avoid the contribution limits that apply to Roth IRAs.

o **Abusive Offsetting Foreign Currency Option Contract Transactions** – These transactions involve two pairs of offsetting foreign currency options. Two of the offsetting options are assigned to a charity, and the taxpayer claims an immediate loss on one option without recognizing the offsetting gain on the other. The Treasury Department and the IRS issued Notice 2003-81 to shut down these transactions.

o **Abusive Contested Liability Transactions** – These transactions involve the purported establishment of trusts to accelerate deductions for liabilities that a taxpayer is contesting under section 461(f). The trusts, however, do not comply with the requirements of that section because the taxpayer either retains control over the trust assets or transferred its own stock or the stock or note of a related party. The Treasury Department and the IRS issued Notice 2003-77 to prevent the use of trusts to accelerate deductions.

o

Abusive Stripping Transactions – These transactions improperly separate income from related deductions. Some of these transactions, for example, are structured to have a tax-indifferent party realize the taxable income while the taxpayer claims deductions related to that income, such as depreciation or rental expenses. The

Treasury Department and the IRS issued Notice 2003-55 to shut down these transactions.

o **Abusive Option Sales to Family Limited Partnerships** – These arrangements involve the purported sale of compensatory stock options to a limited partnership owned by the taxpayer's family members to avoid income and employment taxes on the exercise of the options. The Treasury Department and the IRS issued Notice 2003-47 to shut down these transactions.

o **Abusive Welfare Benefit Funds** – These transactions are designed to avoid the applicable deduction limits on contributions to welfare benefit funds. Taxpayers claim that the benefits are being provided under a collective bargaining agreement. The Treasury Department and the IRS issued Notice 2003-24 stop these abuses and further addressed these transactions in final regulations issued July 2003.

o **Abusive Offshore Deferred Compensation Arrangements** – These transactions are designed to avoid income and employment taxes by utilizing a purported lease of the right to a taxpayer's services in the United States through a foreign leasing company. The proceeds of the leasing arrangement are transferred to an offshore trust maintained on behalf of the taxpayer. The Treasury Department and the IRS issued Notice 2003-22 to shut down these abusive offshore employee leasing arrangements.

o **Abusive Producer Owned Reinsurance Company ("PORC") Arrangements** – These insurance arrangements involve a foreign corporation established to reinsure the policies sold by a taxpayer in connection with the sale of products or services. The taxpayers utilize various exemptions of income for insurance companies to divert portions of the premiums paid to the PORC and pay little or no tax on the diverted funds. The Treasury Department and the IRS issued Notice 2002-70 to shut down these arrangements.

o **Abusive Lease-In/Lease-Out ("LILO") Transactions** – LILOs involve a lease of property from a tax-indifferent party (e.g., a foreign party or a tax-exempt party), and a simultaneous lease of the same property back to the tax-indifferent party to generate substantial deductions of the lease payments. The Treasury Department and IRS issued Rev. Rul. 2002-69 to supersede earlier guidance issued to shut down these transactions.

o **Abusive Partnership Straddle Tax ("Eliminator") Transactions** – These transactions involve the use of a straddle, a tiered partnership structure, a transitory partner, and the partnership allocation rules to generate purported permanent non-economic tax losses for the taxpayer. The Treasury Department and the IRS issued Notice 2002-50 to shut down these transactions.

o **Abusive Passthrough Entity Straddle Transactions** – These transactions involve the use of a straddle, one or more transitory S corporation shareholders, and the rules of subchapter S to allow a taxpayer to claim an immediate loss while deferring an offsetting gain. The Treasury Department and the IRS issued Notice 2002-65 to shut down these transactions.

o **Abusive Common Trust Fund Straddle Transactions** – These transactions involve the use of a common trust fund that invests in economically offsetting gain and loss positions in foreign currencies and allocates the gain to one or more tax-indifferent parties and the losses to the taxpayer. The Treasury Department and the IRS issued Notice 2003-54 to shut down these transactions.

o **Abusive 401(k) Accelerated Deductions** – These transactions involve claims by employers of accelerated deductions for contributions to retirement plans on compensation expected to be earned by participants in future years. The Treasury Department and the IRS issued Rev. Rul. 2002-46 to expand earlier guidance identifying these listed transactions.

o **Abusive Notional Principal Contracts or Contingent Swaps** – These transactions involve the use of a notional principal contract to claim current deductions for periodic payments made by a taxpayer while disregarding the accrual of a right to receive offsetting payments in the future. The Treasury Department and the IRS issued Notice 2002-35 to stop these abuses.

o **Abusive Inflated Basis ("CARDS") Transactions** – These transactions involve the use of a loan assumption agreement to claim an inflated basis in assets. The assets are sold for fair market value and the taxpayer claims a significant loss, arguing that the entire principal amount of the loan is included in taxpayer's basis. The Treasury Department and the IRS issued Notice 2002-21 to shut down these transactions.

o **Abusive Section 302/318 "Basis Shift" Transactions** – These transactions involve an abuse of the attribution rules to increase the basis of the stock held by the taxpayer through a redemption of stock held by a tax-indifferent party (typically, a foreign entity). The taxpayer claims a loss on the sale of its stock based on its position that the basis of the redeemed stock is added to the basis of stock the taxpayer sold. The Treasury Department and the IRS issued Notice 2001-45 to shut down these transactions.

After reading the above descriptions of just some of the abusive tax transactions that make their way into the tax system, you should come to realize that the practice of tax is not only fraught with those who would exploit it but relies urgently upon those who respect it.

417

Chapter 12 - Questions

1. Define tax planning.

2. Define tax reporting.

Appendix A – Sample Individual Tax Return Preparation Tax Engagement Letter

Date

Client name
Client Address

Dear Client:

This letter is to confirm and specify the terms of our [my] engagement with you and to clarify the nature and extent of the services we [I] will provide.

We [I] will prepare your [Year] joint federal income tax return, and the mutually agreed-upon income tax returns for the states of _____ (collectively, the "returns"). This engagement pertains only to the [Year] tax year, and our [my] responsibilities do not include preparation of any other tax returns that may be due to any taxing authority. Our [my] engagement will be complete upon the delivery of the completed returns to you. Thereafter, you will be solely responsible to file the returns with the appropriate taxing authorities.

Please note that any person or entity subject to the jurisdiction of the United States (includes individuals, corporations, partnerships, trusts, and estates) having a financial interest in, or signature or other authority over, bank accounts, securities, or other financial accounts having a value exceeding $10,000 in a foreign country shall report such a relationship. Although there are some limited exceptions, filing requirements also apply to taxpayers that have direct or indirect control over a foreign or domestic entity with foreign financial accounts, even if the taxpayer does not have foreign account(s). For example, a corporate-owned foreign account would require filings by the corporation *and* by the individual corporate officers with signature authority. Failure to disclose the required information to the U.S. Department of the Treasury may result in substantial civil and/or criminal penalties.

If you and/or your entity have a financial interest in any foreign accounts, you are responsible for providing our firm with all the information necessary to prepare FinCEN Form 114 (formerly Form TD-F-90-22.1) required by the U.S. Department of the Treasury on or before June 30 of each tax year. If you do not provide our [my] firm with information regarding any interest you may have in a foreign account, we [I] will not be able to prepare any of the required disclosure statements.

Your returns may be selected for review by one or more than one taxing authority. Any proposed adjustments by the examining agent are subject to certain rights of appeal. In the event of such government tax examination, we [I] will be available upon your written request to represent you during the examination and/or during any appeal. Any such representation will be the subject of, and governed by, a separate engagement letter.

Appendix A: Sample Tax Engagement Letter

We [I] will prepare the returns from information which you will furnish to us [me]. It is your responsibility to provide all the information required for the preparation of complete and accurate returns. We [I] will furnish you with questionnaires and/or worksheets as needed to guide you in gathering the necessary information. Your use of such forms will assist us [me] in keeping our [my] fee to a minimum. To the extent we [I] render any accounting and/or bookkeeping assistance, it will be limited to those tasks we [I] deem necessary for preparation of the returns.

The timeliness of your cooperation is essential to our [my] ability to complete this engagement. Specifically, we [I] must receive sufficient information from which to prepare your returns within a reasonable period of time prior to the applicable filing deadline. Accordingly, if we [I] do not receive information from you, as noted above, by _____, it may be necessary for us [me] to pursue an extension of the due date of your returns, and we [I] reserve the right to suspend our [my] services or withdraw from this engagement.

We [I] will not audit or otherwise verify the data you submit. Accordingly, our [my] engagement cannot be relied upon to disclose errors, fraud, or other illegal acts that may exist. However, it may be necessary to ask you for clarification of some of the information you provide, and we [I] will inform you of any material errors, fraud, or other illegal acts that come to our [my] attention.

You are responsible for maintaining an adequate and efficient accounting system, for safeguarding assets, for authorizing transactions, and for retaining supporting documentation for those transactions, all of which will, among other things, help assure the preparation of proper returns. Furthermore, you are responsible for evaluating the adequacy and results of the services we [I] provide.
The law provides various penalties and interest that may be imposed when taxpayers underestimate their tax liability. You acknowledge that any such understated tax, and any imposed interest and penalties, are your responsibility, and that we [I] have no responsibility in that regard. If you would like information on the amount or circumstances of these penalties, please contact us [me].

We [I] may encounter instances where the tax law is unclear, or where there may be conflicts between the taxing authorities' interpretations of the law and other supportable positions. In those instances, we [I] will outline for you each of the reasonable alternative courses of action, including the risks and consequences of each such alternative. In the end, we [I] will adopt, on your behalf, the alternative which you select after having considered the information provided by us [me].

Without disclosure in the return itself of the specific position taken on a given issue, we [I] must have a reasonable belief that the position(s) satisfies the substantial-authority standard and that the position will be held to be the correct position upon examination by taxing authorities. If we [I] do not have that reasonable belief, we [I] must be satisfied that there is at least a reasonable basis for the position, and in such a case, the position must be formally disclosed on Form 8275 or 8275-R, which form would be filed as part of the return. If we [I] do not believe there is a reasonable basis for the position, either the position cannot be taken or we [I] cannot sign the return. In order for us [me] to make these determinations, we [I] must rely on the accuracy and completeness of the relevant information you provide to us [me], and, in the event we [I] and/or you are assessed penalties due to our [my] reliance on inaccurate, incomplete, or misleading information you supplied to us [me] (with or without your knowledge or intent), you will indemnify us [me], defend us [me], and hold us [me] harmless as to those penalties

We [I] will also provide you with interim and year-end tax planning services on issues that you specifically bring to our [my] attention in writing. Our [my] ability to provide you with appropriate guidance on such issues will be entirely dependent on the timeliness, accuracy, and completeness of the relevant information bearing on the issue which we [I] will rely on you to provide to us [me]. Although we [I] may orally discuss tax planning issues with you from time to time, such discussions will not constitute advice upon which we [I] intend for you to rely for any purpose. Rather, any advice upon which we [I] intend for you to rely, and upon which you will rely, will be embodied in a written report or correspondence from us [me] to you, and any such writing will supersede any prior oral representations between the parties on the issue.

Our [my] fees for this engagement are not contingent on the results of our [my] services. Rather, our [my] fees for this engagement, including tax planning, preparation of your returns, and any representation of your interests during an examination by a taxing authority and/or any subsequent appeal, will be based on our [my] standard hourly rates, as set forth on the attached rate sheet. In addition, you agree to reimburse us [me] for any of our [my] out-of-pocket costs incurred in connection with the performance of our [my] services. We [I] estimate that our [my] fee for these services will range from approximately _____ to _____. You acknowledge that this range is not a limit to the total fees we [I] may charge for our [my] services, and that our [my] fees may actually exceed that range. However, in the event that we [I] encounter unusual circumstances that would require us [me] to expand the scope of the engagement, and/or if we [I] anticipate our [my] fees to exceed the aforementioned range, we [I] will adjust our [my] estimate, and obtain your prior approval before continuing with the engagement.

Prior to commencing our services, we [I] require that you provide us [me] with a retainer in the amount of _____. The retainer will be applied against our [my] final invoice, and any unused portion will be returned to you upon our [my] collection of all outstanding fees and costs related to this engagement. Our [my] fees and costs will be billed monthly, and are payable upon receipt. Invoices unpaid 30 days past the billing date may be deemed delinquent, and are subject to a late fee of 1.0% per month. We [I] reserve the right to suspend our [my] services or to withdraw from this engagement in the event that any of our [my] invoices are deemed delinquent. In the event that any collection action is required to collect unpaid balances due us [me], you agree to reimburse us [me] for our [my] costs of collection, including attorneys' fees.

If we [I] elect to terminate our [my] services for nonpayment, or for any other reason provided for in this letter, our [my] engagement will be deemed to have been completed upon written notification of termination, even if we [I] have not completed your return. You will be obligated to compensate us [me] for all time expended, and to reimburse us [me] for all of our out-of-pocket costs, through the date of termination.

You should retain all the documents, canceled checks and other data that form the basis of income and deductions. These may be necessary to prove the accuracy and completeness of the returns to a taxing authority. You have the final responsibility for the income tax returns and, therefore, you should review them carefully before you sign them.

In connection with this engagement, we [I] may communicate with you or others via email transmission. As emails can be intercepted and read, disclosed, or otherwise used or communicated by an unintended third party, or may not be delivered to each of the parties to whom they are directed and only to such parties, we [I] cannot guarantee or warrant that emails from us [me] will be properly delivered and read only by the addressee. Therefore, we [I] specifically disclaim and waive any liability or responsibility whatsoever for interception or unintentional disclosure of emails transmitted by us [me] in connection with the performance of this engagement. In that regard, you agree that we [I] shall have no liability for any loss or damage to any person or entity resulting from the use of email transmissions, including any consequential, incidental, direct, indirect, or special damages, such as loss of revenues or anticipated profits, or disclosure or communication of confidential or proprietary information.

It is our [my] policy to retain engagement documentation for a period of seven years, after which time we [I] will commence the process of destroying the contents of our [my] engagement files. To the extent we [I] accumulate any of your original records during the engagement, those documents will be returned to you promptly upon completion of the engagement, and you will provide us [me] with a receipt for the return of such records. The balance of our [my] engagement file, other than a copy of your income tax return, which we [I] will provide to you at the conclusion of the engagement, is our [my] property, and we [I] will provide copies of such documents at our [my] discretion, unless required by law, and if compensated for any time and costs associated with the effort.

[For married clients filing joint returns.]Because the income tax returns we [I] are [am] to prepare in connection with this engagement are joint returns, and because you will each sign those returns, you are each our [my] client. You each acknowledge that there is no expectation of privacy from the other concerning our [my] services in connection with this engagement, and we [I] are [am] at liberty to share with either of you, without the prior consent of the other, any and all documents and other information concerning preparation of your returns. We [I] will require, however, that any request for documents or other information be communicated to us [me] in written form. You also acknowledge that unless we [I] are [am] notified otherwise in advance and in writing, we [I] may construe an instruction from either of you to be an instruction on your joint behalf. Absent a contrary written instruction in the future, from either or both of you, we [I] will

communicate with either or both of you at the following mailing address:
_____.

In the event we [I] are [am] required to respond to a subpoena, court order, or other legal process for the production of documents and/or testimony relative to information we [I] have obtained and/or prepared during the course of this engagement, you agree to compensate us [me] at our [my] hourly rates, as set forth above, for the time we [I] expend in connection with such response, and to reimburse us [me] for all of our [my] out-of-pocket costs incurred in that regard.

In the event that we [I] are [am] or may be obligated to pay any cost, settlement, judgment, fine, penalty, or similar award or sanction as a result of a claim, investigation, or other proceeding instituted by any third party, and if such obligation is or may be a direct or indirect result of any inaccurate, incomplete, or misleading information that you provide to us [me] during the course of this engagement (with or without your knowledge or intent), you agree to indemnify us [me], defend us [me], and hold us [me] harmless as against such obligation.

You agree that any dispute (other than our [my] efforts to collect an outstanding invoice) that may arise regarding the meaning, performance, or enforcement of this engagement or any prior engagement that we [I] have performed for you, will, prior to resorting to litigation, be submitted to mediation, and that the parties will engage in the mediation process in good faith once a written request to mediate has been given by any party to the engagement. Any mediation initiated as a result of this engagement shall be administered within the county of [County and State], by [Name of Mediation Organization], according to its mediation rules, and any ensuing litigation shall be conducted within said county, according to [State] law. The results of any such mediation shall be binding only upon agreement of each party to be bound. The costs of any mediation proceeding shall be shared equally by the participating parties.

Any litigation arising out of this engagement, except actions by us [me] to enforce payment of our [my] professional invoices, must be filed within one year from the completion of the engagement, notwithstanding any statutory provision to the contrary.

Our [my] liability relating to the performance of the services rendered under this letter is limited solely to direct damage sustained by you. In no event shall we [I] be liable for the consequential, special, incidental, or punitive loss, damage, or expense caused to you or to any third party (including without limitation, lost profits, opportunity costs, etc.). Notwithstanding the foregoing, our [my] maximum liability relating to services rendered under this letter (regardless of form of action, whether in contract, negligence or otherwise) shall be limited to the fees received by us [me] for this engagement. The provisions set forth in this paragraph shall survive the completion of the engagement.

Notwithstanding anything contained herein, both accountant and client agree that regardless of where the client is domiciled and regardless of where this Agreement is physically signed, this Agreement shall have been deemed to have been entered into at

423

Appendix A: Sample Tax Engagement Letter

Accountant's office located in [County], [State], USA, and [County], [State], USA, shall be the exclusive jurisdiction for resolving disputes related to this Agreement. This Agreement shall be interpreted and governed in accordance with the Laws of [State].

This engagement letter is contractual in nature and includes all of the relevant terms that will govern the engagement for which it has been prepared. The terms of this letter supersede any prior oral or written representations or commitments by or between the parties. Any material changes or additions to the terms set forth in this letter will only become effective if evidenced by a written amendment to this letter, signed by all of the parties.

If, after full consideration and consultation with counsel if so desired, you agree to authorize us [me] to prepare your personal income tax returns pursuant to the terms set forth above, please execute this letter on the line below designated for your signature, and return the original of this executed letter to this office along with a completed copy of the enclosed tax organizer and the supporting documentation requested therein. You should keep a copy of this fully executed letter for your records. If this firm does not receive from you the original of this letter, in fully executed form, but receives from you a completed copy of the enclosed tax organizer and/or supporting documentation requested therein, then such receipt by this office shall be deemed to evidence your acceptance of all of the terms set forth above. If, however, this office receives from you no response to this letter, then this office will not proceed to provide you with any professional services, and will not prepare your income tax returns.

Thank you for your attention to this matter, and please contact me with any questions that you may have.

Very truly yours,

[Firm Contact]
[Title]

ACCEPTED AND AGREED:

_____   _____
[Name of Signatory #1]   Date

_____   _____
[Name of Signatory #2]   Date

Appendix B – Circular 230

Treasury Department
Circular No. 230
(Rev. 6-2014)
Catalog Number 16586R
www.irs.gov

Regulations Governing Practice before the Internal Revenue Service

---

Department
of the
Treasury

Internal
Revenue
Service

Title 31 Code of Federal Regulations,
Subtitle A, Part 10,
published (June 12, 2014)

31 U.S.C. §330. Practice before the Department

(a) Subject to section 500 of title 5, the Secretary of the Treasury may —

(1) regulate the practice of representatives of persons before the Department of the Treasury; and

(2) before admitting a representative to practice, require that the representative demonstrate —

(A) good character;

(B) good reputation;

(C) necessary qualifications to enable the representative to provide to persons valuable service; and

(D) competency to advise and assist persons in presenting their cases.

(b) After notice and opportunity for a proceeding, the Secretary may suspend or disbar from practice before the Department, or censure, a representative who —

(1) is incompetent;

(2) is disreputable;

(3) violates regulations prescribed under this section; or

(4) with intent to defraud, willfully and knowingly misleads or threatens the person being represented or a prospective person to be represented.

The Secretary may impose a monetary penalty on any representative described in the preceding sentence. If the representative was acting on behalf of an employer or any firm or other entity in connection with the conduct giving rise to such penalty, the Secretary may impose a monetary penalty on such employer, firm, or entity if it knew, or reasonably should have known, of such conduct. Such penalty shall not exceed the gross income derived (or to be derived) from the conduct giving rise to the penalty and may be in addition to, or in lieu of, any suspension, disbarment, or censure of the representative.

(c) After notice and opportunity for a hearing to any appraiser, the Secretary may —

(1) provide that appraisals by such appraiser shall not have any probative effect in any administrative proceeding before the Department of the Treasury or the Internal Revenue Service, and

(2) bar such appraiser from presenting evidence or testimony in any such proceeding.

(d) Nothing in this section or in any other provision of law shall be construed to limit the authority of the Secretary of the Treasury to impose standards applicable to the rendering of written advice with respect to any entity, transaction plan or arrangement, or other plan or arrangement, which is of a type which the Secretary determines as having a potential for tax avoidance or evasion.

(Pub. L. 97–258, Sept. 13, 1982, 96 Stat. 884; Pub. L. 98–369, div. A, title I, §156(a), July 18, 1984, 98 Stat. 695; Pub. L. 99–514, §2, Oct. 22, 1986, 100 Stat. 2095; Pub. L. 108–357, title VIII, §822(a)(1), (b), Oct. 22, 2004, 118 Stat. 1586, 1587; Pub. L. 109–280, title XII, §1219(d), Aug. 17, 2006, 120 Stat. 1085.)

Table of Contents

Paragraph 1. The authority citation for 31 CFR, part 10 continues to read as follows:

Authority: Sec. 3, 23 Stat. 258, secs. 2-12, 60 Stat. 237 et. seq.; 5 U.S.C. 301, 500, 551-559; 31 U.S.C. 321; 31 U.S.C. 330; Reorg. Plan No. 26 of 1950, 15 FR 4935, 64 Stat. 1280, 3 CFR, 1949-1953 Comp., p. 1017.

§ 10.0 Scope of part.

(a) This part contains rules governing the recognition of attorneys, certified public accountants, enrolled agents, enrolled retirement plan agents, registered tax return preparers, and other persons representing taxpayers before the Internal Revenue Service. Subpart A of this part sets forth rules relating to the authority to practice before the Internal Revenue Service; subpart B of this part prescribes the duties and restrictions relating to such practice; subpart C of this part prescribes the sanctions for violating the regulations; subpart D of this part contains the rules applicable to disciplinary proceedings; and subpart E of this part contains general provisions relating to the availability of official records.

(b) *Effective/applicability date.* This section is applicable beginning August 2, 2011.

Subpart A — Rules Governing Authority to Practice

§ 10.1 Offices.

(a) *Establishment of office(s).* The Commissioner shall establish the Office of Professional Responsibility and any other office(s) within the Internal Revenue Service necessary to administer and enforce this part. The Commissioner shall appoint the Director of the Office of Professional Responsibility and any other Internal Revenue official(s) to manage and direct any office(s) established to administer or enforce this part. Offices established under this part include, but are not limited to:

(1) The Office of Professional Responsibility, which shall generally have responsibility for matters related to practitioner conduct and shall have exclusive responsibility for discipline, including disciplinary proceedings and sanctions; and

(2) An office with responsibility for matters related to authority to practice before the Internal Revenue Service, including acting on applications for enrollment to practice before the Internal Revenue Service and administering competency testing and continuing education.

(b) Officers and employees within any office established under this part may perform acts necessary or appropriate to carry out the responsibilities of their office(s) under this part or as otherwise prescribed by the Commissioner.

(c) *Acting.* The Commissioner will designate an officer or employee of the Internal Revenue Service to perform the duties of an individual appointed under paragraph (a) of this section in the absence of that officer or employee or during a vacancy in that office.

(d) *Effective/applicability date.* This section is applicable beginning August 2, 2011, except that paragraph (a)(1) is applicable beginning June 12, 2014.

§ 10.2 Definitions.

(a) As used in this part, except where the text provides otherwise —

(1) *Attorney* means any person who is a member in good standing of the bar of the highest court of any state, territory, or possession of the United States, including a Commonwealth, or the District of Columbia.

(2) *Certified public accountant* means any person who is duly qualified to practice as a certified public accountant in any state, territory, or possession of the United States, including a Commonwealth, or the District of Columbia.

(3) *Commissioner* refers to the Commissioner of Internal Revenue.

(4) *Practice before the Internal Revenue Service* comprehends all matters connected with a presentation to the Internal Revenue Service or any of its officers or employees relating to a taxpayer's rights, privileges, or liabilities under laws or regulations administered by the Internal Revenue Service. Such presentations include, but are not limited to, preparing documents; filing documents; corresponding and communicating with the Internal Revenue Service; rendering written advice with respect to any entity, transaction, plan or arrangement, or other plan or arrangement having a potential for tax avoidance or evasion; and representing a client at conferences, hearings, and meetings.

(5) *Practitioner* means any individual described in paragraphs (a), (b), (c), (d), (e), or (f) of §10.3.

(6) A *tax return* includes an amended tax return and a claim for refund.

(7) *Service* means the Internal Revenue Service.

(8) *Tax return preparer* means any individual within the meaning of section 7701(a)(36) and 26 CFR 301.7701-15.

(b) *Effective/applicability date.* This section is applicable on August 2, 2011.

§ 10.3 Who may practice.

(a) *Attorneys.* Any attorney who is not currently under suspension or disbarment from practice before the Internal Revenue Service may practice before the Internal Revenue Service by filing with the Internal Revenue Service a written declaration that the attorney is currently qualified as an attorney and is authorized to represent the party or parties. Notwithstanding the preceding sentence, attorneys who are not currently under suspension or disbarment from practice before the Internal Revenue Service are not required to file a written declaration with the IRS before rendering written advice covered under §10.37, but their rendering of this advice is practice before the Internal Revenue Service.

(b) *Certified public accountants.* Any certified public accountant who is not currently under suspension or disbarment from practice before the Internal Revenue Service may practice before the Internal Revenue Service by filing with the Internal Revenue Service a written declaration that the certified public accountant is currently qualified as a certified public accountant and is authorized to represent the party or parties. Notwithstanding the preceding sentence, certified public accountants who are not currently under suspension or disbarment from practice before the Internal Revenue Service are not required to file a written declaration with the IRS before rendering written advice covered under §10.37, but their rendering of this advice is practice before the Internal Revenue Service.

(c) *Enrolled agents.* Any individual enrolled as an agent pursuant to this part who is not currently under suspension or disbarment from practice before the Internal Revenue Service may practice before the Internal Revenue Service.

(d) *Enrolled actuaries.*

(1) Any individual who is enrolled as an actuary by the Joint Board for the Enrollment of Actuaries pursuant to 29 U.S.C. 1242 who is not currently under suspension or disbarment from practice before the Internal Revenue Service may practice before the Internal Revenue Service by filing with the Internal Revenue Service a written declaration stating that he or she is currently qualified as an enrolled actuary and is authorized to represent the party or parties on whose behalf he or she acts.

(2) Practice as an enrolled actuary is limited

to representation with respect to issues involving the following statutory provisions in title 26 of the United States Code: sections 401 (relating to qualification of employee plans), 403(a) (relating to whether an annuity plan meets the requirements of section 404(a) (2)), 404 (relating to deductibility of employer contributions), 405 (relating to qualification of bond purchase plans), 412 (relating to funding requirements for certain employee plans), 413 (relating to application of qualification requirements to collectively bargained plans and to plans maintained by more than one employer), 414 (relating to definitions and special rules with respect to the employee plan area), 419 (relating to treatment of funded welfare benefits), 419A (relating to qualified asset accounts), 420 (relating to transfers of excess pension assets to retiree health accounts), 4971 (relating to excise taxes payable as a result of an accumulated funding deficiency under section 412), 4972 (relating to tax on nondeductible contributions to qualified employer plans), 4976 (relating to taxes with respect to funded welfare benefit plans), 4980 (relating to tax on reversion of qualified plan assets to employer), 6057 (relating to annual registration of plans), 6058 (relating to information required in connection with certain plans of deferred compensation), 6059 (relating to periodic report of actuary), 6652(e) (relating to the failure to file annual registration and other notifications by pension plan), 6652(f) (relating to the failure to file information required in connection with certain plans of deferred compensation), 6692 (relating to the failure to file actuarial report), 7805(b) (relating to the extent to which an Internal Revenue Service ruling or determination letter coming under the statutory provisions listed here will be applied without retroactive effect); and 29 U.S.C. § 1083 (relating to the waiver of funding for nonqualified plans).

(3) An individual who practices before the Internal Revenue Service pursuant to paragraph (d) (1) of this section is subject to the provisions of this part in the same manner as attorneys, certified public accountants, enrolled agents, enrolled retirement plan agents, and registered tax return preparers.

(e) *Enrolled retirement plan agents* —

(1) Any individual enrolled as a retirement plan agent pursuant to this part who is not currently under suspension or disbarment from practice before the Internal Revenue Service may practice before the Internal Revenue Service.

(2) Practice as an enrolled retirement plan agent is limited to representation with respect to issues involving the following programs: Employee Plans Determination Letter program; Employee Plans Compliance Resolution System; and Employee Plans Master and Prototype and Volume Submitter program. In addition, enrolled retirement plan agents are generally permitted to represent taxpayers with respect to IRS forms under the 5300 and 5500 series which are filed by retirement plans and plan sponsors, but not with respect to actuarial forms or schedules.

(3) An individual who practices before the Internal Revenue Service pursuant to paragraph (e) (1) of this section is subject to the provisions of this part in the same manner as attorneys, certified public accountants, enrolled agents, enrolled actuaries, and registered tax return preparers.

(f) *Registered tax return preparers.*

(1) Any individual who is designated as a registered tax return preparer pursuant to §10.4(c) of this part who is not currently under suspension or disbarment from practice before the Internal Revenue Service may practice before the Internal Revenue Service.

(2) Practice as a registered tax return preparer is limited to preparing and signing tax returns and claims for refund, and other documents for submission to the Internal Revenue Service. A registered tax return preparer may prepare all or substantially all of a tax return or claim for refund of tax. The Internal Revenue Service will prescribe by forms, instructions, or other appropriate guidance the tax returns and claims for refund that a registered tax return preparer may prepare and sign.

(3) A registered tax return preparer may represent taxpayers before revenue agents, customer service representatives, or similar officers and employees of the Internal Revenue Service (including the Taxpayer Advocate Service) during an examination if the registered tax return preparer signed the tax return

or claim for refund for the taxable year or period under examination. Unless otherwise prescribed by regulation or notice, this right does not permit such individual to represent the taxpayer, regardless of the circumstances requiring representation, before appeals officers, revenue officers, Counsel or similar officers or employees of the Internal Revenue Service or the Treasury Department. A registered tax return preparer's authorization to practice under this part also does not include the authority to provide tax advice to a client or another person except as necessary to prepare a tax return, claim for refund, or other document intended to be submitted to the Internal Revenue Service.

(4) An individual who practices before the Internal Revenue Service pursuant to paragraph (f) (1) of this section is subject to the provisions of this part in the same manner as attorneys, certified public accountants, enrolled agents, enrolled retirement plan agents, and enrolled actuaries.

(g) *Others.* Any individual qualifying under paragraph §10.5(e) or §10.7 is eligible to practice before the Internal Revenue Service to the extent provided in those sections.

(h) *Government officers and employees, and others.* An individual, who is an officer or employee of the executive, legislative, or judicial branch of the United States Government; an officer or employee of the District of Columbia; a Member of Congress; or a Resident Commissioner may not practice before the Internal Revenue Service if such practice violates 18 U.S.C. §§ 203 or 205.

(i) *State officers and employees.* No officer or employee of any State, or subdivision of any State, whose duties require him or her to pass upon, investigate, or deal with tax matters for such State or subdivision, may practice before the Internal Revenue Service, if such employment may disclose facts or information applicable to Federal tax matters.

(j) *Effective/applicability date.* Paragraphs (a), (b), and (g) of this section are applicable beginning June 12, 2014. Paragraphs (c) through (f), (h), and (i) of this section are applicable beginning August 2, 2011.

§ 10.4 Eligibility to become an enrolled agent, enrolled retirement plan agent, or registered tax return preparer.

(a) *Enrollment as an enrolled agent upon examination.* The Commissioner, or delegate, will grant enrollment as an enrolled agent to an applicant eighteen years of age or older who demonstrates special competence in tax matters by written examination administered by, or administered under the oversight of, the Internal Revenue Service, who possesses a current or otherwise valid preparer tax identification number or other prescribed identifying number, and who has not engaged in any conduct that would justify the suspension or disbarment of any practitioner under the provisions of this part.

(b) *Enrollment as a retirement plan agent upon examination.* The Commissioner, or delegate, will grant enrollment as an enrolled retirement plan agent to an applicant eighteen years of age or older who demonstrates special competence in qualified retirement plan matters by written examination administered by, or administered under the oversight of, the Internal Revenue Service, who possesses a current or otherwise valid preparer tax identification number or other prescribed identifying number, and who has not engaged in any conduct that would justify the suspension or disbarment of any practitioner under the provisions of this part.

(c) *Designation as a registered tax return preparer.* The Commissioner, or delegate, may designate an individual eighteen years of age or older as a registered tax return preparer provided an applicant demonstrates competence in Federal tax return preparation matters by written examination administered by, or administered under the oversight of, the Internal Revenue Service, or otherwise meets the requisite standards prescribed by the Internal Revenue Service, possesses a current or otherwise valid preparer tax identification number or other prescribed identifying number, and has not engaged in any conduct that would justify the suspension or disbarment of any practitioner under the provisions of this part.

(d) *Enrollment of former Internal Revenue Service employees.* The Commissioner, or delegate, may grant enrollment as an enrolled agent or enrolled retirement plan agent to an applicant who, by virtue of past service and technical experience in the Internal Revenue Service, has qualified for such enrollment and who has not engaged in any conduct that would justify the suspension or disbarment of any practitioner under the provisions of this part, under the following circumstances:

(1) The former employee applies for enrollment on an Internal Revenue Service form and supplies the information requested on the form and such other information regarding the experience and training of the applicant as may be relevant.

(2) The appropriate office of the Internal Revenue Service provides a detailed report of the nature and rating of the applicant's work while employed by the Internal Revenue Service and a recommendation whether such employment qualifies the applicant technically or otherwise for the desired authorization.

(3) Enrollment as an enrolled agent based on an applicant's former employment with the Internal Revenue Service may be of unlimited scope or it may be limited to permit the presentation of matters only of the particular specialty or only before the particular unit or division of the Internal Revenue Service for which the applicant's former employment has qualified the applicant. Enrollment as an enrolled retirement plan agent based on an applicant's former employment with the Internal Revenue Service will be limited to permit the presentation of matters only with respect to qualified retirement plan matters.

(4) Application for enrollment as an enrolled agent or enrolled retirement plan agent based on an applicant's former employment with the Internal Revenue Service must be made within three years from the date of separation from such employment.

(5) An applicant for enrollment as an enrolled agent who is requesting such enrollment based on former employment with the Internal Revenue Service must have had a minimum of five years continuous employment with the Internal Revenue Service during which the applicant must have been regularly engaged in applying and interpreting the provisions of the Internal Revenue Code and the regulations relating to income, estate, gift, employment, or excise taxes.

(6) An applicant for enrollment as an enrolled retirement plan agent who is requesting such enrollment based on former employment with the Internal Revenue Service must have had a minimum of five years continuous employment with the Internal Revenue Service during which the applicant must have been regularly engaged in applying and interpreting the provisions of the Internal Revenue Code and the regulations relating to qualified retirement plan matters.

(7) For the purposes of paragraphs (d)(5) and (6) of this section, an aggregate of 10 or more years of employment in positions involving the application and interpretation of the provisions of the Internal Revenue Code, at least three of which occurred within the five years preceding the date of application, is the equivalent of five years continuous employment.

(e) *Natural persons.* Enrollment to practice may be granted only to natural persons.

(f) *Effective/applicability date.* This section is applicable beginning August 2, 2011.

§ 10.5 Application to become an enrolled agent, enrolled retirement plan agent, or registered tax return preparer.

(a) *Form; address.* An applicant to become an enrolled agent, enrolled retirement plan agent, or registered tax return preparer must apply as required by forms or procedures established and published by the Internal Revenue Service, including proper execution of required forms under oath or affirmation. The address on the application will be the address under which a successful applicant is enrolled or registered and is the address to which all correspondence concerning enrollment or registration will be sent.

(b) *Fee.* A reasonable nonrefundable fee may be charged for each application to become an enrolled agent, enrolled retirement plan agent, or registered tax return preparer. See 26 CFR part 300.

(c) *Additional information; examination.* The Internal Revenue Service may require the applicant, as a condition to consideration of an application, to file additional information and to submit to any written or oral examination under oath or otherwise. Upon the applicant's written request, the Internal Revenue Service will afford the applicant the opportunity to be heard with respect to the application.

(d) *Compliance and suitability checks.*

(1) As a condition to consideration of an application, the Internal Revenue Service may conduct a Federal tax compliance check and suitability check. The tax compliance check will be limited to an inquiry regarding whether an applicant has filed all required individual or business tax returns and whether the applicant has failed to pay, or make proper arrangements with the Internal Revenue Service for payment of, any Federal tax debts. The suitability check will be limited to an inquiry regarding whether an applicant has engaged in any conduct that would justify suspension or disbarment of any practitioner under the provisions of this part on the date the application is submitted, including whether the applicant has engaged in disreputable conduct as defined in §10.51. The application will be denied only if the results of the compliance or suitability check are sufficient to establish that the practitioner engaged in conduct subject to sanctions under §§10.51 and 10.52.

(2) If the applicant does not pass the tax compliance or suitability check, the applicant will not be issued an enrollment or registration card or certificate pursuant to §10.6(b) of this part. An applicant who is initially denied enrollment or registration for failure to pass a tax compliance check may reapply after the initial denial if the applicant becomes current with respect to the applicant's tax liabilities.

(e) *Temporary recognition.* On receipt of a properly executed application, the Commissioner, or delegate, may grant the applicant temporary recognition to practice pending a determination as to whether status as an enrolled agent, enrolled retirement plan agent, or registered tax return preparer should be granted. Temporary recognition will be granted only in unusual circumstances and it will not be granted, in any circumstance, if the application is not regular on its face, if the information stated in the application,

if true, is not sufficient to warrant granting the application to practice, or the Commissioner, or delegate, has information indicating that the statements in the application are untrue or that the applicant would not otherwise qualify to become an enrolled agent, enrolled retirement plan agent, or registered tax return preparer. Issuance of temporary recognition does not constitute either a designation or a finding of eligibility as an enrolled agent, enrolled retirement plan agent, or registered tax return preparer, and the temporary recognition may be withdrawn at any time.

(f) *Protest of application denial.* The applicant will be informed in writing as to the reason(s) for any denial of an application. The applicant may, within 30 days after receipt of the notice of denial of the application, file a written protest of the denial as prescribed by the Internal Revenue Service in forms, guidance, or other appropriate guidance. A protest under this section is not governed by subpart D of this part.

(f) *Effective/applicability date.* This section is applicable to applications received on or after August 2, 2011.

§ 10.6 Term and renewal of status as an enrolled agent, enrolled retirement plan agent, or registered tax return preparer.

(a) *Term.* Each individual authorized to practice before the Internal Revenue Service as an enrolled agent, enrolled retirement plan agent, or registered tax return preparer will be accorded active enrollment or registration status subject to renewal of enrollment or registration as provided in this part.

(b) *Enrollment or registration card or certificate.* The Internal Revenue Service will issue an enrollment or registration card or certificate to each individual whose application to practice before the Internal Revenue Service is approved. Each card or certificate will be valid for the period stated on the card or certificate. An enrolled agent, enrolled retirement plan agent, or registered tax return preparer may not practice before the Internal Revenue Service if the card or certificate is not current or otherwise valid. The card or certificate is in addition to any notification that may be provided to each individual who obtains a preparer tax identification number.

(c) *Change of address.* An enrolled agent, enrolled retirement plan agent, or registered tax return preparer must send notification of any change of address to the address specified by the Internal Revenue Service within 60 days of the change of address. This notification must include the enrolled agent's, enrolled retirement plan agent's, or registered tax return preparer's name, prior address, new address, tax identification number(s) (including preparer tax identification number), and the date the change of address is effective. Unless this notification is sent, the address for purposes of any correspondence from the appropriate Internal Revenue Service office responsible for administering this part shall be the address reflected on the practitioner's most recent application for enrollment or registration, or application for renewal of enrollment or registration. A practitioner's change of address notification under this part will not constitute a change of the practitioner's last known address for purposes of section 6212 of the Internal Revenue Code and regulations thereunder.

(d) *Renewal.*

(1) *In general.* Enrolled agents, enrolled retirement plan agents, and registered tax return preparers must renew their status with the Internal Revenue Service to maintain eligibility to practice before the Internal Revenue Service. Failure to receive notification from the Internal Revenue Service of the renewal requirement will not be justification for the individual's failure to satisfy this requirement.

(2) *Renewal period for enrolled agents.*

(i) All enrolled agents must renew their preparer tax identification number as prescribed by forms, instructions, or other appropriate guidance.

(ii) Enrolled agents who have a social security number or tax identification number that ends with the numbers 0, 1, 2, or 3, except for those individuals who received their initial enrollment after November 1, 2003, must apply for renewal between November 1, 2003, and January 31, 2004. The renewal will be effective April 1, 2004.

(iii) Enrolled agents who have a social security number or tax identification number that ends with the numbers 4, 5, or 6, except for those individuals who received their initial enrollment after November 1, 2004, must apply for renewal between November 1, 2004, and January 31, 2005. The renewal will be effective April 1, 2005.

(iv) Enrolled agents who have a social security number or tax identification number that ends with the numbers 7, 8, or 9, except for those individuals who received their initial enrollment after November 1, 2005, must apply for renewal between November 1, 2005, and January 31, 2006. The renewal will be effective April 1, 2006.

(v) Thereafter, applications for renewal as an enrolled agent will be required between November 1 and January 31 of every subsequent third year as specified in paragraph (d)(2)(i), (d)(2)(ii), or (d)(2)(iii) of this section according to the last number of the individual's social security number or tax identification number. Those individuals who receive initial enrollment as an enrolled agent after November 1 and before April 2 of the applicable renewal period will not be required to renew their enrollment before the first full renewal period following the receipt of their initial enrollment.

(3) *Renewal period for enrolled retirement plan agents.*

(i) All enrolled retirement plan agents must renew their preparer tax identification number as prescribed by the Internal Revenue Service in forms, instructions, or other appropriate guidance.

(ii) Enrolled retirement plan agents will be required to renew their status as enrolled retirement plan agents between April 1 and June 30 of every third year subsequent to their initial enrollment.

(4) *Renewal period for registered tax return preparers.* Registered tax return preparers must renew their preparer tax identification number and their status as a registered tax return preparer as prescribed by the Internal Revenue Service in forms, instructions, or other appropriate guidance.

(5) *Notification of renewal.* After review and approval, the Internal Revenue Service will notify

the individual of the renewal and will issue the individual a card or certificate evidencing current status as an enrolled agent, enrolled retirement plan agent, or registered tax return preparer.

(6) *Fee.* A reasonable nonrefundable fee may be charged for each application for renewal filed. See 26 CFR part 300.

(7) *Forms.* Forms required for renewal may be obtained by sending a written request to the address specified by the Internal Revenue Service or from such other source as the Internal Revenue Service will publish in the Internal Revenue Bulletin (see 26 CFR 601.601(d)(2)(ii)(b)) and on the Internal Revenue Service webpage (www.irs.gov).

(e) *Condition for renewal*: continuing education. In order to qualify for renewal as an enrolled agent, enrolled retirement plan agent, or registered tax return preparer, an individual must certify, in the manner prescribed by the Internal Revenue Service, that the individual has satisfied the requisite number of continuing education hours.

(1) *Definitions.* For purposes of this section —

(i) *Enrollment year* means January 1 to December 31 of each year of an enrollment cycle.

(ii) *Enrollment cycle* means the three successive enrollment years preceding the effective date of renewal.

(iii) *Registration year* means each 12-month period the registered tax return preparer is authorized to practice before the Internal Revenue Service.

(iv) *The effective date of renewal* is the first day of the fourth month following the close of the period for renewal described in paragraph (d) of this section.

(2) *For renewed enrollment as an enrolled agent or enrolled retirement plan agent —*

(i) *Requirements for enrollment cycle.* A minimum of 72 hours of continuing education credit, including six hours of ethics or professional conduct, must be completed during each enrollment cycle.

(ii) *Requirements for enrollment year.* A minimum of 16 hours of continuing education credit, including two hours of ethics or professional conduct, must be completed during each enrollment year of an enrollment cycle.

(iii) *Enrollment during enrollment cycle —*

(A) *In general.* Subject to paragraph (e)(2)(iii) (B) of this section, an individual who receives initial enrollment during an enrollment cycle must complete two hours of qualifying continuing education credit for each month enrolled during the enrollment cycle. Enrollment for any part of a month is considered enrollment for the entire month.

(B) *Ethics.* An individual who receives initial enrollment during an enrollment cycle must complete two hours of ethics or professional conduct for each enrollment year during the enrollment cycle. Enrollment for any part of an enrollment year is considered enrollment for the entire year.

(3) *Requirements for renewal as a registered tax return preparer.* A minimum of 15 hours of continuing education credit, including two hours of ethics or professional conduct, three hours of Federal tax law updates, and 10 hours of Federal tax law topics, must be completed during each registration year.

(f) *Qualifying continuing education —*

(1) *General —*

(i) *Enrolled agents.* To qualify for continuing education credit for an enrolled agent, a course of learning must —

(A) Be a qualifying continuing education program designed to enhance professional knowledge in Federal taxation or Federal tax related matters (programs comprised of current subject matter in Federal taxation or Federal tax related matters, including accounting, tax return preparation software, taxation, or ethics); and

(B) Be a qualifying continuing education program consistent with the Internal Revenue Code and effective tax administration.

(ii) *Enrolled retirement plan agents.* To qualify for continuing education credit for an enrolled retirement plan agent, a course of learning must —

(A) Be a qualifying continuing education program designed to enhance professional knowledge in qualified retirement plan matters; and

(B) Be a qualifying continuing education program consistent with the Internal Revenue Code and effective tax administration.

(iii) *Registered tax return preparers.* To

Treasury Department Circular No. 230

qualify for continuing education credit for a registered tax return preparer, a course of learning must —

(A) Be a qualifying continuing education program designed to enhance professional knowledge in Federal taxation or Federal tax related matters (programs comprised of current subject matter in Federal taxation or Federal tax related matters, including accounting, tax return preparation software, taxation, or ethics); and

(B) Be a qualifying continuing education program consistent with the Internal Revenue Code and effective tax administration.

(2) *Qualifying programs* —

(i) *Formal programs.* A formal program qualifies as a continuing education program if it —

(A) Requires attendance and provides each attendee with a certificate of attendance;

(B) Is conducted by a qualified instructor, discussion leader, or speaker (in other words, a person whose background, training, education, and experience is appropriate for instructing or leading a discussion on the subject matter of the particular program);

(C) Provides or requires a written outline, textbook, or suitable electronic educational materials; and

(D) Satisfies the requirements established for a qualified continuing education program pursuant to §10.9.

(ii) *Correspondence or individual study programs (including taped programs).* Qualifying continuing education programs include correspondence or individual study programs that are conducted by continuing education providers and completed on an individual basis by the enrolled individual. The allowable credit hours for such programs will be measured on a basis comparable to the measurement of a seminar or course for credit in an accredited educational institution. Such programs qualify as continuing education programs only if they —

(A) Require registration of the participants by the continuing education provider;

(B) Provide a means for measuring successful completion by the participants (for example, a written

examination), including the issuance of a certificate of completion by the continuing education provider;

(C) Provide a written outline, textbook, or suitable electronic educational materials; and

(D) Satisfy the requirements established for a qualified continuing education program pursuant to §10.9.

(iii) *Serving as an instructor, discussion leader or speaker.*

(A) One hour of continuing education credit will be awarded for each contact hour completed as an instructor, discussion leader, or speaker at an educational program that meets the continuing education requirements of paragraph (f) of this section.

(B) A maximum of two hours of continuing education credit will be awarded for actual subject preparation time for each contact hour completed as an instructor, discussion leader, or speaker at such programs. It is the responsibility of the individual claiming such credit to maintain records to verify preparation time.

(C) The maximum continuing education credit for instruction and preparation may not exceed four hours annually for registered tax return preparers and six hours annually for enrolled agents and enrolled retirement plan agents.

(D) An instructor, discussion leader, or speaker who makes more than one presentation on the same subject matter during an enrollment cycle or registration year will receive continuing education credit for only one such presentation for the enrollment cycle or registration year.

(3) *Periodic examination.* Enrolled Agents and Enrolled Retirement Plan Agents may establish eligibility for renewal of enrollment for any enrollment cycle by —

(i) Achieving a passing score on each part of the Special Enrollment Examination administered under this part during the three year period prior to renewal; and

(ii) Completing a minimum of 16 hours of qualifying continuing education during the last year of an enrollment cycle.

(g) *Measurement of continuing education coursework.*

(1) All continuing education programs will be measured in terms of contact hours. The shortest recognized program will be one contact hour.

(2) A contact hour is 50 minutes of continuous participation in a program. Credit is granted only for a full contact hour, which is 50 minutes or multiples thereof. For example, a program lasting more than 50 minutes but less than 100 minutes will count as only one contact hour.

(3) Individual segments at continuous conferences, conventions and the like will be considered one total program. For example, two 90-minute segments (180 minutes) at a continuous conference will count as three contact hours.

(4) For university or college courses, each semester hour credit will equal 15 contact hours and a quarter hour credit will equal 10 contact hours.

(h) *Recordkeeping requirements.*

(1) Each individual applying for renewal must retain for a period of four years following the date of renewal the information required with regard to qualifying continuing education credit hours. Such information includes —

(i) The name of the sponsoring organization;

(ii) The location of the program;

(iii) The title of the program, qualified program number, and description of its content;

(iv) Written outlines, course syllibi, textbook, and/or electronic materials provided or required for the course;

(v) The dates attended;

(vi) The credit hours claimed;

(vii) The name(s) of the instructor(s), discussion leader(s), or speaker(s), if appropriate; and

(viii) The certificate of completion and/or signed statement of the hours of attendance obtained from the continuing education provider.

(2) To receive continuing education credit for service completed as an instructor, discussion leader, or speaker, the following information must be maintained for a period of four years following the date of renewal —

(i) The name of the sponsoring organization;

(ii) The location of the program;

(iii) The title of the program and copy of its content;

(iv) The dates of the program; and

(v) The credit hours claimed.

(i) *Waivers.*

(1) Waiver from the continuing education requirements for a given period may be granted for the following reasons —

(i) Health, which prevented compliance with the continuing education requirements;

(ii) Extended active military duty;

(iii) Absence from the United States for an extended period of time due to employment or other reasons, provided the individual does not practice before the Internal Revenue Service during such absence; and

(iv) Other compelling reasons, which will be considered on a case-by-case basis.

(2) A request for waiver must be accompanied by appropriate documentation. The individual is required to furnish any additional documentation or explanation deemed necessary. Examples of appropriate documentation could be a medical certificate or military orders.

(3) A request for waiver must be filed no later than the last day of the renewal application period.

(4) If a request for waiver is not approved, the individual will be placed in inactive status. The individual will be notified that the waiver was not approved and that the individual has been placed on a roster of inactive enrolled agents, enrolled retirement plan agents, or registered tax return preparers.

(5) If the request for waiver is not approved, the individual may file a protest as prescribed by the Internal Revenue Service in forms, instructions, or other appropriate guidance. A protest filed under this section is not governed by subpart D of this part.

(6) If a request for waiver is approved, the individual will be notified and issued a card or certificate evidencing renewal.

(7) Those who are granted waivers are required to file timely applications for renewal of enrollment or registration.

(j) *Failure to comply.*

(1) Compliance by an individual with the requirements of this part is determined by the Internal Revenue Service. The Internal Revenue Service will provide notice to any individual who fails to meet the continuing education and fee requirements of eligibility for renewal. The notice will state the basis for the determination of noncompliance and will provide the individual an opportunity to furnish the requested information in writing relating to the matter within 60 days of the date of the notice. Such information will be considered in making a final determination as to eligibility for renewal. The individual must be informed of the reason(s) for any denial of a renewal. The individual may, within 30 days after receipt of the notice of denial of renewal, file a written protest of the denial as prescribed by the Internal Revenue Service in forms, instructions, or other appropriate guidance. A protest under this section is not governed by subpart D of this part.

(2) The continuing education records of an enrolled agent, enrolled retirement plan agent, or registered tax return preparer may be reviewed to determine compliance with the requirements and standards for renewal as provided in paragraph (f) of this section. As part of this review, the enrolled agent, enrolled retirement plan agent or registered tax return preparer may be required to provide the Internal Revenue Service with copies of any continuing education records required to be maintained under this part. If the enrolled agent, enrolled retirement plan agent or registered tax return preparer fails to comply with this requirement, any continuing education hours claimed may be disallowed.

(3) An individual who has not filed a timely application for renewal, who has not made a timely response to the notice of noncompliance with the renewal requirements, or who has not satisfied the requirements of eligibility for renewal will be placed on a roster of inactive enrolled individuals or inactive registered individuals. During this time, the individual will be ineligible to practice before the Internal Revenue Service.

(4) Individuals placed in inactive status and individuals ineligible to practice before the Internal Revenue Service may not state or imply that they are eligible to practice before the Internal Revenue Service, or use the terms enrolled agent, enrolled retirement plan agent, or registered tax return preparer, the designations "EA" or "ERPA" or other form of reference to eligibility to practice before the Internal Revenue Service.

(5) An individual placed in inactive status may be reinstated to an active status by filing an application for renewal and providing evidence of the completion of all required continuing education hours for the enrollment cycle or registration year. Continuing education credit under this paragraph (j) (5) may not be used to satisfy the requirements of the enrollment cycle or registration year in which the individual has been placed back on the active roster.

(6) An individual placed in inactive status must file an application for renewal and satisfy the requirements for renewal as set forth in this section within three years of being placed in inactive status. Otherwise, the name of such individual will be removed from the inactive status roster and the individual's status as an enrolled agent, enrolled retirement plan agent, or registered tax return preparer will terminate. Future eligibility for active status must then be reestablished by the individual as provided in this section.

(7) Inactive status is not available to an individual who is the subject of a pending disciplinary matter before the Internal Revenue Service.

(k) *Inactive retirement status.* An individual who no longer practices before the Internal Revenue Service may request to be placed in an inactive retirement status at any time and such individual will be placed in an inactive retirement status. The individual will be ineligible to practice before the Internal Revenue Service. An individual who is placed in an inactive retirement status may be reinstated to an active status by filing an application for renewal and providing evidence of the completion of the required continuing education hours for the enrollment cycle or registration year. Inactive retirement status is not available to an individual who is ineligible to practice before the Internal Revenue Service or an individual who is the subject of a pending disciplinary matter under this part.

(l) *Renewal while under suspension or disbarment.* An individual who is ineligible to practice before the Internal Revenue Service by virtue of disciplinary action under this part is required to conform to the requirements for renewal of enrollment or registration before the individual's eligibility is restored.

(m) *Enrolled actuaries.* The enrollment and renewal of enrollment of actuaries authorized to practice under paragraph (d) of §10.3 are governed by the regulations of the Joint Board for the Enrollment of Actuaries at 20 CFR 901.1 through 901.72.

(n) *Effective/applicability date.* This section is applicable to enrollment or registration effective beginning August 2, 2011.

§ 10.7 Representing oneself; participating in rulemaking; limited practice; and special appearances.

(a) *Representing oneself.* Individuals may appear on their own behalf before the Internal Revenue Service provided they present satisfactory identification.

(b) *Participating in rulemaking.* Individuals may participate in rulemaking as provided by the Administrative Procedure Act. See 5 U.S.C. § 553.

(c) *Limited practice* —

(1) *In general.* Subject to the limitations in paragraph (c)(2) of this section, an individual who is not a practitioner may represent a taxpayer before the Internal Revenue Service in the circumstances described in this paragraph (c)(1), even if the taxpayer is not present, provided the individual presents satisfactory identification and proof of his or her authority to represent the taxpayer. The circumstances described in this paragraph (c)(1) are as follows:

(i) An individual may represent a member of his or her immediate family.

(ii) A regular full-time employee of an individual employer may represent the employer.

(iii) A general partner or a regular full-time employee of a partnership may represent the partnership.

(iv) A bona fide officer or a regular full-time employee of a corporation (including a parent, subsidiary, or other affiliated corporation), association, or organized group may represent the corporation, association, or organized group.

(v) A regular full-time employee of a trust, receivership, guardianship, or estate may represent the trust, receivership, guardianship, or estate.

(vi) An officer or a regular employee of a governmental unit, agency, or authority may represent the governmental unit, agency, or authority in the course of his or her official duties.

(vii) An individual may represent any individual or entity, who is outside the United States, before personnel of the Internal Revenue Service when such representation takes place outside the United States.

(2) *Limitations.*

(i) An individual who is under suspension or disbarment from practice before the Internal Revenue Service may not engage in limited practice before the Internal Revenue Service under paragraph (c)(1) of this section.

(ii) The Commissioner, or delegate, may, after notice and opportunity for a conference, deny eligibility to engage in limited practice before the Internal Revenue Service under paragraph (c)(1) of this section to any individual who has engaged in conduct that would justify a sanction under §10.50.

(iii) An individual who represents a taxpayer under the authority of paragraph (c)(1) of this section is subject, to the extent of his or her authority, to such rules of general applicability regarding standards of conduct and other matters as prescribed by the Internal Revenue Service.

(d) *Special appearances.* The Commissioner, or delegate, may, subject to conditions deemed appropriate, authorize an individual who is not otherwise eligible to practice before the Internal Revenue Service to represent another person in a particular matter.

(e) *Fiduciaries.* For purposes of this part, a fiduciary (for example, a trustee, receiver, guardian, personal representative, administrator, or executor) is considered to be the taxpayer and not a representative of the taxpayer.

(f) *Effective/applicability date.* This section is applicable beginning August 2, 2011.

§ 10.8 Return preparation and application of rules to other individuals.

(a) *Preparing all or substantially all of a tax return.* Any individual who for compensation prepares or assists with the preparation of all or substantially all of a tax return or claim for refund must have a preparer tax identification number. Except as otherwise prescribed in forms, instructions, or other appropriate guidance, an individual must be an attorney, certified public accountant, enrolled agent, or registered tax return preparer to obtain a preparer tax identification number. Any individual who for compensation prepares or assists with the preparation of all or substantially all of a tax return or claim for refund is subject to the duties and restrictions relating to practice in subpart B, as well as subject to the sanctions for violation of the regulations in subpart C.

(b) *Preparing a tax return and furnishing information.* Any individual may for compensation prepare or assist with the preparation of a tax return or claim for refund (provided the individual prepares less than substantially all of the tax return or claim for refund), appear as a witness for the taxpayer before the Internal Revenue Service, or furnish information at the request of the Internal Revenue Service or any of its officers or employees.

(c) *Application of rules to other individuals.* Any individual who for compensation prepares, or assists in the preparation of, all or a substantial portion of a document pertaining to any taxpayer's tax liability for submission to the Internal Revenue Service is subject to the duties and restrictions relating to practice in subpart B, as well as subject to the sanctions for violation of the regulations in subpart C. Unless otherwise a practitioner, however, an individual may not for compensation prepare, or assist in the preparation of, all or substantially all of a tax return or claim for refund, or sign tax returns and claims for refund. For purposes of this paragraph, an individual described in 26 CFR 301.7701-15(f) is not treated as having prepared all or a substantial portion of the document by reason of such assistance.

(d) *Effective/applicability date.* This section is applicable beginning August 2, 2011.

Treasury Department Circular No. 230

§ 10.9 Continuing education providers and continuing education programs.

(a) *Continuing education providers —*

(1) *In general.* Continuing education providers are those responsible for presenting continuing education programs. A continuing education provider must —

(i) Be an accredited educational institution;

(ii) Be recognized for continuing education purposes by the licensing body of any State, territory, or possession of the United States, including a Commonwealth, or the District of Columbia;

(iii) Be recognized and approved by a qualifying organization as a provider of continuing education on subject matters within §10.6(f) of this part. The Internal Revenue Service may, at its discretion, identify a professional organization, society or business entity that maintains minimum education standards comparable to those set forth in this part as a qualifying organization for purposes of this part in appropriate forms, instructions, and other appropriate guidance; or

(iv) Be recognized by the Internal Revenue Service as a professional organization, society, or business whose programs include offering continuing professional education opportunities in subject matters within §10.6(f) of this part. The Internal Revenue Service, at its discretion, may require such professional organizations, societies, or businesses to file an agreement and/or obtain Internal Revenue Service approval of each program as a qualified continuing education program in appropriate forms, instructions or other appropriate guidance.

(2) *Continuing education provider numbers —*

(i) *In general.* A continuing education provider is required to obtain a continuing education provider number and pay any applicable user fee.

(ii) *Renewal.* A continuing education provider maintains its status as a continuing education provider during the continuing education provider cycle by renewing its continuing education provider number as prescribed by forms, instructions or other appropriate guidance and paying any applicable user fee.

(3) *Requirements for qualified continuing education programs.* A continuing education provider must ensure the qualified continuing education program complies with all the following requirements —

(i) Programs must be developed by individual(s) qualified in the subject matter;

(ii) Program subject matter must be current;

(iii) Instructors, discussion leaders, and speakers must be qualified with respect to program content;

(iv) Programs must include some means for evaluation of the technical content and presentation to be evaluated;

(v) Certificates of completion bearing a current qualified continuing education program number issued by the Internal Revenue Service must be provided to the participants who successfully complete the program; and

(vi) Records must be maintained by the continuing education provider to verify the participants who attended and completed the program for a period of four years following completion of the program. In the case of continuous conferences, conventions, and the like, records must be maintained to verify completion of the program and attendance by each participant at each segment of the program.

(4) *Program numbers* —

(i) *In general.* Every continuing education provider is required to obtain a continuing education provider program number and pay any applicable user fee for each program offered. Program numbers shall be obtained as prescribed by forms, instructions or other appropriate guidance. Although, at the discretion of the Internal Revenue Service, a continuing education provider may be required to demonstrate that the program is designed to enhance professional knowledge in Federal taxation or Federal tax related matters (programs comprised of current subject matter in Federal taxation or Federal tax related matters, including accounting, tax return preparation software, taxation, or ethics) and complies with the requirements in paragraph (a)(2)of this section before a program number is issued.

(ii) *Update programs.* Update programs may use the same number as the program subject to update. An update program is a program that instructs on a change of existing law occurring within one year of the update program offering. The qualifying education program subject to update must have been offered within the two year time period prior to the change in existing law.

(iii) *Change in existing law.* A change in existing law means the effective date of the statute or regulation, or date of entry of judicial decision, that is the subject of the update.

(b) *Failure to comply.* Compliance by a continuing education provider with the requirements of this part is determined by the Internal Revenue Service. A continuing education provider who fails to meet the requirements of this part will be notified by the Internal Revenue Service. The notice will state the basis for the determination of noncompliance and will provide the continuing education provider an opportunity to furnish the requested information in writing relating to the matter within 60 days of the date of the notice. The continuing education provider may, within 30 days after receipt of the notice of denial, file a written protest as prescribed by the Internal Revenue Service in forms, instructions, or other appropriate guidance. A protest under this section is not governed by subpart D of this part.

(c) *Effective/applicability date.* This section is applicable beginning August 2, 2011.

Subpart B — Duties and Restrictions Relating to Practice Before the Internal Revenue Service

§ 10.20 Information to be furnished.

(a) *To the Internal Revenue Service.*

(1) A practitioner must, on a proper and lawful request by a duly authorized officer or employee of the Internal Revenue Service, promptly submit records or information in any matter before the Internal Revenue Service unless the practitioner believes in good faith and on reasonable grounds that the records or information are privileged.

(2) Where the requested records or information are not in the possession of, or subject to the control of, the practitioner or the practitioner's client, the practitioner must promptly notify the requesting Internal Revenue Service officer or employee and the practitioner must provide any information that the practitioner has regarding the identity of any person who the practitioner believes may have possession or control of the requested records or information. The practitioner must make reasonable inquiry of his or her client regarding the identity of any person who may have possession or control of the requested records or information, but the practitioner is not required to make inquiry of any other person or independently verify any information provided by the practitioner's client regarding the identity of such persons.

(3) When a proper and lawful request is made by a duly authorized officer or employee of the Internal Revenue Service, concerning an inquiry into an alleged violation of the regulations in this part, a practitioner must provide any information the practitioner has concerning the alleged violation and testify regarding this information in any proceeding instituted under this part, unless the practitioner believes in good faith and on reasonable grounds that the information is privileged.

(b) *Interference with a proper and lawful request for records or information.* A practitioner may not interfere, or attempt to interfere, with any proper and lawful effort by the Internal Revenue Service, its officers or employees, to obtain any record or information unless the practitioner believes in good faith and on reasonable grounds that the record or information is privileged.

(c) *Effective/applicability date.* This section is applicable beginning August 2, 2011.

§ 10.21 Knowledge of client's omission.

A practitioner who, having been retained by a client with respect to a matter administered by the Internal Revenue Service, knows that the client has not complied with the revenue laws of the United States or has made an error in or omission from any return, document, affidavit, or other paper which the client submitted or executed under the revenue laws of the United States, must advise the client promptly of the fact of such noncompliance, error, or omission. The practitioner must advise the client of the consequences as provided under the Code and regulations of such noncompliance, error, or omission.

§ 10.22 Diligence as to accuracy.

(a) *In general.* A practitioner must exercise due diligence —

(1) In preparing or assisting in the preparation of, approving, and filing tax returns, documents, affidavits, and other papers relating to Internal Revenue Service matters;

(2) In determining the correctness of oral or written representations made by the practitioner to the Department of the Treasury; and

(3) In determining the correctness of oral or written representations made by the practitioner to clients with reference to any matter administered by the Internal Revenue Service.

(b) *Reliance on others.* Except as modified by §§10.34 and 10.37, a practitioner will be presumed to have exercised due diligence for purposes of this section if the practitioner relies on the work product of another person and the practitioner used reasonable care in engaging, supervising, training, and evaluating the person, taking proper account of the nature of the relationship between the practitioner and the person.

Treasury Department Circular No. 230   § 10.22 — Page 19

(c) *Effective/applicability date.* Paragraph (a) of this section is applicable on September 26, 2007. Paragraph (b) of this section is applicable beginning June 12, 2014.

§ 10.23 Prompt disposition of pending matters.

A practitioner may not unreasonably delay the prompt disposition of any matter before the Internal Revenue Service.

§ 10.24 Assistance from or to disbarred or suspended persons and former Internal Revenue Service employees.

A practitioner may not, knowingly and directly or indirectly:

(a) Accept assistance from or assist any person who is under disbarment or suspension from practice before the Internal Revenue Service if the assistance relates to a matter or matters constituting practice before the Internal Revenue Service.

(b) Accept assistance from any former government employee where the provisions of § 10.25 or any Federal law would be violated.

§10.25 Practice by former government employees, their partners and their associates.

(a) *Definitions.* For purposes of this section —

(1) *Assist* means to act in such a way as to advise, furnish information to, or otherwise aid another person, directly, or indirectly.

(2) *Government employee* is an officer or employee of the United States or any agency of the United States, including a special Government employee as defined in *18 U.S.C. 202(a)*, or of the District of Columbia, or of any State, or a member of Congress or of any State legislature.

(3) *Member of a firm* is a sole practitioner or an employee or associate thereof, or a partner, stockholder, associate, affiliate or employee of a partnership, joint venture, corporation, professional association or other affiliation of two or more practitioners who represent nongovernmental parties.

(4) *Particular matter involving specific parties* is defined at 5 CFR 2637.201(c), or superseding post-employment regulations issued by the U.S. Office of Government Ethics.

(5) *Rule* includes Treasury regulations, whether issued or under preparation for issuance as notices of proposed rulemaking or as Treasury decisions, revenue rulings, and revenue procedures published in the Internal Revenue Bulletin (see *26 CFR 601.601(d)(2)(ii)(b)*).

(b) *General rules —*

(1) No former Government employee may, subsequent to Government employment, represent anyone in any matter administered by the Internal Revenue Service if the representation would violate *18 U.S.C. 207* or any other laws of the United States.

(2) No former Government employee who personally and substantially participated in a particular matter involving specific parties may, subsequent to Government employment, represent or knowingly assist, in that particular matter, any person who is or was a specific party to that particular matter.

(3) A former Government employee who within a period of one year prior to the termination of Government employment had official responsibility for a particular matter involving specific parties may not, within two years after Government employment is ended, represent in that particular matter any person who is or was a specific party to that particular matter.

(4) No former Government employee may, within one year after Government employment is ended, communicate with or appear before, with the intent to influence, any employee of the Treasury Department in connection with the publication, withdrawal, amendment, modification, or interpretation of a rule the development of which the former Government employee participated in, or for which, within a period of one year prior to the termination of Government employment, the former government employee had official responsibility. This paragraph (b)(4) does not, however, preclude any former employee from appearing on one's own behalf or from representing a taxpayer before the Internal Revenue Service in connection with a particular matter involving specific

parties involving the application or interpretation of a rule with respect to that particular matter, provided that the representation is otherwise consistent with the other provisions of this section and the former employee does not utilize or disclose any confidential information acquired by the former employee in the development of the rule.

(c) *Firm representation* —

(1) No member of a firm of which a former Government employee is a member may represent or knowingly assist a person who was or is a specific party in any particular matter with respect to which the restrictions of paragraph (b)(2) of this section apply to the former Government employee, in that particular matter, unless the firm isolates the former Government employee in such a way to ensure that the former Government employee cannot assist in the representation.

(2) When isolation of a former Government employee is required under paragraph (c)(1) of this section, a statement affirming the fact of such isolation must be executed under oath by the former Government employee and by another member of the firm acting on behalf of the firm. The statement must clearly identify the firm, the former Government employee, and the particular matter(s) requiring isolation. The statement must be retained by the firm and, upon request, provided to the office(s) of the Internal Revenue Service administering or enforcing this part.

(d) *Pending representation.* The provisions of this regulation will govern practice by former Government employees, their partners and associates with respect to representation in particular matters involving specific parties where actual representation commenced before the effective date of this regulation.

(e) *Effective/applicability date.* This section is applicable beginning August 2, 2011.

§ 10.26 Notaries.

A practitioner may not take acknowledgments, administer oaths, certify papers, or perform any official act as a notary public with respect to any matter administered by the Internal Revenue Service and for which he or she is employed as counsel, attorney, or agent, or in which he or she may be in any way interested.

§ 10.27 Fees.

(a) *In general.* A practitioner may not charge an unconscionable fee in connection with any matter before the Internal Revenue Service.

(b) *Contingent fees* —

(1) Except as provided in paragraphs (b)(2), (3), and (4) of this section, a practitioner may not charge a contingent fee for services rendered in connection with any matter before the Internal Revenue Service.

(2) A practitioner may charge a contingent fee for services rendered in connection with the Service's examination of, or challenge to —

(i) An original tax return; or

(ii) An amended return or claim for refund or credit where the amended return or claim for refund or credit was filed within 120 days of the taxpayer receiving a written notice of the examination of, or a written challenge to the original tax return.

(3) A practitioner may charge a contingent fee for services rendered in connection with a claim for credit or refund filed solely in connection with the determination of statutory interest or penalties assessed by the Internal Revenue Service.

(4) A practitioner may charge a contingent fee for services rendered in connection with any judicial proceeding arising under the Internal Revenue Code.

(c) *Definitions.* For purposes of this section —

(1) *Contingent fee* is any fee that is based, in whole or in part, on whether or not a position taken on a tax return or other filing avoids challenge by the Internal Revenue Service or is sustained either by the Internal Revenue Service or in litigation. A contingent fee includes a fee that is based on a percentage of the refund reported on a return, that is based on a percentage of the taxes saved, or that otherwise depends on the specific result attained. A contingent fee also includes any fee arrangement in which the practitioner will reimburse the client for all or a portion of the client's fee in the event

that a position taken on a tax return or other filing is challenged by the Internal Revenue Service or is not sustained, whether pursuant to an indemnity agreement, a guarantee, rescission rights, or any other arrangement with a similar effect.

(2) *Matter before the Internal Revenue Service* includes tax planning and advice, preparing or filing or assisting in preparing or filing returns or claims for refund or credit, and all matters connected with a presentation to the Internal Revenue Service or any of its officers or employees relating to a taxpayer's rights, privileges, or liabilities under laws or regulations administered by the Internal Revenue Service. Such presentations include, but are not limited to, preparing and filing documents, corresponding and communicating with the Internal Revenue Service, rendering written advice with respect to any entity, transaction, plan or arrangement, and representing a client at conferences, hearings, and meetings.

(d) *Effective/applicability date.* This section is applicable for fee arrangements entered into after March 26, 2008.

§ 10.28 Return of client's records.

(a) In general, a practitioner must, at the request of a client, promptly return any and all records of the client that are necessary for the client to comply with his or her Federal tax obligations. The practitioner may retain copies of the records returned to a client. The existence of a dispute over fees generally does not relieve the practitioner of his or her responsibility under this section. Nevertheless, if applicable state law allows or permits the retention of a client's records by a practitioner in the case of a dispute over fees for services rendered, the practitioner need only return those records that must be attached to the taxpayer's return. The practitioner, however, must provide the client with reasonable access to review and copy any additional records of the client retained by the practitioner under state law that are necessary for the client to comply with his or her Federal tax obligations.

(b) For purposes of this section — Records of the client include all documents or written or electronic materials provided to the practitioner, or obtained by the practitioner in the course of the practitioner's representation of the client, that preexisted the retention of the practitioner by the client. The term also includes materials that were prepared by the client or a third party (not including an employee or agent of the practitioner) at any time and provided to the practitioner with respect to the subject matter of the representation. The term also includes any return, claim for refund, schedule, affidavit, appraisal or any other document prepared by the practitioner, or his or her employee or agent, that was presented to the client with respect to a prior representation if such document is necessary for the taxpayer to comply with his or her current Federal tax obligations. The term does not include any return, claim for refund, schedule, affidavit, appraisal or any other document prepared by the practitioner or the practitioner's firm, employees or agents if the practitioner is withholding such document pending the client's performance of its contractual obligation to pay fees with respect to such document.

§ 10.29 Conflicting interests.

(a) Except as provided by paragraph (b) of this section, a practitioner shall not represent a client before the Internal Revenue Service if the representation involves a conflict of interest. A conflict of interest exists if —

(1) The representation of one client will be directly adverse to another client; or

(2) There is a significant risk that the representation of one or more clients will be materially limited by the practitioner's responsibilities to another client, a former client or a third person, or by a personal interest of the practitioner.

(b) Notwithstanding the existence of a conflict of interest under paragraph (a) of this section, the practitioner may represent a client if —

(1) The practitioner reasonably believes that the practitioner will be able to provide competent and diligent representation to each affected client;

(2) The representation is not prohibited by law; and

(3) Each affected client waives the conflict of

interest and gives informed consent, confirmed in writing by each affected client, at the time the existence of the conflict of interest is known by the practitioner. The confirmation may be made within a reasonable period of time after the informed consent, but in no event later than 30 days.

(c) Copies of the written consents must be retained by the practitioner for at least 36 months from the date of the conclusion of the representation of the affected clients, and the written consents must be provided to any officer or employee of the Internal Revenue Service on request.

(d) *Effective/applicability date.* This section is applicable on September 26, 2007.

§ 10.30 Solicitation.

(a) *Advertising and solicitation restrictions.*

(1) A practitioner may not, with respect to any Internal Revenue Service matter, in any way use or participate in the use of any form of public communication or private solicitation containing a false, fraudulent, or coercive statement or claim; or a misleading or deceptive statement or claim. Enrolled agents, enrolled retirement plan agents, or registered tax return preparers, in describing their professional designation, may not utilize the term "certified" or imply an employer/employee relationship with the Internal Revenue Service. Examples of acceptable descriptions for enrolled agents are "enrolled to represent taxpayers before the Internal Revenue Service," "enrolled to practice before the Internal Revenue Service," and "admitted to practice before the Internal Revenue Service." Similarly, examples of acceptable descriptions for enrolled retirement plan agents are "enrolled to represent taxpayers before the Internal Revenue Service as a retirement plan agent" and "enrolled to practice before the Internal Revenue Service as a retirement plan agent." An example of an acceptable description for registered tax return preparers is "designated as a registered tax return preparer by the Internal Revenue Service."

(2) A practitioner may not make, directly or indirectly, an uninvited written or oral solicitation of employment in matters related to the Internal Revenue Service if the solicitation violates Federal or State law or other applicable rule, e.g., attorneys are precluded from making a solicitation that is prohibited by conduct rules applicable to all attorneys in their State(s) of licensure. Any lawful solicitation made by or on behalf of a practitioner eligible to practice before the Internal Revenue Service must, nevertheless, clearly identify the solicitation as such and, if applicable, identify the source of the information used in choosing the recipient.

(b) *Fee information.*

(1)(i) A practitioner may publish the availability of a written schedule of fees and disseminate the following fee information —

(A) Fixed fees for specific routine services.

(B) Hourly rates.

(C) Range of fees for particular services.

(D) Fee charged for an initial consultation.

(ii) Any statement of fee information concerning matters in which costs may be incurred must include a statement disclosing whether clients will be responsible for such costs.

(2) A practitioner may charge no more than the rate(s) published under paragraph (b)(1) of this section for at least 30 calendar days after the last date on which the schedule of fees was published.

(c) *Communication of fee information.* Fee information may be communicated in professional lists, telephone directories, print media, mailings, and electronic mail, facsimile, hand delivered flyers, radio, television, and any other method. The method chosen, however, must not cause the communication to become untruthful, deceptive, or otherwise in violation of this part. A practitioner may not persist in attempting to contact a prospective client if the prospective client has made it known to the practitioner that he or she does not desire to be solicited. In the case of radio and television broadcasting, the broadcast must be recorded and the practitioner must retain a recording of the actual transmission. In the case of direct mail and e-commerce communications, the practitioner must retain a copy of the actual communication, along with a list or other description of persons to whom the communication was mailed or otherwise distributed. The copy must be retained by the practitioner for a period of at least 36 months from the date of the last transmission or use.

(d) *Improper associations.* A practitioner may not, in matters related to the Internal Revenue Service, assist, or accept assistance from, any person or entity who, to the knowledge of the practitioner, obtains clients or otherwise practices in a manner forbidden under this section.

(e) *Effective/applicability date.* This section is applicable beginning August 2, 2011.

(Approved by the Office of Management and Budget under Control No. 1545-1726)

§ 10.31 Negotiation of taxpayer checks.

(a) A practitioner may not endorse or otherwise negotiate any check (including directing or accepting payment by any means, electronic or otherwise, into an account owned or controlled by the practitioner or any firm or other entity with whom the practitioner is associated) issued to a client by the government in respect of a Federal tax liability.

(b) *Effective/applicability date.* This section is applicable beginning June 12, 2014.

§ 10.32 Practice of law.

Nothing in the regulations in this part may be construed as authorizing persons not members of the bar to practice law.

§ 10.33 Best practices for tax advisors.

(a) *Best practices.* Tax advisors should provide clients with the highest quality representation concerning Federal tax issues by adhering to best practices in providing advice and in preparing or assisting in the preparation of a submission to the Internal Revenue Service. In addition to compliance with the standards of practice provided elsewhere in this part, best practices include the following:

(1) Communicating clearly with the client regarding the terms of the engagement. For example, the advisor should determine the client's expected purpose for and use of the advice and should have a clear understanding with the client regarding the form and scope of the advice or assistance to be rendered.

(2) Establishing the facts, determining which facts are relevant, evaluating the reasonableness of any assumptions or representations, relating the applicable law (including potentially applicable judicial doctrines) to the relevant facts, and arriving at a conclusion supported by the law and the facts.

(3) Advising the client regarding the import of the conclusions reached, including, for example, whether a taxpayer may avoid accuracy-related penalties under the Internal Revenue Code if a taxpayer acts in reliance on the advice.

(4) Acting fairly and with integrity in practice before the Internal Revenue Service.

(b) *Procedures to ensure best practices for tax advisors.* Tax advisors with responsibility for overseeing a firm's practice of providing advice concerning Federal tax issues or of preparing or assisting in the preparation of submissions to the Internal Revenue Service should take reasonable steps to ensure that the firm's procedures for all members, associates, and employees are consistent with the best practices set forth in paragraph (a) of this section.

(c) *Applicability date.* This section is effective after June 20, 2005.

§ 10.34 Standards with respect to tax returns and documents, affidavits and other papers.

(a) *Tax returns.*

(1) A practitioner may not willfully, recklessly, or through gross incompetence —

(i) Sign a tax return or claim for refund that the practitioner knows or reasonably should know contains a position that —

(A) Lacks a reasonable basis;

(B) Is an unreasonable position as described in section 6694(a)(2) of the Internal Revenue Code (Code) (including the related regulations and other published guidance); or

(C) Is a willful attempt by the practitioner to understate the liability for tax or a reckless or intentional disregard of rules or regulations by the practitioner as described in section 6694(b)(2) of the Code (including the related regulations and other published guidance).

(ii) Advise a client to take a position on a tax return or claim for refund, or prepare a portion of a tax return or claim for refund containing a position, that —

(A) Lacks a reasonable basis;

(B) Is an unreasonable position as described in section 6694(a)(2) of the Code (including the related regulations and other published guidance); or

(C) Is a willful attempt by the practitioner to understate the liability for tax or a reckless or intentional disregard of rules or regulations by the practitioner as described in section 6694(b)(2) of the Code (including the related regulations and other published guidance).

(2) A pattern of conduct is a factor that will be taken into account in determining whether a practitioner acted willfully, recklessly, or through gross incompetence.

(b) *Documents, affidavits and other papers* —

(1) A practitioner may not advise a client to take a position on a document, affidavit or other paper submitted to the Internal Revenue Service unless the position is not frivolous.

(2) A practitioner may not advise a client to submit a document, affidavit or other paper to the Internal Revenue Service —

(i) The purpose of which is to delay or impede the administration of the Federal tax laws;

(ii) That is frivolous; or

(iii) That contains or omits information in a manner that demonstrates an intentional disregard of a rule or regulation unless the practitioner also advises the client to submit a document that evidences a good faith challenge to the rule or regulation.

(c) *Advising clients on potential penalties* —

(1) A practitioner must inform a client of any penalties that are reasonably likely to apply to the client with respect to —

(i) A position taken on a tax return if —

(A) The practitioner advised the client with respect to the position; or

(B) The practitioner prepared or signed the tax return; and

(ii) Any document, affidavit or other paper submitted to the Internal Revenue Service.

(2) The practitioner also must inform the client of any opportunity to avoid any such penalties by disclosure, if relevant, and of the requirements for adequate disclosure.

(3) This paragraph (c) applies even if the practitioner is not subject to a penalty under the Internal Revenue Code with respect to the position or with respect to the document, affidavit or other paper submitted.

(d) *Relying on information furnished by clients.* A practitioner advising a client to take a position on a tax return, document, affidavit or other paper submitted to the Internal Revenue Service, or preparing or signing a tax return as a preparer, generally may rely in good faith without verification upon information furnished by the client. The practitioner may not, however, ignore the implications of information furnished to, or actually known by, the practitioner, and must make reasonable inquiries if the information as furnished appears to be incorrect, inconsistent with an important fact or another factual assumption, or incomplete.

(e) *Effective/applicability date.* Paragraph (a) of this section is applicable for returns or claims for refund filed, or advice provided, beginning August 2, 2011. Paragraphs (b) through (d) of this section are applicable to tax returns, documents, affidavits, and other papers filed on or after September 26, 2007.

§ 10.35 Competence.

(a) A practitioner must possess the necessary competence to engage in practice before the Internal Revenue Service. Competent practice requires the appropriate level of knowledge, skill, thoroughness, and preparation necessary for the matter for which the practitioner is engaged. A practitioner may become competent for the matter for which the practitioner has been engaged through various methods, such as consulting with experts in the relevant area or studying the relevant law.

(b) *Effective/applicability date*. This section is applicable beginning June 12, 2014.

§ 10.36 Procedures to ensure compliance.

(a) Any individual subject to the provisions of this part who has (or individuals who have or share) principal authority and responsibility for overseeing a firm's practice governed by this part, including the provision of advice concerning Federal tax matters and preparation of tax returns, claims for refund, or other documents for submission to the Internal Revenue Service, must take reasonable steps to ensure that the firm has adequate procedures in effect for all members, associates, and employees for purposes of complying with subparts A, B, and C of this part, as applicable. In the absence of a person or persons identified by the firm as having the principal authority and responsibility described in this paragraph, the Internal Revenue Service may identify one or more individuals subject to the provisions of this part responsible for compliance with the requirements of this section.

(b) Any such individual who has (or such individuals who have or share) principal authority as described in paragraph (a) of this section will be subject to discipline for failing to comply with the requirements of this section if—

(1) The individual through willfulness, recklessness, or gross incompetence does not take reasonable steps to ensure that the firm has adequate procedures to comply with this part, as applicable, and one or more individuals who are members of, associated with, or employed by, the firm are, or have, engaged in a pattern or practice, in connection with their practice with the firm, of failing to comply with this part, as applicable;

(2) The individual through willfulness, recklessness, or gross incompetence does not take reasonable steps to ensure that firm procedures in effect are properly followed, and one or more individuals who are members of, associated with, or employed by, the firm are, or have, engaged in a

pattern or practice, in connection with their practice with the firm, of failing to comply with this part, as applicable; or

(3) The individual knows or should know that one or more individuals who are members of, associated with, or employed by, the firm are, or have, engaged in a pattern or practice, in connection with their practice with the firm, that does not comply with this part, as applicable, and the individual, through willfulness, recklessness, or gross incompetence fails to take prompt action to correct the noncompliance.

(c) *Effective/applicability date*. This section is applicable beginning June 12, 2014.

§ 10.37 Requirements for written advice.

(a) *Requirements*.

(1) A practitioner may give written advice (including by means of electronic communication) concerning one or more Federal tax matters subject to the requirements in paragraph (a)(2) of this section. Government submissions on matters of general policy are not considered written advice on a Federal tax matter for purposes of this section. Continuing education presentations provided to an audience solely for the purpose of enhancing practitioners' professional knowledge on Federal tax matters are not considered written advice on a Federal tax matter for purposes of this section. The preceding sentence does not apply to presentations marketing or promoting transactions.

(2) The practitioner must—

(i) Base the written advice on reasonable factual and legal assumptions (including assumptions as to future events);

(ii) Reasonably consider all relevant facts and circumstances that the practitioner knows or reasonably should know;

(iii) Use reasonable efforts to identify and ascertain the facts relevant to written advice on each Federal tax matter;

(iv) Not rely upon representations, statements, findings, or agreements (including projections, financial forecasts, or appraisals) of the taxpayer or any other person if reliance on them would be unreasonable;

(v) Relate applicable law and authorities to facts; and

(vi) Not, in evaluating a Federal tax matter, take into account the possibility that a tax return will not be audited or that a matter will not be raised on audit.

(3) Reliance on representations, statements, findings, or agreements is unreasonable if the practitioner knows or reasonably should know that one or more representations or assumptions on which any representation is based are incorrect, incomplete, or inconsistent.

(b) *Reliance on advice of others*. A practitioner may only rely on the advice of another person if the advice was reasonable and the reliance is in good faith considering all the facts and circumstances. Reliance is not reasonable when—

(1) The practitioner knows or reasonably should know that the opinion of the other person should not be relied on;

(2) The practitioner knows or reasonably should know that the other person is not competent or lacks the necessary qualifications to provide the advice; or

(3) The practitioner knows or reasonably should know that the other person has a conflict of interest in violation of the rules described in this part.

(c) *Standard of review.*

(1) In evaluating whether a practitioner giving written advice concerning one or more Federal tax matters complied with the requirements of this section, the Commissioner, or delegate, will apply a reasonable practitioner standard, considering all facts and circumstances, including, but not limited to, the scope of the engagement and the type and specificity of the advice sought by the client.

(2) In the case of an opinion the practitioner knows or has reason to know will be used or referred to by a person other than the practitioner (or a person who is a member of, associated with, or employed by the practitioner's firm) in promoting, marketing, or recommending to one or more taxpayers a partnership or other entity, investment plan or arrangement a significant purpose of which is the avoidance or evasion of any tax imposed by the Internal Revenue Code, the Commissioner, or delegate, will apply a reasonable practitioner standard, considering all

facts and circumstances, with emphasis given to the additional risk caused by the practitioner's lack of knowledge of the taxpayer's particular circumstances, when determining whether a practitioner has failed to comply with this section.

(d) *Federal tax matter.* A Federal tax matter, as used in this section, is any matter concerning the application or interpretation of---

(1) A revenue provision as defined in section 6110(i)(1)(B) of the Internal Revenue Code;

(2) Any provision of law impacting a person's obligations under the internal revenue laws and regulations, including but not limited to the person's liability to pay tax or obligation to file returns; or

(3) Any other law or regulation administered by the Internal Revenue Service.

(e) *Effective/applicability date.* This section is applicable to written advice rendered after June 12, 2014.

§ 10.38 Establishment of advisory committees.

(a) *Advisory committees.* To promote and maintain the public's confidence in tax advisors, the Internal Revenue Service is authorized to establish one or more advisory committees composed of at least six individuals authorized to practice before the Internal Revenue Service. Membership of an advisory committee must be balanced among those who practice as attorneys, accountants, enrolled agents, enrolled actuaries, enrolled retirement plan agents, and registered tax return preparers. Under procedures prescribed by the Internal Revenue Service, an advisory committee may review and make general recommendations regarding the practices, procedures, and policies of the offices described in §10.1.

(b) *Effective date.* This section is applicable beginning August 2, 2011.

Subpart C — Sanctions for Violation of the Regulations

§ 10.50 Sanctions.

(a) *Authority to censure, suspend, or disbar.* The Secretary of the Treasury, or delegate, after notice and an opportunity for a proceeding, may censure, suspend, or disbar any practitioner from practice before the Internal Revenue Service if the practitioner is shown to be incompetent or disreputable (within the meaning of §10.51), fails to comply with any regulation in this part (under the prohibited conduct standards of §10.52), or with intent to defraud, willfully and knowingly misleads or threatens a client or prospective client. Censure is a public reprimand.

(b) *Authority to disqualify.* The Secretary of the Treasury, or delegate, after due notice and opportunity for hearing, may disqualify any appraiser for a violation of these rules as applicable to appraisers.

(1) If any appraiser is disqualified pursuant to this subpart C, the appraiser is barred from presenting evidence or testimony in any administrative proceeding before the Department of Treasury or the Internal Revenue Service, unless and until authorized to do so by the Internal Revenue Service pursuant to §10.81, regardless of whether the evidence or testimony would pertain to an appraisal made prior to or after the effective date of disqualification.

(2) Any appraisal made by a disqualified appraiser after the effective date of disqualification will not have any probative effect in any administrative proceeding before the Department of the Treasury or the Internal Revenue Service. An appraisal otherwise barred from admission into evidence pursuant to this section may be admitted into evidence solely for the purpose of determining the taxpayer's reliance in good faith on such appraisal.

(c) *Authority to impose monetary penalty —*

(1) *In general.*

(i) The Secretary of the Treasury, or delegate, after notice and an opportunity for a proceeding, may impose a monetary penalty on any practitioner who engages in conduct subject to sanction under paragraph (a) of this section.

(ii) If the practitioner described in paragraph (c)(1)(i) of this section was acting on behalf of an employer or any firm or other entity in connection with the conduct giving rise to the penalty, the Secretary of the Treasury, or delegate, may impose a monetary penalty on the employer, firm, or entity if it knew, or reasonably should have known of such conduct.

(2) *Amount of penalty.* The amount of the penalty shall not exceed the gross income derived (or to be derived) from the conduct giving rise to the penalty.

(3) *Coordination with other sanctions.* Subject to paragraph (c)(2) of this section —

(i) Any monetary penalty imposed on a practitioner under this paragraph (c) may be in addition to or in lieu of any suspension, disbarment or censure and may be in addition to a penalty imposed on an employer, firm or other entity under paragraph (c)(1)(ii) of this section.

(ii) Any monetary penalty imposed on an employer, firm or other entity may be in addition to or in lieu of penalties imposed under paragraph (c)(1)(i) of this section.

(d) *Authority to accept a practitioner's consent to sanction.* The Internal Revenue Service may accept a practitioner's offer of consent to be sanctioned under §10.50 in lieu of instituting or continuing a proceeding under §10.60(a).

(e) *Sanctions to be imposed.* The sanctions imposed by this section shall take into account all relevant facts and circumstances.

(f) *Effective/applicability date.* This section is applicable to conduct occurring on or after August 2, 2011, except that paragraphs (a), (b)(2), and (e) apply to conduct occurring on or after September 26, 2007, and paragraph (c) applies to prohibited conduct that occurs after October 22, 2004.

§ 10.51 Incompetence and disreputable conduct.

(a) *Incompetence and disreputable conduct.* Incompetence and disreputable conduct for which a practitioner may be sanctioned under §10.50 includes, but is not limited to —

(1) Conviction of any criminal offense under the Federal tax laws.

(2) Conviction of any criminal offense involving dishonesty or breach of trust.

(3) Conviction of any felony under Federal or State law for which the conduct involved renders the practitioner unfit to practice before the Internal Revenue Service.

(4) Giving false or misleading information, or participating in any way in the giving of false or misleading information to the Department of the Treasury or any officer or employee thereof, or to any tribunal authorized to pass upon Federal tax matters, in connection with any matter pending or likely to be pending before them, knowing the information to be false or misleading. Facts or other matters contained in testimony, Federal tax returns, financial statements, applications for enrollment, affidavits, declarations, and any other document or statement, written or oral, are included in the term "information."

(5) Solicitation of employment as prohibited under §10.30, the use of false or misleading representations with intent to deceive a client or prospective client in order to procure employment, or intimating that the practitioner is able improperly to obtain special consideration or action from the Internal Revenue Service or any officer or employee thereof.

(6) Willfully failing to make a Federal tax return in violation of the Federal tax laws, or willfully evading, attempting to evade, or participating in any way in evading or attempting to evade any assessment or payment of any Federal tax.

(7) Willfully assisting, counseling, encouraging a client or prospective client in violating, or suggesting to a client or prospective client to violate, any Federal tax law, or knowingly counseling or suggesting to a client or prospective client an illegal plan to evade Federal taxes or payment thereof.

(8) Misappropriation of, or failure properly or promptly to remit, funds received from a client for the purpose of payment of taxes or other obligations due the United States.

(9) Directly or indirectly attempting to influence, or offering or agreeing to attempt to influence, the official action of any officer or employee of the Internal Revenue Service by the use of threats, false accusations, duress or coercion, by the offer of any special inducement or promise of an advantage or by the bestowing of any gift, favor or thing of value.

(10) Disbarment or suspension from practice as an attorney, certified public accountant, public accountant, or actuary by any duly constituted authority of any State, territory, or possession of the United States, including a Commonwealth, or the District of Columbia, any Federal court of record or any Federal agency, body or board.

(11) Knowingly aiding and abetting another person to practice before the Internal Revenue Service during a period of suspension, disbarment or ineligibility of such other person.

(12) Contemptuous conduct in connection with practice before the Internal Revenue Service, including the use of abusive language, making false accusations or statements, knowing them to be false, or circulating or publishing malicious or libelous matter.

(13) Giving a false opinion, knowingly, recklessly, or through gross incompetence, including an opinion which is intentionally or recklessly misleading, or engaging in a pattern of providing incompetent opinions on questions arising under the Federal tax laws. False opinions described in this paragraph (a)(13) include those which reflect or result from a knowing misstatement of fact or law, from an assertion of a position known to be unwarranted under existing law, from counseling or assisting in conduct known to be illegal or fraudulent, from concealing matters required by law to be revealed, or from consciously disregarding information indicating that material facts expressed in the opinion or offering material are false or misleading. For purposes of this paragraph (a)(13), reckless conduct is a highly unreasonable omission or misrepresentation involving an extreme departure from the standards of ordinary care that a practitioner should observe under the circumstances. A pattern of conduct is a factor that will be taken into account in determining whether a practitioner acted knowingly, recklessly, or through gross incompetence. Gross incompetence

includes conduct that reflects gross indifference, preparation which is grossly inadequate under the circumstances, and a consistent failure to perform obligations to the client.

(14) Willfully failing to sign a tax return prepared by the practitioner when the practitioner's signature is required by Federal tax laws unless the failure is due to reasonable cause and not due to willful neglect.

(15) Willfully disclosing or otherwise using a tax return or tax return information in a manner not authorized by the Internal Revenue Code, contrary to the order of a court of competent jurisdiction, or contrary to the order of an administrative law judge in a proceeding instituted under §10.60.

(16) Willfully failing to file on magnetic or other electronic media a tax return prepared by the practitioner when the practitioner is required to do so by the Federal tax laws unless the failure is due to reasonable cause and not due to willful neglect.

(17) Willfully preparing all or substantially all of, or signing, a tax return or claim for refund when the practitioner does not possess a current or otherwise valid preparer tax identification number or other prescribed identifying number.

(18) Willfully representing a taxpayer before an officer or employee of the Internal Revenue Service unless the practitioner is authorized to do so pursuant to this part.

(b) *Effective/applicability date.* This section is applicable beginning August 2, 2011.

§ 10.52 Violations subject to sanction.

(a) A practitioner may be sanctioned under §10.50 if the practitioner —

(1) Willfully violates any of the regulations (other than §10.33) contained in this part; or

(2) Recklessly or through gross incompetence (within the meaning of §10.51(a)(13)) violates §§ 10.34, 10.35, 10.36 or 10.37.

(b) *Effective/applicability date.* This section is applicable to conduct occurring on or after September 26, 2007.

§ 10.53 Receipt of information concerning practitioner.

(a) *Officer or employee of the Internal Revenue Service.* If an officer or employee of the Internal Revenue Service has reason to believe a practitioner has violated any provision of this part, the officer or employee will promptly make a written report of the suspected violation. The report will explain the facts and reasons upon which the officer's or employee's belief rests and must be submitted to the office(s) of the Internal Revenue Service responsible for administering or enforcing this part.

(b) *Other persons.* Any person other than an officer or employee of the Internal Revenue Service having information of a violation of any provision of this part may make an oral or written report of the alleged violation to the office(s) of the Internal Revenue Service responsible for administering or enforcing this part or any officer or employee of the Internal Revenue Service. If the report is made to an officer or employee of the Internal Revenue Service, the officer or employee will make a written report of the suspected violation and submit the report to the office(s) of the Internal Revenue Service responsible for administering or enforcing this part.

(c) *Destruction of report.* No report made under paragraph (a) or (b) of this section shall be maintained unless retention of the report is permissible under the applicable records control schedule as approved by the National Archives and Records Administration and designated in the Internal Revenue Manual. Reports must be destroyed as soon as permissible under the applicable records control schedule.

(d) *Effect on proceedings under subpart D.* The destruction of any report will not bar any proceeding under subpart D of this part, but will preclude the use of a copy of the report in a proceeding under subpart D of this part.

(e) *Effective/applicability date.* This section is applicable beginning August 2, 2011.

Subpart D — Rules Applicable to Disciplinary Proceedings

§ 10.60 Institution of proceeding.

(a) Whenever it is determined that a practitioner (or employer, firm or other entity, if applicable) violated any provision of the laws governing practice before the Internal Revenue Service or the regulations in this part, the practitioner may be reprimanded or, in accordance with §10.62, subject to a proceeding for sanctions described in §10.50.

(b) Whenever a penalty has been assessed against an appraiser under the Internal Revenue Code and an appropriate officer or employee in an office established to enforce this part determines that the appraiser acted willfully, recklessly, or through gross incompetence with respect to the proscribed conduct, the appraiser may be reprimanded or, in accordance with §10.62, subject to a proceeding for disqualification. A proceeding for disqualification of an appraiser is instituted by the filing of a complaint, the contents of which are more fully described in §10.62.

(c) Except as provided in §10.82, a proceeding will not be instituted under this section unless the proposed respondent previously has been advised in writing of the law, facts and conduct warranting such action and has been accorded an opportunity to dispute facts, assert additional facts, and make arguments (including an explanation or description of mitigating circumstances).

(d) *Effective/applicability date.* This section is applicable beginning August 2, 2011.

§ 10.61 Conferences.

(a) *In general.* The Commissioner, or delegate, may confer with a practitioner, employer, firm or other entity, or an appraiser concerning allegations of misconduct irrespective of whether a proceeding has been instituted. If the conference results in a stipulation in connection with an ongoing proceeding in which the practitioner, employer, firm or other entity, or appraiser is the respondent, the stipulation may be entered in the record by either party to the proceeding.

(b) *Voluntary sanction*

(1) *In general.* In lieu of a proceeding being instituted or continued under §10.60(a), a practitioner or appraiser (or employer, firm or other entity, if applicable) may offer a consent to be sanctioned under §10.50.

(2) *Discretion; acceptance or declination.* The Commissioner, or delegate, may accept or decline the offer described in paragraph (b)(1) of this section. When the decision is to decline the offer, the written notice of declination may state that the offer described in paragraph (b)(1) of this section would be accepted if it contained different terms. The Commissioner, or delegate, has the discretion to accept or reject a revised offer submitted in response to the declination or may counteroffer and act upon any accepted counteroffer.

(c) *Effective/applicability date.* This section is applicable beginning August 2, 2011.

§ 10.62 Contents of complaint.

(a) *Charges.* A complaint must name the respondent, provide a clear and concise description of the facts and law that constitute the basis for the proceeding, and be signed by an authorized representative of the Internal Revenue Service under §10.69(a)(1). A complaint is sufficient if it fairly informs the respondent of the charges brought so that the respondent is able to prepare a defense.

(b) *Specification of sanction.* The complaint must specify the sanction sought against the practitioner or appraiser. If the sanction sought is a suspension, the duration of the suspension sought must be specified.

(c) *Demand for answer.* The respondent must be notified in the complaint or in a separate paper attached to the complaint of the time for answering the complaint, which may not be less than 30 days from the date of service of the complaint, the name and address of the Administrative Law Judge with whom the answer must be filed, the name and address of the person representing the Internal Revenue Service to whom a copy of the answer must be served, and that a decision by default may be rendered against the respondent in the event an answer is not filed as required.

(d) *Effective/applicability date.* This section is applicable beginning August 2, 2011.

§ 10.63 Service of complaint; service of other papers; service of evidence in support of complaint; filing of papers.

(a) *Service of complaint.*

(1) *In general.* The complaint or a copy of the complaint must be served on the respondent by any manner described in paragraphs (a) (2) or (3) of this section.

(2) *Service by certified or first class mail.*

(i) Service of the complaint may be made on the respondent by mailing the complaint by certified mail to the last known address (as determined under section 6212 of the Internal Revenue Code and the regulations thereunder) of the respondent. Where service is by certified mail, the returned post office receipt duly signed by the respondent will be proof of service.

(ii) If the certified mail is not claimed or accepted by the respondent, or is returned undelivered, service may be made on the respondent, by mailing the complaint to the respondent by first class mail. Service by this method will be considered complete upon mailing, provided the complaint is addressed to the respondent at the respondent's last known address as determined under section 6212 of the Internal Revenue Code and the regulations thereunder.

(3) *Service by other than certified or first class mail.*

(i) Service of the complaint may be made on the respondent by delivery by a private delivery service designated pursuant to section 7502(f) of the Internal Revenue Code to the last known address (as determined under section 6212 of the Internal Revenue Code and the regulations there under) of the respondent. Service by this method will be considered complete, provided the complaint is addressed to the respondent at the respondent's last known address

as determined under section 6212 of the Internal Revenue Code and the regulations thereunder.

(ii) Service of the complaint may be made in person on, or by leaving the complaint at the office or place of business of, the respondent. Service by this method will be considered complete and proof of service will be a written statement, sworn or affirmed by the person who served the complaint, identifying the manner of service, including the recipient, relationship of recipient to respondent, place, date and time of service.

(iii) Service may be made by any other means agreed to by the respondent. Proof of service will be a written statement, sworn or affirmed by the person who served the complaint, identifying the manner of service, including the recipient, relationship of recipient to respondent, place, date and time of service.

(4) For purposes of this section, *respondent* means the practitioner, employer, firm or other entity, or appraiser named in the complaint or any other person having the authority to accept mail on behalf of the practitioner, employer, firm or other entity or appraiser.

(b) *Service of papers other than complaint.* Any paper other than the complaint may be served on the respondent, or his or her authorized representative under §10.69(a)(2) by:

(1) mailing the paper by first class mail to the last known address (as determined under section 6212 of the Internal Revenue Code and the regulations thereunder) of the respondent or the respondent's authorized representative,

(2) delivery by a private delivery service designated pursuant to section 7502(f) of the Internal Revenue Code to the last known address (as determined under section 6212 of the Internal Revenue Code and the regulations thereunder) of the respondent or the respondent's authorized representative, or

(3) as provided in paragraphs (a)(3)(ii) and (a)(3)(iii) of this section.

(c) *Service of papers on the Internal Revenue Service.* Whenever a paper is required or permitted to be served on the Internal Revenue Service in connection with a proceeding under this part, the paper will be served on the Internal Revenue Service's authorized representative under §10.69(a)(1) at the address designated in the complaint, or at an address provided in a notice of appearance. If no address is designated in the complaint or provided in a notice of appearance, service will be made on the office(s) established to enforce this part under the authority of §10.1, Internal Revenue Service, 1111 Constitution Avenue, NW, Washington, DC 20224.

(d) *Service of evidence in support of complaint.* Within 10 days of serving the complaint, copies of the evidence in support of the complaint must be served on the respondent in any manner described in paragraphs (a)(2) and (3) of this section.

(e) *Filing of papers.* Whenever the filing of a paper is required or permitted in connection with a proceeding under this part, the original paper, plus one additional copy, must be filed with the Administrative Law Judge at the address specified in the complaint or at an address otherwise specified by the Administrative Law Judge. All papers filed in connection with a proceeding under this part must be served on the other party, unless the Administrative Law Judge directs otherwise. A certificate evidencing such must be attached to the original paper filed with the Administrative Law Judge.

(f) *Effective/applicability date.* This section is applicable beginning August 2, 2011.

§ 10.64 Answer; default.

(a) *Filing.* The respondent's answer must be filed with the Administrative Law Judge, and served on the Internal Revenue Service, within the time specified in the complaint unless, on request or application of the respondent, the time is extended by the Administrative Law Judge.

(b) *Contents.* The answer must be written and contain a statement of facts that constitute the respondent's grounds of defense. General denials are not permitted. The respondent must specifically admit or deny each allegation set forth in the complaint, except that the respondent may state that the respondent is without sufficient information to admit or deny a specific allegation. The respondent, nevertheless, may not deny a material allegation in the complaint that the respondent knows to be true, or state that the respondent is without sufficient information to form a belief, when the respondent possesses the required information. The respondent also must state affirmatively any special matters of defense on which he or she relies.

(c) *Failure to deny or answer allegations in the complaint.* Every allegation in the complaint that is not denied in the answer is deemed admitted and will be considered proved; no further evidence in respect of such allegation need be adduced at a hearing.

(d) *Default.* Failure to file an answer within the time prescribed (or within the time for answer as extended by the Administrative Law Judge), constitutes an admission of the allegations of the complaint and a waiver of hearing, and the Administrative Law Judge may make the decision by default without a hearing or further procedure. A decision by default constitutes a decision under §10.76.

(e) *Signature.* The answer must be signed by the respondent or the respondent's authorized representative under §10.69(a)(2) and must include a statement directly above the signature acknowledging that the statements made in the answer are true and correct and that knowing and willful false statements may be punishable under 18 U.S.C. §1001.

(f) Effective/applicability date. This section is applicable beginning August 2, 2011.

§ 10.65 Supplemental charges.

(a) *In general.* Supplemental charges may be filed against the respondent by amending the complaint with the permission of the Administrative Law Judge if, for example —

(1) It appears that the respondent, in the answer, falsely and in bad faith, denies a material allegation of fact in the complaint or states that the respondent has insufficient knowledge to form a belief, when the respondent possesses such information; or

(2) It appears that the respondent has knowingly

introduced false testimony during the proceedings against the respondent.

(b) *Hearing.* The supplemental charges may be heard with other charges in the case, provided the respondent is given due notice of the charges and is afforded a reasonable opportunity to prepare a defense to the supplemental charges.

(c) *Effective/applicability date.* This section is applicable beginning August 2, 2011.

§ 10.66 Reply to answer.

(a) The Internal Revenue Service may file a reply to the respondent's answer, but unless otherwise ordered by the Administrative Law Judge, no reply to the respondent's answer is required. If a reply is not filed, new matter in the answer is deemed denied.

(b) *Effective/applicability date.* This section is applicable beginning August 2, 2011.

§ 10.67 Proof; variance; amendment of pleadings.

In the case of a variance between the allegations in pleadings and the evidence adduced in support of the pleadings, the Administrative Law Judge, at any time before decision, may order or authorize amendment of the pleadings to conform to the evidence. The party who would otherwise be prejudiced by the amendment must be given a reasonable opportunity to address the allegations of the pleadings as amended and the Administrative Law Judge must make findings on any issue presented by the pleadings as amended.

§ 10.68 Motions and requests.

(a) *Motions* —

(1) *In general.* At any time after the filing of the complaint, any party may file a motion with the Administrative Law Judge. Unless otherwise ordered by the Administrative Law Judge, motions must be in writing and must be served on the opposing party as provided in §10.63(b). A motion must concisely specify its grounds and the relief sought, and, if appropriate, must contain a memorandum of facts and law in support.

(2) *Summary adjudication.* Either party may move for a summary adjudication upon all or any part of the legal issues in controversy. If the non-moving party opposes summary adjudication in the moving party's favor, the non-moving party must file a written response within 30 days unless ordered otherwise by the Administrative Law Judge.

(3) *Good Faith.* A party filing a motion for extension of time, a motion for postponement of a hearing, or any other non-dispositive or procedural motion must first contact the other party to determine whether there is any objection to the motion, and must state in the motion whether the other party has an objection.

(b) *Response.* Unless otherwise ordered by the Administrative Law Judge, the nonmoving party is not required to file a response to a motion. If the Administrative Law Judge does not order the nonmoving party to file a response, and the nonmoving party files no response, the nonmoving party is deemed to oppose the motion. If a nonmoving party does not respond within 30 days of the filing of a motion for decision by default for failure to file a timely answer or for failure to prosecute, the nonmoving party is deemed not to oppose the motion.

(c) *Oral motions; oral argument* —

(1) The Administrative Law Judge may, for good cause and with notice to the parties, permit oral motions and oral opposition to motions.

(2) The Administrative Law Judge may, within his or her discretion, permit oral argument on any motion.

(d) *Orders.* The Administrative Law Judge should issue written orders disposing of any motion or request and any response thereto.

(e) *Effective/applicability date.* This section is applicable on September 26, 2007.

§ 10.69 Representation; ex parte communication.

(a) *Representation.*

(1) The Internal Revenue Service may be represented in proceedings under this part by an attorney or other employee of the Internal Revenue Service. An attorney or an employee of the Internal

Revenue Service representing the Internal Revenue Service in a proceeding under this part may sign the complaint or any document required to be filed in the proceeding on behalf of the Internal Revenue Service.

(2) A respondent may appear in person, be represented by a practitioner, or be represented by an attorney who has not filed a declaration with the Internal Revenue Service pursuant to §10.3. A practitioner or an attorney representing a respondent or proposed respondent may sign the answer or any document required to be filed in the proceeding on behalf of the respondent.

(b) *Ex parte communication.* The Internal Revenue Service, the respondent, and any representatives of either party, may not attempt to initiate or participate in ex parte discussions concerning a proceeding or potential proceeding with the Administrative Law Judge (or any person who is likely to advise the Administrative Law Judge on a ruling or decision) in the proceeding before or during the pendency of the proceeding. Any memorandum, letter or other communication concerning the merits of the proceeding, addressed to the Administrative Law Judge, by or on behalf of any party shall be regarded as an argument in the proceeding and shall be served on the othe party.

(c) *Effective/applicability date.* This section is applicable beginning August 2, 2011.

§ 10.70 Administrative Law Judge.

(a) *Appointment.* Proceedings on complaints for the sanction (as described in §10.50) of a practitioner, employer, firm or other entity, or appraiser will be conducted by an Administrative Law Judge appointed as provided by *5 U.S.C. 3105.*

(b) *Powers of the Administrative Law Judge.* The Administrative Law Judge, among other powers, has the authority, in connection with any proceeding under §10.60 assigned or referred to him or her, to do the following:

(1) Administer oaths and affirmations;

(2) Make rulings on motions and requests, which rulings may not be appealed prior to the close of a hearing except in extraordinary circumstances and at the discretion of the Administrative Law Judge;

(3) Determine the time and place of hearing and regulate its course and conduct;

(4) Adopt rules of procedure and modify the same from time to time as needed for the orderly disposition of proceedings;

(5) Rule on offers of proof, receive relevant evidence, and examine witnesses;

(6) Take or authorize the taking of depositions or answers to requests for admission;

(7) Receive and consider oral or written argument on facts or law;

(8) Hold or provide for the holding of conferences for the settlement or simplification of the issues with the consent of the parties;

(9) Perform such acts and take such measures as are necessary or appropriate to the efficient conduct of any proceeding; and

(10) Make decisions.

(c) *Effective/applicability date.* This section is applicable on September 26, 2007.

§ 10.71 Discovery.

(a) *In general.* Discovery may be permitted, at the discretion of the Administrative Law Judge, only upon written motion demonstrating the relevance, materiality and reasonableness of the requested discovery and subject to the requirements of §10.72(d)(2) and (3). Within 10 days of receipt of the answer, the Administrative Law Judge will notify the parties of the right to request discovery and the timeframe for filing a request. A request for discovery, and objections, must be filed in accordance with §10.68. In response to a request for discovery, the Administrative Law Judge may order —

(1) Depositions upon oral examination; or

(2) Answers to requests for admission.

(b) *Depositions upon oral examination —*

(1) A deposition must be taken before an officer duly authorized to administer an oath for general purposes or before an officer or employee of the Internal Revenue Service who is authorized to administer an oath in Federal tax law matters.

(2) In ordering a deposition, the Administrative Law Judge will require reasonable notice to the opposing party as to the time and place of the deposition. The opposing party, if attending, will be provided the opportunity for full examination and cross-examination of any witness.

(3) Expenses in the reporting of depositions shall be borne by the party at whose instance the deposition is taken. Travel expenses of the deponent shall be borne by the party requesting the deposition, unless otherwise authorized by Federal law or regulation.

(c) *Requests for admission.* Any party may serve on any other party a written request for admission of the truth of any matters which are not privileged and are relevant to the subject matter of this proceeding. Requests for admission shall not exceed a total of 30 (including any subparts within a specific request) without the approval from the Administrative Law Judge.

(d) *Limitations.* Discovery shall not be authorized if —

(1) The request fails to meet any requirement set forth in paragraph (a) of this section;

(2) It will unduly delay the proceeding;

(3) It will place an undue burden on the party required to produce the discovery sought;

(4) It is frivolous or abusive;

(5) It is cumulative or duplicative;

(6) The material sought is privileged or otherwise protected from disclosure by law;

(7) The material sought relates to mental impressions, conclusions, of legal theories of any party, attorney, or other representative, or a party prepared in the anticipation of a proceeding; or

(8) The material sought is available generally to the public, equally to the parties, or to the party seeking the discovery through another source.

(e) *Failure to comply.* Where a party fails to comply with an order of the Administrative Law Judge under this section, the Administrative Law Judge may, among other things, infer that the information would be adverse to the party failing to provide it, exclude the information from evidence or issue a decision by default.

(f) *Other discovery.* No discovery other than that specifically provided for in this section is permitted.

(g) *Effective/applicability date.* This section is applicable to proceedings initiated on or after September 26, 2007.

§ 10.72 Hearings.

(a) *In general* —

(1) *Presiding officer.* An Administrative Law Judge will preside at the hearing on a complaint filed under §10.60 for the sanction of a practitioner, employer, firm or other entity, or appraiser.

(2) *Time for hearing.* Absent a determination by the Administrative Law Judge that, in the interest of justice, a hearing must be held at a later time, the Administrative Law Judge should, on notice sufficient to allow proper preparation, schedule the hearing to occur no later than 180 days after the time for filing the answer.

(3) *Procedural requirements.*

(i) Hearings will be stenographically recorded and transcribed and the testimony of witnesses will be taken under oath or affirmation.

(ii) Hearings will be conducted pursuant to *5 U.S.C. 556.*

(iii) A hearing in a proceeding requested under §10.82(g) will be conducted de novo.

(iv) An evidentiary hearing must be held in all proceedings prior to the issuance of a decision by the Administrative Law Judge unless —

(A) The Internal Revenue Service withdraws the complaint;

(B) A decision is issued by default pursuant to §10.64(d);

(C) A decision is issued under §10.82 (e);

(D) The respondent requests a decision on the written record without a hearing; or

(E) The Administrative Law Judge issues a decision under §10.68(d) or rules on another motion that disposes of the case prior to the hearing.

(b) *Cross-examination.* A party is entitled to present his or her case or defense by oral or documentary evidence, to submit rebuttal evidence, and to conduct cross-examination, in the presence of the Administrative Law Judge, as may be required for a full and true disclosure of the facts. This paragraph (b) does not limit a party from presenting evidence contained within a deposition when the Administrative Law Judge determines that the deposition has been obtained in compliance with the rules of this subpart D.

(c) *Prehearing memorandum.* Unless otherwise ordered by the Administrative Law Judge, each party shall file, and serve on the opposing party or the opposing party's representative, prior to any hearing, a prehearing memorandum containing —

(1) A list (together with a copy) of all proposed exhibits to be used in the party's case in chief;

(2) A list of proposed witnesses, including a synopsis of their expected testimony, or a statement that no witnesses will be called;

(3) Identification of any proposed expert witnesses, including a synopsis of their expected testimony and a copy of any report prepared by the expert or at his or her direction; and

(4) A list of undisputed facts.

(d) *Publicity* —

(1) *In general.* All reports and decisions of the Secretary of the Treasury, or delegate, including any reports and decisions of the Administrative Law Judge, under this subpart D are, subject to the protective measures in paragraph (d)(4) of this section, public and open to inspection within 30 days after the agency's decision becomes final.

(2) *Request for additional publicity.* The Administrative Law Judge may grant a request by a practitioner or appraiser that all the pleadings and evidence of the disciplinary proceeding be made available for inspection where the parties stipulate in advance to adopt the protective measures in paragraph (d)(4) of this section.

(3) *Returns and return information* —

(i) *Disclosure to practitioner or appraiser.* Pursuant to *section 6103(l)(4) of the Internal Revenue Code,* the Secretary of the Treasury, or delegate, may disclose returns and return information to any practitioner or appraiser, or to the authorized representative of the practitioner or appraiser, whose rights are or may be affected by an administrative action or proceeding under this subpart D, but solely for use in the action or

proceeding and only to the extent that the Secretary of the Treasury, or delegate, determines that the returns or return information are or may be relevant and material to the action or proceeding.

(ii) *Disclosure to officers and employees of the Department of the Treasury.* Pursuant to *section 6103(l)(4)(B) of the Internal Revenue Code* the Secretary of the Treasury, or delegate, may disclose returns and return information to officers and employees of the Department of the Treasury for use in any action or proceeding under this subpart D, to the extent necessary to advance or protect the interests of the United States.

(iii) *Use of returns and return information.* Recipients of returns and return information under this paragraph (d)(3) may use the returns or return information solely in the action or proceeding, or in preparation for the action or proceeding, with respect to which the disclosure was made.

(iv) *Procedures for disclosure of returns and return information.* When providing returns or return information to the practitioner or appraiser, or authorized representative, the Secretary of the Treasury, or delegate, will —

(A) Redact identifying information of any third party taxpayers and replace it with a code;

(B) Provide a key to the coded information; and

(C) Notify the practitioner or appraiser, or authorized representative, of the restrictions on the use and disclosure of the returns and return information, the applicable damages remedy under *section 7431 of the Internal Revenue Code,* and that unauthorized disclosure of information provided by the Internal Revenue Service under this paragraph (d)(3) is also a violation of this part.

(4) *Protective measures* —

(i) *Mandatory protection order.* If redaction of names, addresses, and other identifying information of third party taxpayers may still permit indirect identification of any third party taxpayer, the Administrative Law Judge will issue a protective order to ensure that the identifying information is available to the parties and the Administrative Law Judge for purposes of the proceeding, but is not disclosed to, or open to inspection by, the public.

(ii) *Authorized orders.*

(A) Upon motion by a party or any other affected person, and for good cause shown, the Administrative Law Judge may make any order which justice requires to protect any person in the event disclosure of information is prohibited by law, privileged, confidential, or sensitive in some other way, including, but not limited to, one or more of the following —

(1) That disclosure of information be made only on specified terms and conditions, including a designation of the time or place;

(2) That a trade secret or other information not be disclosed, or be disclosed only in a designated way.

(iii) *Denials.* If a motion for a protective order is denied in whole or in part, the Administrative Law Judge may, on such terms or conditions as the Administrative Law Judge deems just, order any party or person to comply with, or respond in accordance with, the procedure involved.

(iv) *Public inspection of documents.* The Secretary of the Treasury, or delegate, shall ensure that all names, addresses or other identifying details of third party taxpayers are redacted and replaced with the code assigned to the corresponding taxpayer in all documents prior to public inspection of such documents.

(e) *Location.* The location of the hearing will be determined by the agreement of the parties with the approval of the Administrative Law Judge, but, in the absence of such agreement and approval, the hearing will be held in Washington, D.C.

(f) *Failure to appear.* If either party to the proceeding fails to appear at the hearing, after notice of the proceeding has been sent to him or her, the party will be deemed to have waived the right to a hearing and the Administrative Law Judge may make his or her decision against the absent party by default.

(g) *Effective/applicability date.* This section is applicable beginning August 2, 2011.

§ 10.73 Evidence.

(a) *In general.* The rules of evidence prevailing in courts of law and equity are not controlling in hearings or proceedings conducted under this part. The Administrative Law Judge may, however, exclude evidence that is irrelevant, immaterial, or unduly repetitious.

(b) *Depositions.* The deposition of any witness taken pursuant to §10.71 may be admitted into evidence in any proceeding instituted under §10.60.

(c) *Requests for admission.* Any matter admitted in response to a request for admission under §10.71 is conclusively established unless the Administrative Law Judge on motion permits withdrawal or modification of the admission. Any admission made by a party is for the purposes of the pending action only and is not an admission by a party for any other purpose, nor may it be used against a party in any other proceeding.

(d) *Proof of documents.* Official documents, records, and papers of the Internal Revenue Service and the Office of Professional Responsibility are admissible in evidence without the production of an officer or employee to authenticate them. Any documents, records, and papers may be evidenced by a copy attested to or identified by an officer or employee of the Internal Revenue Service or the Treasury Department, as the case may be.

(e) *Withdrawal of exhibits.* If any document, record, or other paper is introduced in evidence as an exhibit, the Administrative Law Judge may authorize the withdrawal of the exhibit subject to any conditions that he or she deems proper.

(f) *Objections.* Objections to evidence are to be made in short form, stating the grounds for the objection. Except as ordered by the Administrative Law Judge, argument on objections will not be recorded or transcribed. Rulings on objections are to be a part of the record, but no exception to a ruling is necessary to preserve the rights of the parties.

(g) *Effective/applicability date.* This section is applicable on September 26, 2007.

§ 10.74 Transcript.

In cases where the hearing is stenographically reported by a Government contract reporter, copies of the transcript may be obtained from the reporter at rates not to exceed the maximum rates fixed by contract between the Government and the reporter. Where the hearing is stenographically reported by a regular employee of the Internal Revenue Service, a copy will be supplied to the respondent either without charge or upon the payment of a reasonable fee. Copies of exhibits introduced at the hearing or at the taking of depositions will be supplied to the parties upon the payment of a reasonable fee (Sec. 501, Public Law 82-137) (65 Stat. 290) (31 U.S.C. § 483a).

§ 10.75 Proposed findings and conclusions.

Except in cases where the respondent has failed to answer the complaint or where a party has failed to appear at the hearing, the parties must be afforded a reasonable opportunity to submit proposed findings and conclusions and their supporting reasons to the Administrative Law Judge.

§ 10.76 Decision of Administrative Law Judge.

(a) *In general* —

(1) *Hearings*. Within 180 days after the conclusion of a hearing and the receipt of any proposed findings and conclusions timely submitted by the parties, the Administrative Law Judge should enter a decision in the case. The decision must include a statement of findings and conclusions, as well as the reasons or basis for making such findings and conclusions, and an order of censure, suspension, disbarment, monetary penalty, disqualification, or dismissal of the complaint.

(2) *Summary adjudication*. In the event that a motion for summary adjudication is filed, the Administrative Law Judge should rule on the motion for summary adjudication within 60 days after the party in opposition files a written response, or if no written response is filed, within 90 days after the motion for summary adjudication is filed. A decision shall thereafter be rendered if the pleadings, depositions, admissions, and any other admissible evidence show that there is no genuine issue of material fact and that a decision may be rendered as a matter of law. The decision must include a statement of conclusions, as well as the reasons or basis for making such conclusions, and an order of censure, suspension, disbarment, monetary penalty, disqualification, or dismissal of the complaint.

(3) *Returns and return information*. In the decision, the Administrative Law Judge should use the code assigned to third party taxpayers (described in §10.72(d)).

(b) *Standard of proof*. If the sanction is censure or a suspension of less than six months' duration, the Administrative Law Judge, in rendering findings and conclusions, will consider an allegation of fact to be proven if it is established by the party who is alleging the fact by a preponderance of the evidence in the record. If the sanction is a monetary penalty, disbarment or a suspension of six months or longer duration, an allegation of fact that is necessary for a finding against the practitioner must be proven by clear and convincing evidence in the record. An allegation of fact that is necessary for a finding of disqualification against an appraiser must be proved by clear and convincing evidence in the record.

(c) *Copy of decision*. The Administrative Law Judge will provide the decision to the Internal Revenue Service's authorized representative, and a copy of the decision to the respondent or the respondent's authorized representative.

(d) *When final*. In the absence of an appeal to the Secretary of the Treasury or delegate, the decision of the Administrative Law Judge will, without further proceedings, become the decision of the agency 30 days after the date of the Administrative Law Judge's decision.

(e) *Effective/applicability date*. This section is applicable beginning August 2, 2011.

§ 10.77 Appeal of decision of Administrative Law Judge.

(a) *Appeal*. Any party to the proceeding under this subpart D may appeal the decision of the Administrative Law Judge by filing a notice of appeal with the Secretary of the Treasury, or delegate deciding appeals. The notice of appeal must include a brief that states exceptions to the decision of Administrative Law Judge and supporting reasons for such exceptions.

(b) *Time and place for filing of appeal*. The notice of appeal and brief must be filed, in duplicate, with the Secretary of the Treasury, or delegate deciding appeals, at an address for appeals that is identified to the parties with the decision of the Administrative Law Judge. The notice of appeal and brief must be filed within 30 days of the date that the decision of the Administrative Law Judge is served on the parties. The appealing party must serve a copy of the notice of appeal and the brief to any non appealing party or, if the party is represented, the non-appealing party's representative.

(c) *Response*. Within 30 days of receiving the copy of the appellant's brief, the other party may file a response brief with the Secretary of the Treasury, or delegate deciding appeals, using the address identified for appeals. A copy of the response brief must be served at the same time on the opposing party or, if the party is represented, the opposing party's representative.

(d) *No other briefs, responses or motions as of right*. Other than the appeal brief and response brief, the parties are not permitted to file any other briefs, responses or motions, except on a grant of leave to do so after a motion demonstrating sufficient cause, or unless otherwise ordered by the Secretary of the Treasury, or delegate deciding appeals.

(e) *Additional time for briefs and responses*. Notwithstanding the time for filing briefs and responses provided in paragraphs (b) and (c) of this section, the Secretary of the Treasury, or delegate deciding appeals, may, for good cause, authorize additional time for filing briefs and responses upon a motion of a party or upon the initiative of

the Secretary of the Treasury, or delegate deciding appeals.

(f) *Effective/applicability date*. This section is applicable beginning August 2, 2011.

§ 10.78 Decision on review.

(a) *Decision on review*. On appeal from or review of the decision of the Administrative Law Judge, the Secretary of the Treasury, or delegate, will make the agency decision. The Secretary of the Treasury, or delegate, should make the agency decision within 180 days after receipt of the appeal

(b) *Standard of review*. The decision of the Administrative Law Judge will not be reversed unless the appellant establishes that the decision is clearly erroneous in light of the evidence in the record and applicable law. Issues that are exclusively matters of law will be reviewed de novo. In the event that the Secretary of the Treasury, or delegate, determines that there are unresolved issues raised by the record, the case may be remanded to the Administrative Law Judge to elicit additional testimony or evidence.

(c) *Copy of decision on review*. The Secretary of the Treasury, or delegate, will provide copies of the agency decision to the authorized representative of the Internal Revenue Service and the respondent or the respondent's authorized representative.

(d) *Effective/applicability date*. This section is applicable beginning August 2, 2011.

§ 10.79 Effect of disbarment, suspension, or censure.

(a) *Disbarment*. When the final decision in a case is against the respondent (or the respondent has offered his or her consent and such consent has been accepted by the Internal Revenue Service) and such decision is for disbarment, the respondent will not be permitted to practice before the Internal Revenue Service unless and until authorized to do so by the Internal Revenue Service pursuant to §10.81.

(b) *Suspension*. When the final decision in a case is against the respondent (or the respondent has offered his or her consent and such consent has been accepted by the Internal Revenue Service) and such decision is for suspension, the respondent will not be permitted to practice before the Internal Revenue Service during the period of suspension. For periods after the suspension, the practitioner's future representations may be subject to conditions as authorized by paragraph (d) of this section.

(c) *Censure*. When the final decision in the case is against the respondent (or the Internal Revenue Service has accepted the respondent's offer to consent, if such offer was made) and such decision is for censure, the respondent will be permitted to practice before the Internal Revenue Service, but the respondent's future representations may be subject to conditions as authorized by paragraph (d) of this section.

(d) *Conditions*. After being subject to the sanction of either suspension or censure, the future representations of a practitioner so sanctioned shall be subject to specified conditions designed to promote high standards of conduct. These conditions can be imposed for a reasonable period in light of the gravity of the practitioner's violations. For example, where a practitioner is censured because the practitioner failed to advise the practitioner's clients about a potential conflict of interest or failed to obtain the clients' written consents, the practitioner may be required to provide the Internal Revenue Service with a copy of all consents obtained by the practitioner for an appropriate period following censure, whether or not such consents are specifically requested.

(e) *Effective/applicability date*. This section is applicable beginning August 2, 2011.

§ 10.80 Notice of disbarment, suspension, censure, or disqualification.

(a) *In general*. On the issuance of a final order censuring, suspending, or disbarring a practitioner or a final order disqualifying an appraiser, notification of the censure, suspension, disbarment or disqualification will be given to appropriate officers and employees of the Internal Revenue Service and interested departments and agencies of the Federal government. The Internal Revenue Service may

determine the manner of giving notice to the proper authorities of the State by which the censured, suspended, or disbarred person was licensed to practice.

(b) *Effective/applicability date*. This section is applicable beginning August 2, 2011.

§ 10.81 Petition for reinstatement.

(a) *In general*. A practitioner disbarred or suspended under §10.60, or suspended under §10.82, or a disqualified appraiser may petition for reinstatement before the Internal Revenue Service after the expiration of 5 years following such disbarment, suspension, or disqualification (or immediately following the expiration of the suspension or disqualification period, if shorter than 5 years). Reinstatement will not be granted unless the Internal Revenue Service is satisfied that the petitioner is not likely to engage thereafter in conduct contrary to the regulations in this part, and that granting such reinstatement would not be contrary to the public interest.

(b) *Effective/applicability date*. This section is applicable beginning June 12, 2014.

§ 10.82 Expedited suspension.

(a) *When applicable*. Whenever the Commissioner, or delegate, determines that a practitioner is described in paragraph (b) of this section, the expedited procedures described in this section may be used to suspend the practitioner from practice before the Internal Revenue Service.

(b) *To whom applicable*. This section applies to any practitioner who, within 5 years prior to the date that a show cause order under this section's expedited suspension procedures is served:

(1) Has had a license to practice as an attorney, certified public accountant, or actuary suspended or revoked for cause (not including a failure to pay a professional licensing fee) by any authority or court, agency, body, or board described in §10.51(a)(10).

(2) Has, irrespective of whether an appeal has been taken, been convicted of any crime under title

26 of the United States Code, any crime involving dishonesty or breach of trust, or any felony for which the conduct involved renders the practitioner unfit to practice before the Internal Revenue Service.

(3) Has violated conditions imposed on the practitioner pursuant to §10.79(d).

(4) Has been sanctioned by a court of competent jurisdiction, whether in a civil or criminal proceeding (including suits for injunctive relief), relating to any taxpayer's tax liability or relating to the practitioner's own tax liability, for —

(i) Instituting or maintaining proceedings primarily for delay;

(ii) Advancing frivolous or groundless arguments; or

(iii) Failing to pursue available administrative remedies.

(5) Has demonstrated a pattern of willful disreputable conduct by—

(i) Failing to make an annual Federal tax return, in violation of the Federal tax laws, during 4 of the 5 tax years immediately preceding the institution of a proceeding under paragraph (c) of this section and remains noncompliant with any of the practitioner's Federal tax filing obligations at the time the notice of suspension is issued under paragraph (f) of this section; or

(ii) Failing to make a return required more frequently than annually, in violation of the Federal tax laws, during 5 of the 7 tax periods immediately preceding the institution of a proceeding under paragraph (c) of this section and remains noncompliant with any of the practitioner's Federal tax filing obligations at the time the notice of suspension is issued under paragraph (f) of this section.

(c) *Expedited suspension procedures.* A suspension under this section will be proposed by a show cause order that names the respondent, is signed by an authorized representative of the Internal Revenue Service under §10.69(a)(1), and served according to the rules set forth in §10.63(a). The show cause order must give a plain and concise description of the allegations that constitute the basis for the proposed suspension. The show cause order must notify the respondent —

(1) Of the place and due date for filing a response;

(2) That an expedited suspension decision by default may be rendered if the respondent fails to file a response as required;

(3) That the respondent may request a conference to address the merits of the show cause order and that any such request must be made in the response; and

(4) That the respondent may be suspended either immediately following the expiration of the period within which a response must be filed or, if a conference is requested, immediately following the conference.

(d) *Response.* The response to the show cause order described in this section must be filed no later than 30 calendar days following the date the show cause order is served, unless the time for filing is extended. The response must be filed in accordance with the rules set forth for answers to a complaint in §10.64, except as otherwise provided in this section. The response must include a request for a conference, if a conference is desired. The respondent is entitled to the conference only if the request is made in a timely filed response.

(e) *Conference.* An authorized representative of the Internal Revenue Service will preside at a conference described in this section. The conference will be held at a place and time selected by the Internal Revenue Service, but no sooner than 14 calendar days after the date by which the response must be filed with the Internal Revenue Service, unless the respondent agrees to an earlier date. An authorized representative may represent the respondent at the conference.

(f) *Suspension—*

(1) *In general.* The Commissioner, or delegate, may suspend the respondent from practice before the Internal Revenue Service by a written notice of expedited suspension immediately following:

(i) The expiration of the period within which a response to a show cause order must be filed if the respondent does not file a response as required by paragraph (d) of this section;

(ii) The conference described in paragraph (e) of this section if the Internal Revenue Service finds that the respondent is described in paragraph (b) of this section; or

(iii) The respondent's failure to appear, either personally or through an authorized representative, at a conference scheduled by the Internal Revenue Service under paragraph (e) of this section.

(2) *Duration of suspension.* A suspension under this section will commence on the date that the written notice of expedited suspension is served on the practitioner, either personally or through an authorized representative. The suspension will remain effective until the earlier of:

(i) The date the Internal Revenue Service lifts the suspension after determining that the practitioner is no longer described in paragraph (b) of this section or for any other reason; or

(ii) The date the suspension is lifted or otherwise modified by an Administrative Law Judge or the Secretary of the Treasury, or delegate deciding appeals, in a proceeding referred to in paragraph (g) of this section and instituted under §10.60.

(g) *Practitioner demand for §10.60 proceeding.* If the Internal Revenue Service suspends a practitioner under the expedited suspension procedures described in this section, the practitioner may demand that the Internal Revenue Service institute a proceeding under §10.60 and issue the complaint described in §10.62. The demand must be in writing, specifically reference the suspension action under §10.82, and be made within 2 years from the date on which the practitioner's suspension commenced. The Internal Revenue Service must issue a complaint demanded under this paragraph (g) within 60 calendar days of receiving the demand. If the Internal Revenue Service does not issue such complaint within 60 days of receiving the demand, the suspension is lifted automatically. The preceding sentence does not, however, preclude the Commissioner, or delegate, from instituting a regular proceeding under §10.60 of this part.

(h) *Effective/applicability date.* This section is generally applicable beginning June 12, 2014, except that paragraphs (b)(1) through (4) of this section are applicable beginning August 2, 2011.

Subpart E — General Provisions

§ 10.90 Records.

(a) *Roster.* The Internal Revenue Service will maintain and make available for public inspection in the time and manner prescribed by the Secretary, or delegate, the following rosters —

(1) Individuals (and employers, firms, or other entities, if applicable) censured, suspended, or disbarred from practice before the Internal Revenue Service or upon whom a monetary penalty was imposed.

(2) Enrolled agents, including individuals —

(i) Granted active enrollment to practice;

(ii) Whose enrollment has been placed in inactive status for failure to meet the requirements for renewal of enrollment;

(iii) Whose enrollment has been placed in inactive retirement status; and

(iv) Whose offer of consent to resign from enrollment has been accepted by the Internal Revenue Service under §10.61.

(3) Enrolled retirement plan agents, including individuals —

(i) Granted active enrollment to practice;

(ii) Whose enrollment has been placed in inactive status for failure to meet the requirements for renewal of enrollment;

(iii) Whose enrollment has been placed in inactive retirement status; and

(iv) Whose offer of consent to resign from enrollment has been accepted under §10.61.

(4) Registered tax return preparers, including individuals —

(i) Authorized to prepare all or substantially all of a tax return or claim for refund;

(ii) Who have been placed in inactive status for failure to meet the requirements for renewal;

(iii) Who have been placed in inactive retirement status; and

(iv) Whose offer of consent to resign from their status as a registered tax return preparer has been accepted by the Internal Revenue Service under §10.61.

(5) Disqualified appraisers.

(6) Qualified continuing education providers, including providers —

(i) Who have obtained a qualifying continuing education provider number; and

(ii) Whose qualifying continuing education number has been revoked for failure to comply with the requirements of this part.

(b) *Other records.* Other records of the Director of the Office of Professional Responsibility may be disclosed upon specific request, in accordance with the applicable law.

(c) *Effective/applicability date.* This section is applicable beginning August 2, 2011.

§ 10.91 Saving provision.

Any proceeding instituted under this part prior to June 12, 2014, for which a final decision has not been reached or for which judicial review is still available is not affected by these revisions. Any proceeding under this part based on conduct engaged in prior to June 12, 2014, which is instituted after that date, will apply subpart D and E of this part as revised, but the conduct engaged in prior to the effective date of these revisions will be judged by the regulations in effect at the time the conduct occurred.

§ 10.92 Special orders.

The Secretary of the Treasury reserves the power to issue such special orders as he or she deems proper in any cases within the purview of this part.

§ 10.93 Effective date.

Except as otherwise provided in each section and Subject to §10.91, Part 10 is applicable on July 26, 2002.

John Dalrymple,
Deputy Commissioner for Services and Enforcement

Approved: June 3, 2014
Christopher J. Meade,
General Counsel

[FR Doc. 2014-13739 Filed 06/09/2014 at 4:15 pm; Publication Date: 06/12/2014]

INDEX

Made in the USA
Monee, IL
05 May 2021